Interpretation of Fundamental Rights in a Multilevel Legal System

An analysis of the European Court of Human Rights and the Court of Justice of the European Union

SCHOOL OF HUMAN RIGHTS RESEARCH SERIES, Volume 46

The titles published in this series are listed at the end of this volume.

Interpretation of Fundamental Rights in a Multilevel Legal System

An analysis of the European Court of Human Rights and the Court of Justice of the European Union

Hanneke Senden

intersentia
Cambridge – Antwerp – Portland

Intersentia Ltd
Trinity House | Cambridge Business Park | Cowley Road
Cambridge | CB4 OWZ | United Kingdom
mail@intersentia.co.uk

Hanneke Senden
Interpretation of Fundamental Rights in a Multilevel Legal System

Cover: Juriah Mosin, Dreamstime.com

Typesetting: Anne-Marie Krens – Tekstbeeld – Oegstgeest

This is the commercial edition of the dissertation published by Intersentia under
ISBN 978-17-8068-027-9

The research for this publication was made possible by a grant from the Netherlands Organisation of Scientific Research (NWO).

British Library Cataloguing in Publication Data. A catalogue record for this book is available from the British Library.

Acknowledgements

Writing my PhD has been a learning experience in many ways. One of the most important lessons learned in this process is that, even if I wrote this thesis myself, the result could not have been what it is today without the help and support of many others. I would like to thank everyone who has been a part of this process in one way or the other.

I am grateful to the International Office from both Leiden University and Boston University for facilitating my stay in Boston. The European courts were far, very far away in Boston, but the distance from Europe helped me to get a good overview of the whole project. This period has therefore been really important for the whole process.

Even though the writing process has had its ups and downs throughout the years, the atmosphere made possible by my colleagues at the Department of Constitutional and Administrative Law in Leiden has been a true highlight! Also colleagues from other departments have contributed to a pleasant experience in Leiden. Weekly lunches, PhD lunches and occasional dinners brought interesting perspectives to the table. All these colleagues have contributed to a valuable time in Leiden. Two names should be mentioned in particular, because I am not sure that I would have ever finished this PhD if it wasn't for them. Janneke, thank you for your devoted guidance, human touch and your faith in me! And Marina, my partner in PhD. The fact that we could share all the laughs, frustrations and more laughs over this project means a lot to me!

Finally, my family and friends. Where would I have been without my friends? Not in Istanbul, Kirchberg, Marrakech, London, Ischgl, Aït-Benhaddou, Cape Town, the Sahara, Cunel, Paris, Stellenbosch, Gerlos and Rabat, that's for sure. Thanks for all these brilliant trips, some more culturally responsible than others, but always great fun! Moreover the lunch dates, sports classes and many long dinners with friends have formed a great distraction from writing my PhD.

Finally, my own and Joep's family have been wonderfully supportive in many perspectives, perhaps most importantly by knowing when to ask and when not to ask about my progress. I should, however, particularly complement my father for trying to make some sense of my project and closely following (and commenting on) any news related to it. All of you, but mostly Mum & Dad and Toos & Joop thanks for your support!

And last but not least: Joep. I know I have complained many times whenever I was stressed that you do not know how hard it is to finish a PhD. I realize now that *I* do not know how hard it is to live with someone who finishes a PhD. And perhaps it is better that I didn't know. Thank you for always making me laugh!

CONTENTS

PART I – INTRODUCTION 1

Chapter 1
Introduction 3
1.1 Interpretation versus application 7
1.2 Interpretative aids 8
1.3 Values in judicial argumentation 10
1.4 Methodology 13
1.5 Outline 13

Chapter 2
Context of legal argumentation in the European Court of Human Rights 15
2.1 Character of the European Convention 16
2.2 ECtHR a constitutional court? 16
2.3 Style of judgment 20
2.4 Subsidiarity 22
2.5 Conclusion 23

Chapter 3
Context of legal argumentation in fundamental rights cases for the Court of Justice of the European Union 25
3.1 The CJEU and Fundamental Rights 26
3.2 The CJEU and the ECHR 33
3.3 Argumentation by the CJEU 35
3.4 Conclusion 39

PART II – THEORETICAL ANALYSIS 41

Chapter 4
Interpretation methods and interpretative principles 43
4.1 Terminology: Method, rule, principle? 44
4.2 Hierarchy of interpretation methods? 47

4.3 Methods of interpretation 50
4.3.1 Textual interpretation 50
4.3.2 Teleological interpretation 55
4.3.3 Systemic or contextual interpretation 59
4.3.4 Subjective or historical interpretation 62
4.3.5 Comparative method of interpretation 66
4.3.6 Conclusion 69
4.4 Principles of interpretation 69
4.4.1 European Court of Human Rights 70
4.4.1.1 Principle of evolutive interpretation 70
4.4.1.2 Principle of practical and effective rights 73
4.4.1.3 Principle of autonomous interpretation 77
4.4.1.4 Democracy in the European Convention system 79
4.4.1.5 Human dignity and personal autonomy 81
4.4.2 Court of Justice of the European Union 82
4.4.2.1 Principle of meta-teleological interpretation 83
4.4.2.2 Principle of effectiveness (*effet utile*) 84
4.4.2.3 Principle of autonomous interpretation 86
4.4.2.4 Principle of evolutive interpretation 87
4.5 Conclusion 89

Chapter 5
Teleological interpretation 91
5.1 A theoretical point of view 92
5.1.1 Interpreting by reference to object and purpose 93
5.1.2 Object and purpose? 97
5.1.3 How to determine the object and purpose 99
5.1.4 Criticism related to method in general 102
5.2 Teleological interpretation in the ECtHR and CJEU 103
5.2.1 CJEU 103
5.2.2 ECtHR 105
5.3 Which way forward? 107
5.4 Conclusion 109

Chapter 6
Comparative interpretation 111
6.1 Comparative interpretation in more detail 112
6.1.1 What is comparative interpretation? 112
6.1.2 General basis for comparative interpretation? 113
6.1.3 'Internal' and 'external' comparative interpretation 115
6.1.4 Purposes of comparative interpretation 117

6.1.5 The distinction between internal and external component revisited 122
6.1.6 Criticism of comparative interpretation 123
6.1.6.1 Criticism of the legitimacy of comparative interpretation as a method of interpretation 123
6.1.6.2 Criticism of the use of comparative interpretation 127
6.1.7 Solutions for addressing the criticism 131
6.2 Comparative interpretation and the ECtHR 135
6.3 Comparative interpretation and the CJEU 138
6.4 Conclusion 142

Chapter 7
Principle of evolutive interpretation 145
7.1 Some preliminary remarks on evolutive interpretation 146
7.2 Evolutive interpretation and international law 149
7.3 Evolutive interpretation and national law 154
7.4 European Court of Human Rights 161
7.4.1 Basis and justification for evolutive interpretation 161
7.4.2 Meaning and nature of evolutive interpretation in the context of the Convention 163
7.4.3 How is evolutive interpretation established? 164
7.4.4 When does the ECtHR rely on evolutive interpretation? 166
7.4.5 Evolution upwards? 168
7.4.6 Conclusion 169
7.5 Court of Justice of the European Union 169
7.6 Conclusion 171

Chapter 8
Principle of autonomous interpretation 173
8.1 Autonomous interpretation and international law 174
8.2 European Court of Human Rights 176
8.3 Court of Justice of the European Union 184
8.4 Conclusion 188

PART III – CASE LAW ANALYSIS 191

European Court of Human Rights – General introduction 193

Chapter 9
Teleological interpretation in the case law of the ECtHR 195
9.1 How can this method of interpretation be recognized? 196
9.2 What does the Court refer to when speaking about object and purpose? 201
9.3 How does the court establish the object and purpose or underlying values? 205
9.3.1 Objective or subjective intention? 205
9.3.2 Which documents play a role in establishing the subjective or objective purpose? 210
9.3.3 What other factors play a role in establishing the subjective or objective purpose? 212
9.4 Role of teleological interpretation in the interpretation process 213
9.5 Relation with other interpretative aids 219
9.6 Conclusion 221

Chapter 10
Comparative interpretation in the case law of the ECtHR 223
10.1 What is comparative interpretation according to the ECtHR? 224
10.2 When is it used in the Court's reasoning? 226
10.2.1 Comparative method in the interpretation phase 226
10.2.1.1 Comparative interpretation used for 'regular' interpretative problems 227
10.2.1.2 Comparative interpretation used to adopt a new interpretation different from the former interpretation 230
10.2.1.3 Comparative interpretation used to argue that the Court should not adopt a specific interpretation 233
10.2.1.4 Comparative interpretation to show textual difference 235
10.2.2 Comparative method in the application phase 237
10.2.3 Specific type of cases? 240
10.2.4 Conclusion 241
10.3 Any justification? 241
10.4 Comparative interpretation – how? 245
10.4.1 Finding a consensus or trend 245
10.4.2 Separate references to international, regional and foreign materials 255
10.4.3 Used to support argument or decisive argument? 259

10.4.4 Does the ECtHR acknowledge the distinction between internal and external materials? 260
10.4.5 Who collects the materials? 261
10.5 Role of comparative reasoning in relation to other methods and principles 262
10.6 Conclusion 264

Chapter 11
Evolutive interpretation in the case law of the ECtHR 267
11.1 Identification of evolutive interpretation in the case law 268
11.2 Why invoked by the Court? 272
11.3 When does evolutive interpretation play a role? 275
11.4 How does the Court find an 'evolution'? 281
11.5 Relation to other interpretative aids 285
11.6 Conclusion 287

Chapter 12
Autonomous interpretation in the case law of the ECtHR 289
12.1 What is autonomous interpretation? 290
12.2 Autonomous interpretation: interpretative principle or method? 292
12.3 Why autonomous interpretation? 293
12.4 When autonomous interpretation? 297
12.5 How is autonomous meaning established? 302
12.6 Conclusion 308

Chapter 13
Interpretation in the case law of the CJEU 311
13.1 The CJEU and the interpretation of fundamental rights 314
13.2 Comparative Interpretation 318
13.2.1 Introduction 318
13.2.2 Role of national constitutional traditions 320
13.2.2.1 The basis for invoking national constitutional traditions 322
13.2.2.2 CJEU and national constitutional traditions 324
13.2.2.3 Advocate General and national constitutional traditions 331
13.2.2.4 Comparing approaches 340
13.2.2.5 The purpose of invoking national constitutional traditions 340
13.2.2.6 Common Traditions? 344
13.2.2.7 Material 347
13.2.2.8 Conclusion 351
13.2.3 Role of the ECHR 352

13.2.4 Role of other international instruments 363
13.2.5 Conclusion 366
13.3 Teleological interpretation 367
13.4 Other interpretation methods and principles 374
13.4.1 Evolutive interpretation 374
13.4.2 Autonomous interpretation 378
13.5 Conclusion 382

PART IV – CONCLUSION 387

Chapter 14
Conclusion 389
14.1 Interpretation methods and interpretative principles 390
14.2 Teleological interpretation 391
14.3 Comparative interpretation 393
14.4 Evolutive interpretation 399
14.5 Autonomous interpretation 401
14.6 General conclusion 402

Samenvatting 405
Bibliography 415
List of cases 433
Index 443
Curriculum vitae 447

Part I

Introduction

CHAPTER 1
INTRODUCTION[1]

Article 7 of the European Charter of Fundamental Rights[2]
Respect for private and family life
Everyone has the right to respect for his or her private and family life, home and communications.

Article 12 of the European Charter of Fundamental Rights
Freedom of assembly and of association
1. Everyone has the right to freedom of peaceful assembly and to freedom of association at all levels, in particular in political, trade union and civic matters, which implies the right of everyone to form and to join trade unions for the protection of his or her interests.
2. Political parties at Union level contribute to expressing the political will of the citizens of the Union.

Article 9 of the European Convention on Human Rights and Fundamental Freedoms[3]
Freedom of thought, conscience and religion
1. Everyone has the right to freedom of thought, conscience and religion; this right includes freedom to change his religion or belief and freedom, either alone or in community with others and in public or private, to manifest his religion or belief, in worship, teaching, practice and observance.
2. Freedom to manifest one's religion or beliefs shall be subject only to such limitations as are prescribed by law and are necessary in a democratic society in the interests of public safety, for the protection of public order, health or morals, or for the protection of the rights and freedoms of others.

---

1 This thesis is written in the framework of the VIDI-project Judicial reasoning in fundamental rights cases – national and European perspectives, supervised by professor J.H. Gerards and funded by the Netherlands Organisation of Scientific Research (NWO).

2 Hereinafter the Charter. The European Charter of Fundamental Rights proclaimed in 2007, OJ 2010/C 83/02. This Charter contains one general limitation clause in Article 52 which provides:
Article 52:
Scope and interpretation of rights and principles
1. Any limitation on the exercise of the rights and freedoms recognized by this Charter must be provided for by law and respect the essence of those rights and freedoms. Subject to the principle of proportionality, limitations may be made only if they are necessary and genuinely meet objectives of general interest recognized by the Union or the need to protect the rights and freedoms of others.

3 Hereinafter the European Convention or the Convention.

Fundamental rights are often drafted in a very general manner. The examples provided above illustrate the vague or broad nature of fundamental rights. This raises many questions regarding the exact meaning of these rights. What kinds of situations are covered by the notion of family life? Does this extend to homosexual relationships? And what kind of activities are within the scope of the notion of private life? The wish of a handicapped person to be able to access a beach? Or the right to freedom of association, does this include the right not to be associated? And what about the right to freedom of religion? Is any religion protected under the scope of this provision? These are some examples of the types of questions that require answers for a proper understanding of the meaning of these fundamental rights. The problem is that there are no easy answers to these questions, because the text of these provisions does not provide much guidance. Moreover, these questions often deal with highly controversial material on which opinions can differ strongly.

If the text is not clear, the question is who determines the meaning of these provisions? By drafting these vaguely worded provisions the legislator or, in the case of treaties, the drafting states leave these matters to be decided by judges in individual cases. As a consequence, in many cases judges are confronted with questions challenging the scope of fundamental rights. The question is how judges decide these questions on the meaning of fundamental rights. In other words, how do they interpret fundamental rights provisions?[4] This question can be understood in two ways. One can look at the material result of the interpretation of specific fundamental rights provisions or one can look at the interpretation process and try to understand how judges have come to a specific interpretation of a fundamental rights provision. While the former question can be highly interesting, the focus of this thesis is on the latter question, namely how specific interpretative conclusions can be justified.

A logical question is how one can establish how judges have come to a specific interpretative decision. Two different phases can be distinguished in the process of decision-making by judges in general, which is valid for the interpretative process as well. On the one hand there is the heuristic part of the process.[5] This refers to the process of finding an answer to the question at hand. Different judges can have different methods for finding an answer, depending on the person of the judge and his or her experience; other factors might play a role as well.[6] It is extremely difficult

4 As indicated by McCormick (2005), p. 121, interpretation can be understood in a wide sense and in a stricter sense. The wider sense understands interpretation to be any act whereby the law is applied to a specific case. The stricter sense means that there is some doubt about the meaning of a term or provision, which needs to be resolved. The term 'interpretation' will be used in the stricter sense throughout this thesis.

5 Smith (2005) p. 77-78. See also McCormick (1978), p. 14-16 and McCormick (2005), p. 208, who speaks about the process of discovery and the process of justification.

6 Smith (2005), p. 77.

if not impossible to get a proper understanding of this heuristic part of judicial decision-making, because even interviews would not provide enough insight into this process. It would require an analysis of the judge's brain to fully understand how this process of finding a specific answer works. This thesis therefore focuses on the second phase of the judge's decision-making process. In its judgment a judge or a court is required to provide reasons for its decision. By providing reasons a judge is required to produce arguments that justify the decision.[7] Outsiders, like other judges, national legislators, lawyers, academics, but also the general public, can assess on the basis of these arguments whether they really provide a justification for the result in a specific judgment. By providing arguments for a specific decision the judicial conclusions can be more easily checked for their quality and persuasiveness. This research will therefore focus on the judicial argumentation or more specifically on the arguments provided for a specific interpretative choice.

Even though an analysis of judicial argumentation can be relevant for any judicial body dealing with fundamental rights, two specific judicial bodies have been selected for the research in this thesis. Both the European Court of Human Rights (ECtHR) and the Court of Justice of the European Union (CJEU),[8] the latter only in cases dealing with fundamental rights, will be analyzed in this thesis. Two reasons can be provided for this choice. First of all, these judicial bodies operate in a complex legal system. National judges need to pay respect to the national context, but European judges need to take account of the European context and also of the national contexts of the different Member States. In addition European judges need to decide matters in individual cases, meaning that the protection of individual citizens plays a role as well. This results in a complex exercise for European judges in which they have to find a way to pay respect to national differences, while at the same time offering effective protection for individuals. This multilevel background for both the ECtHR and CJEU increases the need for sound judicial reasoning. The reasoning needs to convince even Member States that might not agree with a specific outcome. The implementation of the judgments of both courts depends to a varying degree on the cooperation of Member States; therefore it is highly important that Member States respect their decisions.[9] Judicial argumentation can play an important role in this respect.

---

7 Smith (2005), p. 78 and McCormick (2005) p. 208.

8 Previously known as the European Court of Justice (ECJ). For the sake of clarity this thesis will employ the current name and abbreviation (Court of Justice of the European Union (CJEU)) even when referring to a period when the Court was still called the European Court of Justice. Furthermore, the focus in this thesis will be solely on the Court of Justice of the European Union. The General Court (previously called the Court of First Instance) will not be part of the research.

9 The ECtHR depends entirely on the (political) willingness of the Contracting States to cooperate. Within the EU context there are some legal mechanisms to force reluctant Member States to comply

The second reason for selecting these two judicial bodies is that their judicial reasoning has been criticized. This criticism has been directed both at their reasoning in general,[10] but also at specific parts of the reasoning, for example the use of interpretation methods.[11] Given the fact that to a large degree the success of both courts depends on the cooperation of national authorities,[12] it is important to confront this criticism and analyze whether improvements can be made with regard to the judicial reasoning.[13]

---

with CJEU judgments. Article 260 TFEU is an example of such a mechanism whereby the Commission may bring a Member State that fails to implement a judgment of the CJEU before the CJEU and request a penalty to be imposed. The question whether the Commission will bring such a case can, however, be highly political. The effectiveness of the judgments of the CJEU thus also depends in large part on the (political) willingness of the Member States to cooperate. The fact that cooperation is not always self-evident can be seen from the critical German attitude, for example, the *Solange* judgments in Germany, where the German Constitutional Court ruled that it will only respect decisions from the CJEU, as long as it provides equivalent protection to the German Basic Law. See, among others, Craig & De Burca (2008), p. 357-363 for a discussion of the critical position of the German Constitutional Court. See also Da Cunha Rodrigues (2010), p. 94.

10 The CJEU is often criticized for its unclear reasoning. See for example: Arnull (2006), p. 623, referring to the uninformative nature of the CJEU judgments; De Waele (2009), p. 369-380, discusses critcism at the CJEU that its reasoning is not clear and includes references to many other authors as well. See also Von Bogdandy (2000), p. 1330, who criticizes the lack of explanation in the reasoning of the CJEU on why certain rights are recognized. General criticism of the ECtHR is often expressed not so much at the reasoning of the ECtHR, but at its judicial approach. Accussations of judicial activism have experienced a recent revival in several countries. See, for example, the critical speech by Lord Hoffmann (2009), where he criticizes the ECtHR for judicial activism and expanding its influence without the required legitimacy. This is part of a more general debate on the role of the ECtHR in the United Kingdom fed by the disagreement with the need to change its regime on voting rights of prisoners at the order of Strasbourg. Also these general disagreements warrant a close look at the reasoning of both Courts.

11 Especially in the context of the ECtHR criticism has been expressed at the use of specific interpretation methods, mainly comparative interpretation. See Carozza (1998); Senden (2009); Drooghenbroek (2009); Heringa (1996). See also: Krisch (2008), p. 206-207, who refers to criticism at the use of evolutive interpretation by the ECtHR.

12 See also Krisch (2008), p. 183-184, who describes the effect of the *Görgülü* judgment of the German Constitutional Court in which the German court indicated that it should ignore judgments from Strasbourg which are incompatible with 'central elements of the domestic legal order, legislative intent, or constitutional provisions'.

13 See also Garlicki (2009), p. 391, who points to the fact that it is important for the succes of the ECtHR, in his argument, to convince national constutitional or supreme courts of the Strasbourg position.

1.1 Interpretation versus application

In order to set some boundaries for this project, it has been decided that it will only deal with a specific part of the judicial reasoning: the interpretation process. This has already been referred to above, but it warrants some more elaborate explanation. One of the presuppositions of this thesis is that there are two phases in answering the question whether a certain right has been violated.[14] A distinction can be made between the interpretation phase and the application phase.[15] In the interpretation phase the meaning of a fundamental right will be defined, which results in a more abstract judicial exercise. It will be determined, for example, what a notion like private life entails, for instance whether hunting activities are covered by this notion. By defining the right in question, the court will in the interpretative phase at the same time decide whether the facts of the case fall within the scope of the specific fundamental right complained of. The facts only play a role in this phase to determine whether they come within the scope of the fundamental right invoked. The application phase will deal with the question whether the right in question has been violated. In this second, application phase, the facts of the case play an important role. The question in the application phase is often whether the limitation of the rights in question was prescribed by law, whether it served a legitimate goal and whether it was necessary in a democratic society or a variety of these requirements.[16]

Both phases serve a different goal in the judicial argumentation and complement each other.[17] By defining the right in question, it becomes possible to argue whether this right has been violated.[18] Without knowing what a certain right means it is difficult to argue that it has been violated. As a result of the different purpose of the two phases, different methods play a role in the respective phases. In the interpretation phase, interpretative aids, like textual, teleological or autonomous interpretation play a role.[19] In the application phase techniques like the margin of appreciation and balancing of rights and interests play an important role.[20] One of the differences

14 See elaborately on this topic: Gerards & Senden (2009).

15 See Gerards & Senden (2009). See also: Vanneste (2010), p. 215-217; Faigman (1992), p. 1530-1534; Harris, O'Boyle & Warbrick (2009), p. 6; Schokkenbroek (2000), p. 1; Bernhardt (1995), p. 1416-1417; Orakhelashvili (2008), p. 285, all of whom refer to the distinction either by explicitly recognizing the distinction or by mentioning the two stages, which indicates that the respective authors at least recognize the two stages.

16 See second paragraph of many ECHR provisions. See also Article 52 of the Charter.

17 Vanneste (2010), p. 214-215; Gerards & Senden (2009).

18 Gerards & Senden (2009).

19 Comparative interpretation is the only method that plays a role in both phases as will be seen later on in Chapter 10. The method is, however, used for different purposes in the two phases.

20 On the margin of appreciation, see Yourow (1996) and Arai-Takahashi (2002). On balancing see, among others: Sottiaux & Van der Schijff (2008). See also Den Houdijker (forthcoming).

between the two phases is that the interpretation phase is, in general, to a larger extent aimed at unifying the meaning of the respective fundamental rights;[21] the meaning of the various fundamental rights should not differ by country. The application of the fundamental rights can differ by country, because of different policy choices for example.[22] The margin of appreciation can thus play a role in the application phase and grant room for specific national considerations, but this technique should not play a role in the interpretation phase. As a result of these different roles, these two phases have been distinguished. It must be admitted that this distinction is not always easy to make, but in this thesis the aim has been to try to make this distinction as strict as possible.

1.2 Interpretative aids

The aim of this thesis is to analyze several interpretative aids used by the CJEU and the ECtHR when interpreting fundamental rights. Textual interpretation, teleological interpretation, evolutive interpretation, but also systemic interpretation, play a role in the interpretation process of both courts. A selection has, however, been made to analyze those interpretative aids that are most relevant in the multilevel context that has been described above. Thus those interpretative aids that help the CJEU and the ECtHR in dealing with the complex exercise of paying respect to national differences and at the same time offer effective protection for individuals. Comparative interpretation, evolutive interpretation, autonomous interpretation and teleological interpretation have been selected for further analysis. This choice will be explained in Chapter 4, but the main reason behind this selection is their specific relevance for judges deciding in a multilevel legal system. Methods like textual interpretation are much less helpful in finding a solution for the complex balance that the CJEU and the ECtHR are confronted with when interpreting fundamental rights provisions. This does not mean that other interpretative aids do not play a role in the judicial reasoning. On the contrary, they do play a role as will be seen in Chapter 4, but their role in this thesis will be limited.

A specific way of reasoning that will not be addressed in the framework of this thesis is the use of precedent, because one can doubt whether it should be classified as a method of interpretation. Rather it could be seen as a specific technique for reasoning that not necessarily plays a role only in the interpretation process. This

21 Vanneste (2010), p. 215.

22 See also Lord Hoffman (2009), p. 12, who indicates that even if one agrees to adopt uniform abstract fundamental rights, this does not mean that one agrees to uniform application of those rights.

form of reasoning, however, does play a role in the judgments of both courts.[23] Even though neither of the two courts is formally bound to obey precedent, precedent does play an important role.[24] On the face of it, the European Convention and its corresponding Protocols seem to provide no reason to conclude that the ECtHR applies a system of precedent in its decisions. The European Convention specifically mentions that judgments have *inter partes* effect,[25] which appears to indicate that the system of precedents will play no role at all in the context of the European Convention. The reality turns out to be rather different.[26] The ECtHR has through the years adopted a system of persuasive precedent. In the case of *Mamatkulov and Askarov* the ECtHR held that: 'While the Court is not formally bound to follow its previous judgments, in the interests of legal certainty and foreseeability it should not depart, without good reason, from its own precedents.'[27] The reference to 'good reason' already indicates that the system is less rigid than the system of *stare decisis* in the UK and USA, because it openly allows for overruling. As noted already, the ECtHR does feel free to depart from its earlier decisions if there are 'cogent',[28] 'good'[29] or 'weighty'[30] reasons to be found for deciding differently. No clarification has been given as to what constitutes cogent, weighty or good reasons. WILDHABER has concluded that there are many differing opinions as to the use of precedent,[31] which might explain the lack of clarity as to what constitutes a weighty reason.

A similar starting point can be detected in the case of the CJEU, where no formal obligation for a system of precedent can be deduced from the EU Treaty. Article 267 TFEU could be read to imply a doctrine of persuasive precedent, by allowing the national court to decide whether a preliminary question is 'necessary'. This has in the course of time indeed been interpreted by the CJEU to mean that if a similar

---

23 For the role of precedent at the CJEU, see: Brown & Kennedy (2000), p. 369-375; Reich (2005), p. 34-35. For the role of analogy in the reasoning of the CJEU, see: Schermers & Waelbroeck (2001), p. 18, who argue that reasoning by analogy is a specific form of systemic interpretation; Langenbucher (1998). For the role of precedent in the ECtHR, see: Harris & O'Boyle & Warbrick (2009), p. 17-18; Leach (2005), p. 165; Balcerzak (2004-2005), p. 137-143; Mowbray (2009); Wildhaber (2000).

24 For the CJEU, see: Brown & Kennedy (2000), p. 369-375; Reich (2005), p. 34-35. For the ECtHR, see: Harris & O'Boyle & Warbrick (2009), p. 17-18; Leach (2005), p. 165; Balcerzak (2004-2005), p. 137-143; Mowbray (2009); Wildhaber (2000).

25 Article 46 European Convention.

26 Gerards (2006), p. 103.

27 ECtHR (GC), *Mamatkulov and Askarov v. Turkey*, judgment of 4 February 2005, *Reports* 2005-I, § 121.

28 ECtHR, *Cossey v. United Kingdom*, judgment of 27 September 1990, *Series* A No. 184, § 35.

29 ECtHR (GC), *Beard v United Kingdom*, judgment of 18 January 2001, *unpublished*, § 81.

30 ECtHR, *Abdulaziz, Cabales and Balkandi v. United Kingdom*, judgment of 28 May 1985, Series A No. 94, § 78.

31 Wildhaber (2000).

question has been addressed by the CJEU, the national courts have the discretion to decide that it might not be necessary to refer a question to the CJEU.[32] This implies that the CJEU follows its own case law, since otherwise every question would have to presented to the CJEU. National courts may, however, be presented with new facts and thus consider it necessary to refer, which could persuade the CJEU to depart from its previous case law.[33] If the CJEU is not convinced by the need for overruling, it has on occasion simply repeated its previous judgments, thereby showing the willingness to follow its own precedent.[34] On other occasions it has clearly stated that a new line had to be followed.[35] On the basis of the literature it is not possible to provide any criteria for what could constitute a reason for the CJEU to overrule its previous reasoning.

The doctrine of precedent plays an important role in the context of both courts.[36] The method, however, does not play a specific role in helping the courts to cope with interpreting in the context of a multilevel legal order. The justification for employing this method of interpretation finds its basis in legal certainty and not in the fact that judgments are pronounced in a multilevel legal system. Therefore there is no reason to discuss this method any further in the thesis.

The strong reliance on this method does show the need for both courts to provide convincing reasoning in its case law, since every case could be used as a precedent for a future case. This means that not only the outcome of the case can serve as a precedent, but also its reasoning. Some examples of cases that illustrate this importance will be discussed throughout this thesis in the context of the discussion on the selected interpretative aids, namely comparative, teleological, evolutive and autonomous interpretation.[37]

1.3 Values in judicial argumentation

In order to analyze the judicial reasoning of the CJEU and the ECtHR when interpreting fundamental rights it is necessary to have some frame of reference for the analysis. There needs to be some understanding of what a proper judicial reasoning requires. That in itself is a topic on which a whole thesis can be written. The question as to what values are important for a judicial reasoning has, therefore, been approached from a more practical perspective. The criticism expressed at the reasoning of the

32 C-283/81,*CILFIT v. Ministero della Sanità* [1982] ECR 3415.

33 C-28/62, *Da Costa en Schaake NV and others v. Administratie der Belastingen* [1963] ECR 61.

34 C-28/62, *Da Costa en Schaake NV and others v. Administratie der Belastingen* [1963] ECR 61

35 C-267/91, *Criminal proceedings against Keck and Mithouard* [1993] ECR I-6097.

36 Supra note 23.

37 See for example the case of ECtHR, *Tyrer v. United Kingdom*, judgment of 25 April 1978, *Series* A No. 26 discussed in Chapters 7 and 11.

CJEU or the ECtHR mainly focuses on two elements. These elements are not necessarily limited to the interpretative stage of judicial reasoning, but they will be discussed from that perspective in the context of this thesis.

One of the criticisms expressed is that it is not clear how the judges have reached their conclusion.[38] Either the judgment is so short that hardly any arguments are provided, or it is not clear how the arguments support the conclusion reached in a specific decision or the arguments are incomprehensible.[39] The aim of a judicial decision is not only to provide a solution in an individual case but, especially in the context of the CJEU and the ECtHR, a judicial decision is meant to contribute to the understanding of the EU or ECHR fundamental rights standards. The CJEU and the ECtHR set the standards for the European Union (EU) or the Council of Europe and their judgments play a vital role in that regard. The previous section already indicated that judgments of both courts have a *de facto erga omnes* effect and thus have a potential impact broader than relating only to the parties in a certain case.[40] Given the importance of cooperation by national authorities and the fact that it is not self-evident that they will cooperate, it is crucial that the judgments convince national authorities.[41] One way to convince national authorities is to make sure that they understand the reasoning and the conclusions drawn in a specific case. This does not mean that they necessarily have to agree with the outcome. The purpose should be to make the reasoning insightful so that outsiders can understand and respect the outcome even if they do not agree. For example, if the ECtHR does not explain or poorly explains why it has come to the conclusion that an evolutive interpretation should be adopted in a specific case, it is difficult to convince reluctant national authorities of this conclusion. It is thus important that a reasoning is insightful and shows why a certain conclusion has been reached.[42]

A related concern is that if it is not clear how a certain conclusion has been reached it is also not clear whether the conclusion is an objective conclusion or whether the person of the judge played an important role. It seems almost trite to say, but the CJEU and the ECtHR should not produce judgments on the basis of their own personal convictions, but on the basis of objective factors. Unlike legislators,

38 Supra notes 10 and 11. Criticism has been expressed at both courts.

39 Supra notes 10 and 11.

40 See for example White (2009), p. 172, who argues in the context of the ECtHR that the audience has become wider than only the parties of a specific judgment.

41 See Gerards (2009), p. 409-410; Garlicki (2009), p. 394. Especially the ECtHR with its ever expanding scope of fundamental rights is facing challenges from the national level. The main criticism is that the ECtHR should stick to the protection of core fundamental rights and not deal with cases that have little to do with the core of fundamental rights. Even though the origin of this criticism most probably does not lie in poor reasoning, sound reasoning might help in diminishing this criticism.

42 Smith (2005), p. 140-141; Pontier (1998), § 2.5; Feteris (1994).

judges have not been democratically elected on the basis of their opinions. It is their job to interpret the law and in principle not to change the law. Times have, however, changed and the judge, especially in fundamental rights cases, is no longer simply *la bouche de la loi*.[43] There is therefore a fine line between interpreting and applying the law and changing the law. Fundamental rights are broadly formulated and thus leave a lot of room for judges to determine the exact meaning. This characteristic increases the potential for criticism of legislating from the bench. This is in itself already a controversial issue, on which opinions differ on where to draw the line. It is, however, open for even more criticism if it is not clear which or whether any objective factors have played a role in the decision-making. Interpretative aids help to provide objective factors to argue for a certain conclusion. These interpretative aids should be applied correctly and carefully, because otherwise it is still not clear whether the conclusion has been based on objective factors. Criticism has, for example, been directed at comparative interpretation, which will be dealt with in Chapter 6, holding that it is always possible to find comparative materials that support your own position in a case.[44] As a result the method becomes open for manipulation, which damages the credibility of the judgment. It should thus be made clear how and why a certain interpretative aid has been used, as this makes the decision verifiable for outsiders. This is not only the case when dealing with comparative interpretation, but it applies to other interpretative aids as well. Objectivity instead of subjectivity is thus an important factor, especially in a field where there is already such a fine line to walk between judicial decision-making and judicial legislating.[45] Because of the fact that both the CJEU and the ECtHR operate in a context in which national differences can play a controversial role, it is necessary to reduce the impact of the person of the judge. This is even more so because both courts are made up of judges from different national settings.[46]

43 Montesquieu.

44 See further section 6.1.6.1.

45 Sudre (2008), p. 172, argues that providing a justification for a decision helps to reduce partiality and arbitrariness. Therefore it is important to study this justification process closely in this thesis.

46 Mainly in the context of the ECtHR criticism has been expressed at the fact that judges from perhaps less democratic countries determine cases on fundamental rights in, for example, the Netherlands and the United Kingdom. See for example the criticism expressed in the report of a British think tank entitled 'Bringing Rights Back Home' (2011), 43-45, which also addresses other problems concerning the judges in Strasbourg. This criticism is often voiced in popular discussions on the ECtHR, as is visible in a recent discussion started by Baudet (2010) in a Dutch newspaper, where he also criticized the fact that foreign (Eastern European) judges determine the standards applicable in the Netherlands. The reason that this criticism is mainly directed at the ECtHR and not at the CJEU, can perhaps be explained by the fact that the CJEU decides as a collegiate body, as will be discussed in Chapter 3. Regardless of one's opinion of this criticism, it is important to take note, because it does present a challenge for the ECtHR that should not be ignored.

In conclusion two factors play an important role, namely that judgments provide an insightful reasoning and that the reasoning is as objective as possible.[47] This latter means that the person of the judge should play as little a role as possible.

1.4 Methodology

Most chapters, especially the chapters on the case law analysis, provide a description of the methodological aspect of that specific part of the research. Some general comments can, however, be made at this stage, which explain the methodology behind this whole research project. The research project has been conducted in three stages.[48] Firstly, a legal theoretical analysis will be made of the selected interpretative methods and principles. Each of the selected interpretative aids will be discussed on the basis of theoretical literature. The requirements for a proper use of each method and the pitfalls of each method will be analyzed. This theoretical analysis will result in questions to be answered in the case law analysis, but also assumptions that will be tested in the case law analysis. The second stage is the case law analysis in which the use of the specific interpretative aid in practice will be discussed. The questions and assumptions developed in the theoretical analysis will form a guide for the case law analysis, but matters that attract attention outside these questions and assumptions will also be discussed. The final stage is the synthesis in which the results from the theoretical and case law analysis will be brought together. The case law analysis might fill gaps left open in the theoretical analysis, but the theoretical analysis might also help to provide solutions for problems encountered in the case law. In this final stage a comparison will also be made between the CJEU and the ECtHR. These courts might be able to learn from each other in enhancing their judicial reasoning. Finally, this synthesis will lead to suggestions for directions in which improvement of the use of the selected interpretative aids should be sought.

1.5 Outline

The methodology as just described has to a large extent determined the outline of this thesis. The first half of the book will be devoted to a theoretical analysis of interpretative aids. The second half of the book will address the case law analysis. Finally, the synthesis will address the results of both the theoretical and case law analysis.

---

47 See also Gerards (2002), § 1.3.

48 The methodology is based on an innovative methodological approach adopted in Gerards (2002) in a thesis concerning the principle of equality.

Before setting out the theoretical analysis, two chapters will provide an introduction to both the ECtHR (Chapter 2) and the CJEU (Chapter 3). This introduction will deal with the adjudicative climate in which these courts have to function. This helps to put the analyses presented in the remainder of the thesis into context. It may also be regarded as a discussion of the 'problematic' of these courts, a notion introduced by LASSER.[49] This notion refers to the fact that each court in its own way tries to deal with its institutional and constitutional challenges.[50] This 'problematic' influences the judicial reasoning of the court in question and as a result it is a relevant aspect to discuss in the context of this thesis.

The theoretical analysis will start with a chapter (Chapter 4) on regularly used interpretative aids. This introduction to different interpretation methods and principles will start with an explanation of the distinction between methods and principles that is used throughout this thesis. Subsequently, brief attention will be paid to a variety of interpretation methods and principles that frequently occur in the case law of both courts. The selected methods and principles will also be addressed. This chapter provides the basis for the ensuing discussion on the theoretical aspects of the four selected interpretative aids in Chapters 5 to 8.

The case law analysis is divided into a discussion of the case law of the ECtHR (in Chapters 9 to 12) and the CJEU (in Chapter 13). For both courts the selection of cases will be explained and the case law will be analyzed on the basis of the questions that have arisen in the theoretical chapter.

Finally a synthesis will try to put the findings into perspective and also try to compare the approaches by the two courts. Can anything be learned? In which areas should improvement be sought?

49 Lasser (2004).

50 See also Gerards (2009), p. 407.

Chapter 2
Context of legal argumentation in the European Court of Human Rights

The European Court of Human Rights is one of the courts closely examined in this thesis. In order to understand and put the discussion of the different interpretative aids used by the ECtHR in context, it is necessary to briefly discuss some general aspects of legal argumentation at the ECtHR.[1] After all, for a proper understanding of the discussion in the remainder of this thesis, it is relevant to have some background on the character of the European Convention and on the ECtHR, its style of reasoning and its position vis-à-vis the national Contracting States. These are general aspects that are not necessarily only relevant in an interpretative context, but can play a role in any discussion on the reasoning of the ECtHR or in other discussions on the ECtHR. These aspects will, however, be discussed from the angle taken in this thesis, namely the interpretation of fundamental rights.

First the character of the European Convention will be introduced, because this characterization has an important impact on the interpretation process adopted by the ECtHR. Secondly, the character of the ECtHR and its judgments will be discussed. The discussion touches upon wider issues, but the question whether the ECtHR can be seen as more constitutional or more aimed at individual justice can have an impact on the style of its argumentation. It is therefore relevant to briefly introduce this discussion as a background to the discussion in this thesis. Thirdly, the style of the judgments will be addressed. As will be seen in the discussion on the ECtHR and the CJEU, the style of their judgments impacts on the reasoning used in their judgments as well. Finally, in a supranational context it is necessary to discuss the relation with the Contracting States and see whether that relation influences the interpretation process by the ECtHR.

---

1 For a more elaborate background on the ECtHR, see for example: Van Dijk van Hoof (2006); Harris & O'Boyle & Warbrick (2009); Ovey & White (2010). See also Gerards (2009), who provides an elaborate background on judicial reasoning by the ECtHR.

2.1 Character of the European Convention

In one of the early judgments on the interpretation of the European Convention, the ECtHR qualified the European Convention as a law-making treaty.[2] This qualification is used to indicate the contrast with treaties that have a more contractual character.[3] One of the principal characteristics of a law-making treaty is that it is designed for a common aim and not designed to create reciprocal obligations.[4] The European Convention is thus designed to achieve the common aim of fundamental rights protection for individuals.

The distinction between more contractual treaties and law-making treaties has been discussed in the context of drafting the VCLT, but it was not considered necessary to include this distinction in the text of the VCLT.[5] Likewise in international legal doctrine not all agree on the relevance of this distinction,[6] but it cannot be denied that the ECtHR considers it relevant. The consequence of this qualification for the interpretation of the European Convention is that the object and purpose of the treaty play an important role in the interpretation of the European Convention.[7] Interpretation of the European Convention should lead to achieving the object and purpose of the European Convention and not lead to an interpretation that would limit the obligations for the Contracting Parties to the greatest possible degree.[8] The consequences of this qualification will be touched upon in the context of discussing the different interpretative aids later on in this thesis, but it is important to realize that it is an important qualification underlying the whole interpretation process of the European Convention.

2.2 ECtHR a constitutional court?

The question whether Strasbourg should be considered a constitutional court has been the subject of much debate.[9] Former president of the ECtHR Wildhaber argues that the ECtHR should by now be considered a constitutional court, or at least a quasi-

2 ECtHR, *Wemhoff v. Germany*, judgment of 27 June 1968, *Series* A No. 7.

3 See for example, Vanneste (2010), p. 58; Schokkenbroek (2000), p. 3; Matscher (1993), p. 66.

4 Vanneste (2010), p. 61.

5 Commentary to articles of Vienna Convention, Yearbook of International Law Commission, 1966-Vol. II, p. 219.

6 See Vanneste (2010), p. 58-60.

7 Schokkenbroek (2000), p. 3; Vanneste (2010), p. 66.

8 Schokkenbroek (2000), p. 3; Vanneste (2010), p. 66, both referring to ECtHR, *Wemhoff v. Germany*, judgment of 27 June 1968, *Series* A No. 7.

9 See for example Garlicki (2009), p. 390, who speaks of controversy surrounding this question. See also Wildhaber (2002) as one of the proponents of this position. See Jackson (2006), p. 777-778 for further references.

constitutional court.[10] GARLICKI takes a more modest stance and claims that there is a constitutional element in the function and the decision-making of the ECtHR.[11] In order to support this assumption he looks at the substance of the European Convention, which deals with fundamental rights often similar to those laid down in national constitutional documents. From a procedural perspective it is important that the ECtHR has been granted the power to adjudicate individual complaints. By means of this individual complaints mechanism the ECtHR has been able to explain the meaning of these often generally worded provisions. The meaning of the Convention should thus be sought in the case law, which has kept the Convention up-to-date and only to a limited extent in the text of the Convention itself. GARLICKI argues that national constitutional courts have been through similar developments and in this sense the ECtHR resembles a constitutional court more closely than traditional international courts.[12] Others have pointed to the remarks made by the ECtHR in its judgments calling the Convention a 'constitutional instrument for the European public order' in order to point to the constitutional character of the ECtHR.[13]

The debate on the question whether the ECtHR should be seen as a constitutional court does not primarily focus on the aspects mentioned above, but the real controversy lies in the question what type of justice should be provided by the ECtHR. Should constitutional justice be provided or should the primary focus be individual justice? This debate mainly gained attention in the process of drafting Protocol 14, which contains some reform measures to cope with the enormous workload of the ECtHR.[14] The question is whether the ECtHR should focus on the more important, more constitutional issues or whether the ECtHR should keep on dealing with all individual complaints. The question has even divided the judges of the ECtHR themselves.[15] Some argue that it is not realistic to expect the ECtHR with its current overload of cases to provide justice in each individual case and claim that the constitutional road is the only way to save the system from collapsing under its own success.[16] It has not only been suggested that a more constitutional approach is necessary to save the system, but also to save the quality and consistency of the Court's reasoning, which

10 Wildhaber (2002), p. 161.

11 Garlicki (2009), p. 390.

12 Garlicki (2009), p. 391.

13 Jackson (2006), p. 761 & 777. See also White (2009), p. 9, referring to case law, but also to interviews with ECtHR judges, where most judges could see at least some constitutional elements in the functioning of the ECtHR.

14 See for example: Greer (2008), p. 684-686 and especially Harmsen (2007), 35-41, for an overview of the different positions in the debate.

15 See Wildhaber (2002), p. 164, who argues for constitutional justice, but acknowledges that some of his fellow judges might not agree with this point of view. See Harmsen (2007), p. 38, who refers to a number of judges opposing the constitutional route.

16 Wildhaber (2002), p. 163; Mahoney (2002-2003).

suffers from the enormous workload.[17] In their view the ECtHR should be given the possibility to concentrate on 'major issues of policy, by curtailing, if not eliminating, the need to deal with certain categories of minor or repetitive violations at the European level'.[18] This view has partly succeeded with the introduction of the new admissibility criterion in Protocol 14, which provides that cases will be declared inadmissible where 'the applicant has not suffered a significant disadvantage, unless respect for human rights as defined in the Convention and the Protocols thereto requires an examination of the application on the merits and provided that no case may be rejected on this ground which has not been duly considered by a domestic tribunal'. Some degree of selection has thus been introduced by Protocol 14, but it provides only a limited possibility to select cases.

Proponents of individual justice argue that a curtailment of the fundamental feature of the system, namely the right of an individual to obtain a judgment of the ECtHR in their view constitutes an 'erosion of the protection of human rights',[19] which will have a strong negative impact in the newer Contracting States. In their view it will give the impression that certain issues are more important than others and that some violations can be tolerated.[20] Two remarks need to be made in response. Firstly, it seems wrong to claim that there is at the moment no hierarchy of rights within the Convention system. Often a distinction is made between violations and serious violations, the latter even being excluded from the qualification 'repetitive case'.[21] Moreover, the existence of non-derogable rights is already in itself a strong indication that some rights are considered more important than others. Secondly, with regard to the claim that a wrong signal will be sent to the newer states, it must be said that a more constitutional mission for the ECtHR does not end the states' obligations under Article 1 of the Convention. Even if the ECtHR will not decide on these violations the state is still under the obligation to provide redress. If a state fails to do so on a systematic basis this could lead the ECtHR to consider these cases of value for the effective protection of human rights and issue for example a pilot judgment,[22] thereby eliminating to a certain extent the fear of sending out the wrong signal. Moreover, one should not forget that the ECtHR does not operate in a vacuum. The whole

---

17 Mahoney (2002-2003).

18 Harmsen (2007), p. 36.

19 *Joint Response to Proposals to Ensure the Future Effectiveness of the European Court of Human Rights*, signed by 74 NGO's in March 2003. Response can be found at: http://web.amnesty.org/library/index/engior610082003.

20 CDDH-GDR(2003)024, 12 September 2003.

21 CM(2003)55, Addendum 2 (restricted), 14 April 2003, Proposal A1.

22 See Resolution Res(2004)3 of the Committee of Ministers of the Council of Europe. See also an information sheet by the registry of the ECtHR on the pilot judgment procedure available at: www.echr.coe.int under 'basic texts'. See also Buyse (2009) for a discussion of the pilot judgment procedure.

protection system of the Council of Europe has a role to play in order to achieve the highest level of protection.

The debate on the way forward for the ECtHR is not as black and white as it might seem from the discussion above. It is important to note that the debate concerns which of these two forms of justice should be emphasized and not whether one or the other should be abandoned.[23] The question is thus where to place the balance. That question does not need to be answered in this thesis. The purpose of showing the debate is the battle between the two functions of the ECtHR. In the current situation constitutional justice is most visible in the functioning of the Grand Chamber. The Grand Chamber will deal with cases selected by a panel of five judges if the case 'raises a serious question affecting the interpretation or application of the Convention or the Protocols thereto, or a serious issue of general importance'.[24] A case may also reach the Grand Chamber if a chamber relinquishes jurisdiction if the case raises a serious question the interpretation or application of the Convention, but also when the chamber fears that its judgment will deviate from earlier cases.[25] It is up to the Grand Chamber to determine whether it is necessary to overrule a previous precedent. The function of the Grand Chamber is to ensure uniformity and to decide the most complex and controversial cases.[26]

The five chambers of the ECtHR are much less engaged in constitutional justice. There are a few mechanisms that help to focus on the most important cases. On the one hand there is the new admissibility criterion that has been mentioned above that helps the Court to get rid of cases which have only minor significance both in terms of damage and in terms of fundamental rights. This provides, however, only a minor selection mechanism. On the other hand there is also the possibility of adopting a pilot judgment when a certain issue concerns many applicants. The respondent state will in such a case be obliged to adopt a national remedy for all applicants.[27] The applicants that have already reached Strasbourg will be obliged to resort to this national remedy first, unless this remedy turns out not to be sufficient.[28] This helps to prevent many repetitive cases in cases of structural problems. Not every repetitive issue is, however, suitable for a pilot judgment. Many cases, for example, concerning the length of their proceedings still reach Strasbourg.[29] Chambers are thus still to

23 Harmsen (2007), p. 41, points to the fact that even though the sharp debate might indicate otherwise, it is mainly a matter of where to place the balance.

24 Article 43 ECHR.

25 Article 30 ECHR.

26 Garlicki (2009), p. 395.

27 Rule 61 of the Rules of Court.

28 Rule 61 of the Rules of Court. For a description of the procedure, see supra note 65.

29 About one third of all violations in Strasbourg concern violations regarding the length of proceedings. See www.echr.coe.int under 'reports'.

a large extent concerned with providing individual redress in cases no matter whether they are minor or repetitive. Only in a small minority of cases can a chamber judgment focus on important interpretation or application issues that contribute to the development of the Convention.

This difference in focus between the Grand Chamber and the chambers is also reflected in their judgments. The judgments of the Grand Chamber can be more abstract and focus more on developing principles underlying the Convention and its provisions, which is more in line with constitutional justice.[30] The chamber judgments on the other hand, are often less abstract and focus more on the facts of the individual case as a result of which individual justice plays a more important role in this regard.[31] The following section will deal more in detail with the style of the judgments.

2.3 Style of judgment

In the more than 50 years since its inception the ECHR has developed its own style of reasoning and its own style of judgment. While other international courts, like the CJEU, have had a clear inspirational model, the ECtHR and its judgments have not been modelled on a particular national legal tradition. In the words of Garlicki the ECtHR and the Convention 'represent a merger of different traditions arising from different legal systems'.[32]

The ECtHR operates from a unified structure,[33] in contrast to the bifurcated structure of the CJEU.[34] The judicial discourse at the CJEU takes place in both the CJEU judgments and the opinion of the Advocate General. In the ECtHR there is only the judgment of the ECtHR and no position of Advocate General has been created. This unified structure is more common in Europe among national constitutional courts, than the bifurcated structure of the CJEU.[35] Each system, however, has its benefits and drawbacks, and it cannot be said that one system should be favoured over the other.

---

30 See for example Harris & O'Boyle & Warbrick, (2009), p. 18, who argue that the judgments of the Grand Chamber are more authoritive and only the Grand Chamber is allowed to overrule precedent and thus develop the principles under the Convention.

31 Gerards (2009), p. discusses the strong case-by-case approach of the ECtHR.

32 Garlicki (2009), p. 391.

33 Since 1998 the entry into force of Protocol 11 when the permanent court was installed and the European Commission on Human Rights was abolished.

34 Terminology from Lasser (2004). Garlicki (2009), p. 391-392, points to an internal dualist structure within the ECtHR, where the Registry plays an important role in the preparation of the judgments, but this is rather different from the bifurcation in the CJEU.

35 Garlicki (2009), p. 389-390.

The ECtHR is generally known for its elaborate judgments.[36] In repetitive cases or cases where only a minor issue plays a role, the judgments can, however, be rather succinct.[37] Even though the ECtHR must address all the admissible complaints there is a tendency to spend relatively more time and effort on the cases that deal with important issues or that contribute to development of the case law on the Convention.[38] GARLICKI implies that the elaborative style is born out of the wish to convince and engage national courts and national authorities, since that is the key to successful implementation of the Convention.[39]

An important feature of the ECtHR judgments is that judges are allowed to write separate opinions, either dissenting of concurring.[40] The majority opinion of the judgment is the result of a collegial decision-making process, in which the minority is allowed to express a separate opinion.[41] As a result the majority opinions suffer to a lesser extent from the need to reach an agreement with all judges, which might result in vague and opaque reasoning.[42] The style of the ECtHR judgments is, however, not similar to that of the United Kingdom Supreme Court, where each justice writes his or her own opinion. The disadvantage of having to reach some sort of consensus in the majority opinion is, thus, not entirely negated in the Strasbourg judgments. The main difference between the majority opinion and the dissenting or separate opinions is its tone. In a dissenting or separate opinion a judge is not constrained by trying to find agreement with fellow judges. A dissenting or separate opinion is therefore often of a much more personal tone than the majority opinions.

By allowing dissenting and separate opinions and by revealing the votes cast in favour or against a violation the ECtHR aims to be transparent about its decision-making.[43] The majority is forced to express itself clearly and provide reasons for its decision, because the separate or dissenting opinions can reveal the controversial issues in an opinion.[44] The possibility of these separate opinions in itself thus provides an interesting tool to enhance judicial reasoning,[45] because if both opinions are published the disagreement will become visible to the outside world. In order to convince this outside world, especially the majority opinion will aim to provide a solid reasoning for its contested conclusions. WHITE and BOUSSIAKOU, relying on

36 Ost (1992), p. 284; Garlicki (2009), p. 391.
37 Garlicki (2009), p. 395.
38 Garlicki (2009), p. 395.
39 Garlicki (2009), p. 394.
40 Article 45 ECHR.
41 White (2009), p. 176.
42 Thomassen (2006), p. 686; Mertens & Vermeulen (2008), p. 52 & 60.
43 White (2009), p. 178; Garlicki (2009), p. 395. In decisions there is no such transparency. In decisions it is only indicated whether the decision was reached by majority or unanimity.
44 Thomassen (2006), p. 686; Mertens & Vermeulen (2008), p. 52 & 60.
45 Thomassen (2006), p. 686; Mertens & Vermeulen (2008), p. 52 & 60.

LASSER'S terminology, refer to this model as the publicly argumentative model.[46] In LASSER's view the legitimacy of this type of argumentative model 'stands or falls in large measure on the logic and argumentation of the signed judgment'.[47] OST similarly argues that dissenting opinions do not undermine the authority and credibility of the judgment, but, if properly reasoned, even reinforce it. In his view if opinions are well reasoned the authority of the judgment will result from 'its intrinsic rationality rather than from an "argument" of authority'.[48] This emphasis on proper reasoning for the legitimacy of the ECtHR makes it even more important to analyze the judicial reasoning of the ECtHR.

2.4 SUBSIDIARITY

In the process of interpretation an important factor that should not be left out of sight is the place of the ECtHR in the European legal landscape. The focus hereby is not so much on the often debated relation between the CJEU and the ECtHR regarding the protection of fundamental rights, but on the relation between the European supranational court and the national authorities.

This relation between the supranational and national authorities has been codified at different places in the European Convention. Articles 1 and 13 provide the duty for national authorities to ensure (at domestic level) the protection of fundamental rights for everyone within their jurisdiction and, in case of an interference, an effective (domestic) remedy. Moreover Article 35, which together with Article 34 provides the criteria for admissibility in Strasbourg, emphasizes the duty for the applicant to first allow the state to find a solution at national level and only as a last resort to proceed to the ECtHR. These provisions reflect the subsidiary nature of the European Convention system by emphasizing the primary role of the Contracting States themselves. Despite the fact that this principle of subsidiarity has not been expressly mentioned in any of the provisions, it has been developed in the case law on the basis of the above mentioned articles.[49]

What does this principle of subsidiarity entail? This is a difficult question to answer due to the fact that the principle has not been explicitly laid down in the European Convention. The principle dates back to the 16th century and was introduced by the Catholic Church. Generally this principle refers to the division of powers between the larger unit and its components; 'the larger unit should assume responsibil-

46 White (2009), p. 178.

47 White (2009), p. 178, quoting Lasser (2004), p. 338.

48 Ost (1992), p. 284.

49 According to Petzold the principle was not even referred to in the discussions leading up to the drafting and adoption of the Convention. Petzold (1993), p. 42. Vande Lanotte (2005), p. 180.

ity for functions only insofar as the smaller unit is unable to do so'.[50] Within the context of the Convention it means that on the one hand this principle determines the 'procedural relationship' between the national authorities and the ECtHR and on the other hand it provides a limit on the ECtHR in exercising its supervisory function. These two functions are clearly visible in the case law of the court and reflect important underlying features of the Convention system. First of all, the Convention is not intended to be exhaustive; it provides a minimum level of protection.[51] Secondly, the ECtHR considers the national authorities to be in a better position 'to strike the balance between the interests of the community and the protection of individual interests'.[52] In these types of cases the ECtHR will only marginally review the acts of the national authorities as it cannot replace these domestic authorities. Finally, according to some authors the purpose of the European Convention is not to achieve uniformity.[53] The European Convention provides a minimum level of protection and States are at liberty to provide a higher level of protection.[54] Contracting States also have discretion with regard to the way they achieve the minimum level of protection.

Are these assumptions also valid for the interpretation process? The differentiation between the Contracting States and the room left for policy or other choices mainly plays a role in the application phase. The interpretation phase often leads to more uniformity as explained in the introductory chapter.[55] This does not leave the short discussion above irrelevant. Even though the principle of subsidiarity might not play an explicit role in the interpretation process, these features of the Convention system do have an impact on the relationship between the national authorities and the ECtHR and that relation does play a role in the interpretation process. It explains why the ECtHR cannot boldly opt for an extensive interpretation of a certain right: the multilevel setting needs to be taken into account and the fact that the ECHR plays a subsidiary role is relevant in that context.

2.5 Conclusion

The aim of this short chapter has been to provide a background to the discussion in this thesis, which will focus on the interpretation process. The discussion of the ECtHR has by no means been limitative – many more aspects can be discussed – but these are the most important aspects to keep in mind when reading the remainder of this

50 Petzold (1993), p. 41. Vande Lanotte (2005), p. 180.
51 Article 53 ECHR under which Contracting States may provide a higher level of protection.
52 Petzold (1993), p. 60. Vande Lanotte (2005), p. 180.
53 Petzold (1993), p. 60. Vande Lanotte (2005), p. 180.
54 Article 53 ECHR.
55 See also Vanneste (2010), p. 215.

thesis. The characterization as a law-making treaty is important for the interpretation by the ECtHR, because it has led to the focus on the object and purpose as will be discussed in the following chapters as well. The constant struggle of the ECtHR between general standard setting and providing individual relief is, furthermore, important, because this is reflected in the style of the judgments. In addition, it might explain the more individual and less abstract approach in many of the judgments. Furthermore, the specific style of the judgments, in which dissenting and separate opinions are allowed, also impact on the judicial reasoning. Finally, subsidiarity is more indirectly relevant to the discussion on the interpretation of fundamental rights. It reminds the ECtHR that it operates in a multilevel setting and that it needs the cooperation of the Contracting states.

The following chapters will first provide a theoretical analysis of different interpretative aids. These aids will be analyzed from a general perspective, but also in the context of the ECtHR and CJEU. The case law analysis will focus in more detail on the practice of the ECtHR and the CJEU in using the selected interpretative aids. Before the theoretical and case law analysis, however, an introduction to the CJEU will be provided in the following chapter.

CHAPTER 3
CONTEXT OF LEGAL ARGUMENTATION IN FUNDAMENTAL RIGHTS CASES FOR THE COURT OF JUSTICE OF THE EUROPEAN UNION

The other court that will be closely studied in this thesis is the Court of Justice of the European Union. The focus will be on the reasoning of the CJEU in fundamental rights cases. In order to fully appreciate the analysis of the CJEU case law that will be provided in the course of this thesis, it is necessary to sketch the context of the legal argumentation of the CJEU. Much has already been written on the CJEU and the development of its fundamental rights case law. This chapter does not aim to summarize all the existing materials.[1] Rather, the purpose of the discussion in this chapter is to highlight those elements that may help put the analysis given in this thesis in the relevant context.

Two aspects are particularly relevant when analyzing the reasoning of the CJEU in fundamental rights cases. Firstly, the role of the CJEU in introducing fundamental rights into the then European Community needs to be addressed. In this discussion attention should also be paid to the more recent developments with regard to fundamental rights in the European Union. Secondly, the argumentative style of the CJEU more in general needs to be explored. This may help one to understand the reasoning of the CJEU in fundamental rights cases. In Chapter 4 a general discussion of the interpretative aids that play a role before the CJEU will provide even more context for the reasoning with regard to the specific interpretative aids that will be studied in this thesis. That chapter will address the different interpretation methods and principles that play a role before the CJEU. By discussing the different interpretative aids that play a role it will be possible to explain more in depth which methods and principles have been chosen for further analysis in this thesis.

---

1 See, among others, on the role of the CJEU in introducing fundamental rights: Craig & De Burca, 2007, chapter 11; De Witte (1999), p. 859-897; Blanke (2006), p. 265-277; Mancini (2000), p., 81-95; Coppel & O'Neill (1992), p. 669-692; Weiler & Lockhart (1995), p. 51-94 & 579-627; Tizzano (2008), p. 125-138; Jacobs (2001), p. 331-341. See furthermore for a discussion of the CJEU among others: Brown & Kennedy (2000); Arnull (2006).

3.1 The CJEU and Fundamental Rights

The story on how fundamental rights found their way into European Union law has been told many times already.[2] It is, however, worth recalling summarily the different stages of the development of fundamental rights in the EU context, focusing on those elements that are of specific interest for the ensuing discussion on the interpretation of fundamental rights by the CJEU. The discussion will also focus on the recent developments in the area of fundamental rights as a result of the entry into force of the Treaty of Lisbon.

The founding treaties of the European Communities did not include a reference to the protection of fundamental rights in general as it was thought that the European Communities were mainly an economic entity with no implications for fundamental rights.[3] The treaties, however, did include a few provisions referring to the right to non-discrimination on the basis of nationality and the right to equal pay for men and women.[4] The division of competences was clear in the sense that the aim of the European Convention on Human Rights was to protect against fundamental rights violations and the aim of the European Communities was to promote economic integration.[5] The fact that these themes could partly overlap at some point in the future, was not anticipated at that time. Already quite soon, however, changes in this attitude became visible. Not long after the CJEU had confirmed the supremacy of the then EC legal order,[6] the CJEU started to change its attitude towards recognizing fundamental rights as part of the EC legal order.[7] In the well-known case of *Stauder*, the CJEU for the first time acknowledged that fundamental rights formed part of the

---

2 See authors mentioned in supra note 1 and in addition see, among others: Alston (1999); Kühling (2006), p. 501-547; McCrudden (2002), p. 1-26.

3 Jacobs (2001), p. 332; Siskova (2008), p. 7. Craig & De Burca suggest that this was a reaction to the failure of establishing a far-reaching European Political Community, Craig & De Burca (2008), p. 380. Mancini (2000), p. 82-83, refers to an explanation given by Weiler, according to which the Member States did not want to include a bill of rights in the original treaties as that would have 'constituted an invitation to extend the powers of the central authorities to the very limits of those rights'. Mancini argues that the Member States did not want to become a victim of this power extending tendency.

4 Tizzano (2008), p. 126 points to these specific rights that were included in the treaties from the outset. The relevance of these rights in an economic union is perhaps at first sight more apparent, rather than the relevance of many other fundamental rights.

5 Jacobs (2001), p. 332; Siskova (2008), p. 7.

6 C-26/62, *NV Algemene Transport- en Expeditie Onderneming van Gend & Loos v. Netherlands Inland Revenue Administration* [1963] ECR 1; C-6/64, *Flaminio Costa v. E.N.E.L* [1964] ECR 585.

7 Kühling (2006), p. 504-505; Rainer (2008), p. 28.

general principles of Community law.[8] This position was later firmly grounded in *Internationale Handelsgesellschaft* and it has been often repeated in subsequent cases.[9] What is interesting in the context of this thesis is that the multilevel nature of the EC legal order played an important role at this stage of the recognition of fundamental rights by the CJEU. The decisions in which the CJEU announced the supremacy of Community law, in combination with the low level of attention to fundamental rights protection at the then European Community level, triggered critical reactions by national constitutional courts.[10] National constitutional courts expressed concerns about the insufficient protection of fundamental rights, while this protection was sufficiently afforded at the national level. As a result, acceptance of the supremacy of EC law would, in the eyes of these national constitutional courts, entail acceptance of a lower level of protection for individuals under this EC regime. Consequently, these constitutional courts in their judgments were reluctant to accept the supremacy of the EC as long as the protection at the EC level did not meet their approval.[11] In order to safeguard the supremacy of Community law the CJEU thus had to enhance the protection of fundamental rights in order to gain support at the national level.[12] Through the judgments of the CJEU the fundamental rights doctrine of the CJEU started to take shape and the interpretation of fundamental rights by the CJEU became more influential. While, at first, national and scholarly concerns focused on the insufficient protection of fundamental rights, as a result of the development of fundamental rights protection by the CJEU, these concerns in more recent times have sometimes even shifted in the opposite direction. According to CAROZZA, these worries consist of fear that the EU fundamental rights law 'could become broad enough to

8 C-29/69, *Erich Stauder v City of Ulm – Sozialamt* [169] ECR 419, p. 425.

9 C-11/70, *Internationale Handelsgesellschaft mbH v. Einfuhr- und Vorratsstelle für Getreide und Futtermittel* [1970] ECR 01125.

10 The challenges were mainly made in Germany and Italy. See for example: Mancini (2000), p. 84-86; Carozza (2004), p. 37; Coppel & O'Neill (1992), p. 670; Lenaerts & De Smijter (2001), p. 276; Kühling (2006), p. 504-505; Siskova (2008), p. 7; Craig & De Burca (2008), p. 381; Blanke (2006), p. 266-267; De Witte (1999), p. 863. De Witte refers to a second explanation why the CJEU had to address questions concerning fundamental rights, namely the 'Community's growing capacity to affect fundamental rights to an extent unforeseen at the time the European Communities were created'. De Witte (1999), p. 866.

11 The most famous judgments in this respect were handed down by the constitutional courts of Germany and Italy in the early 70s after the initial judgments by the CJEU recognizing the protection of fundamental rights. Mancini (2000), p. 85. He also refers to the fact that the German constitutional court already in the late 60s before the first fundamental rights judgments by the CJEU expressed concerns about the protection of fundamental rights within the EC.

12 Weiler (1999), p. 107-108.

constrain the otherwise constitutionally permissible choices of the Member States and therefore unduly interfere with their autonomy and sovereignty'.[13]

Thus, the CJEU constantly has to operate between these two concerns, a phenomenon which has been qualified as a manifestation of the more generally 'ambivalent constitutionalism', which lies at the core of the European Union.[14] The exercise in finding a balance between the two concerns by the CJEU necessitates the need for sound argumentation, among others, when interpreting fundamental rights.[15] Given the important role that argumentation plays in convincing all actors concerned that the CJEU has found a proper balance between harmonization and diversity, a close examination of the use of a number of interpretation methods is warranted in this context.

Apart from the fact that the development of the fundamental rights doctrine has created the tension mentioned above, the fundamental rights development in the EU is important from another perspective as well. After all, the development can also lead to changes in case law, legislation and legal practice at the national level. Member States can even be forced to provide protection in areas where their national constitutions do not offer protection. The influence within the area of fundamental rights thus works both ways. The Member States, mostly the national constitutional courts, keep the CJEU alert to provide a sufficient level of protection. In turn, the CJEU can bring about change in the fundamental rights protection at the national level. This dialogue between the CJEU and national courts within the field of fundamental rights thus is a good example of the mutual influences between legal orders at different levels and it provides an interesting background for the analysis in this thesis.

The fact that the influence of fundamental rights works both ways can perhaps partly be explained by the fact that, throughout the years, the CJEU has expanded the reach of its fundamental rights doctrine to cover also actions by Member States. In the early years fundamental rights mainly played a role in proceedings challenging EC legislation or administrative measures by the EC. This could involve challenges to directives or regulations, but also challenges to the actions of the Commission in, for example, staff cases.[16] Challenges to administrative acts of the EC often con-

---

13 Carozza (2004), p. 38.

14 Carozza (2004), p. 38, referring to contributions of De Burca and Eeckhout, which discuss the ambivalent character of constitutionalism at the EU level. He argues that the debate is not about human rights *per se*, but about finding the proper balance between human rights protection at the European level and respecting the autonomy of the Member States.

15 Weiler (1999), p. 102, in this context discusses the fact that fundamental rights protection in a multilevel system can be a unifying force, but also a source of tension. The meaning of fundamnetal rights often differs by country and given that fundamental rights concern fundamental (moral) values, the definition of fundamental rights by the CJEU can be a source of tension. Moreover, it may feed suspicion of extending the jurisdiction of the CJEU.

16 See for a more detailed account: Craig & De Burca (2008), p. 389 et seq.

cerned acts of the Commission in competition proceedings.[17] In subsequent years the CJEU extended the scope of fundamental rights to cover not only actions by the European institutions.[18] The CJEU held that Member States are also bound by EU fundamental rights when they are acting 'within the scope of application of EC law'.[19] This means, among others, that Member States are required to respect EU fundamental rights when applying and implementing EU law.[20] Also when Member States derogate from EU law they are bound to respect fundamental rights. Does the fact that fundamental rights apply to both EU actions and actions of the Member States matter for the interpretative process? Is the interpretation to be given a different one when it concerns the interpretation of a fundamental right that is applied by a Member State or by one of the EU institutions? Although the specific actor may be relevant in the adjudicative background as a whole, since it does determine the context in which a decision is made, for the interpretation of a specific fundamental right it will probably not matter. Even when it concerns the actions by Member States the CJEU is interpreting *EU* fundamental rights, and the meaning of these fundamental rights is the same for the whole EU. The application of these rights, as distinguished from their interpretation (see Chapter 1 above), on the other hand, might depend on the specific context in which the rights are applied.[21]

For another reason, the specific character of the fundamental rights development in the EU legal system is relevant as well. Given the fact that no references were made to fundamental rights in the original treaties, the CJEU had to find a different basis to introduce fundamental rights within the existing situation. General principles of Community law provided an opening for the CJEU to read fundamental rights into the then Community system. National constitutional traditions, the European Convention on Human Rights and other international instruments formed sources of inspiration for establishing these unwritten principles.[22] What these sources mean and how the CJEU invoked these sources, will be explained in detail in the chapter on the analysis of the case law of the CJEU.

---

17 See Craig & De Burca (2008), p. 391-394.

18 Coppel & O'Neill distinguish in this context between the defensive use of fundamental rights, which the CJEU did in its early years when this doctrine only applied to Community acts and offensive use of fundamental rights, which encompasses extending the scope of fundamental rights to acts of Member States as well. See Coppel & O'Neill (1992), p. 673.

19 Craig & De Burca (2008), p. 395.

20 See Craig & De Burca (2008), p. 395 et seq for an overview.

21 See Gerards (2011), on the intensity of review by the CJEU.

22 Blanke (2006), p. 267; Craig & De Burca (2008), p. 383; Siskova (2008), p. 8.

The CJEU had played a pioneering role[23] in the area of fundamental rights for two decades when, in the 1992 Treaty of Maastricht, the Member States decided to codify the practice of the CJEU.[24] The Treaty of Maastricht, by which also the EU was established, provided in Article F that the EU shall respect fundamental rights 'as guaranteed by the European Convention for the Protection of Human Rights and Fundamental Freedoms signed in Rome on 4 November 1950 and as they result from the constitutional traditions common to the Member States, as general principles of Community law'.[25] The subsequent Treaty of Amsterdam (1998), which changed the numbering to Article 6 instead of Article F, added that the EU 'is founded on the principles of liberty, democracy, respect for human rights and fundamental freedoms, and the rule of law, principles which are common to the Member States'.[26] With the ratification of Article F EU, later Article 6 EU, fundamental rights have been explicitly recognized by the Member States as forming part of the EU legal order. Problematic is that the formula of Article 6 EU, which is based on the case law, is rather open ended. JACOBS has argued that the provision, despite certain positive aspects, lacks legal certainty since, for example, it does not clarify which rights or which traditions shall be respected.[27] In this context, BESSELINK has pointed to problems concerning the limitations of the various principles mentioned, when no limitations clauses have been provided for.[28] The open ended nature of this provision is important in the context of interpretation, since it leaves much room for the CJEU to define and interpret fundamental rights. As a result, it is even more important for the CJEU to provide sound reasoning to support its interpretation in fundamental rights cases in order to guard itself against losing authority due to non-transparent judicial interpretation. The question whether the CJEU does meet the expectations in this

---

23 Jacobs (2001), p. 340, cites a report in which reference is made to the pioneering work of the CJEU. See for a critical discussion of the role of the CJEU in these first decades, the discussion between Coppel & O'Neill on the one side and Weiler & Lockhart on the other side: Coppel & O'Neill (1992), p. 669; Weiler & Lockhart (1995), p. 51 & 579.

24 Earlier reference to fundamental rights was made in the preamble to the Single European Act, which provides: 'Determined to work together to promote democracy on the basis of the fundamental rights recognized in the constitutions and laws of the Member States, in the Convention for the Protection of Human Rights and Fundamental Freedoms and the European Social Charter, notably freedom, equality and social justice.' In 1977 the European Parliament, Council and Commission formulated a joint declaration in which they recognized the importance of fundamental rights and the sources of fundamental rights as recognized by the CJEU (OJ 1977/C 103/1). See also: Dörte Hempfing (2004), p. 14; Lenaerts & De Smijter (2001), p. 275

25 Article F (2), Treaty of Maastricht, 1992.

26 Article 6(1) Treaty of Amsterdam.

27 Jacobs (2001), p. 339.

28 Besselink (1998), p. 635.

respect and provides a sufficient explanation for its interpretative choices will be discussed in the case law analysis in Chapter 13.

A significant step forward in granting more visibility to fundamental rights in the EU has been the drafting of the EU Charter of Fundamental Rights.[29] The Charter also aimed to increase the legitimacy of the EU by introducing its own bill of rights.[30] Initially the Charter was not binding and the significance was limited to the political level. As a result of the entry into force of the Lisbon Treaty, the Charter has been given the same status as the treaties. By now, thus, the Charter has been granted a legally binding status. This means that the Charter from now on really is one of the starting points for the CJEU when dealing with fundamental rights cases. In the context of interpretation the existence of the text might play an important role. Before the existence of the Charter, the CJEU often made references to its own case law precedents. Whenever the CJEU considered it necessary to deviate from established precedent, it either had to provide a proper reasoning to justify a different outcome or distinguish the case on the basis of the factual situation. Of course this put a certain burden on the CJEU to argue carefully, but generally it did not prove to be too difficult to argue that the factual situations in two separate cases were different. In this regard, it is important that it has been argued by some scholars that courts are subject to a 'higher argumentative burden' when they have to base their reasoning on binding legal texts instead of solely on legal precedents.[31] This assertion is based on the assumption that all the words in the relevant legal text have 'the force of law and will not be presumed as a coincidental creature of law'.[32] Of course, broadly formulated fundamental rights provisions still leave much room for courts and thereby somewhat diminish the argumentative burden, but even such broad provisions have a limit to their scope. In that sense the fact that the Charter has become binding will clearly play a role in the CJEU's interpretative process.

A relevant question that can be posed in this respect is to what extent the text of the Charter can potentially increase the argumentative burden for the CJEU. To be able to answer this question it is necessary to take a closer look at the wording of the provisions entered into the Charter. The text of the Charter as approved in 2000[33] consists of a wide range of fundamental rights.[34] Most of these rights do not contain any innovation as to the existing situation before the adoption of the

29 Lenaerts & De Smijter (2001), p. 273; Weiler (2000), p. 95.

30 See Conclusions of the European Council in Cologne 3 and 4 June 1999, Annex IV (150/99 REV 1).

31 See Lutzhoeft (2009), p. 11.

32 Lutzhoeft (2009), p. 11. He claims that even if this assertion 'is false, words still call for a definition which tends to be abstract and general, thereby going beyond mere case-to case reasoning'.

33 The text was reaffirmed in 2007 with some slight modifications in some procedural provisions (OJ 2007/C 303/01). This modified version became binding in 2009 (OJ 2010/C 83/02).

34 See De Burca (2001) on the drafting process of the Charter.

Charter,[35] but represent a codification of the existing situation. The preamble also hints in this direction by speaking of 'reaffirming' rights.[36] For many rights it is indeed true that they either resemble rights contained in the European Convention on Human Rights or rights recognized in the constitutional traditions of the Member States or rights already recognized in the case law of the CJEU. What is important to note is that the wording of the Charter rights is not the same as the wording of, for example, the European Convention.[37] According to LENAERTS & DE SMIJTER the drafting of the Convention has taken 'over the basic idea behind fundamental rights states in well-known texts, but without actually copying the latter'.[38] The new and often updated description of these rights has become even more open-ended than fundamental rights provisions generally are.[39] Within the interpretative context the broad framing of these rights might put only a limited argumentative burden, as discussed above, on the CJEU to explain its reasoning in the light of the text of the Charter.

Even though the broad framing of the Charter might not make it very difficult for the CJEU to argue one way or the other, this of course does not mean that there are no other factors forcing the CJEU to explain itself properly. The introductory chapter already indicated that the multilevel background increases the need for sound judicial reasoning. Even though the CJEU in its early judgments pronounced the autonomy of the EU legal order and its supremacy, this does not mean that its judgments are always automatically implemented by national authorities.[40] With each judgment the CJEU thus needs to convince national authorities and gain respect for its judgment. In that respect it is necessary that the CJEU explains clearly how it has reached a specific conclusion. The point here is, however, to show the potentially limited influence of the Charter on the interpretation process in terms of the textual interpretation and the resulting need to use other interpretative aids, such as will be discussed in Chapter 4 below.

---

35 Reich (2005), p. 217, refers to the fact that in the field of solidarity rights the Charter does contain some innovations.

36 See Reich (2005), p. 217.

37 See Lenaerts & De Smijter (2001), p. 281; White (2008), p. 147-148

38 See Lenaerts & De Smijter (2001), p. 281.

39 Lenaerts & De Smijter (2001), p. 282, refer to this new formulation as unconditional and unlimited. See also White (2008), p. 147-148. Article 2 of the EU Charter provides a good example of the open ended character of the Charter rights:
Article 2:
Right to life
1. Everyone has the right to life.
2. No one shall be condemned to the death penalty, or executed.

40 Supra note 9 (Chapter 1).

3.2 The CJEU and the ECHR

Thus, it is clear that fundamental rights have gradually become more prominent at the EU stage. This increasing attention for the protection of fundamental rights within the EU has important consequences for the relation of the EU with the European Convention on Human Rights. In section 3.1 it was mentioned that at their inception the existence of both a Council of Europe and the then European Communities were not considered to result in any significant overlap. This perception has changed dramatically over the years. Especially now that the Charter has become binding, the question on the relation between the EU and the European Convention becomes increasingly more relevant. In 1999 Spielmann argued that the EU had entered into competition with the Council of Europe when it came to fundamental rights.[41] As a result, the relationship between the EU and the ECHR is rather complicated. Already quite early in the process of developing fundamental rights the CJEU has accorded a special status to the European Convention.[42] In the subsequent codification of the practice of the CJEU in Article 6 TEU, the special status of the European Convention as a source of inspiration was retained by the Member States. The European Convention has also served as a source of inspiration for the EU Charter. This is reflected in the Council decision[43] that provided for the creation of the Charter and in the preamble to the Charter itself, which provides:

> This Charter reaffirms, with due regard for the powers and tasks of the Community and the Union and the principle of subsidiarity, the rights as they result, in particular, from the constitutional traditions and international obligations common to the Member States, the Treaty on the European Union, the Community Treaties, the European Convention for the Protection of Human Rights and Fundamental Freedoms, the Social Charters adopted by the Community and by the Council of Europe and the case-law of the Court of Justice of the European Communities and of the European Court of Human Rights.[44]

The Charter moreover provides in Article 52(3) that the rights in the Charter which correspond with Convention rights shall be given the same meaning as in the Convention context. Lock has posed the question whether this provision should be interpreted to mean that the case law of the ECtHR has become binding on the CJEU.[45] If that

41 Spielmann (1999), p. 760.

42 See, for more detail, Chapter 13 on the case law analysis.

43 Conclusions of the European Council in Cologne 3 and 4 June 1999, Annex IV (150/99 REV 1).

44 Preamble of EU Charter of Fundamental Rights.

45 Lock (2009), p. 383-387. See also: Hempfing (2004). Mancini (2000), p. 90-91, refers to authors on both sides of the discussion. In his view the majority considers the European Convention to be an integral part of Community law. The problem is, when comparing these views, that some refer to the case law of the ECHR and some only to the Convention.

were the case, a hierarchy between the two courts would have been created, with the ECtHR at the top of that hierarchy.[46] He elaborately argues that the ECtHR case law is an interpretative aid for the CJEU when interpreting the Charter, but if it should have been considered binding, he argues that it would have been expressly provided for by the Member States.[47] LENAERTS & DE SMIJTER come to a different conclusion and claim that the case law of the ECtHR has become 'an integral part of the meaning and scope of these rights'[48] and that, as a result, the CJEU is obliged to follow the ECtHR case law. They, however, do not address the consequences that this would have for the relationship between these two courts. Apart from the more political consequences in terms of status, an obligation to follow the case law of the ECtHR would have quite an impact on the interpretative process before the CJEU. Others again consider the CJEU not to be bound by the ECtHR case law, unless the EU accedes to the European Convention.[49] In their view both courts are regarded as co-existing equals.[50] This status of mutually respecting courts has been confirmed by the ECtHR in its *Bosphorus* jurisprudence.[51] The ECtHR acknowledged that the level of fundamental rights protection in the EU is equivalent to that under the Convention.[52] As the ECtHR indicates in its judgment, 'equivalent' means comparable and not identical.[53] The CJEU is thus allowed (within the boundaries of 'equivalent') to give its own interpretation and it is not obliged to strictly follow the Strasbourg case law, at least according to the ECtHR.

---

46 Lock (2009), p. 383.

47 Lock (2009), p. 386-387.

48 Lenaerts & De Smijter (2001), p. 99.

49 See for example: Jacobs (2007), p. 208; Douglas-Scott (2006); Hempfing (2004); Reich (2005), p. 220, claiming that Lenaerts & De Smijter exaggerate.

50 Lock (2009), p. 386. See also: Douglas-Scott (2006).

51 See Lock (2009), p. 380. In the case of ECtHR (GC), *Bosphorus HavaYollari Turizm Ve Ticaret Anonim Śirketi v. Ireland*, judgment of 30 June 2005, *Reports* 2005-VI, the ECtHR addressed the responsibility of Member States for powers transferred to international organizations. The ECtHR held that if Member States act under obligations from an international organization this might be justified if that organization provides equivalent protection for human rights (equivalent to the protection under the Convention). The ECtHR also held that the EU provided this equivalent protection. If no equivalent protection is provided, the Member States will be held responsible under the European Convention.

52 ECtHR, 30 June 2005, ECtHR (GC), *Bosphorus HavaYollari Turizm Ve Ticaret Anonim Śirketi v. Ireland*, judgment of 30 June 2005, *Reports* 2005-VI, § 165.

53 ECtHR (GC), *Bosphorus HavaYollari Turizm Ve Ticaret Anonim Śirketi v. Ireland*, judgment of 30 June 2005, *Reports* 2005-VI, § 155.

Finally, it is interesting to note that the institutional relation between these courts is a purely informal one at the time of writing of this thesis.[54] The relationship, as has been said above, might be formalized in the near future now that the entry into force of both Protocol 14 on the side of the European Convention and the Treaty of Lisbon on the side of the EU have made accession of the EU to the European Convention possible. Discussions on the institutional aspects of this accession are already taking place at a political level, amongst others, in the European Parliament.[55] The exact shape of this future accession is not clear at the time of writing, but the chances that it will happen, after some unsuccessful attempts in the past, have significantly increased with the acceptance of these two documents.

It is important to keep this complex and changing relationship between these two Courts in mind as a background to the discussion in this thesis, because it does determine the multilevel context in which both Courts have to adjudicate. It is, however, questionable whether the potential accession of the EU to the ECHR will have a direct impact on the use of the interpretation methods and principles by the CJEU.

3.3 Argumentation by the CJEU

As a background to the discussion in this thesis on the reasoning of the CJEU in fundamental rights cases, it is useful to have some understanding of the reasoning of this court in general. For that reason, this section will address the CJEU's style of reasoning, its main argumentative techniques and some elements that determine the argumentative context. In Chapter 4, closer attention will be paid to the interpretation methods and principles used by the CJEU. Therefore, this section will merely serve as an introduction. Its aim is to discuss a number of aspects that determine the context in which the CJEU has to operate.

National courts, be they constitutional courts, supreme courts or any other type of court, develop their style of reasoning within a specific legal tradition in a national setting. Their style will thus be heavily influenced by the context of that specific country. The CJEU had to develop a style of reasoning as a European court in an organization composed of Member States, which have different legal traditions and, as a result, different styles of judicial reasoning.[56] This not only influences the legal

54 Douglas-Scott (2006), p. 652. One element of this informal relationship is the visits by a delegation from one of the courts to another court. See www.echr.coe.int under the heading 'official visits'. The last visit took place in January 2011 when a delegation from Strasbourg visited the CJEU.

55 See: Draft report on the institutional aspects of the accession of the European Union to the European Convention for the Protection of Human Rights and Fundamental Freedoms (2009/2241(INI)).

56 See for example: Due (1999), p. 73-74.

argumentative methods used by the CJEU itself, but it also has the effect of making the CJEU vulnerable to criticism.[57]

In its search for a suitable judicial style, it is clear that the CJEU has been strongly influenced by the continental and more particularly the French way of judicial reasoning.[58] This French influence can be seen by two related characteristics, namely the style of the judgments of the CJEU and the existence of an Advocate General.[59] Judgments by the CJEU are rather brief and succinctly reasoned.[60] This is especially visible if its cases are compared to judgments of highest courts in other legal traditions, like that of the United Kingdom.[61] Although the CJEU has moved away from extremely terse (single sentence) judgments over the years, its judgments have remained rather brief.[62] In particular, the judgments often lack an elaborate reasoning by the CJEU in a particular case. In the context of the interpretation of fundamental rights this has been noted in particular by VON BOGDANDY, who has criticized the lack of reasoning on *why* certain rights are really recognized by the CJEU.[63]

To some extent, this brevity is compensated by the more elaborate reasoning of the Advocate General.[64] The role of Advocate General, according to Article 252 TFEU, is to act in 'complete impartiality and independence, to make, in open court, reasoned submissions on cases which, in accordance with the Statute of the Court of Justice, require his involvement'.[65] In their opinions the Advocates General are not bound to address only those questions relevant for deciding the case in the narrow sense, but the Advocate General can dwell on other questions raised by the case as well.[66] The Advocate General can, for example, show different solutions to the case and the consequences of a different reasoning.[67] LOTH has qualified this difference

57 See for example Brown (2000) who discusses the way in which English and Scottish lawyers perceive the CJEU, p. 54-55.

58 See among others: Lasser (2004), p. 103 & p. 347-348; Arnull (2006), p. 622; Fennelly (1997), p. 658; Brown (2000), p. 55.

59 See for an elaborate discussion: Lasser (2004),

60 Lasser (2004), p. 104 et seq; Brown (2000), p 55; Due (1999), p. 79.

61 Brown (2000), p. 55.

62 Brown (2000), p. 54-55; Lasser (2004), p. 305 & p. 318; Shapiro (1999), p. 326; Loth also points to the fact that the CJEU has tried to improve the French example, Loth (2009), p. 274. Arnull (2006), p. 623 refers to the fact that the judgments are 'by common law standards, spectacularly uninformative'.

63 Von Bogdandy (2000), p. 1330.

64 See, among others, on the Advocate General: Brown (2000), chapter 4; Sharpston (2008), p. 20-33; Ritter (2005-2006), p. 751-774.

65 Since the Treaty of Nice there is no longer the requirement that every case should be accompanied by an opinion of an Advocate General. In some minor judgments an opinion is not considered to be necessary.

66 Brown (2000), p. 67-68. See also Ritter (2006), p. 759.

67 Burrows & Greaves (2007), p. 28-29.

in the style of reasoning as the distinction between 'authoritive decision-making and substantial debate', whereby the CJEU has to *decide* in an authoritive manner, while the Advocate General can contribute to the substantial *debate*.[68] This explains why the Advocate General often is in a position to elaborate on the different issues at stake, while the CJEU will often not do so.

Although there are clear similarities between the French argumentative approach and the style of argumentation of the CJEU, an important difference with the French system is that the opinions of the CJEU's Advocate Generals are always published, while this is not the case in the French legal tradition.[69] This means that the internal discourse between the Advocate General and the court, as LASSER has qualified it, remains confidential in the French situation, while in the case of the CJEU this discourse is more visible and transparent.[70] By publishing both the judgment and the opinion of the Advocate General more insight is thus granted into the judicial kitchen of the CJEU. As a result both the judgment and the opinions will be analyzed in this thesis. Both can shed light on the way the Court of Justice as an institution approaches the interpretation of fundamental rights.

Apart from the added transparency, the availability and publication of opinions of the Advocate Generals is beneficial for the interpretation process in another way as well. The opinion by the Advocate General is an advice to the Court; the judges are not obliged to follow it. In practice, however, the CJEU often does follow the Advocate General.[71] According to BURROWS & GREAVES, the opinion really forms the starting point for deliberation of the judges. In that sense the Advocate General can be quite influential.[72] BURROWS & GREAVES argue that the added value of the opinion consists of the dialogical relationship between the Advocate General and the CJEU.[73] They view this relationship as an 'ongoing conversation on the interpretation of Community law'.[74] The Advocate General thus contributes to the quality of the reasoning in the collegial judgments of the CJEU.[75]

---

68 Loth (2009), p. 274.

69 Lasser (2004); see also Pinna (2009), p. 178, who argues that the argumentative legitimacy of the French Supreme Court is reduced as a result of this lack of publication.

70 Lasser (2004). See also Sharpston (2008), p. 23.

71 According to Burrows & Greaves (2007), p. 291, the CJEU only occasionally reaches a decision that is fundamentally different from the opinion of the Advocate General.

72 Burrows & Greaves (2007), p. 30. See also Brown (2000), p. 69.

73 Burrows & Greaves (2007), p. 292-293.

74 Burrows & Greaves (2007), p. 293. They do, however, also suggest that there is no longer a need for the position of Advocate General in a mature European Union, p. 297-298. This suggestion is contested by Sharpston (2008), p. 32, who argues that the expanding jurisdiction of the CJEU opens up new territory, which needs to be interpreted.

75 Burrows & Greaves (2007), p. 293. See also Ritter (2006), p. 763.

Another characteristic feature of the form of the CJEU judgments that has been derived from the continental legal systems is that the CJEU decides as a collegiate body.[76] Decisions are taken by the court as a whole and there is no possibility for dissenting or concurring opinions.[77] This naturally has an impact on the style of reasoning, since all judges have to agree with the final judgment. This is often noted as one of the disadvantages of a system without the possibility of dissenting opinions, since the need for consensus often results in equivocal and vague reasoning.[78] As a result judgments are often less clear and provide less guidance to its audience than might have been the case if the court was not forced to make any concessions in order to gain a consensus.[79] In this context, the existence of opinions of the Advocate General counterbalances this lack of dissenting opinions to a modest extent. A dissenting opinion, however, provides a more powerful force to enhance the court's reasoning, since the dissenting judge is actually part of the body making the final decision. Moreover, a dissenting opinion is written with knowledge of the decision to be taken by the majority. The dissenting judge is therefore able to highlight which specific points in the reasoning are controversial. An Advocate General is obliged to write his opinion in advance of the judgment of the CJEU and is therefore not guided by the debate of the majority. His opinion is a taste of what might be the line of reasoning of the CJEU, but the CJEU could also argue entirely differently and the focus in its reasoning could be different as well. The opinion of the Advocate General is thus not able to fully compensate for the lack of dissenting opinions. The reasoning of the CJEU in its interpretative process is thus strongly influenced by the collegiate decision-making.

Another aspect that is relevant to the CJEU's style of argumentation has been briefly discussed in the introductory chapter. Both courts to be discussed in this thesis operate in a multilevel legal system and subsidiarity therefore plays some role. In the argumentation in fundamental rights cases, the CJEU hardly ever directly invokes references to subsidiarity. Nevertheless, according to CAROZZA, subsidiarity does play an implicit role.[80] It does so in two ways. Firstly, the CJEU relies on national constitutional traditions and thereby to a certain extent respects national traditions at EU level.[81] Secondly, the CJEU does vary its scope of review depending on the type

---

76 Brown (2000), p. 54; Due (1999), p. 78;

77 Brown (2000), p. 54; Due (1999), p. 78.

78 Brown (2000), p. 55; Thomassen (2006), p. 686; Mertens & Vermeulen (2008), p. 52 & 60.

79 It is often noted that the possibility of dissenting opinions forces the majority to forcefully and convincingly defend their argument. This possibility thus provides a stimulating force to improve the judicial reasoning. See Brennan (1986), p. 430; Thomassen (2006), p. 686; Mertens & Vermeulen (2008), p. 52.

80 Carozza (2003), p. 53-56.

81 Carozza calls this subsidiarity at work. Carozza (2003), p. 54-55.

of action under examination. In some cases more room is left to national authorities, while in other cases the CJEU has adopted a more strict intensity of review depending, among others, on 'the rights and interests that are at stake'.[82] This latter form of subsidiarity concerns the application of fundamental rights and will not be further explored in this thesis. The first, implicit, role of subsidiarity, however, will be addressed more fully in this thesis, since the importance of national sources to the interpretation by the CJEU will be analyzed.

Finally, one could question whether the nature of the procedure before the CJEU influences the reasoning of the court. Questions on EU law find their way to the CJEU mainly by two distinct procedures, i.e. by way of preliminary questions by national courts (Article 267 TFEU) or by way of an appeal to a direct challenge brought before the General Court (previously known as the Court of First Instance) on the basis of Article 256 in conjunction with Article 263 TFEU. According to CAROZZA a difference in intensity of review can be distinguished whether the challenge concerns actions by EU bodies or Member States. In his view the intensity of review is the strictest when it concerns EU actions. GERARDS, on the contrary, has argued that the intensity of review depends on a larger number of factors.[83] The intensity of review, however, mainly concerns the application stage of the reasoning, i.e. the stage in which the CJEU examines the reasonableness of an interference with a fundamental right. The question is whether elements relating to the nature of the procedure are also relevant at the interpretation stage. It has already been argued earlier in this chapter that the CJEU will most likely not interpret the meaning of fundamental rights differently, regardless of the context.[84] Thus the meaning of the notion of, for example, private life, will be the same throughout the EU, even though the application of this right to the facts of a specific case might differ depending on different factors. Therefore, the analysis provided in this thesis will proceed on the theoretical presumption that the nature of the procedures in which questions of interpretation of fundamental rights are at stake, do not matter.

3.4 CONCLUSION

The aspects that have been discussed in this chapter determine the specific setting within which the CJEU has to operate. Both the background of the CJEU's fundamental rights case law and the relevant features of its argumentative approach and

82 See Gerards (2011), p. 100. Carozza (2003), p. 55 claims that the intensity of review depends on the type of action that is under review.

83 See Gerards (2011), p. 91-101.

84 See section 3.1.

judicial tradition will serve as a background for the discussions in the remainder of this thesis and might help one to understand certain differences between the two respective courts. The following chapter will continue to provide a background for the subsequent in-depth case law analysis, but the focus will shift towards the interpretative process by discussing in general the different interpretation methods and principles that play a role. Together these chapters will help one to understand the context in which the selected interpretation methods and principles are used.

Part II

Theoretical analysis

Chapter 4
Interpretation Methods and Interpretative Principles

Any meaningful discussion of interpretation methods and principles will have to start by outlining the existing methods and principles being used in the interpretation process of the courts under analysis in this thesis. This chapter will start by describing the terminology that will be adopted throughout this thesis. In the literature on interpretation a wide variety of terms are used to refer to different interpretative aids. For the benefit of the subsequent analysis a distinction will be made between interpretation methods and interpretative principles. Subsequently, in section 4.2 attention will be paid to the debate in academic literature on whether there is any hierarchy among interpretative aids. Subsequent to this theoretical discussion the interpretation methods will be discussed, followed by a discussion of the most commonly found principles of interpretation. These are methods and principles of interpretation that are regularly used in the case law of both the ECtHR and the CJEU. The section aims to provide a broad overview of the analysis that has been made in academic literature on the interpretative aids used by those courts. The interpretative aids will all be briefly discussed from the perspective of legal theoretical literature, both in general and more specifically in relation to the ECtHR and the CJEU. Some references to case law will be made in order to disclose the way in which the interpretative aids are founded in the case law. A thorough case law analysis will be provided in part III of this thesis. At the end of this chapter, the selection of methods and principles for the analysis in this thesis will be set out. After a discussion of the different methods and principles it will be easier to justify the choice for further analysis of a selected number of methods and principles. The selected interpretative aids will be discussed rather briefly in this chapter in order to avoid too much overlap with the subsequent chapters.[1]

Apart from theoretical literature on interpretation (methods), the Vienna Convention on the Law of Treaties[2] (VCLT) will play an important role in the context of this

1 Teleological interpretation, comparative interpretation, evolutive interpretation and autonomous interpretation have been selected for this thesis.

2 Vienna Convention on the Law of Treaties, Vienna, 22 May 1969, entry into force 27 January 1980 (VCLT or Vienna Convention). The Vienna Convention entered into force after the adoption of the ECHR and the then EC treaties. The VCLT does not have retroactive effect and is technically not binding on the CJEU and the ECtHR. The Vienna Convention, however, is generally considered to reflect the customary rule on treaty interpretation and as a result this convention is relevant to the interpretation process of both courts. The ECHR has even explicitly acknowledged that it will be guided by the provisions from the Vienna Convention.

chapter. Both the CJEU and the ECtHR have to deal with the interpretation of an international treaty and operate as such in the context of the VCLT. The chapter will show to what extent the VCLT plays a role in the interpretative process of both of these courts.

4.1 Terminology: Method, rule, principle?

In the literature on treaty interpretation in general and on interpretation by the Court of Justice of the European Union (CJEU) or the European Court of Human Rights (ECtHR) more in particular, there is no common approach as to the terminology used. A *method* of interpretation in the eyes of one author could be a *principle* of interpretation in the view of another author and vice versa.[3] This difference can be illustrated by taking the difference between Matscher and Leach as an example.[4] Both refer to the European Convention as a living instrument, but qualify the nature of this interpretative aid differently. Matscher refers to it as a method of interpretation, while Leach considers the living instrument to be an interpretative principle. Yet other authors have referred to different terminology by speaking of, among others, rules or canons of interpretation. In order to provide a useful overview and to avoid any confusion, it will therefore be necessary to first offer an explanation of how the terminology will be used throughout this thesis. While it may seem to be a matter of labels, the qualification can help one to get a better understanding of the nature of the specific interpretative aids and thereby also the role of these interpretive aids in the judicial reasoning. This will become clear once the distinction has been explained.

Based on the literature the following approach seems to provide the clearest distinction between the various terms.[5] A difference will be made between *methods* and *principles* of interpretation.[6] In order to qualify as a method of interpretation, the interpretative aid must be a technique which is used to justify a particular line

3 This confusion is partly caused by the lack of clarity between interpretation and application, which has been explained in the introduction, Chapter 1.
4 Matscher (1993), p. 68-70; Leach (2005), p. 164.
5 Among others: ECtHR: Ost (1992); Merrills (1993); Matscher (1993); Leach (2005); Ovey & White (2006). CJEU: Llorens (1999); Brown & Kennedy (2000); Vincenzi & Fairhurst (2002); Lasok (2004).
6 To some extent this distinction seems to be visible as well in a short discussion on the subject by Fennelly (1996-1997), p. 662. He claims that one should distinguish between 'the guiding interpretative principle deployed in search of the meaning of legal texts ... and the range of particular techniques and source materials upon which reliance may be placed'. Bossuyt (2005), p. 78-79, does not explain the distinction he makes, but he does adhere to a similar distinction. Mertens de Wilmars (1990), makes the distinction between methods of interpretation and foundations that serve as a source of inspiration in the interpretation process (p. 11). This distinction is not elaborately explained, but seems to be similar to the distinction made in this thesis.

of reasoning or a particular outcome.[7] This technique clarifies which substantive argument has been used in order to support a specific decision and which helps the judge to objectify the reasoning underlying this decision. The reference to objectivity here refers to objectivity in relation to the person of the judge and not in relation to the elements that play a role in the interpretation methods; some elements might entail a certain subjectivity, but this is generally in relation to the drafters of the legal text.[8]

Thus, depending on the choice of specific interpretation method, a legally relevant substantive argument will always play a role in a judge's reasoning. The element that constitutes the core of an interpretation method has been recognized as granting authority to a certain reasoning on the basis of different reasons, depending on the theory behind the interpretation method.[9] Textual interpretation, for example, is a method whereby the ordinary or technical meaning of the text of the provision in question is decisive.[10] The substantive element that thus plays a role when using this method of interpretation is the text of the provision. For reasons that will be discussed in section 4.3.1 the text can be regarded as an authoritative basis for interpretation according to this interpretation method. The main point to be noted here is that the method determines which element justifies the outcome of the interpretation. Similar arguments can be made about, for example, systemic interpretation or teleological interpretation. A method of interpretation thus provides a technique which leads to an objectified argument for a reasoning in a certain direction.

A principle of interpretation on the other hand has a different function. It serves as an objective or aim that can be taken into account when interpreting a provision with the help of an interpretation method. A principle of interpretation does not provide an element that will help to determine the meaning of a provision. It will generally provide an aim that is sought after when interpreting provisions of a certain treaty, thus it does not refer to the purpose of a specific provision, but the purpose of the treaty as a whole.[11] For example, the principle of effective interpretation does not reveal which elements should play a role in the reasoning, but it does provide a general objective for the interpretation process, namely that the interpretation based on whichever interpretation method should be effective. Similarly, the principle of

---

7 See McCormick & Summers (1991), p. 511-512. They do not speak about 'technique', but about 'arguments'. The term technique has been chosen here, because it makes the distinction with the interpretative principles more clear.

8 See the discussion in the chapter on teleological interpretation, Chapter 5.

9 In American literature on interpretation methods there is strong disagreement on which elements on which elements may be taken into consideration by judges when interpreting law, for example in the debate on comparative interpretation, which will be discussed more elaborately in Chapter 6.

10 McCormick & Summers (1991), p. 512.

11 See also Lasser (2004), p. 208.

evolutive interpretation entails an objective, namely interpretation in line with changes over time in society. The principle itself does not indicate which substantive arguments should be taken into consideration in obtaining that objective and therefore it should be distinguished from a *method* of interpretation. For both principles that have just been mentioned, various interpretation methods could be invoked to reach the goal that has been set by the principles. Perhaps unavoidably, there will be some interpretative principles that have a more natural link with certain interpretation methods, but in general the interpretative principles are not strictly linked to the use of a specific interpretation method. Given the role of interpretative principles of providing a purpose for the interpretation process, they cannot by themselves support the choice for a specific interpretation. For example, a judge cannot solely on the basis of the principle of effective interpretation justify a certain interpretation. Interpretation methods are needed to base the reasoning on one of the recognized elements, such as text or system. The interpretative principles can help to make a choice between the potentially diverging outcomes resulting from different methods of interpretation. Both principles and methods of interpretation thus complement each other, but each fulfils a different role in the judicial reasoning.

The existence of interpretative principles has also been discussed by LASSER in the context of the CJEU.[12] It is not clear whether he supports the same distinction in function between interpretation methods and principles, but he does provide a basis for the use of interpretative principles. He distinguishes on the one hand the use of micro-teleological arguments, which is the use of teleological interpretation in its everyday modus by using references to the object and purpose of a provision or the treaty as a whole to justify the interpretation of a specific term.[13] On the other hand he distinguishes meta-teleological arguments, which is argumentation on the basis of principles that have been derived from the treaty system as a whole, in his case 'the EU legal structure as a whole'.[14] These are the meta-teleological principles that resemble the principles that have been described above. They find their basis in the object and purpose of the treaty system as a whole. This also explains why interpretative principles can be different for each treaty system. One of the questions to be answered by the case law analysis therefore is whether meta-teleological interpretation is also used in relation to interpretative principles outside the EU context, i.e. in the framework of the ECtHR.

The present distinction serves as a basis for the classification of interpretative aids throughout this thesis. The precise meaning of the distinction between methods and

12 Lasser (2004).
13 Lasser (2004), p. 208.
14 Lasser (2004), p. 208.

principles will become clearer in the course of the discussion of specific interpretation methods and principles. Firstly, the following section will deal with the question whether some methods or principles are regarded as more important than other methods or principles. Subsequently, several relevant interpretation methods and principles will be discussed.

4.2 HIERARCHY OF INTERPRETATION METHODS?

The distinction discussed in the previous section between methods and principles revealed that different (types of) arguments can have a different function in the interpretative process. This section will address the question whether different interpretation methods can differ in terms of argumentative force. The question can be put differently by asking whether some theoretical hierarchy amongst interpretation methods can be said to exist. This theoretical discussion is relevant as a background for the analysis of the use of the different aids by the CJEU and the ECtHR and the force they accord to the interpretative aids.

The starting point for a discussion on the hierarchy of interpretation methods in the context of treaty interpretation should focus on the Vienna Convention. Article 31 VCLT provides the general rule of treaty interpretation, which holds: 'A treaty shall be interpreted in good faith in accordance with the ordinary meaning to be given to the terms of the treaty in their context and in the light of its object and purpose'.[15] In its second and third section this article provides what should be considered to constitute the 'context' and what can be taken into account apart from the context.[16]

---

15 This provision reflects a compromise between three schools of interpretation. The first considered the text of the treaty to be decisive. The second school focused on the intention of the drafters. The final school focused on the object and purpose of the treaty. Shaw (2008), p. 933; Bossuyt (2005), p. 77. See for an overview of the drafting of the Vienna Convention and the period leading to this drafting process: Orakhelashvili (2008), p. 301-316.

16 *Article 31 VCLT:*
General rule of interpretation
1. A treaty shall be interpreted in good faith in accordance with the ordinary meaning to be given to the terms of the treaty in their context and in the light of its object and purpose.
2. The context for the purpose of the interpretation of a treaty shall comprise, in addition to the text, including its preamble and annexes:
(*a*) any agreement relating to the treaty which was made between all the parties in connection with the conclusion of the treaty;
(*b*) any instrument which was made by one or more parties in connection with the conclusion of the treaty and accepted by the other parties as an instrument related to the treaty.
3. There shall be taken into account, together with the context:
(*a*) any subsequent agreement between the parties regarding the interpretation of the treaty or the application of its provisions;

In its commentary to the Vienna Convention the International Law Commission (ILC) argued that Article 31 VCLT should not be read as establishing a hierarchy of interpretative norms.[17] The ILC held that logic determined the order in which references to the different interpretation methods were presented and not any hierarchy.[18] This does not mean that the rules on treaty interpretation in the VCLT are devoid of any hierarchy. First of all, Article 32 VCLT refers to 'supplementary' means of interpretation.[19] This means that the interpretation methods included in this article are only to be used if the methods mentioned in Article 31 VCLT do not lead to a clear meaning of the term or provision that requires interpretation. Secondly, the ILC does consider textual interpretation to be the prime method of interpretation.[20] The primacy granted to the text of the treaty provision, thus, means that textual interpretation is, even if this is not explicitly acknowledged by the ILC, at the top of the hierarchy of interpretation methods. Any reasoning based on this method will therefore be considered to have strong argumentative force.

As has already been said, theoretical discussions on (national) interpretation methods could be relevant for the context of treaty interpretation as well. The question may be asked whether any hierarchy has been established in the context of national interpretation methods.[21] An interesting example of an attempt to bring order or

---

(*b*) any subsequent practice in the application of the treaty which establishes the agreement of the parties regarding its interpretation;

(*c*) any relevant rules of international law applicable in the relations between the parties.

4. A special meaning shall be given to a term if it is established that the parties so intended.

17 See: Commentary to articles of Vienna Convention, Yearbook of International Law Commission, 1966- Vol. II, p. 220. The International Law Commission was involved in drafting the VCLT and its commentary reflects many considerations throughout the drafting process that can help one to understand the final version of the VCLT.

18 See: Commentary to articles of Vienna Convention, Yearbook of International Law Commission, 1966- Vol. II, p. 220. See also Aust (2007), p. 234.

19 *Article 32 VCLT:*
Supplementary means of interpretation
Recourse may be had to supplementary means of interpretation, including the preparatory work of the treaty and the circumstances of its conclusion, in order to confirm the meaning resulting from the application of article 31, or to determine the meaning when the interpretation according to article 31:
(*a*) leaves the meaning ambiguous or obscure; or
(*b*) leads to a result which is manifestly absurd or unreasonable.

20 See for reference to the primacy of the text: articles of Vienna Convention, Yearbook of International Law Commission, 1966- Vol. II, p. 220; Bernhardt (1967), p. 495-496; Orakhelashvili (2008), p. 309.

21 According to Alexy no one has succeeded in drafting a catalogue accepted by everyone. Alexy (1989), p. 247. Franken in the Dutch context claims that textual and historical interpretation should take precedence in case of multiple options, since these methods emphasize the fact that a judge is bound by the law. Franken (2003), p. 199.

hierarchy into interpretation methods has been presented by a group of scholars known as the Bielefelder Kreis.[22] After a study of the use of interpretation methods in many different jurisdictions, they presented a very simple model of the order in which different interpretation methods should be considered.[23] First, linguistic arguments should be considered; secondly, systemic arguments; and, finally, teleological arguments. Only if the interpretative result is not clear enough should one proceed to the next interpretation method. Thus, according to this model, teleological interpretation may only be used if textual and systemic interpretation do not provide a clear result. The question is, however, whether and when it is possible to conclude if a result from textual interpretation is clear. After all, the use of systemic or teleological interpretation might show that the result is not that clear. Nonetheless, apart from this problem the model is useful to show that reasoning based on some methods is sometimes granted more argumentative force than others.[24]

Both in theoretical literature and in literature on treaty interpretation, no clear hierarchy among interpretation methods has been found to exist, even though textual interpretation is often regarded as the primary method of interpretation (which is perhaps understandable when interpreting a legal text). The problem for our purpose is that interpretation beyond the purely textual or grammatical meaning of treaty notions is often necessary, precisely because the text of treaty provisions is often rather vague. Fundamental rights are generally broadly formulated. An example of this broad formulation is Article 8 ECHR: 'everyone has the right to respect for his private and family life, his home and correspondence'. Especially the term private life is a broad term that needs further interpretation; textual interpretation might not be very helpful in that case. Furthermore, the fact that, in the Vienna Convention, textual interpretation, systemic interpretation and teleological interpretation are all mentioned as part of the general rule of interpretation might be an indication that the ILC did not intend to create a hierarchy of interpretation methods. It only shows that arguments based on these methods should be given primary consideration.

It will be interesting to see in the case law analysis whether the ECtHR and the CJEU distinguish between the argumentative force of different interpretation methods and whether some form of hierarchy is visible in their argumentation.

---

22 See MacCormick & Summer (1991) for the outcomes of the study of this group of scholars from different countries.

23 MacCormick & Summer (1991), p. 531.

24 The study by Bielefelder Kreis revealed that in many jurisdictions textual arguments have a strong force in justification. MacCormick & Summer (1991), p. 533.

4.3 Methods of interpretation

There are two ways to start a discussion on interpretation methods, namely either by taking national constitutional theory as a point of departure, or by starting from the general international rules of interpretation. The introduction to this thesis and to this particular chapter already indicated that both the European Court of Human Rights and the Court of Justice of the European Union are international courts showing strong similarities with national constitutional courts.[25] Therefore, both angles can be legitimate starting points. Given, however, that these courts are international courts by origin, the starting point of the following discussion will be the international rules of interpretation, supplemented with relevant aspects of national (constitutional) theory of interpretation.

As discussed above, general international rules of interpretation have been codified in the Vienna Convention on the Law of Treaties (VCLT).[26] The relevant provisions for treaty interpretation are Articles 31, 32 and 33 of the Vienna Convention. Certain methods of interpretation can be deduced from these provisions. These methods will be discussed first, and subsequently, an overview will be given of methods that do not directly derive from the VCLT, but which are relevant in treaty interpretation.

4.3.1 Textual interpretation

Article 31 of the Vienna Convention, as has been said above, clearly emphasizes the primacy of the text when dealing with treaty interpretation. This primacy stems from the view that the text reflects the authentic expression of the intention of the parties, therefore 'the starting point of interpretation is the elucidation of the meaning of the text, not an investigation *ab initio* into the intentions of the parties'.[27] This authentic expression of the parties is relevant in the context of treaty interpretation, since it is a way to 'establish and preserve the original consensus between State-parties'.[28] In a national context, textual interpretation is valued since it pays respect to the legislator who drafted the legislation. The legislator is democratically elected and as such represents the will of the people.[29] Moreover, in light of the separation of

25 See for the CJEU: Helfer (2003-2004), p, 199-201. For the ECtHR, see Gerards (2009), p. 409.

26 See: Commentary to articles of Vienna Convention, Yearbook of International Law Commission, 1966- Vol. II; Bernhardt (1967), p. 491; Bernhardt (1988), p. 65; Aust (2000), p. 185-186; McRae (2002), p. 210; Slotboom (2001), p. 576.

27 ILC Commentary to Article 27 of Vienna Convention, Yearbook at 220 (par. 11).

28 Orakhelashvili (2008), p. 318, claims that this primacy of the text is a *direct* consequence of this need to preserve the original consensus.

29 MacCormick & Summers (1991), p. 534, briefly describe the underlying values of textual interpretation.

powers the judge should respect the products of the legislator and not take the position of the legislator.[30] The CJEU operates in a composite legal order, but the structure of the legal order resembles to a limited extent the classical functions of a state, in the sense that the EU has a representative body, the European Parliament, an executive body, the Commission and the Council, and a judicial body, the CJEU.[31] These arguments relating to the role of the judge and hence the respect that a judge should pay to the language used by the legislator could therefore play a role before the CJEU that is similar to a national context. The ECtHR does not operate in a similar structure and therefore these arguments do not play much of a role before the ECtHR.[32] A different argument can, however, be made for the ECtHR. The ECtHR depends, among others, on the national legislator for the effectiveness of its judgments. As a result the ECtHR will try to respect and even engage in a dialogue with the national legislators.[33] One way to show respect for national legislators is by paying respect to the text of the provisions which they have ratified and thus employ the textual method of interpretation.

The idea behind textual interpretation is to establish the ordinary or technical meaning of a notion.[34] The main problem that has been stressed in view of the textual method is that words in themselves do not have an ordinary meaning.[35] A strictly textual approach may therefore be considered arbitrary, as it leaves much latitude to the interpreter. Article 31 of the Vienna Convention can however be read to contain a more moderate version of textual interpretation, by including the words 'in their context'. This contextual method of interpretation will be discussed in more detail below.

Given the primacy granted to this method in theory and the problems of the method, it is interesting to see briefly how the CJEU and ECtHR have dealt with this interpretative method in practice and how valuable this method is to these courts.

Already before the Vienna Convention entered into force, the ECtHR in the *Golder* case[36] determined that it should be guided by Articles 31-33 of the VCLT.[37] In

---

30 MacCormick & Summers (1991), p. 534, briefly describe the underlying values of textual interpretation

31 See for a more detailed discussion Lenaerts (2005), p. 563-565.

32 See Gerards (2009), p. 414, who argues that the ECtHR does not have any constitutional counterparts like in a national system. The ECtHR pays respect and enters into a dialogue with the national legislator (and national courts as well), according to Gerards. This is, however, not equivalent to a constitutional counterpart.

33 Gerards (2009), p. 414.

34 MacCormick & Summers (1991), p. 512-513.

35 Lauterpacht (1949), p. 53; McRae (2002), p. 209 referring to McLauchlan.

36 ECtHR, *Golder v United Kingdom*, judgment of 21 February 1975, *Series* A No. 18, § 29. This case concerned the question whether Article 6 of the European Convention contained a right of access to a court.

subsequent cases it has therefore (often) taken the text of the European Convention to be its starting point, which has at times been expressly stated by the ECtHR.[38] It is however apparent from the case law that textual interpretation alone is never sufficient to provide a clear interpretation of the provisions of the ECHR.[39] The case of *Johnston,*[40] for example, concerned the question whether Article 12 of the European Convention, which grants the right to marry, also included a right to divorce. Basing itself on the meaning of the notion of marriage, the ECtHR held that no right to divorce could be derived from Article 12. This judgment is a good illustration of the approach taken by the ECtHR. The text of Article 12 in itself is rather clear (only referring to the right to marry), but the ECtHR continued and corroborated its finding by looking at the context and the object and purpose of the provision in question. Thereby it sent the message that the text is important, but an interpretation based on several interpretation methods may be more convincing. In many cases where the text is less clear than in the case of *Johnston,* reference to other interpretation methods will simply be necessary. Textual interpretation in those cases will only play a marginal role. Examples can be found in cases concerning the interpretation of Article 8 of the European Convention, which provides that everyone's private and family life should be respected. Textual interpretation would in this respect not be very helpful in determining the meaning of private life. Textual interpretation cannot provide much guidance in deciding whether the right to a person's reputation should be covered by the right to respect for someone's private life, or whether a transsexual should be able to have his or her gender change officially recognized as part of the right to protection of one's private life.

The approach described above shows the limits on the applicability of the textual approach, especially in the context of these vaguely drafted provisions. Another characteristic of the European Convention that limits the usefulness of the textual interpretation is the fact that there are two authentic language versions of the European Convention: the English and the French. If these language versions differ the ECtHR has stated that it must 'interpret them in a way that will reconcile them as far as possible'.[41] In reconciling the two language versions the ECtHR considers it im-

---

37 Repeated in: ECtHR, *Ireland v. United Kingdom*, judgment of 18 January 1978, *Series* A No. 25; ECtHR, *Lithgow and others v United Kingdom*, judgment of 8 July 1986, *Series* A No. 102; ECtHR, *Witold Litwa v. Poland*, judgment of 4 April 2000, *Reports* 2000-III; ECtHR (GC), *Banković and others v. Belgium and others*, decision of 12 December 2001, Reports 2001-VII.

38 ECtHR, *Witold Litwa v. Poland*, judgment of 4 April 2000, *Reports* 2000-III.

39 This has also been defended in the literature by Ost (1992).

40 ECtHR, *Johnston and others v Ireland*, judgment of 18 December 1986, *Series* A No. 112, § 52.

41 ECtHR, *Wemhoff v. Germany*, judgment of 27 June 1968, *Series* A No. 7.

portant that, due to the nature of the European Convention (a law-making treaty),[42] the interpretation that best 'realizes the aim and achieves the object of the treaty' must be adopted. In other words: the interpretation which best protects the fundamental individual rights. At times, textual interpretation could even be 'overruled' by the need to ensure protection of the fundamental individual rights.[43] Ost discusses the example of *Wemhoff* where the ECtHR argued that a 'purely grammatical interpretation would [result in an interpretation] that would not conform to the intention of the High Contracting Parties. It is inconceivable that they should have intended to permit their judicial authorities, at the price of release of the accused, to protract proceedings beyond a reasonable time. This would, moreover, be flatly contrary to the provision in Article 6 (1)'.[44] In conclusion one could say that the textual interpretation, due to the specific characteristics of the European Convention, plays only a limited role in the interpretation process of the ECtHR and the text will generally only serve as a starting point.

The CJEU, on the contrary, has never explicitly referred to the Vienna Convention in any of its judgments.[45] In the literature it is generally assumed that the CJEU employs the textual method of interpretation,[46] on occasion applying it to show the limits of its own competence.[47] Some authors would even assert that the textual method of interpretation is the main method of interpretation employed by the CJEU.[48] The main line in the literature, however, is to show the limits of the textual method in the case law of the CJEU. Several characteristics of EU law have been mentioned in that regard, most importantly: the multilingual character on the one hand and the general and open-ended nature of EU law on the other hand.[49] This could explain the fact that the CJEU has displayed a willingness to disregard the wording

42 This special characteristic has been repeated in ECtHR, *Ireland v UK*, judgment of 18 January 1978, Series A No. 25, § 239. According to Matscher (1993), p.66, this is a controversial distinction. In the discussion on the different interpretative principles this characteristic plays a role as well, as will be seen in the second part of this chapter.

43 Ost (1992), p. 289, referring to the *Wemhoff* case, ECtHR, *Wemhoff v. Germany*, judgment of 27 June 1968, *Series* A No. 7.

44 ECtHR, *Wemhoff v. Germany*, judgment of 27 June 1968, *Series* A No. 7, § 4-5.

45 Slotboom claims that the CJEU has suggested that it does interpret EC law in the light of the Vienna Convention. Slotboom (2001), p. 577.

46 Lasok & Millet (2004); Schermers & Waelbroeck, (2001); Arnull (2006); Brown & Kennedy (2000); Vincenzi & Fairhurst (2002).

47 C-245/97, *Germany v. Commission* [2000] ECR I-11621, § 72; C-310/98, *Met-Trans and Sagpol* [2000] ECR I-1797, § 32 and § 46.

48 Schermers & Waelbroeck, (2001).

49 See, for the multilingual character: Jacobs (2003), p. 298-299; Shelton (1996-1997), p. 631-632. See Janssen (2005), p. 173 for the argument that textual interpretation is not very helpful given the open ended character of EU provisions.

by allowing the contextual and teleological interpretations to prevail or at least not to overemphasize the importance of the wording of the text.[50] This can be demonstrated by the famous approach in the *Van Gend en Loos* judgment,[51] repeated in many subsequent cases, where the CJEU stated that for determining the scope of a certain provision it is necessary 'to consider the spirit, the general scheme and wording' of a provision.[52] At first sight this statement seems reflective of the status of the text when interpreting EU law, though one should keep in mind that the reliance on the text is much stronger in the case of secondary EU law, which is often much more precisely worded.[53] What is moreover important is that from this line, one should not draw the conclusion that this reflects a fixed hierarchy among different interpretation methods. The CJEU uses diverse approaches and it selects the approach it 'consider[s] most appropriate in the circumstances'.[54]

A particular feature of EU law, as has been mentioned above, is the fact that all official languages are equally authentic.[55] This complicates textual interpretation as differences will inevitably arise. The textual interpretation method in this type of case will at most be able to provide an indication for determining the scope of the provision in question, though in some cases that might not even be possible. Often the CJEU selects the most 'liberal interpretation consonant with the objectives of the provision'; however, examples of different approaches can be found as well.[56] The connection in all these differing approaches appears to be the crucial role played by the teleological approach, to be discussed below.

In the context of fundamental rights protection the role of textual interpretation in the case law of the CJEU was virtually non-existent until very recently. This is understandable, since no binding legal text containing a catalogue of fundamental rights existed in the EU context. The EU Charter on Fundamental Rights became binding only in December 2009. As a result of this, textual interpretation might take on a more prominent role in the interpretation of fundamental rights. The question is only how prominent this role will be, because a characteristic of fundamental rights is that they are vaguely worded.

50 E.g. C-22/70, *Commission v. Council (ERTA)*, [1971] ECR 263.

51 C-26/62, *Van Gend en Loos v. Administratie der Belastingen* [1963] ECR 3.

52 C-26/62, *Van Gend en Loos v. Administratie der Belastingen* [1963] ECR 3, 12.

53 Lasok & Millett (2004), § 659.

54 Arnull (2006), p. 617.

55 Jacobs (2003), p. 302-303, calls this the fiction of equal plurilingual authority, because he claims that the legislator did not devote its collective attention to all language versions. So it is a fiction to say that the legislator has approved all language versions.

56 Lasok & Millet (2004), § 662, p. 382-3855, where examples of a more teleological approach, but also other approaches are discussed.

The aim of this short overview was to show that both courts take textual interpretation seriously, but due to a number of characteristics, the nature of fundamental rights and the multilingual treaties, the usefulness of this method of interpretation may be somewhat limited.

4.3.2 Teleological interpretation

'A treaty shall be interpreted in good faith in accordance with the ordinary meaning to be given to the terms of the treaty in their context and in the light of its object and purpose' according to Article 31 of the VCLT.' The latter part of the sentence is a clear confirmation of the acceptance of the teleological interpretation method within the framework of the Vienna Convention. The commentary claims that this has been included for reasons of common sense and good faith.[57] This was probably inspired by the often heard claim that 'the determination of the ordinary meaning cannot be done in the abstract' and thus the object and purpose should be considered to determine the meaning.[58] Teleological interpretation assumes that legislation or a treaty has been drafted in order to realize a specific social goal.[59] This method aims to realize this purpose for which the measure was designed.[60] The question is how one can 'find' this object and purpose that should guide the interpretation. Different approaches have been established. On the one hand, some authors focus on the subjective object and purpose, meaning that the object and purpose of a piece of legislation is the real purpose the author(s) had in mind when creating the text.[61] On the other hand, some authors consider the object and purpose to be the intent of the 'reasonable author'.[62] This will be elaborately discussed in the chapter on teleological interpretation, but it is important to realize that object and purpose are a normative construction and thus 'not a matter of empirical findings'.[63] The fact that there is no clear method to find the object and purpose leaves much latitude for the judge when employing this method. Some have in this context pointed to the danger of judges being overly creative and going into the realm of treaty amendment.[64] This is why judges should be careful when employing this method of interpretation.

---

57 Commentary to articles of Vienna Convention, Yearbook of International Law Commission, 1966-Vol. II

58 Aust (2000), p. 188.

59 Barak (2005), p. 148.

60 Barak (2005), p. 88.

61 Barak, (2005), p. 120; MacCormick and Summers (1991), p. 520.

62 Barak (2005), p. 148.

63 Alexy (1989), p. 241. See also Barak (2005), p. 89.

64 McRae (2002), p. 222, referring to the danger of sliding into treaty amendment instead of treaty interpretation.

In this context the Vienna Convention limits the teleological method of interpretation by giving primacy to the text, which basically means that the object and purpose 'cannot be invoked to contradict the text'.[65]

The means used to establish the object and purpose will be influenced by the question whether one takes a subjective or objective approach. Depending on the approach chosen, the means could be taken as broad or as narrow as one wishes them to be. For example, this method could correspond completely with a textual method of interpretation if one takes the text to evidence the object and purpose of a certain treaty.[66] On the other hand, if other, even extrinsic,[67] means are allowed to be taken into account, the result could be the exact opposite of the result deriving from a textual interpretation. Given this latitude for judges in determining the object and purpose and the different sources that are potentially available for judges to find this object and purpose, it is necessary for the court to clearly justify the choices made in employing teleological interpretation in order to avoid any suspicion of subjectiveness on the part of the judge.

The section on the division between methods and principles already referred to the difference between meta-teleological interpretation and micro-teleological interpretation.[68] Meta-teleological interpretation refers to arguments based on meta-teleological principles, which will be explained more clearly in section 4.4.2.1. Argumentation in this case thus falls into the category of principles, as described above. Micro-teleological arguments are arguments based on the technique as described at the beginning of this section and as such micro-teleological interpretation can be considered a method of interpretation. The focus in this version of teleological interpretation is on the object and purpose of a specific provision or a piece of legislation and not the nature of the treaty system as a whole.[69] When speaking about teleological interpretation in this thesis, reference is made to micro-teleological interpretation. If reference is made to the principle of meta-teleological interpretation this will be stated explicitly.

In section 4.3.1 it has become clear that for the European systems, for several reasons, the textual method has only a limited role to play. The object and purpose are much

65 Jacobs (1969), p. 338.

66 This position is taken by the ILC in its Commentary to articles of Vienna Convention, Yearbook of International Law Commission, 1966- Vol. II, p. 220.

67 Jacobs (1969), p. 337. He does not explain this term, but from the context one can discern what he means when referring to extrinsic means. Intrinsic means are 'the text and related documents'; extrinsic means are therefore means that lie outside the realm of the treaty. Unfortunately he does not provide an example of this latter type of means.

68 These concepts have been described by Lasser (2004).

69 Lasser (2004), p. 207-208.

more important in deciding on the interpretation of a certain provision. This method plays an important role in coping with the challenges of decision-making in a multilevel legal system. Teleological interpretation and the principle of meta-teleological interpretation allow the supranational courts to take into account the character of the treaty and its provisions. On the one hand, the principle of meta-teleological interpretation serves as a basis for many interpretative principles that are helpful in a multilevel legal system, which will be shown when discussing these principles below. The characteristic of the European Convention, for example, as a law-making treaty helps to defend the approach of the ECtHR that the European Convention should not be interpreted in a manner that would restrict the obligations of the Contracting States to the greatest degree.[70] On the other hand, a micro-teleological approach allows the judges to take the purpose of the treaty into account when interpreting a specific provision. By taking into account the purpose of the treaty even when interpreting specific terms, helps to take note of the multilevel characteristic of the European systems even in those specific cases. This method will be part of the extensive research throughout this thesis, which means that only a summary overview of teleological interpretation needs to be provided here.

The CJEU is widely known for applying the teleological method of interpretation. It is this approach that has subjected the CJEU to accusations of judicial activism.[71] This is not the place to discuss whether these accusations have any truth in them or not, but it is important to keep in mind that the approach chosen by the CJEU has not been accepted without resistance.[72] The famous statement in the *Van Gend en Loos* case[73] is reflective of the importance attached to the object and purpose. The CJEU does not refer to object and purpose, but instead refers to the spirit of the treaty.[74] Reference to the spirit of the treaty is one of the main considerations for the CJEU when determining the scope of a provision. Contrary to the systemic approach,[75] which considers the place of a provision in the relation to other parts of the Treaty depending on the context, the teleological method considers 'the whole purpose, the aims and objectives of the Community and the Union'.[76] The CJEU has not seen itself limited by the text of the treaties, among others due to its multi-

70 Interpreting in a restrictive manner in favour of state sovereignty used to be the common approach in treaty interpretation. Bernhardt (1999), p. 14.

71 Llorens (1999), p. 382.

72 In the theoretical discussion on the different interpretation methods and principles employed by the CJEU, the accusations of judicial activism directed at the CJEU will be addressed as well.

73 C-26/62, *Van Gend en Loos v. Administratie der Belastingen* [1963] ECR 3.

74 C-26/62, *Van Gend en Loos v. Administratie der Belastingen* [1963] ECR 3.

75 This method of interpretation will be discussed in the following section 4.3.3.

76 Vincenzi & Fairhurst, (2002), p. 107.

lingual character, which has on occasion led the CJEU to overrule the wording of a certain provision.[77] A more detailed account of when the CJEU uses this method will be given below. Many questions will need to be answered in order to get a complete picture of the use of teleological interpretation, among others when will this method be applied and in what cases will this method be left aside? How can the object and purpose be determined? Which documents will be taken into account in this process? The preamble provides many indications of the objectives of the EU Treaty[78] and one may wonder whether this is often taken into consideration when determining the object and purpose. The same question could be raised for the *travaux préparatoires*.

The nature of the European Convention allows for the ECtHR to apply the teleological method as the system of the European Convention is based on the aim to progressively improve the protection of fundamental rights throughout Europe. The ECtHR has stressed this in the cases of *Wemhoff* and *Golder* by stating that the character of the European Convention as a law-making treaty warrants an interpretation 'that is most appropriate in order to realize the aim and achieve the object of the treaty, not that which would restrict to the greatest possible degree the obligations undertaken by the Parties'.[79] The focus on the role of the European Convention as a bill of rights[80] has firmly established the importance of the teleological method of interpretation within the ECtHR. This also follows from the *Soering* and *Kjeldsen* judgments which state that any interpretation has to be in conformity with the 'general spirit of the Convention'.[81] Similar to the CJEU this has in some cases led the ECtHR to override the result of a textual interpretation,[82] but in many cases this method will simply confirm the wording of a particular provision.

Teleological interpretation features in virtually all judgments of the ECtHR, and object and purpose have constantly been 'identified as the "protection of individual human rights" and the "maintenance and promotion of the ideals and values of a democratic society"'.[83] This is still rather vague and abstract; the case law analysis

---

77 E.g. C-22/70 *Commission* v. *Council (ERTA)*, [1971] ECR 263 and Vincenzi & Fairhurst, (2002), p. 107.

78 The same applies to the EU Treaty.

79 ECtHR, *Wemhoff v. Germany*, judgment of 27 June 1968, *Series* A No. 7, § 8; ECtHR, *Golder v United Kingdom*, judgment of 21 February 1975, Series A No. 18, § 36.

80 Harris, O'Boyle & Warbrick (2009), p. 6.

81 ECtHR, *Soering v United Kingdom*, judgment of 7 July 1989, *Series* A No. 161, § 87, quoting from ECtHR, *Kjeldsen, Busk Madsen and Pederson v Denmark*, judgment of 7 December 1976, *Series* A No. 23, § 53

82 Ost (1992), p. 293.

83 Harris, O'Boyle & Warbrick (2009), p. 5-6.

will disclose in more detail how this has been applied in concrete situations. In these concrete situations, how will a less abstract object and purpose be defined? Which sources will be taken into account? Is the ECtHR consistent in using the different means to establish the object and purpose? If yes, can any criteria be extracted? These and other questions will be dealt with in the course of this thesis, specifically in Chapters 5 and 9.

4.3.3 Systemic or contextual interpretation

The basis for the systemic or contextual method of interpretation in the context of treaty interpretation can also be traced back to the first sentence of Article 31 of the Vienna Convention, which provides that the wording must be read in its context. The term 'contextual interpretation' has in the literature been used interchangeably with the term 'systemic interpretation'. Since both seem to refer to the same method, the terms will be used interchangeably throughout this thesis. In order to determine the interpretation to be given to a specific provision, when applying this method, regard must be had to the bigger picture in which the provision is placed: the context. According to the Vienna Convention the context includes (in addition to the text, including its preamble and annexes): firstly, 'any agreement relating to the treaty which was made between all the parties in connection with the conclusion of the treaty'[84] and secondly 'any instrument which was made by one or more parties in connection with the conclusion of the treaty and accepted by the other parties as an instrument related to the treaty'.[85] The underlying consideration here is that the context cannot be based on any unilateral documents; all parties should have had some direct or indirect influence.[86] While these documents, referred to in Article 31 VCLT, can certainly be relevant, systemic interpretation could also be seen in a more limited manner. By looking at, for example, the place of the provision in the system of the treaty, or by looking at treaty elements like headings and paragraphs, the context could be determined as well.

The main advantage of contextual interpretation is that it can provide the necessary support for the textual interpretation method; some would even say that the textual interpretation necessarily involves employing the systemic method of interpretation,

84 Article 31 Vienna Convention.

85 Article 31 Vienna Convention.

86 Commentary to articles of Vienna Convention, Yearbook of International Law Commission, 1966-Vol. II. See also Orakhelashvili (2008), p. 342-343, who refers to examples from practice that underline this requirement that instruments should represent some form of agreement between states in order to be considered as a relevant part of the context.

since a term cannot be fully understood in the abstract.[87] The assumption behind systemic interpretation is that the system is made up of a coherent set of legal rules and systemic interpretation is meant to guard this coherence.[88] Different provisions cannot be seen entirely separately from each other or from, for example, the preamble and thus have to be interpreted by taking them into account. The structure of the system as a whole thus influences the way in which the specific provisions should be understood.[89]

The question is to what extent this method can be used to interpret a specific notion. To put it differently, what is the relation with textual interpretation? According to ORAKHELASHVILI, contextual interpretation can only play a limited role and it does not have 'primary relevance in interpreting the treaty text'.[90] Only if 'the meaning of the word or phrase positively admits of more than one signification, raises the issue of compatibility with the object and purpose, or undermines the meaning of another clause in the same treaty' is there, in his view, room for contextual interpretation.[91] Thus, only in a limited number of situations can contextual interpretation be used to deviate from the ordinary meaning of the provision in question.[92]

The method of systemic interpretation has been adopted by the ECtHR as early as in the *Belgian Linguistic* judgment[93] and subsequently in the *Golder* case.[94] In the case of *Golder* the ECtHR stated that 'the provisions of the Convention and its Protocols must be examined as a whole'[95] and 'the process of interpretation is a unity, a single combined operation'.[96] In other words, the provisions of the European Convention and its Protocols must be interpreted in relation to each other. Most often

87 Aust (2000), p. 188. Orakhelashvili (2008), p. 339 considers systemic interpretation to be a ramification of textual interpretation.

88 This method is also used by national judges, in that context reference is made to the need to maintain the coherence of the system. These arguments are, however, also valid in the context of treaty interpretation. See MacCormick & Summer (1991), p. 535; Franken (2003), p. 198; Cliteur (2005), p. 169.

89 See Orakhelashvili (2008), p. 340 who refers to the fact that mutually contradictory outcomes should be prevented. Cliteur (2005), p. 169.

90 Orakhelashvili (2008), p. 340.

91 Orakhelashvili (2008), p. 340.

92 Orakhelashvili (2008), p. 340.

93 ECtHR, *Case "Relating to certain aspects of the laws on the use of languages in education in Belgium" v. Belgium*, judgment of 23 July 1968, *Series* A No. 6, A/6, § 1.

94 ECtHR, *Golder v United Kingdom*, judgment of 21 February 1975, *Series* A No. 18, § 30; recently confirmed in among others ECtHR, *Witold Litwa v. Poland*, judgment of 4 April 2000, *Reports* 2000-III, § 58.

95 ECtHR, *Case "Relating to certain aspects of the laws on the use of languages in education in Belgium" v. Belgium*, judgment of 23 July 1968, *Series* A No. 6, § 1.

96 ECtHR, *Golder v United Kingdom*, judgment of 21 February 1975, *Series* A No. 18, § 30.

this method has been used when a certain matter was governed in detail by a specific Protocol which had not (yet) been ratified by the respondent state in question.[97] In other cases this method has been used where more than one provision of the European Convention could govern the matter. The ECtHR has dealt with these cases by regarding the European Convention as a whole. It has held that that interpretation must 'be in harmony with the logic of the Convention'.[98] This entails that, if a right is not recognized under a specific provision, the ECtHR cannot read this right into a more general provision, since that would undermine the coherence of the European Convention. The case of *Schalk and Kopf* presents a clear example of this approach.[99] The question in this case was whether Contracting States are obliged to allow for same-sex couples to marry. The applicants argued their case from the perspective of Article 12 of the European Convention, under which they argued that their right to marry was violated. They also invoked Article 14 in conjunction with Article 8, under which they argued that they were discriminated against on the basis of their sexual orientation. The ECtHR held that since Article 12 ECHR did not oblige Contracting States to open marriage up for same-sex couples this choice is left to the Contracting States. In the context of Article 14 and Article 8 the ECtHR held that:

> [T]he Convention is to be read as a whole and its Articles should therefore be construed in harmony with one another ... Having regard to the conclusion reached above, namely that Article 12 does not impose an obligation on Contracting States to grant same-sex couples access to marriage, Article 14 taken in conjunction with Article 8, a provision of more general purpose and scope, cannot be interpreted as imposing such an obligation either.[100]

Even though the ECtHR has stated that the Convention and its Protocols must be considered as a whole, the context it looks at will differ from case to case. Sometimes it can mean simply looking at the other paragraphs of the provision in question; on other occasions it stretches to cover the European Convention and the Protocols itself.

The systemic method of interpretation is frequently used by the CJEU as well, which is quite understandable considering that EU law consists of an extensive body of primary and secondary legislation. The importance of this method is already apparent from the above repeated statement in the *Van Gend en Loos* judgment[101] where the CJEU referred to the spirit, general scheme and wording of a provision as relevant

97 Merrils (1993), p. 73; Ovey & White (2006), p. 44.

98 ECtHR, *Leander v Sweden*, judgment of 26 March 1987, *Series* A No. 116, § 78.

99 ECtHR, *Schalk and Kopf v. Austria*, judgment of 24 June 2010, *unpublished.*

100 ECtHR, *Schalk and Kopf v. Austria*, judgment of 24 June 2010, *unpublished*, § 101.

101 C-26/62, *Van Gend en Loos v. Administratie der Belastingen* [1963] ECR 3.

for determining the scope of the provision. The provision in question should thus be interpreted in relation to the treaty as a whole, for example, by taking the place of a provision in a particular chapter under consideration and or by looking at the EU system as a whole.[102] According to BROWN & KENNEDY 'it is natural to stress the interrelationship of the individual Treaties and their provisions as component parts of the total scheme'.[103]

The question is whether this method is also relevant in the context of the interpretation of fundamental rights. REICH has argued that 'systemic interpretation makes little sense in legal systems that do not rely on codification,... [because] judge made law cannot aim to be systematic, since there is no theoretical reference point to which interpretation could turn'.[104] While it is not true that the whole EU system is based on judge-made law, the fundamental rights doctrine in the EU was until recently entirely based on judge-made law.[105] The entry into force of the EU Charter might make reference to this method of interpretation valuable or even necessary.

4.3.4 Subjective or historical interpretation[106]

By applying the subjective or historical method of interpretation a court or judge tries to discover the intentions of the author of the text.[107] In the context of treaty interpretation the term 'subjective' interpretation is often used,[108] yet in some national contexts the term 'historical' interpretation is more regularly used for referring to the same method of interpretation.[109] For the purpose of this thesis the term 'historical' interpretation will be employed, since it illustrates most clearly what type of argument plays a role in this kind of interpretation. Reference is made to the intention the drafters had when they drafted the text, which is an historical argument. The term 'subjective' interpretation leaves out this historical aspect and only focuses

102 Many different examples from the case law of the CJEU can be given; however due to lack of space, reference is made to Brown & Kennedy (2000), p. 334 where some examples from the case law have been enumerated.

103 Brown & Kennedy (2000), p. 334.

104 Reich (2005), p. 29.

105 See Chapter 3 for a more detailed explanation.

106 Villiger (2009), p. 421, employs this terminology. Toufayan (2005), p. 7, also uses both terms interchangeably.

107 Bernhardt (1995), p. 1420; Brown & Kennedy (200), p. 330; Llorens (1999), p. 379; Vincenzi & Fairhurst (2002), p. 103

108 See for example, Ayral (2003), p. 15; Aust (2007), p. 231; Orakhelashvili (2008), p. 304.

109 See for example, in the Dutch context: Franken (2003), p. 196; Janssen (2005), p. 191; Cliteur (2005), p. 171; Smith (2005), p. 145-146.

on the intention of the drafters, which could also change over time and be derived from, for example, subsequent actions.[110]

While the text is regarded as a factor that reflects the intention of the drafters, adherents of this method of interpretation also take note of other documents that reveal the intention of the drafters, which in some cases can be more important than the text.[111] Beside the text of a treaty, the most important other document that reflects the intention of the drafters of a treaty is the *travaux préparatoires*.[112] The Vienna Convention allows for these documents to play a role in the interpretation process, but only as a supplementary means of interpretation.[113] This means that they may only be resorted to if the text of the provision remains unclear even after using the primary interpretation methods contained in Article 31 VCLT.[114] Given the position of one of the crucial elements of this interpretation method in the Vienna Convention, one can conclude that this method is not given a prominent role.

There are several reasons why the *travaux préparatoires* have only been given a supplementary role in the VCLT. Most authors emphasize the fact that the *travaux préparatoires* must be used carefully.[115] One of the problems is that often the *travaux* are not publicly accessible, which raises the question whether in those cases

110 Historical interpretation closely resembles subjective teleological interpretation as discussed in Chapter 5. It is discussed separately because it is often recognized in its own right in theoretical literature.

111 McRae (2002), p. 216.

112 See Bernhardt (1995), p. 1419, who notes that this method of interpretation prevailed for a long period before the drafting of the Vienna Convention on the Law of Treaties. McRae (2002), p. 216, also refers to the *travaux préparatoires* as important evidence of the intention of the drafters. See also Aryal (2003), p. 15, referring to Lauterpacht who argued that the *travaux préparatoires* are a 'legitimate and desirable means to ascertain the intentions of the parties'. Orakhelashvili (2008), p. 384, is more sceptical of the relevance of the *travaux préparatoires* and argues that they reflect the intentions of the parties at the preparatory stage, but not their intentions with regard to the final text.

113 *Article 32 VCLT:*
Supplementary means of interpretation
Recourse may be had to supplementary means of interpretation, including the preparatory work of the treaty and the circumstances of its conclusion, in order to confirm the meaning resulting from the application of Article 31, or to determine the meaning when the interpretation according to Article 31:
(a) leaves the meaning ambiguous or obscure; or
(b) leads to a result which is manifestly absurd or unreasonable.

114 Orakhelashvili (2008), p. 383 is rather absolute in his statement. He also refers to judicial practice that reveals that the ICJ often found reference to the *travaux préparatoires* not necessary or even not possible given the secondary status of these documents in the VCLT, see p. 387- 389. Aust (2007), p. 245, however, defends the statement that even if the ordinary meaning of a provision is clear, if the ordinary meaning is in contradiction with the *travaux préparatoires*, these latter documents will be used to 'correct' the ordinary meaning. According to his opinion, this is also the way these documents are used in practice.

115 Aust (2007), p. 247. See also: Villiger (2009), p. 446; Bernhardt (1999), p. 14-15.

they may be resorted to. The VCLT does not provide any guidance on this question, so each court should decide for itself whether non-publicly accessible *travaux* may be relied upon.[116] As will be shown below, this question seems to be answered in the negative by the CJEU. Furthermore, even if they are accessible, *travaux préparatoires* are notoriously unreliable.[117] Reference is made to the incompleteness of the *travaux*, the fact that they are often contradictory or that they contain self-serving statements for political purposes.[118] As a result the *travaux* can be misleading and should be used carefully.

A final problematic aspect of relying on *travaux préparatoires* is whether they should be used in the context of multilateral treaties where states may accede at a later stage, like the EU or the ECHR.[119] The states that accede to a treaty at a later stage have not been able to influence the *travaux préparatoires*. Both AUST and ARYAL agree with the ILC that *travaux préparatoires* can also be invoked in cases between parties that did not take part in the preparatory negotiation process.[120] In their view, parties acceding to a treaty either had the opportunity to take notice of the *travaux préparatoires* because they are publicly available or the parties could have requested to see the travaux before acceding to the treaty.[121] Therefore the travaux can be relied upon even in the case of multilateral treaties. BERNHARDT, however, argues that in the context of multilateral treaties *travaux préparatoires* should have a minor role.[122] These problematic aspects affect the historical method of interpretation, because the *travaux préparatoires* play such a crucial role in the context of this method.[123] The method, therefore, does not play a very prominent role in the interpretation of the treaties central to this thesis as will be discussed below.

The use of this method of interpretation in respect of the ECHR system is also rather limited due to the specific nature of this system, namely a system progressively trying to reach a certain goal.[124] This feature shows an inherent inclination towards a more dynamic kind of interpretation rather than a historical one. Already in its early cases the ECtHR has referred to the European Convention as a living instrument, thereby

116 Orakhelashvili (2008), p. 383.

117 Aryal (2003), p. 37; Orakhelashvili (2008), p. 383-386; McRae (2002), p. 218.

118 See, among others, Orakhelashvili (2008), p. 383-384.

119 See Aust (2007), p. 247; Aryal (2003), p. 40-41.

120 Commentary to articles of Vienna Convention, Yearbook of International Law Commission, 1966-Vol. II, p. 223. See also: Aust (2007), p. 247; Aryal (2003), p. 40-41

121 Commentary to articles of Vienna Convention, Yearbook of International Law Commission, 1966-Vol. II, p. 223.

122 Orakhelashvili (2008), p. 387, referring to Bernhardt (1963). See also Bernhardt (1999), p. 14.

123 Bernhardt (1999), p. 14-15.

124 This follows amongst others from the wording of the preamble referring to 'further realization of human rights' and to 'the first steps for the collective enforcement'.

reducing the relevance of the historical interpretation.[125] This phrase has been repeated in numerous subsequent cases and has become one of the fundamental features of the European Convention.

Within the confines of the system of the European Convention the *travaux préparatoires* are the main (if not only) representatives of the historical method of interpretation. Despite the fact that the principle of dynamic interpretation[126] contradicts the historical interpretation, the ECtHR has made use of the *travaux préparatoires* on some occasions.[127] In order to get a feeling of how the ECtHR uses the *travaux préparatoires* as an element of the historical interpretation, reference will be made to some cases of the ECtHR. In the *Johnston*[128] case the *travaux préparatoires* served to show the limits of interpretation for the ECtHR. The ECHR held that a right to divorce could not be read into the European Convention as no such intention could be deduced from the *travaux préparatoires*. On different occasions the ECHR referred to the *travaux préparatoires* in order to support an interpretation already sustained by other interpretation methods.[129] In some instances where reference is made to the *travaux*, this is done by the dissenting judges to a certain case in order to support (generally) a more restrictive interpretation.[130] Of course for many issues the *travaux préparatoires* do not provide any help, simply because the drafters could not anticipate all societal developments. This factor, beside the principle of evolutive interpretation clearly limits the usefulness of the *travaux préparatoires*.

This quick glance at the case law warrants the question whether there are any reasons behind the decision whether to resort to the *travaux préparatoires* or not. It would also be relevant to analyze in the case law when the ECtHR ignores or sidesteps the *travaux préparatoires* and in what kind of situations it respects them. The question is whether there is a consistent line in this respect. Even though historical interpretation will not be part of the case law analysis, these questions are also relevant in the context of evolutive interpretation, because if the *travaux préparatoires* are applied this means that there is no room for an evolutive approach.

---

125 ECtHR, *Tyrer v. United Kingdom*, judgment of 25 April 1978, *Series* A No. 26, § 31.

126 This principle will be discussed in the following section.

127 See Lawson (1996) for an elaborate account of the role of the *travaux préparatoires* in the 80s and 90s.

128 ECtHR 18 December 1986, *Johnston and others v Ireland*, A/112, § 52.

129 For example: ECtHR (GC), *Banković and others v. Belgium and others*, decision of 12 December 2001, *Reports* 2001-VII, § 65; ECtHR, *Kjeldsen, Busk Madsen and Pederson v Denmark*, judgment of 7 December 1976, *Series* A No. 23, § 50; ECtHR, *Le Compte, Van Leuven and De Meyere v Belgium*, judgment of 23 June 1981, *Series* A No. 34, § 65.

130 See for example the dissenting opinion of Judge Thór Vilhjálmsson in the case of ECtHR, *Sigurdur A. Sigurjónsson v. Iceland*, judgment of 30 June 1993, *Series* A No. 264.

Within the EU legal system the role of the historical interpretation method is even more limited. Due to 'the dynamic character of the Treaties as laying down programs for the future the reference to the *travaux préparatoires* tends to diminish as the dates of concluding the Treaties recede into the past'.[131] Not only does this specific feature of the Treaties play a role in the use of historical interpretation, the accessibility of the *travaux préparatoires* is a highly important limitation in the context of the CJEU, as indicated above. There are no published *travaux préparatoires* of the Treaties, which has led Judge *Kutscher* to state that: 'Documents which are not generally accessible must, ..., be ruled out as aids to interpretation for constitutional reasons'.[132] This seems to be the line taken by the CJEU, as hardly any reference to the *travaux préparatoires* can be found. Interpretation concerning secondary legislation, however, might involve a reference to the subjective intention of the parties, as the preparatory documents are sometimes available for secondary legislation.[133] For reasons of transparency, preparatory works are more regularly published and it has been asserted that this might change the approach of the CJEU in the future.[134] The question is whether that statement is true, because publishing the *travaux préparatoires* does not change the dynamic character of EU law.

In conclusion, one could say that the historical method of interpretation in the context of these European systems is limited to the question whether the courts refer to the *travaux préparatoires* in their interpretation in order to shed any light on the (subjective) intentions of the drafting parties. It is clear that due to the characteristics of both systems this method plays a limited role. Despite that limited role it would be interesting, as has been mentioned above, to get more insight into the role of these documents in the interpretation process. Historical interpretation as a method will not be studied more closely in this thesis, but the role of the *travaux préparatoires* will be addressed in the context of evolutive interpretation and teleological interpretation.

4.3.5 Comparative method of interpretation

The comparative method of interpretation has been developed by supranational courts like the CJEU and ECtHR and does not follow from the Vienna Convention.[135] Comparative interpretation means interpretation where the judge in question uses

131 Brown & Kennedy, (2000), p. 332.

132 Arnull (2006), p. 614 referring to a report of a Conference in 1976.

133 Brown & Kennedy (2000) p. 333; Llorens (1999), p. 379; Schermers & Waelbroeck, (2001), p. 16; Lasok, & Millet, (2004), § 671.

134 Arnull (2006), p. 615.

135 One could argue that one version of comparative interpretation does flow from the Vienna Convention, but that argument will be explored in the context of Chapter 6.

foreign or international materials in order to find the meaning of a specific provision.[136] Under this method reference can be made to the laws of Member States, as well as laws of third countries, or treaties that are outside the framework of the treaty in question. There is no common understanding of which materials can and cannot be relied on in the context of comparative interpretation.[137] Also the purposes of relying on these materials may differ. Foreign materials can be used to support a certain interpretation, but they can also be decisive in establishing a certain interpretation, the choice depending on the court employing this method. Both the CJEU and the ECtHR have mainly referred to the laws of the Member States in order to support a specific interpretation, so this section will focus on that type of comparative interpretation.[138]

Why has this method been invoked by the supranational courts under study? One possible explanation might be that relying on the laws of the Member States to argue in favour of or against a specific interpretation may help in engaging the Member States in the enterprise of fundamental rights protection in Europe. It certainly helps the supranational courts to check whether sufficient ground can be found for a specific interpretation. The supranational courts are, on the one hand, faced with a mix of Member States that differ on many levels, for example, socially and culturally. On the other hand, effective protection of fundamental rights requires a high level of protection for all individuals within the jurisdiction of the respective court. This constitutes a certain tension, since it will not always be easy to convince all Member States of the need to afford a specific type of protection. The use of comparative interpretation might prevent the CJEU and ECtHR from running ahead of the Member States and as a result risk losing its credibility.

The comparative method will be discussed in detail in Chapter 6. For that reason, only a short introduction will be provided here in order to indicate what is meant when the respective courts resort to this method.

In the context of the European Convention, the comparative method of interpretation (also referred to as the 'consensus method')[139] is one of the most important methods in the interpretation process. The term 'consensus' refers to a crucial element of the method, i.e. the laws of the Contracting States will be compared in order to check whether a consensus on a certain issue can be found. If this consensus can be found, the ECtHR will adopt the interpretation in line with the consensus. If, however, no such consensus can be found, Contracting States will often be able to decide for

136 Alexy (1989), p. 239.

137 See section 6.1.1.

138 Chapter 6 will explore other versions of comparative interpretation as well.

139 For example: Heringa, (1996).

themselves whether they will provide protection or not (or in some cases the ECtHR will adopt an autonomous interpretation; see for a discussion section 4.4.1.3 below). In the case of *Schalk and Kopf,* for example, the ECtHR had to decide whether Article 12 of the European Convention entailed an obligation to allow for same-sex marriages.[140] In order to be able to answer that question, the ECtHR took into account the situation in the different Contracting States and concluded that no consensus could be found concerning the acceptation of same-sex marriages.[141] This sounds rather straightforward, but if one examines the way the ECHR has employed this method in its case law, many questions arise. What can be considered a consensus? Is this established on the basis of a simple majority? Are there any criteria for establishing a consensus? Could the use of the consensus approach lead to a lower degree of protection after the accession of many new Contracting States? How does the comparison itself take place? Is there a checklist that will be applied in each instance of comparing? Will all Contracting States be considered? Is the consequence of the existence or non-existence of a consensus always the same? When will national differences (not) be allowed? It is questions such as these that will be considered in more detail in Chapters 6 and 10 of this thesis.

The involvement of the comparative method in the general interpretation process before the CJEU is often less explicit in its judgments. In the context of interpretation of EU law in general it has been said that notions of EU law have an independent meaning, but that inspiration may be drawn from national interpretations.[142] In the specific context of fundamental rights the comparative method of interpretation plays a rather prominent role, because the CJEU introduced the whole concept of fundamental rights into, at that time, Community law by labelling them general principles of Community law, derived from the constitutional traditions of Member States.[143] In other words, the domestic constitutions serve as one of the sources for the concept of fundamental rights in EU law. This again raises many questions, some similar to the ones noted above for the ECtHR and some different. How does the CJEU determine whether something can be considered common to the constitutional traditions of the Member States? Will a majority be sufficient to support the finding of a common principle? What is the effect of the enlargement of the EU on this consensus finding? How does the comparison take place? Who undertakes the comparison: the CJEU, Advocate General or maybe a third body? What if no common tradition can be found? What is or might be the influence of the EU Charter on this method? This

140 ECtHR, *Schalk and Kopf v. Austria*, judgment of 24 June 2010, *unpublished.*

141 ECtHR, *Schalk and Kopf v. Austria*, judgment of 24 June 2010, *unpublished*, § 58.

142 Llorens (1999), p. 380.

143 See Chapters 3 and 13.

is just a short and by no means exhaustive insight into the kind of questions that come up and that will be discussed in Chapters 6 and 13.

4.3.6 Conclusion

In the previous sections a short overview of different interpretation methods has been presented, most of which have their basis in the Vienna Convention. The aim has been to indicate briefly what the methods entail and to what extent the use of these methods is relevant in the context of fundamental rights interpretation by (supra)national courts. Teleological interpretation and comparative interpretation both seem to play an important role in the interpretation of fundamental rights before the CJEU and the ECtHR. Other interpretation methods, like textual interpretation, systemic interpretation or historical interpretation, often appear to provide outside boundaries for the interpretation of fundamental rights, but they may be less helpful in determining the specific meaning of a provision. For example, the often vaguely worded fundamental rights provisions can have many different meanings, so textual interpretation is hardly helpful, except when the linguistic opposite of the wording of the provision is argued. In that case textual interpretation can often be used to set the boundaries of what can be achieved by means of interpretation. Historical interpretation plays only a limited role in the context of both the CJEU and the ECtHR, since both courts deal with treaties with a dynamic character. Systematic interpretation, however, does play a more prominent role in the interpretation process. This method helps the courts to understand the provisions in their context and respect the treaty as a coherent whole instead of a collection of separate provisions.

4.4 Principles of interpretation

The second part of this chapter will provide an overview of the most important principles of interpretation employed by the ECtHR or the CJEU. Most bodies interpreting treaties use similar interpretation methods, which are often methods that are also regularly employed in a national context. The use of interpretative principles depends, much more than is the case with interpretation methods, on the context of the specific treaty. Interpretative principles, as explained in section 4.1, entail an objective of the interpretative process. They are, therefore, closely related to the character of the treaty in question. As a result it depends on the specific treaty as to which interpretative principles are relevant. Some interpretative principles, thus, might not play any role in a specific treaty context, for example, the principle of uniform interpretation; not every treaty might aim towards harmonization. A discussion of the different principles that play a role in the context of the CJEU and the ECtHR is necessary to complete the interpretative framework of both courts, which exists for both interpretation methods and principles. As has been said, contrary to interpretative principles, interpretation methods do not say much about the character of a treaty. For that reason, adding interpretative principles to the framework of interpretation helps to emphasize the specific character of a particular treaty.

The preliminary understanding that not every court employs the same interpretative principles explains why the second part of this chapter is structured on the basis of the two courts and not, like the first part, on the basis of interpretative principles. For both the CJEU and the ECtHR the most important interpretative principles found in the literature will be discussed; the list is not intended to be exhaustive. The aim is to discuss briefly what these interpretative principles entail and, insofar as is possible, their relation with interpretation methods. The chapter will provide an overview of a number of principles, not all of which will be used for the analysis in this thesis. The selection of principles and methods to be examined specifically for the case law of the CJEU and the ECtHR will be explained at the end of the present chapter (section 4.5).

4.4.1 European Court of Human Rights

The ECtHR has developed several principles that play an important guiding role in the interpretation process. Some of these principles are qualified in the literature as interpretation methods (e.g. autonomous interpretation), but on the basis of the distinction made in section 4.1, for the purpose of the analysis in this thesis, these interpretative aids are qualified as interpretative principles. The most relevant ones within the context of interpretation will be discussed in this chapter.

4.4.1.1 Principle of evolutive interpretation

The European Convention on Human Rights provides long-term guarantees against human rights violations in Europe. Societies do, however, change over the course of time, which could result in changes in societal and human rights standards as well. If the meaning of these Convention guarantees were fixed at the time of the adoption of the Convention, the Convention runs the risk of losing its relevance in modern society. A certain degree of flexibility when interpreting the Convention would help the European Court of Human Rights to keep the Convention alive. The ECtHR has incorporated this flexibility into the Convention system by qualifying the Convention as a living instrument which needs to be interpreted in light of present-day conditions.[144] This is called the evolutive approach or is referred to as the 'living instru-

144 The first time that the ECtHR recognized this principle was in the case of ECtHR, *Tyrer v. United Kingdom*, judgment of 25 April 1978, *Series* A No. 26.

ment doctrine'. Both concepts are used interchangeably by the ECtHR,[145] but this thesis will adhere to the term 'evolutive interpretation'. In this section the recognition of evolutive interpretation and the basis for this interpretative principle will briefly be discussed. Chapter 7 will address the meaning of the principle of evolutive interpretation in more detail.

The question is how this principle found its way into the reasoning of the ECtHR. After all, the text of the Convention itself does not explicitly provide for an evolutive approach. The preamble does refer to 'the maintenance and further realization of human rights', but that is a rather broad reference that does not explicitly refer to an evolutive approach. Despite this lack of clear textual support the ECtHR has consistently said in its case law that the Convention is a living instrument that should be interpreted in an evolutive manner. Indeed, the concept is entirely developed in the case law. The first case in which the ECtHR recognized an evolutive approach was in 1978, in *Tyrer v United Kingdom.*[146] In this case a schoolboy complained about corporal punishment and claimed that this violated Article 3 of the Convention (prohibition of torture and inhuman or degrading treatment). The boy was sentenced to three strokes of the birch on his bare posterior in the presence of his father. The question before the ECtHR was whether this constituted degrading treatment. Without providing any reasons for invoking a new approach, the ECtHR recalled that 'the Convention is a living instrument which must be interpreted in light of present-day conditions'. It is not entirely clear whether the evolutive approach had a major influence on the outcome of the *Tyrer* case, but the ECtHR did decide that the corporal punishment constituted degrading treatment. More important for the present discussion is that the qualification of the Constitution as a living instrument has become a standard part of the reasoning in many subsequent cases and it has developed into one of the most important concepts in the interpretation process of the ECtHR.[147]

The principle of evolutive interpretation provides a good example of one of the interpretative aids that are referred to in different qualifications by various authors. In section 4.1 the example has already been given of MATSCHER who, contrary to LEACH, qualifies evolutive interpretation as an interpretation *method.*[148] HELFER and RIGAUX also understand evolutive interpretation to be an interpretation *method,*[149] while PREBENSEN seems to acknowledge that evolutive interpretation should be qualified differently by referring to the 'doctrine' and 'principle' of evolutive interpretation.[150] These differences create confusion, most importantly regarding

145 Mowbray (2005), p. 64.
146 ECtHR, *Tyrer v. United Kingdom*, judgment of 25 April 1978, *Series* A No. 26.
147 Prebensen (2000), p. 1123; Mowbray (2005), p. 60.
148 Matscher (1993), p. 68-70; Leach (2005), p. 164.
149 Helfer (1993); Rigaux (1998), p. 41.
150 Prebensen (2000), p. 1123- 1124, 1126. See also summarily Jacot-Guillarmod (1995), p. 61.

the role that evolutive interpretation plays in the reasoning of judgments. As has been explained in section 4.1, a method of interpretation provides a technique that leads to an interpretative outcome, while a principle of interpretation only provides an objective for the interpretative process. Qualifying evolutive interpretation as a method of interpretation, thus, wrongly implies that a judge with the help of this principle alone can interpret a specific provision. An interpretative principle, however, can play an important role in the interpretative process, but only as a supplement to one or several interpretation methods.

Interestingly, the fact that the ECtHR introduced an evolutive approach through its case law did not attract much controversy.[151] This does, however, not mean that there are no debates on evolutive interpretation; the case is quite the contrary. The debates on evolutive interpretation focus on *how* the ECtHR invokes evolutive interpretation in its cases.[152] Evolutive interpretation, in short, means that provisions of the Convention will be interpreted in accordance with contemporary standards. The principle does not give much guidance as to which element should be taken into account when interpreting in an evolutive manner, unlike textual or systematic interpretation. One could argue that the reference to present-day conditions is equal to a reference to the situation in the different Contracting States. That is, however, a limited understanding of present-day conditions. It would be analytically more helpful to regard the relation between 'present-day conditions' and looking at different Contracting States as a strong link between a version of comparative interpretation and the principle of evolutive interpretation. Thus, a better perspective would be to view this as an example of the interconnectedness between interpretation methods and principles, since separating this method and principle respects their different roles. Moreover, in theory different interpretation methods could play a role in determining the present-day conditions. For example, the contemporary meaning of a certain term may have changed,[153] or the object and purpose could be viewed in a contemporary light. There might, for instance, be a different understanding of the purpose of the protection of one's private life in 2010 than what would have been the purpose of protecting one's private life in 1960. Furthermore, the adoption of a new protocol could lead to a different context, which through a systemic interpretation could have an impact on a specific interpretation.

A related question is whether the principle of evolutive interpretation is used in practice to supplement these interpretation methods or whether it is mainly used in

151 Prebensen (2000), p. 1124.

152 See for example Mowbray (2005), p. 71; Matscher (1993), p. 69-70; Bernhardt (1999), p. 21-23, refers to some critical questions, but also to some problems that are directed at the interconnectedness with comparative interpretation.

153 Linderfalk (2008), p. 111, discusses that with the passing of time words are given new meanings.

combination with comparative interpretation. The case law analysis provided in Chapter 11 will be able to provide an answer to this question.

In this thesis, most attention will be paid to the question what it really means to take an evolutive approach. In Chapter 7 a theoretical perspective will be taken in order get a basic understanding of the different aspects that play a role in evolutive interpretation. The role of evolutive interpretation in the interpretative framework will also be addressed. Chapter 11 will subsequently deal with the case law analysis and shed some more light on the evolutive approach in practice. The question is whether the ECtHR addresses all concerns that emerge from the theoretical analysis or whether there are areas for improvement.

4.4.1.2 Principle of practical and effective rights

The special nature of the European Convention as a law-making treaty granting rights to individual citizens, compels a different approach towards the rights that have been laid down in the document than would be the case for purely contractual treaties.[154] The ECtHR has explicitly acknowledged this special character of the European Convention by stating in *Wemhoff* that 'given that it is a law-making treaty, it is also necessary to seek the interpretation that is most appropriate in order to realize the aim and achieve the object of the treaty, not that which would restrict to the greatest possible degree the obligations undertaken by the Parties'.[155] The ECtHR has adopted, among others, the principle of practical and effective rights in order to ensure the relevance of the enumerated rights and to prevent the document from becoming a dead letter. Numerous cases contain a reference to this doctrine by stating that the European Convention does not protect rights that are theoretical and illusory, but serves to protect rights that are practical and effective.[156] This description by the ECtHR already indicates that it is an objective that is taken into consideration when interpreting Convention rights, but not a technique on how to interpret these rights. Some consider teleological interpretation to be synonymous with effective interpreta-

154 See among others Matscher (1993), p. 66; Greer (2006), p. 195-196; Mahony (1990), p. 65; Rietiker (2010), p. 246, who all argue that the ECtHR has a character distinct from reciprocal contractual treaties between states.

155 ECtHR, *Wemhoff v. Germany*, judgment of 27 June 1968, *Series* A No. 7.

156 A HUDOC-search over the first six months of 2010 rendered at least 30 judgments in which the ECtHR invoked a reference to the principle of practical and effective rights. The ECtHR did not in all these cases invoke these references in the interpretative phase, but for example, in ECtHR, *Rantsev v. Cyprus and Russia*, judgment of 7 January 2010, *unpublished* and in ECtHR, *Vanjak v Croatia*, judgment of 14 January 2010, *unpublished*, the ECtHR did invoke this principle in the interpretative phase.

tion,[157] but others consider it to be an aspect of teleological interpretation.[158] The latter qualification is in line with the division described earlier in this chapter and respects the role that the method and this principle play in the interpretation process. The ECtHR seems to agree with this position, since in *Stoll* they referred to the '*principle* whereby the Convention is intended to guarantee rights that are not theoretical or illusory, but practical and effective'.[159]

The use of this principle is not confined to one particular right. It is a general principle, which is applicable to all rights laid down in the European Convention.[160] The ECtHR has even applied it to the institutional provisions of the Convention in order to prevent rigid legal formalism from occurring.[161] In the case of *Klass and others*, for example, the ECtHR held that the concept of 'victim' as contained in Article 34 of the European Convention (then Article 25) must be applied in a manner that renders the Convention enforcement machinery effective. The ECtHR emphasized that: 'The procedural provisions of the Convention must, in view of the fact that the Convention and its institutions were set up to protect the individual, be applied in a manner which serves to make the system of individual applications efficacious.'[162]

The European Convention itself does not provide any basis for the principle; it has been introduced and developed in the case law of the ECtHR. This does not mean that it is a principle that only features in ECtHR case law. On the contrary, it is a recognized principle of treaty interpretation more generally.[163] It has not been included explicitly in the VCLT, but according to the commentary to the VCLT, the principle of practical and effective rights is embodied in the reference to 'good faith' and 'object and purpose' contained in Article 31 VCLT.[164] The use of this principle is also visible in the case law of, for example, the International Court of Justice and the Inter-American Court of Human Rights.[165] Nevertheless, the principle of practical

157 Aust (2007), p. 231.

158 See Fitzmaurice (2010), p. 202.

159 ECtHR (GC), *Stoll v. Switzerland,* judgment of 10 December 2007, *unpublished.*

160 Schokkenbroek (2000), p. 7.

161 See Merrils (1993), p. 113-114; Schokkenbroek (2000), p. 2.1 8.

162 ECtHR, *Klass and others v Germany*, judgment of 6 September 1978, *Series* A No. 28, § 34.

163 Fitzmaurice (2010), p. 202 refers to the fact that this principle has been acknowledged by the International Law Commission. In the context of treaty interpretation, this principle is often referred to as the principle of 'effet utile' or the principle of 'effectiveness', which is similar to the principle of practical and effective rights. Given that the ECtHR uses the terminology of 'practical and effective rights' this terminology will be used here as well.

164 See: Commentary to articles of Vienna Convention, Yearbook of International Law Commission, 1966- Vol. II, p. 219.

165 See Rietiker (2010), p. 256.

and effective rights 'has taken its most prominent place' in the context of the European Convention.[166]

The commentary by the ILC already provided a justification for the use of the principle of practical and effective rights, namely that this is inherent to interpreting a treaty in good faith in line with the object and purpose of a treaty. The ECtHR has provided a similar justification for its use of the principle of practical and effective rights.[167] In *Soering* the ECtHR held that: 'the object and purpose of the Convention as an instrument for the protection of individual human beings require that its provisions be interpreted and applied so as to make its safeguards practical and effective'.[168] Along the same lines, the ECtHR held in *Osman* that interpretation of Convention provisions must be compatible with 'the requirements of Article 1 of the Convention and the obligations of Contracting States under that Article to secure the practical and effective protection of the rights and freedoms laid down therein'.[169] Both justifications, one more explicit than the other, refer to the object of the European Convention, namely the protection of fundamental rights for individual human beings. Interestingly, the principle of meta-teleological interpretation, as explained in section 4.1, thus plays an important role in this justifying the use of the principle of effectiveness.

As has been mentioned, the principle of practical and effective rights has been developed in the case law of the ECtHR and it is therefore useful to discuss one of these cases as an illustration of what this principle actually entails. The *Airey* case constitutes a famous example of the application of the principle of practical and effective rights.[170] The case concerned a woman who wanted to obtain a decree of judicial separation from her abusive husband. Due to her low income she was unable to pay the costs of such legal proceedings and since there was no legal aid available this left her without any access to court. The ECtHR concluded that there was a positive obligation on the Irish state to provide legal assistance for Ms. Airey in order to ensure her effective access to court. An important element in this case is that it clearly shows

---

166 According to Rietiker (2010), p. 256, who refers to Koskenniemi, who argues that in the context of human rights treaties the principle of practical and effective rights has been used to a wider extent than in the context of other treaties.

167 Schokkenbroek (2000) referring to the case of ECtHR, *Soering v. United Kingdom*, judgment of 7 July 1989, *Series* A No. 161, § 87 and ECtHR *McCann and others v United Kingdom*, judgment of 27 September 1995, Series A No. 324, § 146.

168 ECtHR, *Soering v. United Kingdom*, judgment of 7 July 1989, *Series* A No. 161, § 87.

169 ECtHR (GC), *Osman v. United Kingdom*, judgment of 28 October 1998, *Reports* 1998-VIII.

170ECtHR, *Airey v. Ireland*, judgment of 9 October 1979, *Series* A No. 32.

that this principle can be used as a basis for the positive obligations doctrine.[171] The ECtHR has often applied this concept in order to establish a positive obligation on the side of the state.[172] The underlying idea is that states cannot offer effective protection by 'simply remaining passive'.[173] Simultaneously, this case exemplifies the perceived risks that are connected to this principle. The principle almost automatically leads to extensive interpretation of the rights laid down in the Convention.[174] This is due to the fact that the emphasis is placed on the question of what *can* be achieved on the basis of these rights and how to ensure their (maximum) effectiveness for the protection of individual human beings.[175] The perspective of the individual leads to an emphasis on extensive interpretation, since that is generally beneficial for the protection of their rights. This perspective is also visible in the ECtHR's judgments, for example in *Vilho Eskelinen*. The ECtHR in this case recalled its case law in order to establish whether an old criterion on the basis of which the court could determine whether Article 6 was applicable to civil servants had to be changed. The ECtHR observed that: 'It is important to note that the Court emphasized that in applying a functional criterion it must adopt a restrictive interpretation, in accordance with the object and purpose of the Convention, of the exceptions to the safeguards afforded by Article 6 § 1 ... This was to limit the cases in which public servants could be denied the practical and effective protection afforded to them.'[176] Adopting a practical and effective approach thus often leads to a restrictive interpretation of the exceptions in the European Convention and an extensive interpretation of the rights therein.[177]

One of the dangers of interpreting in a practical and effective manner is therefore that it stretches beyond interpretation into law making, since it seems to provide 'a *carte blanche* for unlimited judicial legislation'.[178] There are, however, limitations to this doctrine which prevent the abovementioned consequences. First of all, one should not forget that this principle is a *principle* of interpretation and therefore the text and system of the Convention still play an important limiting role when it actually comes to determining the meaning of certain Convention notions.[179] In the case

171 See also Mowbray (2005), p. 72, who refers to the case of ECtHR, *Marckx v. Belgium*, judgment of 13 June 1979, *Series* A No. 31.

172 Mowbray (2005), p. 72.

173 Mowbray (2005), p. 78.

174 Vande Lanotte (2005), p. 183; Schokkenbroek (2000), p. 6; Merrills (1993), p. 102.

175 Merrills (1993), p. 106, where he even asserts that the aim of the Convention is to ensure *maximum* effectiveness.

176 ECtHR (GC), *Vilho Eskelinen and others v. Finland*, judgment of 19 April 2007, *unpublished*, § 48.

177 See also Vande Lanotte (2005), p. 183, who refers to ECtHR (GC), *Mamatkulov and Askarov v. Turkey*, judgment of 4 February 2005, *Reports* 2005-I.

178 Merrills (1993), p. 119.

179 Merrills (1993), p. 199-120.

of *Johnston,* for example, the question was posed whether effective protection of family life (Article 8 ECHR) imposed a positive obligation on the state to permit divorce.[180] The ECtHR held that, since it concluded under Article 12 of the Convention that it did not entail a right to divorce, the interpretation of Article 8 could not be isolated from the interpretation of Article 12. Thus the system of the European Convention prevented the ECtHR from adopting a rather extensive interpretation. Moreover, the object and purpose and the relation with the Contracting States play an important role in the interpretation process and can limit the judicial discretion under the principle of practical and effective rights.[181]

Despite the danger of judicial law making, the principle itself has not been subjected to much criticism in academic literature. This could be the result of sensible use of the principle by the ECtHR.[182] The principle in itself is widely accepted, even beyond the context of the European Convention as has been discussed above, but the use of this principle in individual cases can be criticized for going too far. If criticism is voiced it could be because in a specific case the reliance on one of the interpretation methods is not convincing to more conservative critics. This might result in criticism being directed at the method of interpretation and not necessarily at the principle of practical and effective interpretation.

Hence, it has been shown that the principle of practical and effective interpretation plays a prominent role in the interpretation process of the ECtHR. The principle has, however, not been selected for further analysis in the context of this thesis – priority has been given to other meta-teleological principles. The purpose of this discussion therefore only has been to briefly provide an overview of the role of this principle in the context of the ECtHR.

4.4.1.3 Principle of autonomous interpretation

One of the characteristics of the interpretation process of the ECtHR is that some notions are granted an autonomous or 'European' meaning.[183] This means that some notions of a Convention provision are granted a 'status of semantic independence: the meaning is not to be equated with the meaning that these very same concepts possess in domestic law'.[184] The description clearly demonstrates that this is a prin-

180 ECtHR, *Johnston and others v. Ireland*, judgment of 18 December 1986, *Series* A No. 112.

181 Merrills (1993), p. 118-120.

182 Mowbray claims that the ECHR has been careful not to impose undue burdens on states. Mowbray (2005), p. 78.

183 Schokkenbroek (2000), 2.1 p. 9; Ost (1992), p. 305.

184 Letsas (2004), p. 282.

ciple of interpretation and not a method of interpretation.[185] The description refers to a goal or objective, namely to grant an autonomous or European meaning, but it does not provide any indication as to what this meaning should be. The content of this autonomous meaning should be established by relying on interpretation methods. A logical follow-up question is which interpretation methods are mostly used to establish an autonomous meaning. This will be analyzed in detail in Chapter 8 from a theoretical perspective and Chapter 12 on the basis of a case law analysis.

The use of the principle of autonomous interpretation can be justified by reference to the Vienna Convention, which provides in Article 31(4) that terms may be given a special meaning. On top of that, regardless of the rules on treaty interpretation, the Vienna Convention has made an exception for treaties adopted in the context of an international organization; in that case the rules of the specific organization prevail.[186] According to GANSHOF VAN DER MEERSCH this provision alone would justify the principle of autonomous interpretation, given the object and purpose of the European Convention, which has been concluded in the context of the Council of Europe.[187]

The ECtHR also justifies the application of this principle in the interpretation process by emphasizing that, if it were to take a different approach, states would be able to circumvent or escape responsibility under the European Convention.[188] It would leave the European Convention dependent on national classifications, which would seriously undermine the credibility of the European Convention as a minimum level of protection of fundamental rights. The case of *Engel*[189] is one of the leading examples of the application of this principle in the case law of the ECtHR. It concerned the question whether penalties for military disciplinary offences could be considered criminal in the sense of Article 6 ECHR. The government claimed that they could not, since national law classified these offences as disciplinary. While respecting the national distinction between disciplinary and criminal charges, the Court did not leave it at that. It established, despite this distinction, its own criteria to ascertain whether something qualified as a criminal charge, regardless of the national classification. The ECtHR has adopted a similar approach in many subsequent cases.

Even though the ECtHR regularly employs the principle of autonomous interpretation, it has not developed a general theory underlying this principle.[190] Neither does

185 For authors referring to autonomous interpretation as a method of interpretation, see Kastanas (1996), p. 344; Matscher (1993), p. 73; Sudre does not classify it as a method of interpretation in so many words, but considers it an interpretative technique. Sudre (1998), p. 94.

186 Article 5 of the Vienna Convention on the Law of Treaties.

187 Ganshof van der Meersch (1988), p. 205.

188 Letsas (2004), p. 282; Sudre (1998), p. 94; Merrils (1993), p. 71.

189 ECtHR, *Engel and others v. the Netherlands*, judgment of 8 June 1976, *Series* A No. 22.

190 Schokkenbroek (2000), p. 9.

the European Convention itself provide any reference to the principle of autonomous interpretation. Likewise, it is difficult to establish exactly how the ECtHR uses this principle: when it is applied and how the autonomous meaning is determined. What interpretation methods play a role in establishing an autonomous meaning? The theoretical chapter on autonomous interpretation will aim to provide a more in-depth analysis of the meaning of and theory behind this principle. The relation with interpretation methods and other principles will be the main focus of the case law analysis in Chapter 12.

4.4.1.4 Democracy in the European Convention system

The preamble of the European Convention expressly refers to an effective political democracy as the best form in order to maintain respect for fundamental rights. Not only the preamble, but also certain provisions contain references to a democratic society. To be more precise certain restrictions on the Convention rights are only allowed when they are 'necessary in a democratic society'.[191] These examples reflect the presence of the concept of democracy in many facets of the Convention.[192]

Several examples of the use of this concept have been discovered in the case law of the ECtHR. First, and most important for our subject, according to some authors democracy is to 'justify and lend shape to, and priority among, the rights and freedoms guaranteed'.[193] In other words: democracy is used as a guiding principle for the interpretation of the vague Convention terms.[194] The problem is that the examples given by these authors usually do not concern the interpretative phase of the judgment, but the application phase.[195] Democracy plays a role in underlining the importance of certain interests that need to be balanced against each other in the application phase. It is understandable that mainly examples of the application phase are discussed, since many ECHR provisions contain an explicit reference to 'democratic society' in the limitation clause. An important function of the notion of democracy is thus to enable the ECtHR to make a distinction between justified and unjustified restrictions of the Convention rights.[196] In this sense democracy plays a role in the application of the European Convention as well. Only in cases on Article 3 First Protocol, which concerns the right to free elections and is consequently directly linked to democracy, does the concept play a role in the interpretation phase. Finally, the concept plays

---

191 See article 8, 9, 10, 11 of the European Convention.

192 Mahony claims that even though it is not mentioned in other articles, democracy is a notion that permeates the whole Convention system. Mahony (1990), p. 64.

193 Marks (1995), p. 231; Vande Lanotte (2005), p. 198.

194 Vande Lanotte (2005), p. 198.

195 See Chapter 1 on an explanation of the distinction between interpretation and application.

196 Marks (1995), p. 231.

a role in 'grounding certain rights that are directly connected to elections'.[197] For example, the eligibility to stand for elected office (*Gitonas v Greece*),[198] the freedom of expression of opposition politicians (*Incal v Turkey*)[199] and participation in European parliamentary election (*Matthews v UK*).[200]

Even if democracy does not usually play an explicit role in the interpretation phase, it is a notion that is strongly intertwined with the protection of human rights. As such it is a background principle that does determine the context of all ECtHR judgments.[201] Indeed, the concept of democracy has been given a prominent place in the Convention by the drafting states.[202] Considering the moment of drafting the Convention, in the aftermath of WWII, it is not surprising that the concept of democracy was used in order to clearly mark the contrast with totalitarianism.[203] The aim of the European Convention was to 'preserve the rule of law and the principles of democracy, and "[to] forestall any trend to dictatorship before it [was] too late."'[204] Throughout the years the concept of democracy has not only been used in order to stress the contrast with totalitarianism, but the concept of democracy has also been used to contrast this concept with a regime in which there is an 'absence of adequate safeguards against arbitrary exercises of power'.[205] Nevertheless, despite the importance of this concept for the development of the European Convention, the ECtHR has not identified a theoretical basis for the model of democracy that it applies.[206]

The aim of briefly referring to the concept of democracy in the context of this chapter has been to show the variety of principles that play an explicit or implicit role in the interpretative framework, even though only a selection of these interpretative principles will be analyzed in the remainder of this thesis.

---

197 Marks (1995), p. 231.

198 ECtHR, *Gitonas v Greece*, judgment of 1 July 1997, *Reports* 1997-IV.

199 ECtHR (GC), *Incal v Turkije*, judgment of 9 June 1998, *Reports* 1998-IV.

200 ECtHR (GC), *Matthews v. United Kingdom*, judgment of 18 February 1999, *Reports* 1999-I. The given examples are discussed by: Mowbray (1999), p. 713.

201 Mahony (1990), p. 64, refers to the Preamble and democracy and human rights on the basis of which he claims that democracy and human rights are inseparable. Furthermore, he argues that indeed democracy can play an implicit role in the interpretation of the European Convention, since 'any theory of interpretation or review by the ECtHR must be compatible with that basic underpinning of political theory [referring back to political democracy which he was referring to in that paragraph]'. Mahony (1990), p. 81.

202 Mowbray (1999), p. 705.

203 Marks (1995), p. 211.

204 See Wheatley (2007), p. 780, quoting from Robertson, Human Rights in Europe (2nd edn, Manchester University Press, 1977).

205 Marks (1995), p. 212.

206 Ten Napel (2009), p. 465; Greer (2000), p. 18; Mowbray (1999), p. 723.

4.4.1.5 Human dignity and personal autonomy

In addition to the concept of democracy there is another substantive principle that plays a role in the interpretation process: the notion of human dignity. This principle has not been explicitly included in the text of the European Convention, but it has found its way into the case law of the ECtHR.[207] In the words of the ECtHR human dignity constitutes the 'very essence' of the European Convention.[208] It is a value or principle underlying all rights protected by the European Convention and as a result the principle plays a role in the interpretation process.[209] According to McCrudden the principle played a role in cases on 'the right to a fair hearing, the right not to be punished in the absence of a legal prohibition, the prohibition of torture and the right to private life'.[210] In recent cases the concept has also been invoked in the context of racial discrimination.[211]

The ECtHR regards human dignity thus as the essence of the European Convention, but there is no general understanding of the content of this concept of human dignity.[212] It would require a thorough analysis of the different cases in which human dignity plays a role in order to get an understanding of the meaning of this concept. That would stretch beyond the purpose of this chapter and this thesis, which merely is to indicate that human dignity has become an important principle in the interpretation process.

In recent cases the concept of personal autonomy has been playing an increasingly important role in the case law of the ECtHR, especially in the context of the interpretation of Article 8, the right to respect for private and family life.[213] The question is whether this notion is a corollary of human dignity or whether it is a separate concept. Both views can be defended and both views can be found in the case law of the ECtHR.[214] Once again, it would go far beyond the purpose of this chapter to discuss the positions in the debate about human dignity and personal autonomy in more detail. The purpose of mentioning the notions of human dignity and personal autonomy in the present context is to indicate that the ECtHR might develop more

---

207 McCrudden (2008), p. 683, indicating that the European Convention is an exception compared to other post-Second World War human rights texts, the majority of which includes explicit references to human dignity.

208 ECtHR, *Pretty v. United Kingdom*, judgment of 29 April 2002, *Reports* 2002-III. See further: McCrudden (2008), p. 683 and Koffeman (2010), p. 6-7.

209 McCrudden (2008), p. 683 and Koffeman (2010), p. 6-7.

210 McCrudden (2008), p. 683.

211 McCrudden (2008), p. 690.

212 McCrudden (2008), p. 724, argues that this is a more general problem connected to the judicial use of the concept of human dignity.

213 See on the concept of personal autonomy the case law of the ECtHR: Koffeman (2010).

214 Koffeman (2010), p. 5-8.

substantive principles that play a role in the interpretation of the provisions of the European Convention. They play a role in the interpretative framework, in addition to interpretative principles like evolutive and autonomous interpretation.

4.4.2 Court of Justice of the European Union

A discussion of the principles that guide the Court of Justice of the European Union and its Advocates General in the interpretation process is much more difficult and complex than is the case for the ECtHR. Several reasons can be put forward to explain this. First of all, the CJEU does not adjudicate in fundamental rights cases only. It has a wide jurisdiction and deals with a highly diverse range of cases. Debates on the interpretation methods and approach adopted by the CJEU therefore not necessarily focus on the interpretation of fundamental rights and are simply not always relevant in the context of fundamental rights. When studying the literature, it is thus necessary to constantly question whether the assumptions are also applicable in the process of interpreting fundamental rights. In some cases it might not even be possible to draw any conclusions without an extensive study of the case law itself. Especially in the context of the CJEU, it is therefore crucial to undertake a thorough case study in order to draw appropriate conclusions – indeed, this will be done for a number of selected principles in Chapter 13.

A second complicating factor is that fundamental rights have a different status in the EU legal order than within the European Convention system. For the CJEU, fundamental rights – being classified as general principles of (EU) law – serve two main functions. On the one hand they serve as guiding interpretative criteria in the interpretation process of all EU law, insofar as they are relevant.[215] On the other hand they figure in a 'much more immediate fashion as a direct yardstick by which to gauge the legality of Community acts'.[216] The difficulty for the present discussion lies in the fact that, within EU law, fundamental rights serve as interpretative criteria, while this research endeavours to establish which interpretative criteria guide the interpretation of exactly these fundamental rights. They are both the question and the answer in this discussion, which does not provide much clarity as to their precise function for the interpretative reasoning by the CJEU.

A final complicating factor is that, with regard to fundamental rights within EU law, many authors do not speak about interpretation. Instead they refer to the elabora-

---

215 AG Omega § 61 Referring as well to Weiler & Lockhart (1995), p. 51 & 579; Reich (2005), p. 32. Steiner (2006), p. 115

216 AG Omega § 61. Referring as well to Weiler & Lockhart (1995), p. 51 & 579 who speak about fundamental rights serving as a principle of validation. Steiner (2006), p. 115.

tion or development of fundamental rights.[217] This could be just a terminological matter due to the fact that fundamental rights within the EU have for a long time not been codified in any binding document. At the same time, due to this different terminology, it is difficult to get a grip on the exact manner of interpretation or development of fundamental rights by the CJEU. How does this Court determine the exact meaning of fundamental rights? Why are some rights protected and others not? The answer to such questions might become easier to discern since the EU Charter on Fundamental Rights became binding in December 2009, but whether this will really be the case depends on the attitude the CJEU will take towards the Charter. The discussion on the interpretation process of these rights has remained somewhat unclear, as has already been said above, due to the function of fundamental rights in the EC system. The discussion generally does not extend beyond the claim that teleological and comparative interpretation play an important role, followed by a discussion of the outcome of the different relevant cases. Therefore it remains vague how the CJEU derives concrete rights by using these different methods and what justifications have been provided for the concrete outcomes.[218]

Due to these factors the discussion below still might leave many questions unanswered. The case law analysis will try to find answers to these questions. The discussion below is interesting nonetheless, since it will provide food for phrasing more specific questions and assumptions that can be tested in the case law analysis.

4.4.2.1 Principle of meta-teleological interpretation

An important factor that becomes clear when researching the interpretation process of the CJEU is that the teleological method plays a crucial role. In section 4.1 mention has already been made of the concepts of micro-teleological interpretation and meta-teleological interpretation. These concepts have been introduced by LASSER.[219] As has been indicated, micro-teleological interpretation is a method of interpretation that is used to establish the object and purpose of a specific provision or piece of legislation, i.e., at a rather concrete level of abstraction. Meta-teleological interpretation takes place at a much higher level of abstraction and deals with the treaty system as a whole. Meta-teleological arguments produce certain principles that underlie the treaty system as a whole and should therefore be taken into account in the interpretation of any provision of the treaty or any other form of legislation under this treaty system.

---

217 See for example: Groussot (2006), p. 11, but he uses both terms; Blanke (2006), p. 267, who refers to the judicial methodology of the development of fundamental rights. Steiner (2006), p. 117.

218 Craig & Burca (2003), p. 337.

219 Lasser (2004).

The meta-teleological principle should thus be distinguished from the micro-teleological principle of interpretation: even though the latter is also employed both by the CJEU and the Advocates General, it is the former that shapes the interpretative approach of both institutions.[220] On the basis of a case law analysis, LASSER has been able to distinguish four meta-purposes that recur in many cases and which also feature in many different discussions on interpretation by the CJEU (not always placed in a similar setting as LASSER does). According to LASSER, effectiveness, uniformity, legal certainty,[221] and legal protection are the meta-purposes sought after by the CJEU. These purposes ensure 'the appropriate nature and structure of the Community legal system'. The problem with the analysis by LASSER for the purpose of this research project is that it does not concentrate on fundamental rights, but on the EU legal system as a whole. It therefore needs to be established in our own case law analysis whether the assumptions of LASSER also hold in a fundamental rights context.

The teleological *method* of interpretation will be discussed in a later chapter. Below, the principles of effectiveness and uniformity will be singled out and discussed in some more detail and they will be related to the other principles and methods of interpretation.[222] One aspect of the principle of uniformity is the 'practice of giving concepts an autonomous Community definition'.[223] The principle of uniformity will therefore be referred to as the principle of autonomous interpretation.

4.4.2.2 Principle of effectiveness (effet utile)

The principle of effectiveness, or *effet utile* as it is also called in the EU context, has been identified by LASSER as one of the main meta-teleological principles.[224] Other authors have employed descriptions in line with this qualification by referring to the principle of effectiveness as an extension or application of the teleological method.[225] Some authors regard the principle of effectiveness and the method of teleological interpretation to be one and the same.[226] However, this qualification whereby the principle of effectiveness and the method of teleological interpretation are considered

---

220 Lasser (2004), p. 209-210.

221 This discourse is closely related to that of uniformity and often appears simultaneously. Lasser (2004), p. 219.

222 Legal protection is not that relevant in the context of interpreting fundamental rights as they offer legal protection themselves. Therefore this meta-purpose cannot provide much guidance for the content of these rights. It seems to be rather a principle of application and in that context relevant for the duties upon courts of the different Member States. This purpose will therefore not be dealt with in the subsequent discussion.

223 Millett (1989), p. 164.

224 Lasser (2004), p. 212.

225 Tridimas (1996), p. 208; Millett (1989), p. 181; Fennelly (1996), p. 674.

226 Reich (2005), p. 30; Groussot (2006), p. 12; Schermers (2001), p. 21.

as one concept ignores that even though principle and method might be closely connected, they have a different role to play in the interpretation process, as has been described in section 4.1. In this thesis, therefore, the principle of effectiveness and the method of teleological interpretation will be considered as related, but separate concepts.

The principle of effectiveness derives from international law and entails that treaty provisions should be interpreted in such a way as to attain its object and purpose and gain practical value.[227] A clear basis for this principle has not been provided in the founding treaties. As has been said, LASSER has justified the use of this principle on the basis of meta-teleological consideration. In other literature on the CJEU, not much attention is given to the question whether any basis can be found for the use of this principle. If any attention is paid to this aspect at all, the fact that it is a recognized principle in international law is regarded as sufficient justification for the use of the principle.[228] Another question is what this principle means in the context of the CJEU. The CJEU has recognized this principle as one of the general principles of law, but it has not provided an explanation of the meaning of this principle.[229] Nor has a clear, detailed description of this principle been provided in the literature. This does not lead much further than that under this principle maximum effect should be granted to EU law, which still remains rather vague. LASSER also refers to the principle of effectiveness as a 'vague and multifarious concept'.[230] His analysis of a number of Advocate General opinions shows a pattern, that when the argument of effectiveness comes into play in an opinion this tilts 'the debate into ever higher levels of Community institutional policy'.[231] Thus the effectiveness of the EU system as a whole is sometimes brought into play. The examples given in the literature often refer to the effectiveness of EU law in relation to the Member States.[232]According to this notion, a certain EU provision cannot be interpreted in such a way that it would grant Member States the opportunity to hamper the effectiveness of EU law. The question is whether, in the context of the interpretation of fundamental rights, the CJEU employs this principle as well and whether, in that context, it also focuses on the effectiveness for the purpose of EU law or effectiveness for the purpose of individual protection. This is difficult to establish on the basis of the literature and should therefore be established on the basis of a case law analysis. It is relevant to analyze if considerations based on the *effet utile* play any role at all in the interpreta-

227 Commentary to articles of Vienna Convention, Yearbook of International Law Commission, 1966-Vol. II, p. 219. See also: Kutscher (1976), p. 39; Millett (1989), p. 180.
228 See for example Brown & Kennedy (2000), p. 343.
229 Tridimas (2005), p. 418.
230 Lasser (2004), p. 212.
231 Lasser (2004), p. 213, where he provides some examples as well.
232 See Tridimas (2005), p. 418-419.

tion of fundamental rights, because the principle seems to provide a useful tool for the supranational judge to argue why in a certain case preference should be attributed to individual protection. In other words, it can provide the European judge with a tool for determining when the balance between the best individual protection and respect for national differences should tilt in the direction of the former.

4.4.2.3 Principle of autonomous interpretation

The principle of autonomous interpretation means that terms of EU law must be given 'an independent and uniform interpretation', independent from the Member States.[233] Or, as the CJEU has put it: terms must be given a 'Community meaning'.[234]

This principle finds its basis in the Vienna Convention on the Law of Treaties, which provides that a term may be given a special meaning.[235] Moreover, Article 5 of the Vienna Convention ensures that account must be taken of the articles of interpretation of the Vienna Convention, but subject to the specific rules of the organization within which the treaty has been adopted, in this case the EU.[236] Although the CJEU never seems to have stated that it considers itself bound by the Vienna Convention, it is still useful to know, since we are dealing with treaty interpretation, that a basis can be found within the general principles of treaty interpretation.

Despite its basis in the Vienna Convention, some additional justification is needed for the employment of the principle by the CJEU. As has been stated above, uniformity is an important consideration in this respect. This argument is relevant in the broader EU law context and plays an important role in that respect, but it is questionable whether in the area of fundamental rights this notion of uniformity is equally relevant. Fundamental rights concern controversial moral and social issues, which can be closely connected to the identity of a state. An autonomous interpretation of fundamental rights may therefore have quite some impact, which could warrant a careful use of the principle of autonomous interpretation in, for example, a moral context.[237] On the other hand a certain level of uniformity might be needed to ensure

233 Millett (1989), p. 177.

234 Reich (2005), p. 27 referring to the CJEU in the case of *Levin* (C-53/81, *D.M. Levin v Staatssecretaris van Justitie* [1982] ECR 01035).

235 Article 31(4) Vienna Convention on the law of treaties. This has also been explained in section 4.4.1.3. dealing with the ECtHR.

236 According to Ganshof van der Meersch this provision in itself allows for an autonomous interpretation in accordance with the object and purpose of the treaty. Ganshof van der Meersch (1988), p. 205.

237 This could be the case in cases like *Grogan* (C-159/90, *The Society for the Protection of Unborn Children Ireland Ltd v Stephen Grogan and others* [1991] ECR I-04685), where the CJEU had to deal with a highly controversial topic like abortion and the spread of information on abortion.

sufficient protection of fundamental rights and therefore autonomous interpretation should not be ruled out *per se*. The amount of caution that should be exercised by the CJEU also depends on the way this autonomous interpretation is established.

Reference has already been made to the fact that the CJEU establishes fundamental rights on the basis of national constitutional traditions. According to KÜHLING, the CJEU does take the constitutional traditions of the Member States into account by resorting to the comparative method when trying to establish an autonomous interpretation.[238] This comparison does not bind the CJEU and the teleological method still plays a role, but in KÜHLING'S view the CJEU would always need to respect the 'core values of a Member State'.[239] In other words the limits of autonomous interpretation will be determined by the Member States. This raises the question whether this is truly autonomous interpretation. Are the national constitutional traditions only used as a starting point or are they decisive in establishing fundamental rights?

In the context of fundamental rights the CJEU is not only confronted with Member States, but also with the interpretations of the ECtHR. In many cases the CJEU adopts the interpretation given by the ECtHR, but in some cases the CJEU has adopted an interpretation autonomous from the ECtHR.[240] These interpretations provide an additional difficulty for the CJEU to take into account, because given the importance of the ECtHR one could argue that the CJEU cannot lightly ignore the interpretations of the ECtHR.[241] It therefore raises interesting questions. The main question is in what kind of situations the CJEU will adopt an approach autonomous from the ECtHR. What kind of justifications is provided when the CJEU interprets autonomously from the ECtHR?

The discussion in the literature provides a rather limited view of how the autonomous interpretation works in the case law practice of the CJEU and more particularly in the context of fundamental rights. A more detailed theoretical discussion and a case law analysis are therefore necessary to find a more detailed answer to the two most prominent questions: What role does the principle of autonomous interpretation play in this context and how is such an autonomous meaning established? Is it truly autonomous interpretation?

4.4.2.4 Principle of evolutive interpretation

Just like in the case of the ECtHR in the context of the EU the question is relevant whether there is some judicial mechanism for the CJEU to keep EU law in line with

238 See for just one example of many: Kühling (2006), p. 505.

239 Kühling (2006), p. 506.

240 Douglas-Scott (2006), p. 648.

241 See also Lasser (2009), p. 216, referring to the pressure the CJEU must feel from the ECtHR.

the needs of a changing society, because the EU is a long-term project which is supposed to resist the test of time. Interestingly enough, evolutive interpretation does not seem to play a very prominent role in the case law of the CJEU.[242] At least on the basis of the literature, it seems correct to conclude that this principle does not play an explicit role. The evolutive character of EU law is often stated as a fact of life, given the nature of EU law as a programme for the future.[243] BROWN refers to 'the dynamic character' of EU law,[244] TRIDIMAS argues that the 'European Community is by its nature a dynamic entity',[245] ALBORS LLORENS states that 'EC law is evolutionary law'[246] and KUTSCHER claims that the character of EU law demands an evolutionary approach.[247] What is striking about these references, when compared to literature on the ECtHR, is that hardly any author qualifies evolutive interpretation as a method of interpretation.[248] Most authors view evolutive interpretation as a characteristic of the EU legal order. This is in line with the division and qualification made in this thesis. As explained in section 4.1 on evolutive interpretation by the ECtHR, the principle does not indicate which substantive argument should be considered in order to interpret a specific provision. It is merely an objective that should be considered when employing different interpretation methods. Viewing evolutive interpretation as a characteristic which is automatically taken into account when interpreting fundamental rights is rather similar to viewing it as an interpretative principle. In both cases one acknowledges that an evolutive approach can or should be taken, but that interpretation methods are needed to provide a range of interpretative options.

It has already been said that the CJEU itself hardly ever refers to evolutive interpretation. It could be that it is considered to be so obvious that an evolutive approach should be taken when interpreting EU law that this is implicit in the reasoning of the CJEU. But even if this is inherent in the CJEU's approach, it is interesting to know exactly how the evolutive interpretation is established. In the EU literature, evolutive interpretation is often linked with the method of teleological interpretation.[249] Is this the only method used to establish evolutive interpretation or do other methods of interpretation play a role as well?

---

242 In literature on the CJEU and evolutive interpretation the term dynamic interpretation is more commonly used; however, for consistency in this thesis the term evolutive interpretation will be used.

243 Brown (2000), p. 332; Groussot (2006), p. 4; Millett (1989), p. 163; Tridimas (1996), p. 205 & 208 where he refers to the dynamic interpretation of EC law.

244 Brown (2000), p. 332.

245 Tridimas (1996), p. 205.

246 Albors Llorens (1999), p. 379.

247 Kutscher (1976), p. 38.

248 Reich (2005), p. 31.

249 See for example Reich (2005), p. 31; Schermers (2001), p. 20-21.

The fact that evolutive interpretation does not play an explicit role in the case law of the CJEU perhaps explains why no specific description of evolutive interpretation is given. This means that, unlike in the ECtHR context, there is no standard phrase that EU law should be interpreted in line with present-day conditions. The exact meaning of evolutive interpretation therefore remains unclear. The theoretical and case law analyses should bring more clarity in this respect.

The previous discussion focused on interpretation before the CJEU in general. An important question in the context of this thesis is, however, whether evolutive interpretation plays any role when interpreting fundamental rights. It is hard to deny that the CJEU has employed an evolutive approach (albeit perhaps not explicitly) in other fields, for example, regarding the increasing role of the European Parliament.[250] The question remains whether the CJEU has considered it appropriate to adopt this approach as well in dealing with fundamental rights? GROUSSOT has argued that 'the CJEU appears as the reflector of common constitutional or legal values rather than the guide of dynamic and new legal trends'.[251] In his view the evolutive approach is linked to the comparative interpretation method, because 'a lack of consensus between the laws of the Member States may impede the elaboration of a general principle'.[252] This finding makes the question by which method the CJEU establishes an evolutive interpretation even more interesting, especially since it was found above that teleological interpretation is mainly associated with evolutive interpretation.

4.5 CONCLUSION

The main aim of this chapter has been to sketch the interpretative framework of the ECtHR and the CJEU. An important distinction has been made between interpretation methods and interpretative principles. Both have an important role to play in the interpretation process and they can often complement each other in order to reach an interpretation of a certain provision. The aim has been to point out the most important interpretation methods that have been discussed in the literature on both European Courts. In addition, for each court the most important interpretative principles have been discussed. Some can be found at both courts, like evolutive and autonomous interpretation, but others, like the principle of human dignity, only play a role at one of the courts.

250 Tridimas (1996), p. 208 uses the case of *Les Verts* (CJEU C-294/83, *Parti écologiste "Les Verts" v. European Parliament* [1986] ECR 01339) as an example.
251 Groussot (2006), p. 132.
252 Groussot (2006), p. 132.

The remainder of this thesis will only deal with two interpretation methods and two interpretative principles that have been selected for further analysis. The criterion for selection has been the question whether these interpretative aids in some way help judges specifically address the multilevel context in which they have to operate. Both courts under analysis in this thesis have to deal with the tension between, on the one hand, providing individual fundamental rights protection, and, on the other hand, trying to respect national legal systems as well.

Teleological interpretation and comparative interpretation have been selected as relevant interpretation methods. Comparative interpretation has been added, since it helps the courts to get a clear picture of what the state of affairs is in the different Member States. This can help the courts to adopt interpretations that might be more easily accepted by the Member States. Teleological interpretation has been selected, since through this method of interpretation judges are able to take into account the multilevel nature of the European systems when interpreting specific terms. The purpose of the system is to protect fundamental rights in a multilevel legal system, namely the EU or the Council of Europe and through teleological interpretation this can be taken into account. Meta-teleological reasoning that has been discussed in this chapter provides a basis for interpretative principles that respect the object and purpose of the system. Meta-teleological reasoning will, however, not be discussed separately, but some of the principles based on this form of reasoning will be discussed. These selected principles are the principles of evolutive and autonomous interpretation. Evolutive interpretation has a strong link with comparative interpretation and therefore a discussion of this method of interpretation would not be complete without also discussing evolutive interpretation. Furthermore, autonomous interpretation is the expression of the above described tension in interpretative terms. Autonomous interpretation means that a uniform European interpretation will be sought in order to provide individuals the same level of protection. It is therefore very interesting to see whether any pattern in the use of this principle can be established on the basis of both the literature on and case law analysis of both courts.

The analysis of these methods and principles will be divided in two stages. First, the interpretative aids will be analyzed on the basis of a theoretical discussion. This theoretical discussion will provide a more thorough analysis of these methods and principles, but it will also raise many questions that will be used as a basis for the subsequent case law analysis. The case law analysis will aim to answer many of the questions raised in the theoretical chapters. In the end this combination of theoretical and case law analysis should reveal which areas are open for improvement.

CHAPTER 5
TELEOLOGICAL INTERPRETATION

This chapter aims to continue the discussion on the teleological method of interpretation that was started in Chapter 4. The idea is to provide more depth to the discussion on this particular method of interpretation. Some more theoretical background should generate information on the basis of which questions can be formulated for the case law analysis. Another aspect that will be dealt with in this chapter is the connection between this specific method of interpretation and the relevant principles of interpretation, like evolutive and autonomous interpretation.

In Chapter 4 the teleological method of interpretation has been briefly introduced. The chapter briefly touched upon the reference to the teleological method in the Vienna Convention. The Vienna Convention formulates teleological interpretation as interpretation according to the object and purpose of a treaty, which is a common way of phrasing this method of interpretation. It has also been shown in that short discussion that the teleological method is widely used by both courts under review in this thesis. The primary purpose of this chapter is to provide a thorough overview of the teleological method. Moreover, the question why this method can be regarded as a legitimate method of interpretation will be discussed.

In Chapter 4 a distinction was introduced between meta-teleological reasoning and micro-teleological reasoning. Meta-teleological reasoning refers to reasoning based on certain principles that have been derived from the object and purpose of a specific treaty. The qualification as meta-teleological interpretation refers to the origin of these principles, namely in the object and purpose of the treaty in question. Micro-teleological interpretation, on the other hand, has been qualified as a method whereby a provision or a specific notion in the treaty is interpreted in light of the object and purpose of the treaty in general or the object and purpose of the provision in question. This micro-teleological reasoning is what is known as teleological interpretation in the sense of being an interpretation method.[1] The following discussion will focus on this understanding of teleological interpretation as a method of interpretation. Meta-teleological interpretation will be addressed by discussing some of the interpretative principles that have been derived from the object and purpose of the treaty. In the context of this thesis evolutive interpretation and autonomous interpretation have been identified as such interpretative principles. They will be discussed in Chapters 7 and 8.

1 See Lasser (2004), p. 207-208.

5.1 A THEORETICAL POINT OF VIEW

The theoretical discussion on the teleological method of interpretation will be structured according to four questions that can be posed with respect to this method of interpretation.[2] As a starting point, the question what it means to interpret according to object and purpose will be discussed in section 5.1.1 Subsequently section 5.1.2 will deal with the expression 'object and purpose'. Thirdly, attention will be drawn to the matter of establishing the object and purpose of a piece of legislation (in this case a treaty) in section 5.1.3. Finally, the criticism or drawbacks of this method will be discussed in section 5.1.4. These questions will be discussed from a theoretical angle, drawing from insights of both the discussions about the national and international contexts.[3] In addition, these insights will be related to the specific context of a multilevel legal order, like the European Convention and the EU. Both the national and international theoretical debates are relevant, since the EU treaty and the European Convention are not 'classical' international treaties and they might have some characteristics that are more similar to a national constitution.[4] Therefore, presenting both international and national views might help to improve the understanding of teleological interpretation before the CJEU and the ECtHR, not least because in both discussions different aspects appear to be emphasized.

---

2 Similar questions have also been posed in the literature. Even though the author does not explicitly ask these questions, Jonas & Saunders try to answer most of the questions posed here in this thesis as well. Jonas & Saunders (2010), p. 577-582. Similarly, Buffard & Zemanek (1998) address questions of terminology and methodology for the use of the notions 'object and purpose'.

3 Even though the notion of interpreting according to 'object and purpose' has existed in some form or another for centuries in international law, the concept of object and purpose has not received much systematic attention and Klabbers claims that little is known about this concept. Klabbers (1997), p. 139-140 and 159. Since 1997 some more attention has been paid to this concept by a few recent authors, but the attention remains somewhat limited. See for some recent contributions: Buffard & Zemanek (1998); Linderfalk (2007); Jonas & Saunders (2010). Therefore the main theoretical elements will derive from a theoretical discussion within a national context.

4 In his article on analogies between constitutional law and international law, Helfer (2003) argues that it can be valuable to learn from discussions in a national constitutional context for problems existing at the international level. One should, however, be careful not to transpose national constitutional solutions too easily. He discusses several themes in which relevant analogies can be found between the national and international level.
The discussion here in this thesis also takes into consideration discussions on teleological interpretation of national legislation. The discussions on teleological interpretation do not always make a clear distinction between constitutions and other national legislation (see for example Barak (2005), p. xi). Therefore discussions on teleological interpretation of legislation might be reflected in the discussion here as well. The discussion will be 'translated' to the supranational context where necessary.

5.1.1 Interpreting by reference to object and purpose

Teleological interpretation starts from the assumption that legislation is rationally drafted with a certain purpose[5] or that legislation serves as an instrument to achieve 'certain legal, social or economic goals'.[6] According to this method, any interpretation has to be compatible with this particular purpose.[7] To put it differently: 'the meaning of a legal rule should be established on the basis of the good the rule aims to promote or the evil it seeks to avert.'[8] It means that the consequences of interpreting a legal text in a certain way must contribute to the realization of the goals and purposes of this legal text.[9] Thus, the purpose of a measure provides an interpreter with an evaluative basis to prefer one interpretation over another.[10] The question is why this legislative purpose should be taken into account. In the light of the division of powers this purpose should play a role when determining the meaning of the text as well. If a judge were to ignore the purpose for which a specific text has been drafted, this judge could be accused of taking the place of the legislator by redesigning the legal text.

This automatically brings up the following question: exactly what purpose should be considered for this type of argument? Should it be the (subjective) purpose of the author of the legislation in question, or a more objective purpose? Different theoretical views have been developed to answer this question and there certainly is not one

---

5 This is the reason why this method is sometimes referred to as purposive interpretation as well, e.g. Barak (2005). Cueto-Rua (1981), p. 178, draws an analogy between a legislator and a carpenter: both use their tools as an instrument to achieve a certain purpose. See further MacCormick (2005), p. 133-134. He emphasizes that legislation does not accidently come into being; 'they are the product of legislative decisions'.

6 Feteris (2005), p. 459. See also Barak (2005), p. 220.

7 Even though teleological interpretation encompasses both the object and purpose of a legislative text, when dealing with the question whether a subjective or objective approach should be taken, generally only the purpose is referred to. This might be explained by the fact that the method is sometimes called: purposive interpretation. Alternatively this might be explained by the claim of Buffard & Zemanek, who claim that within 'traditional teleological interpretation the distinction is superfluous'. Buffard & Zemanek (1998), p. 323. A short discussion, however, on the notion of object and purpose will follow in the next section of this chapter.

8 Feteris (2005), p. 460 paraphrasing Fuller, 'Positivism and the Fidelity to the Law- A Reply to Professor Hart', 71 *Harvard Law Review* 1958, 630-672.

9 Feteris (2005), p. 460-461; see also MacCormick (2005), p. 134. The latter author considers this interpretation method a manifestation of consequentialist reasoning, which he discusses in his book on legal reasoning. It would stretch beyond the purpose of this thesis to discuss consequentialism here.

10 MacCormick and Summers (1991), p. 514.

correct answer.[11] In itself this is already a complicated matter to be dealing with, but it is further complicated by the lack of a generally accepted definition of subjective and objective purpose of a piece of legislation. In order to provide a convincing answer to the question posed above, it is therefore necessary to first explain what will be regarded as subjective and objective purpose in the context of this thesis.

Some authors conceive the subjective purpose of a piece of legislation to be the real purpose the author(s) (or drafters) had in mind when creating the text.[12] It is a historical and static fact that cannot really change in time.[13] Societies, however, do develop, therefore situations might occur which were not foreseen by the drafters. In some situations it might be possible to make an educated guess as to what the purpose of the drafters would have been had they taken these developments into account. The term 'subjective purpose', however, does not refer to the purpose the author[14] of the legal text would have had if he/she had thought about such a matter. This is considered a 'hypothetical intent', which is deemed to fall under the scope of the concept of 'objective purpose'.[15] This form of hypothetical intent does not reflect the true intent of the author of the legal text, because it is a guess about what this author would have intended if certain circumstances would have occurred.[16] Only the real purpose or true intent of the author counts as the subjective purpose. The meaning of the notion of 'subjective intent', however, is still debated. LINDERFALK, for example, appears to regard subjective purpose as a slightly broader concept than the 'real purpose' or 'true intent' of the author.[17] By claiming that it is not

11 See Barak (2005b), p. 93, for references to some discussions on the question whether the purpose is subjective or objective. MacCormick & Summers (1991), p. 519, also refer to the fact that the question whose purpose should be taken into consideration is a hotly disputed issue.

12 Barak (2005), p. 120, this purpose of the authors includes: 'the values, objectives, interests, policy, aims and function that the authors sought to realize'. MacCormick and Summers (1991), p. 520. See also: Jonas & Saunders (2010), p. 581.

13 Barak (2005), p. 120.

14 Barak (2005), p. 120 argues that when the author of a legal text is a collective body, the shared purpose or intent of that entity counts and not the purpose or intent of all its individual members.

15 Barak (2005), p. 121.

16 Barak (2005), p. 121, refers to three forms of hypothetical intent. Only the first can, in some circumstances count as subjective purpose, because in that case it will come as close as possible to the real intent. According to Barak the first sense refers to the situation where the real intent is unknown, but where the hypothetical intent can be established on the basis of the legal community's life experience. The second way to understand hypothetical intent, is when the author never thought about a certain fact, but if she or he had, then the author would have had this in mind. In this case one should guess at the intent of the author and therefore this cannot be qualified as the subjective purpose. The third way of understanding hypothetical intent is the intent the author 'would have had as a reasonable person'. Only the first understanding can count as the real intent and thus as the subjective purpose.

17 Linderfalk (2007), p. 205 and 228-229 (footnote 6).

possible to reconstruct the intent of the author with absolute certainty, he also includes a rational reconstruction of the purpose of the original legislator. The fact that the real purpose of the original legislator will sometimes have to be based on a reconstruction of 'the legal community's life experience' is not denied by those who adhere to a strict explanation of the subjective purpose.[18] The question is, however, whether according to LINDERFALK a hypothetical reconstruction of the purpose of the original legislator is also included under the term 'subjective purpose', i.e., a reconstruction of what the legislator or drafter would have thought if they had thought about the matter. That is the point where LINDERFALK could differ from other authors, but it does not become clear whether that is what he proposes. Thus, in fact it is not possible to say for certain whether LINDERFALK really adheres to a broader understanding of the subjective purpose, or whether he just confuses hypothetical (and thus objective) intent and subjective intent. Regardless of this debate, the notion of 'subjective intent' will for the purpose of this thesis be considered to be the purpose the original author had in mind when drafting the treaty. Even though this may be a reconstruction of the actual purpose, a hypothetical intent will not be included under the concept of 'subjective purpose'.

It might be interesting to note that some scholars have claimed that the subjective purpose of the author at the time of creating the legislation does not form part of the teleological method of interpretation, since they only consider the objective purpose to be relevant for teleological interpretation.[19] This does not necessarily mean that the purpose the original lawmaker had in mind cannot play any role in the interpretation process at all. In the context of the Vienna Convention reference has been made to three schools of interpretation: the textual school, the subjective school and the teleological school.[20] The textual school emphasizes the importance of the text in treaty interpretation. The subjective school considers the intentions of the parties to be of primary importance. This closely resembles the subjective purpose that has been discussed in the context of this chapter.[21] The teleological school only refers to the objective purpose as discussed below, and considers the subjective intent to be irrelevant to teleological interpretation.

The concept of objective purpose has been described by many to constitute the intent of the 'reasonable author'[22] or an 'ideally rational author'[23] of a legal text. ALEXY considers objective teleological arguments to be based on 'rational aims or

18 See Barak (2005), p. 121.
19 Smith (2005), p. 152. Jacobs makes the same distinction. Jacobs (1969), p. 303.
20 See, among others, Shaw (2008), p. 932-933; Vanneste (2010), p. 221-225.
21 Vanneste (2010), p. 223, indeed argues that this method has a strong teleological component.
22 Barak (2005), p. 148.
23 MacCormick & Summers (1991), p. 520.

on objectively prescribed aims in the framework of the valid legal order'.[24] BARAK adds that the objective purpose reflects 'the need of society' and is an 'expression of a social ideal'.[25] It is clear that the objective purpose is thus 'disassociated from the original lawmaker'.[26] The objective purpose is, however, not disassociated from the text of the treaty to be interpreted; in fact the objective purpose can only be achieved if the text allows this.[27]

The preference for one of the two different concepts of purpose depends on one's view of the importance of each of these concepts. One's view on the importance again depends on one's position in the theoretical debate on the proper role of the judge in the legal order.[28] In general one could say that in a view where the subjective intention prevails, the role of the judge in the interpretation process is rather narrow. By using the intention of the author of the text in determining the meaning of a certain term the judge has to respect the role of the original legislator and supposedly limit its own discretion.[29] This prevents a judge from becoming too activist. Adherents of the more objective component of teleological interpretation have a different perception of the role of the judge. They allow a judge to establish what a rational lawmaker would consider the purpose to be, which might have even changed over time, as will be discussed below. The judge in this view is thus granted much more discretion to establish the object and purpose in comparison to a judge who is only allowed to determine the purpose the original lawmaker had in mind.[30]

The preference for either the subjective or the objective purpose also depends on the type of legislative text that needs to be interpreted. BARAK holds that in constitutional interpretation the objective purpose should prevail.[31] While the focus of this thesis is on supranational treaties, this statement has some relevance, since the European Convention and the EU treaties are sometimes considered to contain constitutional elements.[32] LINDERFALK, on the other hand, in discussing teleological interpretation of treaties, claims that in treaty interpretation only the subjective purpose should be taken into account, because of the specific role of the treaty parties in

---

24 Alexy (1989), p. 241.
25 Barak (2005), p. 148.
26 Linderfalk (2007), p. 228-229.
27 Barak (2005), p. 148.
28 For a good overview see Barak (2005), p. 221 et seq.
29 The term supposedly is used since *Dworkin* has shown that this method leaves a lot of implications to be made by the judge. Dworkin (1986), ch. 9.
30 See also Vanneste (2010), p. 225.
31 Barak (2005), p. 96.
32 See for example Helfer (2003), p. 199-201 where he discusses the constitutional character of the European Union. On the ECtHR see Gerards (2009), p. 409-412, with further references.

international law.[33] A different position has been taken by BERNHARDT, who focuses on the interpretation of international human rights treaties. In his view this type of treaties requires an objective teleological approach, due to their special character.[34] The question is which position is most relevant for the treaties that the CJEU and ECtHR are supposed to interpret when dealing with fundamental rights. This is, however, a matter that cannot be determined on a general basis for both legal orders at the same time. Therefore the relation between the subjective and objective purpose will be discussed below, when dealing with both legal orders separately (see section 5.2).

5.1.2 Object and purpose?

In the discussion above on the meaning of the teleological method of interpretation, no attention was paid to the expression 'object and purpose' itself. While this concept is also part of teleological interpretation at a national level, much more discussion on this expression has taken place in an international context.[35] Therefore, before dealing with the question how to establish the object and purpose, it is important to give the meaning of this concept a moment of thought.

Within international law, reference to the object and purpose of a treaty is a common approach, but the notion itself remains rather vague. One of the main questions is whether the object and purpose are distinct or synonymous notions,[36] and whether they can change over time. This is mainly relevant in order to be as transparent as possible about this method of interpretation. If the meaning of the different notions involved is clear, it is much easier to check whether this method is applied in a legitimate manner.

International practice does not provide many clues as to the meaning of the expression 'object and purpose'. Within the scholarly debate, two alternatives have been defended. On the one hand the position has been taken that the notions 'object' and 'purpose' can be used interchangeably and that no distinction between the two should be made.[37] This position is mainly based on English and German theoretical discussions. The expression 'object and purpose' should thus be considered to refer

33 Linderfalk (2007), p. 205. This claim is supported by Klabbers, who claims that object and purpose can only be 'the result of parties' intentions'. Klabbers (1997), p. 150. Linderfalk even claims that the distinction between objective and subjective purpose does not exist in international law.

34 Bernhardt (1988), p. 68 and 71.

35 See for example: Klabbers (1997); Buffard & Zemanek (1997); Linderfalk (2007), p. 207-211.

36 Klabbers (1997), p. 140; Buffard & Zemanek (1997), p. 342; Linderfalk (2007), p. 207-211.

37 Position has been taken by Klabbers (1997), p. 144-148, who refers to many different authors as well.

to one notion, which is the general aim of a treaty.[38] On the other hand it has been argued, based on the French theoretical debate, that the two notions should be distinguished. According to BUFFARD & ZEMANEK 'purpose' refers to the aim of a treaty and 'object' refers to the 'legal instruments created for achieving the aim'.[39] According to this view, connecting the 'object' to the 'purpose' of a treaty provides a link between the aim of the treaty and its actual provisions and is therefore a restraint on unfettered interpretation.[40] On this 'bifurcated' reading of object and purpose, however, other views have been expressed as well. KLABBERS has considered, for example, the object to refer to an 'immediate goal' and the purpose to refer to a more distant goal.[41]

While both positions seem to have some value, it seems that in the international debate the former reflects the view of the majority.[42] In the context of this thesis object and purpose will therefore be used as a single notion. It is interesting to consider this point in the case law analysis and try to find out whether the European Courts make a distinction.

A different matter is whether the object and purpose remain the same over time. This question is strongly connected to the issue of taking a subjective or objective teleological approach. If a subjective approach should prevail, it seems inherently impossible that the object and purpose can change with the passage of time. Subjective teleological interpretation, as has been determined above, refers to the intent of the original legislator and will therefore not change over time. In cases where an objective teleological approach is followed, reference will be made to the rational or reasonable legislator. Perceptions of what the rational or reasonable legislator thinks or intends can change in time and therefore the object and purpose ascribed to a treaty may change.[43] This phenomenon has been called 'emergent' purpose.[44] The extent of the change depends on the level of abstraction at which the object and purpose are discussed. The higher the level of abstraction, the more stable an object and purpose are. Therefore a more abstract object and purpose will not change much throughout the existence of a treaty. At a lower level of abstraction the object and purpose might

38 Buffard & Zemanek (1998), p. 323.

39 Buffard & Zemanek (1998), p. 332.

40 Buffard & Zemanek (1998), p. 332.

41 Klabbers referring to Elisabeth Zoller, *La bonne foi en droit international public*, 1977. Klabbers (1997), p. 144-145.

42 See mainly references by Klabbers (1997), 145-148.

43 Linderfalk also acknowledges that the object and purpose of a treaty can be subject to change, but is unsure in which cases this could be the case. Linderfalk (2007), p. 211.

44 Orakhelashvili (2008), p. 344; Vanneste (2010), p. 224; Jacobs (1969), p. 320, argues that the doctrine of emergent purpose is widely recognized in the context of interpretation of constitutional documents.

change in time, because when interpreting a provision the context of the legal issue that needs to be resolved needs to be taken into account. Both the legal issue and the context are subject to change and can therefore influence the object and purpose of a treaty.[45] When reviewing the case law of both the ECtHR and the CJEU it is interesting to try to find out whether the object and purpose have gone through a change and whether this has been justified in some way or another by the respective courts.

5.1.3 How to determine the object and purpose

The question of how to determine the object and purpose is closely tied to the previous question on whether the subjective or objective reading of purpose should be adhered to. Depending on the choice of subjective or objective approach, different indicators might play a role in establishing the object and purpose. Subjective purpose refers to the actual purpose of the author of the legal text, while the objective purpose involves a search for the purpose of a reasonable author. It is therefore relevant to reflect on the different theoretical views on what can be considered an appropriate way to establish the (subjective or objective) object and purpose.

While both national and international theoretical literature on the teleological method have been consulted, for this discussion the international context will be most relevant. The national context is really different with regard to the type of documents that can and should be considered in determining object and purpose. Despite the fact that the European Convention and the EU treaty are particular kinds of treaties, they remain international treaties that have been established in a manner distinct from national constitutions. The role and reliability of, for example, preparatory documents, like *travaux préparatoires,* is different from the role and reliability of preparatory documents in the national context.[46] Guidance on how to establish object and purpose should therefore be found in international legal theory, rather than in legal theory that is directed at national or constitutional interpretation. This matter has, however, not been extensively addressed in international law literature.[47] As a result this section will only provide a rather general overview of different aspects that could play a role in determining which documents may be consulted for the purpose of teleological

45 Klabbers (1997), p. 149-150.

46 *Travaux préparatoires* are often referred to as not reflecting the intentions of the parties in a reliable manner. Moreover, the fact that some State Parties join later and are not represented in the *travaux préparatoires* is an additional factor leaving them less relevant. Both factors differ from a national context. See Orakhelashvili (2008), p. 382-387, on a critical dicussion of the value of the *travaux préparatoires*.

47 Klabbers (1997), p. 156.

interpretation. The next sections, dealing with both courts individually, will address the specific situation of each court.

As often in the context of this thesis, the Vienna Convention provides a good starting point for a discussion on how to determine the object and purpose of a treaty. Articles 31 and 32 of the Vienna Convention refer to different types of documents that can be consulted in the interpretation process. These include agreements or instruments created after the conclusion of the treaty and accepted by all parties and subsequent agreements or practice between the parties. The preparatory works only have a subsidiary place in the interpretation process. The category of supplementary means of interpretation appears not to be limited. Many different documents could be included on the basis of this provision.[48] The commentary to this provision, however, refers almost exclusively to the *travaux préparatoires*.[49] It therefore seems that on the basis of this provision mainly the *travaux préparatoires* are allowed as a secondary source in the interpretation process. In order not to exclude relevant evidence, the term *travaux préparatoires* has not been defined and a general reference has been chosen.[50]

The question whether a subjective or objective teleological approach will be taken to interpret a certain treaty determines to some extent the documents that may be taken into consideration. For a subjective approach, the *travaux préparatoires* play a significant role, since they reflect the intentions of the original legislators.[51] The fact that preparatory works are regarded as supplementary tools for interpretation reveals their limited relevance in the interpretation process. This implies that the Vienna Convention, at least, does not support an entirely subjective approach.[52]

In order to establish the objective purpose, and also to some extent the subjective purpose, the text of the treaty plays a significant role. The main elements of the text of the treaty that should be considered are the title, the preliminary provisions, but also the preamble of a treaty.[53] They provide strong indicators of its object and

---

48 Aust (2000), p. 200.

49 Commentary to articles of Vienna Convention, Yearbook of International Law Commission, 1966-Vol. II, p. 222-223.

50 Commentary to articles of Vienna Convention, Yearbook of International Law Commission, 1966-Vol. II, p. 223.

51 Villiger (2009), p. 444, indicates that the *travaux préparatoires* are often relied upon to take a subjective approach. See also Barak (2005), p. 135-136 and 140, referring to the legislative history as a factor that helps to establish the subjective purpose.

52 McDougal claims that the reference to object and purpose in the Vienna Convention does not support reference to the 'actual subjectivities of the parties', but that the text reflects the real object and purpose. McDougal (1967), p. 272-273.

53 Klabbers (1997), p. 156-157; Buffard & Zemanek (1998), p. 328. The Vienna Convention also refers to the relevance of the preamble in art. 31.

purpose.[54] The category of documents that is relevant to establish the objective purpose of a treaty can, however, be much broader than the text and its preamble. While other documents might be accepted when establishing the objective purpose, the further removed the documents are from the actual text of the treaty, the more important it is that a proper explanation is given why these documents are consulted. After all, a (too) lenient approach to the use of different documents might generate accusations of judicial activism. The only problem is that no general guideline can be given as to what can be considered as 'too lenient'. This depends on one's perspective on the role of the judge. How to deal with this problem will be discussed below.

A different aspect that, rather obviously, plays a role in determining the most appropriate documents for reference, is the availability of documents. The availability not only has consequences for the type of documents that can be consulted, but also for the interpretative approach that will be taken (objective or subjective). If, for example, the *travaux préparatoires* have not been published, they cannot be consulted, which means that a subjective approach seems hardly possible. Especially in the case of multilateral treaties where not all parties have taken part in the negotiation process, it might not be reasonable to use the *travaux préparatoires* to establish the object of the treaty. More recent parties to the treaty cannot be held to comply with documents they have never been able to discuss.[55] In this context it should be noted that DWORKIN has argued against the use of authorial (legislative) intent in interpreting legislation, albeit in the national context rather than in the context of international law, mainly because of the problems involved in basing authorial intent on legislative history.[56] These difficulties primarily arise in the context of establishing the subjective purpose. In the context of establishing the objective purpose the availability of (preparatory) documents is not much of an issue, because of the prominent role of the preamble, the text, the title and general clauses of a treaty.

Apart from these factors, KLABBERS holds that common sense and intuition can be 'useful indicators' of object and purpose.[57] This is probably true and these indicators might be helpful, but they are far from being objective indicators. Reliance on common sense and intuition makes an interpretation entirely dependent on the person of the judge. That is not a very desirable situation and preference should be given to objective indicators that lie outside the person of the judge. Common sense

54 See Klabbers (1997), p. 156, who lists several indicators of the object and purpose on the basis of an analysis of cases by international courts. See also: Villiger (2009), p. 428; Orakhelashvili (2008), p. 343.

55 Aust (2000), p. 199.

56 Dworkin (1986), ch. 9; MacCormick (2005), p. 135, referring to Dworkin; Barak (2005), p. 228, also referring to Dworkin.

57 Klabbers (1997), p. 155.

and intuition may lead to the right direction, but references to documents are still always needed in order to test or support that initial assumption.

5.1.4 Criticism related to method in general

It has already been mentioned casually before, but it is such an important aspect that it warrants a separate discussion: the critique on the teleological method of interpretation. In the literature the main point of critique is that this method could lead the judge into the realm of treaty amendment instead of treaty interpretation.[58] This is mainly the case when judges try to establish the objective purpose of a treaty.[59] The subjective purpose reflects the purpose of the drafters and as a result interpretation taking into account only subjective purpose will not lead to accusations of judicial legislating. As has already been said above, this is different for the objective purpose, since that notion reflects the purpose of a rational legislator and refers to the needs of society. People might have different views on what would be the purpose of a rational lawmaker and the needs of society. If judges adopt a progressive view on what would be the purpose of a rational legislator this may lead judges to adopt a progressive or extensive interpretation of the treaty in question and invoke accusations of judicial legislating.[60] An additional factor is that the objective purpose can change over time, as explained in section 5.1.2. This 'extreme' form of teleological interpretation entails that judges will establish the *present* purpose of the treaty, rather than the historical aims.[61] Especially in situations where the present objective purpose deviates from the subjective (historical) purpose, judges could be criticized for revising the treaty. Others have warned against the risk of slipping into policy making.[62] Both statements refer to the same fear, namely that of judicial activism.[63] This fear of activism concerns only the actual use of the method and not the method itself, which is considered an essential part of treaty interpretation.[64] VANNESTE even argues that as a result of the 'open texture' of fundamental rights provisions reference to the object and

58 McRae (2002), p. 222; Shaw (2008), p. 933; Villiger (2009), p. 428.

59 Vanneste (2010), p. 225.

60 See Bernhardt (1995), p. 1420.

61 Orakhelashvili (2008), p. 343.

62 Hartley (2003), p. 79-80. See also Vanneste (2010), p. 225, referring to Jacobs (1969), p. 343.

63 See Tridimas (1996), p. 199-200, for criticism on the use of teleological interpretation by the CJEU. See also Albors Llorens (1999), p. 373, referring to the criticism directed at the teleological approach by the CJEU.

64 Benhardt (1995), p. 1420, argues that some form of teleological interpretation is necessary for treaty interpretation (he argues against using teleological interpretation to interpret the treaty in its most extensive meaning). See also Shaw (2008), p. 933, who argues that treaty interpretation has to take the object and purpose into account.

purpose is essential to establish an interpretation.[65] Any suggestions for improving this method of interpretation should therefore concern the actual use of this method.

The question then is what can be regarded in this context as judicial activism. It is almost impossible to answer this question in a neutral manner. The difficulty lies in the vagueness of the term 'activism'. It is a term that is often used in the legal debate, but which has not been clearly defined and thus remains fuzzy. The term is strongly linked to the perception of the role of the judge in the judicial process.[66] The meaning of judicial activism is therefore dependent on one's (theoretical) view of the proper role of the judge. Someone with a traditional view on the role of the judge has a different perception of activism than someone with a view on the role of the judge based on constitutional dialogue.[67] Trying to determine what would be regarded as judicial activism in the context of teleological interpretation would thus entail imposing a certain theoretical view of the role of the judge. That is, however, not the purpose of this chapter. It is necessary to emphasize what can be learned from this, namely that judicial activism is not a neutral or objective term.

If that is the case, how can accusations of judicial activism be prevented when determining the scope of fundamental rights? Due to the normative and subjective character of the criticism of judicial activism, such accusations can never be fully prevented. They can be reduced to a minimum, however, if the method is applied in a careful manner. By providing a reasoning that covers all aspects of a teleological argument, it is much harder to accuse a judge of activism, regardless of the definition of activism that is used. At least someone claiming these accusations would have to provide more than the general claim of judicial activism, which makes it harder to defend these accusations. What this entails for the actual interpretation process will be dealt with after the separate discussions of both courts.

5.2 Teleological interpretation in the ECtHR and CJEU

5.2.1 CJEU

In Chapter 4 a short introduction to the use of the teleological method of interpretation by the CJEU has been provided. Reference was made to the famous statement of the CJEU that, when interpreting a certain provision, it is necessary 'to consider the spirit, the general scheme and wording' of that provision.[68] The teleological method of interpretation is frequently employed by the judges and Advocates General and it

65 Vanneste (2010), p. 253.

66 See model developed by Cohn & Kremnitzer (2005).

67 For an elaborate explanation see the model of Cohn & Kremnitzer (2005).

68 As first stated in: C-26/62, *Van Gend en Loos v. Administratie der Belastingen* [1963] ECR 3, 12.

has become a hallmark of the adjudication process before the CJEU. The observation that the method plays such an important role in the interpretation process is interesting,[69] but a crucial question for our purpose is whether this is also the case when the CJEU deals with fundamental rights. It has been noted before that discussions in the literature on the interpretation methods of the CJEU seldom deal with the interpretation of fundamental rights. This complicates a discussion of the role of interpretation methods when interpreting fundamental rights without a thorough case law analysis.

Fundamental rights have a special status within EU law.[70] The main sources for establishing these fundamental rights are the European Convention on the one hand and the common traditions of the Member States on the other hand. Due to the importance of common traditions in this respect, the comparative method plays a central role when interpreting fundamental rights.[71] The question is, then, whether the comparative method is considered sufficient in this regard by the CJEU or whether there is still a role to play for the teleological method of interpretation. According to different authors, the CJEU should not apply a purely comparative approach. The results of the comparative analysis will have to be considered in the light of the object and purpose of the EU treaty before a certain interpretation will be accepted.[72] In this context the teleological method clearly plays a role, but the relation with the comparative method is not entirely obvious. What if both methods contradict each other? Will the teleological method ultimately prevail, or will the CJEU respect the common traditions on fundamental rights? It is interesting to examine this relation between the two methods in the context of fundamental rights, which will be done in detail in Chapter 13.

Since the teleological method plays a role in the context of fundamental rights too, some further questions should be dealt with as well. The two most important ones are: how are the object and purpose established and does the CJEU take a subjective or objective approach? These questions are intertwined, since the answer to the first to some extent determines the answer to the second. In addition, the question arises as to what kind of documents the CJEU takes into account when applying the teleological method. Some references have been made to the type of

---

69 Brown & Kennedy (2000), p. 339; Tridimas (1996), p. 204; Arnull (2006), p. 612; Millett (1989), p. 170-171; Albors Llorens (1999), p. 382.

70 See Chapter 3. The introduction of fundamental rights into the EU legal order can be qualified as an example of a teleological approach as well. Reading fundamental rights into the general principles of the then community law can be justified by the object and purpose of the community itself. The question is whether the CJEU justified the introduction of fundamental rights by using teleological arguments. This will be seen in the case law analysis in Chapter 13.

71 See Chapter 13.

72 Kühling (2006), p. 506; Blanke (2006), p. 268.

documents that have been consulted for establishing the object and purpose of the former EC treaties.[73] The preamble and opening provisions are important factors in determining the object and purpose. Some substantive provisions even refer to more detailed aims.[74] It is not a subject that has received much attention and it is therefore difficult to draw any conclusions with regard to the use of other material on the basis of this information. A type of material that has been discussed by many authors is the *travaux préparatoires*.[75] The role of this material has been discussed briefly in Chapter 4, the main conclusion from that discussion being that the *travaux préparatoires* of most of the treaties have never been published, which is why they do not play a role in the interpretation process.[76] This conclusion has important implications for the use of the teleological method of interpretation by the CJEU, namely that a subjective approach is hardly possible or acceptable. The CJEU should really adopt an objective teleological approach and as a consequence not attach much value to the intentions of the original legislator.[77]

5.2.2 ECtHR

Despite the fact that it is primarily the CJEU that is well-known for its use of the teleological method, it is a central feature in the interpretation process of the ECtHR too.[78] In its interpretation process the ECtHR often emphasizes the object and purpose of the European Convention in order to justify a certain interpretation.[79] If the method plays such a vital role in the interpretation process, it is necessary to discuss its theoretical meaning and validity in more detail.

Bernhardt has argued that the special nature of human rights treaties requires the ECtHR to take an objective approach to interpretation.[80] The ECtHR has confirmed this in its own case law by claiming that it does not consider itself bound by the understanding of the parties at the time of ratification.[81] A further indication of a mainly objective teleological approach is the strong emphasis on an evolutive approach. This approach will be discussed separately in Chapter 7 hereinafter. For now it is interesting to note the link with this principle of interpretation and its influence on the ECtHR's objective teleological approach. The ECtHR does not limit

73 Arnull (2006), p. 612; Brown & Kennedy (2000), p. 339.
74 Arnull (2006), p. 612.
75 Hartley (2006), p. 79; Albors Llorens (1999), p. 379.
76 See Kutscher (1976), p. 21.
77 Hartley (2006), p. 79; Kutscher (1976), p. 38.
78 Ost (1992), p. 292; Matscher (1993), p. 65.
79 Schokkenbroek (2000), p. 4.
80 Bernhardt (1988), p. 68 & 71. Confirmed by Orakhelashvili (2003), p. 535.
81 Bernhardt (1988), p. 68-69; Orakhelashvili (2003), p. 535; Ovey & White (2006), p. 46.

itself to a purely objective teleological approach; however, this is a point which will be developed further below in relation to its use of the *travaux préparatoires*.

The crucial document in establishing the object and purpose of the ECtHR must be the preamble.[82] The preamble to the European Convention clearly states the aims of the European Convention, which according to some are so obvious that simply common sense would be enough to establish them.[83] The literature does not refer to much more than the preamble as the main indicator of the object and purpose of the European Convention. One would, however, expect that, over the years of its activity, the ECtHR in one or the other case relied on other documents to establish the object and purpose of the European Convention or one of its provisions. The literature does not really provide an answer to this question. If the case law analysis indicates that the ECtHR has indeed relied on other documents in addition to the preamble, some questions become relevant. Have these documents been internal to the European Convention, or have they referred to external documents? What justifications have been provided if other documents than the preamble have been consulted? These are relevant questions that should be considered in the case law analysis, since they shed light on how the ECtHR uses teleological interpretation.

The academic literature did devote attention to the use of one other type of document in the context of the interpretation process, namely the *travaux préparatoires*.[84] The role of these documents will also be discussed in the chapter on the principle of evolutive interpretation (Chapter 7). Here it may suffice to say that the role of the *travaux préparatoires* will be rather limited, but cannot be ignored. The *travaux* have been published and have in some cases been consulted by the ECtHR, as will further be explained in the case law chapter (Chapter 9). Only in some cases have they played a decisive role in the interpretation process. Against this background one cannot defend that the ECtHR relies on an exclusively objective teleological approach. It seems from the examples that have been provided in the literature on the limits of the evolutive approach that the *travaux préparatoires* will be decisive, or at least important, in cases where a certain interpretation would lead to the protection of a new right.[85] One could read from this that the ECtHR adopts a subjective teleological approach when the court itself feels that the boundaries of its own interpretative role have been reached. It will be interesting to see whether other situations can be found in which the preparatory works play an important role, which is one of the questions that have been studied in the case law analysis.

82 Harris (1995), p. 6; Gerards (2007), p. 15 refering to Ost and Prebensen; Sudre (1998), p. 111.
83 Klabbers (1997), p. 155.
84 See for example: Orakhelashvili (2003), p. 537; Ost (1992), p. 289; Ovey & White (2006), p. 40.
85 Prebensen (2000). For further discussion see Chapter 6.

In his discussion of the evolutive approach of the ECtHR, PREBENSEN claims that reference to the *travaux préparatoires* has been made when no common ground could be found among the different Contracting States. This link between the two methods is an interesting one to consider in the case law analysis as well, since it would imply that the use of the *travaux préparatoires* is linked to the outcome of the comparative method. Only in those cases would a subjective approach be considered.

The criticism of the ECtHR for using the interpretation method has manifested itself in accusations of judicial activism. Some rather harsh criticism has been voiced by dissenting judges in the ECtHR. Judge FITZMAURICE, for example, has pleaded strongly in favour of a subjective teleological approach and considered the intentions of the parties to be the only guide in order to establish the object and purpose.[86] Such accusations of judicial activism are, different from the criticism levelled at the CJEU, not necessarily only directed against the use of the teleological method. Still, improvements in the interpretation process should also concern this method of interpretation in order to enhance the interpretation process as a whole.

Just as for the CJEU, thus, there are many questions that have remained unanswered (or have only been rather vaguely addressed) in the literature on the theoretical use and desirability of the method. The case law analysis can provide some interesting answers to these questions, mainly on the questions how the ECtHR establishes the object and purpose and what documents play a role in that process. Before presenting the results of the case law analysis, however, some suggestions for improving this method of interpretation will be discussed first.

5.3 WHICH WAY FORWARD?

The chapter on comparative interpretation, Chapter 6, will show that many suggestions for improvement of the use of comparative interpretation have been given in the literature.[87] This can be mainly attributed to the fact that the comparative method itself is highly contested and that suggestions really need to be presented to enhance the legitimacy of the method as such. Such harsh criticism has not been levelled at the teleological method of interpretation. Hardly anyone objects as a matter of principle to the use of this method of interpretation for determining the meaning of a (part of a) legal text. What has been criticized is the use of this method; more specifically the use of the objective (emergent) purpose has led to accusations of judicial legislating and judicial activism, as indicated in section 5.1.4. It is difficult to rebut such accusations, since it is not clear what the source of these accusations is. Judicial

86 Ost (1992), p. 292.
87 See section 6.1.7.

activism is a rather vague term and therefore the source of the accusation can be a variety of things; it could be that someone is unhappy with the judgment or its outcome, or that someone actually thinks the judge has gone beyond his or her role.[88]

Given the importance of the method for the interpretation process of both courts, it is important to try to address this criticism. After all, that might help to enhance the legitimacy of the use of the method. It should, however, be emphasized that it is not possible to completely eliminate accusations of activism, especially because of the normative and subjective character of many of such accusations. The question whether a judge has acted within the confines of his or her role, depends on the perception one has of the proper role of a judge, which may be a different one for different scholars. These differences are inherent to any legal system, which means that they will not disappear by improving the method of teleological interpretation. The challenge for judges is thus not to try to have everyone agree on a specific interpretation, but to use their interpretation methods in such a way that even critics agree that the interpretation has been established in an acceptable manner.

This chapter has shown that answering specific questions as to the use of the teleological interpretation method by the courts can shed light on the use of teleological interpretation. Most importantly, the question how the object and purpose of a treaty are established should be answered in any judgment relying on teleological reasons. Providing insight into how the object and purpose are established makes it easier to assess whether the court has overstepped its boundaries, for example, by relying on documents that should not play a role in the interpretation process. By being rather vague about the object and purpose the court can also read a broad range of notions into a certain provision. If the court is clearer about the object and purpose, this might restrain the court and keep it from reading too much into the object and purpose. The question is, however, whether such care as to asking and answering these questions is really visible in the interpretative practice of the CJEU and the ECtHR. Do these courts justify their choice for a specific object and purpose? How explicit are their choices when using teleological arguments? Are they clear on the documents they use for determining the object and purpose?

This constitutes the main respect in which improvements to the courts' reasoning can possibly be made. Specific suggestions can only be made after a case law analysis that provides more insight into the practice of establishing the object and purpose. This does not mean that paying attention to this aspect will silence all critics, but critics might have less reason to criticize the interpretation process and be forced to argue on substantive issues. That would already be an achievement.

88 Cohn & Kremnitzer (2005).

5.4 Conclusion

This chapter has indicated that teleological interpretation is a generally valued method of interpretation. In its non-controversial version it provides a tool for understanding the meaning of the text against the background of the intention of the parties who drafted the treaty. In its more controversial version it still provides a background to interpret the treaty, but the connection with the intentions of the original parties is missing. The purpose of the treaty or one of its provisions in that case is then determined in an objective manner, which means that it might even change over time. Some argue that only the objective purpose has a place in the interpretation of international human rights treaties, but the question is whether that corresponds with the actual practice of teleological interpretation by supranational courts such as the CJEU and the ECtHR. Legal literature on both European Courts has found that the objective purpose plays an important role in the context of teleological interpretation, but it remains rather unclear how this object and purpose are established. That is a vital question to be answered in the case law analysis, especially since it has been indicated that the key to reducing criticism might be related to clarifying how the object and purpose are established.

Chapter 6
Comparative interpretation

Recent years have shown a great deal of scholarly interest in the use of comparative law by judges.[1] The debate on this method of interpretation is rather broad and therefore this chapter will not reflect all aspects of that debate. Given the topic of this book, the focus will be on comparative interpretation in the field of fundamental rights, which is one of the areas where judges have been quite willing to look across borders.[2] The discussion will draw on both national and international discourse on the method and its use.

The term 'comparative interpretation' will be used in this book, rather than the term 'consensus interpretation' or 'common ground method'. These latter terms have been used in the ECtHR context, but the term 'comparative interpretation' fits better in a wider context. The term 'comparative interpretation' has been used in the context of the general debate on this form of interpretation in judicial decisions. Therefore the general terminology will be used, rather than the specific ECtHR terminology.

The chapter will first deal with different aspects of the general debate on comparative interpretation. This discussion will take place against the background of supranational adjudication. For that reason, some specifically national aspects have been left out of the discussion. Many aspects of the general discourse on comparative interpretation are also relevant for both European Courts, but the second part of this chapter will address some more specific aspects that are relevant only for either the CJEU or the ECtHR. Especially in the latter part of this chapter, dealing with both European Courts, it will be become clear that many questions remain and need to be addressed in the case law analysis.

The aim of this chapter is to discuss the answers that have been given in academic literature to several theoretical questions on comparative interpretation. What does comparative interpretation mean? Why do courts invoke this method? How can the

1 See for a selection of the articles produced on this topic: Slaughter (1994); Choudhry (1998); Harding (2003); Slaughter (2003); Tushnet (2003); Dorsen (2005); Jackson (2005); Waldron (2005); Young (2005); Higgins (2006); Tsen-Ta Lee (2007); Khushal Murkens (2008).

2 See Kentridge (2004), p. 235, who argues that the field of human rights is particularly suitable for comparison, among others, because many human rights derive from their common ancestor, the Universal Declaration of Human Rights. See also: McCrudden (2003); Örücü (2003); McCrudden (2007). Also many of the articles referred to in the previous footnote focus on constitutional law and constitutional rights.

use of this method be justified? What is the role of this method in the interpretative framework? Has any criticism been expressed? This discussion will help one to understand the benefits and pitfalls of this method. A thorough analysis of the theoretical literature on this interpretation method will result in raising more specific and refined questions that provide the basis for the case law analysis in subsequent chapters. A better understanding of the theoretical aspects of the method, in combination with information as to its use in the case law of the courts under study, will ultimately help in suggesting areas for improvement.

6.1 Comparative interpretation in more detail

6.1.1 What is comparative interpretation?

Comparative interpretation refers to the fact that judges sometimes make references to or use arguments based on materials or information derived from foreign legal systems.[3] This entails that, by means of a comparative study, one or more foreign solutions to an interpretation problem will be considered.[4] In general this often occurs in the case of a new interpretation of a specific right or when courts are confronted with the question whether a certain right exists within their jurisdiction (the creation of a new right).[5] When applying this method of interpretation, it is not the text or purpose of the provision, but the outcome of a comparative study that supports a certain choice of interpretation. In other words, the comparative analysis justifies or supports a certain line of reasoning in a specific case.

Comparative interpretation is the common name for a variety of different methods of employing foreign materials in judgments. There is no uniform way of applying comparative interpretation. Due to this lack of a blueprint for the use of the method, every court may have a different conception of what it entails. This difference can be, for example, at the level of the sources to be used for the comparison, but it can also be that different courts use comparative interpretation for different purposes. The common denominator is, however, that the argument invoked by a judge is based on or inspired by at least one foreign source. An explanation for the variety in the forms of comparative reasoning could be that the method has mainly been developed

3 Alexy (1989), p. 239.

4 Llorens (1999), p. 380. Comparable descriptions can be found in: Brown (2000), p. 337; Harris (1995), p. 9; Ovey and White (2006), p. 48; Matscher (1993), p. 74; Ost (1992), p. 305; Schermers, (2001), p. 13-15.

5 Gerards (2006), p. 112. This is also the case in the United States; see for example the use of foreign materials in Lawrence v Texas. In this case the question was whether it was unconstitutional to prohibit consensual homosexual private conduct. The Supreme Court concluded that it was.

in judicial practice.[6] The subsequent academic discussion struggles to 'make sense of [a] relatively fast-moving' form of judicial reasoning.[7]

The following sections will address some more specific aspects of what it means to employ comparative interpretation. Even though there is not one version of this method, some general remarks can be made on this method of interpretation.

6.1.2 General basis for comparative interpretation?

There are only a few international treaties or constitutional documents that explicitly allow for comparative arguments to be taken into consideration. A famous example is the South African constitution, which contains a specific section that allows (some argue: requires)[8] the Constitutional Court to take international and other foreign experiences into account when interpreting the constitution.[9] Most courts, however, do not operate on the basis of a document that explicitly allows for taking foreign experiences into account. The question whether a basis for this practice exists should therefore be answered in the specific context of each particular court as there might be implicit factors within the system in which a particular court functions that allow for this form of reasoning.

Due to the fact that the courts central to this thesis are supranational courts interpreting treaties, the provisions in the Vienna Convention should briefly be considered. In Chapter 4 it was briefly stated that the Vienna Convention does not mention the comparative method of interpretation, but that statement should not be understood as to mean that it does not *allow* for such interpretation. The Vienna Convention in Article 31(3)(c) provides that 'any relevant rules of interpretation law applicable in the relations between the parties' shall be taken into account when interpreting a treaty.[10] This indicates that international and supranational courts do have to take 'international' materials into account, but the extent of this provision is not entirely clear. First of all, what kind of international rules are referred to under this provision? There is no definite answer to this question, but a convincing argument has been made to understand this as a reference to 'all rules that spring from any

6 McCrudden (2007), p. 372.

7 McCrudden (2007), p. 372.

8 Huscroft speaks about the mandatory approach in the South African Constitution. Huscroft (2006), p. 6.

9 § 39 (1). See also Huscroft (2006), p. 6; Bentele (2008), p. 7. Huscroft also refers to the New Zealand Constitution and argues that they have a permissive approach.

10 See elaborately on this provision McLachlan (2005). He discusses the principle of systemic integration (principle that all treaties are part of the system of international law and must be interpreted against that background), which underlies this provision and provides some examples of the use of this principle in the recent practice of international courts. It would stretch too far beyond the purpose of this thesis to discuss this principle in depth; therefore this principle will only be mentioned.

of the formal sources of international law'.[11] This means that the reference includes 'treaties, customary norms and general principles of international law'.[12] Some authors have adopted a more limited understanding of this reference and exclude one of these sources.[13] No basis for such exclusion can be found in the text, object and purpose or the intention of the drafters of the Vienna Convention, which is the reason why doing so would be somewhat arbitrary.[14] A second question is what can be understood by the reference to 'the parties'. Does this refer to the parties to the specific dispute or all the parties to the treaty that requires interpretation? Traditionally, the reference to 'the parties' has been understood to mean all the parties to the treaty that had to be interpreted.[15] LINDERFALK has noticed a change in understanding of this provision towards reading the reference to 'the parties' as a reference to the parties to the specific dispute.[16] For the purpose of this section it is not necessary, however, to provide a definitive answer to these questions raised by Article 31(3)(c). It is sufficient to show that this provision provides only a limited basis for using comparative material. First of all, this is true because following the traditional understanding of Article 31(3)(c) only those international rules ratified by all parties can be used for interpretative purposes. This will be the case especially for a multilateral treaty that leaves only a limited number of materials. Moreover, the provision does not provide a clear basis for references to national law. Article 31(3)(c) accordingly provides only a limited basis for comparative interpretation.

An important question that should thus be answered when looking at both European systems is whether the respective treaties provide a more explicit legal basis for invoking comparative arguments. This will be discussed when addressing the European Court of Human Rights and Court of Justice of the European Union later in this theoretical chapter (see sections 6.2 and 6.3 respectively). In the chapters on the case law analysis this question will also be addressed in order to understand what the ECtHR and the CJEU themselves consider to be the basis for their use of comparative arguments (see Chapters 10 and 13).

---

11 Linderfalk (2007), p. 177.

12 Orakhelashvili (2008), p. 366.

13 Linderfalk (2007), p. 177-178, discusses some authors that have adopted a more limited understanding of this provision.

14 Linderfalk (2007), p. 177-178.

15 Linderfalk (2008), p. 345. See also Orakhelashvili (2008), p. 368.

16 Linderfalk (2008), p. 345. He invokes different interpretation methods, such as text, context and the object and purpose, to argue that the Vienna Convention, in his view, only supports the traditional understanding.

6.1.3 'Internal' and 'external' comparative interpretation

In order to understand comparative interpretation it is necessary to address what is actually meant with 'references to a foreign source'. What kinds of sources are referred to and what does the term 'foreign' stand for in the context of comparative interpretation? Often, when invoking foreign references, judges rely on foreign court decisions or international documents, mainly treaties. Depending on how comfortable judges in a specific jurisdiction are with referring to foreign materials the list of foreign sources could be longer or shorter. Part of the answer on what counts as 'foreign' depends on the specific context in which the method is used. Nevertheless, some general, more abstract remarks can be made. In this thesis, a distinction will be made between an internal and an external component of comparative interpretation for two reasons.[17] First of all, such a distinction might provide an analytical tool in the discussion on comparative interpretation before international or supranational courts.[18] Secondly, it is questionable whether both forms of comparative interpretation can be employed on the basis of the same justification, a question that will be explored further in section 6.1.5 below, which will make clear that the justification for the choice of either an internal or an external comparison will depend on the purposes for which comparative interpretation is employed. Therefore there might be cases in which both components are in need of a different justification, as will be seen below. Some further background is, however, needed before this argument can be clarified in more detail.

The *internal component* means, on the one hand, that the comparative study limits itself to a comparison between the countries that fall within the jurisdiction of the court in question. For the courts central to this thesis that means a comparison between the Member States of either the European Union or the Contracting States to the European Convention of Human Rights.

---

17 The literature has not explicitly discussed this distinction. This could perhaps be because many discussions on comparative interpretation focus on national constitutional courts and as a result this distinction is much less relevant. Bernhardt (1999), p. 36, argues that comparative law normally refers to comparison of national law, but that a different dimension should be added for references to international law. This is thus a different distinction, but at least he acknowledges as well that comparative law might have different dimensions.

18 A different analytical tool in discussing comparative interpretation has been introduced by Slaughter (1994), p. 103-112. She distinguishes between horizontal, vertical and mixed vertical-horizontal communication between courts. Horizontal refers to courts that are of similar status, like national courts referring to other national courts. Vertical refers to courts of different status, like a reference by the ECtHR to the United States Supreme Court. Mixed vertical-horizontal communication refers to, for example, the fact that 'supranational tribunals can serve as a conduit for [national] horizontal communication'.

The *external component* of comparative interpretation refers to the use of sources that are not covered by the internal component of this method. In general that means reliance on documents or on information derived from outside the jurisdiction of the court in question. References under the external component can either consist of references to other national jurisdictions, like the United States or Canada, or references to international documents, either treaties or soft law instruments, like 'Guidelines for Community Noise' issued by the World Health Organization.[19] None of these sources of law are within the jurisdiction of either the ECtHR or the CJEU and they may therefore be qualified as external sources. References to Council of Europe documents also count as external references for both courts. This is particularly important in the context of the ECtHR. Even though the membership of the Council of Europe and the European Convention overlap, Council of Europe instruments are like any international legal instrument and only bind the parties that have ratified the specific instrument. Therefore these instruments can be considered as external to the ECHR.

The question which sources are external and which are internal can be answered differently for both the ECtHR and the CJEU. Including references to, for example, Russian law and Turkish law in a comparison fall, in the case of the ECtHR, within the internal component, while for the CJEU it would fall into the external component. The jurisdiction for both courts is different, which implies that the division between the internal and external component of comparative interpretation will also be a different one.

As has been mentioned before, the relevance of this distinction is related to the justification provided for invoking this method of interpretation.[20] The question is whether both components can rely on a similar justification. Perhaps a different or more elaborate justification may be necessary when invoking references under the external component. This question can only be answered in relation to a discussion of the different purposes of comparative interpretation, since the answer depends on the purpose for which comparative interpretation is used. The following section will therefore first consider different purposes of comparative interpretation; subsequently, we will return to the question of justification.

---

19 This was the case in ECtHR, *Fägerskiöld v. Sweden*, decision of 26 February 2008, *unpublished*.

20 The fact that in the United States the search for a consensus among the 52 states is much less controversial than looking for a broader consensus in Western civilization is already a small indication that there is a relevant difference between these two components. See for a discussion on this method and the lack of controversy of a national consensus in the USA: Jacobi (2005), p. 2. The situation is however not entirely comparable, since the Supreme Court is a national constitutional court and the present discussion concerns supranational courts.

6.1.4 Purposes of comparative interpretation

Various purposes for invoking comparative arguments have been identified in the literature. A preliminary remark should, however, be made. The discussion here does not concern references to international or foreign materials compelled by the facts of the case. Therefore comparative references for the purpose of explaining a foreign contract, for example, will not be included.[21] The use of comparative material that is relevant for this study concerns those cases where the court in principle is not forced to look at comparative arguments, but does do so on its own accord.

In some instances references to foreign materials are included only for rhetorical purposes[22] or, as Justice Scalia has called it, for 'ornamentation'.[23] In these instances the reference to foreign materials is not different from a reference to 'Shakespeare or the Bible'[24] or 'a newspaper article or a law review article'.[25] This kind of reference can be seen as part of a certain style of elaborate writing, without having a substantive meaning. This type of use is generally not controversial, although some authors have argued that if this is the actual and only purpose of the reference, then it has no place in judicial reasoning.[26]

A second common purpose of comparative interpretation is to draw inspiration from courts that have dealt with similar problems.[27] Even though the implementation and application of fundamental rights differs according to the country, there seems to be a strong agreement on the existence of 'general principles of human and constitutional rights'.[28] Most constitutions and international human rights treaties contain rather similar lists of rights.[29] Constitutional courts and also international human rights tribunals are often confronted with similar factual situations that present similar interpretative problems. From that perspective it might be helpful to look abroad to find and design creative solutions for interpretative problems in one's own legal system.[30] Moreover, it might shed some light on 'new' issues which might already

---

21 McCrudden (2007), p. 377 lists different categories of cases where judges resort to international or foreign law on the basis of the facts of the case. He concludes that these instances are not controversial.

22 McCrudden (2007), p. 378.

23 Yoo (2004), p. 2.

24 McCrudden (2007), p. 378.

25 Yoo (2004), p. 3.

26 McCrudden (2007), p. 391 referring to Justice Scalia in *Roper v Simmons* (2005).

27 Slaughter (2003) referring to Justice Ginsburg, p. 199. See also McCrudden (2003), p. 9, referring to Justice Barak of the Supreme Court of Israel.

28 McCrudden (2007), p. 372.

29 McCrudden (2007), p. 372.

30 Slaughter (2003), p. 201.

have been addressed in other legal systems,[31] such as new technological challenges to the current fundamental rights protection. Comparative interpretation thus provides a way to learn and benefit from other experiences.[32] Foreign materials employed for this purpose have only persuasive value, which means that these materials will only be used to support a certain solution (which can be based on other arguments as well) and do not have any binding force. Nevertheless, this is still a controversial way to use comparative arguments. CHOUDHRY, for example, refers to the argument advanced by legal hegemonists who claim that the USA has nothing to learn from foreign experiences.[33] Likewise, US Supreme Court Justice Thomas has argued in *Knight v Florida* that the fact that you need to resort to foreign materials may weaken the court's own argument.[34]

Thirdly, a related, though somewhat separate function of comparative interpretation is that it provides an opportunity for judges to 'test his or her value-judgment against the judgments of other judges who have grappled with similar provisions'.[35] In this case the emphasis is not on the learning factor of foreign experiences, but on the simple fact that foreign courts have taken a similar path. If judges are able to show that courts in different jurisdictions have chosen a similar solution, this might help to increase the objectivity of a particular decision.[36] Especially in the field of fundamental rights, where provisions are drafted in a very general manner, judges can be easily accused of being overly judicially creative in their interpretation process.[37] Using comparative arguments to indicate that other judges have considered a similar solution can be one way to objectify the chosen solution in a specific case. A different way of viewing this purpose is to argue that sometimes foreign or international citations can add authority to a particular decision.[38] Many courts in the world have, for example, included references to the United States Supreme Court in their decision as a way to enhance the force of their argument.[39]

---

31 Tsen-Ta Lee (2007), p. 149.

32 Tsen-Ta Lee (2007), p. 149; Bentele (2008), p. 8.

33 Choudhry (1998), p. 832.

34 *Knight v Florida*.

35 Kentridge (2004), p. 236.

36 See for a similar argument on objectifying the decision of judges: Jackson (2005), p. 119. See also Kentridge (2004), p. 236. McCrudden (2003), p. 1 refers to term 'distancing devices' which has been introduced by Raz. McCrudden argues that a continuing concern for human rights judges is to interpret 'independent of the personal taste of the judges'.

37 Kentridge (2004), p. 236.

38 Slaughter (2003), p. 201; Slaughter (1994), p. 119. Even though Scalia does not support this type of argument, he considers that this can be a purpose of comparative references, Scalia (2004), p. 309.

39 See Fontana (2001), p. 549, referring to Chief-Justice Rehnquist who remarked that new constitutional courts in their early days often looked to the USA to develop their own law.

Depending on whether a court employs the comparative method in a decisive or persuasive manner, this can be a more or less controversial form of comparative interpretation as well. Both proponents and opponents of comparative interpretation agree that decisive use of foreign material is inappropriate, but some strong critics of this method even find persuasive or informative use of foreign materials inappropriate.[40] In their view either the references to foreign material are decisive (which is unacceptable in their view) or they have no place in a judicial opinion, since they are irrelevant.[41]

Fourthly, references to foreign materials can be used to keep up with 'evolving national and international standards'.[42] This does not mean that courts necessarily have to follow this development. The fact that there are clear tendencies (sort of consensus) among different human rights standards, however, might be a reason for a court to ask 'why the laws of other nations have developed as they have and, further, to identify the material differences between those nations and the court's own jurisdiction that demand a different approach'.[43] An example of using comparative interpretation for this purpose can be found in some of the death penalty (Eighth Amendment) cases in the United States Supreme Court. In the case of *Roper* v. *Simmons* the Supreme Court had to address the question whether it was constitutional to impose the death penalty on a juvenile offender who was at the time of committing the crime older than 15, but younger than 18.[44] In answering that question the majority took different factors into account, such as the developments within the different states, but they also looked outside the United States.[45] The majority of the Justices of the Supreme Court observed that:

> Our determination that the death penalty is disproportionate punishment for offenders under 18 finds confirmation in the stark reality that the United States is the only country in the world that continues to give official sanction to the juvenile death penalty. This reality does not become controlling for the task of interpreting the Eight Amendment remains our responsibility. [reference is also made to the United Nations on the Rights of the Child] ... only seven countries other than the United States have executed juvenile offenders since 1990: Iran,

40 Bentele (2008), p. 9. See also Sitaraman (2009), p. 27 who discusses authoritative use of foreign law and claims that this is a rather controversial form of comparative interpretation. He provides the example of the Argentina Supreme Court in the 1920s as one of the rare examples of this type of comparative interpretation.

41 Dorsen (2005), p. 522.

42 Tsen-Ta Lee (2007), p. 151.

43 Tsen-Ta Lee (2007), p. 152.

44 *Roper v Simmons* 2005. The death penalty had already been declared unconstitutional for juvenile offenders of 15 years or younger in *Stanford v Kentucky* (1989).

45 A similar approach was taken in *Atkins v Virginia* (2003) where the Supreme Court had to answer the question whether it was constitutional to execute mentally retarded persons.

> Pakistan, Saudi Arabia, Yemen, Nigeria, the Democratic Republic of Congo and China. Since then each of these countries has either abolished capital punishment for juveniles or made public disavowal of the practice. In sum it is fair to say that the United States now stands alone in a world that has turned its face against the juvenile death penalty... The opinion of the world community, while not controlling our outcome, does provide respected and significant confirmation for our own conclusions.[46]

Even though the majority opinion seems to grant only a confirmatory status to the (unanimous) world opinion and stresses this more than once,[47] the reference to the opinion of the world community here was rather controversial. In a dissenting opinion, Justice O'Connor held that it is legitimate to take foreign materials into account, but she argued that in this case the national consensus was not clear, and therefore foreign materials could not serve a confirmatory role. Justice Scalia, one of the main opponents to the use of modern foreign materials in judicial opinions,[48] moreover argued in his dissenting opinion to the case that the reference to the world opinion was more than just confirmatory. He observed that:

> Though the views of our own citizens are essentially irrelevant to the Court's decision today, the views of other countries and the so-called international community take center stage.[49]

Moreover, he argued that:

> More fundamentally, ..., the basic premise of the Court's argument --that American law should conform to the laws of the rest of the world-- ought to be rejected out of hand.[50]

This example from the US case law clearly shows that using comparative arguments for confirmatory purposes can be quite controversial, even more so when the world opinion is less clear-cut as was the case in *Roper v Simmons*. In the European context such a search for consensus seems to be less controversial.[51] On the contrary, it is often argued that the existence of a consensus might increase the acceptance of an

---

46 *Roper v Simmons* (2005).

47 Brand argues that the place of the reference to foreign materials in this opinion did put special emphasis on this material, since it was placed just before the final statement in the case. Brand (2006-2007), p. 429.

48 See for example Scalia (2004); Dorsen (2005). Scalia only considers old English law to be a legitimate foreign source for interpretation.

49 *Roper v Simmons* (2005), dissenting opinion Scalia.

50 *Roper v Simmons* (2005), dissenting opinion Scalia. Also discussed in Choudhry (2006), p. 3.

51 The term 'consensus' here refers to an 'internal' consensus, namely a consensus composed of Member States of the organization in question. The distinction between internal and external comparative interpretation has been addressed earlier in this chapter; see section 6.1.3. and will be addressed in more detail in section 6.1.5.

interpretation by either the CJEU or the ECtHR, depending of course on how these courts establish a consensus.[52] The fact that a consensus takes account of the legal situation in the Member States, as set out by the democratically elected legislature, helps to increase the acceptance of the interpretation by these supranational courts. It helps to build a bridge between the national and supranational level by engaging the Member States in their reasoning.[53] This is considered especially valuable in a multilevel legal context where the success of the supranational legal order to some extent depends on the cooperation of and acceptance by the Member States.

Finally, comparative interpretation can be helpful in situations where, for example, due to a newly enacted bill of rights or treaty or constitution there is not yet a rich body of case law.[54] This is what happened in South Africa and some argue that this is one of the reasons why Canada has a very open attitude towards foreign materials.[55] For the European Courts, this purpose may seem to be of less relevance, given that the treaties they have to deal with are already well-established. Nevertheless, the Court of Justice of the European Union may use this purpose as a justification for comparative interpretation in using the rather new EU Charter of Fundamental Rights, for example by using references to Council of Europe materials that may be helpful to explain the meaning of specific provisions on social and economic rights.

An important question resulting from this discussion relates to which purpose is or which purposes are important for the ECtHR and CJEU. Probably, more than one of the purposes discussed here can be found relevant to the context of these courts, but an interesting question might be if one of them is more important and pertinent than others. Such issues will be addressed below on the basis of theoretical literature, but the issues will also be discussed in Chapters 10 and 13 on the basis of a case law analysis.

Firstly, however, now that different purposes of comparative interpretation have been identified, the question why it is important to distinguish between the internal and external component of comparative interpretation should be addressed.[56]

---

52 Carozza (1998), p. 1227-1228, discusses the fact that the effectiveness of the ECtHR judgments depends on the acceptance by Member States. Especially in the early years it was helpful in that respect to ground the controversial decisions in the practice of the Member States themselves.

53 Mahoney (2004), p. 147; Lenaerts (2003), p. 879.

54 McCrudden (2003), p. 14; Harding (2003), p. 414.

55 Harding (2003), p. 414. The Charter of Rights in Canada is of a rather recent date, namely 1982.

56 The overview presented here is not exhaustive. It represents a description of the purposes mostly mentioned in the literature or most relevant for the discussion. See further, for example, Sitaraman (2009) who discusses nine different purposes of comparative interpretation with varying degrees of controversy. See also Markesinis & Fedtke (2005), who discuss seven different purposes of comparative interpretation.

6.1.5 The distinction between internal and external component revisited

The previous discussion highlighted different purposes of comparative interpretation. The question is how this affects the debate on the justification of the use of either the internal or the external component of comparative interpretation. If the first purpose of drawing inspiration is concerned, for example, this does not seem to make much of a difference. When judges rely on comparative interpretation in order to draw inspiration from solutions that have been adopted in different legal systems, after all, it does not really matter whether they derive such inspiration from external or internal sources. The purpose of drawing inspiration can justify both the use of the internal component and external component of comparative interpretation. It is, however, important that a justification is provided for the documents or instruments referred to for this purpose. That may be more difficult in the context of external comparative interpretation.

A different situation arises when judges are looking for a trend or a consensus in order to support a certain argument, like in the example of *Roper v Simmons* that has been discussed in section 6.1.4. The question in this case was whether imposing the death penalty on a minor who was between 15 and 18 years old when committing a crime was contrary to the Eight Amendment which prohibits cruel and unusual punishment. In its reasoning the Supreme Court referred to a national consensus, i.e. a comparison of the legislation of the different states. This reference to a national consensus can be regarded as what has been called in this thesis the internal component of comparative interpretation. The reference to a national consensus as such was not controversial at all in this judgment. The only question was whether the national consensus had sufficiently evolved to draw any conclusions from it.[57] On the basis of several other arguments the majority of the Supreme Court finally concluded that imposing the death penalty in this situation would violate the Eighth Amendment, including a reference to an international consensus to support that view. This is thus an example of the external component of comparative interpretation. As explained in the previous section, the use of exactly this external material was highly controversial in both academia and in practice, which proves that it really makes a difference if either internal or external sources are being used if comparative interpretation serves a confirmatory purpose.

How can this difference in acceptance between the use of internal and external comparative interpretation be explained? Most likely, basing a new or extended right on the basis of an 'internal' consensus is considered to be justified by the fact that the consensus is formed by the Member States that fall within the jurisdiction of the

57 See dissent by O'Connor, who considers that there was no sufficient evidence of a strong change in the national consensus since the last judgment on the same subject matter.

court in question. The court in question takes into account the practice in its own legal order. This territorial aspect cannot, however, justify the search for an external consensus. A different justification is therefore needed in order to legitimately employ the external comparative method for the purpose of finding a consensus.

On what legitimate basis may a court then take into account such purely external references? What kind of justification can be given for doing so? An attempt will be made to provide an answer to this question in section 6.1.7 of this chapter. Subsequently, the case law analysis in Chapters 10 and 13 should provide more insight into the use of external and internal references by both courts, more specifically in whether the courts acknowledge that a different justification is needed for these different components.

6.1.6 Criticism of comparative interpretation

There has been quite some criticism on the use of comparative interpretation. The criticism to be discussed in this section will focus on general criticism that can be distilled from the different theoretical discussions on comparative interpretation. The discussions on the ECtHR and CJEU will reveal some specific criticisms directed at the use of the method by these courts.

The criticism can be divided into roughly two categories. On the one hand, there are those who criticize the use of comparative interpretation *per se*. They claim that this is not a legitimate method of interpretation at all. On the other hand, there are those who criticize the current use of the method and focus on methodological issues. The two categories are related, but deserve separate attention, since not every solution might be able to silence critics on both sides.

6.1.6.1 Criticism of the legitimacy of comparative interpretation as a method of interpretation

The most fundamental criticism voiced against comparative interpretation is that it should not be used as a method of interpretation at all. This criticism has mainly been expressed in the context of national discussions on the legitimacy of comparative interpretation. This means that if this criticism were to be translated to the context of the European supranational courts it would be directed mainly to the external component of this method, since in the national context the discussion focuses on the use of foreign or international (thus external) materials. Most famous for its strong opposition against the use of comparative interpretation is the United States.[58] The opposition identifies two major objections against the use of comparative references as an interpretative tool. First of all, some people argue that invoking foreign materials constitutes a 'threat' to the sovereignty of the legal system of the court employing these references.[59] This threat might be realistic if courts were to refer to foreign materials as binding precedent.[60] There are, however, no known examples of courts relying on foreign precedents as binding. Foreign precedents are at the most regarded as providing persuasive force of argument.[61] Assuming that opponents of comparative interpretation also consider persuasive references a threat to national sovereignty, what is it that they are afraid of? Opponents mainly appear to be concerned about the lack of democratic legitimacy of these foreign materials, which 'have no democratic provenance, they have no democratic connection to this legal system, to this constitutional system, and thus lack democratic accountability as legal materials'.[62] For example, Chief Justice Roberts of the US Supreme Court focused on the lack of democratic legitimacy of the foreign judge of a particular case that was being referred to: '[n]o President accountable to the people appointed that judge, and no Senate accountable to the people confirmed that judge, and yet he's playing a role in shaping a law that binds the people in this country...'[63] The main problem according to the opponents is thus that no one can be held accountable for the arguments based on foreign references.[64]

The question is, of course, whether this criticism (or perhaps a different version of it), may also be relevant for the ECtHR and the CJEU. After all, it can hardly be

58 The main judicial characters in this discussion in the United States are Justice Breyer defending the use of comparative references and Justice Scalia passionately trying to eradicate this type of reasoning. The difference in opinion is mainly due to a different theory of constitutional interpretation. Their view of what the constitution is plays an important role here as well. Scalia considers that constitution to be a code of detailed historical rules, while Breyer considers the constitution to be a charter of principles. In the latter case it might make more sense to look abroad to other constitutions that have dealt with the same broad principles. This discussion of the nature of the document does not play any role in Europe and therefore this is not a relevant difference for the general discussion in this thesis. For differing views on what is the Constitution, see Barber & Fleming (2007).

59 Choudhry (2006), p. 7-8; Bentele (2008), p. 8-9. Tsen-Ta Lee (2007), p. 133; Tushnet (2003), p. 257. A similar argument has been presented in Dammann (2001), p. 531. At one point a bill had been introduced to prohibit judges from incorporating foreign references in their judgments. The text was never adopted, but is an indication of the strong opposition. Choudhry (2006), p. 11.

60 Bentele (2008), p. 9.

61 Slaughter (1994), p. 124; Bentele (2008), p. 9, who claims that courts consider foreign law to provide *at most* persuasive reasons.

62 Choudhry (2006), p. 8, citing from Dorsen (2005), p.540.

63 Choudhry (2006), p. 9, referring to Roberts. See also: McCrudden (2007), p. 389.

64 McCrudden describes a similar argument. He speaks about 'circumventing national democratic controls'. McCrudden (2007), p. 389.

the 'sovereignty' of these European systems or their democratic legitimacy that is being threatened. Rather one could argue that the sovereignty of the States could be limited by the fact that a European consensus could force a minority of States in a certain direction. One might also contend that *national* sovereignty is being limited when a consensus *outside* Europe is used to determine the direction in which Europe is heading. The question is, however, whether the perceived threat to national sovereignty in the European context is typically associated with comparative interpretation as such, or whether it is an inherent aspect of any form of interpretation taking place in a supranational legal order. After all, whether an interpretation by the CJEU or ECtHR is based on a teleological argument or a comparative argument does not matter for the fact that a specific State in some situations no longer has the last say on fundamental rights issues. In the European situation this 'threat' to national sovereignty is thus not necessarily specific for comparative interpretation.

If the European Courts, however, invoke references to international and foreign materials and use them as a basis for a far-reaching or controversial interpretation, they run the risk that Member States will complain about introducing obligations that they never agreed to.[65] This risk may arise in particular when supranational courts rely on the external component of comparative interpretation, since in that case materials foreign to the Member States play a role in the final interpretation. In that sense, relying on foreign or international material could present a threat to sovereignty.[66] The discussion below in the following section will deal with this problem in more detail.

The second objection put forward by opponents of the use of comparative arguments concerns the role of the judge and judicial activism.[67] As has been explained before, in Chapter 5, the notion of judicial activism is often used to express discontent with a judicial decision, which renders the term rather subjective.[68] Therefore, the term will be used here only to illustrate the type of rhetoric used to direct criticism at this method.

Under the objection of judicial activism, opponents show themselves concerned that judges overstep the borders of the proper judicial role by looking beyond the

65 Like Turkey in the case of ECtHR (GC), *Demir and Baykara v. Turkey*, judgment of 12 November 2008, *unpublished*. See Chapter 10 for a full discussion of this case.

66 McCrudden discusses this argument in the national context and claims that reliance on not accepted international obligations circumvents the democratic mechanism designed to approve these international obligations. McCrudden (2007), p, 390.

67 Choudhry (2006), p. 6-7; this argument is advanced by Justice Scalia in his conversation with justice Breyer on the use of foreign material in US Supreme Court cases, Dorsen (2005).

68 Cohn and Kremnitzer (2005), p. 334. See also Chapter 5 for a more extensive discussion.

national borders.[69] There are two aspects to this argument. First of all, the question is whether comparative material can be a legitimate source of constitutional interpretation. The answer depends on which theory of interpretation one adheres to. Originalists, for example, do not consider comparative interpretation to be a legitimate method of interpretation. In their view judges in the interpretation process should strive to find the original meaning of the constitutional provision, i.e. the meaning the provision had at the time it was adopted. Comparative references cannot shed any light on the meaning of these constitutional provisions and, as a result, they arguably cannot be considered to constitute a legitimate method of interpretation. In the originalists' view, judges should refrain from invoking foreign materials in their reasoning, since otherwise they would go beyond their role as a judge. Yet other interpretative schools consider comparative interpretation to be a legitimate method of interpretation.[70] This means that it is really dependent on one's theoretical starting point if one regards the use of comparative interpretation *per se* to stretch beyond the proper role of the judge. Accusations of judicial activism are therefore difficult to address. Just mentioning the justification for comparative interpretation and addressing the methodological concerns that will be discussed below, might not convince these strong opponents that comparative interpretation is a legitimate interpretation method within their own theoretical framework. It might convince them that, however, within a different theoretical framework, comparative interpretation is a legitimate method of interpretation.

A third objection to comparative interpretation is related to criticism of the use of this method. Crudely put, some argue that relying on (objective) comparative references masks the fact that judges are actually imposing their own (subjective) legal preferences.[71] Judges can simply pick the references that support their own opinion and use these references as a justification for this result.[72] In this sense the method 'permits courts to achieve desired results while pretending they are engaged in a legal enterprise'.[73] The problem, according to opponents, is basically that comparative

69 McCrudden refers to this argument as well and describes that comparative references upset the balance between constraint and discretion by granting more discretion to judges. McCrudden (2007), p. 387.

70 For example the interpretative theory that focuses on a moral reading of the constitution. Dworkin is one of the most famous proponents of this theory. It has also been called the 'philosophical approach'. See, for example, Fleming & Barber (2007), p. 26-33.

71 Choudhry (2006), p. 6-7 and Dorsen (2005), p. 531, where Justice Scalia refers to the fear of manipulation.

72 This phenomenon has been called 'cherry-picking'. See for example: McCrudden (2003), p. 5 & (2007), p. 388; Bentele (2008), p. 13-14; Tsen-Ta Lee (2007), p. 147; Dorsen (2005), p. 530, where Justice Breyer acknowledged that there is a certain element of selectivity in the citations of foreign sources.

73 Choudhry (2006), p. 7.

arguments can be used to support any argument. This criticism is strongly intertwined with criticism of the methodological aspects of comparative interpretation. The difference is that some point to the methodological shortcomings, but still think it is an appropriate method of interpretation, even though it should be improved. Others consider the methodological shortcomings to constitute a reason to dismiss the whole method. The difference is thus one of consequences, but not necessarily one of substance. The following section will deal more in detail with the methodological problems that are connected with the use of comparative arguments.

6.1.6.2 Criticism of the use of comparative interpretation

The previous section already showed that there are serious methodological concerns regarding comparative interpretation. The problem is that no consistent application of this method has been developed, which leads to all sorts of criticism. Generally, the criticism of the use of the method can be divided into two categories. The first category of criticism is directed against the use of the comparative method for all the purposes listed in section 6.1.4. The second category is more limited and is directed at the specific use of the comparative method when it is applied to find a consensus or a trend. The criticism in this latter category has most prominently been expressed in the context of the European Courts. It will, however, be addressed in the more general discussion here, since the criticism applies to both courts in a similar fashion.

The main problem that has been noted in this first category is a problem of selecting the relevant sources.[74] The question is how judges can select foreign sources without being accused of 'looking over the heads of the crowd and picking out his friends'.[75] This phenomenon has also been described as the risk of 'cherry-picking', which refers to the fact that, without any guidance on where to look, judges can just pick the cherries they like best.[76] Of course, it is impossible for judges to analyze every relevant national judgment or piece of legislation, not only because of a simple lack of time, but also due to lack of accessibility. A certain amount of selectivity will therefore always be present in any use of comparative interpretation.[77] The question is, however, how to avoid accusations of *deliberate* cherry-picking. As has been explained in the previous section, these accusations can ultimately affect the legitimacy of the method. The problem of cherry-picking has not only been mentioned with regard to the sources used for comparative interpretation, but also with regard to the 'sub-

74 McCrudden (2007), p. 388; Tsen-Ta Lee (2003), p. 145; Bentele (2008), p. 12-14.

75 McCrudden (2007), p. 388 referring to Scalia in *Roper v Simmons*.

76 Supra note 72.

77 Tsen-Ta Lee (2007), p. 145.

stantive issues concerning which the court is willing to look at comparative material'.[78] This criticism has been voiced most strongly by Justice Scalia in the American context. He claims that the proponents of comparative interpretation only use this type of argumentation when it suits their purposes.[79] He claims that once a court starts invoking this method, it should be consistent and always invoke this method, no matter which substantive issue it is dealing with. The Supreme Court has not used this type of reasoning in abortion cases and Justice Scalia claims that this is because comparative material would not support the majority opinion on abortion issues.[80] In cases on the death penalty, however, the Supreme Court has been willing to look abroad and has found support for its position in foreign materials. Such differences in approach seem to support the concern expressed by Justice Scalia.

The problem of deliberate cherry-picking has been noted as one of the concerns of this method in the European Courts as well.[81] Whether this is really an issue in the European Courts, however, is an aspect that can only be answered in the case law analysis. Specific attention will thereby be paid to the question whether comparative interpretation is reserved for certain types of substantive issues or whether it is used in a wide variety of cases.

A different problem often noted in relation to comparative interpretation is that there is a danger of misunderstanding or misinterpreting foreign materials.[82] This danger is rarely presented as an argument against the use of this method as such; rather, it is regarded as one of the challenges any court has to confront when applying it. The proper understanding of legal materials creates a particular problem when legal materials in a different language are involved.[83] Either judges have to use reliable translations into, most likely, English or French, or they are limited to studying systems of which they are familiar with the language. But even leaving the language obstacles aside, it is difficult to correctly understand legal concepts in a foreign system. A correct understanding does not only require knowledge of the foreign legal system, but also an understanding of the particular social, cultural and political context of this legal system.[84] This does not make comparative interpretation impossible, but it does call for a careful approach to comparative materials.[85] The question then

78 McCrudden (2007), p. 388.
79 McCrudden (2007), p. 388.
80 McCrudden (2007), p. 388.
81 See Gerards (2006), p. 120.
82 Bentele (2008), p. 14. Markesinis & Fedtke (2005), p. 112-116 referring to the problems that one might not have precise information and not always up-to-date information. Tsen-Ta Lee downplays this argument. He argues that judges should be careful when citing foreign law as in other cases where they are dealing with an area they do not know much about. Tsen-Ta Lee (2007), p. 148.
83 Bentele (2008), p. 14.
84 Kahn-Freud (1974), p. 27; Bernhardt (1999), p. 34; Baudenbacher (2003), p. 524.
85 Tsen-Ta Lee (2007), p. 148.

arises whether the court in question has sufficient resources to undertake a thorough examination of the comparative materials. Alternatively, such an analysis might be left to a different actor, for example the parties arguing the case.[86] If that is done, however, questions may again arise as to the objectivity of the materials that are being advanced by the parties, once again evoking a risk of cherry-picking.

One further category of criticism is directed at the specific way comparative interpretation is used in order to find an (evolving) consensus.[87]As mentioned above, this criticism has mainly been expressed in the context of the European Courts. The problem is that it is unclear how a consensus will be established.[88] Which countries will be taken into consideration; all Member States, some Member States, other countries or international material? What is being compared; is it legislation, case law, policies or anything else? What is necessary to constitute a consensus; is a real consensus needed or is a majority sufficient? What are the consequences of finding a consensus? A lack of transparency on how judges employ this form of comparative reasoning may have the result that judges can be accused of cherry-picking in this context as well.

An additional problem is that, without some kind of guideline, it is easy to play with the 'level of generality' at which a consensus is being sought.[89] If the question is whether a certain right exists in different countries, this can be framed either at a very specific level or at a rather abstract level. Depending on the specific issue or specific question, framing a right more specifically or more broadly can influence the finding of a consensus. This can be clarified with an example from the United States Supreme Court. In *Washington v. Glucksberg* the Supreme Court had to decide whether the state of Washington could constitutionally ban assisted suicide.[90] Chief Justice Rehnquist wrote the majority opinion and asked whether the history and traditions of the United States supported a 'right to commit suicide, which itself includes a right to assistance in doing so'.[91] He thus framed the right on a rather abstract level and concluded that no support could be found – as a result he found that the ban should be held to be constitutional. Justice O'Connor, in her concurring opinion, framed the right at a lower level of abstraction and claimed that the question

86 Bentele refers to the advantage of parties including comparative materials in their argument. Bentele (2008), p. 17.

87 The relation with evolutive interpretation will be discussed in Chapter 7.

88 Carozza (1998), p. 1224-1225; Heringa (1996), p. 139. It is hard to find an explicit discussion of this specific question in the context of the CJEU.

89 See for a general discussion on different levels of generality: Tribe & Dorf (1993).

90 *Washington v Glucksberg*. See for a discussion on the level of generality issue in this case, Fleming (2006), p. 120-123.

91 Justice Rehnquist.

was whether 'a mentally competent person who is experiencing great suffering [has] a constitutionally cognizable interest in controlling the circumstance of his or her imminent death'.[92] Even though she did not think that this case concerned 'great suffering', she concluded that support could be found for such a more specific right in the history and traditions of the United States. This example shows that the framing of the question can have an important impact on the finding of a consensus. Therefore it is important that this aspect is taken into consideration when employing this form of comparative interpretation.

A final problem with the search for a consensus has been expressed in the context of the ECtHR. The problem is that the search for a consensus,[93] a common ground or common denominator, in practice does not entail that there should be absolute agreement among all the consulted sources, nor that all Member States have to adhere to the same practice.[94] As a result, Member States who belong to a numerical minority could be forced to adhere to an interpretation that is based on the practice in other Member States that together form some kind of numerical majority. If only a limited number of Member States can constitute a 'consensus', this could be problematic for reasons of sovereignty and legitimacy that have been referred to above. This makes it more difficult to use the method to attain one of the purposes noted in section 6.1.4, i.e. to increase the acceptance by involving the Member States. When an interpretation is based on the practice of only a small group of Member States, it might not increase the acceptance of that interpretation in the other Member States. The problem of acceptance could also present itself when there is a clear consensus of a considerable number of Member States, yet one or more Member States explicitly take a different position. These Member States might not easily accept an interpretation based on a consensus. A reasoning based on different arguments or different interpretation methods could be preferable in those situations.[95]

This problem of acceptance can be even more apparent when courts rely on an external consensus. The problem has already been briefly referred to above in section 6.1.5. A consensus based on international materials might include materials that have not been signed or ratified by all the Member States in question, or it might include soft law instruments.[96] Despite the fact that states might have expressly rejected these international instruments, parts of them can become binding upon states in an indirect manner, i.e. through comparative interpretation by the ECtHR or the CJEU. The question is whether Member States will accept this type of reasoning in all circum-

---

92 Justice O'Connor.

93 The use of this term is misleading, but is often used and therefore will be used here as well.

94 *Roper v Simmons* was a rare example in this respect.

95 Carozza (1997), p. 1228-1229; Jacobi (2005), p. 80-81; Gerards (2006), p. 117.

96 Drooghenbroeck (2009), p. 811.

stances. At least it puts courts to the task of explaining why this type of consensus is really relevant for their reasoning. An important question therefore also is whether the European Courts, if they do use this type of external comparative interpretation, provide sufficient reasoning as justification.

6.1.7 Solutions for addressing the criticism

What do these criticisms mean? Should the comparative method of interpretation be abandoned as a whole, or are there any solutions that can address this criticism in a satisfactory manner? The majority of commentators on comparative interpretation do not call for a total ban on the use of the method. They rather focus on trying to reduce the methodological shortcomings that have been mentioned above. Especially in the context of multilevel adjudication this method can provide a bridge between the supranational and national level. The challenge is thus to discover why and how comparative interpretation should be considered.[97]

The methodology and normative underpinnings of comparative interpretation, according to CHOUDHRY, have not been sufficiently addressed in discussions on comparative interpretation.[98] In his view, 'to say that courts 'rely upon' or 'use' foreign jurisprudence because it is 'useful' or 'helpful'', does not explain *why* or *how* such jurisprudence is helpful'.[99] The explanation that relying on foreign materials can be helpful, also fails to justify why it might be appropriate to seek support for a specific reasoning in international or foreign materials. 'In short, the practice of comparative constitutional law has outgrown the conceptual apparatus that legal actors use to make sense of it'.[100] In other words, there is a desperate need for a justification for the different purposes of comparative interpretation.

From this perspective, improvements to comparative interpretation can be suggested at two levels: firstly, at a theoretical level, trying to develop a justification for using this method, and secondly, at a practical level, in order to mitigate the shortcomings of this interpretation method. This section will address one of the attempts that have been made to address the first challenge, namely the theoretical challenge. Suggestions for improvement on a practical level will be discussed in Chapters 10 and 13, after the case law analysis has shed more light on the problems that actually present themselves in the application of the method by the European Courts.

97 Choudhry (2006), p. 3.
98 Choudhry (2006), p. 14. He speaks more in general about constitutional migration, but this includes constitutional interpretation as well.
99 Choudhry (2006), p. 10.
100 Choudhry (2006), p. 10.

An interesting attempt to justify comparative interpretation that has gained broader attention has been made by CHOUDHRY.[101] He argues for a specific mode of comparative interpretation, which is called dialogical interpretation.[102] Dialogical interpretation is a mode of comparative interpretation under which the court that invokes comparative references, engages in a dialogue with the comparative materials.[103] This entails that comparative references under this mode are used as a means for self-reflection. By 'comprehending a foreign system as being organized around a core set of normative and factual assumptions [this] leads to a deeper understanding of that system'.[104] At the same time it increases self-understanding about the normative and factual assumptions underlying the judge's own system. This mode of interpretation contains three steps for judges to apply. First, a judge has to identify the assumptions underlying its own legal system. The presumption is that if courts engage in the question why other courts reason in a particular way, courts will turn that question onto themselves as well. The second step involves 'comparing the assumptions underlying the domestic and comparative jurisprudence'.[105] The main question to be answered here, by the court, is why are there any differences or similarities? Finally, the court, in the third step, has to make a choice between different interpretative options. After the first two steps a judge will be able to justify whether it will embrace the similarities or the differences found. This means that the judge will either argue that there are too many differences and, accordingly, the approach of the foreign legal system does not fit with the underlying values of the legal system of the country in question, or these steps could lead the judge to conclude that there are important similarities and that the foreign solution does fit within the legal system he is dealing with. Whichever option is chosen, the judge's reasoning will be based on an increased understanding of his own system.

One of the main advantages of this dialogical mode of comparative interpretation is that it is not based on controversial normative claims like, for example, universalist interpretation. This latter mode of interpretation is based on the premise that trans-

101 Choudhry (1998); Choudhry (2006). See also Harding (2003), Jackson (2005) and McCrudden (2007) who also discuss some form of dialogical interpretation. He builds on similar ideas advanced by Glendon, Ewald and Frankenberg. Choudhry (1998), p. 836.

102 He also presents two other modes for comparative interpretation, namely universalist interpretation and genealogical interpretation. Dialogical interpretation, however, is the mode he is advocating. Universalist interpretation is based on the assumption that there are certain transcendent legal principles and courts can use comparative interpretation to find these principles. Genealogical interpretation relies on the link that exists between particular countries and justifies comparative interpretation from that perspective. This link can, for example, be between a former colony and its former ruler. Choudhry (1998).

103 Choudhry (1998), p. 836.

104 Choudhry (1998), p. 837.

105 Choudhry (1998), p. 857.

cendent legal principles exist and that, for that reason, comparative materials may always be relevant to understanding one's own legal system.[106] Dialogical interpretation does not seem to make any normative claims as to a universality of legal norms or principles, rather focusing on comparative interpretation as a means to stimulate self-understanding.[107]

There are several jurisdictions in which this mode of interpretation is already applied in some form; South Africa and Canada are two common examples.[108] The case of *The Queen v Keegstra* of the Canadian Supreme Court provides a good example to illustrate the dialogical mode of interpretation.[109] This case concerned a high school teacher who was fired for expressing wilful hatred against Jews in the classroom. The teacher challenged the Statute on which his conviction was based as violating his freedom of expression. Chief Justice Dickson writing for the majority held the Statute to be constitutional. He did agree that the Statute violated the teacher's freedom of expression, but on the basis of Section 1 of the Canadian Charter, he found that interferences were allowed as long as they were prescribed by law and justifiable in a free and democratic society. The Court in *Keegstra* thus had to address the question whether the statute was justified in a free and democratic society. Next to various considerations based on the Charter itself, for example relating to the harm caused to society by the talk and on the objective of the statute in question, the Canadian Court discussed foreign materials to help it to find an answer to the question whether the infringement was justified. Chief Justice Dickson first extensively discussed the American approach to hate speech by looking at American precedents and the literature discussing this American approach. He subsequently explicitly addressed the reasons for looking at the American approach and why it did not consider this approach applicable to the Canadian situation:

> The question that concerns us in this appeal is not, of course, what the law is or should be in the United States. But is important to be explicit as to the reasons why or why not American experience may be useful in the s. 1 analysis of [the statute]. In the United States, a collection of fundamental rights has been constitutionally protected for over two hundred years. The resulting practical and theoretical experience is immense and should not be overlooked by Canadian courts. On the other hand, we must examine American constitutional law with a critical eye ... Canada and the United States are not alike in every way, nor have the documents entrenching human rights in our two countries arisen in the same context. It is only common sense to recognize that, just as similarities will justify borrowing from the American experience, differences may require that Canada's constitutional vision depart

---

106 Choudhry (1998), p. 890.

107 Choudhry (1998), p. 892.

108 See Choudhry (1998), p. 855-865 and Harding (2003), p. 413-417 who discuss examples of this dialogical method in practice.

109 *The Queen v Keegstra* (1990). See also Harding (2003), p. 425-426.

> from that endorsed in the United States ... Equally, I am unwilling to embrace various categorizations and guiding rules generated by American law without careful consideration of their appropriateness to Canadian constitutional theory. Though I have found the American experience tremendously helpful in coming to my own conclusions regarding this appeal, and by no means reject the whole of the First Amendment doctrine, in a number of respects I am dubious as to the applicability of this doctrine in the context of a challenge to hate propaganda legislation.[110]

The majority opinion continued to explain why it would not be appropriate to follow the American approach, concluding that:

> Where section 1 operates to accentuate a uniquely Canadian vision of a free and democratic society ... we must not hesitate to depart from the path taken in the United States ... such independence of vision protects rights and freedoms in a different way ... the special role given [to] equality and multiculturalism in the Canadian Constitution necessitate a departure from the view, reasonably prevalent in America at present, that the suppression of hate propaganda is incompatible with the guarantee of free of expression.[111]

What becomes clear by these quotations is that the American approach helped the judges understand the main values underlying the Canadian system and how they shape their own approach to protecting human rights. The majority opinion also cited international materials and showed that these materials valued the same principles that 'infused' the Canadian Charter.[112] The emphasis was thus on understanding the characteristics of the Canadian legal system by looking at other approaches.

The dialogical mode of interpretation raises an important question with regard to the extent of this interpretative mode. Is this mode of interpretation relevant for all the purposes of comparative interpretation that have been discussed in section 6.1.4 or is this only relevant for some of these purposes? The aim of the dialogical mode of interpretation is to justify the relevance of comparative argumentation in specific cases. As has been mentioned by CHOUDRY, the fact that foreign experiences might be helpful may not provide a sufficient justification to use comparative interpretation in particular situations. However, when looking for a consensus, or when looking for inspiration to support a certain solution at national level, the dialogical mode is helpful, since it stresses that it is necessary to explain why this foreign experience or reasoning is relevant (or not) in one's own legal system. This can only be explained on the basis of a reason coming from one's own system.

---

110 *The Queen v Keegstra* (1990).
111 *The Queen v Keegstra* (1990).
112 *The Queen v Keegstra* (1990).

On the other hand, when the purpose of looking abroad is to find a rich body of case law, because, for example, there is a vacuum left by a dark period in history in one's own jurisdiction, then there is not really a need to apply dialogical interpretation.[113] In the case of South Africa, for example, after the end of the Apartheid era there was a need for neutral case law, which could not be found in South Africa itself.[114] The whole purpose of looking abroad in this situation was to fill this vacuum and use the experience from abroad. Self-reflection would have been almost contradictory in these circumstances and thus dialogical interpretation would not make sense in this context.

If the purpose is to simply show that others have taken a similar path and to use that as an additional argument to support a certain interpretation, which is based on other interpretative arguments, then there is no need or use to resort to the dialogical mode of interpretation either. It is the numerical information that is relevant then, not so much the substance of the solution that has been found in these foreign systems. However, if the argument becomes more substantial than solely providing a numerical example of other systems that have adopted a similar solution, dialogical interpretation becomes increasingly relevant. Once again, dialogical interpretation may then help to explain why substantive arguments from foreign systems can be relevant for one's own system based on reasons from within one's system.

Dialogical interpretation, in conclusion, thus may be relevant when there is a need to justify the use of substantive solutions from another legal system. The fact that these solutions are 'helpful' is not sufficient to explain why these foreign solutions may play an important role in the interpretation of provisions of one's own legal system.

The question is whether this mode of interpretation is also relevant for the CJEU and the ECtHR. That question will be tentatively answered after a discussion of these specific systems in section 6.4. A more informed answer will be provided after the case law analysis.

6.2 Comparative interpretation and the ECtHR

The general discussion has provided various insights that are also relevant for comparative interpretation by the ECtHR. The present discussion will add some specific insights on the use of comparative interpretation in the Convention system. Questions that were left unresolved or insufficiently resolved for the ECtHR in the general discussion on the use of the method relate to whether any basis for comparative

113 McCrudden (2003), p. 14.
114 Bentele (2008), p. 6.

interpretation can be found in the Convention and to whom undertakes the comparison – is it the judges themselves, is it a special research unit or is it even an external party? The main question that still needs to be answered, moreover, is what role comparative interpretation plays in relation to other interpretative methods and principles in the interpretative framework of the ECtHR.

The preamble of the European Convention on Human Rights provides that it is 'resolved, as the governments of European countries which are like-minded and have a common heritage of political traditions, ideals, freedom and the rule of law, to take the first steps for the collective enforcement of certain of the rights stated in the Universal Declaration'. This statement provides some justification for the ECtHR to make comparative references,[115] but it seems to provide a basis only for the internal component of comparative interpretation. The reference to European countries and their common heritage cannot really be seen as a basis for invoking references from outside the context of the European Convention. The text of the Convention, thus, does not seem to provide an additional basis for relying on the external component of comparative interpretation. The question is whether the ECtHR in its reasoning provides a basis for this component of comparative interpretation. This question will be addressed as part of the case law analysis.

A second question to be addressed relates to *who* undertakes the comparative study? This is not a subject that has received much attention in scholarly literature, but it is important for the use of this method. In previous years the ECtHR appears to have had hardly any resources for systematic comparative research at its disposal.[116] Comparative research took place in a rather informal manner, depending on the knowledge of the judges themselves.[117] In recent years, a research unit has been established, which undertakes comparative studies.[118] It is not entirely clear, however, whether this research unit is sufficiently equipped to undertake systematic and thorough comparative studies; in particular, it is relevant that systematic studies are only conducted in respect to cases to be decided by the Grand Chamber, which only constitute a small proportion of all the cases decided by the Court.[119] The role of the parties and third parties, like NGOs, should not be forgotten either. They can

115 Ost (1992), p. 305.

116 Bernhardt (1999), p. 35; Mahoney (2004), p. 148.

117 Bernhardt (1999), p. 35.

118 See the website of the ECtHR : http://www.echr.coe.int under "The Court". The judge-rapporteur in a specific case decides whether the research unit will be asked to draw up a comparative study. See Myjer (2005), p. 1058 and (2007), p. 567, discussing the procedure before the Grand Chamber.

119 Mahoney writes in 2004, when the unit was already established, that the court does not have the facilities or staff to undertake proper comparative research.

provide valuable contributions in terms of comparative interpretation.[120] MAHONEY even claims that this is one of the successes of the institution of intervention.[121] These observations on *who* performs a comparative study lead to an additional methodological question, namely the question as to *when* comparative materials are used by the ECtHR in its judgments. Are comparative materials considered to be an integral part of every case; are references only made in cases where one of the parties refers to comparative materials; or is there even a more arbitrary explanation for their use, namely that it depends on the individual judges' knowing of any relevant comparative materials?[122] This question has not been given much attention in scholarly literature, but it is relevant to know whether there is any consistency in the use of comparative interpretation. Given the case load of the ECtHR it is highly unlikely that a comparative study will be done for every case, not even now that the judges no longer have to conduct comparative studies themselves. Even for a research unit it would be too much to supply comparative information in every case. The question thus remains whether any pattern can be found in the use of comparative interpretation.

Finally, an important aspect that should be discussed is the role of comparative interpretation in relation to other interpretative methods and principles in the interpretative framework of the ECtHR. It is hard to ignore the close relation between comparative interpretation and evolutive interpretation. The ECtHR uses comparative interpretation to establish present-day circumstances.[123] In other words, comparative interpretation may be used to provide the evidence that is needed to substantiate an evolutive interpretation. The principle of evolutive interpretation in itself cannot generate a result: it points in the direction of a certain outcome or approach. In combination with comparative interpretation, it is possible to put some flesh on the bones of this approach. Both interpretative aids thus perform complementary functions in the interpretative framework. Examples of this interaction will be discussed in the chapters on the case law analysis. It will be shown there that the ECtHR mostly looks for a consensus to establish present-day circumstances.[124] Whether this consensus will be considered to be a sufficient basis to support a novel interpretation will depend on the strength of interpretative arguments that point in a different direction. Some general situations that indicate the limits of an evolutive approach, and thus the limits of the comparative evidence, will be discussed in Chapter 7.

BERNHARDT has argued, furthermore, that comparative interpretation could also play a useful role in relation to autonomous interpretation.[125] He has contended

120 Bernhardt (1999), p. 36; Mahoney (2004), p. 149.
121 Mahoney (2004), p. 149.
122Bernhardt (1999), p. 35.
123 Prebensen (2000), p. 1128; Mahoney (2004), p. 139.
124 Helfer (1993), p. 134-135; Rigaux (1998), p. 41.
125 Bernhardt (1999), p. 37.

that comparative considerations should be only one element in the whole interpretation process, stressing that their role should be more prominent than it presently is.[126] The question as to the present role of comparative interpretation in relation to autonomous interpretation will be discussed in Chapter 10. The more theoretical question whether comparative interpretation should play a role in substantiating an autonomous interpretation will be discussed in the chapter on autonomous interpretation.

The case law analysis will take the relation between the different methods and principles as one of its focal points. Only after this analysis, conclusions can be reached as to whether the use of this method can be improved.

6.3 Comparative interpretation and the CJEU

The CJEU has been referred to as a 'working laboratory for comparative law'.[127] The fact that the judges and Advocates General come from different legal systems and the fact that the cases to be decided by the CJEU are rooted in different legal systems have lead the CJEU, according to some, to almost naturally adopt a comparative approach.[128] The question can be raised, however, as to whether there is a concrete legal basis for the CJEU to rely on comparative materials in interpreting the EU treaties. Can an explicit reference be found in the TFEU or is there any other basis for comparative interpretation? A subsequent question is how the CJEU employs this method in the context of fundamental rights, especially if seen in relation to the question as to who supplies the comparative materials. Finally, the relation of comparative interpretation with the other methods and principles discussed in this thesis should be addressed in the context of the CJEU too.

One of the problems in answering all of these questions is that the CJEU is not very explicit in its use of comparative interpretation.[129] Indeed, the method has often been mentioned in academic literature, but it has not been analyzed at a sufficiently detailed level to answer all the questions that have been raised in the context of this chapter. This section will therefore be able to provide a basic theoretical analysis, but at the same time it will raise more questions than it will be able to answer.

---

126 Bernhardt (1999), p. 37.

127 Hilf (1986), p. 550, referring to Pescatore. See also Lenaerts (2003), p. 876.

128 Lenaerts (2003), p. 874, who also adds that the multilingual character of EU law leads the CJEU to adopt a comparative approach. See also Colneric (2007), p. 316.

129 Lenaerts (2003), p. 873, points to this problem. Colneric (2007), p. 316, argues that the use of the comparative method by the CJEU can be compared with the tip of an iceberg.

General discussions on the use of comparative materials by the CJEU have pointed to Article 19 TEU as a basis for a comparative approach.[130] This provision grants jurisdiction to the CJEU to ensure that the law is observed. When interpreting and applying the treaty the CJEU needs to make sure that the law is observed. The argument holds that comparative arguments help to establish what 'the law' is. In the context of fundamental rights a specific basis for comparative arguments is provided in Article 6(3) TEU, which states that the national constitutional traditions and the European Convention are a source for EU fundamental rights.[131] Article 6 TEU is only relevant for the practice of the CJEU since the early 90s when this provision was included in the treaty. Article 19 TEU, on the other hand, provides a very broad justification for the use of comparative interpretation. The question is whether the CJEU in its case law provides a justification for its use of comparative arguments. This will probably be the case in its case law after the coming into existence of Article 6(3) TEU, because this provision provides a clear basis at least for the use of internal comparative interpretation. The question is therefore mainly directed at the case law from before 1992 and aims to find out whether the CJEU provided a justification for its comparative approach in those cases.

In the introduction on the CJEU (provided in Chapter 3), attention has already been drawn to the fact that references to national constitutional traditions and other international instruments play an important role in the process of establishing the meaning of fundamental rights by the CJEU. The question is how the CJEU uses this comparative method. It has been noted in this regard that the CJEU is not explicit in its use of comparative interpretation.[132] It is therefore difficult to draw any conclusions on the use of the method on the basis of theoretical literature alone.[133] It is clear that the CJEU refers, at least, to national constitutional traditions and the European Convention, but that still raises many questions. What are these national constitutional traditions? Is a consensus required? LENAERTS has argued that the CJEU is looking for the solution which best suits the EU, but the question is whether that is also the goal of the comparative method in the context of fundamental rights.[134] Does the CJEU look at all Member States or just a limited number? Do they rely on other materials as well? These are just a number of questions that cannot be fully

130 See Lenaerts (2003), p. 876-877. See also Wasensteiner (2004), p. 30. Article 19 TEU is the equivalent of former Article 220 EC.

131 Lenaerts (2003), p. 877 and Singer & Engel (2007), p. 499, make a similar point. Reference is also made to Article 340 TFEU, which concerns non-contractual liability. This provision explicitly refers to comparative interpretation.

132 Lenaerts (2003), p. 873, points to this problem. Colneric (2007), p. 316, argues that the use of the comparative method by the CJEU can be compared with the tip of an iceberg.

133 See Wasensteiner (2004), p. 41.

134 Lenaerts (2003), p. 879.

answered at this moment, but which will be further explored in the chapter presenting the results of the case study.

An important source of external comparative interpretation at the CJEU is the European Convention. Literature suggests that references to the ECHR and its corresponding case law play an important role in the reasoning of the CJEU. It is, however, not clear exactly how these references play a role and to what extent they are used in the reasoning of the CJEU. Are they used as inspiration or simply incorporated in the reasoning? These aspects have not received much attention in the literature. One aspect that has received much attention is the question why the CJEU relies on the European Convention. Legal commentaries suggest that there may be more strategic underlying reasons for paying particular respect to Strasbourg.[135] These reasons can mainly be found in the complex relationship between the EU, the European Convention on Human Rights and to some extent also the Member States of the EU. Until the CJEU had entered the field of fundamental rights, there was hardly any overlap of jurisdiction. This changed when the CJEU started to introduce fundamental rights in the EU. This resulted in jurisdictional overlap between the European Court of Human Rights and the CJEU, which had to be dealt with in a satisfactory manner.[136] Given that the ECtHR is a specialized court which already dealt with fundamental rights adjudication at the time the CJEU started to engage in this type of adjudication, it seems quite natural that the CJEU in principle adheres to the interpretations provided by the ECtHR. This is true, even though this might be less obvious in terms of international public law since this case law is not binding for the EU.[137] More important than the binding character of the ECHR is that the ECtHR and the CJEU are considered to be both 'engaged in a common project of European integration'.[138] Both courts are interested in finding common fundamental rights norms.[139] As a result it is easier for the CJEU to take account of the case law of the ECtHR, which represents rights accepted by all Member States, than to delve into a comparison between the different Member States. A judgment by a well-respected international court grants much authority to the reasoning of the Court. Moreover, it provides a rather objective input, since not one Member State's approach is favoured.

Another, related reason to approve the approach of the European Convention is that the EU Member States are at the same time Contracting States to the European Convention. As a result they can be held responsible for fundamental rights violations

---

135 See among others: Jacobs (2007), p. 209 & 211; Douglas-Scott (2006), p. 652-653.
136 Douglas-Scott (2006), p. 652.
137 Jacobs (2007), p. 208; Reich (2005), p. 214.
138 Douglas-Scott (2006), p. 653.
139 Douglas-Scott (2006), p. 653.

which follow from the implementation of EU law or any other action of the EU.[140] The CJEU would put Member States in a rather difficult situation if it were to interpret EU law in conflict with the case law of the ECHR.[141] Apart from the fact that it would be difficult, it would also be highly impractical and counterproductive if two different standards of fundamental rights protection were in force at the same time.

It has also been argued that the references to the ECHR have helped the EU gain legitimacy, since it lacked a catalogue of fundamental rights of its own.[142] By incorporating references to the ECHR the EU has been able to establish itself as a 'fully established democratic community which respects human rights'.[143]

Thus, from a strategic perspective (i.e. in order to gain more authority for the protection of fundamental rights at the EU level and to prevent a clash of jurisdictions), it is logical and justifiable that the CJEU has opted for respecting the ECHR. But still questions remain as to the way in which the CJEU relies on references to the European Convention and the ECtHR.

A relevant question in order to get a full understanding of the use of this method is also who undertakes a comparative study. From the literature it becomes clear that the Advocate General has an important role to play in this regard.[144] The question is to what extent the CJEU relies on the study by the Advocate General. Furthermore, it is interesting to get a grasp of how the Advocate General uses the comparative method. In addition to the role of the Advocate General, reference is made in theoretical literature to the research and documentation unit, which undertakes comparative studies for the benefit of the CJEU judgments.[145] This unit operates on a request by the CJEU and prepares a note on the comparative study on a certain subject.[146] The notes are not public documents and it is thus difficult to get an understanding of how this study is undertaken.[147] This difficulty is increased by the fact that the CJEU is rarely explicit in its references to comparative materials, as has been noted before. As a result it is impossible for an outsider to understand which materials have been used, which countries have been taken into account, etc. This lack of transparency does not add to the argumentative force of this method. The question is whether the case law reveals a similar picture or whether in the actual use of the

140 See cases like ECtHR (GC), *Matthews v. United Kingdom*, judgment of 18 February 1999, *Reports* 1999-I; ECtHR (GC), *Senator Lines GmbH v. Austria and others*, decision of 10 March 2004, *Reports* 2004-IV; ECtHR (GC), *Bosphorus HavaYollari Turizm Ve Ticaret Anonim Śirketi v. Ireland*, judgment of 30 June 2005, *Reports* 2005-VI.

141 Jacobs (2007), p. 209. Van den Berghe (2010).

142 Douglas-Scott (2006), p. 653.

143 Douglas-Scott (2006), p. 653.

144 See Faircloth Peoples (2008). Colneric (2007), p. 316.

145 Singer & Engel (2007), p. 508-511.

146 Singer & Engel (2007), p. 508-511.

147 Singer & Engel (2007), p. 508-511.

method the CJEU and its Advocates General provide insight into the comparative materials that play a role when using this method.

A final aspect of this method that should be addressed is its relation with the other method and principles under discussion in this thesis, because that helps to understand the interpretative framework of the CJEU. Not many references are made to the relation of comparative interpretation and other interpretative aids. LENAERTS has discussed the relation between teleological interpretation and comparative interpretation. He claims that the CJEU uses comparative interpretation to build a bridge between the solution that best suits the object of the EU and that is still acceptable to the Member States.[148] Especially in a multilevel legal order, this is a valuable connection between these two methods. The remarks, however, have been made in the context of the comparative interpretation by the CJEU in general and not in the specific area of fundamental rights. The question is thus whether these conclusions apply to that area as well. The case law analysis should help to answer this question.

Once the case law analysis has clarified how the CJEU uses comparative interpretation, there is another question that should be answered. The question is whether the coming into force of the Charter on Fundamental Rights will change the use of comparative interpretation. It will only be possible to answer this question when the present use of comparative interpretation has been discussed in more detail in the case law analysis.

6.4 CONCLUSION

This chapter aimed to provide an overview of what the method of comparative interpretation entails and which challenges are presented by this method. Two different versions of comparative interpretation have been identified, namely internal comparative interpretation and external comparative interpretation. This distinction has proven to be important, because a different justification can be necessary for the different versions. In the literature many references have been made to the use of internal comparative interpretation by both European Courts. In the context of the ECtHR this version has been justified by reference to the Preamble which refers to the 'common heritage' of the European states. For the CJEU, Article 6 TEU provides a clear basis for an internal comparison, since express reference is made therein to constitutional traditions of the Member States. The fact that these courts rely on an internal comparison has not been subject to heavy criticism, but the way in which these courts use references to an internal comparison has been heavily criticized. Many methodological issues have been raised in the current chapter, which need to be addressed in the case law analysis.

148 Lenaerts (2003), p. 879.

External comparative interpretation, on the other hand, is highly controversial in theoretical literature on the use of foreign sources by national courts. In discussions on the use of this version of comparative interpretation by the European Courts this method does not seem equally controversial, but it is fair to add that this version of comparative interpretation has not received as much attention as the internal version. The main question that has been posed in the debates on external comparative interpretation is what justification can be found to legitimize the use of foreign materials. Even though the use of external materials is not as controversial in the European debate as it is, for example, in the American debate, it is useful to learn from this debate and enhance the legitimacy of arguments based on external comparative interpretation.

Dialogical interpretation has been suggested as a relevant option for both European Courts to enhance the legitimacy of comparative interpretation. The fact that references to foreign materials can be helpful is not enough to justify the use of these materials; therefore a different justification is needed. Dialogical interpretation is based on the idea that looking at foreign systems helps a judge to learn about the values underlying his or her own system. Looking at foreign systems thus eventually leads to arguments based on one's own system to choose one interpretation or the other and this choice is then not based on arguments coming from a foreign system. As a result dialogical interpretation can be helpful in justifying the use of foreign (external) materials, but it can also explain why a certain trend among the Member States of either the EU or the Council of Europe will be followed, while other trends will be ignored. In both cases the reasons for doing that will come from the system itself. The question whether this is actually a relevant solution can only be answered after a thorough analysis of the present situation. Only then will it be possible to see if dialogical interpretation would fit the interpretative framework of these courts or whether a different answer would be more suitable.

CHAPTER 7
PRINCIPLE OF EVOLUTIVE INTERPRETATION

In Chapter 4 the guiding principles in the interpretative framework of both European Courts have been identified. Evolutive interpretation is one of these principles, which derive from a meta-teleological perspective on the treaty in question. The aim of this chapter will be to shed some light on the principle of evolutive interpretation. What does evolutive interpretation mean? How and when can an evolutive interpretation be established? Why do judges sometimes resort to evolutive interpretation? Can any conclusions be drawn on the nature of this interpretative aid? What is the relation of this principle with other interpretative principles and methods discussed in this thesis? Answers to these questions will provide a better understanding of this interpretative principle. The present chapter will take a theoretical perspective on these questions and Chapters 11 and 13 will address these and other questions on the basis of a case law analysis.

In order to be able to understand the theoretical discussion of the principle, it is necessary to provide a preliminary understanding of evolutive interpretation. The problem with evolutive interpretation is that most people can imagine what it might mean, but no one seems to have a clear understanding of what it actually entails. This chapter therefore aims to clarify the meaning and implications of the principle. It will start from the presumption that evolutive interpretation refers to the fact that judges might interpret a treaty in light of (legal) circumstances 'prevailing at the time of interpretation'.[1] This presumption will be developed more fully throughout this chapter, but as a common starting point it may help to place the discussion in context.

Another aspect that should be addressed at the beginning of this chapter is the nature of evolutive interpretation. According to the division made between interpretation methods and principles in Chapter 4, evolutive interpretation should be considered as an interpretative principle. After all, as has been explained in section 4.4.1.1, evolutive interpretation refers to the general objective that the text in question is not interpreted in a static, but in a dynamic manner. The understanding of a text can thus change over time, according to evolutive interpretation. This changed understanding

1 This is part of a description provided by the ICJ in *Legal Consequences for States of the Continued Presence of South Africa in Namibia (South West Africa) notwithstanding Security Council Resolution 276 (1970),* Advisory Opinion, I.C.J. Reports 1971, p. 16, § 53.

can be the result of, for example, technical changes, moral changes or cultural changes. Thus, evolutive interpretation as such does not provide a substantive argument on which a choice for a specific interpretation can be based.[2] It refers to a goal that should be reached, rather than providing a technique that can be used to establish an evolutive interpretation. In order to take an evolutive approach, a court will need one or more interpretation methods to provide a basis for an interpretation in the concrete case at hand. Thus, evolutive interpretation needs to be achieved by, for example, using textual interpretation, teleological interpretation or comparative interpretation. The question is whether in the academic literature on evolutive interpretation, the nature of this interpretative aid is discussed and what the outcome of that discussion is. That is one of the aspects that will be discussed in this chapter.

This chapter will present some theoretical observations from both an international law perspective and a national (constitutional) law perspective. It is appropriate to do so, since the European Court of Human Rights as well as the Court of Justice of the European Union are international (supranational) courts, but both courts also have characteristics of national constitutional courts.[3] Subsequently, the discussion on evolutive interpretation as used by both courts, which has already been briefly introduced in Chapter 4, will be continued. In section 7.1, the academic literature will be explored on the evolutive approach taken by both the CJEU and the ECtHR, addressing the questions that have been posed at the beginning of this introduction. The discussion will, however, remain a theoretical one. The case law analysis provided in Chapters 11 and 13 will address in more detail the use of evolutive interpretation in the case law of both courts. It can be noted here that there will be an imbalance in the discussion of the theoretical literature on the use of the principle by the respective courts. This is unavoidable, since the approach by the ECtHR has been subjected to much more theoretical analysis than that of the CJEU.

7.1 Some preliminary remarks on evolutive interpretation

Before discussing evolutive interpretation from both an international and national perspective, there is one element relevant for the discussion that needs to be addressed. It has been mainly discussed in national literature on evolutive interpretation, but in the context of this thesis it will be relevant for the discussion from an international perspective as well.

2 This point is also made by Scalia (1997), p. 45.

3 See Mahoney (1990), p. 59, who acknowledges as well that national constitutional discussions can be relevant for a discussion on the ECHR. See also Helfer (2003) for a discussion on the analogies between international courts, like the ECtHR and national constitutional courts.

Evolutive interpretation has been introduced above as interpretation in light of (legal) circumstances 'prevailing at the time of interpretation'.[4] This might seem to leave little room for different forms of evolutive interpretation. Nevertheless, discussions on the question whether evolutive interpretation is allowed have led to an understanding by some that evolutive interpretation can roughly be divided in two different forms.[5] The first form has been called 'meaning originalism' which means that by applying this form of evolutive interpretation the meaning of the provision stays the same, but the application can change according to the needs of the time.[6] This means in practice that, for example, the meaning of the provision on freedom of expression will stay the same, but that this protection will also be afforded to people expressing themselves through new media, like the internet.[7] KAVANAGH has described this first form of evolutive interpretation as a way to take account of 'changes in the social environment' or 'changes in social facts'.[8] In general, technological, scientific and economic developments are often mentioned as examples of the type of changes that can be taken into account under this form of evolutive interpretation. The underlying idea is that these developments do not change the values that a certain provision is intended to protect. A constitution would become a dead letter if these kinds of developments could not be taken into account.[9] By only looking at the application of the provision in an evolutive manner, the original understanding of the drafters of the provision is respected. That is why this form of evolutive interpretation is acceptable even for originalists.[10]

The second form of evolutive interpretation concerns taking into account 'changes in the moral values'.[11] Morals can change in society over time as well. Many people have, for example, different attitudes than 50 years ago towards homosexual relationships. The question is who should decide to take these changes into account. Should judges be able to decide for themselves to take account of these changes when

4 Supra note 1.

5 These two forms are in one way or another recognized by Scalia (1997), p. 45 and Kavanagh (2003), p. 80. Roosevelt III (2006), p. 52 only recognizes one of these forms.

6 The term is introduced by Roosevelt III (2006), p. 52. Roosevelt III (2006), p. 52, introduces the terms 'application originalists' and 'meaning originalists' . The latter indicates that the meaning of the constitution stays the same, but the application might change. 'Application originalists' on the other hand indicates that both the meaning and the application remain the same. Kavanagh (2003), p. 82-83, is skeptical of the explanation provided by, what Roosevelt III calls, meaning originalists. She claims that even if the application changes (often this means that it is applied in a broader context) this does involve moral change.

7 Scalia (1997), p. 45.

8 Kavanagh (2003), p. 80-81, quoting Lawrence Lessig when speaking of 'changes in social facts'.

9 Kavanagh (2003), p. 81.

10 Scalia (1997), p. 45.

11 Kavanagh (2003), p. 80.

interpreting constitutional provisions? Or should the Member States as treaty legislators determine whether the fundamental rights protection should be extended to also cover these changes in moral values? The difference with regard to the first form of evolutive interpretation is that in the first form the developments are more of a factual nature; it is hard to deny the role of the internet in modern society, while in this second form the developments are of a moral nature and the question whether these developments should be protected depends on a (potentially controversial) value judgment. The underlying assumption of those that criticize this form of evolutive interpretation is that interpretation in light of these moral developments in society actually changes the original meaning of the provision in question.[12] The question is thus who should be able to determine that these changes in the moral values of society have an impact on the meaning of fundamental rights provisions. Depending on one's answer to that question, some people will find this second form of evolutive interpretation to be legitimate, while others will find this form unacceptable. The different views on the question whether a judge may take these moral changes into account in the interpretation process make this second form of evolutive interpretation a more controversial one.

The division between the two forms of evolutive interpretation presented here is not as black and white as it seems. There might be overlap between the two forms of evolutive interpretation. In practice therefore it might be better to present it as two ends of a scale with many points in between. The purpose of the division has been to show that one of the forms is not controversial, while the other one is. When further on in the discussion reference is made to the 'extent' of evolutive interpretation, reference is really being made to one of these points between evolutive interpretation as taking into account developments in social facts on the one hand and moral values on the other. A 'narrow' version of evolutive interpretation in this sense means that only developments in social facts are taken into account, while a 'broad' version of evolutive interpretation indicates that both developments in moral values and social facts will be taken into account.

A final question that warrants attention before discussing evolutive interpretation from the specific perspective of the courts under study is what it means to interpret in an evolutive manner for the level of protection afforded. Does interpreting fundamental rights in an evolutive manner automatically entail a higher level of protection? In other words, does evolutive interpretation always mean progress? When the notion of evolutive interpretation is mentioned, it is often related to change and development, though not many authors have addressed this question explicitly. One of the opponents

12 This argument is made by Scalia (1997), p. 45-46.

of evolutive interpretation has argued that, apart from some exceptions, evolutive interpretation is used to argue for more personal freedom and consequently it results in more restrictions on the government.[13] That would be an indication that an evolutive interpretation generally leads to a higher level of protection, but it is questionable whether this is not a theoretical presumption that might be rebutted by studying the case law in which the principle is actually applied. Indeed, there may be good reason to question the presumption that evolutive interpretation always implies a higher level of protection. By allowing an evolutive interpretation of a specific right, this might come into conflict with the fundamental rights of another person. For example, if in present-day society there is a trend towards more protection of the private life of celebrities and this trend finds its way into legal judgments, this might result in a lower protection for the freedom of expression of the press. The question whether a higher level of protection is afforded therefore depends on one's perspective on the case and the side one is taking. However, whether or not evolutive interpretation implies progression in the sense of offering additional rights protection, will be an interesting element to investigate in relation to the case law of the courts under study, the CJEU and the ECtHR.

7.2 Evolutive interpretation and international law

The rules of interpretation provided by the Vienna Convention on the Law of Treaties have already been introduced in other chapters.[14] It should be recalled that these rules serve as the generally accepted international rules of interpretation.[15] In that light it is warranted to discuss whether these rules allow for evolutive interpretation.

The text of the articles of the Vienna Convention on treaty interpretation already provides some clues for the present discussion. The general rule laid down in Article 31 of the Vienna Convention provides that: 'A treaty shall be interpreted in good faith in accordance with the ordinary meaning to be given to the terms of the treaty in their context and in the light of its object and purpose'.[16] This article further provides that the following elements are part of the context as well and should therefore be taken into account:

13 Scalia (1997), p. 41-42, who argues that evolutive interpretation as a result does not increase flexibility, but increases inflexibility. This argument results from his perspective, namely that of the government and not the individual.

14 Mainly Chapter 4.

15 Commentary to articles of Vienna Convention, Yearbook of International Law Commission, 1966-Vol. II; Bernhardt (1967), p. 491; Bernhardt (1988), p. 65; Aust (2000), p. 185-186; McRae (2002), p. 210; Slotboom (2001), p. 576.

16 Art. 31 VCLT.

> (*a*) any subsequent agreement between the parties regarding the interpretation of the treaty or the
> application of its provisions;
> (*b*) any subsequent practice in the application of the treaty which establishes the agreement of the
> parties regarding its interpretation[17]

By referring to *subsequent* agreement or practice, these sections indicate that a certain form or extent of evolutive interpretation is allowed by the Vienna Convention. A further indication that an evolutive approach is permitted by the Vienna Convention is that the *travaux préparatoires* are stated to be a *supplementary* means of interpretation, which only come into play if the general rule of interpretation, as laid down in Article 31 of the Vienna Convention, does not provide a sufficient answer to the interpretative question.[18] Subsequent practice or agreement will thus be considered before recourse is sought in the *travaux préparatoires.*[19]

The relevant question for the topic of evolutive interpretation is what subsequent agreement or subsequent practice can be held to mean.[20] The concept of 'subsequent agreement' appears to refer to some sort of agreement to modify the treaty, which, however, does not need to be as formal as an amendment to the treaty.[21] According to AUST this agreement 'can take various forms', like a decision, a resolution, a declaration or a memorandum of understanding.[22] It seems warranted to conclude that this element does require some activity by the State Parties, but it is not really clear in which form such activity should take place or whether consent by all parties is necessary to be able to speak of 'subsequent agreement'.

'Subsequent practice', on the other hand, requires some action as well, as is implied by the term *practice*. However, this notion is less explicit and seems to require action of a different manner. Subsequent practice refers to the way the treaty is applied by states in reality, which might differ from the wording of the treaty itself. AUST argues that this is one of the most important elements of treaty interpretation and states that it is well-established in the jurisprudence of international tribunals.[23] Unfortunately, it is not entirely clear what kind of practice is considered to be relevant, for

17 Art. 31 3 a & b VCLT.

18 Art. 32 VCLT. Letsas (2010), p. 257, argues that this indicates that an evolutive approach is considered more important than a static approach.

19 Bossuyt (2005), p. 81; Shaw (2008), p. 935; Bernhardt (1995), p. 1419-1421

20 The listing of both concepts separately suggests that these are two different concepts. Orakhelashvili, however, claims that there is not much difference between subsequent agreement and subsequent practice for the purpose of interpretation. Orakhelashvili (2008), p. 355.

21 Aust (2007), p. 239.

22 Aust (2007), p. 239-240 discusses different examples.

23 Aust (2007), p. 241.

example if the notion only refers to enacted legislation, or to judicial practice or factual practice by states as well. For subsequent practice to be relevant as an element of treaty interpretation it is not necessary that all states are actually engaged in that practice; tacit agreement on the reasonableness of the practice appears to be sufficient.[24] VILLIGER adds that no state should raise an objection, so the lack of an objection might be understood as tacit agreement.[25]

While these two elements indicate that evolutive interpretation is not alien to international law and to the Vienna Convention, they only provide a limited basis for evolutive interpretation. 'Subsequent agreement' is a very narrow form of evolutive interpretation, since it requires active agreement from the states on the topic to be interpreted. That will hardly ever be the case. 'Subsequent practice' provides more leeway, because it does not require an explicit agreement and tacit acceptance of a practice is sufficient to provide a basis for interpretation. However, this still makes it a difficult basis for interpretation. Tacit agreement implies that states should not object to a certain practice, but the question is whether adopting a different approach qualifies as an objection. For example, if some states within the EU of Council of Europe adopt a different approach, does this qualify as an objection against the approach by other states, and can this be considered as an objection to evolutive interpretation? Given the size of both organizations there is a realistic chance that there is some diversity in the practice of the Member States. From that perspective, the interpretative principles contained in the Vienna Convention provide a rather limited and rather unclear basis for evolutive interpretation.

These elements contained in Article 31 of the Vienna Convention are, however, not the only indications that an evolutive approach is allowed under international law. Several authors refer to the Namibia Advisory Opinion in which the International Court of Justice concluded that 'an international instrument has to be interpreted and applied within the framework of the entire legal system prevailing at the time of interpretation'.[26] Implicit in this conclusion is a reference to Article 31(3)(c) VCLT,

---

24 Aust (2007) p. 243; Villiger (2009), p. 431.

25 Villiger (2009), p. 431.

26 Paragraph 53 of *Legal Consequences for States of the Continued Presence of South Africa in Namibia (South West Africa) notwithstanding Security Council Resolution 276 (1970)*, Advisory Opinion, I.C.J. Reports 1971, p. 16, provides: '... the Court is bound to take into account the fact that the concepts embodied in Article 22 of the Covenant-"the strenuous conditions of the modern world" and "the well-being and development" of the peoples concerned-were not static, but were by definition evolutionary, as also, therefore, was the concept of the "sacred trust". The parties to the Covenant must consequently be deemed to have accepted them as such. That is why, viewing the institutions of 1919, the Court must take into consideration the changes which have occurred in the supervening half-century, and its interpretation cannot remain unaffected by the subsequent development of law, through the Charter of the United Nations and by way of customary law. Moreover, an international instrument has to be interpreted and applied within the framework of the entire legal system prevailing

but also a rather explicit reference to the notion of evolutive interpretation.[27] In addition, BERNHARDT has argued that the prominent role of teleological interpretation for treaty interpretation brings along a certain evolutive influence.[28] He claims that if treaties are drafted with the purpose of ensuring long-lasting commitments to guarantee fundamental rights, it is contrary to that purpose to ignore new developments when interpreting that treaty.[29] These arguments provide an interesting theoretical basis for the use of evolutive interpretation, since they do not necessarily require agreement among the Member States for an evolutive approach to be established. The question is what elements do need to be present in order to establish an evolutive approach. That aspect is not clear for both of these theoretical bases. Nevertheless, both arguments show that some form of evolutive interpretation is accepted under international law.

The words 'some form of' evolutive interpretation have been deliberately chosen here to indicate that while there might be general agreement that evolutive interpretation can play a role in treaty interpretation, it is often debated how far a court may take this evolutive approach.[30]

It is difficult to make general comments on the extent of evolutive interpretation, since, according to CHRISTOFFERSEN, the extent will depend on the 'specific treaty's terms and nature and object as well as the parties' intention', but also the facts of the case.[31] The parties' intention, in this quote from CHRISTOFFERSEN, seems to refer to the intention of the original State Parties. Thus the question whether they intended the treaty to have an evolutive meaning can influence the extent of evolutive interpretation.

Even though not much can be said in general about the extent of evolutive interpretation, some authors have signalled areas of concern connected to the use of evolutive interpretation in treaty interpretation.[32] First of all, the legitimacy of evolutive interpretation is closely related to the understanding of the role of an

---

at the time of the interpretation.'

27 Bernhardt (1999), p. 16 and Christoffersen (2009), p. 48 referring to an Advisory Opinion of 1971. Prebensen (2000) also refers to this Advisory Opinion and uses it to show that the approach by the ECtHR is not new in international law.

28 Bernhardt (1999), p. 16.

29 Bernhardt (1999), p. 16-17. This viewpoint is supported by Wessel (2004), who argues that treaties in which dynamic obligations (meaning obligations that have been designed for an ongoing relationship) have been laid down must be interpreted differently from end-game treaties. This latter type of treaty has, for example, been designed to end a conflict.

30 Bernhardt (1999), p. 16, considers this to be the real problem.

31 Christoffersen (2009), p. 49-50, referring to McLachlan.

32 Bernhardt (1999), p. 21-24.

international judge.[33] If one considers that an international judge should be a very cautious and conservative one, then one will probably have a stricter view of the extent of permissible evolutive interpretation. This close relation is due to the fact that by interpreting in an evolutive manner, an international judge to some degree may change the law. As has been explained in section 7.1, adopting an evolutive approach can in some situations lead a judge to an interpretation that goes beyond the original understanding of the provision in question. A modest use of evolutive interpretation will probably not generate discussions on the division of competences between the State Parties (as legislators of treaties) and an international or supranational court. Depending on the degree of evolutive interpretation, however, the question might arise whether the decision to adopt a new evolutive approach is still within the province of an international or supranational court or should be left to the State Parties.[34] It is in this debate that accusations of judicial activism are sometimes made.[35] However, as also has been explained in relation to other interpretative principles and methods, the term judicial activism is in itself not very helpful in this context, since it is a rather vague term and different people have different conceptions of this term.[36] A discussion using the term judicial activism as a starting point might therefore lead to confusion, because not everybody has a similar understanding of this term. It would be more constructive to discuss the question what the limits of an evolutive approach should be, taking into account the particular position of international and supranational courts and the potentially far-reaching effects of evolutive interpretation.

Secondly, some criticism is levelled that is of special relevance for human rights treaties, which is arguably the most prominent area where evolutive interpretation plays a role in international law.[37] It is sometimes argued that when interpreting human rights treaties the practice of states at the domestic level plays a crucial role, especially if it is held that an evolutive approach is acceptable if a 'widespread practice' exists.[38] Inter-state practice is much less important to determining such widespread practice than national practices are.[39] This can certainly put the international judge in a challenging position, since he will have to answer the delicate

33 Bernhardt (1999), p. 22.
34 Mahony (1990), p. 60.
35 Mahony (1990), p. 62.
36 Cohn and Kremnitzer (2005), p. 334.
37 Bernhardt (1999), p. 12, claims it is the most important area where this principle plays a role; Christoffersen (2009), p. 48, does not deny this, but claims it is not the only area.
38 Bernhardt (1999), p. 23. Prebensen (2000), p. 1126, claims that this is only natural in the context of human rights treaties.
39 Bernhardt (1999), p. 23.

question when it is legitimate to conclude that such a 'widespread practice' exists.[40] This concern is related to the previous one, but it addresses the question when there is enough proof to legitimize an evolutive interpretation. There is no magic formula to answer the question when a widespread practice can be said to exist; it depends on the specific treaty context, possibly even on the specific case. Therefore this matter will be discussed more in depth when discussing the respective courts.

Finally, it is interesting to note that while not much discussion focuses on the question of exactly how to establish an evolutive interpretation, the reference to state practice indicates that comparative arguments will most likely play a role. This may help to explain the strong link between evolutive and comparative interpretation which is addressed at several places throughout this thesis. This link will be discussed below when addressing the question how both European Courts establish an evolutive interpretation.

In conclusion one can say that international law in itself does allow for evolutive interpretation. A narrow version can be based directly on the Vienna Convention, but the ICJ approach allows for a broader version of evolutive interpretation. Most important for evolutive interpretation, however, is the context of the specific treaty. It is relevant in that regard whether there is a basis for evolutive interpretation in the specific treaty, what kind of treaty it is, the text of the provisions and other factors that might indicate that an evolutive approach can be adopted under a specific treaty regime. It is good to acknowledge that there is general support for evolutive interpretation in international law, but it is also widely accepted that this form of reasoning has to fit the treaty context. That can only be determined on a treaty-by-treaty basis.

The debates in international law did reveal possible areas of concern that might be relevant for the interpretation of any treaty, namely the role of the international judge and the level of proof required for an evolutive interpretation. These aspects also should receive attention in the analysis of the use of evolutive interpretation before both European Courts. The next section will first address the theoretical discussion from a national perspective.

7.3 Evolutive interpretation and national law

It has already been mentioned that both the Court of Justice of the European Union and the European Court of Human Rights have some features in common with a national constitutional court.[41] Therefore a theoretical discussion on national constitu-

40 Bernhardt (1999), p. 23.
41 Supra note 25 (Chapter 4).

tional matters can be relevant in furthering our understanding of evolutive interpretation. Many national constitutional courts are confronted with the question whether they should interpret the constitution in light of the intention of the drafters of the document or in light of current circumstances.[42] In some countries this debate leads to more controversy than in others,[43] but the question appears to be relevant for most, if not all, constitutional courts.

References to evolutive interpretation are often captured in metaphors, like the 'living constitution'[44] or the constitution as a 'living tree'.[45] These metaphors indicate that a constitution is not static and can grow or develop over time though judicial interpretation.[46] The opponents of this type of reasoning do not focus on metaphors, perhaps because the image of a 'dead constitution'[47] would probably not attract many supporters. Opponents of an evolutive approach are often termed originalists, named after the specifically American 'originalist' theory of constitutional interpretation.[48] There are different versions of originalism, but a common characteristic is that they all consider that the constitution has a fixed meaning, which is based on either original meaning, original intentions or hypothetical intentions.[49] One would assume that much of the debate focuses on the question whether an evolutive approach is legitimate, but this does not seem to be the case. All originalists, even US Supreme Court Justice Scalia, acknowledge that some development should be allowed for or, at least, is inevitable in constitutional interpretation.[50] This is the first form of evolutive interpretation as discussed in section 7.1, where it is explained that this

---

42 See Jackson (2006), p. 927-937, who discusses the German, Canadian and Australian experience.

43 See, for example, the difference between the USA and Canada. In the latter an evolutive approach to constitutional law is hardly controversial. See for example Miller (2009), p. 332.

44 This is the American metaphor; see Rehnquist (2006), p. 401.

45 This is the Canadian metaphor; see Jackson (2006), p. 926.

46 Kavanagh (2003), p. 55-56. See also Huscroft (2004), p. 417; Scalia (1997), p. 38. This discussion concerns the debate between those who adhere to a living constitution and originalists. In the USA at least there are also those that do not engage in the rhetoric of this debate. Scholars like Dworkin focus on a moral reading of the constitution. This could lead to the same interpretation as the one based on an evolutive approach, but scholars taking this moral approach will support their reasoning by relying on moral arguments and not on arguments referring to the living constitution.

47 Term referred to by Rehnquist (2006), p. 401.

48 Justice Scalia is the most famous proponent of this theory. See for example: Scalia (1997) or Scalia (1989).

49 Waluchow (2007), p. 52-73.

50 Rehnquist (2006), p. 402; Jackson (2006), p. 942. See also Scalia (1989), p. 861-864, where he discusses the fact that originalism in its purest form is a medicine that many find too hard to swallow. He admits that he is a so-called faint-hearted originalist by discussing the hypothetical example of whether a statute permitting flogging as a punishment (which was not considered cruel and unusual punishment at the time of the Framers) would now be ruled unconstitutional.

uncontroversial form concerns taking into account changes in social facts. It has been mentioned there that changes in technology or other changes of a more factual nature may be taken into account in all readings of evolutive interpretation. The debate on evolutive interpretation thus focuses on the second form of evolutive interpretation, namely whether judges are allowed to take changes in moral values into account.

It is difficult to discuss these issues relating to the extent of evolutive interpretation in a general manner, since the debate on evolutive interpretation is closely connected to the role of the judge in a specific constitutional system.[51] The difference between the USA and Canada may exemplify that the attitude towards evolutive interpretation depends on the national context. In Canada, there is hardly any controversy on evolutive interpretation.[52] It is accepted as a form of interpretation without much discussion or resistance. In the USA, on the other hand, there is much debate over the concept of evolutive interpretation.[53] Judging solely by the age of the bills of rights in these countries, one might expect that evolutive interpretation would not be much of a problem in the USA, because their bill of rights is over two hundred years old and evolutive interpretation of any extent could thus be highly relevant. One might expect it to be a controversial matter in Canada where the charter on fundamental rights is barely 30 years old. Given that the reverse is true, there must be other factors that play a role in determining to what extent evolutive interpretation is accepted in a national legal system.

Various authors have stated that, for example, the nature of a constitution and the authority granted to a constitution in a specific country could influence the extent of legitimate evolutive interpretation.[54] Another factor that plays an important role is the role of the judge in a specific society and the perceived democratic legitimacy of a judge.[55] Both factors are related, since one's views on the nature of the constitution influences one's perspective of the role of the judge in constitutional interpretation. A constitution, but also a bill of rights,[56] defines and limits the power of a government. It depends on one's view of what a constitution is trying to protect whether one considers that a judge should easily defer to the legislator in constitutional

51 Jackson (2006), p. 925.

52 Miller (2009), p. 332.

53 The clearest example of this controversy being the opposition of Scalia against evolutive interpretation, Scalia (1997), p. 45.

54 Waluchow (2007), p. 53 argues that 'theories of constitutional interpretation [...] are not easily separated from theories concerning the very nature, point and authority of constitutions'.

55 Jackson (2006), p. 925 argues that different views on 'democratic legitimacy, rule of law, judicial constraint and judicial competence' have an impact on the discussion on evolutive interpretation.

56 In some countries a separate constitution and bill of rights exist, but in others this is combined in one document. Both are part of the constitutional make up of a country in the broad sense and therefore they will be treated as equal for the discussions here. Waluchow (2007), p. 53, also uses both terms interchangeably.

cases or whether a judge should be able to have more leeway in deciding constitutional cases. WALUCHOW illustrates this difference by discussing the fictional Judges Ronnie and Antonin.[57] Judge Ronnie believes the constitution aims to protect minorities against the will of the majority. From that perspective Judge Ronnie might not consider himself strictly bound by the will of the legislator as a representative of the will of the majority. Judge Antonin, on the other hand, thinks that the constitution is designed to protect everyone from the arbitrary exercise of government power. As a result Judge Antonin has more respect for the will of the legislator and is careful not to display arbitrary judicial activism himself. This general example may explain the connection between the view of the nature of a constitution and the perceived proper role of the judge.

The nature of a constitution can also refer to the character of the constitution, which can be relevant for the discussion on evolutive interpretation. In the debate in the USA, for example, opponents and proponents of evolutive interpretation have different views on the character of the constitution. Some regard the constitution as a 'narrow set of negative restraints on policy makers',[58] while others view the constitution as a set of abstract constitutional principles, which have a 'broader reach than the framers' concrete intentions'.[59] Those who support the latter view, might be more inclined to leave room for judicial evolutive interpretation, because these abstract principles might change over time. The question is whether such stark contrasts exist in the European context as well. Even if the contrasts are not as strong, differences with regard to the nature of the constitution might have an impact on the extent of evolutive interpretation one finds acceptable.

The second aspect that influences the attitude towards evolutive interpretation, as mentioned above, is the role of a judge.[60] This is often discussed in the context of the concerns on evolutive interpretation, which will be addressed below.

The remainder of this section will address a number of arguments for and against evolutive interpretation that can be distilled from the national debate about constitutional interpretation. Not much attention has been paid in the literature on national constitutional law to the advantages of evolutive interpretation.[61] Some advantages

57 See Waluchow (2007), p. 53 for a more extensive illustration.

58 Barber & Fleming (2007), p. 21.

59 Barber & Fleming (2007), p. 21.

60 One could imagine, for example, that historical attitudes towards the judiciary and the legislator also play a role or that other more sociological factors could play a role as well, but that would require a whole different type of research.

61 Miller (2009), p. 331-332, does address the point that in the Canadian context there has not been much reason to defend the evolutive (sometimes also called 'progressive') approach, due to lack of challenges to this approach.

have, however, been briefly mentioned. First of all, it has been argued that an evolutive approach enables judges to adapt the constitution to 'modern needs and circumstances'.[62] It ensures that the constitution stays effective even if it was drafted generations ago. It thus, secondly, provides for some flexibility when interpreting the constitution. The constitution does not become stuck in rigid historical interpretation.[63] Finally, it has been argued that it is the task of judges to do *justice*. According to some scholars, that means that they have to be open to, or even actively consider, the possibility for improvement and therefore should be willing to adopt an evolutive approach.[64]

The concerns about evolutive interpretation, on the other hand, have been discussed extensively.[65] The most important concern is somewhat similar to that in international law concerning the impact of the use of the method in relation to the role and the competence of the judge. The question is how far a judge should be allowed to change the constitution by means of (evolutive) interpretation. The basis for this concern is the division of powers between the judiciary and the legislature. Originalists fear that the (non-elected) judiciary will develop into a third legislative branch, which is not considered to be acceptable from a constitutional perspective.[66] Changes to the constitution should be made by the democratically elected legislator (or by any other competent organ, depending on the constitutional system of the relevant state), but they are not within the province of the courts. An additional aspect is that judgments of highest courts can, generally, only be overturned by the legislator through constitutional amendment, which in most constitutional systems is a cumbersome matter and therefore in most situations not a realistic option.[67] If courts change the meaning of the constitution by means of interpretation and such change is considered unacceptable by the democratically legitimized organs, this means that it can be very difficult to undo the consequences of the court's decisions. Arguments have been advanced to mitigate this criticism, which will be addressed below, but it is difficult to completely rebut this concern, since it ultimately depends in large part on the constitutional conception of the role of the judge. It does, however, challenge proponents of an evolutive approach (judges and academics alike) to show that there are certain constraints on evolutive reasoning – it should not be regarded as a licence for 'unlimited moral adjudication by a free-wheeling judiciary'.[68]

---

62 Kavanagh (2003), p. 56.
63 Jackson (2006), p. 958. Huscroft (2004), p. 415, refers to the need for flexibility as well.
64 Kavanagh (2003), p. 68.
65 Among others: Rehnquist (2006), Scalia (1989) and (1997).
66 Kavanagh (2003), p. 69.
67 Huscroft (2004), p. 415, refers to this cumbersome process. See also article V of the United States Constitution for an example of the amendment process in one specific constitutional context.
68 Kavanagh (2003), p. 72.

A number of arguments have been raised to show that there are certain constraints for judges when they invoke an evolutive approach, which should mitigate the concerns of opponents of evolutive interpretation that evolutive interpretation leads a judge to go beyond his or her legitimate role. In this context it is useful to recall the metaphor discussed at the beginning of this section, namely 'living constitution' and 'living tree'. It has been argued in constitutional theory that the latter metaphor is a more appropriate reflection of evolutive interpretation.[69] The understanding of the constitution as a 'living tree' indicates that the constitution can grow, but that it is at the same time grounded in its roots: 'the tree is rooted in past and present institutions, but must be capable of growth to meet the future'.[70] This aspect is missing in the 'living constitution' metaphor, which perhaps explains to a certain extent the fear for unguided judicial reasoning in constitutional systems where this metaphor prevails as a means to describe evolutive interpretation.[71] Such metaphors themselves cannot be regarded as real constraints, they just represent a concept. In theoretical literature, however, several actual constraints have been mentioned in order to show that judges will not simply impose their own moral conceptions when invoking evolutive interpretation. The most important constraint is the text of the constitution itself. Even if the constitution is drafted in a general manner, the constitution cannot be interpreted to mean just anything.[72] Judges have to interpret a constitutional provision within the context of the text and structure of the constitution.[73] Furthermore, precedents impose an important constraint on courts as well. Of course, the extent to which this will really be the case will depend on whether the court in question does indeed adhere to some form of system of precedent. Both the European Court of Human Rights and the Court of Justice of the European Union for reasons of legal certainty, whilst not formally obliged to respect precedent, at least try to adhere to their own precedents.[74] Therefore they can be expected to find some restraint in the need to carefully connect each novel interpretation to the decisions and judgments the courts already rendered in the past.

A final general constraint that has been mentioned is that judges have to adjudicate within a specific legal culture.[75] This is perhaps not a constraint in the legal sense,

69 Jackson (2006), p. 941-954.

70 Jackson (2006), p. 948.

71 Choudhry (2006), p. 19-20, briefly refers to the value of the right metaphor in shaping thought about a specific issue.

72 Kavanagh (2003), p. 70.

73 Huscroft (2004), p. 427, speaks about limits inherent to the Charter or Constitution. He also refers to Dworkin who refers to constraints of structure and precedent as well, p. 428.

74 See in the context of the CJEU: Brown & Kennedy (2000), p. 369-370. In the context of the ECtHR: Mowbray (2009), p. 180, who cites an official of the ECtHR Registry, who claims that the ECtHR adheres to a limited form of *stare decisis*.

75 Kavanagh (2003), p. 71.

such as the constraints constituted by the constitution and by precedent, but it rather can be considered to come down to 'professional pressures' or 'internal constraints on judicial decision-making'.[76] Justice Brennan of the United States Supreme Court has called this constitutional integrity.[77] Every legal culture has specific norms on, for example, how to decide a case or 'the degree of deference that should be accorded to parliament'.[78] Judges have to adjudicate within their particular legal and constitutional cultures and they will thereby be restrained in their (evolutive) reasoning.

Another argument against evolutive interpretation that has sometimes been brought forward is that there is no general guiding principle for evolutive interpretation and that, as a result, the whole process of evolutive interpretation is unclear.[79] The lack of clarity in the process can lead to a lack of clarity with regard to the solution that is adopted on the basis of an evolutive approach. If it is unclear how judges have reached a certain (perhaps controversial) interpretation this might affect the force of the argument and ultimately it might affect the willingness to accept the interpretation. To be more precise, it is unclear, according to SCALIA, whether a judge should consult the 'chats at the country club' or Aristotle when interpreting a constitutional text in an evolutive manner.[80] The problem for SCALIA seems to be that each theory of interpretation incorporating an evolutive perspective on the constitution holds a different view of what documents and developments should be considered as constituting sufficient foundation for evolutive interpretation.[81] He seems to imply that this could mean that every judge trying to interpret the 'living constitution' will be taking different elements into account and as a result it becomes an unguided, unpredictable and unprincipled form of interpreting a constitution. At a certain level, SCALIA might be correct in the sense that judges should try to be consistent in the elements they consult in order to establish an evolutive interpretation and they should provide sound reasons to consult certain documents or materials. The fact, however, that different theories can exist on which documents or developments should be taken into account and different theories might emphasize different elements in these documents, should not in itself render evolutive interpretation useless. It does require

76 Kavanagh (2003), p. 71.

77 See Brennan (1989), p. 435, who argues that judges are limited by precedents, the text to be interpreted, regard for the public opinion and institutional integrity. See also Huscroft (2004), p. 428, referring to Brennan. See also De Blois (1994), p. 41-42, who points to similar factors that relate to the legal cultural environment of the judge, which limit their freedom of discretion.

78 Kavanagh (2003), p. 71.

79 Scalia (1997), p. 44-45.

80 Scalia (1997), p. 45.

81 Scalia (1997), p. 45, this becomes especially clear when he claims that originalists might not always agree, but at least they agree on what they are looking for.

proponents of an evolutive approach to address this criticism. The question is how judges in the European Courts establish an evolutive interpretation and whether that is done in a consistent and reasonable manner.

The discussion on evolutive interpretation in the national context has provided some interesting insights that are relevant for the discussion on the use of the method of evolutive interpretation by both European Courts. Firstly, the discussion showed that the permissible extent of evolutive interpretation depends on many different factors, such as the nature of the constitution or charter to be interpreted and the national perception of the role of the judge. Secondly, two major drawbacks of evolutive interpretation have been discussed. One notable concern is that it is not clear in situations where judges take an evolutive approach, how far judges may take this approach. In addition, concerns have been voiced against the fact that it is unclear how judges reach an evolutive interpretation. It has also become clear that more specific answers on the question what evolutive interpretation entails should be answered in the context of the relevant court. The remainder of this chapter will aim to provide some theoretical answers to questions that are left open. Chapters 11 and 13 will subsequently address how both courts deal with evolutive interpretation in practice.

7.4 European Court of Human Rights

The previous general theoretical discussion made two aspects of evolutive interpretation very clear. First of all, both in the international and national discussion the context of the specific treaty or constitution is crucial for answering many questions on evolutive interpretation. Secondly, the main concern with evolutive interpretation, again also in the national and international context, is that the judge should not overstep its role. The aim of this section on the European Court of Human Rights is to answer the questions that have been listed in the introduction to this chapter and to discuss the limits of evolutive interpretation in the context of the European Convention.

7.4.1 Basis and justification for evolutive interpretation

Even though some references to evolutive interpretation can be found in the Vienna Convention, the discussion in section 7.2 revealed that this Convention only provides a limited basis for such interpretation. The question is therefore whether the specific European Convention context offers a more general basis for the use of this interpretative principle. The introduction to evolutive interpretation in Chapter 4 already mentioned that the preamble of the European Convention refers to the 'maintenance and further realization of human rights and fundamental freedoms'.[82] The same phrase has been incorporated in Article 1 of the Statute of Council of Europe. Although this does not provide a very clear or explicit basis for evolutive interpretation, at least the term 'further realization' may be understood to have an evolutive connotation. A further indication that an evolutive approach is warranted under the Convention system is provided by the text of the Convention itself. According to PREBENSEN, the Convention is drafted in the present tense and it contains rather general standards that should be defined by judicial interpretation.[83] This has led PREBENSEN to assume that the drafters could not have expected the open-ended provisions in the Convention to be treated as 'fossilized instruments'.[84] Others have argued that it was the intention of the drafters to guarantee the protection of Convention rights for the future and that, for that reason, an evolutive approach is needed.[85] In addition, it has been argued that the object and purpose of the European Convention (or human rights treaties more in general) require an evolutive approach as they would otherwise more or less be defeated.[86] Some have criticized this argument. In the view of FITZMAURICE, evolutive interpretation goes beyond the classical starting point of international law, i.e. the notion that state consent should play an important role in its interpretation.[87] In her view the argument based on the special nature of human rights treaties is not sufficient to justify an approach that is contrary to this notion of state consent. A different justification would thus be necessary to justify evolutive interpretation. Nevertheless, most authors seem to accept that an evolutive approach can be based on the general aims underlying the Convention as a whole. One of the oft-noted advantages of an evolutive approach is that it offers a tool to make the Convention into an effective human rights treaty. The principle of effective protection in that sense provides a basis for an evolutive approach, since an interpretation that is according to present day standards and opinions will be essential to ensure that the Convention rights are applied in a practical and effective manner.[88] These are theoretical explanations for the basis of evolutive interpretation in the Convention system. Chapter 11 will try to analyze whether the ECtHR itself has felt the need to explain the basis of evolutive interpretation.

---

82 Preamble of the ECHR.

83 Prebensen (2000), p. 1124-1125.

84 Prebensen (2000), p. 1125.

85 Ovey & White (2006), p. 47; Mahony (1990), p. 65. Christoffersen (2009). In this context it should be noted that Prebensen argues that an originalist interpretation of the convention would be practically impossible. Prebensen (2000), p. 1125.

86 Mahony (1990), p. 65. Harris (1995), p. 7; Van der Meersch (1988), p. 202.

87 Fitzmaurice (2008), p. 132.

88 Bernhardt (1999), p. 23.

7.4.2 Meaning and nature of evolutive interpretation in the context of the Convention

In Chapter 4, the ECtHR's characteristic reference to an evolutive approach has already been introduced. The ECtHR claims that the Convention is a 'living instrument; which should be 'interpreted in light of present-day conditions'.[89] The introduction on evolutive interpretation by the ECtHR indicated that the nature of this concept is understood in slightly different ways by different authors.[90] The focus in this chapter will be on those authors that imply that evolutive interpretation is not an interpretation method, but plays a distinctive role in the interpretation process as a guiding principle.[91] PREBENSEN is one of the authors that seems to embrace this position.[92] In his elaborate discussion on evolutive interpretation, he qualifies it as a *principle* or a *doctrine* of interpretation.[93] Moreover, he argues that the ECtHR in establishing an evolution often resorts to comparative arguments.[94] This seems to indicate that evolutive interpretation does need support from other types of arguments, or at least that other interpretative methods are needed to establish an outcome that fits in well with the general idea of evolution. In the same vein, MAHONEY has acknowledged that an evolutive approach needs 'some methodology or evidence' in order to be effected in a concrete case placed before the Court.[95]

However, only a few authors do make some kind of a distinction between methods and principles of interpretation. The troubling consequences of this lack of any distinction have already been pointed out earlier, in section 4.1.[96] When such a distinction is omitted, the distinct role of methods and principles will not be fully appreciated and as a result the two concepts may be confused. For example, the *principle* of evolutive interpretation may be confused with the *method* of comparative interpretation.[97] This is problematic, since each of these concepts has its particular characteristics, aims and values, but also its own particular problematic aspects. All of these should be assessed and valued in their own right. By confusing concepts, the critique on the comparative interpretation may find its way into the discussion

89 ECtHR, *Tyrer v. United Kingdom*, judgment of 25 April 1978, *Series* A No. 26.
90 See section 4.4.1.1.
91 Prebensen (2000); see for example: p. 1123 and Mowbray (2005); see for example: p. 71.
92 Prebensen (2000), p. 1123.
93 Prebensen (2000), p. 1123-1124, 1126
94 Prebensen (2000), p. 1127. Mowbray (2005), p. 69 also refers to evolutive interpretation as a doctrine and principle and refers to comparative interpretation as factors that the court takes into account.
95 Mahoney (1990), p. 73. He claims that the ECtHR has found this objective evidence in a comparative approach.
96 See section 4.1.
97 Helfer (1993), p. 134-135; Rigaux (1998), p. 41; Janssen (2003), p. 187 , De Blois (1994), p. 55; Van de Lanotte (2005), p. 194.

on evolutive interpretation. This might be problematic if the specific criticism levelled at comparative interpretation is not really pertinent to the principle of evolutive interpretation, especially if the criticism is so serious that it invites completely abandoning or avoiding the principle. The same may be true for criticism that is aimed at the principle of evolutive interpretation, but which is directed at the method of comparative interpretation. It is thus very important to carefully distinguish between principles and methods, in particular between the principle of evolutive interpretation and the method of comparative interpretation.

The main question that results from this discussion is whether the ECtHR itself acknowledges the difference in nature between evolutive interpretation as an interpretative principle supporting interpretation methods. Even though the ECtHR might not address that question explicitly, some indicative answers may be found in its case law. For example, it might be examined if the ECtHR always refers to an interpretation method when trying to establish an evolutive interpretation and, if so, which interpretation method. If this is carefully done, it may be gleaned from this if the ECtHR does in fact distinguish between the evolutive principle as providing general guidance to its interpretation and the methods of interpretation as providing the tools to translate the general notions underlying the Convention into a concrete interpretation of a provision in a case at hand. The discussion above already indicated that comparative interpretation generally plays an important role in the Court's case law and it may be expected that there is at least a close connection between comparative and evolutive interpretation. The following section will discuss a theoretical perspective on how the ECtHR establishes an evolutive interpretation. An interesting question is whether the assumptions discussed in the literature correspond with the results of the case law analysis.

7.4.3 How is evolutive interpretation established?

In the previous section, it was argued that in order to establish an evolutive interpretation one or more interpretation methods are needed. Often evolutive interpretation is linked to comparative interpretation.[98] On the basis of the literature on the Court's interpretative methods, it would seem reasonable to conclude that other interpretation methods only play a limited role in the context of evolutive interpretation.[99] Even though it is not often mentioned as a relevant method in establishing an evolutive interpretation, micro-teleological interpretation could in theory play a role as well

98 Mahony (1990), p. 73-74; Prebensen (2000), p. 1128.

99 Some authors argue that the consensus only serves as a rhetorical instrument and that the ECtHR is not really interested in an evolution towards a common standard. Letsas (2007), p. 79.

in establishing an evolutive interpretation.[100] Through the course of time the object and purpose of a provision might change and thus an evolutive approach can be supported by a changed understanding of the object and purpose of a specific provision. In that case the evolutive approach would be supported by a teleological interpretation and not a comparative interpretation. Despite the fact that a case law analysis should reveal the actual practice of the ECtHR in establishing an evolutive interpretation, it seems warranted to conclude for now that comparative interpretation plays the main part in this regard and not teleological interpretation.

The next question is then how comparative interpretation can be used by the Court as an instrument to establish an evolutive interpretation. Most authors claim that the ECtHR relies on the internal component of comparative interpretation to find a consensus among the Contracting States.[101] Attention has already been devoted to the fact that it is not clear how the ECtHR employs references to an internal consensus.[102] The most important concern for the present discussion is that it is not clear when there is a sufficient consensus for an evolutive interpretation. Is a majority of Contracting States sufficient or is there another requirement? This is also an aspect that can be analyzed in the Court's case law.

Assuming that the ECtHR does rely on a consensus to establish an evolutive approach, this can be criticized from a perspective of the need for substantial reasoning in fundamental rights cases. Behind the reliance on conditions in the Contracting States to establish an evolutive interpretation lies a presumed respect for state sovereignty.[103] In the view of one author this respect can be motivated by the following consideration: 'it is better to defer to state consent which is a valid source of state obligation than to allow individual judges to impose new obligations upon sovereign states'.[104] This argument resembles the argument in the national context that judges should in some cases defer to the democratic legislator, who has a stronger legitimacy than the courts to determine 'new' rights and obligations. However, LETSAS has argued that this is not a valid argument in the context of fundamental rights.[105] The content of fundamental rights in his view should not be determined by sovereign states and the eventuality of their agreement or disagreement on certain issues, but on the basis

100 See Chapter 5 for a discussion of micro-teleological interpretation.

101 The authors do not qualify their description as internal comparative interpretation, but it does boil down to that type of comparative interpretation. See: Bernhardt (1999), p. 20; Mahoney (2000), p. 69; Rigaux (1998), p. 41; Helfer (1993), p. 135. For a description of internal comparative interpretation, see Chapter 6.

102 A number of practical concerns on the practice of invoking consensus arguments have been noted in section 6.1.6.2.

103 See section 6.1.4. on comparative interpretation.

104 Letsas (2007), p. 72.

105 Letsas (2007), p. 73.

of substantive arguments.[106] Therefore, according to LETSAS, consensus should not play a role in determining an evolutive interpretation. He has even argued that in the reasoning of the ECtHR an internal consensus does not really determine the evolutive interpretation. In his view, the ECtHR establishes the evolutive interpretation by looking for a 'moral truth of ECHR rights'. In LETSAS' view this conclusion can be drawn for three reasons.[107] First of all, he argues that the ECtHR does not take a comparative study seriously, which would have been the case, in his view, if they did fully rely on a consensus. Secondly, he argues that the reasoning of the ECtHR is based on substantive arguments and not arguments based on a common denominator. Finally, he argues that the ECtHR emphasizes the value of an evolutive approach by arguing that it leads to 'a better understanding of ECHR rights'.[108] These three factors lead LETSAS to conclude that the ECtHR does not rely on the common denominator when establishing an evolutive approach. This is interesting in the light of the view taken by different authors, who claim that evolutive interpretation is based on comparative interpretation. It will be interesting to see if the ECtHR itself pays attention to this specific issue of the reasonableness of using a comparative approach to establish evolutive interpretation, either expressly or implicitly (i.e. by just using comparative interpretation without showing evident concern for the lack of substantive reasoning). This particular aspect will therefore be part of the case law analysis in Chapter 11.

7.4.4 When does the ECtHR rely on evolutive interpretation?

While the previous section dealt with the question as to the methods that the ECtHR employs to establish an evolutive approach, the question here is in what cases and circumstances the ECtHR uses an evolutive approach. Not much guidance can be found in the literature on the type of situations in which the ECtHR refers to evolutive interpretation. PREBENSEN distinguishes three situations in which evolutive interpretation plays a role in the interpretation process.[109] In two of those situations the ECtHR adopts an evolutive interpretation and in one of these situations there appear to be reasons to opt for a different interpretation. The majority of cases where the ECtHR adopts an evolutive approach is where this is in line with the text, context, and object and purpose of the provision in question.[110] In these cases, according to PREBENSEN the ECtHR relies on a 'sufficient degree of convergence' between the Contracting

106 Letsas (2007), p. 73.
107 Letsas (2007), p. 79.
108 Letsas (2007), p. 79.
109 Prebensen (2000), p, 1128-1136.
110 Prebensen (2000), p. 1128.

States; thus a consensus among a significant number of Contracting States.[111] This has been mentioned most often as the primary method to establish an evolutive interpretation in the previous section. The argument made by PREBENSEN is that in this type of case the text, object and purpose, and context do not present any obstacle for taking an evolutive approach. The evolutive approach in these cases thus supports or underlies the use of other means of interpretation, which may also be taken as a sign that the comparative method is not the only one to be used in establishing an evolutive interpretation. In the second type of case, the ECtHR relies on an evolutive approach, while supplementary means, often the *travaux préparatoires*, point towards a different direction. PREBENSEN discusses some important cases in this respect and concludes that these show the prudence of the ECtHR in dealing with *travaux préparatoires*. In his view, it would be improper to grant decisive weight to the *travaux préparatoires* when the primary means of interpretation do not indicate an interpretation, because the *travaux préparatoires* are not necessarily the clearest expression of the intention of the drafters and not all present Contracting States participated in the drafting process.[112] Thus, an important hypothesis might be that the ECtHR may overrule the normal function of supplementary means of interpretation if it favours an evolutive approach. Whether this hypothesis is a correct one, will be examined in the context of the case law analysis.[113]

The final situation distinguished by PREBENSEN is when evolutive interpretation is outweighed by primary means of interpretation. In these cases the ECtHR considers that adopting an evolutive interpretation would imply that it would go beyond its role and might lead to a creation of rights that were originally not included in the European Convention. One of the examples provided by PREBENSEN is the case of *Johnston*. In this case the question was whether Article 12, which includes a right to marry, also included a right to divorce. The ECtHR held that the text of this provision referred only to the marriage as such and not its dissolution. It put most emphasis, however, on the object and purpose of the provision as they could be gleaned from the *travaux préparatoires*, and which revealed that a right to divorce was deliberately omitted by the drafters of the Convention. PREBENSEN argues that the reason for the Court not to use an evolutive approach in this case was that the text of Article 12 was very clear and prevented a different interpretation; the *travaux préparatoires* thus only played a supplementary role. The question is whether these are the only categories

111 Prebensen (2000), p. 1128.

112 Prebensen (2000), p. 1135-1136.

113 Letsas (2010), p. 265, argues that it is not clear why the ECtHR relies on an originalist interpretation in the case of ECtHR (GC), *Banković and others v. Belgium and others*, decision of 12 December 2001, Reports 2001-VII, § 19-22, 58, 63 and 65, in which reference is made to the *travaux préparatoires*.

visible in the case law or whether a different division should be made on the basis of the analysis in Chapter 11.

Apart from showing different situations in which the ECtHR seems to rely on the principle of evolutive interpretation, the division made by PREBENSEN also indicates the limits which the ECtHR seems to have set itself for employing this approach. It becomes clear, for example, that the ECtHR does not adopt an evolutive interpretation if the primary means of interpretation, i.e. the text, context, and object and purpose, would contradict this evolutive interpretation. This does limit the ECtHR to some extent in pursuing an evolutive approach, but it does leave some leeway as well, since one can differ, for example, about the exact meaning of the text or the exact intention of the drafters. Furthermore, reference has already been made to the fact that many authors signal that the existence of some sort of consensus plays an important role in establishing an evolutive approach. This provides an additional limit to the Court's use of the evolutive principle, since it will not be easy to rely on the principle if there is clearly no consensus visible on what the 'new' interpretation should be. Chapter 10, in which an analysis is made of the case law on comparative interpretation, will also deal with the question whether any trend can be found on when the ECtHR considers a consensus sufficiently established.

7.4.5 Evolution upwards?

In the general theoretical part the question was already put forward whether an evolutive interpretation automatically generates a higher level of protection of the fundamental right that is being interpreted. It is interesting to see whether anything can be said about this in the specific context of the ECHR. The term evolutive (interpretation) refers to a gradual development of societal and legal standards. In the general international context, as well as in the Council of Europe, this may refer to an upward adjustment of the fundamental rights protection, but it may equally be conceivable that application of this principle leads to a negative adjustment of the rights protection. It is questionable, however, whether this is really desirable from the perspective of fundamental rights protection and whether such lowering of standards will be accepted by the ECtHR. Put differently: is it really to be expected that the ECtHR uses the principle as a basis for taking a more restrictive approach towards individual rights protection, if that reflects the state of affairs in Europe as it has evolved over time? In the light of the enlargement of the Council of Europe with many new democracies and the present day challenges posed, among others by terrorism, this is not just a theoretical issue. The principle of evolutive interpretation itself is neutral in this respect and, as a result, it is impossible to conclude on the basis of its sheer meaning whether the possibility of 'levelling down' should be included or excluded. It is therefore necessary to consider whether other factors within the Convention system might offer an answer to this question. The literature does not provide any decisive answer to this question.[114] Some authors claim that it is a realistic possibility, which is proven by the fact that 'levelling down' in some situations actually has taken place in the case law of the ECHR.[115] More recently, however, a number of authors have claimed that such use of the principle is out of the question since the preamble of the Convention supports a one-way dynamic by referring to the 'maintenance and further realization' of the Convention rights.[116] PREBENSEN adds in the context of this discussion that the enlargement of the Council of Europe with many new democracies will probably not lead to a devolution of standards, although it might slow down the evolution towards effective protection of (new) rights.[117] Especially since various authors seem to disagree on this issue, it will be interesting to see whether the ECtHR has expressed itself on this issue in its case law, in order to find out if and to what extent the ECtHR is aware of this risk of lowering the level of protection and, if so, how it deals with it.

7.4.6 Conclusion

Much has been written about the importance of evolutive interpretation in the interpretative framework of the ECtHR. Specific answers can, however, not be given to the questions that have been raised. For example, it is clear that comparative interpretation plays an important role in relation to evolutive interpretation, but exactly what role this is cannot be established on the basis of the theoretical literature alone. Also, the situations in which the ECtHR establishes an evolutive interpretation are not really clear from the literature. Hopefully the approach of this thesis, in which specific questions are formulated on the basis of a theoretical analysis, will help to elucidate specific aspects of the ECtHR's approach, in particular the meaning and use of the principle of evolutive interpretation.

7.5 Court of Justice of the European Union

In stark contrast to the abundant literature on evolutive interpretation at the ECtHR, not much has been written on evolutive interpretation at the CJEU in general, nor in the context of its case law on fundamental rights. However, section 4.4.2.4 already referred to the way in which evolutive interpretation is incorporated in the EU system

---

114 See Vande Lanotte (2005), p. 195 for many references.

115 Vande Lanotte (2005) referring to the case of ECtHR, *Soering v. United Kingdom*, judgment of 7 July 1989, *Series* A No. 161, p. 195. Also Prebensen (2000), p. 1136.

116 Schokkenbroek (2000), p. 17; Vande Lanotte (2005) 195; Prebensen (2000), p. 1137; Mahony (1990), p. 67.

117 Prebensen (2000), p. 1137.

as a whole. In academic literature, reference is often made to the dynamic character of the Treaties or the evolutionary nature of EU law.[118] The programmatic nature of EU law as a project for the future to enhance European integration legitimizes an evolutive approach to interpretation. The changing objectives of the EU and the broadening of the aim of European integration to fields beyond purely economic integration allow, if not require, the CJEU to take an evolutive approach.[119] Apart from this positive basis for an evolutive approach, there is also a negative reason to rely on an evolutive approach, being that a static or originalist approach is often not possible for the CJEU. The simple reason for this is that the *travaux préparatoires* of many EU treaties are still not accessible and cannot be used as a basis for interpretation.[120] This accessibility problem also directs the CJEU in the direction of an evolutive approach, rather than an originalist approach.

An important question is whether the CJEU applies an evolutive approach in the context of fundamental rights as well. One could argue that introducing fundamental rights into the EU system already evidences an evolutive approach by the CJEU.[121] The codification of the fundamental rights case law of the CJEU in Article 6 of the Treaty of Maastricht on the one hand, and in the Charter on Fundamental Rights on the other indicates that the Member States approve of this evolutive approach by the CJEU. The question then becomes whether this evolutive approach will change now that the Charter on Fundamental Rights has become binding. Will the CJEU take a strict approach to the text or an evolutive approach and read the text in light of changing circumstances? It is difficult to predict an answer to that question as the text is of a relatively recent date and it is not yet necessary to interpret the text in the light of changed circumstances. However, the preamble of the Charter does provide food for arguing that the CJEU will adopt an evolutive approach when dealing with the rights included in the Charter. Reference is made to the fact that the Member States are 'resolved to share a peaceful future based on common values'. Moreover, the preamble refers to the fact that according to the drafters of the Charter, 'it is necessary to strengthen the protection of fundamental rights in the light of changes in society, social progress and scientific and technological developments by making those rights more visible in a Charter'. Both citations indicate that the Charter is focused on the future and that changes in, among others, society and science might influence the protection of fundamental rights. This is not clear proof that the CJEU will adopt an evolutive approach, but it could be an indication.

118 See for example: Millett (1989), p. 163 & p. 171; Brown (2000), p. 332; Reich (2005), p. 25 & p. 31; Arnull (2006), p. 621; Schermers (2001), p. 12 & p. 21; Tridimas (1996), p. 205; Pollicino (2004), p. 289.

119 Pollicino (2004), p. 289. See also Maduro (2007), p. 12.

120 Arnull (2006), p. 614-615.

121 Maduro (2007), p. 11.

Several questions still remain to be answered as regards the use of evolutive interpretation by the CJEU, which have not been addressed explicitly in legal literature. For example: When does the CJEU use evolutive interpretation, how does it establish an evolutive interpretation and which methods play a role in this regard? The case law analysis might provide more insight here, but it is probable that the CJEU will not be expressly employing an evolutive approach.

Some assumptions, however, have been made in the literature which do shed some light on the interpretative approach of the CJEU. For example, many authors notice a close relation between evolutive interpretation and teleological interpretation, and some have even gone so far as to consider the two concepts to be equivalent.[122] Even though there may indeed be a close link between the teleological method and the evolutive principle, it is not clear from the literature how and to what extent teleological interpretation may help the CJEU to establish an evolutive meaning. Is teleological interpretation used as a basis for evolutive interpretation, or is it the other way around? The former might be the case if the CJEU accepts that an evolutive approach is warranted by reference to the object and purpose of the treaties. If this were found to be the case, it would not yet provide an answer to the question which methods are used to establish an evolutive interpretation. After all, the approach then used by the Court would be one of meta-teleological reasoning, rather than a strictly evolutive one. In that case, the principles of meta-teleological interpretation and evolutive interpretation may seem to be placed on the same level, or evolutive interpretation may even be regarded as part of the general and overarching principle of meta-teleological interpretation. This is different if teleological interpretation actually does help to establish the evolutive interpretation in a certain case, i.e. if micro-teleological reasoning is used. The exact role of teleological interpretation and its relation to evolutive interpretation is therefore of particular interest for the case study. Similarly, it should be examined what role other interpretation methods might play in establishing an evolutive interpretation to fundamental rights. Given the importance of comparative interpretation in the context of fundamental rights before the CJEU, it is legitimate in particular to ask whether comparative interpretation also plays a role in establishing an evolutive interpretation.

7.6 CONCLUSION

The aim of this chapter has been to address several theoretical questions on evolutive interpretation in order to get a better understanding of evolutive interpretation as an interpretative aid. In general international law, evolutive interpretation is regarded as a common interpretative concept. The Vienna Convention provides a limited

122 Reich (2005), p. 25 and p. 31.

foundation for evolutive interpretation, but reference has also been made to the Namibia advisory opinion of the International Court of Justice as a basis for evolutive interpretation. More specifically, the preamble and the text of the European Convention have been mentioned as factors that support an evolutive approach in the context of the European Convention. In the context of the EU, the programmatic nature of the treaties as a design for the future has been mentioned as the most important indication that an evolutive approach is warranted. The question is whether both courts in their case law address the basis for their evolutive approach.

Evolutive interpretation has been qualified in this thesis as an interpretative principle. This qualification is often not explicitly made in the literature. Some authors seem to implicitly recognize the different nature of evolutive interpretation in relation to interpretation methods, but even then the difference is not really addressed. Often evolutive interpretation is regarded as an interpretation method, just like any other. The question is whether the ECtHR and the CJEU in their case law show any concern for the nature of evolutive interpretation.

The advantages of evolutive interpretation are often taken for granted and discussions focus on the criticism voiced against evolutive interpretation. In general theoretical literature there are two main points of criticism. First, the opponents are concerned how far a judge can take evolutive interpretation. Several constraints for judges have been mentioned in this regard, but these constraints only mitigate the concern. The second criticism is that there is no guiding principle for evolutive interpretation. As a result the use of this principle is unclear and that reduces the force of this argument. These concerns need to be addressed. Both concerns show that it is not clear how an evolutive interpretation is established. In the discussion on the specific courts it became clear that for both courts the question how evolutive interpretation is established could not be clearly answered either. The case law analysis should provide some clarification in this respect. Comparative interpretation seems to play an important role in the context of the ECtHR, while teleological interpretation seems to be important in the context of the CJEU. Chapters 11 and 13 will test these theoretical assumptions. A clear understanding of how evolutive interpretation is established will also help reduce the criticism that has been voiced against this interpretative principle.

Chapter 8
Principle of autonomous interpretation

The final theoretical analysis will be devoted to autonomous interpretation. Autonomous interpretation has been explained in Chapter 4 as interpretation that is independent from the meaning granted to terms and notions as contained in international texts or in domestic law. Just like the principle of evolutive interpretation, autonomous interpretation is one of the general interpretative principles that derives from a meta-teleological approach to the treaty in question. This means that the object and purpose of the treaty structure as a whole can be said to warrant an autonomous approach.[1] As a result the reasons for adopting an autonomous approach could differ slightly per treaty, depending on the specific object and purpose of each particular treaty. Both the question what autonomous interpretation means exactly and on what basis this principle of interpretation is invoked will be discussed in this chapter.

An important difference can be noted between autonomous interpretation and the other interpretative aids discussed in this thesis. Autonomous interpretation is a concept that is mainly developed in case law and which has not been the subject of much theoretical debate. As a result, the general theoretical discussion on this interpretative principle in this chapter is rather limited. In addition, while for the other interpretation methods and principles national theoretical discussions proved relevant, this is different in the context of autonomous interpretation. Autonomous interpretation inherently appears to be a phenomenon that is not particularly relevant in national constitutional interpretation. After all, it is clear from the definition provided that it concerns interpretation that is independent of the interpretation accorded to a term in domestic law. This already indicates that such a principle can hardly be relevant at the national level. The focus of this chapter therefore will be on the role of autonomous interpretation before the supranational courts and, as far as any materials are available, on the theoretical discussion on the principle in international law.

The objective of this chapter is to see whether it is possible to get a better understanding of how autonomous interpretation can be established in theory, and to determine which questions and hypothesis can be formulated for further investigation in the case law of the court. This chapter will focus on the question what methods of interpretation may help the courts to establish an autonomous interpretation and

1 Lasser (2004), p. 208.

in what situations autonomous interpretation can be used. These and other remaining questions will subsequently be addressed in more depth in the case law analysis.

8.1 Autonomous Interpretation and International Law

Since autonomous interpretation mainly plays a role in the context of international law, it is interesting to see if any (theoretical) foundations for the use of this interpretative principle can be found at the level of international law. The logical starting point to search for such foundations is the Vienna Convention. Indeed, two bases for autonomous interpretation can be found in the Vienna Convention. Firstly, Section 4 of Article 31 of the Vienna Convention, which contains the general rules on treaty interpretation, provides that, in exception to the general rule that the ordinary meaning of a specific term must prevail, a 'special meaning' may be attributed to a term if the parties so intended.[2] The 'special meaning' could in the interpretation process for the ECtHR and CJEU exist in the attribution of an autonomous meaning. The indication that the parties intended such a special meaning can, for example, be found in the object and purpose of a treaty. The second justification can be found in an article unrelated to interpretation, namely Article 5 of the Vienna Convention. This article provides that when interpreting the constituent instrument of an international organization or any treaty adopted within an international organization, the special rules of this organization may be taken into account.[3] Within the context of the EU and the European Convention this allows for an autonomous approach to interpretation. Various authors have emphasized this second justification as an important basis for autonomous interpretation within the Vienna Convention.[4] However, regardless of the relative importance of either of these bases, it is clear that they do not contradict or exclude each other. Rather, they can be seen in combination, thus constituting a proper justification for developing a general principle of autonomous interpretation.

In the context of a different type of international treaty than the human rights treaties on which this thesis focuses, attention has been paid to autonomous interpretation as well. Autonomous interpretation is also used in the context of the United Nations Convention on Contracts for the International Sale of Goods (CISG). The situation is somewhat different from the situation before the ECtHR and CJEU. Under the CISG

---

2 Article 31 § 4 reads: 'A special meaning shall be given to a term if it is established that the parties so intended.' See for example, Aust (2000), p. 204.

3 Article 5 of the Vienna Convention reads: 'The present Convention applies to any treaty which is the constituent instrument of an international organization and to any treaty adopted within an international organization without prejudice to any relevant rules of the organization.'

4 See most importantly: Ganshof van der Meersch (1988), p. 205. See further: Vande Lanotte (2005), p. 186; Matscher (1993), p. 71; Kastanas (1996), p. 344.

there is no supranational court to address interpretative matters, so interpretations have to be provided by national courts. This might create the risk of divergent interpretations of the treaty provisions, since there is no single body responsible for giving a clear and autonomous meaning to their text. For that reason, some authors have argued that in the context of the CISG the solution to guarantee an autonomous interpretation would be to establish a supranational court.[5] To a certain extent, this seems to be of little help for the present discussion, of which the focus is precisely on autonomous interpretation at supranational courts. However, the desire to create a supranational body may be considered to express the general need for autonomous interpretation of treaty provisions in order to avoid divergent case law and divergent interpretations on the domestic level. Autonomous interpretation in this context is strongly motivated by a wish for uniformity. To that extent, the CISG example may serve to stress the need and the justifiability of using a general principle of autonomous interpretation by supranational courts that already exist.

The special character of autonomous interpretation has been stressed by GEBAUER. While he sometimes refers to the notion as a method of interpretation, he does acknowledge that it has a rather distinct character.[6] He argues that autonomous interpretation is 'a principle of interpretation that gives preference to a particular kind of teleological and systematic argument in interpreting a legal text'.[7] Autonomous interpretation accordingly is based on the treaty's own system and objectives. GEBAUER'S statement thus not only stresses the character of autonomous interpretation as a principle, rather than a method of interpretation, but also provides an indication as to how an autonomous interpretation can be established. GEBAUER and others also indicate that comparative interpretation may play a role in establishing an autonomous interpretation as well.[8] Thus, autonomous interpretation should not be taken so strictly as to mean that drawing any inspiration from national legal orders to find a proper interpretation is unacceptable. Although it seems to be accepted that the interpretational result should not be dominated by the interpretation adopted in one of the Member States, DIEDRICH has suggested that finding some sort of consensus is acceptable under an autonomous interpretation.[9] In the context of the CISG, for example, autonomous interpretation could be based on an analysis of the legal systems of a number of the states that are a party to the Convention. In the case law analysis, the question as to whether in the context of the CJEU and ECtHR the same understanding of establishing autonomous interpretation can be found will be further explored.

5 See Gebauer (2000), p. 684; Diedrich (1996), p. 336.
6 Gebauer (2000), p. 684 & p. 687
7 Gebauer (2000), p. 687.
8 Gebauer (2000), p. 690; Diedrich (1996), p. 324.
9 Diedrich (1996), p. 324.

8.2 European Court of Human Rights

The meaning of the principle of autonomous interpretation has already been discussed in Chapter 4 together with the justification provided for the use of this interpretative principle. The aim of the present chapter is not to duplicate that discussion, but rather to elaborate on the different types of autonomous interpretation. Moreover, the aim is to try to answer the question when the ECtHR will use the instrument of autonomous interpretation, how it can establish autonomous interpretation and what kind of criticism has been directed at this form of interpretation.

Before addressing these questions it is important to clarify one aspect of autonomous interpretation, namely its relation to the margin of appreciation doctrine. Often these two instruments are considered as each other's opposites, since autonomous interpretation seems to be inspired by a desire for uniformity, whereas the margin of appreciation is expressly intended to enable the Court to respect national differences, and to allow for divergence and variety in the national protection of fundamental rights.[10] The two instruments, however, have clearly different functions in the adjudication process of the ECtHR. Autonomous interpretation, as implied by the terminology, is a concept used in the interpretation process and concerns the applicability of Convention rights to the facts of the case presented to the Court.[11] The doctrine of the margin of appreciation, on the other hand, plays a role in the process of establishing whether a certain right has been violated and in assessing the justification that has been advanced by the national authorities. They therefore in principle do not stand in any meaningful relation to each other, which allows for omission of the doctrine from the remainder of this chapter. Nevertheless, it remains a relevant question for the case law analysis whether the ECtHR always adheres to this division or whether in some cases it might grant a margin of appreciation in order to avoid an autonomous interpretation.

Even though the concept of autonomous interpretation seems rather clear, there is no common conception of the qualification 'autonomous interpretation' in scholarly literature.[12] Should all terms of the European Convention be qualified as autonomous or does this qualification apply only to some Convention terms and not to others? While some authors consider the former to be correct, other authors have proposed a distinction between different types of autonomous concepts. These different types

10 See, for example, Ost (1992), p. 306, who argues that if states are granted a large margin of appreciation, the ECtHR will be less inclined to adopt an autonomous interpretation.

11 Sudre, p. 108.

12 Sudre discusses the different understandings of autonomous concepts, Sudre (1998), p. 96-98.

can be divided into two categories.[13] On the one hand, some scholars adhere to a 'weak'[14] concept of autonomy or *l'autonomie organique*,[15] which is based on the idea that any interpretation coming from an international body that is specifically charged with the interpretation of a treaty or convention can be considered autonomous.[16] Put differently, in this view the fact that an international autonomous body interprets the Convention is enough to consider the interpretation of all Convention terms autonomous. On the other hand, adherents of 'strong'[17] autonomy or *l'autonomie substantielle*[18] do not take such a broad stance. In their view, one can only speak of 'autonomous' interpretation if the Convention term is expressly and intentionally interpreted in a real 'European' way, disconnected from the national qualification. This does not mean that national qualifications cannot play a role in determining this interpretation. The national qualification of the Member State in question is used as a starting point and the national qualifications of all Contracting States can play a role if the ECtHR uses a comparative interpretation to establish the autonomous meaning.[19] In the case of strong autonomy, the specific interpretation (even if based on a national example) will be adapted to the European system and will be granted a European flavour.

It is the latter conception of autonomous interpretation that is most often referred to in the literature. Within this conception there is one more distinction to be made. This distinction is a rather subtle one, but it is necessary in order to be exact about the understanding of autonomous interpretation. There are those that consider Convention terms to be autonomous solely if the ECtHR has expressly qualified its interpretation or the Convention terms as such.[20] Some, however, take a slightly broader

---

13 Vande Lanotte has made a different classification. On the one hand he distinguishes 'semi-autonomous' terms and on the other 'autonomous' terms. He starts from the presumption that all terms are autonomous, because an international body is charged with the interpretation of these terms. The semi-autonomous terms are those terms in the Convention that refer back to national law (like 'prescribed by law' which has been laid down in art. 8-11). He seems to imply that autonomous terms are all other terms in the European Convention, of which some have been explicitly classified as such. Vande Lanotte (2005), p. 187-191.

14 Schokkenbroek (2000), p. 13.

15 Sudre (1998), p. 99; Vande Lanotte (2005), p. 187-188.

16 Kastanas (1996), p. 344.

17 Schokkenbroek (2000), p. 13.

18 Sudre (1998), p. 99.

19 This is visible in ECtHR, *Engel and others v. the Netherlands*, judgment of 8 June 1976, *Series* A No. 22.

20 Sudre provides a list of terms that have been expressly qualified as autonomous: arrest; civil rights and obligations; criminal charge; witness; charge; penalty; possessions. See Sudre (1998), p. 96-97. Letsas on the other hand provides a different list of terms that have been expressly qualified as autonomous by the ECHR. Some of the terms overlap, but others differ: civil rights and obligations; criminal charge; possessions; association; victim; civil servant; lawful detention; home. See Letsas

perspective by attributing the qualification autonomous also to terms that have been given a specific Convention meaning, even though the ECtHR has not expressly qualified this meaning in its case law as autonomous.[21] Both perspectives seem acceptable, but for the current research it is most useful to focus on what the ECtHR itself qualifies as autonomous terms, since that reveals most about how this principle is used by the ECtHR.[22] Although the findings of the analysis may be relevant for the broader category described in the literature as well, the analysis will therefore focus on the label provided by the ECtHR.

Why does the ECtHR employ this principle of interpretation in its interpretation process? A short indication of possible reasons and explanations was already given in the introduction on autonomous interpretation in Chapter 4. Various authors have provided different explanations, but the bottom line of most explanations seems to be rather similar. By employing an autonomous interpretation the ECtHR establishes a certain level of minimum uniformity or harmonization in a specific area,[23] which is, according to the preamble, one of the objectives of the European Convention.[24] This uniformity ensures that fundamental rights will be granted effective protection, since the (minimum) level of protection does not depend on the national qualification of these rights in the various states. Put differently, the Court may favour an autonomous interpretation in order to avoid the creation of different levels of protection throughout the Contracting States of the European Convention.[25] Contracting States will not be able to exclude their citizens from the protection provided by certain Convention rights by classifying or interpreting them more narrowly.[26]

Apart from the concerns relating to the effective protection of fundamental rights, some authors have stressed the strategic relevance of the principle of autonomous interpretation for the ECtHR itself. An autonomous interpretation provides the ECtHR with a possibility to emphasize its jurisdictional power, by interpreting a specific term in such a way that the national qualification cannot be used to escape from European

---

(2004), p. 283. Sudre notes that he is surprised that in the doctrine a broader notion of autonomous interpretation exists, Sudre (1998), p. 97-98.

21 Distinction explained by Sudre (1998), p. 96. See also: Vanneste (2010), p. 233-234.

22 Sudre notes that it is not clear why the ECtHR qualifies some terms as autonomous, so the choices of the ECtHR in explicitly qualifying a term as autonomous might not be the result of a specific approach. Sudre (1998), p. 98.

23 Ost (1992), p. 305; Schokkenbroek (2000), p. 2.1-10; Matscher (1993), p. 73; Ovey & White (2006), p. 43; Kastanas (1996), p. 346-347; Ganshof van der Meersch (1988), p. 204; Vande Lanotte (2005), p. 186; Gerards (2008), p. 18; Kastanas (1996), p. 346.

24 Matscher (1993), p. 73.

25 Ryssdall (1996), p. 23.

26 Letsas (2004), p. 281-282; Gomez-Arostegui (2005), p. 159.

protection.[27] The ECtHR has the final say in determining whether a certain legal term falls within the scope of the European Convention and if a complaint about an interference with a Convention right is admissible *ratione materiae*. If a specific term does come within the scope of the European Convention, this means that the ECtHR will have jurisdiction to conclude whether a violation has occurred.[28] It thus affects the autonomous or sovereign position of the Contracting States, since even in the process of classifying certain legal situations as being relevant under the Convention they are subject to the control of Strasbourg. The ECtHR can therefore expand both its jurisdiction and, accordingly, its control over national legal systems, by using the instrument of autonomous interpretation to widen the scope of the fundamental rights provisions.[29] Such an approach may clearly have quite an impact on the Contracting States.

Given the importance of the principle of autonomous interpretation for the ECHR system, the questions become relevant as to when the ECtHR will choose an autonomous approach and how it will establish such an autonomous interpretation. A very general indication of when the ECtHR will resort to an autonomous interpretation can be found in the text of the ECHR. The text of some provisions refers back to national law, like Article 12, which stipulates that the right to marry is governed by national laws.[30] In the context of this type of provision it is to be expected that the ECtHR will not employ an autonomous approach, given the explicit reference to national law.[31] The question is whether a more specific indication can be found as to when the ECtHR applies an autonomous approach. SUDRE contends that the ECtHR appears to resort to an autonomous approach as soon as there is a classification dispute.[32] This means that there is a dispute as to how a certain legal concept should be classified. Two or more conceptions of one legal concept might exist and there is disagreement about which is the correct one in the context of the ECHR.[33] In the case of *Engel*, for example, the applicant argued that a disciplinary sanction fell within the concept of a criminal charge, while the respondent state argued that the concept

27 Vande Lanotte (2005), p. 186-187; Schokkenbroek (2000), p. 11; Kastanas (1996), p. 346.

28 Sudre (1998), p. 107.

29 Sudre (1998), p. 113.

30 *Article 12 ECHR:*
Men and women of marriageable age have the right to marry and to found a family, according to the national laws governing the exercise of this right.

31 Gerards (2011), p. 33.

32 This has been noted by Letsas as well. Letsas (2004), p. 284.

33 Letsas (2004), p. 288.

of a criminal charge did not include disciplinary sanctions.[34] The ECtHR finally adopted an autonomous interpretation to determine which conception of the term criminal charge should be adhered to in the context of the European Convention. What is peculiar about these disputes in comparison with other cases before the ECtHR is that they concern a disagreement at an 'earlier stage' in the argument or at a different level.[35] In the majority of the cases the applicants argue that the respondent state has not provided the necessary conditions to exercise their rights under the ECHR. In this particular type of case the disagreement does not concern the conditions necessary to respect the Convention rights, but the question whether certain categories should be excluded from the protection afforded under the Convention.[36]

The question when the ECtHR invokes an autonomous interpretation, however, is still not fully answered. In principle a classification dispute could arise for any of the provisions, but the ECtHR has not adopted an autonomous approach for all provisions. LETSAS argues that these disputes generally concern 'distinctively legal concepts' like 'criminal charge', 'civil rights and obligations' and 'lawful detention'.[37] He argues that these are technical legal terms, generally included in legal sources, that only obtain their full meaning if placed in a legal context (unlike a notion such as 'life', which does not only or mainly gain meaning in a legal context).[38] National legislatures have often made deliberate choices in classifying these terms in a certain way and this might conflict with the views of Strasbourg, which is why they adopt an autonomous approach.

One could derive from this analysis by LETSAS that in cases where the interpretation concerns notions with an almost 'moral' content and meaning, like 'religion', 'private life' or 'life' more generally, the ECtHR would not adopt an autonomous approach. Assuming that this is a deliberate choice by the ECtHR, one could question whether this is a logical choice. No explanation has been provided in the literature as to the reasons why the ECtHR would seem to reserve autonomous interpretation for rather technical terms. Such an approach might be explained, however, by the implications of autonomous interpretation. The underlying assumption could be that there are more differences between Contracting States on moral issues and that Contracting States feel more strongly about moral issues than about more 'technical'

34 ECtHR, *Engel and others v. the Netherlands*, judgment of 8 June 1976, *Series* A No. 22. See also Letsas (2004), p. 281 & p. 288 for a discussion of this case in the context of autonomous interpretation.

35 Letsas (2004), p. 283, speaks of a 'conceptual sub-level'. Vanneste (2010), p. 234, has, however, classified this distinction as 'artificial'.

36 Sudre, p. 103.

37 Letsas (2004), p. 285.

38 Letsas (2004), p. 285. Matscher (1993), p. 70. Harris, O'Boyle & Warbrick (1995), p. 16: this passage has not been included in the most recent version of Harris, O'Boyle & Warbrick (2009).

aspects of the Convention. As discussed above, autonomous interpretation may easily intrude on the sovereignty of Contracting States in the sense that the ECtHR, by relying on its own qualification, may declare itself competent to deal with all kinds of sensitive national cases that fall within the scope of the provision as defined by the ECtHR. Since this may be difficult to accept for the states, especially if they tend to define certain rights or notions more narrowly, the ECtHR might be inclined to adopt such an autonomous approach only in those areas where it thinks that there will be no strong resistance in the states to a uniform understanding. The question is whether any clues can be found, first of all for the assumption that autonomous interpretation applies mainly to more technical terms and, secondly, as regards the underlying reasons for adopting such an approach.

In his discussion on when the ECtHR relies on autonomous interpretation, SUDRE further argues that in his view the ECtHR will rely on autonomous interpretation when the rights in question are closely related to the rule of law principle.[39] Without defining his understanding of the rule of law, he argues that autonomous interpretation helps to ensure the effectiveness of the rule of law.[40] SUDRE considers that Article 5 (right to liberty and security), Article 6 (right to a fair trial) and Article 7 (no punishment without law) are intimately connected to the rule of law; thus one may infer from these provisions that the rule of law in his view, is closely connected to a fair trial in a broad sense.[41] The fact that most of the concepts that have been qualified as autonomous concern Articles 5 and 6 of the Convention seems to provide some support for this assertion. An autonomous approach has, however, also been adopted in the context of Article 1 First Protocol (protection of property) and Article 11 (freedom of assembly and association). These provisions are, in SUDRE'S view, not closely connected to the rule of law and they thus do not seem to support his argument. The argument by SUDRE raises the question whether the ECtHR indeed predominantly employs an autonomous approach when interpreting rights closely related to the rule of law. The difficulty is that, in order to answer that question, one would need to know what the concept 'rule of law' means, both in SUDRE's view and in the view of the ECtHR, which requires a further study that is beyond the scope of this thesis. It is more feasible and suitable, therefore, to just explore whether the ECtHR expressly refers to the rule of law to justify an autonomous approach and if it does so, whether it provides an explanation for doing so. Indeed, this exploration will be undertaken in the case law analysis discussed in Chapter 12.

---

39 Sudre claims that the ECtHR in its case law confirms that analysis (referring to ECtHR, *Deweer v. Belgium*, judgment of 27 February 1980, *Series* A No. 35). Sudre (1998), p. 116-117.

40 Sudre (1998), p. 116.

41 Sudre (1998), p. 115.

The second question that should be answered is how an autonomous interpretation can be established by the ECtHR, in particular what methods of interpretation it can use in this respect. When discussing the basis for relying on an autonomous interpretation, the relevance of teleological interpretation has already been mentioned. This type of reasoning, which refers to the object and purpose of the Convention as a whole to justify the use of certain interpretative principles, has been identified as a meta-teleological approach in Chapter 4 and will not play a concrete role in the interpretation of a specific provision.[42] (Micro-)teleological interpretation, on the other hand, may certainly play a role in establishing an autonomous meaning. It will be relevant to examine in the case law analysis whether teleological arguments actually play a role in determining the autonomous meaning of a provision. Both LETSAS and SUDRE discuss the role of comparative interpretation as a means of establishing an autonomous interpretation.[43] Both authors refer to comparative interpretation in the sense of consensus interpretation, meaning that the ECtHR endeavours to establish some kind of consensus that can be used as a basis for an autonomous interpretation.[44] SUDRE points out that this seems to be rather paradoxical.[45] The ECtHR wants to take a uniform approach by adopting an autonomous interpretation precisely because there is no uniform understanding of a certain notion. At the same time the ECtHR bases this autonomous interpretation on the existence of a consensus among the Contracting States. One could question whether the use of comparative interpretation is really contrary to the idea behind autonomous interpretation. Perhaps one's view on this may depend on one's precise understanding of autonomous interpretation. Autonomous interpretation refers to interpretation that is independent of a notion's meaning in domestic law, but does that refer to one domestic system in particular, or to the meaning in any domestic system? The latter understanding of autonomous interpretation would be hard to defend, because it would mean that a supranational court would have to force itself to establish an interpretation that does not exist in any of the Contracting States. According to OST an entirely autonomous approach is never possible, since in that situation the ECtHR would run the risk of 'detaching itself from reality'.[46] The more logical explanation would seem to be that autonomous interpretation concerns interpretation independent of the particular understanding of a notion in the respondent State. In that perspective it could be valuable to find some

42 See page 4.1. and 4.4.2.1. for a more elaborate description on meta-teleological principles.

43 See also Gerards (2008), p. 18.

44 Sudre (1998), p. 118; Letsas (2004), p. 295-296. Vanneste (2010), p. 238-239 also claims that this method plays an important role in establishing an autonomous interpretation.

45 Sudre (1998), p. 118.

46 Ost (1992), p. 305 & 308, argues that an autonomous interpretation completely detached from all national qualifications would be illegitimate, because the preamble refers to the 'common heritage' on which the Convention is built. See also: Gomez-Arostegui (2005), p. 159.

basis for a certain interpretation in the Contracting States as long as that does not diminish the character of autonomous interpretation, by relying on only a few Contracting States. Then, a comparative interpretation could be acceptable as a method to arrive at an autonomous understanding of the notion.

How a consensus can be established using comparative interpretation is discussed in the context of comparative interpretation. The present chapter is concerned with the question which methods have been identified as playing a role in establishing an autonomous interpretation. The exact role of the consensus is, however, not clear. LETSAS argues that the ECtHR when establishing an autonomous interpretation does seriously look for a common ground, but establishes an autonomous meaning based on moral truth.[47] In his view the ECtHR does not really use comparative interpretation, but uses substantive arguments to support a certain interpretation. LETSAS concludes that the ECtHR in some cases lacks real interest in the outcome of the consensus, which leads him to assume that the ECtHR does not actually rely on this consensus in establishing autonomous interpretation. After all, if the consensus argument really played a role, the judges of the Court in LETSAS' view would have given a better explanation of the link between the consensus found and the interpretation chosen. This challenge by LETSAS provides an interesting background for the case law analysis, in which it should be analyzed which role consensus plays in establishing an autonomous interpretation. An additional question to be examined for the case law of the ECtHR is whether there are other methods which help to determine an autonomous interpretation, if it turns out that consensus indeed is not really or not always decisive. Perhaps examples can be found of cases where the ECtHR invoked arguments based on micro-teleological interpretation, textual interpretation or systemic interpretation.

A final matter that should be dealt with in this chapter relates to the criticism that has been voiced as regards the use of this interpretative approach. Some of the dissenting judges within the ECHR have been critical of the application of the principle of autonomous interpretation.[48] This criticism has been directed in particular at the role of the comparative method in establishing an autonomous meaning to notions and terms contained in the Convention.[49] The bottom line of this criticism is that the Court may show itself to be too activist when extensively using the instrument of autonomous interpretation.[50] Especially since extensive autonomous interpretation can have far-reaching implications for the national legal order and for the

47 Letsas (2004), p. 297.

48 See Letsas and Ost referring to judge Matscher. Letsas (2004), p. 285; Ost (1992), p. 307.

49 Ost (1992), p. 307.

50 This danger is also highlighted by Matscher in his extra-judicial writings. Matscher (1993), p. 73.

Court's jurisdiction, this is a concern that should be taken seriously.[51] In the discussion on the teleological method, the issue of judicial activism has been briefly discussed and the conclusions reached in this respect are equally relevant in the context of autonomous interpretation. The accusations of activism depend on one's perception of the role of the judge and may therefore never be entirely avoided. A consistent and transparent reasoning in which it is made very clear for which reasons and on which grounds an autonomous interpretation is chosen, may reduce the force of these accusations and may thereby strengthen the legitimacy of the argument made on the basis of the autonomous approach.

8.3 Court of Justice of the European Union

In the interpretation of fundamental rights by the CJEU, the concept of autonomous interpretation plays a role as well. Various aspects of this interpretation have already been briefly touched upon in Chapter 4. The aim of this chapter is to delve deeper into the role of autonomous interpretation in the context of the development of fundamental rights principles by the CJEU. To do so, however, it is first useful to set out the different types of autonomous interpretation and the reason for the use of this principle by the CJEU.

Reference has already been made to the understanding that autonomous interpretation indicates that the chosen interpretation is independent of that given to similar notions and terms in the Member States. However, that is not the only version of autonomous interpretation that is relevant in the context of the CJEU's case law. In the field of fundamental rights the relation with the ECtHR cannot be ignored. When discussing autonomous interpretation of fundamental rights in the EU context, 'autonomy' can also be related to a definition that is independent of the meaning provided by the ECtHR, as well as from the meaning given in domestic law. Especially Douglas-Scott has viewed autonomous interpretation in light of this relation between the two European Courts.[52] The discussion below will address both forms of autonomous interpretation.

The discussion on the principle of autonomous interpretation in the context of the ECtHR has shown that one of the main aims of this principle is uniformity. In an organization that is aimed at closer cooperation, integration and harmonization, such as the EU, uniformity plays a crucial role.[53] If only looking at the preamble of the

51 See Gerards, who highlights the impact of the autonomous approach. Gerards (2008), p. 19.

52 Douglas-Scott (2006), p. 648.

53 Lasser (2004), p. 215-219, who has identified uniformity as one of the meta-teleological purposes of the EU.

founding treaties, a strong argument can already be made for uniformity, considering statements like: 'an ever closer union', 'to strengthen the unity of their economies', 'ensure their harmonious development', 'process of European integration' and the recurrence of the word 'common'.[54] The subsequent developments of the EU appear to enhance and strengthen this argument for uniformity. Given the overriding importance of uniformity as regards core notions and principles of EU law, autonomous interpretation seems to constitute a vital principle for the interpretation process of the CJEU. After all, autonomous interpretation is an important vehicle to arrive at uniform definitions which are independent of particular domestic legal systems. In addition, the CJEU itself has stated that such interpretation may find a basis in the fact that '... Community law uses terminology which is peculiar to it'.[55] The interpretation of the term 'worker' may exemplify the importance of a uniform and autonomous interpretation by the CJEU. The CJEU held that this term should be given a 'Community meaning', because otherwise Member States could 'eliminate at will the protection afforded by the Treaty to certain categories of person'.[56] Indeed, a similar justification is provided by the ECtHR when adopting an autonomous interpretation, as has been expounded in section 8.2 above. Finally, and apart from this need for uniformity and the efficacy of the EU's four freedoms, autonomous interpretation provides the CJEU with an opportunity 'to claim ultimate authority over the meaning and scope' of these terms.[57] From the perspective of the CJEU's position as a supranational court, too, autonomous interpretation will therefore constitute an essential principle underlying and guiding the definition of fundamental rights.

Considering the nature and aims of the European Union, these considerations seem to constitute a legitimate justification for employing autonomous interpretation. There, however, appears to be one catch, being that the European Union originally was not expressly concerned with fundamental rights at all. On the contrary, in the early years of the European Economic Community, fundamental rights were considered entirely outside the scope of EEC law. Only gradually have they found their way into the European project, resulting only recently in adopting a fundamental rights catalogue as a binding part of EU law by means of the Lisbon Treaty. This development has clear implications for the role of the principle of autonomous interpretation regarding the interpretation of fundamental rights. While the desire for uniformity can be considered to constitute a legitimate basis for an autonomous approach to economic provisions in the Treaty, as has been shown above, the situation is different when

---

54 See preamble of the then EC and EU treaty.

55 C-283/81,*CILFIT v. Ministero della Sanità* [1982] ECR 3415, § 19. Arnull (2006), p. 608.

56 C-75/63 Unger v Bestuur [1964] ECR 1977. See furthermore Craig & De Burca (2003), p. 705 and Barnard (2000), p. 133 both referring to CJEU cases that have dealt with the Community meaning of the term 'worker'.

57 Craig & De Burca (2003), p. 706, referring to AG Mancini.

fundamental rights are at play. In fact, the CJEU has long refrained from imposing one uniform version of fundamental rights that must be accepted in all Member States. Instead it respects diversity between the different national cultures, traditions and identities, only striving to protect as common values those principles which are already widely shared and accepted throughout the European Union.[58] Thus, the common values and traditions among the different Member States, combined with the definition of rights provided by the European Convention on Human Rights and the case law of the ECtHR, provide the basis for the fundamental rights that are protected within the EU.[59] This comparative element inherent to the interpretation of fundamental rights within the EU, in addition to the CJEU's reliance on the interpretation of rights provided by the ECtHR, seems to exclude or at least severely limit the role of autonomous interpretation of fundamental rights by the CJEU.[60] Precisely these factors have led VON BOGDANDY to state that fundamental rights are the least autonomous part of EU law.[61] It has already been argued in the context of the ECtHR that using a comparative approach to establish an autonomous meaning, does not have to be contrary to the idea behind an autonomous approach. It depends on the way the comparative method is used.[62]

In this regard, it is therefore a relevant question whether the CJEU applies only a comparative approach when defining the meaning of fundamental rights notions. This is not to be expected, as it has already been mentioned in section 6.3 that the CJEU does not blindly copy the results of the comparative method, but rather will consider and sometimes re-define these results in the light of the object and purpose of the EU.[63] This could certainly have implications for the role of autonomous interpretation. If a common ground approach is not unquestioningly and uncritically applied, fundamental rights notions could be granted a specific EU flavour by the CJEU. KÜHLING even speaks about an 'autonomous specification' of fundamental rights based on the common traditions in the Member States. The approach might thus be not as strictly autonomous as in other fields of EC law, but there still may be a role for it.

An interesting question is, however, if the CJEU will choose a similar autonomous stance as regards the meaning of notions that have already been interpreted and explained by the ECtHR. DOUGLAS-SCOTT argues that only in a few cases the CJEU has taken a different approach than the ECtHR and has adopted its own, 'autonomous'

58 As can be seen in the preamble of the Charter of Fundamental Rights of the European Union (2000).

59 Art. 6 TEU.

60 Reich (2005), p. 29 claims that Community law in the case of fundamental rights encourages the comparative argument; he seems to imply that this occurs to the detriment of the autonomous approach.

61 Von Bogdandy (2000), p. 1333; Douglas-Scott (2006), p. 652.

62 See section 8.2.

63 See among others: Kühling (2006), p. 506; Blanke (2006), p. 268.

interpretation.[64] Apparently, it feels less free to deviate from the authoritative interpretation that has been given by a specialized human rights court, and which are themselves based on interpretative principles and methods such as teleological, evolutive and autonomous interpretation, than from interpretations given by domestic authorities. However, the case law analysis will have to disclose if it is really true that there is a difference between autonomous interpretation in relation to domestic law and autonomous interpretation in relation to the ECtHR's case law. An additional question that may be raised in this respect is whether the entry into force of the Treaty of Lisbon will change anything. Article 52(3) of the now binding Charter provides that, as regards rights that are both contained in the ECHR and in the Charter, the meaning of the rights as contained in the Charter shall be the same as that under the European Convention. This would seem to imply that there is hardly any room for an autonomous approach by the CJEU, but a contra-indication may be that the CJEU is allowed to provide more protection than is already offered by the ECHR. As far as the interpretation given by the CJEU is more protective, such an interpretation may then be autonomous indeed. Although there is only limited case law in which the Charter has been applied thus far, the case law analysis will pay some attention to the question if the fundamental rights case law of the CJEU has been given more 'body' through the binding Charter, or if the approach remains a rather reluctant and strongly comparative one.

The previous sections already provided some indication as to how an autonomous interpretation is established by the CJEU. A main role is played by comparative argumentation, but other arguments may be relevant as well. It was mentioned, for example, that the CJEU can consider a consensus in the light of the object and purpose of the EU and can decide to adapt the outcome of an exercise in comparative interpretation to fit better with the aims and objectives of EU law. Thus, teleological arguments may play an interesting role in this context.[65] The examples of autonomous interpretation in relation to the interpretation provided by the ECtHR that have been given by Douglas-Scott also reveal that the CJEU sometimes relies on teleological arguments.[66] In the chapter relating to the case law approach used by the CJEU, it will be examined exactly how and to what extent such methods are used in order to arrive at an autonomous meaning of fundamental rights notions.

---

64 Douglas-Scott (2006), p. 648.

65 In the broader EU context teleological arguments also play a role in establishing an autonomous interpretation: Millett (1989), p. 177; Lenearts (2003), p. 894.

66 Douglas-Scott (2006), p. 648.

Even though some authors claim that the fundamental rights context is the least autonomous area of EU law, reasons have been listed to assume that autonomous interpretation does play some role in this context. Therefore, assuming that there is some form of autonomous interpretation, a subsequent question is in what types of cases and in which circumstances does the CJEU employ such an autonomous approach. It has been submitted in scholarly literature on other fields of EU law that this will be the case in particular if the national systems diverge on a certain issue and it will be interesting to test whether that reason is also valid for adopting an autonomous approach in fundamental rights cases.

A final point that should be considered in this chapter is whether and in which respects the principle has been the subject of criticism. Probably because of the limited importance of the principle, the literature relating to fundamental rights interpretation by the CJEU shows hardly any criticism that is specifically related to this principle of interpretation. However, in analogy to the criticism discussed in relation to the ECtHR, it may be supposed that the use of an autonomous approach by the CJEU can evoke accusations of judicial activism. Before any such accusations can be addressed or suggestions for improvement can be made, however, it is necessary to gain more insight into the exact use of this interpretative principle by the CJEU. For that reason, the question as to possible criticism as regard the use of autonomous interpretation by the CJEU will only be answered after an in-depth analysis has been provided of the relevant case law in Chapter 13.

8.4 Conclusion

For both the CJEU and the ECtHR, the autonomous approach appears to have added value. Problematic is that the principle remains some sort of enigma. A general justification for the use of this principle is provided in the Vienna Convention, which allows for a 'special meaning' to be given to specific terms. The respective courts have, however, mainly referred to arguments based on the need to ensure that Member States do not avoid protection provided by fundamental rights. Scholars have for both courts also identified a strategic reason for invoking an autonomous approach, namely that it confirms their position as supranational judge vis-à-vis the Member States.

The main problem with autonomous interpretation is that, at least from the theoretical literature and the analyses made thus far, it is not clear when the ECtHR and the CJEU invoke an autonomous interpretation and how they establish an autonomous meaning. Several suggestions have been made in order to find a pattern in the terms that the ECtHR qualifies as autonomous. According to one author, autonomous terms are mainly technical legal terms, but they are terms that have a close relation with the rule of law according to another author. Reference has also been made to the fact that the ECtHR often adopts an autonomous meaning when there is a dispute over the classification of a legal concept. None of these explanations, however, really discloses a coherent approach by the ECtHR. The case law analysis should help in getting more grip on the question when the ECtHR adopts an autonomous interpretation. The fundamental rights approach by the CJEU has been referred to as the least autonomous area of EU law, but the question is whether that image will be confirmed by the case law analysis.

According to theoretical analyses, the main method to establish an autonomous meaning is comparative interpretation. This might seem strange in the context of autonomous interpretation, but the aim of the comparison in these cases is not to adopt an interpretation which is entirely detached from *any* legal system, but which is detached from a *specific* legal system. In the case law analysis, further answers will be presented to the question whether this is really the method employed in the case law or whether different methods have also been employed to establish an autonomous meaning.

This chapter furthermore aimed to provide a more fully-fledged theoretical understanding of autonomous interpretation. This has been only partly successful, since many aspects remain unclear. If there is one aspect that has become clear throughout this chapter it is the need for a thorough case law analysis. The case law analysis is needed to get a proper understanding of this principle and its role in the interpretative framework of both European Courts.

Part III

Case law analysis

European Court of Human Rights – General introduction[1]

The results of the analysis made of the case law of the European Court of Human Rights on the interpretation of the Convention will be presented in four different chapters, each one dedicated to one of the selected interpretative aids that have been discussed in the theoretical analysis.

One general issue needs to be addressed before dealing with the analysis on each specific method or principle, namely the selection of cases. Throughout the years, the ECtHR has produced a vast amount of cases. The aim of this research has been to undertake a qualitative analysis and not a quantitative analysis of the Court's case law. Several criteria have been used to make a selection of cases which would provide relevant information as to the application of the interpretative aids under study by the ECtHR. Firstly, all Grand Chamber judgments and decisions since 1998 have been summarily reviewed, selecting those in which an interpretative issue played a substantive role. Secondary sources have been used as a basis for the remainder of these selection angles. A second criterion has been to select all landmark cases on any of the Convention provisions, either substantive or procedural, on the basis of several secondary sources.[2] Not all of these cases appeared to concern matters of interpretation. The initial selection therefore was narrowed in order to include only those cases in the analysis in which an interpretative issue could be found. Thirdly, the resulting selection has been broadened by adding a number of more recent cases on the basis of case notes that indicated that the case concerned an interpretative issue.[3] Finally, the selection has been supplemented with judgments dealing with Article 8 and Article 1 Protocol 1. This has been done because the theoretical analysis indicated that in these cases the selected interpretation methods and principles often play a role, which would ensure that at least some cases featured the selected interpretative aids. This selection has also been made on the basis of secondary literature dealing with these

---

1 The case law analysis includes judgments until 31.12.2010.

2 Several chapters and articles on the interpretative approach of the ECtHR have been used to select landmark judgments that featured in most of these chapters: Schokkenbroek (2000); Ost (1992); Harris, O'Boyle & Warbrick (1995).

3 Case notes which appear in European Human Rights Cases. A journal publishing a selection of ECtHR and CJEU cases, but its main focus is on ECtHR cases.

specific provisions.[4] Again, only those cases dealing with an interpretative issue have been selected.

This approach has resulted in a representative selection of cases that have been used for the case law analysis. When analyzing the cases in detail to answer the questions raised in the theoretical analysis, some cases in which interpretative issues had been found when selecting the cases, proved not to add much in terms of an analysis of interpretation methods and principles. This did not turn out to be problematic, however, now that sufficient cases were left for a thorough case law analysis.

An additional complication for the case law selection was that it sometimes proved to be challenging to determine whether one could really speak of an interpretative issue. The distinction between interpretation and application discussed in the introduction served as a framework for this selection, but this distinction is not always strictly adopted in the actual judgments. Some cases in which the interpretation and application phase were seriously mixed have not been added to the selection.[5] Those cases were not suitable for an analysis of the interpretation methods and principles of the ECtHR.

The final selection has been analyzed on the basis of the four selected interpretation methods and principles. Both majority opinions and dissenting and concurring opinions were included in this analysis. As indicated in the general introduction on the ECtHR in Chapter 2, the dissenting and concurring opinions shed much light on the discussions taking place among the judges and are therefore relevant for a discussion of judicial argumentation.

It has already been said at the beginning of this introduction that each chapter will be dealing with one of the selected interpretative aids. Chapter 9 will therefore address teleological interpretation, Chapter 10 comparative interpretation, Chapter 11 evolutive interpretation and Chapter 12 autonomous interpretation. Each chapter will be structured along the most important questions that need to be answered for that specific method or principle, which have been introduced in Chapters 5-8. Thus, the analysis of the theoretical literature will form a starting point for these different discussions.

---

4 Vande Lanotte (2005); EVRM Rechtspraak en Commentaar.

5 See, for example the case of ECtHR (GC) *Hirst (No.2.) v. United Kingdom*, judgment of 6 October 2005, *Reports* 2005-IX. This judgment contains a mix of aspects that belong to the interpretative phase, like a short reference to the *travaux préparatoires* and the context of the Convention, but it is heavily mixed with references to the margin of appreciation and proportionality. The two phases are thus not clearly separated; thus even though one could argue that this case does contain an interpretative element, the case has not been selected.

Chapter 9
Teleological interpretation in the case law of the ECtHR

In the theoretical chapter on teleological interpretation it became clear that this is an important method of interpretation. References to the object and purpose of the Convention or its provisions have an important role to play in the interpretation process. Two versions of this method were discovered. On the one hand, the object and purpose can refer to the intention of the original drafting states, which is considered to be the subjective version of teleological interpretation. On the other hand, the object and purpose can also be established by relying on what rationally can be considered to be the purpose of a specific provision or the Convention. This is referred to as the objective version of teleological interpretation. The theoretical analysis revealed that many authors consider the objective version to be the most important one in fundamental rights adjudication and some even consider that there is no room at all for the subjective version when dealing with fundamental rights.[6] The question is whether in practice objective teleological interpretation plays a leading role and whether there is any space for subjective teleological interpretation.

Before delving into the case law analysis, it is important to recall from section 4.3.2 an aspect that is relevant as a background to the analysis of teleological interpretation at the ECtHR. It has already been pointed out that in addition to the characterization of the Convention as a system for the protection of human rights, the ECtHR has also characterized the Convention as a 'law-making treaty'.[7] That entails, according to the ECtHR, seeking 'the interpretation that is most appropriate in order to realize the aim and achieve the object of the treaty, not that which would restrict to the greatest possible degree the obligations undertaken by the Parties'.[8] As a result of this characterization, exceptions to the Convention have to be interpreted in a restricted manner.[9] This characterization also increases the importance of teleo-

6 See section 5.1.1.

7 ECtHR, *Wemhoff v. Germany*, judgment of 27 June 1968, *Series* A No. 7, § 8; ECtHR, *Golder v. United Kingdom*, judgment of 21 February 1975, *Series* A No. 18, § 36. See for example section 4.3.2 as well.

8 ECtHR, *Wemhoff v. Germany*, judgment of 27 June 1968, *Series* A No. 7, § 8.

9 See for example: ECtHR (GC), *Pellegrin v. France*, judgment of 8 December 1999, *Reports* 1999-VIII, § 64; ECtHR (GC), *Demir and Baykara v. Turkey*, judgment of 12 November 2008, *unpublished*, § 146. See among others: Vande Lanotte (2005), p. 183.

logical interpretation in the context of the ECtHR, which is important as a background for the following analysis.

In the theoretical chapter on teleological interpretation, several questions have been identified that should be answered on the basis of the case law analysis. By doing so, more in-depth information can be provided as to its legitimacy and its actual use by the ECtHR. The following questions will be addressed hereinafter: How has teleological interpretation been identified in the cases (section 9.1)? What is meant when the ECtHR refers to the object and purpose (section 9.2)? How are they established (section 9.3)? What role does this method play in the interpretation process (section 9.4)? And what is its relation with other interpretative aids (section 9.5)?

9.1 How can this method of interpretation be recognized?

There are different ways to recognize teleological reasoning in the judgments of the ECtHR or even in judgments in general. Referring to the 'object and purpose' of either a provision or a Convention in general, is the dominant form used to refer to teleological interpretation.[10] The ECtHR fits this general description perfectly; many cases where some form of teleological interpretation can be detected do indeed contain references to the 'object and purpose' of the Convention.[11]

10 See Chapter 5 on the theoretical analysis of teleological interpretation.

11 ECtHR, *Soering v. United Kingdom*, judgment of 7 July 1989, *Series* A No. 161, § 87; ECtHR, *James and others v. United Kingdom*, judgment of 21 February 1986, *Series* A No. 98, § 42; ECtHR, *Golder v. United Kingdom*, judgment of 21 February 1975, *Series* A No. 18, § 34-36; ECtHR, *Öztürk v. Germany*, judgment of 21 February 1984, *Series* A No. 73, § 49-50; ECtHR, *Johnston and others v. Ireland*, judgment of 18 December 1986, *Series* A No. 112, § 51-52; ECtHR, *Engel and others v. the Netherlands*, judgment of 8 June 1976, *Series* A No. 22, § 81; ECtHR, *König v. Germany*, judgment of 28 June 1978, *Series* A No. 27, § 88-89; ECtHR, *Loizidou v. Turkey (preliminary objections)*, judgment of 23 March 1995, *Series* A No. 310, § 62, 72, 73, 75, 88, 89; ECtHR, *Wemhoff v. Germany*, judgment of 27 June 1968, *Series* A No. 7, § 8; ECtHR, *Witold Litwa v. Poland*, judgment of 4 April 2000, *Reports* 2000-III, § 61; ECtHR, *Case "Relating to certain aspects of the laws on the use of languages in education in Belgium" v. Belgium*, judgment of 23 July 1968, *Series* A No. 6, § 3-6; ECtHR (GC), *Öneryildiz v. Turkey*, judgment of 30 November 2004, *Reports* 2004-XII, § 69, 124; ECtHR (GC), *Chassagnou and others v. France*, judgment of 29 April 1999, *Reports* 1999-III, § 100; ECtHR (GC), *Mamatkulov and Askarov v. Turkey*, judgment of 4 February 2005, *Reports* 2005-I, § 101, 108, 123; ECtHR (GC), *Bosphorus HavaYollari Turizm Ve Ticaret Anonim Śirketi v. Ireland*, judgment of 30 June 2005, *Reports* 2005-VI, § 154; ECtHR (GC), *Kudla v. Poland*, judgment of 26 October 2000, *Reports* 2000-XI, § 152; ECtHR (GC), *Ferrazzini v. Italy*, judgment of 12 July 2001, Reports 2001-VII, § 24; ECtHR (GC), *Martinie v. France*, judgment of 12 April 2006, Reports 2006-VI, § 30; ECtHR (GC), *Saadi v. United Kingdom*, judgment of 29 January 2008, *unpublished*, § 62-63-66; ECtHR (GC), *Jussila v. Finland*, judgment of 23 November 2006, *unpublished*, § 36; ECtHR (GC), *Stoll v. Switzerland*, judgment of 10 December 2007, *unpublished*, § 60; ECtHR (GC), *Banković and others v. Belgium and others*, decision of 12 December 2001, *Reports*

One of the first cases where reference was made by the ECtHR to the 'object and purpose' was *Golder*.[12] In this judgment the ECtHR had to determine whether Article 6 of the Convention contained a right of access to courts or tribunals, since this is not explicitly mentioned in the article itself. Before the Court elaborately answered that question, it first clarified its interpretative approach by referring to the Vienna Convention on the Law of Treaties (VCLT). The Convention being a codification of 'generally accepted principles of international law', the Court considered that its interpretation should be guided by the rules of the VCLT as laid down in Articles 31 to 33.[13] Without expressly referring to the particular article from the VCLT,[14] the European Court did refer literally to the text of Article 31(1) of the VCLT when justifying its interpretative approach to Article 6, which included a reference to teleological interpretation.

> This is not an extensive interpretation forcing new obligations on the Contracting States: it is based on the very terms of the first sentence of Article 6 para. 1 read in its context and having regard to the object and purpose of the Convention.[15]

The Court seems to have included the indirect reference to Article 31 of the VCLT to provide a legitimate or at least a generally accepted framework for its interpretation process, which could serve as a starting point for its own interpretative approach. On later occasions the Court repeated its reference to the rules from the VCLT by stating that it would interpret a certain provision or phrase "in their context and in light of its object and purpose".[16]

2001-XII, § 56; ECtHR (GC), *Stec and others v. United Kingdom*, decision of 6 July 2005, *Reports* 2005-X, § 53; ECtHR (GC), *Ilaşcu and others v. Moldova and Russia*, decision of 4 July 2001, *unpublished*; ECtHR (GC), *Maaouia v. France*, judgment of 5 October 2000, *Reports* 2000-X, § 38; ECtHR (GC), *Pellegrin v. France*, judgment of 8 December 1999, *Reports* 1999-VIII, § 64; ECtHR, *Marckx v. Belgium*, judgment of 13 June 1979, *Series* A No. 31, § 31.

12 ECtHR, *Golder v. United Kingdom*, judgment of 21 February 1975, *Series* A No. 18; in ECtHR, *Ringeisen v. Austria*, judgment of 16 July 1971, *Series* A No. 13, reference was made to object and purpose by dissent.

13 ECtHR, *Golder v. United Kingdom*, judgment of 21 February 1975, *Series* A No. 18, § 29. For the text of the provisions, see supra note 198 and 201.

14 As has been noted the Court at the beginning of its reasoning referred to the relevant articles from the VCLT and declared that it would be guided by them.

15 ECtHR, *Golder v. United Kingdom*, judgment of 21 February 1975, *Series* A No. 18, § 36.

16 ECtHR (GC), *Demir and Baykara v. Turkey*, judgment of 12 November 2008, *unpublished*, § 65; ECtHR, *Rantsev v. Cyprus and Russia*, judgment of 7 January 2010, *unpublished*, § 273-274; ECtHR, *Johnston and others v. Ireland*, judgment of 18 December 1986, *Series* A No. 112, § 51; ECtHR, *Loizidou v. Turkey (preliminary objections)*, judgment of 23 March 1995, *Series* A No. 310, § 73; ECtHR (GC), *Banković and others v. Belgium and others*, decision of 12 December 2001, *Reports* 2001-XII, § 55; ECtHR (GC), *Mamatkulov and Askarov v. Turkey*, judgment of 4 February 2005,

On many occasions after the *Golder* judgment the Court referred to the object and purpose without explicitly basing itself on the VCLT.[17] This difference appears to have no influence on the application of the teleological method, which is understandable as the reference to the VCLT mainly seems to have been made in order to introduce the interpretation methods mentioned in those provisions into the Convention framework. The reference to the VCLT thus only serves as a basis for relying on teleological interpretation.

Another indication that teleological interpretation has been used is a reference to the 'aim' of a provision or Convention. While less frequent, the Court applies this term in its case law as well. Good examples can be found in sections such as the following ones:

> To determine the scope of the "right to education", within the meaning of the first sentence of Article 2 of the Protocol, the Court must bear in mind the aim of this provision.[18]

Reports 2005-I, § 123; ECtHR (GC), *Saadi v. United Kingdom*, judgment of 29 January 2008, *unpublished*, § 62; ECtHR, *Witold Litwa v. Poland*, judgment of 4 April 2000, *Reports* 2000-III, § 59.

17 ECtHR, *Soering v. United Kingdom*, judgment of 7 July 1989, *Series* A No. 161, § 87; ECtHR, *James and others v. United Kingdom*, judgment of 21 February 1986, *Series* A No. 98, § 42; ECtHR, *Öztürk v. Germany*, judgment of 21 February 1984, *Series* A No. 73, § 49-50; ECtHR, *Engel and others v. the Netherlands*, judgment of 8 June 1976, *Series* A No. 22, § 81; ECtHR, *König v. Germany*, judgment of 28 June 1978, *Series* A No. 27, § 88-89; ECtHR, *Wemhoff v. Germany*, judgment of 27 June 1968, *Series* A No. 7, § 8; ECtHR, *Case "Relating to certain aspects of the laws on the use of languages in education in Belgium" v. Belgium*, judgment of 23 July 1968, *Series* A No. 6, § 3-6; ECtHR (GC), *Öneryildiz v. Turkey*, judgment of 30 November 2004, *Reports* 2004-XII, § 69-124; ECtHR (GC), *Chassagnou and others v. France*, judgment of 29 April 1999, *Reports* 1999-III, § 100; ECtHR (GC), *Bosphorus HavaYollari Turizm Ve Ticaret Anonim Śirketi v. Ireland*, judgment of 30 June 2005, *Reports* 2005-VI, § 154; ECtHR (GC), *Kudla v. Poland*, judgment of 26 October 2000, *Reports* 2000-XI,§ 152; ECtHR (GC), *Ferrazzini v. Italy*, judgment of 12 July 2001, Reports 2001-VII, § 24; ECtHR (GC), *Martinie v. France*, judgment of 12 April 2006, Reports 2006-VI, § 30; ECtHR (GC), *Saadi v. United Kingdom*, judgment of 29 January 2008, *unpublished*, § 62-63-66; ECtHR (GC), *Jussila v. Finland*, judgment of 23 November 2006, *unpublished*, § 36; ECtHR (GC), *Stoll v. Switzerland*, judgment of 10 December 2007, *unpublished*, § 60; ECtHR (GC), *Stec and others v. United Kingdom*, decision of 6 July 2005, *Reports* 2005-X, § 53; ECtHR (GC), *Ilaşcu and others v. Moldova and Russia*, decision of 4 July 2001, *unpublished*, p. 17; ECtHR (GC), *Maaouia v. France*, judgment of 5 October 2000, *Reports* 2000-X, § 38; ECtHR (GC), *Pellegrin v. France*, judgment of 8 December 1999, *Reports* 1999-VIII, § 64; ECtHR, *Marckx v. Belgium*, judgment of 13 June 1979, *Series* A No. 31, § 31.

18 ECtHR, *Case "Relating to certain aspects of the laws on the use of languages in education in Belgium" v. Belgium*, judgment of 23 July 1968, *Series* A No. 6, § B.3.

> The inequality between Contracting States which the permissibility of such qualified acceptances might create would, moreover, run counter to the aim, as expressed in the Preamble to the Convention ... .[19]

The terminology the Court uses to refer to the aim of a provision is somewhat different from cases where express reference is made to the object and purpose, but in principle it appears to stand for the same thing. Aim or purpose, as well as the well-known term of 'object and purpose' both refer to the goal that the Convention or a provision is designed to achieve.

Teleological interpretation can finally be seen in cases where reference is made to the "spirit", "essence" or "underlying principles" of the Convention or one of its provisions, as in the following examples:

> Extradition in such circumstances, while not explicitly referred to in the brief and general wording of Article 3, would plainly be contrary to the spirit and intendment of the Article (..).[20]

> The very essence of the Convention is respect for human dignity and human freedom.[21]

> However it flows from the very essence of this procedural right that it must be open to individuals to complain of alleged infringements of it in Convention proceedings.[22]

> Although no previous case has established as such any right to self-determination as being contained in Article 8 of the Convention, the Court considers that the notion of personal autonomy is an important principle underlying the interpretation of its guarantees.[23]

These quotations indicate that the Court took into account the underlying values or principles that the Convention or a specific provision aims to protect. It will construct the right in question in such a manner that it respects the underlying values of the provision.

---

19 ECtHR, *Loizidou v. Turkey (preliminary objections)*, judgment of 23 March 1995, *Series* A No. 310, § 77.

20 ECtHR, *Soering v. United Kingdom*, judgment of 7 July 1989, *Series* A No. 161, § 88. See also § 87. ECtHR (GC), *Ilaşcu and others v. Moldova and Russia*, decision of 4 July 2001, *unpublished*, p. 16.

21 ECtHR, *Pretty v. United Kingdom*, judgment of 29 April 2002, *Reports* 2002-III, § 65.

22 ECtHR, *Cruz Varas and others v. Sweden*, judgment of 20 March 1991, *Series* A No. 201, § 99. Reference to the essence of a right has also been made in ECtHR (GC), *Christine Goodwin v. United Kingdom*, judgment of 11 July 2002, *Reports* 2002-VI, § 99 and 101 and ECtHR (GC), *I v. United Kingdom*, judgment of 11 July 2002, *Reports* 2002-VI, § 79 and 81.

23 ECtHR, *Pretty v. United Kingdom*, judgment of 29 April 2002, *Reports* 2002-III, § 61.

In some cases teleological interpretation is used at a different level in the interpretative framework. Earlier in this thesis reference was made to meta-teleological interpretation.[24] This term refers to interpretative principles of which the use is justified by reference to the object and purpose of the Convention as a whole. This is a more abstract form of using teleological interpretation, because teleological interpretation is used to justify another interpretative aid and not a particular interpretation of a Convention provision. This form of teleological interpretation is visible in those cases where reference is made to the need to interpret the Convention in a practical and effective manner. The Court claims that this practical and effective approach to interpretation follows from the object and purpose of the Convention:

> The Convention is intended to guarantee not rights that are theoretical and illusory but rights that are practical and effective.[25]
>
> Taking the parties' arguments as a whole, the Court reiterates, firstly, that its approach to the interpretation of Article 2 is guided by the idea that the object and purpose of the Convention as an instrument for the protection of individual human beings requires its provisions to be interpreted and applied in such a way to make its safeguards practical and effective.[26]
>
> Interpretation in these cases thus entails a reference to a teleological view on the Convention as a whole and can be identified by a reference to the need to interpret the Convention in a practical and effective manner.[27]

All these indicators have been taken into account when analyzing in which cases the Court employs a teleological method of interpretation.[28] On the basis of these indica-

24 See sections 4.1., 4.3.2. and 4.4.2.1.

25 ECtHR, *Airey v. Ireland*, judgment of 9 October 1979, *Series* A No. 32, § 24

26 ECtHR (GC), *Öneryildiz v. Turkey*, judgment of 30 November 2004, *Reports* 2004-XII, § 69.

27 See for a similar approach also: ECtHR (GC), *Micallef v. Malta*, judgment of 15 October 2009, *unpublished,* § 81; ECtHR, *Rantsev v. Cyprus and Russia*, judgment of 7 January 2010, *unpublished,* § 275; ECtHR (GC), *Demir and Baykara v. Turkey*, judgment of 12 November 2008, *unpublished,* § 66.

28 A category of cases that does not provide much insight into teleological interpretation and has therefore not been included in the list of categories is where the Court states that a certain act or right can be considered sufficient for the purpose of the Convention provision. The only indication for teleological interpretation is the fact that the word purpose is used, but for the rest there is no indication that teleological interpretation played any role in these cases. See among others: ECtHR, *Rotaru v. Romania*, judgment of 4 May 2000, Reports 2000-V, § 38 and 44; ECtHR, *Gasus Dosier- und Fördertechnik GmbH v. the Netherlands*, judgment of 23 February 1995, *Series* A No. 306B, § 53; ECtHR, *Matos e Silva, Lda, and others v. Portugal*, judgment of 16 September 1996, *Reports* 1996-IV, § 75; ECtHR (GC), *Iatridis v. Greece*, judgment of 25 March 1999, *Reports* 1999-II, § 54; ECtHR (GC), *Beyeler v. Italy*, judgment of 5 January 2000, *Reports* 2000-I, § 100; ECtHR, *Tre Traktörer Aktiebolag v. Sweden*, judgment of 7 July 1989, *Series* A No. 159, § 53; ECtHR, *Gaygusuz v. Austria*,

tors the conclusion can be drawn that the Court indeed applied teleological interpretation in many cases. The difference in terminology seems to be based on linguistic choices and does not point to a different form of teleological interpretation. In order to keep matters clear when referring to teleological interpretation in this chapter, the terms 'object' and 'purpose' will be used, but this also includes cases where the Court, for example, refers to the 'aim' of the Convention or one of its provisions. The rest of the chapter will be dedicated to the actual use of this method by the Court.

9.2 What does the Court refer to when speaking about object and purpose?

A logical next step in the analysis of the Court's use of the teleological interpretation method is to uncover what the terms that have been identified above actually refer to. In other words, what does the Court refer to when it speaks about the 'object' or 'purpose' of the Convention or any of its provisions? The answer might be obvious at first hand, but the question actually concerns whether the reference is substantiated in any way by the Court. This only plays a role when the Court uses abstract indicators like object and purpose, spirit, aim, etc. In cases where the Court literally refers to underlying principles or values, the question whether the reference is substantiated does not play a role. After all, the reference to principles and values is already a substantive reference, as can be seen, for example, in the case of *Pretty*. In *Pretty* the Court held that 'the notion of personal autonomy is an important principle underlying the interpretation of the guarantees' of Article 8.[29] This type of case will thus not be addressed in this section. The focus will be on those cases where the reference of the Court to teleological interpretation through one of the indicators referred to above, is not readily substantiated.

On the basis of the analysis, two types of cases can be distinguished in which teleological interpretation is used. On the one hand there is a range of cases in which the teleological method of interpretation does not extend beyond a mere reference to the indicators.[30] On the other hand there is a whole set of cases where the reference

judgment of 16 September 1996, *Reports* 1996-IV, § 41; ECtHR, *Gillow v. United Kingdom*, judgment of 24 November 1986, *Series* A 109, § 46; ECtHR, *Buckley v. United Kingdom*, judgment of 25 September 1996, *Reports* 1996-IV, § 54; ECtHR, *Koua Poirrez v. France*, judgment of 30 September 2003, *Reports* 2003-X, § 37.

29 ECtHR, *Pretty v. United Kingdom*, judgment of 29 April 2002, *Reports* 2002-III, § 61.

30 ECtHR, *König v. Germany*, judgment of 28 June 1978, *Series* A No. 27, § 88-89; ECtHR (GC), *Ilaşcu and others v. Moldova and Russia*, decision of 4 July 2001, *unpublished*, p. 16-17; ECtHR, *Engel and others v. the Netherlands*, judgment of 8 June 1976, *Series* A No. 22, § 81; ECtHR, *Öztürk v. Germany*, judgment of 21 February 1984, *Series* A No. 73, § 49-50; ECtHR (GC), *Ferrazzini v. Italy*,

to object or purpose has been more or less substantiated.[31] In the former set of cases the use of these terms remains devoid of any substance and the reference seems to be merely there for rhetorical purposes. This can be illustrated by the following quotations from the Court's case law:

> To regard the imposition of such a duty as constituting in itself an interference with possessions for the purposes of Article 1 Protocol No. 1 would be giving the Article a far-reaching interpretation going beyond its object and purpose.[32]

> Moreover, regard being had to the object and purpose of the Convention, the responsibility of a Contracting Party may also arise when as a consequence of military action - whether lawful or unlawful - it exercises effective control of an area outside its national territory.[33]

In these cases the Court leaves the reader in doubt about the exact object and purpose of the Convention, while on face value they play some role in the interpretation process. This somewhat obscures the Court's reasoning on the provision in question,

---

judgment of 12 July 2001, Reports 2001-VII, § 24; ECtHR (GC), *Jussila v. Finland*, judgment of 23 November 2006, *unpublished*, § 36; ECtHR (GC), *Martinie v. France*, judgment of 12 April 2006, Reports 2006-VI, § 30; ECtHR (GC), *Pellegrin v. France*, judgment of 8 December 1999, *Reports* 1999-VIII, § 64; ECtHR, *Van der Mussele v. Belgium*, judgment of 23 November 1983, *Series* A No. 70, § 49; ECtHR, *Costello-Roberts v. United Kingdom*, judgment of 25 March 1993, *Series* A No. 247-C, § 36.

31 ECtHR (GC), *Saadi v. United Kingdom*, judgment of 29 January 2008, *unpublished*, § 63, 66; ECtHR, *Case "Relating to certain aspects of the laws on the use of languages in education in Belgium" v. Belgium*, judgment of 23 July 1968, *Series* A No. 6, § B5, 6, 8; ECtHR, *Soering v. United Kingdom*, judgment of 7 July 1989, *Series* A No. 161, § 87, 88; ECtHR, *Loizidou v. Turkey (preliminary objections)*, judgment of 23 March 1995, *Series* A No. 310, § 72, 73, 75, 77; ECtHR, *Witold Litwa v. Poland*, judgment of 4 April 2000, *Reports* 2000-III, § 59, 61; ECtHR (GC), *Mamatkulov and Askarov v. Turkey*, judgment of 4 February 2005, *Reports* 2005-I, § 101; ECtHR (GC), *Chassagnou and others v. France*, judgment of 29 April 1999, *Reports* 1999-III, § 100; ECtHR (GC), *Stoll v. Switzerland*, judgment of 10 December 2007, *unpublished*, § 60-61; ECtHR (GC), *Kudla v. Poland*, judgment of 26 October 2000, *Reports* 2000-XI, § 152; ECtHR, *Johnston and others v. Ireland*, judgment of 18 December 1986, *Series* A No. 112, § 52; ECtHR, *James and others v. United Kingdom*, judgment of 21 February 1986, *Series* A No. 98, § 42; ECtHR, *Golder v. United Kingdom*, judgment of 21 February 1975, *Series* A No. 18, § 34; ECtHR, *Marckx v. Belgium*, judgment of 13 June 1979, *Series* A No. 31, § 31; ECtHR (GC), *Öneryildiz v. Turkey*, judgment of 30 November 2004, *Reports* 2004-XII, § 69; ECtHR, *Niemietz v. Germany*, judgment of 16 December 1992, *Series* A No. 251-B, § 31; ECtHR, *Futro v. Poland*, decision of 12 December 2000, *unpublished*, § 3.

32 ECtHR, *Van der Mussele v. Belgium*, judgment of 23 November 1983, *Series* A No. 70, § 49. In this case the question arose whether the fact that a duty prescribed by law can involve a certain outlay for the person bound to perform constituted an interference with the possessions of that person.

33 ECtHR (GC), *Ilaşcu and others v. Moldova and Russia*, decision of 4 July 2001, *unpublished*, p. 17. In this case the Court had to answer the question whether Russia could be held responsible for violations of the Convention in Transdniestria in Moldova.

since a particular interpretation is then based on an object and purpose that have not explicitly been identified. Moreover, the exact function of the teleological interpretation in this type of case is unclear. When analyzing these cases it is not possible to assess whether teleological interpretation was actually considered to be relevant in determining the meaning of a Convention notion. For the purpose of this chapter, namely analyzing the use and role of the teleological method, this type of case is therefore not particularly helpful. A more elaborate discussion of the consequences and desirability of this way of using teleological interpretation will follow in the conclusion of this chapter. For now the focus will be on the second category of cases, i.e. the cases where the Court does provide some insight into the use of this method.

Fortunately, the Court has in the majority of cases put some flesh on the references to the teleological method.[34] This provides much more insight into the way the Court incorporates this method into its reasoning. Again, this collection of cases can be divided into two types. First, there are cases where the Court confines itself to the provision in question. As can be seen from the examples below, the underpinnings are still rather thin, but at least there is some elaboration on the meaning of the object and purpose of the Convention provision.

> The Court, like the Commission, considers that such an interpretation best reconciles the language of the English and French texts, having regard to the object and purpose of Article 1 Protocol 1, which is primarily to guard against the arbitrary confiscation of property.[35]

> [T]he Court emphasizes that such detention must be compatible with the overall purpose of Article 5, which is to safeguard the right to liberty and ensure that no-one should be dispossessed of his or her liberty in an arbitrary fashion.[36]

> According to the express terms of Article 8 of the Convention, "everyone has the right to respect for his private life and family life, his home and correspondence". This provision by itself in no way guarantees either a right to education or a personal right of parents relating to the education of their children: its object is essentially that of protecting the individual against arbitrary interference by the public authorities in his private family life.[37]

Even though this does not seem like a very elaborate account of the object or purpose of the provision at hand, these references are helpful for unravelling the meaning of the teleological method in the Court's case law. After all, with these short explanations the Court provides the reader with indications as to the frame of reference from which

34 Supra note 31.

35 ECtHR, *James and others v. United Kingdom*, judgment of 21 February 1986, *Series* A No. 98, § 42.

36 ECtHR (GC), *Saadi v. United Kingdom*, judgment of 29 January 2008, *unpublished*, § 66.

37 ECtHR, *Case "Relating to certain aspects of the laws on the use of languages in education in Belgium" v. Belgium*, judgment of 23 July 1968, *Series* A No. 6, § B7.

it approached the interpretative problem. Already such a short elaboration sets some boundaries for the interpretative process; by invoking this teleological insight the Court indicates that it will stay within these limits when interpreting the provision. By doing so it provides some guidance to the national authorities as well, since it indicates in which direction the Court will look for an answer to the interpretative problem. This makes it easier to see which role the teleological method played in the final interpretation – a point that will be addressed more elaborately below.

In many cases the Court furthermore deals with the object or purpose of the Convention as a whole. This almost automatically results in much more general explanations of the object or purpose of the Convention:

> In addition, any interpretation of the rights and freedoms guaranteed has to be consistent with the general spirit of the Convention, an instrument designed to maintain and promote the ideals and values of a democratic society.[38]
>
> The object and purpose of the Convention as an instrument for the protection of individual human beings require that its provisions be interpreted and applied so as to make its safeguards practical and effective, as part of the system of individual applications.[39]
>
> If Contracting States were able, at their discretion, by classifying an association as "public" or "para-administrative", to remove it from the scope of Article 11, that would give them such latitude that it might lead to results incompatible with the object and purpose of the Convention, which is to protect rights that are not theoretical or illusory but practical and effective.[40]
>
> Given that it is a law-making treaty, it is also necessary to seek the interpretation that is most appropriate in order to realize the aim and achieve the object of the treaty, not that which would restrict to the greatest possible degree the obligations undertaken by the Parties.[41]

These examples show that, on a very general level, the meaning of the object or purpose of the Convention provides a frame of reference for the interpretation of the Convention provisions as well. In contrast with the type of case where the object and purpose of a certain Convention *provision* are discussed, the framework in the cases discussed here is extremely wide and hardly provides any substantive information as to the interpretative process. The added value of this teleological element should be sought at a 'meta-level', where it may serve as a justification for the application

38 ECtHR, *Soering v. United Kingdom*, judgment of 7 July 1989, *Series* A No. 161, § 87.

39 ECtHR (GC), *Mamatkulov and Askarov v. Turkey*, judgment of 4 February 2005, *Reports* 2005-I, § 101.

40 ECtHR (GC), *Chassagnou and others v. France*, judgment of 29 April 1999, *Reports* 1999-III, § 100.

41 ECtHR, *Wemhoff v. Germany*, judgment of 27 June 1968, *Series* A No. 7, § 8.

of other interpretative aids.[42] In addition, by referring to the object and purpose of the Convention as a whole, the Court is granted an opportunity to show the Contracting States that it is not straying its own competence, but that this approach to the Convention rights is inherent to the Convention. Reference to the object and purpose of the Convention can as such be a way for the Court to indicate that its approach was intended by the parties when accepting the Convention. To some extent this is visible in the final three quotations that have been provided above. Referencing to the object and purpose in this manner might make some interpretations more acceptable to the Contracting States. The question is whether this argument still holds when the Court relies on an evolutive interpretation of the object and purpose of the Convention, but that will be discussed in the following section.

9.3 How does the Court establish the object and purpose or underlying values?

In the process of analyzing the Court's use of teleological interpretation, one of the most important aspects is the manner in which the Court establishes the object or purpose. How does the Court determine the object of a certain provision or its underlying values? To answer this question it is not necessary to retain the distinction made above between the different types of case. The only set of cases that will not be discussed here, is the set in which the Court has not substantiated the reference to teleological arguments. In all other cases the question of how the Court determined its teleological viewpoint is a highly interesting one.

Different elements deserve attention in this regard. In the theoretical chapter on the teleological method of interpretation these aspects have been identified. Important questions that have arisen as a result of the theoretical discussion are: whether the Court invokes the subjective or objective purpose of the Convention or one of its provisions and which documents the Court refers to when establishing the object or underlying values of the Convention or the fundamental rights it protects. These two aspects will be discussed in this section and should provide an overview of the Court's approach; in addition, the role of a number of different factors that have been found in examining the court's case law will be discussed.

9.3.1 Objective or subjective intention?

It should be recalled that the significance of the teleological method has been discussed in the theoretical chapter. This discussion revealed that the underlying justification for teleological reasoning is that it is assumed that legislating is a rational and pur-

42 See Lasser (2004), p. 206-208 and section 4.1.

posive activity. Interpreting the legislative text, in this case the Convention, should not lead to defeating the purpose of the legislative text.[43] Instead it should try to interpret the provision in such a way that it respects the purpose of the legislative text at hand. This raises the question which purpose should be sought after: the subjective purpose of the original legislator or drafter, or the objective purpose of a rational legislator? As has been explained in section 5.1.3, there is no right or wrong answer to this question; it appeared from the theoretical literature that it depends on one's perspective which approach is being favoured. However, in practice it makes quite some difference which perspective is taken and therefore it is interesting to discover which purpose the Strasbourg Court tries to respect.

In the majority of cases the Court seems to take into account the objective purpose of the Convention or the provision at hand.[44] The Court in these cases does not pay any attention or at least does not grant any weight to the intention of the drafters of the Convention. This lack of any reference to the purpose of the drafters of the Convention supports the conclusion that the Court has taken an objective perspective of the purpose of the Convention and its provisions. Examples of the use of an objective purpose can be seen in quotations such as these:

> Furthermore, private life, in the Court's view, includes a person's physical and psychological integrity; the guarantee afforded by Article 8 of the Convention is primarily intended to ensure the development, without outside interference, of the personality of each individual in his relations with other human beings. There is therefore a zone of interaction of a person with others, even in a public context, which may fall within the scope of 'private life'.[45]

---

43 See section 5.1.1.

44 ECtHR (GC), *Mamatkulov and Askarov v. Turkey*, judgment of 4 February 2005, *Reports* 2005-I; ECtHR, *Soering v. United Kingdom*, judgment of 7 July 1989, *Series* A No. 161; ECtHR (GC), *Öneryildiz v. Turkey*, judgment of 30 November 2004, *Reports* 2004-XII; ECtHR (GC), *Chassagnou and others v. France*, judgment of 29 April 1999, *Reports* 1999-III; ECtHR, *Witold Litwa v. Poland*, judgment of 4 April 2000, *Reports* 2000-III; ECtHR, *Case "Relating to certain aspects of the laws on the use of languages in education in Belgium" v. Belgium*, judgment of 23 July 1968, *Series* A No. 6, § B7; ECtHR, *Marckx v. Belgium*, judgment of 13 June 1979, *Series* A No. 31; ECtHR, *Niemietz v. Germany*, judgment of 16 December 1992, *Series* A No. 251-B, § 31; ECtHR (GC), *Saadi v. United Kingdom*, judgment of 29 January 2008, *unpublished*; ECtHR, *Golder v. United Kingdom*, judgment of 21 February 1975, *Series* A No. 18; ECtHR, *Wemhoff v. Germany*, judgment of 27 June 1968, *Series* A No. 7; ECtHR (GC), *Osman v. United Kingdom*, judgment of 28 October 1998, *Reports* 1998-VIII, § 116; ECtHR, *P.G. and J.H. v. United Kingdom*, judgment of 25 September 2001, *Reports* 2001-IX, § 56-60; ECtHR, *Von Hannover v. Germany*, judgment of 24 June 2004, *Reports* 2004-VII, § 50-53; ECtHR, *Pretty v. United Kingdom*, judgment of 29 April 2002, *Reports* 2002-III, § 61; ECtHR, *Botta v. Italy*, judgment of 24 February 1998, *Reports* 1998-I, § 32; ECtHR, *Futro v. Poland*, decision of 12 December 2000, *unpublished*, § 3.

45 ECtHR, *Von Hannover v. Germany*, judgment of 24 June 2004, *Reports* 2004-VII, § 50.

> Although no previous case has established as such any right to self-determination as being contained in Article 8 of the Convention, the Court considers that the notion of personal autonomy is an important principle underlying the interpretation of its guarantees.[46]

In these cases the Court clearly refrained from making any reference to the original purpose of the drafters. On rare occasions the Court has even explicitly ignored the subjective approach and preferred the objective approach, as in the case of *Sigurdur A. Sigurjónsson v. Iceland*.[47] This case concerned the question whether a taxi driver could be obliged to be a member of a professional association. The ECtHR had to determine whether this constituted a violation of Article 11 (the right to freedom of association and assembly). In order to answer this question the ECtHR had to determine whether Article 11 also included a right not to be associated. The respondent government argued that Article 11 did indeed include a right not to be associated, but this right was rather limited in their view. They supported their argument by referring to an earlier judgment in the case of *Young, James and Webster v. United Kingdom*.[48] In that case it had cited the *travaux préparatoires*, which 'showed that a general rule, modelled on Article 20 para. 2 of the 1948 United Nations Universal Declaration of Human Rights, that no one may be compelled to belong to an association, had deliberately been omitted from the Convention'.[49] If this was deliberately omitted by the drafters, so the argument by the respondent government went, then Article 11 should not be interpreted in such a broad manner as to render this passage nugatory. The ECtHR dismissed this argument by recalling that the precedent in which the *travaux préparatoires* were cited, did not attach decisive weight to the *travaux préparatoires*. It subsequently concluded that a negative right to association, i.e. the right not to be a member of an association, indeed fell within the scope of Article 11. What is interesting about this case is that the Court in *Young, James and Webster* established only a limited version of a negative right under Article 11. In *Sigurdur* the Court went further and adopted the right which had been deliberately omitted. The subjective intention of the drafters of the Convention was thus explicitly ignored in this case.

The conclusion that the Court mainly adheres to an objective teleological approach is also supported by the fact that the Court has regularly adopted an evolutive approach in its interpretation process. This evolutive approach assumes that the Convention should be interpreted according to present-day conditions and not the conditions at the time of drafting of the Convention. This approach is clearly in contradiction with

46 ECtHR, *Pretty v. United Kingdom*, judgment of 29 April 2002, *Reports* 2002-III, § 61.
47 ECtHR, *Sigurdur A. Sigurjónsson v. Iceland*, judgment of 30 June 1993, *Series* A No. 264.
48 ECtHR, *Young James and Webster v. United Kingdom*, judgment of 13 August 1981, *Series* A No. 44.
49 ECtHR, *Sigurdur A. Sigurjónsson v. Iceland*, judgment of 30 June 1993, *Series* A No. 264, § 33.

the approach that aims to discover the subjective purpose of the Convention. Chapter 11 will deal with evolutive interpretation and its role in the Court's case law. The present purpose was to indicate that this might be one of the reasons why the Court in its teleological reasoning not often considers the subjective purpose of the Convention.

As has already been hinted at above, there is a small number of cases in which the Court does take the subjective intentions of the drafting states into account.[50] Sometimes reference is made to the *travaux préparatoires* when establishing the object and purpose. In other cases reference is made to the intentions of the drafting Contracting States without explicitly discussing the *travaux préparatoires*. Examples of both uses of the *travaux* can be found in the following quotations:

> The object of Article 13, as emerges from the *travaux préparatoires*, is to provide a means whereby individuals can obtain relief at national level for violations of their Convention rights before having to set in motion the international machinery of complaint before the Court.[51]
>
> One reason why the signatory Governments decided to 'take the first steps for the collective enforcement of certain of the Rights stated in the Universal Declaration' was their profound belief in the rule of law.[52]

In these cases the Court clearly tries to invoke the purpose of the original legislator and use that purpose as a frame of reference for interpretation in these individual cases. It is interesting to know why in these cases the Court resorts to the subjective teleological approach. Unfortunately, in none of these cases does the Court provide any clues to answer this question. In *Johnston* the Court had to address the question whether Article 12 included not only the right to marry, but also the right to divorce. The *travaux préparatoires* were helpful for the Court's final interpretation, since they

---

50 ECtHR, *Golder v United Kingdom*, judgment of 21 February 1975, Series A No. 18; ECtHR (GC), *Kudla v. Poland*, judgment of 26 October 2000, *Reports* 2000-XI; ECtHR, *Johnston and others v. Ireland*, judgment of 18 December 1986, *Series* A No. 112; ECtHR, *Case "Relating to certain aspects of the laws on the use of languages in education in Belgium" v. Belgium*, judgment of 23 July 1968, *Series* A No. 6, § B5,6; ECtHR (GC), *Banković and others v. Belgium and others*, decision of 12 December 2001, Reports 2001-VII, § 19-21, 58, 63 and 65; ECtHR, *Soering v. United Kingdom*, judgment of 7 July 1989, *Series* A No. 161, § 103; ECtHR, *Loizidou v. Turkey (preliminary objections)*, judgment of 23 March 1995, *Series* A No. 310, § 71, where the ECtHR did hold that the intention of the drafters should not be the sole argument taken into account.

51 ECtHR (GC), *Kudla v. Poland*, judgment of 26 October 2000, *Reports* 2000-XI, § 152. A similar consideration can be found in ECtHR, *Johnston and others v. Ireland*, judgment of 18 December 1986, *Series* A No. 112, § 52: "Moreover, the foregoing interpretation of Article 12 is consistent with the object and purpose as revealed by the travaux préparatoires."

52 ECtHR, *Golder v United Kingdom*, judgment of 21 February 1975, Series A No. 18, § 34.

revealed that the drafters explicitly excluded a right to divorce. The *travaux préparatoires* in this case supported the textual interpretation. The same can be said for the *Belgian Linguistic* case in which the reference to the *travaux préparatoires* supported the textual considerations as well, as is evidenced by the following paragraphs:

> The second sentence of Article 2 of the Protocol does not guarantee a right to education; this is clearly shown by its wording. The second sentence of Article 2 of the Protocol does not guarantee a right to education; this is clearly shown by its wording:
>
> '... In the exercise of any functions which it assumes in relation to education and to teaching, the State shall respect the right of parents to ensure such education and teaching in conformity with their own religious and philosophical convictions.'
>
> This provision does not require of States that they should, in the sphere of education or teaching, respect parents' linguistic preferences, but only their religious and philosophical convictions. To interpret the terms 'religious' and 'philosophical' as covering linguistic preferences would amount to a distortion of their ordinary and usual meaning and to read into the Convention something which is not there. Moreover the 'preparatory work' confirms that the object of the second sentence of Article 2 was in no way to secure respect by the State of a right for parents to have education conducted in a language other than that of the country in question.

It can, however, not be derived from this that the Court tends to resort to the subjective intentions of the drafters if it wants to justify a strictly textual or narrow interpretation. In *Kudla* the reference to the *travaux préparatoires* simply seems to support the whole argument of the Court, rather than only a specific reading of the text of the provision.[53] In that case the Court employed the subjective approach to find extra support in general and the *travaux préparatoires* could afford this support. This approach is difficult to explain since these cases are not exceptionally controversial, nor are they in any other way different from the cases where the Court opted for an objective teleological approach. For example, in *Pretty* the Court had to address a similar type of interpretative question to the one in *Johnston*. Here the question was whether Article 2 included the right to die, which is exactly the opposite of the right to life. In this case the Court did not call upon the *travaux préparatoires*, but it stuck to a mainly textual interpretation and concluded that this right could not be considered to be included in the article. While the situations are not the same, the interpretative problem presented by the cases was similar, making it difficult to understand why the Court adopted a different approach in both types of case. An explanation could be that the *travaux préparatoires* in the case of *Johnston* (on Article 12) provided support for the Court, while the *travaux préparatoires* in the case of *Pretty* (on Article

53 ECtHR (GC), *Kudla v. Poland*, judgment of 26 October 2000, *Reports* 2000-XI, § 152:

2) did not. More likely, however, is that the Court just does not really apply a consistent approach towards the use of methods of interpretation and picks those methods which seem to be most convincing in the case at hand.

It might therefore be warranted to conclude that there is not really a coherent policy behind the reference to the objective or subjective purpose of the Convention. With very few clues from the Court itself it is hard to draw definite conclusions. Judging by the frequency of the cases in which the Court tries to find an objective purpose, it seems legitimate to conclude that the Court has a preference for the objective purpose, while at the same time it does not rule out the subjective approach.

9.3.2 Which documents play a role in establishing the subjective or objective purpose?

In cases where the Court has substantiated the reference to the object or purpose of the Convention or where the Court has referred to the underlying values of the provision of the Convention, the Court has sometimes supported its findings by making reference to specific documents. Already in *Golder* the Court stated that 'the preamble is generally very useful for the determination of the "object" and "purpose" of the Convention.'[54] In some others cases the preamble has been invoked in the same manner:

> The inequality between Contracting States which the permissibility of such qualified acceptances might create would, moreover, run counter to the aim, as expressed in the Preamble to the Convention, to achieve greater unity in the maintenance and further realization of human rights.[55]

> It would hardly be compatible with the underlying values of the Convention, that 'common heritage of political traditions, ideals, freedom and the rule of law' to which the Preamble refers, were a Contracting State knowingly to surrender a fugitive to another State where there were substantial grounds for believing that he would be in danger of being subjected to torture, however heinous the crime allegedly committed.[56]

In the case of *United Communist Party of Turkey*, the Court used the preamble in a more covert way to emphasize the importance of democracy throughout the whole Convention.[57] In the Court's view the preamble reflects the fundamental value of

---

54 ECtHR, *Golder v United Kingdom*, judgment of 21 February 1975, Series A No. 18, § 34.

55 ECtHR, *Loizidou v. Turkey (preliminary objections)*, judgment of 23 March 1995, *Series* A No. 310, § 77.

56 ECtHR, *Soering v. United Kingdom*, judgment of 7 July 1989, *Series* A No. 161, § 88.

57 ECtHR (GC), *United Communist Party of Turkey and others v. Turkey*, judgment of 30 January 1998, *Reports* 1998-I, § 25 refering to § 45.

democracy in the Convention context. It is the importance of democracy in the Convention that makes the protection of political parties fall within the scope of Article 11:

> Democracy is without doubt a fundamental feature of the European public order ... That is apparent, firstly, from the Preamble to the Convention, which establishes a very clear connection between the Convention and democracy by stating that the maintenance and further realization of human rights and fundamental freedoms are best ensured on the one hand by an effective political democracy and on the other by a common understanding and observance of human rights ... The Preamble goes on to affirm that European countries have a common heritage of political tradition, ideals, freedom and the rule of law. The Court has observed that in that common heritage are to be found the underlying values of the Convention ...; it has pointed out several times that the Convention was designed to maintain and promote the ideals and values of a democratic society ... .[58]

In the previous section, the *travaux préparatoires* have already been mentioned. These documents are only used in a small number of cases, namely when the Court tries to determine the subjective purpose of the Convention. What may be added to the discussion of this use in the previous section is that it might seem to be rather easy for the Court to refer to the *travaux préparatoires*, as if they constitute one clear document that reveals *the* purpose of the drafting states. In reality this is not the case and referring to the *travaux préparatoires* might be less transparent than it seems at first sight. There was not one single purpose of the original framers of the Convention and if the Court refers to the object as revealed by the *travaux préparatoires* this is still in many cases an interpretation of these materials by the Court.

The Court has made use of other documents in its reasoning as well. However, it usually does not do so in the context of teleological reasoning, but mainly in the context of comparative reasoning, which will be discussed in Chapter 10. In the teleological context the Court has really limited itself to the preamble and the *travaux préparatoires*.

The positive side of the references made to either the preamble or the *travaux préparatoires* is that the Court at least tried to legitimize how they determined the object or purpose or underlying value. In many cases the Court does not refer to any document at all, which makes it more difficult to understand where a particular object or value comes from.

58 ECtHR (GC), *United Communist Party of Turkey and others v. Turkey*, judgment of 30 January 1998, *Reports* 1998-I.

9.3.3 What other factors play a role in establishing the subjective or objective purpose?

The limited number of cases in which the Court seeks support from a document, like the preamble or *travaux préparatoires*, indicates that there have to be other factors that play a role for the Court when establishing the object and purpose of the Convention. At least, that would have to be the case if the Strasbourg Court wants to provide some insight into how it determines the object of the Convention or the underlying values of a certain provision. There are some judgments in which this is not really the case and where the reader is left in doubt about how the Court determined the purpose.[59] This lack of transparency makes it difficult for the reader to fully understand the logic of the Court's reasoning.

In many cases the Court, however, tries to increase the transparency of its reasoning by relying heavily on precedent in establishing the object and purpose of the Convention as a whole or of specific provisions.[60] Hereby the Court does provide some justification for construing the object or purpose in a certain way or for relying on a specific underlying value. The reference to precedents ensures continuity in the Court's approach. This is clearly visible in cases where the Court relies on the teleological justification for its practical and effective approach. In all these cases the Court refers to precedents that state the same:

---

59 ECtHR, *Pretty v. United Kingdom*, judgment of 29 April 2002, *Reports* 2002-III; ECtHR (GC), *Saadi v. United Kingdom*, judgment of 29 January 2008, *unpublished*; ECtHR, *Wemhoff v. Germany*, judgment of 27 June 1968, *Series* A No. 7; ECtHR, *James and others v. United Kingdom*, judgment of 21 February 1986, *Series* A No. 98.

60 ECtHR, *Loizidou v. Turkey (preliminary objections)*, judgment of 23 March 1995, *Series* A No. 310, § 72; ECtHR, *Witold Litwa v. Poland*, judgment of 4 April 2000, *Reports* 2000-III, § 60; ECtHR, *Niemietz v. Germany*, judgment of 16 December 1992, *Series* A No. 251-B, § 31; ECtHR, *Futro v. Poland*, decision of 12 December 2000, *unpublished*, § 3; ECtHR, *Soering v. United Kingdom*, judgment of 7 July 1989, *Series* A No. 161, § 87; ECtHR (GC), *Mamatkulov and Askarov v. Turkey*, judgment of 4 February 2005, *Reports* 2005-I, § 101; ECtHR (GC), *Öneryildiz v. Turkey*, judgment of 30 November 2004, *Reports* 2004-XII, § 69; ECtHR (GC), *Chassagnou and others v. France*, judgment of 29 April 1999, *Reports* 1999-III, § 100; ECtHR, *P.G. and J.H. v. United Kingdom*, judgment of 25 September 2001, *Reports* 2001-IX, § 56; ECtHR, *Stjerna v. Finland*, judgment of 25 November 1994, *Series* A No. 299-B, § 37; ECtHR, *Von Hannover v. Germany*, judgment of 24 June 2004, *Reports* 2004-VII, § 50; ECtHR, *Airey v. Ireland*, judgment of 9 October 1979, *Series* A No. 32, § 24; ECtHR (GC), *Osman v. United Kingdom*, judgment of 28 October 1998, *Reports* 1998-VIII, § 116; ECtHR, *Cruz Varas and others v. Sweden*, judgment of 20 March 1991, *Series* A No. 201, § 94; ECtHR, *Botta v. Italy*, judgment of 24 February 1998, *Reports* 1998-I, § 32; ECtHR, *Smirnova v. Russia*, judgment of 24 July 2003, *Reports* 2003-IX, § 95.

> [T]he object and purpose of the Convention as an instrument for the protection of individual human beings requires its provisions to be interpreted and applied in such a way as to make its safeguards practical and effective.[61]

In cases concerning specific provisions, such continuity is less obvious. Especially in cases concerning Article 8 the Court regularly relies on precedents. One needs to look carefully at the precedents that the Court refers to in order to check whether the precedent supports the Court's own reasoning or whether it indirectly expands the scope of the right in question. This 'danger' can be explained by the cases of *Pretty* and *Evans*. In the case of *Pretty* the Court stated that the 'notion of personal autonomy' was an important principle underlying Article 8 of the Convention.[62] In *Evans* the Court stated by referring to *Pretty* that Article 8 included a 'right to personal autonomy'.[63] The Court did not explain the seeming expansion in *Evans* and pretended that it arose directly from the *Pretty* case. It does not need much explanation why there is quite a difference between a notion and a right, and that the Court silently seems to have expanded the scope of Article 8 in this example. This can happen in more cases if the Court relies as heavily on precedents as it currently does.

9.4 Role of Teleological Interpretation in the Interpretation Process

The analysis discussed until now has already given some idea of the role of teleological interpretation, but this role still warrants some more in-depth analysis. The role of teleological interpretation in the interpretative reasoning of the Court is not easy to define. This could largely be the result of the fact that teleological interpretation plays different roles in the case law and it also does do so at different levels of abstraction. The ensuing discussion will explain the different roles and thus will complete the picture of teleological interpretation.

As has been explained in the theoretical part of this thesis, broadly three different functions can be distinguished for teleological interpretation. In some cases teleological interpretation functions as one of the arguments or as the sole argument in favour of a certain interpretation.[64] In other cases reference to teleological interpretation

61 ECtHR (GC), *Öneryildiz v. Turkey*, judgment of 30 November 2004, *Reports* 2004-XII, § 69.

62 ECtHR, *Pretty v. United Kingdom*, judgment of 29 April 2002, *Reports* 2002-III Pretty § 61.

63 ECtHR (GC), *Evans v. United Kingdom*, judgment of 10 April 2007, *unpublished*, § 71.

64 See: ECtHR (GC), *United Communist Party of Turkey and others v. Turkey*, judgment of 30 January 1998, *Reports* 1998-I; ECtHR, *Soering v. United Kingdom*, judgment of 7 July 1989, *Series* A No. 161; ECtHR, *Johnston and others v. Ireland*, judgment of 18 December 1986, *Series* A No. 112; ECtHR, *Witold Litwa v. Poland*, judgment of 4 April 2000, *Reports* 2000-III; ECtHR (GC), *Ilaşcu*

seems to have only a symbolic or rhetorical function in the sense that it does not seem to play an actual role in the decision of the Court; or at least not one that is visible for the reader.[65] The final category is where teleological interpretation influences the approach by the Court on a rather abstract level. It may play such a role, for example, when the Court wants to justify an autonomous approach or if it wants to support the conclusion that the Convention should be interpreted in a practical and effective manner. The example below will illustrate the three categories.

As said, the first category of cases is constituted by those where teleological interpretation functions like any other interpretation method, such as systematic interpretation or textual interpretation. This means that the teleological argument is used in order to establish the meaning of one of the Convention provisions or an aspect thereof. As an example the case of *Soering* can be mentioned, where the Court had to determine whether extraditing a person to a territory where the person would be faced with a real risk of exposure to torture could fall within the scope of Article 3 of the

and others v. Moldova and Russia, decision of 4 July 2001, *unpublished*; ECtHR, *Niemietz v. Germany*, judgment of 16 December 1992, *Series* A No. 251-B; ECtHR, *Golder v United Kingdom*, judgment of 21 February 1975, Series A No. 18; ECtHR (GC), *Kudla v. Poland*, judgment of 26 October 2000, *Reports* 2000-XI; ECtHR, *James and others v. United Kingdom*, judgment of 21 February 1986, *Series* A No. 98; ECtHR, *Van der Mussele v. Belgium*, judgment of 23 November 1983, *Series* A No. 70; ECtHR, *Futro v. Poland*, decision of 12 December 2000, *unpublished*; ECtHR (GC), *Saadi v. United Kingdom*, judgment of 29 January 2008, *unpublished*; ECtHR, *Case "Relating to certain aspects of the laws on the use of languages in education in Belgium" v. Belgium*, judgment of 23 July 1968, *Series* A No. 6, § B3 & B6; ECtHR, *Loizidou v. Turkey (preliminary objections)*, judgment of 23 March 1995, *Series* A No. 310, § 62, § 75 and 77 § 88-89; ECtHR, *Pretty v. United Kingdom*, judgment of 29 April 2002, *Reports* 2002-III, § 61 and 65; ECtHR (GC), *Jussila v. Finland*, judgment of 23 November 2006, *unpublished*, § 36.

65 ECtHR, *Van der Mussele v. Belgium*, judgment of 23 November 1983, *Series* A No. 70, § 37; ECtHR (GC), *Stoll v. Switzerland*, judgment of 10 December 2007, *unpublished*, § 60; ECtHR (GC), *Banković and others v. Belgium and others*, decision of 12 December 2001, Reports 2001-VII, § 65; ECtHR, *Pretty v. United Kingdom*, judgment of 29 April 2002, *Reports* 2002-III Pretty 54 (?). See also: ECtHR, *Rotaru v. Romania*, judgment of 4 May 2000, Reports 2000-V, § 38 and 44; ECtHR, *Gasus Dosier- und Fördertechnik GmbH v. the Netherlands*, judgment of 23 February 1995, *Series* A No. 306B, § 53; ECtHR, *Matos e Silva, Lda, and others v. Portugal*, judgment of 16 September 1996, *Reports* 1996-IV, § 75; ECtHR (GC), *Iatridis v. Greece*, judgment of 25 March 1999, *Reports* 1999-II, § 54; ECtHR (GC), *Beyeler v. Italy*, judgment of 5 January 2000, *Reports* 2000-I, § 100; ECtHR, *Tre Traktörer Aktiebolag v. Sweden*, judgment of 7 July 1989, *Series* A No. 159, § 53; ECtHR, *Gaygusuz v. Austria*, judgment of 16 September 1996, *Reports* 1996-IV, § 41; ECtHR, *Gillow v. United Kingdom*, judgment of 24 November 1986, *Series* A 109, § 46; ECtHR, *Buckley v. United Kingdom*, judgment of 25 September 1996, *Reports* 1996-IV, § 54; ECtHR, *Koua Poirrez v. France*, judgment of 30 September 2003, *Reports* 2003-X, § 37.

Convention.[66] The Court concluded that it could and it thereby relied heavily on a teleological interpretation of the provision. It held that:

> Extradition in such circumstances, while not explicitly referred to in the brief and general wording of Article 3, would be plainly contrary to the spirit and intendment of the Article, ...[67]

In another example, the case of *Johnston*, the Court had to decide whether a right to divorce could be derived from Article 12 of the Convention.[68] In answering that question, the Court relied on the ordinary meaning of the text and the context of the provision. Additionally, the Court held that:

> Moreover, the foregoing interpretation of Article 12 is consistent with its object and purpose as revealed by the *travaux préparatoires*.[69]

There are few cases in which the Court expresses itself on the persuasive force of teleological interpretation. In *United Communist Party of Turkey* the text of the provision already supported the conclusion that political parties came within the scope of Article 11, but the Court continued and held that:

> However, even more persuasive than the wording of Article 11, in the Court's view, is the fact that political parties are a form of association essential to the proper functioning of democracy. In view of the importance of democracy in the Convention system, there can be no doubt that political parties come within the scope of Article 11.[70]

The emphasis on the strength of the teleological argument would seem to suggest that that argument was decisive in determining the scope of Article 11.

In other cases the Court employs teleological arguments to argue against a very broad interpretation of the Convention. Here generally only the teleological method plays a role like in the case of *Futro*, for example:

---

66 ECtHR, *Soering v. United Kingdom*, judgment of 7 July 1989, *Series* A No. 161.
67 ECtHR, *Soering v. United Kingdom*, judgment of 7 July 1989, *Series* A No. 161, § 88.
68 ECtHR, *Johnston and others v. Ireland*, judgment of 18 December 1986, *Series* A No. 112.
69 ECtHR, *Johnston and others v. Ireland*, judgment of 18 December 1986, *Series* A No. 112, § 52.
70 ECtHR (GC), *United Communist Party of Turkey and others v. Turkey*, judgment of 30 January 1998, *Reports* 1998-I, § 25.

> [T]he Court recalls that Article 1 of Protocol No. 1 aims at securing the peaceful enjoyment of existing possessions and that it does not guarantee a right to acquire property nor a right to restitution of property.[71]

The examples show that teleological interpretation in the first category of cases has a varying degree of influence, depending on the case in question. It ranges from highly influential or even decisive in some cases to supporting an interpretation together with other interpretation methods. No trend can be discerned on when teleological interpretation is more influential. Apparently this depends on the arguments and material available in a specific case. Another observation is that teleological interpretation is often employed at a very concrete level. It is used to establish the meaning of a particular right laid down in the Convention; this use is contrary to the third category of cases, which will be discussed below, where the teleological interpretation plays a role at a much more abstract level.

The second category of cases is those where the Court at some point in its reasoning refers to the object or purpose of the Convention or one of its provisions, but does not substantiate this teleological reference in any visible manner. The reference to teleological interpretation might indicate that the Court took a teleological approach, but failed to express so in its reasoning. The Court in these cases typically considers that:

> [T]he Court will have regard to all the circumstances of the case in light of the underlying objectives of Article 4 ... .[72]

Or

> [T]he meaning which best reconciles the texts, having regard to the object and purpose of the treaty, is to be adopted.[73]

Another group of cases within this category only refers to the teleological method of interpretation when concluding that a certain right is a right for the purpose of one of the Convention provisions. An example can be found in the case of *Gaygusuz* where the Court concluded that:

---

71 ECtHR, *Futro v. Poland*, decision of 12 December 2000, *unpublished,* § 3. Similar approach in ECtHR, *Van der Mussele v. Belgium*, judgment of 23 November 1983, *Series* A No. 70, § 49; ECtHR (GC), *Ilaşcu and others v. Moldova and Russia*, decision of 4 July 2001, *unpublished*, p. 16.

72 ECtHR, *Van der Mussele v. Belgium*, judgment of 23 November 1983, *Series* A No. 70, § 37.

73 ECtHR (GC), *Stoll v. Switzerland,* judgment of 10 December 2007, *unpublished,* § 60.

> [T]he right to emergency assistance- in so far as provided for in the applicable legislation- is a pecuniary right for the purposes of Article 1 of Protocol No. 1.[74]

In this type of judgment the ECtHR does not substantiate the object or purpose of the Convention or a particular provision in these cases. As a result there is no possibility to check how the Court has come to its conclusion that the specific situation is covered by the Convention.

All the cases in this second category have in common that the Court hints at teleological interpretation, but does not explicate whether it has actually used this method in the interpretative process in these cases. As a result the role of teleological interpretation is unclear in these cases.

Arguably the most important role for teleological interpretation is not at the concrete level of determining an interpretation of one of the Convention rights or a Convention term, but at a more abstract level. In short it entails that the Court has created a teleological framework which helps it to interpret the Convention and its provisions. It requires some explanation in order to fully understand this point. The starting point is that the Court has repeatedly emphasized the 'special character [of the Convention] as a treaty for the collective enforcement of human rights and fundamental freedoms'.[75] Two consequences follow from this characterization, both of which have been most explicitly articulated in the cases of *Soering* and *Mamatkulov*.[76] The first is that:

> [O]bject and purpose of the Convention as an instrument for the protection of individual human beings require that its provisions be interpreted and applied so as to make its safeguards *practical* and *effective* (emphasis added).[77]

---

74 ECtHR, *Gaygusuz v. Austria*, judgment of 16 September 1996, *Reports* 1996-IV, § 41.

75 ECtHR, *Soering v. United Kingdom*, judgment of 7 July 1989, *Series* A No. 161, § 87. See also ECtHR, *Loizidou v. Turkey (preliminary objections)*, judgment of 23 March 1995, *Series* A No. 310; ECtHR (GC), *Mamatkulov and Askarov v. Turkey*, judgment of 4 February 2005, *Reports* 2005-I; ECtHR, *Cruz Varas and others v. Sweden*, judgment of 20 March 1991, *Series* A No. 201. ECtHR (GC), *Demir and Baykara v. Turkey*, judgment of 12 November 2008, *unpublished* alludes to this characterization, but only states that the Convention is first and foremost a system for the protection of human rights', § 66.

76 ECtHR, *Soering v. United Kingdom*, judgment of 7 July 1989, *Series* A No. 161, § 87; ECtHR (GC), *Mamatkulov and Askarov v. Turkey*, judgment of 4 February 2005, *Reports* 2005-I, § 100.

77 ECtHR, *Soering v. United Kingdom*, judgment of 7 July 1989, *Series* A No. 161, § 87; ECtHR (GC), *Mamatkulov and Askarov v. Turkey*, judgment of 4 February 2005, *Reports* 2005-I, § 101. See also ECtHR (GC), *Bosphorus HavaYollari Turizm Ve Ticaret Anonim Śirketi v. Ireland*, judgment of 30 June 2005, *Reports* 2005-VI, § 154; ECtHR, *Loizidou v. Turkey (preliminary objections)*, judgment of 23 March 1995, *Series* A No. 310, § 72. The early Belgian Linguistic case already stated that the object and purpose of the Convention was to provide effective protection, ECtHR, *Case "Relating*

This requirement that rights should be practical and effective has become a very important principle in the case law of the Court.[78] It has guided the interpretation of many Convention rights by providing a benchmark for the concrete interpretation of these provisions. In determining the appropriate interpretation the Court is thus guided by the general consideration that the interpretation has to fulfil the requirements of being practical and effective. Moreover, it has proven to be a basis for justifying other interpretative principles, namely autonomous and evolutive interpretation. The chapters dealing with these interpretative principles will also deal with this issue, but in order to understand the role of teleological interpretation the issue has to be discussed here as well. The case of *Chassagnou* clearly justifies autonomous interpretation on the basis of the need to achieve a practical and effective interpretation:

> If Contracting States were able, at their discretion, by classifying an association as "public" or "para-administrative", to remove it from the scope of Article 11, that would give them such latitude that it might lead to results incompatible with the object and purpose of the Convention, which is to protect rights that are not theoretical or illusory but practical and effective.[79]

Thus, the Court finds that if it in some situations does not adopt an autonomous approach, it risks surrendering the applicability of the ECHR to the 'sovereign will'[80] of the Contracting States and that might reduce the Convention to a paper tiger. A similar justification has been provided for evolutive interpretation. The Court explicitly linked evolutive interpretation with the need for practical and effective protection in the case of *Stec*:

> Since the Convention is first and foremost a system for the protection of human rights, the Court must have regard to the changing conditions within the respondent State and within

to certain aspects of the laws on the use of languages in education in Belgium" v. Belgium, judgment of 23 July 1968, *Series* A No. 6, § B5.

78 Supra note 935 where some examples of this principle in the case law of the ECtHR are mentioned.

79 ECtHR (GC), *Chassagnou and others v. France*, judgment of 29 April 1999, *Reports* 1999-III, § 100. In the following cases the link with the object and purpose has been made as well, but the Court has not literally referred to the terms pratical and effective. ECtHR, *Öztürk v. Germany*, judgment of 21 February 1984, *Series* A No. 73, § 49; ECtHR, *König v. Germany*, judgment of 28 June 1978, *Series* A No. 27, § 88; ECtHR, *Engel and others v. the Netherlands*, judgment of 8 June 1976, *Series* A No. 22, § 81; ECtHR (GC), *Ferrazzini v. Italy*, judgment of 12 July 2001, Reports 2001-VII, § 24.

80 ECtHR, *Öztürk v. Germany*, judgment of 21 February 1984, *Series* A No. 73, § 49; ECtHR, *Engel and others v. the Netherlands*, judgment of 8 June 1976, *Series* A No. 22, § 81.

> Contracting States generally, and must interpret and apply the Convention in a manner which renders its rights practical and effective, not theoretical and illusory.[81]

The presumption by the Court in the case of evolutive interpretation is that human rights standards evolve over time and that there is a need to keep them up to date in order to avoid the Convention turning into a dead letter. A teleological approach to the Convention thus generates some further interpretative principles, which play an important role in the interpretation process.

The second consequence of the characterization of the Convention as a system for the protection of human rights is that any interpretation:

> [H]as to be consistent with the "general spirit of the Convention, an instrument designed to maintain and promote the ideals and values of a democratic society".[82]

As a result the whole underlying approach to the interpretation of any aspect of the rights protected in the Convention can be said to be teleological in nature. It is difficult to tell whether teleological interpretation plays an important role in the interpretative process under this second strand of the consequences, because if it were to be taken into consideration it would be more implicit.

Teleological interpretation thus plays different roles at different levels of abstraction. It is both a 'regular' interpretation method and a method that generates a whole framework of interpretative principles. The level of influence of teleological interpretation in the first category is not always easy to discern and it varies per case. Teleological interpretation in the final category has a strong influence on the interpretative process since it generates important and characteristic interpretative principles, such as evolutive and autonomous interpretation.

9.5 Relation with other interpretative aids

The final category of cases discussed in the previous section serves as a good prelude for the discussion on the relation of teleological interpretation with other interpretative aids, mainly those discussed elsewhere in this thesis. Now that the different roles of

81 ECtHR (GC), *Stec and others v. United Kingdom*, decision of 6 July 2005, *Reports* 2005-X, § 47. A rather similar statement has been made in ECtHR (GC), *Mamatkulov and Askarov v. Turkey*, judgment of 4 February 2005, *Reports* 2005-I, § 121. Link also made in ECtHR, *Airey v. Ireland*, judgment of 9 October 1979, *Series* A No. 32, § 26.

82 ECtHR, *Soering v. United Kingdom*, judgment of 7 July 1989, *Series* A No. 161, § 87; ECtHR (GC), *Mamatkulov and Askarov v. Turkey*, judgment of 4 February 2005, *Reports* 2005-I, § 101.

teleological interpretation have been discussed it is clear that teleological interpretation serves as a basis for autonomous and evolutive interpretation. The Court has not explicitly invoked this method to establish the autonomous or evolutive meaning of the Convention, so the main role for teleological interpretation is to justify the reliance on these interpretative aids.

The teleological approach to the Convention has been translated by the Court in the principle that rights should be interpreted in a practical and effective manner. This principle has played an important role in advancing the protection afforded by the Convention.[83] Like the interpretative principles mentioned above, autonomous and evolutive interpretation, the principle of effective interpretation interacts with teleological interpretation on an abstract level.

On a more concrete level there is not really a clear relation between teleological interpretation and other interpretative methods. The Court invokes teleological interpretation along with different other interpretative methods, such as textual interpretation, systematic interpretation or comparative interpretation.[84] In some cases the methods support the same conclusion, while in others they point in conflicting directions. Interestingly, while the Court may in some cases overrule, for example, a textual interpretation (or at least go beyond the clear wording), there are no cases where a teleological interpretation is overruled by arguments from other interpretation methods, at least none where teleological interpretation had been explicitly invoked. This does not mean that an interpretation is always in line with the object and purpose of the provision of the Convention. The dissenting opinion in *Pellegrin*, for example, argues that the approach taken in *Pellegrin*, which claimed to be in line with the object and purpose of the Convention, is not very consistent with the object and purpose of the Convention.[85] However, the fact that the Court never openly disregards teleological considerations does show that the method is important to the Court. Comparative arguments may be disregarded[86] or the original intent of the drafters may have been overturned,[87] but teleological interpretations have not been dismissed in an explicit manner. Thus, the Court really makes an effort to interpret the terms of the

83 Supra note 937 and see in addition: Leach (2005), p. 165; Christoffersen (2009), p. 55; Ovey & White (2006), p. 47; Vanneste (2010), p. 312-317; Vande Lanotte (2005), p. 183; Gerards (2010), p. 16-19.

84 See Chapter 4 for a discussion of those methods.

85 ECtHR (GC), *Pellegrin v. France*, judgment of 8 December 1999, *Reports* 1999-VIII, dissenting opinion by Tulkens, Fischbach, Casadevall and Thomassen.

86 Some examples: ECtHR (GC), *Chapman v. United Kingdom*, judgment of 18 January 2001, *Reports* 2001-I; ECtHR, *Schalk and Kopf v. Austria*, judgment of 24 June 2010, *unpublished*.

87 This was implicit in ECtHR, *Sigurdur A. Sigurjónsson v. Iceland*, judgment of 30 June 1993, *Series* A No. 264; see discussion in section 10.2.1.1.

Convention in line with the object and purpose of the various Convention provisions. Whether the Court always succeeds in doing so in a satisfactory manner is matter for debate. Finally, there does not appear to be a clear relation between teleological interpretation and other interpretation methods, although the Court does seem to value teleological interpretation as one of the more important interpretation methods.

9.6 Conclusion

While taking stock of the case law analysis, a few things have become clear. First of all, teleological interpretation plays a role at different levels of abstraction. This has already been found to be one of the results of the theoretical analysis, but this analysis was based on the theory of Lasser which does not expressly concern the ECtHR. The case law analysis has confirmed the theoretical assumption that the ECtHR also invokes meta-teleological principles. The reference to the fact that the interpretation of the Convention needs to be practical and effective serves as a justification for both autonomous interpretation and evolutive interpretation. This is an important function of teleological interpretation that takes place at a rather abstract level.

At a more concrete level teleological interpretation also plays a role in the interpretation of the Convention provisions. One of the aspects that played a role in the theoretical analysis is the question whether the ECtHR tries to establish the subjective or objective purpose of the Convention or its provisions. The analysis showed that in the majority of cases the ECtHR prefers the objective purpose. Only in a few cases does the ECtHR refer to the *travaux préparatoires* to establish the subjective intention of the original drafters. These instances all concerned the object and purpose of a specific provision and not the Convention as a whole. The only problem that emerged from the analysis is that it is not clear in what kind of situations the ECtHR relies on the objective and the subjective purpose. Similar interpretative problems have led to different approaches, which renders it difficult to understand the actual use of the method.

Another aspect that does not help to get much insight into the use of this method is that it is often not really clear how the ECtHR establishes the object and purpose. The ECtHR generally only briefly indicates what it considers the object and purpose to be, and that is it. Or in some cases there is no indication of what the object and purpose are and only by mentioning these terms it is clear to the outsider that teleological interpretation must have played some role. The ECtHR would provide more insight into its conclusions if it was more open about the use of teleological interpretation. In practice, moreover, there are hardly any discussions between dissenters and the majority opinion on the object and purpose in a specific case. Providing more insight into this method, or having a clear debate on it between dissenters and the majority, might clarify the use of the method, even though it may also make it more vulnerable to criticism.

CHAPTER 10
COMPARATIVE INTERPRETATION IN THE CASE LAW OF THE ECTHR

Comparative interpretation as a method of interpretation has led to quite some debate, as can be seen in the theoretical analysis on this method in Chapter 6. In order to streamline the discussion of the method, a distinction was proposed in that chapter between internal comparative interpretation and external comparative interpretation. If the ECtHR takes materials from Contracting States into account, this means that it relies on internal comparative interpretation, but if materials from, for example, the United Nations, the Council of Europe or the United States are taken into consideration, this constitutes external comparative interpretation. It has been explained that each of these two components requires a different justification. One of the main questions defined for the case law analysis accordingly is whether the ECtHR in practice acknowledges the need to distinguish between external and internal comparative interpretation and the need for a different justification for each component. Moreover, even if this distinction is not made, it is interesting to see what kind of justification is provided for looking at comparative material. Especially the justification for taking these materials into account is a controversial topic and the question is whether the theoretical debate on the justification of comparative interpretation is reflected in the case law.

Another aspect that warrants attention is the search for a consensus. The ECtHR is known for relying on this particular form of comparative interpretation, but its use remains somewhat of an enigma. One of the questions raised by the theoretical analysis is whether there is any methodology to be discovered in the case law as to when and how to use the consensus method or whether the reference to the existence of a consensus is really as case-based as is assumed in the academic analysis.

These are, however, not the only topics to be discussed. The aim of this chapter is to present a comprehensive overview of comparative interpretation in the case law of the ECtHR. Therefore section 10.1 will discuss the meaning of comparative interpretation, which it has according to the ECtHR in the cases under study. Subsequently, section 10.2 will discuss when this method is used. The justifications for relying on comparative interpretation will be discussed in section 10.3. An important aspect is how comparative interpretation is used and what kinds of materials are referred to, which will be addressed in section 10.4. Finally, section 10.5 will discuss the relation between comparative interpretation and the other interpretative methods and principles discussed in this thesis.

10.1 What is comparative interpretation according to the ECtHR?

The notion 'comparative method' might seem rather straightforward, but it does warrant some explanation in order to understand the scope of the discussion on this method. In the theoretical chapter on comparative interpretation this issue has been addressed as well,[1] but it is important to revisit this question and look at it from the perspective of the Court. The understanding of different concepts in the literature might not always coincide with the understanding by the Court itself. For a full understanding of the reasoning of the Court it is crucial to try to distil the Court's answer to the question what it considers comparative interpretation to be. A complete answer to this question can only be given at the end of this chapter, but a short discussion of some elements can serve as a useful introduction.

In the case law analyzed in this thesis, the Court hardly ever expressly employs the terms 'comparative method', 'comparative reasoning' or 'comparative interpretation'.[2] The Court seems to prefer to refer to elements that indicate a comparative approach over explicitly labelling the method it is using. The Court thus in its reasoning makes mention of international treaties, national laws etc., without necessarily explicitly qualifying this as comparative reasoning.

Only on rare occasions, such as in the Grand Chamber judgment in *Demir and Baykara*, does the Court extensively discuss its use of the comparative method. For other interpretation methods such a methodological account is very rare as well.[3] Due to the significance of the *Demir and Baykara* case for this chapter, it may be useful to present some background information on the case itself. The case arose out of a complaint that the applicants as civil servants were denied sufficient protection under Article 11 of the Convention.[4] In its judgment the Chamber heavily relied on some provisions of the European Social Charter, which had not been ratified by

---

1 See section 6.1.1.

2 Only the term 'comparative interpretation' has been found once in a partly dissenting opinion by judge Thór Vilhjálmsson in ECtHR, *Marckx v. Belgium*, judgment of 13 June 1979, *Series* A No. 31.

3 Most famous example is ECtHR, *Golder v United Kingdom*, judgment of 21 February 1975, Series A No. 18.

4 The *Demir & Baykara*-case concerned a union for civil servants that had concluded a collective agreement with a local government. The local government, however, failed to meet its obligations under the collective agreement. The union went to court to try to enforce the collective agreement. The Court of Cassation finally determined that civil servants did not have a right to form a union and as a result they did not have the power to conclude legally binding collective agreements. The union complained in Strasbourg about a violation of their rights under Article 11 ECHR. ECtHR (GC), *Demir and Baykara v. Turkey*, judgment of 12 November 2008, *unpublished.*

Turkey.[5] Before the Grand Chamber Turkey objected to this practice of interpreting the Convention on the basis of instruments that the respondent government had not ratified, Turkey considered that the Court could not 'by means of an interpretation of the Convention, ... create for Contracting States new obligations that were not provided for in the Convention'.[6] The Grand Chamber elaborately responded to this 'invitation' of the Turkish government and, before deciding on the merits of the case, it dealt with the methodological aspects of the case. The ECtHR did not in so many words mention 'comparative interpretation', but it referred to the method as 'interpretation in light of international texts and instruments'. The Court in this case unanimously articulated its understanding of the comparative method as follows:

> The Court, in defining the meaning of terms and notions in the text of the Convention, can and must take into account elements of international law other than the Convention, the interpretation of such elements by competent organs, and the practice of European States reflecting their common values. The consensus emerging from specialized international instruments and from the practice of contracting States may constitute a relevant consideration for the Court when it interprets the provisions of the Convention in specific cases.[7]

This probably comes closest to a definition of the comparative method in the entire case law of the Court. Most importantly for the question what the method entails, one can discern in the quoted considerations that, according to the Court, the comparative method encompasses the use of all non-Convention material.[8] An interpretation based on Council of Europe material is therefore in the eyes of the Court an expression of the comparative method as well. Furthermore, the unanimous decision shows that the use and application of this method is far from contested within the Court. Indeed, it is a well-accepted form of reasoning. While this observation may not be very helpful towards a full understanding of the meaning of this method, it is an important aspect to keep in mind.

In *Demir and Baykara*, the ECtHR ultimately concluded that in order to find the consensus referred to in the citation above, it was not necessary that the respondent State had ratified all the relevant instruments. 'A continuous evolution in norms and principles applied in international law'[9] or a common ground in the Member States of the Council of Europe appears to provide a sufficient basis for the Court to give a novel interpretation to one of the terms contained in the Convention.

---

5 ECtHR, *Demir & Baykara v. Turkey*, judgment of 21 November 2006, *unpublished*, § 35; ECtHR (GC), *Demir and Baykara v. Turkey*, judgment of 12 November 2008, *unpublished*, § 53-54.
6 ECtHR (GC), *Demir and Baykara v. Turkey*, judgment of 12 November 2008, *unpublished*, § 54.
7 ECtHR (GC), *Demir and Baykara v. Turkey*, judgment of 12 November 2008, *unpublished*, § 85.
8 ECtHR (GC), *Stec and others v. United Kingdom*, decision of 6 July 2005, *Reports* 2005-X, the ECtHR also made this clear in a more indirect manner.
9 ECtHR (GC), *Demir and Baykara v. Turkey*, judgment of 12 November 2008, *unpublished*, § 86.

Even though the case provides some clarity on certain aspects of the comparative method, it also raises many questions as well as leaving certain matters open for discussion. An analysis of the use of this method in the Court's case law is therefore still warranted.

10.2 When is it used in the Court's reasoning?

In contrast with, for example, teleological interpretation or textual interpretation, the comparative method is not solely a method of interpretation. Its use is wider than purely for determining the scope of a particular right, because the method is also sometimes used for determining the margin of appreciation. This makes the method more difficult to grasp, because it is more complicated to draw conclusions on the basis of the diffuse application of this method. The focus of this chapter is on the comparative method as a method of interpretation, but it is necessary to at least briefly discuss some examples of the other roles of the comparative method in order to demarcate the scope of comparative interpretation. This distinction between the various functions of the comparative method is often underexposed, but it is relevant when assessing whether there are any shortcomings in the current use of this method by the Court as a method of interpretation. The following section will therefore first analyze comparative interpretation in the interpretative phase and the different functions that comparative interpretation has in that context. Subsequently, some examples of the comparative method in the application phase will be discussed. The final aspect that will be discussed in this section is the question whether the Court relies on comparative interpretation in specific types of cases or whether it uses this method randomly.

10.2.1 Comparative method in the interpretation phase

There are many ways in which the Court relies on the comparative method in the interpretative phase, which complicates categorizing the different roles of the comparative method. The division discussed below is a reflection of the trends that can be found in the case law. It is not a strict division into categories and there might be cases that do not fit neatly into the categories. However, the fact that those cases might be found does not defeat the usefulness of the categories drawn up here as they are mainly meant to reflect general trends and cannot be tailored to fit every case. The discussion in this section will be structured along the lines of the main functions of comparative interpretation. Within these broad categories there might be differences with regard to the role of comparative interpretation in a specific case.

10.2.1.1 Comparative interpretation used for 'regular' interpretative problems

The first category of cases is those where comparative arguments are employed in cases where the Court is simply presented with an interpretative question that has not been conclusively answered in earlier cases. The Court in these cases invoked comparative arguments either on their own or along with arguments based on other interpretation methods.

In the case of *Sigurdur A. Sigurjónsson* the Court used a comparative argument to interpret the scope of Article 11 of the Convention.[10] The case, which has already been discussed in relation to teleological interpretation in section 9.1.3, concerned the compulsory membership of a professional association, raising the question whether Article 11 encompassed a negative right not to join an association. This question had not yet been decisively answered by the Court and needed to be addressed in order to understand the exact meaning of Article 11. The government relied on the *travaux préparatoires* which showed that an explicit reference to a negative right not to join an association had been deliberately left out of the text of Article 11 of the Convention.[11] The Court recalled that the precedent[12] invoked by the Icelandic government took the *travaux préparatoires* into account, but the precedent did not attach decisive importance to these *travaux préparatoires.* The ECtHR subsequently discussed the situation in Member States of the Council of Europe and at the international level.

> Compulsory membership of this nature, which, it may be recalled, concerned a private-law association, does not exist under the laws of the great majority of the Contracting States. On the contrary, a large number of domestic systems contain safeguards which, in one way or another, guarantee the negative aspect of the freedom of association, that is the freedom not to join or to withdraw from an association.

---

10 ECtHR, *Sigurdur A. Sigurjónsson v. Iceland*, judgment of 30 June 1993, *Series* A No. 264, § 35. In the case of ECtHR, *Johnston and others v. Ireland*, judgment of 18 December 1986, *Series* A No. 112 the Court made use of the comparative method in a similar fashion. One of the questions the Court was presented with was whether Article 8 required states to ensure that illegitimate children were placed in a similar social and legal position to legitimate children. The main argument for the Court to conclude that the states were under such a positive obligation was the fact that the Preamble to the European Convention on the Legal Status of Children born out of Wedlock provided that: 'In a great number of member States of the Council of Europe efforts have been, or are being, made to improve the legal status of children born out of wedlock by reducing the differences between their legal status and that of children born in wedlock which are to the legal and social disadvantage of the former.' (§ 74) The Court emphasized the importance of these changes to the legal status of illegitimate children in the Member States by adding that it could not 'but be influenced by these developments'. (§ 74)

11 ECtHR, *Sigurdur A. Sigurjónsson v. Iceland*, judgment of 30 June 1993, *Series* A No. 264, § 33.

12 ECtHR, *Young James and Webster v. United Kingdom*, judgment of 13 August 1981, *Series* A No. 44.

A growing measure of common ground has emerged in this area also at the international level.[13]

After this discussion on the situation in the Contracting States and at an international level, the Court concluded that the Convention had to be interpreted in light of present-day conditions. Thus it found that Article 11 also entailed a negative right of association.[14] One of the judges, Judge Thór Vilhjálmsson, did not agree with this outcome and claimed that Article 11 could not be construed to conclude a negative right to association.[15] He took a different approach by emphasizing the difference in nature between the negative and positive freedom of association. Unfortunately, he did not address or comment on the use of the comparative method in this case.

Another example of the Court's reliance on comparative arguments in order to underpin a new approach is the case of *Zolotukhin v. Russia*.[16] In this case the Court was forced to explain the meaning of the term 'ne bis in idem' contained in Article 4 Protocol 7 (the right not be tried twice for the same offence). In previous cases three different approaches had been developed. Depending on which precedent was followed, the notion of 'idem' could either refer to the same facts, to the same legal qualification or to the fact that essential elements had to be the same.[17] The Grand Chamber found that these different approaches led to legal uncertainty, which ran counter to the aim of Article 4 Protocol 7 and therefore a 'harmonized interpretation' had to be adopted.[18] In order to find this harmonized interpretation the Court looked at decisions of other international courts. After discussing the variety of ways the right is formulated in different international instruments, the Court invoked a specific reference to the case law of the Court of Justice of the European Union and the Inter-American Court of Human Rights in which they addressed the same question. Both courts held that 'idem' referred to 'the identity of the material acts' and not the legal classification of those acts.[19] This approach is favourable to the perpetrator in the sense that it provides more legal certainty. The ECtHR subsequently held that a more restrictive approach was not necessary under the text of Article 4 Protocol 7 and concluded that 'idem' must be understood to refer to the same or substantially the

13 ECtHR, *Sigurdur A. Sigurjónsson v. Iceland*, judgment of 30 June 1993, *Series* A No. 264, § 35.

14 ECtHR, *Sigurdur A. Sigurjónsson v. Iceland*, judgment of 30 June 1993, *Series* A No. 264, § 35.

15 ECtHR, *Sigurdur A. Sigurjónsson v. Iceland*, judgment of 30 June 1993, *Series* A No. 264, dissenting opinion by Thór Vilhjálmsson.

16 ECtHR (GC), *Zolotukhin v. Russia*, judgment of 10 February 2009, *unpublished*. For other recent examples see, among others, ECtHR, *Rantsev v. Cyprus and Russia*, judgment of 7 January 2010, *unpublished*; ECtHR, *M.C. v. Bulgaria*, judgment of 4 December 2003, *Reports* 2003-XII.

17 ECtHR (GC), *Zolotukhin v. Russia*, judgment of 10 February 2009, *unpublished*, § 70-77.

18 ECtHR (GC), *Zolotukhin v. Russia*, judgment of 10 February 2009, *unpublished*, § 78.

19 ECtHR (GC), *Zolotukhin v. Russia*, judgment of 10 February 2009, *unpublished*, § 79 referring back to § 37 and § 40.

same facts. The interpretative choice of the ECtHR in this case was clearly based on the approach of the Court of Justice of the European Union and the Inter-American Court of Justice.

In the case of *Demir & Baykara* the Court did not only address the methodological aspects of the comparative method, but it also made extensive use of it in its reasoning on the merits of the case. One of the matters put before the Court was whether civil servants could invoke the protection guaranteed by Article 11 of the Convention.[20] The Grand Chamber argued that exceptions to the freedom of association had to be narrowly construed and that civil servants could not be excluded *per se* from the protection of Article 11. It supported this conclusion by reference to, among others, European practice and it concluded that 'the right of public servants to join trade unions is now recognized by all Contracting States'.[21] Even though the Court here did not literally mention the existence of a consensus, the fact that all Contracting States adopted the same approach strongly indicated that there was a consensus.[22]

In the case of *James and Others*[23] the Court used the lack of a consensus or common principle to argue *against* a too narrow understanding of the exceptions to the right to property. The applicant argued that Article 1 of the First Protocol only allowed for deprivation of property if the property was taken for a public purpose, consequently compulsory transfer of property between private parties was not justified by this provision.[24] The Court did not agree and explained that the text of the Convention did not warrant such a narrow interpretation of the exceptions right to property. Moreover, the Court emphasized that 'no common principle can be identified in the constitutions, legislation and case-law of the Contracting States that would warrant understanding the notion of public interest as outlawing compulsory transfer between private parties'.[25] Therefore it held that the fact that property was compulsorily transferred between private parties was not *per se* against the public purpose exception in Article 1 Protocol 1.

These examples show that the interpretative problem can concern a vital aspect of the provision in question, like in the *Zolotukhin* case, or only a term that is less

20 ECtHR (GC), *Demir and Baykara v. Turkey*, judgment of 12 November 2008, *unpublished,* § 96.

21 ECtHR (GC), *Demir and Baykara v. Turkey*, judgment of 12 November 2008, *unpublished,* § 106.

22 In *Loizidou* the Court did not literally speak of a consensus either but concluded that there was uniform and consistent state practice which supported the argument the Court was trying to make. ECtHR, *Loizidou v. Turkey (preliminary objections)*, judgment of 23 March 1995, *Series* A No. 310, § 80 and 82.

23 ECtHR, *James and others v. United Kingdom*, judgment of 21 February 1986, *Series* A No. 98.

24 Article 1 First Protocol provides: 'Every natural or legal person is entitled to the peaceful enjoyment of his possessions. No one shall be deprived of his possessions except *in the public interest* and subject to the conditions provided for by law and by the general principles of international law... (emphasis added)'.

25 ECtHR, *James and others v. United Kingdom*, judgment of 21 February 1986, *Series* A No. 98, § 40.

often invoked, like in the *Demir & Baykara* case. In all these situations comparative arguments play a role in the final interpretative outcome.

10.2.1.2 Comparative interpretation used to adopt a new interpretation different from the former interpretation

There is also a category of cases where the Court is faced with an interpretative problem that has been addressed before, but where the current interpretation is challenged on the basis of comparative arguments. Comparative arguments in such cases can perform two functions. Either comparative arguments provide a substantial basis for a new interpretation or comparative arguments can be used to argue only that a new approach is necessary. In the latter function comparative arguments do not necessarily play a role in determining the new approach to be taken, but only serve as proof that a new approach is warranted. Examples of both functions will be discussed in this section, starting first with the category of cases where comparative arguments are used to justify overruling a (often well-established) precedent.

A clear example of comparative arguments that lead to the overruling of a precedent is the case of *Micallef*.[26] In this case the ECtHR was presented with the question whether injunction proceedings were protected by Article 6 of the Convention. Until this case was placed before the Court, it had always concluded that injunction proceedings were not covered by Article 6. In *Micallef*, however, the Court considered that:

> there is widespread consensus amongst Council of Europe member States, which either implicitly or explicitly provide for the applicability of Article 6 guarantees to interim measures, including injunction proceedings ... Similarly, as can be seen from its case-law ... , the Court of Justice of the European Communities ("CJEU") considers that provisional measures must be subject to the guarantees of a fair trial, particularly to the right to be heard.[27]

The widespread consensus and the approach taken by the CJEU clearly provided one of the reasons for the ECtHR to adopt a new approach towards the applicability of Article 6 in injunction proceedings. The criteria set out in the new approach were, however, not justified by a direct reference to the comparative arguments. In this case the comparative arguments thus clearly served to indicate that a new approach was justified in the light of the developments in the Contracting States and in other European organizations, like the EU. In other cases, like *Demir & Baykara*[28] and

26 See for an unsuccessful attempt ECtHR (GC), *Ferrazzini v. Italy*, judgment of 12 July 2001, Reports 2001-VII.

27 ECtHR (GC), *Micallef v. Malta*, judgment of 15 October 2009, *unpublished*, § 78.

28 ECtHR (GC), *Demir and Baykara v. Turkey*, judgment of 12 November 2008, *unpublished*.

Mamatkulov,[29] comparative arguments served both as a reason for the Court to adopt a new approach, but comparative arguments also served as a substantial argument to justify the content of the new approach.[30]

In many cases the Court did not explicitly overrule its previous approach, but it adopted a new interpretation based (in part) on comparative arguments, which is the second and most important function of comparative interpretation in this category. The most famous example of adopting a new interpretation on the basis of comparative arguments is presented by the so-called transsexuality cases.[31] Given the exemplary character of these cases, the whole line of case law will be discussed here. Over a period of 16 years the Court received several applications on the same subject matter, namely whether states could be obliged to ensure legal recognition of the gender change of transsexuals. The question was whether such a positive obligation could be inferred from Article 8 of the Convention. In *Rees* the Court was confronted with the issue for the first time.[32] The Court rejected the comparative argument of the applicant and the Commission in favour of finding such a positive obligation and simply claimed that it was not persuaded.[33] After concluding that no violation of Article 8 could be found, the Court ended by stating that the 'need for appropriate legal measures should be kept under review having regard particularly to scientific and societal developments'.[34] In the subsequent case dealing with this matter, *Cossey,*[35] the Court indeed addressed these developments in the following manner:

> There have been certain developments since 1986 in the law of some member States of the Council of Europe. However, the reports accompanying the resolution adopted by the European Parliament on 12 September 1989 ... and Recommendation 1117 (1989) adopted by the Parliamentary Assembly of the Council of Europe on 29 September 1989 – both of which seek to encourage harmonization of laws and practices in this field- reveal, as the Government

29 ECtHR (GC), *Mamatkulov and Askarov v. Turkey*, judgment of 4 February 2005, *Reports* 2005-I.

30 See also ECtHR, *Marckx v. Belgium*, judgment of 13 June 1979, *Series* A No. 31; ECtHR (GC), *Christine Goodwin v. United Kingdom*, judgment of 11 July 2002, *Reports* 2002-VI; ECtHR (GC), *Scoppola v. Italy (No. 2),* judgment of 17 September 2009, *unpublished.*

31 ECtHR, *Rees v. United Kingdom*, judgment of 17 October 1986, *Series* A No. 106; ECtHR, *Cossey v. United Kingdom*, judgment of 27 September 1990, *Series* A No. 184; ECtHR, *Sheffield & Horsham v. United Kingdom*, judgment of 30 July 1998, *Reports* 1998-V; ECtHR (GC), *Christine Goodwin v. United Kingdom*, judgment of 11 July 2002, *Reports* 2002-VI; ECtHR (GC), *I v. United Kingdom*, judgment of 11 July 2002, *Reports* 2002-VI. ECtHR, *B. v. France*, judgment of 25 March 1993, *Series* A No. 232-C, is one of the transsexual cases as well but this case was decided on different grounds and the comparative method did not play an important role.

32 ECtHR, *Rees v. United Kingdom*, judgment of 17 October 1986, *Series* A No. 106.

33 ECtHR, *Rees v. United Kingdom*, judgment of 17 October 1986, *Series* A No. 106, § 41-42.

34 ECtHR, *Rees v. United Kingdom*, judgment of 17 October 1986, *Series* A No. 106, § 47.

35 ECtHR, *Cossey v. United Kingdom*, judgment of 27 September 1990, *Series* A No. 184.

> pointed out, the same diversity of practice as obtained at the time of the Rees judgment. Accordingly this is still, having regard to the existence of little common ground between Contracting States, an area in which they enjoy a wide margin of appreciation.[36]

It thus concluded that not enough had changed to allow it to find a different conclusion on the existence of a positive obligation, but again it stressed that the issue should be kept under review.[37] The dissenters all claimed that the developments had been sufficient to justify a different conclusion than in *Rees* and that some consensus could now be found.[38]

The story continued in *Sheffield and Horsham* where the Court again took note of the developments that had taken place since the earlier judgments. The Court was less definite in dismissing the comparative argument, but it did not yet consider the time to be ripe to adopt a different approach:

> As to legal developments in this area, the Court has examined the comparative study which has been submitted by Liberty. However, the Court is not fully satisfied that the legislative trends outlined by the amicus suffice to establish the existence of any common European approach to the problems created by the recognition in law of post-operative gender status.[39]

Thus, according to the majority of the Court there was still no consensus, yet again the dissenters argued the opposite and claimed that there was sufficient consensus to establish a positive obligation.[40]

The Grand Chamber in the case of *Christine Goodwin*[41] finally put an end to the story and confirmed the existence of the long awaited positive obligation. The Court still concluded that there was no common European approach, but that was attributed to the number of Contracting States.[42] Contrary to what the Court did in the previous cases, it took into account the developments that took place outside

---

36 ECtHR, *Cossey v. United Kingdom*, judgment of 27 September 1990, *Series* A No. 184. § 40

37 ECtHR, *Cossey v. United Kingdom*, judgment of 27 September 1990, *Series* A No. 184, § 32.

38 See the dissenting opinion in ECtHR, *Cossey v. United Kingdom*, judgment of 27 September 1990, *Series* A No. 184 by Martens and the joint dissenting opinion by Palm, Foighel and Pekkanen.

39 ECtHR, *Sheffield & Horsham v. United Kingdom*, judgment of 30 July 1998, *Reports* 1998-V, § 57.

40 See the joint partly dissenting opinion in ECtHR, *Sheffield & Horsham v. United Kingdom*, judgment of 30 July 1998, *Reports* 1998-V by Bernhardt, Thór Vilhjálmsson, Spielmann, Palm, Wildhaber, Makarczyk, Voicu and dissenting opinion by Casadevall.

41 ECtHR (GC), *Christine Goodwin v. United Kingdom*, judgment of 11 July 2002, *Reports* 2002-VI; ECtHR (GC), *I v. United Kingdom*, judgment of 11 July 2002, *Reports* 2002-VI is similar, decided on the same date, but Christine Goodwin has become the landmark judgment.

42 ECtHR (GC), *Christine Goodwin v. United Kingdom*, judgment of 11 July 2002, *Reports* 2002-VI, § 85: 'While this would remain the case, the lack of such a common approach among forty-three Contracting States with widely diverse legal systems and traditions is hardly surprising.'

Europe and concluded that an international trend existed in favour of legal recognition of gender change.[43]

This line of cases provides an interesting example of the reliance of the Court on comparative material in order to adopt a new approach. Many more aspects of the Court's use of this method in these cases can be analyzed, but that will be done in different parts of this chapter.

In other cases the ECtHR has also referred to comparative arguments, either to support or to argue against taking a new approach. In the case of *Schalk & Kopf*, for example, the applicants argued that Article 12 of the Convention had to be interpreted in an evolutive manner and should now be considered to include a right to same-sex marriage as well.[44] The ECtHR did not agree and held that there was no consensus on same-sex marriage in Europe:

> Although, as it noted in Christine Goodwin, the institution of marriage has undergone major social changes since the adoption of the Convention, the Court notes that there is no European consensus regarding same-sex marriage. At present no more than six out of forty-seven Convention States allow same-sex marriages.[45]

The Court thus found that the comparative argument in this case did not provide sufficient support for a new interpretation, neither did other interpretation methods provide for a justification for a new interpretation of Article 12.

As can be seen from the examples provided above, it is mainly in this category of cases that comparative arguments are strongly linked with an evolutive approach to the Convention, either to explicitly accept or explicitly reject an evolutive approach.

10.2.1.3 Comparative interpretation used to argue that the Court should not adopt a specific interpretation

An interesting set of cases are those where comparative arguments are used to indicate that the issue is not ripe for interpretation by the Court. The most famous example is *Vo*[46] where the Court had to decide whether the term 'everyone' in Article 2 of the Convention also covered an embryo or a foetus. The Court resorted to comparative interpretation and concluded that there existed no European consensus as to the question when life begins. The only common ground that could be found was that a foetus belonged to the human race. Due to this lack of consensus the Court did

43 ECtHR (GC), *Christine Goodwin v. United Kingdom*, judgment of 11 July 2002, *Reports* 2002-VI, § 85.

44 ECtHR, *Schalk and Kopf v. Austria*, judgment of 24 June 2010, *unpublished*, § 57.

45 ECtHR, *Schalk and Kopf v. Austria*, judgment of 24 June 2010, *unpublished*, § 58.

46 ECtHR (GC), *Vo v. France*, judgment of 8 July 2004, *Reports* 2004-VIII.

not feel competent to decide the abstract question on the status of a foetus and granted the Contracting States a margin of appreciation on the question when life begins.[47] Here the Court, oddly enough, invoked the margin of appreciation in the interpretation phase, whereas this doctrine normally only plays a role in respect to the justification of an interference, i.e. in the phase of application.[48] The exceptionally controversial nature of the case seems to have led the Court to an equally exceptional approach, whereby the comparative arguments are used as an indicator whether it is 'safe' to pronounce itself on the issue.

The case of *Vo* is, however, not the only case in which this approach has been taken. In *Kimlya* the Court adopted a similar approach.[49] The Court was presented with the question whether Scientology could be considered a religion in the sense of Article 9 of the Convention. The Court held that 'in the absence of any European consensus on the religious nature of Scientology teachings, and being sensitive to the subsidiary nature of its role, the Court considers that it must rely on the position of the domestic authorities in the matter and determine the applicability of Article 9 of the Convention accordingly'.[50] Again the Court used comparative arguments to indicate that it did not feel competent to answer an abstract question related to the scope of Convention provision and deferred to the Russian authorities. Their actions indicated that the Russian authorities believed that Scientology was a religion.[51]

An interesting difference between these two cases is the extent of the proof of the existence of a consensus. The question what kind of proof the Court uses to substantiate its comparative arguments will be discussed in section 10.4. It can, however, already be noted here that in the case of *Vo* the Court indeed made an effort to show that there was no consensus. In the case of *Kimlya* on the other hand, the Court did not go beyond the above quoted statement, namely that there was no consensus. Initially the Court did provide some proof that matters were controversial throughout Europe by making the following remark:

> Many European countries, including Belgium, France, Germany and the United Kingdom, have refused to grant Scientology religious recognition, whereas such recognition has been obtained through the courts in other States, such as Spain and Portugal.

47 ECtHR (GC), *Vo v. France*, judgment of 8 July 2004, *Reports* 2004-VIII, § 82 and 85.
48 Gerards & Senden (2009).
49 ECtHR, *Kimlya and others v. Russia*, judgment of 1 October 2009, *unpublished,* § 79.
50 ECtHR, *Kimlya and others v. Russia*, judgment of 1 October 2009, *unpublished,* § 79.
51 ECtHR, *Kimlya and others v. Russia*, judgment of 1 October 2009, *unpublished,* § 80-81.

Two months after the original judgment this sentence has been deleted ('rectified') by the Registry in accordance with Rule 81 of the Rules of Court.[52] Rule 81 allows for errors to be corrected, but one might wonder whether that also applies to deleting parts of a justification, which does not seem to be obviously wrong. On the contrary, deleting the sentence has diminished the force of the argument made by the Court. Therefore one may wonder what was behind the decision to delete the sentence, but that is not really relevant for the purposes of this section, being to show that the comparative arguments used by the Court need not be very convincing in order for the Court not to feel competent to adopt a position.

10.2.1.4 Comparative interpretation to show textual difference

A different comparative argument is presented by cases where the Court relies on foreign material to emphasize the textual difference with the European Convention. In these cases the Court seems to want to corroborate a textual argument that a certain aspect is not included in the text of a Convention provision by indicating that it is explicitly included in the text of other, similar, treaties or conventions. In *Burghartz*,[53] for example, the Court had to determine whether a complaint on a refusal to change the family name was applicable under Article 8 of the Convention. In addressing that question the Court emphasized that:

> Unlike some other international instruments, such as the International Covenant on Civil and Political Rights (Article 24 para. 2), the Convention on the Rights of the Child of 20 November 1989 (Articles 7 and 8) or the American Convention on Human Rights (Article 18), Article 8 of the Convention does not contain any explicit provision on names.[54]

The fact that these treaties did include an explicit provision on names strengthened the ECtHR's argument that it could not be held to be automatically included in the text of the Convention. This does not, however, mean that a certain right or obligation cannot be read into the Convention, it just entails that such an argument should rest on a different basis. In *Soering* the Court made that point abundantly clear by stating that:

---

52 Rule 81 (Rectification of errors in decisions and judgments): Without prejudice to the provisions on revision of judgments and on restoration to the list of applications, the Court may, of its own motion or at the request of a party made within one month of the delivery of a decision or a judgment, rectify clerical errors, errors in calculation or obvious mistakes.

53 ECtHR, *Burghartz v. Switzerland*, judgment of 22 February 1992, *Series* A No. 280-B.

54 ECtHR, *Burghartz v. Switzerland*, judgment of 22 February 1992, *Series* A No. 280-B, § 24. Similar arguments have been advanced in ECtHR (GC), *Vo v. France*, judgment of 8 July 2004, *Reports* 2004-VIII, § 75.

> [T]he fact that a specialized treaty should spell out in detail a specific obligation attaching to the prohibition of torture does not mean that an essentially similar obligation is not already inherent in the general terms of Article 3 of the European Convention.[55]

The Court subsequently relied on the 'spirit and intendment'[56] of the provision to vindicate the inherent obligation.

A similar argument was adopted in the case of *Cruz Varas* in which the Court had to decide whether a state could be held accountable for not respecting an interim measure imposed by the then Commission. The text of the Convention did not contain a reference to interim measures, but the measure was based on the Rules of Procedure of the former Commission. The Court indicated the limits of the Convention by pointing to other treaties that did contain a clause on interim measures:

> While this approach argues in favor of a power of the Commission and Court to order interim measures to preserve the rights of parties in pending proceedings, the Court cannot but note that unlike other international treaties or instruments the Convention does not contain a specific provision with regard to such measures (see, inter alia, Article 41 of the Statute of the International Court of Justice; Article 63 of the 1969 American Convention on Human Rights; Articles 185 and 186 of the 1957 Treaty establishing the European Economic Community).[57]

The Court seems to have referred to comparative arguments to provide extra force to the argument that the Convention does not contain a provision on interim measures by pointing to the fact that other treaties have addressed the matter. Subsequently the ECtHR addressed the question whether an obligation to respect interim measures could be inferred from the obligation for Contracting States under then Article 25 of the Convention not to hinder the effectiveness of an individual's rights to petition (presently Article 34).[58] The Court finally concluded that this was not the case.

The comparative arguments in this category of cases thus do not support a specific interpretation, but they do strengthen the ECtHR's argument that certain rights were not originally included in the Convention. The Court does not make clear in these cases, however, why it calls upon additional support from similar treaties when the text of the Convention alone already offers a strong indication that a certain obligation or right is not included. The obvious explanation is that the Court apparently does not consider the text to be evident and therefore seeks additional support. Whether that is the whole answer is, however, difficult to tell from the cases.

---

55 ECtHR, *Soering v. United Kingdom*, judgment of 7 July 1989, *Series* A No. 161, § 88.
56 ECtHR, *Soering v. United Kingdom*, judgment of 7 July 1989, *Series* A No. 161, § 88.
57 ECtHR, *Cruz Varas and others v. Sweden*, judgment of 20 March 1991, *Series* A No. 201, § 94.
58 ECtHR, *Cruz Varas and others v. Sweden*, judgment of 20 March 1991, *Series* A No. 201, § 97.

10.2.2 Comparative method in the application phase

It has already been explained at the beginning of this section that comparative arguments do not only play a role in the interpretation phase of a judgment.[59] The focus of this thesis is the interpretation phase, but in order to get a better understanding of the role of comparative arguments, this section will briefly address some examples of its use in the application phase.

In the case of *Evans* the Court had to deal with a conflict between the rights of two individuals. In connection with her treatment for cancer, Ms. Evans had to have her ovaries removed, but the growth of the cancer did allow for time to remove some eggs from Ms. Evans so that she could still have her own biological child once her ovaries were removed. Due to the cancer she would have to wait two years before having the embryos planted back into her uterus, so the eggs would have to be stored. She was advised against freezing her unfertilized eggs, because this had a lower chance of success and was not performed at the clinic she attended. She therefore agreed to have her eggs fertilized with the sperm of her then partner J, whom also consented to have the created embryos stored for a period of a maximum of 10 years. Half a year later the relationship broke down and J wanted to have the embryos destroyed. In accordance with the law both partners had to consent to storing the embryos and this consent could be withdrawn at any time by one of the partners. Ms. Evans (the applicant) argued that destroying the embryos would violate her right to become a biological parent under Article 8 of the Convention, while there is also the right of J not to become a biological parent against his will. The ECtHR argued that the right to respect for the decision to become or not become a parent is covered by Article 8 of the Convention. In order to determine whether the English legislation that ordered the destruction of the embryos if one of the partners withdrew his or her consent, violated the Convention the Court first addressed the extent of the margin of appreciation for the Contracting States. This is where the Court invoked comparative arguments. The Court held that:

> Where, however, there is no consensus within the Member States of the Council of Europe, either as to the relative importance of the interest at stake or as to the best means of protecting it, particularly where the case raises sensitive moral or ethical issues, the margin will be wider …

59 This has been explicitly acknowledged by Judge Finlay Geoghegan in her concurring opinion in ECtHR (GC), *A, B and C v. Ireland*, judgment of 16 December 2011, *unpublished.* This judgment, however, dealt with the use of this argument in the application phase, which is outside the scope of this thesis.

> In addition, while the Court is mindful of the applicant's submission to treat the comparative law data with caution, it is at least clear, and the applicant does not contend otherwise, that there is no uniform European approach in this field. Certain States have enacted primary or secondary legislation to control the use of IVF treatment, whereas in others this is a matter left to medical practice and guidelines. While the United Kingdom is not alone in permitting storage of embryos and in providing both gamete providers with the power freely and effectively to withdraw consent up until the moment of implantation, different rules and practices are applied elsewhere in Europe. It cannot be said that there is any consensus as to the stage in IVF treatment when the gamete providers' consent becomes irrevocable ...
>
> While the applicant contends that her greater physical and emotional expenditure during the IVF process, and her subsequent infertility, entail that her Article 8 rights should take precedence over J's, it does not appear to the Court that there is any clear consensus on this point either. The Court of Appeal commented on the difficulty of comparing the effect on J of being forced to become the father of the applicant's child and that on the applicant of being denied the chance to have genetically-related offspring ..., and this difficulty is also reflected in the range of views expressed by the two panels of the Israeli Supreme Court in *Nachmani* and in the United States case-law ...
>
> In conclusion, therefore, since the use of IVF treatment gives rise to sensitive moral and ethical issues against a background of fast-moving medical and scientific developments, and since the questions raised by the case touch on areas where there is no clear common ground amongst the Member States, the Court considers that the margin of appreciation to be afforded to the respondent State must be a wide one ... .[60]

The lengthy quotation from this judgment indicates that the comparative arguments disclosed a clear lack of consensus on the specific issue, as a result of which the Contracting States were granted a wide margin of appreciation. The case of *Dickson* showed a similar approach, whereby the existence of a consensus determined the extent of the margin of appreciation.[61]

A different role for comparative arguments in relation to the examination of a justification for an interference can be seen in the case of *Yumak and Sadak*.[62] The electoral threshold for parliamentary elections in Turkey was 10%. The applicants in the case complained that this threshold interfered with the free expression of the opinion of the people in the choice of the legislature and relied on Article 3 of

60 ECtHR (GC), *Evans v. United Kingdom*, judgment of 10 April 2007, *unpublished*, § 77-81.

61 ECtHR (GC), *Dickson v. United Kingdom*, judgment of 4 December 2007, *unpublished*. See also ECtHR (GC), *A, B and C v. Ireland*, judgment of 16 December 2011, *unpublished*. In this judgment on abortion issues, the Grand Chamber invoked a reference to the existence of a consensus in a discussion on the extent of the margin of appreciation. In this case the existence of a strong consensus did not limit the margin of appreciation according to the majority of the Grand Chamber. A number of dissenting judges commented on this conclusion by the Grand Chamber.

62 ECtHR (GC), *Yumak & Sadak v. Turkey*, judgment of 8 July 2008, *unpublished*.

Protocol 1. The Court indicated that Contracting States have a large margin of appreciation in designing their own electoral system, but the question was whether this threshold was proportionate. In order to answer that question the Court invoked references to other European systems.

> The Court observes that electoral thresholds are not unknown among European electoral systems and that there are different kinds which vary according to the type of election and the context within which they are used. Analysis of the electoral thresholds adopted in the member States shows that, apart from Turkey, only three States have opted for high thresholds. Liechtenstein has fixed the level at 8%, and the Russian Federation and Georgia at 7%. A third of the States impose a 5% threshold and 13 of them have chosen a lower figure. The other States which have a proportional representation system do not use thresholds. Thresholds also vary according to whether they apply to a party or a coalition, and some countries have adopted thresholds for independent candidates... .[63]
>
> The large variety of situations provided for in the electoral legislation of the member States of the Council of Europe shows the diversity of the possible options. It also shows that the Court cannot assess any particular threshold without taking into account the electoral system of which it forms a part, although the Court can agree with the applicants' contention that an electoral threshold of about 5% corresponds more closely to the member States' common practice. However, it has already been pointed out that any electoral legislation must be assessed in the light of the political evolution of the country concerned, so that features that would be unacceptable in the context of one system may be justified in the context of another, at least so long as the chosen system provides for conditions which will ensure the "free expression of the opinion of the people in the choice of the legislature" ... That is why the Court must now assess the effects of the correctives and other safeguards with which the impugned system is attended.[64]

The Court thus used comparative arguments to assess whether the threshold was exceptional, which it was. For that reason, it found it necessary to take a close look at the correctives and safeguards provided by the Turkish system. The Court finally concluded that the threshold was indeed excessively high, but given the political context and the safeguards provided there was no violation of Article 3 Protocol 1.

These examples show that comparative arguments can play an important role in the application phase. They also make clear that the aim of the use of these arguments in this phase is quite a different one than in the phase of interpretation. In relation to the examination of a justification, comparative arguments are either used as a basis for determining the intensity of review, or in connection with the test of proportionality.

63 ECtHR (GC), *Yumak & Sadak v. Turkey*, judgment of 8 July 2008, *unpublished*, § 129.
64 ECtHR (GC), *Yumak & Sadak v. Turkey*, judgment of 8 July 2008, *unpublished*, § 132.

10.2.3 Specific type of cases?

The question as to *when* the Court uses comparative interpretation can also be looked at from a different angle, namely whether the Court has used this method mainly in specific *types* of cases. The examples discussed above already indicate that the Court uses the method in a wide variety of cases. The method has been invoked to interpret various Convention rights: the right to life,[65] the prohibition of torture,[66] prohibition of forced labour,[67] right to liberty,[68] right to a fair trial,[69] right to respect for private and family life,[70] freedom of expression,[71] freedom of assembly and association,[72] right to marry[73] and some procedural provisions of the Convention.[74] No clear line can be found in the case law as to when the Court considers it warranted to invoke comparative arguments. That is, however, not a specific character of comparative interpretation; teleological interpretation is also invoked in many different cases. Both are flexible methods and are therefore suitable to be applied in a broad variety of cases without there necessarily being a coherent strategy behind the use of such methods in specific cases. Furthermore, it also depends on the specific facts and circumstances of each case whether the Court considers it appropriate or necessary to resort to comparative interpretation.

Despite the fact that there is no clear trend in the use of the comparative method, there is one provision that is often interpreted on the basis of comparative arguments, namely Article 8, which protects the right to respect for private and family life. This provision is overrepresented in the case law on comparative interpretation that has been analyzed for the purposes of this thesis.[75] The very broad character of this

65 ECtHR, *Al-Saadoon and Mufdhi v. United Kingdom*, judgment of 2 March 2010, *unpublished.*

66 ECtHR (GC), *T v. United Kingdom*, judgment of 16 December 1999, *unpublished*; ECtHR (GC), *Selmouni v. France*, judgment of 28 July 1999, *Reports* 1999-V; ECtHR, *Soering v. United Kingdom*, judgment of 7 July 1989, *Series* A No. 161

67 ECtHR, *Van der Mussele v. Belgium*, judgment of 23 November 1983, *Series* A No. 70.

68 ECtHR (GC), *Saadi v. United Kingdom*, judgment of 29 January 2008, *unpublished.*

69 ECtHR (GC), *Pellegrin v. France*, judgment of 8 December 1999, *Reports* 1999-VIII; ECtHR (GC), *Vilho Eskelinen and others v. Finland*, judgment of 19 April 2007, *unpublished.*

70 Transsexual cases, but also ECtHR, *M.C. v. Bulgaria*, judgment of 4 December 2003, *Reports* 2003-XII.

71 ECtHR (GC), *Stoll v. Switzerland,* judgment of 10 December 2007, *unpublished.*

72 ECtHR (GC), *Demir and Baykara v. Turkey*, judgment of 12 November 2008, *unpublished*; ECtHR, *Sigurdur A. Sigurjónsson v. Iceland*, judgment of 30 June 1993, *Series* A No. 264

73 ECtHR, *Schalk and Kopf v. Austria*, judgment of 24 June 2010, *unpublished*; ECtHR, *Johnston and others v. Ireland*, judgment of 18 December 1986, *Series* A No. 112.

74 ECtHR (GC), *Mamatkulov and Askarov v. Turkey*, judgment of 4 February 2005, *Reports* 2005-I.

75 See the transsexuals cases discussed in section 10.2.1.1. See also: ECtHR, *Schalk and Kopf v. Austria*, judgment of 24 June 2010, *unpublished*; ECtHR, *Marckx v. Belgium*, judgment of 13 June 1979, *Series* A No. 31; ECtHR, *M.C. v. Bulgaria*, judgment of 4 December 2003, *Reports* 2003-XII.

provision could be part of the explanation. The Court itself has not provided any indication as to why it appreciates comparative arguments so much in the context of Article 8.[76] As a result only the tendency as such can be inferred from the cases.

10.2.4 Conclusion

This section aimed to show the different functions comparative arguments can have in the case law of the ECtHR. Within the different categories discussed, the first two are the most common. This means that comparative arguments are most often when the Court wants to support a 'regular' interpretative solution or when the Court is challenged to adopt a new approach that deviates from its former approach. In this latter category the relation with evolutive interpretation plays an important role, which will be addressed in Chapter 11 as well.

10.3 Any justification?

Many justifications can be adduced in favour of the use of comparative arguments in judicial reasoning; they have been discussed in a general fashion in the theoretical analysis (see section 6.1.4). Here, the question is pertinent whether the Court itself has provided any justifications. Indeed, it has appeared from the case law analysis that the Court in some cases has provided a general explanation why it considers comparative arguments justifiable in interpreting the Convention.

Firstly, the Court has invoked the Vienna Convention on the Law of Treaties to account for either looking at the Contracting States or taking international material into consideration.[77] In *Cruz Varas* the Court explained that subsequent state practice was an important factor that could be taken into account:

> Subsequent practice could be taken as establishing the agreement of Contracting States regarding the interpretation of a Convention provision [Court refers to Soering and the VCLT

76 The Court in *Johnston* did say that in comparison to Article 12, Article 8 did lend itself more to an evolutive interpretation. Perhaps the wide use of the comparative method for interpreting Article 8 should be seen in this context. ECtHR, *Johnston and others v. Ireland*, judgment of 18 December 1986, *Series* A No. 112, § 57.

77 ECtHR, *Cruz Varas and others v. Sweden*, judgment of 20 March 1991, *Series* A No. 201; ECtHR (GC), *Saadi v. United Kingdom*, judgment of 29 January 2008, *unpublished*; ECtHR (GC), *Banković and others v. Belgium and others*, decision of 12 December 2001, Reports 2001-VII; ECtHR (GC), *Mamatkulov and Askarov v. Turkey*, judgment of 4 February 2005, *Reports* 2005-I; ECtHR (GC), *Demir and Baykara v. Turkey*, judgment of 12 November 2008, *unpublished*.

> art. 31(b)] but not to create new rights and obligations which were not included in the Convention at the outset.[78]

The approach ultimately failed in this case, but that did not defeat the general statement that subsequent state practice was a relevant consideration in the interpretation process. While *Cruz Varas* provided an argument for relying on comparative material from the Contracting States, however, it did not explain reliance on international material. The Court provided a more express justification for reliance on international material based on the Vienna Convention in *Banković*.[79] When setting out the general interpretative approach to the case, the Court observed that:

> Moreover, Article 31 § 3 (c) indicates that account is to be taken of "any relevant rules of international law applicable in the relations between the parties". More generally, the Court recalls that the principles underlying the Convention cannot be interpreted and applied in a vacuum. The Court must also take into account any relevant rules of international law when examining questions concerning its jurisdiction and, consequently, determine State responsibility in conformity with governing principles of international law, although it must remain mindful of the Convention's special character as a human rights treaty. The Convention should be interpreted as far as possible in harmony with other principles of international law of which it forms part.[80]

The Court thus did not only rely on the Vienna Convention on the Law of Treaties to justify the use of comparative international material, but it also claimed that is has to be mindful of the context in which the Court is operating.[81] Or to put in the words of the Court: it has to take into account 'the international law background'.[82] It is important to note in the context of the distinction made between external and internal comparative interpretation in the theoretical chapter that an additional justification is provided for relying on external or international materials. This does not mean to

78 ECtHR, *Cruz Varas and others v. Sweden*, judgment of 20 March 1991, *Series* A No. 201, § 100. The general statement that subsequent state practice can be relevant has been reconfirmed by the Court in general terms in ECtHR (GC), *Banković and others v. Belgium and others*, decision of 12 December 2001, Reports 2001-VII, § 56.

79 ECtHR (GC), *Banković and others v. Belgium and others*, decision of 12 December 2001, Reports 2001-VII, § 57.

80 ECtHR (GC), *Banković and others v. Belgium and others*, decision of 12 December 2001, Reports 2001-VII, § 57. A similar statement has been made in ECtHR (GC), *Mamatkulov and Askarov v. Turkey*, judgment of 4 February 2005, *Reports* 2005-I, § 111.

81 Dissent in *Saadi* also confirms that Convention is not interpreted in a vacuum and that it applies 'in conjunction with the other international fundamental rights protection instruments'. ECtHR (GC), *Saadi v. United Kingdom*, judgment of 29 January 2008, *unpublished*, joint partly dissenting opinion by Rozakis, Tulkens, Kovler, Hajiyev, Spielmann and Hirvelä.

82 ECtHR (GC), *Saadi v. United Kingdom*, judgment of 29 January 2008, *unpublished*, § 63; ECtHR (GC), *Demir and Baykara v. Turkey*, judgment of 12 November 2008, *unpublished*, § 76.

say that the ECtHR expressly embraces this distinction, an issue that will be discussed further in section 10.4.4, but it does indicate that it at least at some level realizes that an additional justification might be necessary to justify relying on materials that are further removed from the European Convention and the Council of Europe.

It can be doubtful, though, whether this combined explanation provides a justification for reliance on all types of international materials. Article 31(c) of the VCLT refers to international law in force between the parties. The question is whether this provision can be interpreted in such a broad manner as to justify reference to any type of international legal instrument. The provision rather seems to imply that in interpreting the Convention the ECtHR needs to take account of obligations of international law that rest upon the Contracting States.[83] The ECtHR itself also seems to adhere to this interpretation of the VCLT in other cases, like *Bosphorus*.[84] In this case Ireland had to obey its obligations under EU law, which the ECtHR considered a legitimate goal to restrict property rights under the European Convention. The ECtHR added that on the basis of Article 31(c) VCLT it had to respect relevant international legal rules, which included the principle of *pacta sunt servanda*.[85] This interpretation makes it doubtful whether this provision or the reference to the international legal context is a sufficient justification for invoking references to, for example, the Inter-American Court of Human Rights or other international instruments which are not applicable between the parties.

A different set of cases provides a more explicit justification for the function of the comparative argument for the Court. In *Polacek*[86] the applicants had relied on a United Nations Human Rights Committee conclusion in their complaint. The Court stressed that it was only competent to apply the European Convention, but added that in interpreting the Convention 'it may find it helpful to be guided by provisions of other international legal instruments'.[87] Similarly in *Pellegrin* the Court turned to the CJEU for helpful guidance.[88]

83 Drooghenbroeck (2009), p. 811.

84 ECtHR (GC), *Bosphorus HavaYollari Turizm Ve Ticaret Anonim ªirketi v. Ireland*, judgment of 30 June 2005, *Reports* 2005-VI.

85 ECtHR (GC), *Bosphorus HavaYollari Turizm Ve Ticaret Anonim ªirketi v. Ireland*, judgment of 30 June 2005, *Reports* 2005-VI, § 150; similarly ECtHR (GC), *Behrami & Behrami v. France*, decision of 2 May 2007, *unpublished*.

86 ECtHR (GC), *Polacek & Polackova v. Czech Republic*, decision of 10 July 2002, *unpublished*, § 45.

87 ECtHR (GC), *Polacek & Polackova v. Czech Republic*, decision of 10 July 2002, *unpublished*, § 45.

88 ECtHR (GC), *Pellegrin v. France*, judgment of 8 December 1999, *Reports* 1999-VIII, § 66. A similar reference can be found in ECtHR (GC), *Vilho Eskelinen and others v. Finland*, judgment of 19 April 2007, *unpublished*, § 60.

A final justification provided for looking at comparative material in the Contracting States and at international level is based on the link between evolutive interpretation and comparative interpretation. This link has already been mentioned above, when discussing the different roles of comparative interpretation. Comparative interpretation may be used by the Court to substantiate arguments based on evolutive interpretation. In *Dangeville* the Court explicitly pointed out that the Convention had to be interpreted in light of comparative material:

> The Convention is a living instrument that must be interpreted in the light of present-day conditions and the notions currently prevailing in democratic States.[89]

Likewise in *Demir and Baykara* the Court observed that 'it has always referred to the "living" nature of the Convention, which must be interpreted in the light of present-day conditions, and that it has taken account of evolving norms of national and international law in its interpretation of Convention provisions'.[90] The principle of evolutive interpretation is thus invoked to justify the use of comparative arguments. The idea that evolutive interpretation helps the ECtHR to keep pace with developments in Contracting States and the Council of Europe can be supported as an explanation and justification for the use of international and foreign material. This explanation is, however, far less convincing when developments at the international level or developments in Australia, New Zealand and the United States of America are mentioned. A separate justification that explains the relevance of looking at these materials would be desirable.

The Court has thus relied on comparative arguments for a variety of reasons. It has done so to receive guidance, to be able to ground an evolutive interpretation in developments occurring within Europe or internationally, or to take the international law background into account. However, these justifications are usually somewhat succinctly mentioned and it can be questioned whether they suffice to legitimize the use of the method by the Court.

---

89 ECtHR, *S.A. Dangeville v. France*, judgment of 16 April 2002, *Reports* 2002-III, § 47. Somewhat similar statements have been made in ECtHR (GC), *I v. United Kingdom*, judgment of 11 July 2002, *Reports* 2002-VI, § 54; ECtHR (GC), *Christine Goodwin v. United Kingdom*, judgment of 11 July 2002, *Reports* 2002-VI; ECtHR, *Cossey v. United Kingdom*, judgment of 27 September 1990, *Series* A No. 184, § 35; ECtHR (GC), *Stec and others v. United Kingdom*, decision of 6 July 2005, *Reports* 2005-X, § 47.

90 ECtHR (GC), *Demir and Baykara v. Turkey*, judgment of 12 November 2008, *unpublished,* § 68.

10.4 Comparative interpretation – how?

An important question that still needs to be answered relates to the way in which the Court invokes comparative arguments or, put differently, the 'how' of comparative interpretation. Reference has already been made to the fact that the Court is sometimes looking for a consensus, but this does not yet provide any information as to what the Court considers to constitute such a consensus. It is also interesting to know what kinds of materials are invoked by the Court when referring to comparative arguments. The examples in previous sections have already provided some insight, but this section will address this issue in more detail. Moreover, it is relevant to know whether the Court only relies on comparative arguments to support other arguments or whether the comparative argument is really the main or decisive argument and actually determines the meaning of the Convention notion at issue. Finally, the question by whom the materials are collected and selected will be addressed.

In section 10.4.1 the search for a consensus or trend will be discussed. This search will be shown to be often limited to finding a consensus or trend among the Contracting States. Section 10.4.2 deals with all other references and how the Court has invoked them. In section 10.4.3 the question will be addressed whether the comparative argument is the main argument or whether it is used to support other arguments. The question whether the Court acknowledged the distinction between external and internal comparative interpretation will be discussed in section 10.4.4. Finally, section 10.4.5 will discuss where the materials come from. In the discussion in the first two sections attention will be paid to the way in which the Court invokes the materials; thus whether it is looking for a consensus or trend or whether it is simply a reference to some comparative materials. Moreover, attention will also be paid to the depth of the comparative reference and the kind of materials that are referred to, in the sense that it will be discussed whether reference has been made to treaties, legislation, case law or other materials.

10.4.1 Finding a consensus or trend

A much criticized aspect of comparative interpretation is the search for a consensus or trend. In most of these cases the ECtHR refers solely to the Member States of the Council of Europe, but in some cases it looks beyond the borders of Europe. The ECtHR sometimes tries to find a trend outside Europe when no trend or consensus was found within Europe. In other cases, however, the ECtHR refers to some international materials to support a trend among the Contracting States. It is not always explicitly stated that the ECtHR is looking for a trend or consensus, but in all the judgments discussed below, the ECtHR is looking for some sort of common standard. In order to get more insight into the way the ECtHR uses this consensus, two main questions need to be answered. Firstly, when does the ECtHR speak of a consensus or trend? Secondly, what kind of evidence is used to support this conclusion? Both questions are intertwined and therefore both aspects are dealt with when discussing some specific cases even though attempts will be made to discuss the two questions separately as much as possible in order to make the discussion more clear.

The first aspect that should be discussed is whether any guideline or standard can be found with regard to when there is enough support to speak of a consensus, trend or common standard. In many cases the Court relies on the situation in the Member States of the Council of Europe.[91] Some of these judgments contain rather general references without much explanation. They generally do not illuminate which countries have been examined or how many countries support a particular approach. Even though the Court should perhaps not be compelled to provide statistically exact numbers, solely stating that 'judicial practice in several of the States shows that'[92] a particular practice has been adopted is rather indefinite.[93] The statement of the

91 ECtHR, *Sigurdur A. Sigurjónsson v. Iceland*, judgment of 30 June 1993, *Series* A No. 264, § 35; ECtHR (GC), *Demir and Baykara v. Turkey*, judgment of 12 November 2008, *unpublished*; ECtHR, *M.C. v. Bulgaria*, judgment of 4 December 2003, *Reports* 2003-XII; ECtHR, *Rees v. United Kingdom*, judgment of 17 October 1986, *Series* A No. 106; ECtHR, *Cossey v. United Kingdom*, judgment of 27 September 1990, *Series* A No. 184; ECtHR, *Sheffield & Horsham v. United Kingdom*, judgment of 30 July 1998, *Reports* 1998-V; ECtHR (GC), *Christine Goodwin v. United Kingdom*, judgment of 11 July 2002, *Reports* 2002-VI; ECtHR (GC), *I v. United Kingdom*, judgment of 11 July 2002, *Reports* 2002-VI; ECtHR, *B. v. France*, judgment of 25 March 1993, *Series* A No. 232-C; ECtHR, *Wemhoff v. Germany*, judgment of 27 June 1968, *Series* A No. 7; ECtHR, *Cruz Varas and others v. Sweden*, judgment of 20 March 1991, *Series* A No. 201; ECtHR, *Niemietz v. Germany*, judgment of 16 December 1992, *Series* A No. 251-B; ECtHR (GC), *Ferrazzini v. Italy*, judgment of 12 July 2001, Reports 2001-VII; ECtHR (GC), *Stec and others v. United Kingdom*, decision of 6 July 2005, *Reports* 2005-X; ECtHR (GC), *Comingersoll S.A. v. Portugal*, judgment of 6 April 2000, *Reports* 2000-IV; ECtHR, *James and others v. United Kingdom*, judgment of 21 February 1986, *Series* A No. 98; ECtHR (GC), *Üner v. the Netherlands*, judgment of 18 October 2006, *Reports* 2006-XII; ECtHR (GC), *Vilho Eskelinen and others v. Finland*, judgment of 19 April 2007, *unpublished*; ECtHR (GC), *Pellegrin v. France*, judgment of 8 December 1999, *Reports* 1999-VIII; ECtHR, *Van der Mussele v. Belgium*, judgment of 23 November 1983, *Series* A No. 70; ECtHR, *Soering v. United Kingdom*, judgment of 7 July 1989, *Series* A No. 161; ECtHR (GC), *Vo v. France*, judgment of 8 July 2004, *Reports* 2004-VIII; ECtHR, *Tyrer v. United Kingdom*, judgment of 25 April 1978, *Series* A No. 26; ECtHR, *Loizidou v. Turkey (preliminary objections)*, judgment of 23 March 1995, *Series* A No. 310; ECtHR, *Öztürk v. Germany*, judgment of 21 February 1984, *Series* A No. 73; ECtHR, *Engel and others v. the Netherlands*, judgment of 8 June 1976, *Series* A No. 22; ECtHR, *König v. Germany*, judgment of 28 June 1978, *Series* A No. 27; ECtHR (GC), *T v. United Kingdom*, judgment of 16 December 1999, *unpublished.*

92 ECtHR (GC), *Comingersoll S.A. v. Portugal*, judgment of 6 April 2000, *Reports* 2000-IV, § 34.

93 See for more references that hardly provide an insight into the material that is relied upon: ECtHR, *Niemietz v. Germany*, judgment of 16 December 1992, *Series* A No. 251-B, § 30; ECtHR, *Cossey v. United Kingdom*, judgment of 27 September 1990, *Series* A No. 184, § 40; ECtHR, *Wemhoff v. Germany*, judgment of 27 June 1968, *Series* A No. 7, § 9; ECtHR, *Öztürk v. Germany*, judgment

ECtHR in *Sigurdur A. Sigurjónsson* only referred to 'a large number of domestic systems'.[94] In addition in *Tyrer* the Court did not even define what the situation in the Contracting States is, even though it claims that it has influenced its decision: 'the Court cannot but be influenced by the developments and commonly accepted standards in the penal policy of the member States of the Council of Europe in this field.'[95] These examples render it rather difficult to understand at what point one can speak of a consensus or trend. A more elaborate example of this type of case can be found in the decision in *Stec*. Previous judgments by the Court had created two distinct lines of case law on the same subject matter. In *Stec*, the Court considered that it was time to remove the confusion and to decide on the new line for future cases.[96] The Court held that:

> The Court's approach to Article 1 of Protocol No. 1 should reflect the reality of the way in which welfare provision is currently organized within the Member States of the Council of Europe. It is clear that within those States, and within most individual States, there exist a wide range of social security benefits designed to confer entitlements which arise as of right. Benefits are funded in a large variety of ways ... Given the variety of funding methods, and the interlocking nature of benefits under most welfare systems, it appears increasingly artificial to hold that only benefits financed by contributions to a specific fund fall within the scope of Article 1 Protocol No. 1.[97]

Without attempting to find a real consensus, the Court limited itself to making a vague reference to 'those States' that showed a variety of approaches to the problem at hand, using this to support its choice for the broadest interpretation of the provision.[98]

---

of 21 February 1984, *Series* A No. 73, § 53; ECtHR (GC), *Ferrazzini v. Italy*, judgment of 12 July 2001, Reports 2001-VII, § 29; ECtHR (GC), *I v. United Kingdom*, judgment of 11 July 2002, *Reports* 2002-VI, § 65; ECtHR (GC), *Christine Goodwin v. United Kingdom*, judgment of 11 July 2002, *Reports* 2002-VI, § 85; ECtHR, *Van der Mussele v. Belgium*, judgment of 23 November 1983, *Series* A No. 70, § 40; ECtHR (GC), *Pellegrin v. France*, judgment of 8 December 1999, *Reports* 1999-VIII, § 62; ECtHR (GC), *Vilho Eskelinen and others v. Finland*, judgment of 19 April 2007, *unpublished*, § 57; ECtHR, *Cruz Varas and others v. Sweden*, judgment of 20 March 1991, *Series* A No. 201, § 100.

94 ECtHR, *Sigurdur A. Sigurjónsson v. Iceland*, judgment of 30 June 1993, *Series* A No. 264, § 35.

95 ECtHR, *Tyrer v. United Kingdom*, judgment of 25 April 1978, *Series* A No. 26, § 31.

96 In the case of *Stec* the Court had to determine whether both contributory and non-contributory benefits were considered 'possession' for the purpose of Article 1 Protocol No. 1. The case law had been contradictory on this point and there were many differences between the way the social system was organized in the different Member States. ECtHR (GC), *Stec and others v. United Kingdom*, decision of 6 July 2005, *Reports* 2005-X.

97 ECtHR (GC), *Stec and others v. United Kingdom*, decision of 6 July 2005, *Reports* 2005-X ,§ 50

98 The decision did include a paragraph that provided some comparative data on the pensionable age of men and women in Europe, but that data dealt with an entirely different question and as a result did not provide any help for the question discussed here.

In other cases the ECtHR does mention specific Contracting States, but it hardly ever refers to all Contracting States.[99] In *Micallef*, for example, references to a 'widespread practice' were used to argue for overruling the ECtHR's previous approach, which was to exclude injunction proceedings from the scope of Article 6 (right to fair trial). In a paragraph devoted to the comparative analysis, reference was made to 23 Contracting States (a relevant number according to the Court) in which injunction proceedings were protected by the guarantees provided by Article 6. In the eyes of the ECtHR this presented a 'widespread practice'. It is questionable whether this is indeed a widespread practice, considering that the European Convention has 47 Contracting States. If these Contracting States, which are not mentioned in *Micallef*, all exclude injunction proceedings from protection under the right to fair trial, the conclusion of the ECtHR comes to stand in an entirely different light (23 against 24 Contracting States). The aim of this remark is not to show that the conclusion of the ECtHR was wrong, but to show that it is difficult to understand the conclusion if only the Contracting States that support the conclusion are discussed. It would be more insightful to discuss the Contracting States that do not support the conclusion as well. This is especially relevant, because the theoretical chapter noted that a Contracting State which has taken an explicit position against the majority position might be less convinced by an argument based on the will of the majority.[100] In that context a discussion of the Contracting States which do not support the consensus, common standard or trend can either be used to support the conclusion of the Court or to show the need for an additional explanation for its conclusion. Moreover, there is the psychological aspect to not mentioning Contracting States. They might consider that they are not taken into account, especially if the ECtHR speaks of a 'relevant number of Contracting States'. After all, who determines which Member State is 'relevant'?

In the case of *M.C. v. Bulgaria*, where the ECtHR had to determine whether 'the Member States' positive obligations under Articles 3 and 8 of the Convention must be seen as requiring the penalization and effective prosecution of any non-consensual sexual act, including in the absence of physical resistance by the victim'.[101] The ECtHR referred to specific Contracting States in order to support the conclusion that the physical resistance of the victim was no longer required in rape cases. The ECtHR stated that most continental European Contracting States held this position, but actual reference was only made to eight Contracting States. The United Kingdom and Ireland

---

99 See ECtHR (GC), *Micallef v. Malta*, judgment of 15 October 2009, *unpublished*; ECtHR, *Schalk and Kopf v. Austria*, judgment of 24 June 2010, *unpublished*; ECtHR (GC), *T v. United Kingdom*, judgment of 16 December 1999, *unpublished*, for examples of cases where the ECtHR refers to an incomplete number of Contracting States.

100 See section 6.1.6.2.

101 ECtHR, *M.C. v. Bulgaria*, judgment of 4 December 2003, *Reports* 2003-XII, § 166.

were discussed separately under the common law countries. The conclusion that states were under a positive obligation to prosecute rape crimes even if there was no physical resistance by the victim was also supported by evidence from external comparative material. Moreover, the ECtHR relied on a Recommendation adopted by the Council of Ministers in which all Member States are represented.[102] Reference was also made to the findings of the International Criminal Tribunal for the former Yugoslavia to show developments in international criminal law. The ECtHR thus relied on different sources to support its conclusion. The purpose of discussing this case is, however, to show that vague references of the ECtHR to 'most European countries influenced by the continental legal tradition' can be quite misleading, if the judgment shows that only eight Contracting States have been analyzed.

In *Schalk & Kopf*, where the ECtHR held that there was not enough consensus to determine that the right to marriage included a right for same-sex couples to marry, the ECtHR also referred to around 22 Contracting States. Here only six Contracting States had adopted legislation to allow for same-sex couples to marry, which was not enough to support a radical turn in Article 12 case law. The ECtHR did discuss other Contracting States where legislative proposals were pending or that had already adopted legislation allowing same-sex couples to legally register their union, but not to marry. Even though the comparative analysis did not provide enough support to find a consensus on Article 12, the ECtHR did witness a growing trend towards legal recognition of same-sex couples and thus determined that these types of relationships were henceforth covered under the notion of 'family life' (Article 8). The question whether some sort of consensus is actually required or whether a mere tendency is enough, thus appears to depend on the specific issue the Court is presented with.

The question whether there is enough support for a consensus or common standard is also complicated by another factor. Should all Contracting States have adopted similar measures or is it sufficient to constitute a consensus that developments can be seen, even though they might not all go in the same direction? This question is related to an issue that has been discussed in the theoretical chapter, namely that this also may depend on the level of abstractness of the question to be answered.[103] If a question is posed at a relatively abstract level it might be easier to find a consensus than in cases where a relatively concrete question is asked. The answer can also be approached from two angles, on the one hand in an abstract manner, namely to conclude that there is a clear tendency towards one specific direction and on the other hand the answer can also be approached in a rather concrete manner by requiring that all Contracting States adopt a similar standard. This can be illustrated by the case

102 ECtHR, *M.C. v. Bulgaria*, judgment of 4 December 2003, *Reports* 2003-XII, § 162.
103 See section 6.1.6.2.

of *T v United Kingdom*.[104] This case concerned an 11-year old boy who had to stand trial for murdering a two-year old boy. He claimed that this constituted inhuman and degrading treatment due to his youth. The Court invoked the general notion of evolutive interpretation to justify its taking the minimum age for criminal responsibility throughout Europe into account.[105] Subsequently, it concluded that no common standard could be found, thereby referring to a number of Contracting States. The overview included about half the Contracting States and showed that a few states had a similarly low age of criminal responsibility as the United Kingdom (7 or 8 years old), while many others had a higher minimum age, varying from 13 years old to 18 years old.[106] The majority in *T* concluded that no common standard could be found on the basis of the Contracting States listed; the United Kingdom had one of the lowest in age (together with only a few other countries), but this did not disproportionately differ from the age limit in the other Contracting States.[107] The dissenting judges did not agree and concluded there was indeed a clear minimum standard.[108] They considered that only a few out of the then 41 Contracting States (not even half of those that were explicitly mentioned in the overview provided by the Court) had such a low age; all the others used a higher minimum age. The dissenters thus adopted a more abstract analysis and pointed to the fact that most states opted for a higher age, even though they did not necessarily all adopt the same minimum age. This example shows that the same comparative materials can lead to opposing conclusions.[109]

A similar problem can be noted in the case of *Sheffield and Horsham* on the right of transsexuals to have their gender change legally recognized.[110] The Court in this case had to decide again on the rights of transsexuals under Article 8 of the Convention. An NGO provided a comparative study outlining different legislative trends throughout Europe.[111] The Court held on the basis of this study that it was: 'not fully satisfied that the legislative trends outlined by *amicus* suffice to establish the existence of any common European approach to the problems created by the recog-

104 See also ECtHR (GC), *V v. United Kingdom*, judgment of 16 December 1999, *Reports* 1999-IX. This is the parallel case to ECtHR (GC), *T v. United Kingdom*, judgment of 16 December 1999, *unpublished.*

105 ECtHR (GC), *T v. United Kingdom*, judgment of 16 December 1999, *unpublished* , § 70.

106 ECtHR (GC), *T v. United Kingdom*, judgment of 16 December 1999, *unpublished* , § 48.

107 ECtHR (GC), *T v. United Kingdom*, judgment of 16 December 1999, *unpublished* , § 72.

108 ECtHR (GC), *T v. United Kingdom*, judgment of 16 December 1999, *unpublished,* dissenting opinion by Judges Pastor Ridruejo, Ress, Makarczyk, Tulkens and Butkevych, § 1.

109 A similar problem can be seen in the discussion on the transsexuals cases; see section 10.2.1.1. for the discussion on the transsexuals cases.

110 ECtHR, *Sheffield & Horsham v. United Kingdom*, judgment of 30 July 1998, *Reports* 1998-V.

111 The judgment itself only contains a very succinct overview of that comparative study.

nition in law of post-operative gender status.'[112] It subsequently outlined in which areas the Court considered that there was no common approach. The dissenters did not agree with this approach and considered that it was impossible to request uniformity in such a highly complex and controversial area. The dissenters continued to consider that:

> ... the essential point is that in these countries, unlike in the United Kingdom, change has taken place – whatever its precise form is – in an attempt to alleviate the distress and suffering of the post-operative transsexual and that there exists in Europe a general trend which seeks in differing ways to confer recognition on the altered sexual identity.[113]

In other words, the fact that different solutions were sought, according to the dissenters, did not matter, but what did matter was that most Contracting States were seeking a solution.

Two other cases from this line of cases on the rights of transsexuals warrant discussion. First of all, in one of the early cases on the rights of transsexuals, namely *Cossey*, the Court had to examine whether sufficient changes had taken place to warrant overruling the case of *Rees*.[114] When discussing the legal developments the Court considered the following:

> There have been certain developments since 1986 in the law of some of the member States of the Council of Europe. However, the reports accompanying [a Resolution by the European Parliament and a Recommendation by the Parliamentary Assembly of the Council of Europe] reveal, ..., the same diversity of practice as obtained at the time of the Rees judgment.[115]

Without mentioning one single development or reference to the law in a State the Court dismissed the developments as not sufficient. At least two of the dissenting judges, however, drew the opposite conclusion from the same materials according to their dissenting opinions.[116] Judge Martens actually supported his conclusion with references to specific developments.[117] By failing to provide support for its

---

112 ECtHR, *Sheffield & Horsham v. United Kingdom*, judgment of 30 July 1998, *Reports* 1998-V, § 57.

113 ECtHR, *Sheffield & Horsham v. United Kingdom*, judgment of 30 July 1998, *Reports* 1998-V, joint partly dissenting opinion by Judges Bernhardt, Thór Vilhjámsson, Spielmann, Palm, Wildhaber, Makarczyk and Voicu.

114 ECtHR, *Cossey v. United Kingdom*, judgment of 27 September 1990, *Series* A No. 184; ECtHR, *Rees v. United Kingdom*, judgment of 17 October 1986, *Series* A No. 106. See section 10.2.1.1. for a more detailed account on the transsexuals cases.

115 ECtHR, *Cossey v. United Kingdom*, judgment of 27 September 1990, *Series* A No. 184, § 40.

116 ECtHR, *Cossey v. United Kingdom*, judgment of 27 September 1990, *Series* A No. 184, joint partly dissenting opinion by Judges MacDonald and Spielmann and dissenting opinion by Martens.

117 ECtHR, *Cossey v. United Kingdom*, judgment of 27 September 1990, *Series* A No. 184, dissenting opinion by Martens § 5.5.

conclusion on the comparative material the majority thus left more room for discussion than perhaps would have been the case if they had paid more attention to show that in their view no consensus existed.

A consensus or trend is mostly based on references to the Contracting States, but not always; in some cases a combination can be found.[118] The case of *Christine Goodwin* presents a famous example of relying solely on an external trend.[119] This case was the last one in the line of transsexual cases and the ECtHR considered that there was still no European consensus on the issue. In the eyes of the ECtHR 'the lack of such a common approach among forty-three Contracting States with widely diverse legal systems and traditions is hardly surprising'.[120] The ECtHR continued and referred to the fact that in their view a clear and uncontested international trend could be found.[121] Reference was made to Singapore, Canada, South Africa, Israel, Australia, New Zealand and almost all states of the United States of America.[122]

The examples discussed have so far indicated that it is not clear when the ECtHR will conclude that a consensus or trend can be found. In *M.C.* ten Contracting States were sufficient, in *Schalk & Kopf* six Contracting States were not enough, while in *Christine Goodwin* no consensus could be found, but evidence from seven foreign countries proved to be sufficient. It thus depends heavily on the specific context and the specific question. The problem is that the lack of standards also leads to different interpretations and outcomes, as indicated by some of the dissents. As a result this might jeopardize the persuasiveness and credibility of this method.

---

118 In some cases in addition to the consensus or trend found in Member States the ECtHR does refer to external materials as well. For example in the case of ECtHR, *M.C. v. Bulgaria*, judgment of 4 December 2003, *Reports* 2003-XII, where the results of Member States were supported with a reference to the ICTY. In *Demir & Baykara* references were made to several international and Council of Europe materials and also to the practice in Member States. ECtHR (GC), *Demir and Baykara v. Turkey*, judgment of 12 November 2008, *unpublished*.

119 ECtHR (GC), *Christine Goodwin v. United Kingdom*, judgment of 11 July 2002, *Reports* 2002-VI. See also: ECtHR (GC), *Scoppola v. Italy (No. 2),* judgment of 17 September 2009, *unpublished*, where the majority relied on a consensus that emerged in Europe and internationally, but reference was made only to external documents. In *Mamatkulov* the ECtHR also only looked at external materials to find an international trend. This was, however, inevitable given that they were seeking an answer that was related to a procedural matter in the context of international or supranational adjudication. Looking at Member States would not have provided any relevant results. ECtHR (GC), *Mamatkulov and Askarov v. Turkey*, judgment of 4 February 2005, *Reports* 2005-I.

120 ECtHR (GC), *Christine Goodwin v. United Kingdom*, judgment of 11 July 2002, *Reports* 2002-VI, § 85.

121 ECtHR (GC), *Christine Goodwin v. United Kingdom*, judgment of 11 July 2002, *Reports* 2002-VI, § 85.

122 ECtHR (GC), *Christine Goodwin v. United Kingdom*, judgment of 11 July 2002, *Reports* 2002-VI, § 55.

The second aspect that should be discussed in this context is the question what these references entail. It has already been said, in the majority of the cases that the consensus or trend is established on the basis of references to Contracting States, sometimes with support from external materials. Only in rare cases is reference made to only external materials. Even then, however, it is not clear on which kind of materials these references are based, such as legislation, case law or other materials. Interestingly, a difference can be noted in this regard between cases in which the Court refers to external or Council of Europe documents and cases in which it refers to the law of the States.

The cases of *Mamatkulov*, *Demir*, *James and others*, *Stec* and *Sigurdur* can serve as good examples of such differences. In *Mamatkulov* the ECtHR referred to external materials to support its conclusion that interim measures are binding on the respondent Contracting States. In the paragraph devoted to the presentation of 'relevant international law and practice', reference was made to the Statute of the International Court of Justice and to excerpts of some of its judgments.[123] Reference was also made to the rule of procedures of the United Nations Committee against Torture, United Nations Human Rights Committee and the Inter-American Court of Human Rights.[124] Not only the relevant parts of their rules of procedure were cited in the judgment, but even excerpts of relevant decisions or judgments were reproduced. When dealing with the question of interim measures, the ECtHR referred back to these observations.[125]

Similarly extensive references to international and Council of Europe materials can be found in the case of *Demir & Baykara*.[126] Several provisions of different Conventions of the International Labour Organization (ILO) were discussed, including references to explanations of these provisions by relevant committees, such as the ILO Committee of Experts.[127] A similar type of reference was made to provisions of the European Social Charter and the explanation provided by the European Committee of Social Rights.[128] In addition relevant provisions of the International Covenant on Civil and Political Rights, the International Covenant on Economic, Social and

123 ECtHR (GC), *Mamatkulov and Askarov v. Turkey*, judgment of 4 February 2005, *Reports* 2005-I, § 46-48.

124 ECtHR (GC), *Mamatkulov and Askarov v. Turkey*, judgment of 4 February 2005, *Reports* 2005-I, § 40-45 & 51-53.

125 ECtHR (GC), *Mamatkulov and Askarov v. Turkey*, judgment of 4 February 2005, *Reports* 2005-I, § 113-117.

126 ECtHR (GC), *Demir and Baykara v. Turkey*, judgment of 12 November 2008, *unpublished.*

127 ECtHR (GC), *Demir and Baykara v. Turkey*, judgment of 12 November 2008, *unpublished,* § 37-39 and 42-44.

128 ECtHR (GC), *Demir and Baykara v. Turkey*, judgment of 12 November 2008, *unpublished,* § 45 and 49-50.

Cultural Rights and the EU Charter on Fundamental Rights were cited.[129] The reference to the Contracting States was both extensive and limited at the same time. The reference did provide an analysis of the situation in the Contracting States by generally discussing the current situation in Europe without mentioning specific Contracting States, but no references were made to the materials from which this information had been drawn.[130] Of course, it would make judgments extremely long if the ECtHR were to discuss per Member State the analyzed materials,[131] but it would be more insightful if the ECtHR in general indicates the type of materials considered: legislation, case law, policy or other materials.

The case of *James and others* provides an example which does provide information on the type of data analyzed.[132] The question was how the notion of 'in the public interest' contained in Article 1 Protocol 1 (the right to property) should be explained. The ECtHR claimed that 'no common principle can be identified in the constitutions, legislation, and case-law of the Contracting States that would warrant understanding the notion of public interest as outlawing compulsory transfer between private parties'.[133] Even though this reference could have been more elaborate on other aspects, it is useful to know the type of materials analyzed for this conclusion.

In a case like *Sigurdur* the ECtHR did not provide any insight at all into the material used. The ECtHR simply stated on the question whether Article 11 includes a right not join an association:

129 ECtHR (GC), *Demir and Baykara v. Turkey*, judgment of 12 November 2008, *unpublished,* § 40-41, 47, 51.

130 ECtHR (GC), *Demir and Baykara v. Turkey*, judgment of 12 November 2008, *unpublished,* § 52. As to the practice of European States, it can be observed that, in the vast majority of them, the right for public servants to bargain collectively with the authorities has been recognized, subject to various exceptions so as to exclude certain areas (disciplinary procedures, pensions, medical insurance, wages of senior civil servants) or certain categories of civil servants who hold exclusive powers of the State (members of the armed forces and of the police, judges, diplomats, career civil servants at federal level). The right of public servants working for local authorities and not holding State powers to engage in collective bargaining in order to determine their wages and working conditions has been recognized in the vast majority of Contracting States. The remaining exceptions can be justified by particular circumstances. Similar in ECtHR (GC), *T v. United Kingdom*, judgment of 16 December 1999, *unpublished.*

131 The case of ECtHR, *M.C. v. Bulgaria*, judgment of 4 December 2003, *Reports* 2003-XII, is an exception in this context. The discussion on the Member States in that case referred to specific provision of national legislation and thus provided insight into the material on which the subsequent conclusion would be based. This case, however, did not address all Member States, but only discussed ten Member States.

132 ECtHR, *James and others v. United Kingdom*, judgment of 21 February 1986, *Series* A No. 98.

133 ECtHR, *James and others v. United Kingdom*, judgment of 21 February 1986, *Series* A No. 98, § 40.

> Compulsory membership of this nature, which, it may be recalled, concerned a private-law association, does not exist under the laws of the great majority of the Contracting States. On the contrary, a large number of domestic systems contain safeguards which, in one way or another, guarantee the negative aspect of the freedom of association, that is the freedom not to join or to withdraw from an association.[134]

No paragraph providing data on which this conclusion is based can be found in the judgment, which renders it difficult to verify the conclusion.

These are some examples of varying degrees of referring to both international data and data on the Contracting States. While more elaborate discussions on the data drawn from the Contracting States are exceptional, they are much more common when reference is made to international materials or Council of Europe treaties. This makes it especially more difficult to understand the conclusions drawn on the basis of references to Contracting States.

10.4.2 Separate references to international, regional and foreign materials

In many different cases the Court relies on international or regional material or material based on foreign jurisdictions as a basis for comparative interpretation.[135] The ECtHR hardly ever relies on references to specific Contracting States without looking for a trend or consensus; therefore the discussion in this section is limited to those instances when the ECtHR, for one of the purposes listed in section 6.1.4 looks at external materials or Council of Europe documents.

134 ECtHR, *Sigurdur A. Sigurjónsson v. Iceland*, judgment of 30 June 1993, *Series* A No. 264, § 35.

135 ECtHR, *Pretty v. United Kingdom*, judgment of 29 April 2002, *Reports* 2002-III Pretty; ECtHR (GC), *Saadi v. United Kingdom*, judgment of 29 January 2008, *unpublished*; ECtHR, *Costello-Roberts v. United Kingdom*, judgment of 25 March 1993, *Series* A No. 247-C; ECtHR (GC), *Selmouni v. France*, judgment of 28 July 1999, *Reports* 1999-V; ECtHR (GC), *Amann v. Switzerland*, judgment of 16 February 2000, *Reports* 2000-II; ECtHR (GC), *Banković and others v. Belgium and others*, decision of 12 December 2001, Reports 2001-VII; ECtHR (GC), *Stoll v. Switzerland,* judgment of 10 December 2007, *unpublished*; ECtHR (GC), *Demir and Baykara v. Turkey*, judgment of 12 November 2008, *unpublished*; ECtHR (GC), *Öneryildiz v. Turkey*, judgment of 30 November 2004, *Reports* 2004-XII; ECtHR, *P.G. and J.H. v. United Kingdom*, judgment of 25 September 2001, *Reports* 2001-IX; ECtHR, *Cruz Varas and others v. Sweden*, judgment of 20 March 1991, *Series* A No. 201; ECtHR, *Soering v. United Kingdom*, judgment of 7 July 1989, *Series* A No. 161; ECtHR, *James and others v. United Kingdom*, judgment of 21 February 1986, *Series* A No. 98; ECtHR, *Marckx v. Belgium*, judgment of 13 June 1979, *Series* A No. 31; ECtHR (GC), *Vilho Eskelinen and others v. Finland*, judgment of 19 April 2007, *unpublished.*

These references have included, but not been limited to: UN documents (mainly treaties and conventions);[136] other (regional) human rights instruments;[137] Council of Europe documents, mainly treaties and materials from the Parliamentary Assembly;[138] material from the European Union, like directives, the EU Charter on Fundamental Rights, judgments from the Court of Justice of the European Union;[139] judgments from other international courts;[140] specialized international treaties;[141] and judgments from foreign jurisdictions.[142]

In *Costello Roberts,* for example, the Court had to determine whether Articles 3 and 8 of the Convention had been violated. The headmaster of a private school had

---

136 For example: ECtHR (GC), *Zolotukhin v. Russia*, judgment of 10 February 2009, *unpublished*, for a reference to the International Covenant on Civil and Political Rights in § 79; ECtHR (GC), *Mamatkulov and Askarov v. Turkey*, judgment of 4 February 2005, *Reports* 2005-I, for a reference to the United Nations Committee against Torture in § 115; ECtHR (GC), *Saadi v. United Kingdom*, judgment of 29 January 2008, *unpublished*, for a reference to the United Nations High Commissioner for Refugee's Programme and the UNHRC Guidelines in § 65; ECtHR (GC), *Selmouni v. France*, judgment of 28 July 1999, *Reports* 1999-V, for a reference to the United Nations Convention against Torture and other Cruel and Inhuman or Degrading Treatment of Punishment in § 97.

137 Mainly references to the American Convention on Human Rights: ECtHR (GC), *Zolotukhin v. Russia*, judgment of 10 February 2009, unpublished, § 79; ECtHR (GC), *Mamatkulov and Askarov v. Turkey*, judgment of 4 February 2005, *Reports* 2005-I, § 116; ECtHR, *Soering v United Kingdom*, judgment of 7 July 1989, *Series* A No. 161, § 108.

138 See for example: ECtHR (GC), *Amann v. Switzerland*, judgment of 16 February 2000, *Reports* 2000-II, referring to the Council of Europe Convention for the Protection of Individuals with regard to Automatic Processing of Personal Data in § 65; ECtHR (GC), *Demir and Baykara v. Turkey*, judgment of 12 November 2008, *unpublished*, referring to, among others, the European Social Charter in § 149; ECtHR, *Marckx v. Belgium*, judgment of 13 June 1979, *Series* A No. 31, referring to the European Convention on the Legal Status of Children born out of Wedlock in § 41; ECtHR, *Koua Poirrez v. France*, judgment of 30 September 2003, *Reports* 2003-X, referring to a Recommendation from the Committee of Ministers in § 39.

139 See for example: ECtHR (GC), *Vilho Eskelinen and others v. Finland*, judgment of 19 April 2007, *unpublished*, referring to the EU Charter and case law of the CJEU in § 60; ECtHR (GC), *Micallef v. Malta*, judgment of 15 October 2009, *unpublished*, referring to case law of the CJEU in § 78; ECtHR, *Schalk and Kopf v. Austria*, judgment of 24 June 2010, *unpublished,* referring to the EU Charter in § 60; ECtHR, *Posti and Rahko v. Finland*, judgment of 24 September 2002, Reports 2002-VII, referring to case law of the CJEU in § 54.

140 See for example: ECtHR, *Rantsev v. Cyprus and Russia*, judgment of 7 January 2010, *unpublished*, referring to judgments of the ICTY in § 280; ECtHR, *M.C. v. Bulgaria*, judgment of 4 December 2003, *Reports* 2003-XII, referring to judgments from the ICTY as well in § 163; ECtHR (GC), *Mamatkulov and Askarov v. Turkey*, judgment of 4 February 2005, *Reports* 2005-I, referring to the case law of the International Court of Justice in § 117.

141 This does not happen often. See for example: ECtHR, *Pretty v. United Kingdom*, judgment of 29 April 2002, *Reports* 2002-III, referring to a judgment from the Canadian Supreme Court in § 66.

142 See for example: ECtHR, *James and others v. United Kingdom*, judgment of 21 February 1986, *Series* A No. 98; ECtHR, *Pretty v. United Kingdom*, judgment of 29 April 2002, *Reports* 2002-III.

inflicted corporal punishment on a schoolboy in accordance with the disciplinary rules. The applicability of the Convention depended on the question whether this treatment invoked the responsibility of the United Kingdom under Article 1 of the Convention. The Court recalled that the Convention should be read as a whole and that it included an obligation for states to secure the right to education. School discipline was, in the view of the Court, not secondary to the educational process and as a result this fell within the responsibility of the respondent state. In order to support its own view the Court stated that:

> That a school's disciplinary system falls within the ambit of the right to education has also been recognized, more recently, in Article 28 of the United Nations Convention of the Rights of Child of 20 November 1989 which entered into force on 2 September 1990 and was ratified by the United Kingdom on 16 December 1991.[143]

The Court substantiated this support based on the United Nations Convention of the Rights of the Child by a reference to the text of the relevant provision, which literally referred to school discipline.[144]

A similar reference was made in *Selmouni*[145] where the Court was struggling to determine whether certain acts amounted to torture under Article 3 of the Convention. The Court held that the distinction between torture and inhuman or degrading treatment was intended to attach a 'special stigma to deliberate inhuman treatment causing very serious and cruel suffering'.[146] Support for this approach was provided by the United Nations Convention against Torture and Other Cruel, Inhuman or Degrading Treatment or Punishment, which embodied the same distinction in its Articles 1 and 16 as was shown by the inclusion of their text in the judgment of the Court.[147]

In Amann[148] the Court, instead, relied on a regional Convention in order to underpin its argument. The Court held that Article 8 of the Convention should not be interpreted narrowly and as a result the storing of data relating to an individual's private life fell within the scope of the provision.

143 ECtHR, *Costello-Roberts v. United Kingdom*, judgment of 25 March 1993, *Series* A No. 247-C, § 27. ECtHR (GC), *Saadi v. United Kingdom*, judgment of 29 January 2008, *unpublished* and ECtHR (GC), *Stoll v. Switzerland,* judgment of 10 December 2007, *unpublished,* equally rely on UN material to support the interpretation in those cases.

144 ECtHR, *Costello-Roberts v. United Kingdom*, judgment of 25 March 1993, *Series* A No. 247-C, § 27.

145 ECtHR (GC), Selmouni v. France, judgment of 28 July 1999, *Reports* 1999-V.

146 ECtHR (GC), Selmouni v. France, judgment of 28 July 1999, *Reports* 1999-V, § 96.

147 ECtHR (GC), Selmouni v. France, judgment of 28 July 1999, *Reports* 1999-V, § 97.

148 ECtHR (GC), Amann v. Switzerland, judgment of 16 February 2000, *Reports* 2000-II.

> That broad interpretation corresponds with that of the Council of Europe's Convention of 28 January 1981 for the Protection of Individuals with regard to Automatic Processing of Personal Data ... whose purpose it is "to secure in the territory of each Party for every individual ... respect for his rights and fundamental freedoms, and in particular his right to privacy, with regard to automatic processing of personal data relating to him" (Article 1), such personal data being defined as "any information relating to an identified or identifiable individual" (Article 2).[149]

Just like in other cases, the Court relied on a specialized treaty, in this case a Council of Europe Convention, to support the interpretation of the general Article 8 of the European Convention.

Whenever the Court invokes references to international materials or materials from foreign jurisdictions, it generally is rather specific in presenting the material. The Court, for example, explicitly invoked a Canadian judgment that dealt with a similar matter as the ECtHR in the case of *Pretty*.[150] Or the Court invokes 'the practice of the Freedom of Association Committee of the Governing Body of the International Labor Office (ILO)', whereby it refers to the exact page where the decision supporting this argument can be found.[151] In a similar way the Court has referred to 'observations of the United Nations Human Rights Committee', while citing some of the observations themselves.[152] It is possible to continue this list, but that might not add anything extra. The important observation to make is that contrasted with references to material from the Contracting States, the references to international material are generally on a much more specific level and allow for much less disagreement on the conclusion to be drawn from them. This difference was also mentioned in the previous section. The case law does not provide any explanation for this difference, but perhaps the Court considers that this somehow increases the legitimacy of referring to these materials in the first place.

---

149 ECtHR (GC), Amann v. Switzerland, judgment of 16 February 2000, *Reports* 2000-II, § 65. The same reference can be found in ECtHR, *P.G. and J.H. v. United Kingdom*, judgment of 25 September 2001, *Reports* 2001-IX, § 57 which dealt with the same subject matter. In *Öneryildiz* the Court refers to European developments reflected in Council of Europe documents, ECtHR (GC), *Öneryildiz v. Turkey*, judgment of 30 November 2004, *Reports* 2004-XII. ECtHR, *Marckx v. Belgium*, judgment of 13 June 1979, *Series* A No. 31 also refers to CoE material (CoM Resolution). In ECtHR, *Pretty v. United Kingdom*, judgment of 29 April 2002, *Reports* 2002-III, § 40 reference is made to a Recommendation of the Parliamentary Assembly of the Council of Europe.

150 ECtHR, *Pretty v. United Kingdom,* judgment of 29 April 2002, *Reports* 2002-III Pretty § 66.

151 ECtHR, *Sigurdur A. Sigurjónsson v. Iceland,* judgment of 30 June 1993, *Series* A No. 264, § 35.

152 ECtHR (GC), *Stoll v. Switzerland,* judgment of 10 December 2007, *unpublished,* § 54 and 42.

10.4.3 Used to support argument or decisive argument?

By now, it has become clear that comparative interpretation in the ECtHR's case law can serve various purposes and it can be used in different ways, which have generally be analyzed as looking for a consensus or by referring to one or a few specific comparative sources. There is one final aspect that needs to be discussed in this context and that is whether the comparative argument is the sole or main argument pleading for a specific interpretation or whether comparative interpretation is used to support other interpretation methods.

In cases like, *M.C.*, *Mamatkulov* and *Vo* the comparative arguments play a crucial role.[153] The comparative argument might not be the only argument provided, but from these judgments it emerges that the comparative argument played a decisive role in these cases. The conclusion is thus almost exclusively built upon the comparative argument. In the majority of cases comparative arguments are used in addition to arguments based on other interpretation methods, like textual interpretation or systemic interpretation.[154] Cases like *Rantsev* and *Van der Mussele*, illustrate this use of comparative arguments, whereby comparative arguments are one of a set of arguments used to argue for a specific conclusion.

It is perhaps not always possible to make this distinction clearly, because it does not always become entirely clear from the presentation whether all arguments played an equal role or not. The main point is to realize that comparative arguments are both used to support an argument or as a decisive argument. This renders it even more important that this method is used in a convincing manner.

---

153 See also ECtHR, *Kimlya and others v. Russia,* judgment of 1 October 2009, *unpublished*; ECtHR (GC), *Demir and Baykara v. Turkey*, judgment of 12 November 2008, *unpublished.* ECtHR (GC), *Christine Goodwin v. United Kingdom*, judgment of 11 July 2002, *Reports* 2002-VI.

154 See for example: ECtHR, *James and others v. United Kingdom,* judgment of 21 February 1986, *Series* A No. 98; ECtHR (GC), *Selmouni v. France*, judgment of 28 July 1999, *Reports* 1999-V; ECtHR (GC), *Amann v. Switzerland*, judgment of 16 February 2000, *Reports* 2000-II; ECtHR (GC), *Saadi v. United Kingdom*, judgment of 29 January 2008, *unpublished*; ECtHR, *Niemietz v. Germany*, judgment of 16 December 1992, *Series* A No. 251-B; ECtHR (GC), *Ferrazzini v. Italy*, judgment of 12 July 2001, Reports 2001-VII; ECtHR (GC), *Stec and others v. United Kingdom*, decision of 6 July 2005, *Reports* 2005-X; ECtHR, *Marckx v. Belgium*, judgment of 13 June 1979, *Series* A No. 31; ECtHR, *Van der Mussele v. Belgium*, judgment of 23 November 1983, *Series* A No. 70; ECtHR, *Soering v. United Kingdom*, judgment of 7 July 1989, *Series* A No. 161; ECtHR, *Costello-Roberts v. United Kingdom*, judgment of 25 March 1993, *Series* A No. 247-C; ECtHR (GC), *Pellegrin v. France*, judgment of 8 December 1999, *Reports* 1999-VIII; ECtHR (GC), *Vilho Eskelinen and others v. Finland*, judgment of 19 April 2007, *unpublished*; ECtHR (GC), *Stoll v. Switzerland,* judgment of 10 December 2007, *unpublished.*

10.4.4 Does the ECtHR acknowledge the distinction between internal and external materials?

The theoretical chapter on comparative interpretation distinguished between the use of internal and external materials. Internal materials are based on the situation in the Member States of the European Convention, while external materials come from countries outside the European Convention or are international or regional in character, such as UN Conventions or EU materials or Council of Europe documents. The reason to make this distinction is that a different justification has to be provided for each of the different sources of materials, as explained in section 6.1.3. The question to be answered in this section is whether the Court considers it necessary to make this distinction as well.

The answer can be rather short: the Court does not seem to think that this distinction is relevant. While indications for such a non-differential approach can already be found in earlier judgments,[155] the Court in the recent case of *Demir and Baykara* clearly implied that the distinction does not matter. In its methodological account of comparative interpretation the Court was presented with a slightly different question, namely whether the fact that a respondent state had not ratified a certain instrument mattered for comparative arguments. The Court answered that question in the negative, considering as follows in doing so:

> The consensus emerging from specialized international instruments and from the practice of contracting States may constitute a relevant consideration for the Court when it interprets the provisions of the Convention in specific cases.[156]

The Court thus treats internal and external material in exactly the same way. Though it does try to provide an extra justification for referring to international materials, as indicated in section 10.3, this justification can only cover references to a limited selection of international materials. Does the fact that the ECtHR does not acknowledge this distinction mean that it is not valid or not relevant in practice? One can argue that that is not the case. The *Demir and Baykara* case might even prove the point that a distinction should be made between different types of material and that these require different justifications. There are good arguments for distinguishing between European materials and non-European materials, which have been discussed

---

155 For example in ECtHR (GC), *I v. United Kingdom*, judgment of 11 July 2002, *Reports* 2002-VI and ECtHR (GC), *Christine Goodwin v. United Kingdom*, judgment of 11 July 2002, *Reports* 2002-VI.

156 ECtHR (GC), *Demir and Baykara v. Turkey*, judgment of 12 November 2008, *unpublished*, § 85. This excerpt has already been quoted above, but it is easier for the discussion not to refer back, but to repeat the statement here as well.

in the theoretical chapter. This distinction could have benefited the ECtHR in providing a convincing answer to the question posed in *Demir and Baykara.*

10.4.5 Who collects the materials?

The material that is used for comparative interpretation has to be carefully collected and selected, since not every piece might be relevant for the case. This process might not seem that interesting, but it can have a strong influence on the comparative argument. The choice for certain materials can be crucial for the argument in question, since the reasoning is naturally only based on the selected materials. If this process is underestimated the Court risks being criticized for cherry-picking or worse of manipulating the comparative argument.[157] It might be impossible to undertake an extensive comparative research for each case before the Court or even for each Grand Chamber judgment, but it is important that the selection process is undertaken carefully. This element of the comparative method might not be very visible in the case law, but perhaps some information can be gained from the case law analysis.

Does the case law provide any insight into who collects the comparative materials? This is hardly ever clarified in the Court's case law. In some cases where one of the parties supplies comparative information or where it is supplied by an intervening third party this has been explicitly mentioned.[158] In most other cases the source of the reference is not clarified. The more recent cases, especially recent Grand Chamber judgments, often include a section on comparative and international material.[159] The extent of the overview in those cases depends on the specific issue,

157 See section 6.1.6.2.

158 See among others: ECtHR (GC), *Mamatkulov and Askarov v. Turkey,* judgment of 4 February 2005, *Reports* 2005-I; ECtHR (GC), *Christine Goodwin v. United Kingdom,* judgment of 11 July 2002, *Reports* 2002-VI; ECtHR (GC), *I v. United Kingdom,* judgment of 11 July 2002, *Reports* 2002-VI; ECtHR (GC), *Banković and others v. Belgium and others,* decision of 12 December 2001, Reports 2001-VII; ECtHR, *Soering v. United Kingdom,* judgment of 7 July 1989, *Series* A No. 161; ECtHR, *James and others v. United Kingdom,* judgment of 21 February 1986, *Series* A No. 98.

159 ECtHR (GC), *Pellegrin v. France,* judgment of 8 December 1999, *Reports* 1999-VIII; ECtHR (GC), *T v. United Kingdom,* judgment of 16 December 1999, *unpublished*; ECtHR (GC), *Chapman v. United Kingdom,* judgment of 18 January 2001, *Reports* 2001-I; ECtHR (GC), *Banković and others v. Belgium and others,* decision of 12 December 2001, Reports 2001-VII; ECtHR (GC), *Christine Goodwin v. United Kingdom,* judgment of 11 July 2002, *Reports* 2002-VI; ECtHR (GC), *I v. United Kingdom,* judgment of 11 July 2002, *Reports* 2002-VI; ECtHR, *Pretty v. United Kingdom,* judgment of 29 April 2002, *Reports* 2002-III; ECtHR, *M.C. v. Bulgaria,* judgment of 4 December 2003, *Reports* 2003-XII; ECtHR (GC), *Vo v. France,* judgment of 8 July 2004, *Reports* 2004-VIII; ECtHR (GC), *Öneryildiz v. Turkey,* judgment of 30 November 2004, *Reports* 2004-XII; ECtHR (GC), *Mamatkulov and Askarov v. Turkey,* judgment of 4 February 2005, *Reports* 2005-I; ECtHR (GC), *Stec and others v. United Kingdom,* decision of 6 July 2005, *Reports* 2005-X; ECtHR (GC), *Vilho Eskelinen and others v. Finland,* judgment of 19 April 2007, *unpublished*; ECtHR (GC), *Stoll v. Switzerland,* judgment of

but also, as shown in section 10.4.2 on the type of material to be discussed. In most cases this material is actually used in the reasoning of the Court, but this is not the case for all of these judgments. This change in the case law can be explained by the fact that a research unit has been set up in the Court. There is not much public information on this unit, but it seems safe to assume that the sections on comparative and international material are based on findings made by this research unit. The setting up of the unit clearly is an improvement, since it enhances the capacity of the Court to do comparative research. Still, an important question that cannot be answered on the basis of the case law is who determines the framework for the research. Or to put it differently: who decides what will be investigated. That may be the unit itself, but it may also be the judge-rapporteur in a particular case. The same lack of clarity exists as to who selects which results are relevant for the case at hand. Thus, even though the existence of the research unit shows that the Court does take comparative interpretation seriously, it is not possible to answer a number of important questions as to its exact functioning on the basis of publicly available information.

10.5 Role of comparative reasoning in relation to other methods and principles

The lengthy analysis of comparative interpretation in this chapter has already dealt with the relationship between comparative interpretation and other interpretative methods on some specific occasions. The aim of the discussion in the current section is to identify the relations that have not yet been mentioned and to briefly recall those that have been touched upon. Specific attention will be paid to the relation between comparative interpretation and those other interpretative aids that are central to this thesis.

In general there is no clear relation between comparative interpretation and other interpretative aids, with one notable exception that will be discussed below. Beyond the fact that in some cases teleological interpretation and comparative interpretation support the same interpretation,[160] there is no relevant relation between these two methods. The only relation that can be discerned from the case law is that both are interpretation methods used by the Court.

A few cases refer to the existence of a connection between autonomous interpretation and comparative interpretation. In *Pellegrin* the Court was struggling with the

10 December 2007, *unpublished*; ECtHR (GC), *Saadi v. United Kingdom*, judgment of 29 January 2008, *unpublished*; ECtHR (GC), *Demir and Baykara v. Turkey*, judgment of 12 November 2008, *unpublished*.

160 ECtHR, *Loizidou v. Turkey* (preliminary objections), judgment of 23 March 1995, *Series* A No. 310; ECtHR, *Niemietz v. Germany*, judgment of 16 December 1992, *Series* A No. 251-B.

question in what situations a civil servant would be covered by the scope of Article 6 and in what situation a civil servant would be excluded.[161] The Court noticed that several Contracting States made a distinction between 'two categories of staff at the service of the State, namely officials under contract and established civil servants'.[162] Furthermore, the Court observed that 'in the current practice of the Contracting States established civil servants and officials under contract frequently perform the same duties'.[163] Despite the fact that both categories frequently performed the same duties the civil servant could not in all States claim protection under Article 6 of the Convention. In order to avoid this inequality the Court decided to adopt an autonomous interpretation. The comparative arguments thus justified or at least spurred the autonomous approach in this case. An entirely different relation to autonomous interpretation was presented in the case of *Stec*.[164] In this case the Court had to adopt an autonomous interpretation of Article 1 of Protocol No. 1. The Court invoked evolutive interpretation and comparative interpretation substantiated the evolutive arguments.[165] The case thus actually represents the interaction between three interpretative aids.

The relation between evolutive interpretation and comparative interpretation has already been touched upon frequently in the course of this chapter and will be discussed in the chapter on evolutive interpretation as well. Indeed, it has been mentioned in the theoretical chapter that some authors do not even distinguish between the two interpretative aids and consider them as one.[166] However, even if they are closely intertwined, it is important to note that comparative interpretation does not only play a role as substantiating evolutive interpretation. It is used for other purposes as well, as has been shown in this chapter. By considering both concepts as one, one would be ignoring those other roles of comparative interpretation. That would be an oversimplification of the interpretative framework established by the Court. So evolutive interpretation and comparative interpretation are strongly related, but they have different functions in the interpretative process.

Finally, the limitations on the comparative method of interpretation are instructive for the relation between this method and two of the key methods of interpretation employed by the Court.[167] These limitations are not related to the persuasiveness

161 ECtHR (GC), *Pellegrin v. France,* judgment of 8 December 1999, *Reports* 1999-VIII.
162 ECtHR (GC), *Pellegrin v. France,* judgment of 8 December 1999, *Reports* 1999-VIII, § 62.
163 ECtHR (GC), *Pellegrin v. France,* judgment of 8 December 1999, *Reports* 1999-VIII, § 62.
164 ECtHR (GC), *Stec and others v. United Kingdom,* decision of 6 July 2005, *Reports* 2005-X. A weaker version is visible in: ECtHR (GC), *Ferrazzini v. Italy*, judgment of 12 July 2001, Reports 2001-VII.
165 ECtHR (GC), *Stec and others v. United Kingdom,* decision of 6 July 2005, *Reports* 2005-X, § 50.
166 Helfer (1993); Rigaux (1998).
167 Systemic and textual interpretation.

of the comparative argument, but reflect the value which the Court attaches to arguments based on the clear text of the Convention or the system or structure of the Convention. If these point in a direction different from the comparative argument, these considerations often take priority over comparative interpretation.[168] For example, in the case of *Üner* the Court had to decide whether the expulsion of a long-term immigrant was allowed under the Convention.[169] The case was finally determined on the question whether the interference with Article 8 was necessary in a democratic society, but the Court did address the scope of Article 8 as well. The Court addressed the question whether an absolute right for long-term immigrants not to be expelled could be derived from Article 8. Even though a number of Contracting States indeed had legislation or policies to that effect and the Parliamentary Assembly of the Council of Europe had issued Recommendations on the issue, the Court held that the structure and text of Article 8 did not allow for such a conclusion.[170]

10.6 Conclusion

This chapter has tried to provide a complete overview of comparative interpretation in the case law of the Court. Some observations are worth recalling here. Comparative arguments are used for different purposes in the interpretation stage. Comparative arguments can be used to support a regular interpretative problem or a change of approach, they can be used to argue that the ECtHR should not interpret a specific aspect of a Convention provision, and they even can be used to show that a certain interpretation is not automatically included in the text of the Convention. The comparative arguments within these different purposes can either be based on a reference to one or a few comparative materials or the argument can be based on the existence of a consensus or trend or lack thereof. In some cases the comparative argument is the main argument and plays a crucial role in the conclusion, while in most cases comparative interpretation is used in addition to other interpretative arguments.

It is interesting to note that in the theoretical analysis comparative interpretation proved to be rather controversial, while the case law does not show signs that this method is considered controversial. Some dissents point in the direction that the actual use of this method can be controversial in specific cases, but the method in itself seems to be universally accepted by the judges of the ECtHR, as can be seen from the unanimous decision in the case of *Demir & Baykara*.

168 ECtHR, *Soering v. United Kingdom*, judgment of 7 July 1989, *Series* A No. 161; ECtHR (GC), *Üner v. the Netherlands*, judgment of 18 October 2006, *Reports* 2006-XII.

169 ECtHR (GC), *Üner v. the Netherlands*, judgment of 18 October 2006, *Reports* 2006-XII.

170 ECtHR (GC), *Üner v. the Netherlands*, judgment of 18 October 2006, *Reports* 2006-XII, § 55.

The main disagreement between judges concerns the question whether one can speak of a consensus or trend in a certain case. An important problem in this context is the fact that it is not clear when there is enough proof for a consensus, as indicated in section 10.4.1. A related problem is that it is not always clear what is sought, in that the Court does not provide an unequivocal answer to the question if all Contracting States have adopted the same solution to a certain development, or if it is sufficient that a trend can be seen from which a minimum standard can be distilled. Both aspects have led to discussions among judges. Disagreement can lead to useful discussions, but some disagreements have underlying causes that can be prevented. It might not be possible to draw up a general standard to determine when one can speak of a consensus. This is not a mathematical exercise and the context of a specific case cannot be ignored. Much could be gained, however, if more insight is provided into the material taken into account for the conclusion and the specific question the ECtHR seeks to answer. The cases of *Sheffield & Horsham v United Kingdom* and *T v United Kingdom* were instructive in this regard, where judges disagreed on what was necessary to constitute a consensus in this case. If the ECtHR is clear on the specific question it seeks to answer, this type of disagreement might be prevented, which ultimately will benefit the credibility of the method.

An aspect that played an important role in the theoretical analysis, but which has not appeared to play a role in the case law, is the distinction between internal and external comparative interpretation and the related need for a different justification. The ECtHR does seem to provide an additional justification for relying on external materials, namely Article 31(c) VCLT, which refers to rules of international law applicable in the relation between the parties and the fact that the ECtHR does not operate in a vacuum. This justification can, however, not explain why in some cases the ECtHR looks at foreign jurisdictions, like the United States of America, or to international treaties that have not been ratified by all parties concerned or international soft law. Indeed, in *Demir and Baykara* the Court even stressed that no difference needs to be made between the different sources. Nevertheless, a different justification is necessary if the ECtHR really wants to convince outsiders of the relevance of these materials for the interpretation of the European Convention. A more specific justification would also help to explain the choice of certain materials. In the international arena different materials can be found that support different positions. A justification is therefore necessary that helps to explain the choice of the chosen materials.

In a few cases the ECtHR justified comparative arguments by calling them helpful. The theoretical analysis indicated that the fact that comparative data can be helpful is not a sufficient justification, because it does not indicate ‘why’ or ‘how’ these materials are helpful.[171] From this perspective an additional justification would be warranted as well.

Both the problem of unclear use of comparative interpretation, mainly when the ECtHR seeks to find a consensus, and the question of finding a justification can have an impact on the credibility and objectivity of this method. This is especially problematic in the context of comparative arguments. Given the wealth of materials available not indicating why certain materials have been taken into consideration leaves this method vulnerable to criticism. Cherry-picking is an often heard term and refers to the fact that support can be found for any argument if you cite the correct material (the 'cherries'). More insight into the use of this method might not entirely prevent this criticism, but it might at least lead to significant reduction.

The method is highly valued as indicated before; the question is therefore how this method can be enhanced. The areas of concern have been identified, but the question is whether any suggestions can be provided for actual improvement. Because comparative interpretation is one method in an interpretative framework, this question will be dealt with after the other methods and principles have been analyzed as well. This question will thus be reserved for the final synthesis.

171 See section 6.1.7.

Chapter 11
Evolutive interpretation in the case law of the ECtHR

Evolutive interpretation is a well-known interpretative aid in the case law of the ECtHR. The theoretical discussion in Chapter 7 already indicated its importance for the interpretation of the European Convention. The theoretical analysis indicated that evolutive interpretation could be seen as a meta-teleological interpretative principle. The question to be answered in this chapter is whether the Court provides any indication to support this conclusion or whether the Court remains silent on the nature of evolutive interpretation as an interpretative aid.

The theoretical analysis further indicated that references to evolutive interpretation will often be justified by invoking the Preamble and the text of the Convention. The Preamble points to further realization of human rights and the text of the Convention is written in the present tense. The question phrased for further analysis in that chapter is whether any express justification is provided by the Court for the use of evolutive interpretation and whether this justification corresponds to the academic explanation.

In order to get a proper understanding of evolutive interpretation it is necessary to analyze the type of situations in which evolutive interpretation is used. Is this interpretative aid used for the interpretation of all Convention provisions, or only for some? Is evolutive interpretation used in different types of situations or only in specific types of situations?

The most controversial aspect of evolutive interpretation is that it is not clear how far a judge may take this interpretative aid. Can a judge rewrite the Convention according to present-day conditions or are there any restraints? Some theoretical limits have been discussed in Chapter 7 and it is highly interesting to see whether the Court is aware of this controversy and how it addresses that aspect of evolutive interpretation. A related concern for evolutive interpretation is that there is no guiding principle. It is not always clear how evolutive interpretation is established. Comparative interpretation seems to play an important role, but this chapter will also investigate whether that is the only way to establish an evolutive interpretation or whether other methods play a role as well.

These questions will be addressed in the course of this chapter in order to get a better understanding of the perspective of the ECtHR on evolutive interpretation.

11.1 Identification of Evolutive Interpretation in the Case Law

In order to provide an overview of the approach of the ECtHR to evolutive interpretation it is necessary to first establish what the Court means by evolutive interpretation. A closely related question is how evolutive interpretation can be identified in the Court's cases. The terms by which the Court refers to evolutive interpretation reveal to a certain extent the meaning of evolutive interpretation. Discussing the two questions separately would lead to unnecessary repetition. Therefore this section will endeavour to answer what evolutive interpretation means to the Court, while revealing simultaneously the indicators for evolutive interpretation.

The Court never extensively explained what it considers to be evolutive interpretation. Yet the case law does provide some indications on how the Court perceives this interpretative aid. A case like *Kress* shows that in the eyes of the Court evolutive interpretation means:

> that the Convention is a living instrument to be interpreted in light of current conditions and of the ideas prevailing in democratic States today.[1]

In other cases the more commonly used term 'present-day conditions' has been linked to the Convention as a living instrument and thus evolutive interpretation:[2]

---

1 ECtHR (GC), Kress v. France, judgment of 7 June 2001, *Reports* 2001-VI, § 70. A similar statement has been made in ECtHR, *Johnston and others v. Ireland*, judgment of 18 December 1986, *Series* A No. 112, § 53: '... the Convention and its Protocols must be interpreted in the light of present-day conditions'. It continued to state the limits of this approach, which will be discussed in section 11.3. below. In ECtHR (GC), *T v. United Kingdom*, judgment of 16 December 1999, *unpublished*, § 70 the Court expressed itself in similar terms as well: 'In doing so, it has regard to the principle, well established in its case-law that, since the Convention is a living instrument, it is legitimate when deciding whether a certain measure is acceptable under one of its provisions to take account of the standards prevailing amongst the Member States of the Council of Europe'. See also: ECtHR, *Van der Mussele v. Belgium*, judgment of 23 November 1983, *Series* A No. 70, § 32.

2 See for example ECtHR, Société Colas Est and others v. France, judgment of 16 April 2002, *Reports* 2002-III, § 41; ECtHR, *Soering v. United Kingdom*, judgment of 7 July 1989, *Series* A No. 161, § 102; dissenting opinion in ECtHR (GC), *Hatton and others v. United Kingdom*, judgment of 8 July 2003, *Reports* 2003-VII, § 2; ECtHR, *Tyrer v. United Kingdom*, judgment of 25 April 1978, *Series* A No. 26, § 31; ECtHR (GC), *Ferrazzini v. Italy*, judgment of 12 July 2001, Reports 2001-VII, § 26; ECtHR, *Sigurdur A. Sigurjónsson v. Iceland*, judgment of 30 June 1993, *Series* A No. 264, § 35; ECtHR, *S.A. Dangeville v. France*, judgment of 16 April 2002, *Reports* 2002-III, § 47; ECtHR (GC), *Demir and Baykara v. Turkey*, judgment of 12 November 2008, *unpublished*, § 68 and § 146; ECtHR (GC), *Banković and others v. Belgium and others*, decision of 12 December 2001, *Reports* 2001-XII, § 64; ECtHR (GC), *Selmouni v. France*, judgment of 28 July 1999, *Reports* 1999-V, § 101; ECtHR (GC), *Mamatkulov and Askarov v. Turkey*, judgment of 4 February 2005, *Reports* 2005-I, § 121; ECtHR (GC), *Vo v. France*, judgment of 8 July 2004, *Reports* 2004-VIII, § 82.

> The Court reiterates that the Convention is a living instrument, which must be interpreted in the light of present-day conditions.[3]

A recurring aspect in all cases is that the Convention provisions have to be interpreted according to present-day circumstances and not 'solely in accordance with the intentions of their authors as expressed more than forty years ago'.[4] The Convention is thus not a static or frozen document, but on the contrary *evolves* with the passage of time.

Evolutive interpretation thus means that the interpretation of the Convention will evolve. An almost inevitable follow-up question is what this element of 'evolution' means. Does evolutive interpretation mean that the interpretation of Convention provisions develops for better or for worse throughout the years? Or does evolutive interpretation mean that increasingly more protection will be afforded in line with changes in society? In other words, will a decrease in human rights standards also be adopted as an evolutive interpretation or will only developments that lead to a higher form of protection be taken into account when relying on evolutive interpretation? The term itself does not provide a conclusive answer to these questions. Fortunately, the matter has been addressed by the Court in a number of cases. The prime example mentioned in most scholarly writings is the case of *Selmouni,* which dealt with the question whether specific ill-treatment had to be qualified as torture or inhuman treatment. In this case the Court, after stating that the Convention is a living instrument, considered that:

> It takes the view that the *increasingly high standards* being required in the area of the protection of human rights and fundamental liberties correspondingly and inevitably requires greater firmness in assessing breaches of the fundamental values of democratic societies.[5]

More recently, the Court confirmed this approach and more explicitly linked evolutive interpretation to these "higher standards":

> … it is appropriate to remember that the Convention is a living instrument which must be interpreted in the light of present-day conditions, and in accordance with developments in international law, so as to reflect *the increasingly high standard* being required in the area of protection of human rights, thus necessitating greater firmness in assessing breaches of fundamental values of democratic societies.[6]

---

3 ECtHR, Société Colas Est and others v. France, judgment of 16 April 2002, *Reports* 2002-III, § 41.

4 ECtHR, Loizidou v. Turkey (preliminary objections), judgment of 23 March 1995, *Series* A No. 310, § 71. The approach is subject to limitations which will be discussed below.

5 ECtHR (GC), Selmouni v. France, judgment of 28 July 1999, *Reports* 1999-V, § 101, emphasis added.

6 ECtHR (GC), Demir and Baykara v. Turkey, judgment of 12 November 2008, *unpublished*, § 146, emphasis added.

The Court thus considers that evolutive interpretation is a means to reflect the increasingly high standards in the area of human rights.[7] The examples confirm that the ECtHR does not consider evolutive interpretation to be a neutral interpretative aid, but should reflect the progress in human rights protection. This conclusion has been confirmed in the dissenting opinion in *Hatton v United Kingdom*, where the dissenters considered that:

> this evolutive interpretation by the Commission and the Court of various Convention requirements has generally been "progressive", in the sense that they have gradually extended and raised the level of protection afforded to the rights and freedoms guaranteed by the Convention to develop the "European public order".[8]

These statements indicate that *in the view of the Court* evolutive interpretation is not neutral, but should be progressive. The question is whether this aim is tenable in every situation as pointed out in the theoretical chapter. Often more protection in one area will mean less protection in another area, because fundamental rights can conflict. Granting more protection for the freedom of expression, for example, might conflict with the right to protect one's privacy, one's reputation or the right not to be discriminated against. The examples from the case law indicate that the fact that this does is not an aspect that the Court acknowledges, at least not explicitly.

So far several indicators of an evolutive approach have been mentioned. Apart from the cases where the Court literally refers to notions such as 'living instrument', 'evolutive interpretation' or any term derived from the word 'evolutive',[9] there are other ways in which the Court signals that it will take an evolutive approach. As indicated above, the Court frequently refers to present-day conditions, but also without

---

7 This is also confirmed in the recent cases of ECtHR (GC), A v. Croatia, judgment of 14 October 2010, *unpublished*; ECtHR, *Mubilanzila Mayeka and Kaniki Mitunga v. Belgium*, judgment of 12 October 2006, *Reports* 2006-XI; ECtHR, *Rantsev v. Cyprus and Russia*, judgment of 7 January 2010, *unpublished.*

8 ECtHR (GC), Hatton and others v. United Kingdom, judgment of 8 July 2003, *Reports* 2003-VII, dissenting opinion by Judges Costa, Ress, Türmen, Zupancic and Steiner.

9 Like 'evolution' ECtHR, Marckx v. Belgium, judgment of 13 June 1979, *Series* A No. 31, § 41; 'evolving' ECtHR, *M.C. v. Bulgaria*, judgment of 4 December 2003, *Reports* 2003-XII, § 155-164, ECtHR (GC), *I v. United Kingdom*, judgment of 11 July 2002, *Reports* 2002-VI, § 54, ECtHR (GC), *Christine Goodwin v. United Kingdom*, judgment of 11 July 2002, *Reports* 2002-VI, § 74; for 'evolutive interpretation' see ECtHR, *Johnston and others v. Ireland*, judgment of 18 December 1986, *Series* A No. 112, § 53-57.

the additional qualification of the Convention as a living instrument.[10] Beside these regularly used references to the Convention as a living instrument or present-day conditions, there are other less frequently used terms that indicate an evolutive approach. When the Court refers to a 'dynamic approach'[11] or to 'changing conditions'[12] it also applies evolutive interpretation. The Court in its case law does not provide any reason to assume that the difference in signalling terms is more than a mere change of words. The terminology is different, but all terms are used alternatively to refer to the same concept, namely an evolutive approach. The common denominator in all the different ways of indicating evolutive interpretation is that the Court refers to an element of change, an element of development, which is the characteristic feature of evolutive interpretation.

One final element still needs to be discussed, because it will also shed light on the real meaning of the concept of evolutive interpretation in the Court's case law, which is whether the Court classifies this interpretative aid as a principle or as a method of interpretation. The Court has never pronounced itself on the character of this interpretative aid. Therefore the issue has to be addressed on the basis of indirect information, i.e. on various indications as to its use in the case law under study.

Although a definitive conclusion as to the classification of evolutive interpretation can best be given at the end of this chapter, the discussion on the meaning of evolutive interpretation in this section warrants at least a preliminary answer. The fact that the Court keeps referring to the Convention as a living instrument and in *Demir & Baykara* referred to the 'living nature'[13] of the Convention can be taken as a clear indication that the Court does not see evolutive interpretation as a technique to establish the meaning of the Convention. It seems to imply that the Court considers

10 ECtHR, Marckx v. Belgium, judgment of 13 June 1979, *Series* A No. 31, § 41; ECtHR (GC), *I v. United Kingdom*, judgment of 11 July 2002, *Reports* 2002-VI, § 55; ECtHR (GC), *Christine Goodwin v. United Kingdom*, judgment of 11 July 2002, *Reports* 2002-VI, § 75; ECtHR, *Johnston and others v. Ireland*, judgment of 18 December 1986, *Series* A No. 112, § 30; ECtHR, *Cossey v. United Kingdom*, judgment of 27 September 1990, *Series* A No. 184, § 35; ECtHR, *F v. Switzerland*, judgment of 18 December 1987, *Series* A No. 128, § 33; ECtHR, *Airey v. Ireland*, judgment of 9 October 1979, *Series* A No. 32, § 26; ECtHR, *James and others v. United Kingdom*, judgment of 21 February 1986, *Series* A No. 98, concurring opinion by Thór Vilhjálmsson.

11 ECtHR (GC), I v. United Kingdom, judgment of 11 July 2002, *Reports* 2002-VI, § 54; ECtHR (GC), *Christine Goodwin v. United Kingdom*, judgment of 11 July 2002, *Reports* 2002-VI, § 74; ECtHR, *Société Colas Est and others v. France*, judgment of 16 April 2002, *Reports* 2002-III, § 41; ECtHR, *Pretty v. United Kingdom*, judgment of 29 April 2002, *Reports* 2002-III, § 54.

12 ECtHR (GC), Stec and others v. United Kingdom, decision of 6 July 2005, *Reports* 2005-X, § 47; ECtHR (GC), *I v. United Kingdom*, judgment of 11 July 2002, *Reports* 2002-VI, § 54, ECtHR (GC), *Christine Goodwin v. United Kingdom*, judgment of 11 July 2002, *Reports* 2002-VI,§ 74.

13 ECtHR (GC), Demir and Baykara v. Turkey, judgment of 12 November 2008, *unpublished*, § 146.

evolutive interpretation to be an aim that it seeks to achieve, but not a method that provides a substantive argument that helps to interpret the Convention.[14] The reference to 'present-day conditions', however, might imply that the Court does view evolutive interpretation as a method whereby these present-day conditions are used as a reference point to establish an evolutive interpretation. At this point in the discussion, an argument can thus be made going either way. The discussion in the following sections will perhaps make it possible to draw more decisive conclusions.

11.2 Why invoked by the Court?

The concept of evolutive interpretation has by now been well-established in the case law of the Court,[15] but what justification has been provided for invoking this interpretative aid? The best starting point for that discussion is the case in which the very concept was introduced into the case law of the Court.

The first case in which the Court referred to evolutive interpretation or at least to what later has become known as evolutive interpretation is the case of *Tyrer*.[16] This case concerned a schoolboy who was sentenced to three strokes of the birch, which were administered to him on the bare posterior and in the presence of his father. He complained that this sentence constituted a breach of Article 3 ECHR (prohibition of inhuman and degrading treatment). In answering the question whether this constituted degrading treatment, the Court, for the first time, classified the Convention as a living instrument that had to be interpreted in light of present-day conditions. Interestingly enough the Court did not provide any reasons for invoking this new approach. It merely stated:

> The Court must also *recall* that the Convention is a living instrument which, as the Commission rightly stressed, must be interpreted in the light of present-day conditions.[17]

Attention should be paid to the word 'recall' as that implies that this concept has been invoked before, which seems to indicate a justification for the use of evolutive interpretation in this case. The fact that the Court itself or the Commission applied evolutive interpretation before could justify the Court's use of this approach. However,

---

14 See Chapter 4.1. on a more detailed discussion of the distinction between interpretation methods and principles that will be adhered to in this thesis.

15 ECtHR, Loizidou v. Turkey (preliminary objections), judgment of 23 March 1995, *Series* A No. 310; ECtHR (GC), *Banković and others v. Belgium and others*, decision of 12 December 2001, *Reports* 2001-XII.

16 ECtHR, Tyrer v. United Kingdom, judgment of 25 April 1978, *Series* A No. 26.

17 ECtHR, Tyrer v. United Kingdom, judgment of 25 April 1978, *Series* A No. 26, § 31. Italics added.

such prior justification cannot be found in the case law of the Court; *Tyrer* is generally acknowledged to be the first case where these evolutive concepts have been invoked.[18] In the quoted passage the Court refers explicitly to the Commission, which suggests that the Commission in this case or in an earlier case relied on the Convention as a living instrument that should be read in light of present-day conditions. The report of the Commission in the *Tyrer* case itself did not mention this approach explicitly; the applicant and government, however, both indirectly evoked an evolutive interpretation by referring to modern development in juvenile punishments and by referring to the fact that not all countries have abolished corporal punishment. The Commission did not address these arguments and was silent on evolutive interpretation, so that cannot explain the Court's reference to evolutive interpretation. Earlier Commission reports reveal that only once, in the context of the interpretation of Article 11, reference has been made by the Commission to the need to keep the interpretation of the Convention in pace with the dynamic international context.[19] This reference shows that the Commission was already welcoming towards an evolutive approach, but it did not provide a thorough justification for the use of evolutive interpretation. While the Court in *Tyrer* could at that time not predict that evolutive interpretation would become a characteristic element of the Strasbourg reasoning, it should at least have properly referred to the precedent that justified the reliance on this new approach to interpretation. Now subsequent case law relied on a precedent that is unclear about the justification for introducing a specific element in the Court's reasoning.

Shortly after the *Tyrer* case the Court applied an evolutive approach in the case of *Airey* as well.[20] In this case the ECtHR did provide some kind of justification for invoking reliance on an evolutive interpretation. The case concerned the question whether in the specific circumstances of that case Article 6 included an obligation for the Contracting States to grant legal aid in order to safeguard an effective right of access to a court. The Court concluded that such an obligation existed in this case and in its reasoning referred to the fact that:

> [T]he Convention must be interpreted in the light of present-day conditions ... and it is designed to safeguard the individual in a real and practical way as regards those areas with which it deals ... .[21]

With the latter remark the Court referred back to an earlier passage in the judgment where the Court held that 'the Convention is intended to guarantee not rights that

18 Vanneste (2010), p. 244; Ost (1992), p. 302; Matscher (1993), p. 68; Christoffersem (2009), 47; Bernhardt (1999), p. 18; Mowbray (2005), p. 60; Prebensen (2000), p. 1123; Mahoney (1990), p. 61.

19 ECHR, Svenska Lokmannaförbundet v. Sweden, report of 27 May 1974, *Series* B. No. 18, p. 39.

20 ECtHR, Airey v. Ireland, judgment of 9 October 1979, *Series* A No. 32.

21 ECtHR, Airey v. Ireland, judgment of 9 October 1979, *Series* A No. 32, § 26.

are theoretical or illusory but rights that are practical and effective'.[22] Evolutive interpretation is thus a way to keep the Convention alive and capable of offering effective protection. The Court often refers to these two aspects, evolutive interpretation and practical and effective protection in one paragraph, but not always expressly connects the two. In the case of *Stec* the ECtHR expressly provided this connection and added another justification:

> Since the Convention is first and foremost a system for the protection of human rights, the Court must have regard to the changing conditions within the respondent State and within Contracting States generally, and must interpret and apply the Convention in a manner which renders its rights practical and effective, not theoretical and illusory.[23]

The Court thus links the need for an evolutive approach to the nature of the system, namely a system to protect human rights. The underlying presumption for the Court must be that human rights reflect fundamental moral standards and, since these standards are subject to progressive change, so too should the standards laid down in the Convention.[24] The fear of provisions becoming a dead letter justifies, where necessary, an evolutive approach. This is not a very elaborate justification, but at least the Court provides more insight into its own reasoning and the underlying reasons for its interpretative approach.

A justification that is less often invoked for relying on evolutive interpretation has been given, among others, in the case of *Vilho Eskelinen*.[25] The Court in this case was contemplating whether to overrule a previous line of cases (*Pellegrin v France*).[26] After extensively discussing the difficulty and practical problems and results of the criterion that had been established in *Pellegrin*, the Court concluded that the previous approach had created uncertainty.[27] The Court considered that:

> While it is in the interest of legal certainty, foreseeability, and equality before the law that the Court should not depart, without good reason, from precedents laid down in previous

22 ECtHR, Airey v. Ireland, judgment of 9 October 1979, *Series* A No. 32, § 24.

23 ECtHR (GC), Stec and others v. United Kingdom, decision of 6 July 2005, *Reports* 2005-X, § 47. A rather similar statement was made in ECtHR (GC), *Mamatkulov and Askarov v. Turkey*, judgment of 4 February 2005, *Reports* 2005-I, § 121. Link also made in ECtHR, *Airey v. Ireland*, judgment of 9 October 1979, *Series* A No. 32, § 26.

24 See section 7.2.

25 ECtHR (GC), Vilho Eskelinen and others v. Finland, judgment of 19 April 2007, *unpublished.*

26 ECtHR (GC), Pellegrin v. France, judgment of 8 December 1999, *Reports* 1999-VIII. This case concerned the question whether Article 6 ECHR was applicable to disputes concerning civil servants.

27 ECtHR (GC), *Vilho Eskelinen and others v. Finland*, judgment of 19 April 2007, *unpublished*, § 55.

> cases, a failure by the Court to maintain a dynamic and evolutive approach would risk rendering it a bar to reform or improvement.[28]

The need to reform or improve the Convention is thus considered an important justification for overruling precedents. This justification nicely ties in with the justification discussed above in the sense that both are related to the concern to keep the Convention protection as effective as possible. The difference between the two lines of cases is therefore not so much the justification, but the function of evolutive interpretation, which is why they are discussed separately. In the first line of cases evolutive interpretation is used to interpret a specific provision and is one of the interpretative aids used to come to an interpretation. In the second line of cases evolutive interpretation is only used to justify a new approach, but it does not necessarily form a part of the interpretative aids that are used to justify the content of the new approach. The different situations in which evolutive interpretation is used, will be discussed in the next section. The point of this section is to show that the nature of the system and the need to ensure practical and effective human rights protection are the prime justifications for an evolutive approach.

11.3 When does evolutive interpretation play a role?

Is there a specific area of the Convention in which evolutive interpretation plays a bigger role than in other areas, or is evolutive interpretation used randomly for all the Convention rights? No clear trend can be distilled from analyzing the case law in which the indicators discussed in section 11.1 have been found. References to evolutive interpretation have been made in all kinds of cases, ranging from the interpretation of Article 1, to Article 12 and even the interpretation of procedural provisions. Evolutive interpretation has, however, often been invoked in the context of the interpretation of Articles 3 and 8 of the Convention. Especially in cases concerning Article 8, the Court seems to be more inclined to rely on evolutive interpretation. The question is whether an explanation can be found for the more frequent reliance on evolutive interpretation in the context of Articles 3 and 8. The Court has itself given some kind of explanation for this tendency, but only with respect to Article 8. In the *Johnston* case, where the Court had to decide whether the right to marry

---

28 ECtHR (GC), *Vilho Eskelinen and others v. Finland*, judgment of 19 April 2007, *unpublished*, § 56. ECtHR (GC), *I v. United Kingdom*, judgment of 11 July 2002, *Reports* 2002-VI, § 54; ECtHR (GC), *Christine Goodwin v. United Kingdom*, judgment of 11 July 2002, *Reports* 2002-VI, § 74. Afterwards in ECtHR (GC), *Demir and Baykara v. Turkey*, judgment of 12 November 2008, *unpublished*, § 153 as well. See also: ECtHR (GC), *Sergey Zolotukhin v. Russia*, judgment of 10 February 2009, *unpublished*, § 78.

included a right to divorce as well, the Court considered that, contrary to Article 12 (right to marriage):

> Article 8, with its reference to the somewhat vague notion of "respect" for family life, might appear to lend itself more readily to an evolutive interpretation than does Article 12.[29]

It is doubtful whether this one statement can serve as a basis for the conclusion that the Court is more willing to apply an evolutive approach to vaguely worded provisions, but it at least explains why an evolutive approach is often adopted when interpreting Article 8. No explanation can, however, be found with regard to the popularity of an evolutive approach in the context of Article 3. The fact that conceptions of what constitutes torture or inhuman or degrading treatment change overtime, might explain that the Court relies regularly on evolutive interpretation in this context. Nevertheless, it does not really explain why this is more often the case in the context of Article 3, because this justification could easily apply to other Convention provisions as well.

A second interpretation of the central question in this section concerns the type of situation in which the Court employs evolutive interpretation. As a result of the meaning of evolutive interpretation, namely that the Convention will be interpreted in light of present-day conditions, this interpretative aid will mainly be invoked when the Court is confronted with a new situation. This new situation arises generally because an applicant invokes the Convention in a situation in which the Convention has not been applied before. Either this is because the situation has not yet been placed before the Court, or it is because an applicant challenges the Court to revisit a situation in which it has previously always denied that the Convention was applicable. In other situations the Court has already dealt with a certain aspect in the context of another Convention article and the application forces the Court to consider whether that approach can be also be adopted in the context of the provision at stake. The case of *Rantsev*, for example, was one of the few occasions where the Court was confronted with the question whether trafficking in human beings was covered by the scope of Article 4 (prohibition of slavery and forced labour).[30] The Court took this opportunity

29 ECtHR, *Johnston and others v. Ireland*, judgment of 18 December 1986, *Series* A No. 112, § 57.

30 ECtHR, *Rantsev v. Cyprus and Russia*, judgment of 7 January 2010, *unpublished*. Similar cases where the Court was confronted with a new situation are, among others: ECtHR, *Marckx v. Belgium*, judgment of 13 June 1979, *Series* A No. 31; ECtHR, *M.C. v. Bulgaria*, judgment of 4 December 2003, *Reports* 2003-XII; ECtHR, *Loizidou v. Turkey (preliminary objections)*, judgment of 23 March 1995, *Series* A No. 310; ECtHR, *Airey v. Ireland*, judgment of 9 October 1979, *Series* A No. 32; ECtHR, *Van der Mussele v. Belgium*, judgment of 23 November 1983, *Series* A No. 70; ECtHR,

to discuss this question in light of the fact that trafficking in human beings had not been a big problem at the time of the conclusion of the Convention, it has grown to be a major problem in present-day society. Even though the text of Article 4 does not make express mention of trafficking, the present-day circumstances led the Court to adopt a new interpretation of Article 4 in which trafficking should be seen as a separate category in addition to 'slavery', 'servitude' or 'forced and compulsory labour', which are expressly laid down in the text of Article 4.

The case of *Ferrazzini* provides a good example of a case where the Court is challenged to revaluate its approach. The applicant in that case complained about the length of the proceedings in a tax dispute. In earlier cases the ECtHR had held that tax proceedings were not covered by Article 6 as they were not covered by the notion of 'civil rights and obligations'. The government therefore argued that Article 6 was not applicable, but the Court recalled that the Convention is a living instrument and that:

> ... it is incumbent on the Court to review whether, in the light of changed attitudes in society as to the legal protection that falls to be accorded to individuals in their relations with the State, the scope of Article 6 § 1 should not be extended to cover disputes between citizens and public authorities as to the lawfulness under domestic law of the tax authorities' decisions.[31]

The Court finally concluded that there was not enough ground to take an evolutive approach and thus tax proceedings were still excluded from the scope of Article 6.

Finally, an example of the last situation discussed above, can be found in the case of *Colas Est*. In this case the Court applied an evolutive approach which was already taken in the context of Article 41 (just satisfaction) to Article 8. The question was whether Article 8 also included a right of respect for a 'company's registered office, branches, or other business premises'.[32] The Court held that it had already concluded in the context of Article 41 that a company could have a right to compensation for

---

Tyrer v. United Kingdom, judgment of 25 April 1978, *Series* A No. 26; ECtHR (GC), *T v. United Kingdom*, judgment of 16 December 1999, *unpublished.*

31 ECtHR (GC), *Ferrazzini v. Italy*, judgment of 12 July 2001, Reports 2001-VII, § 26. Similar cases where the Court was requested to review its own approach are, among others: ECtHR (GC), *Stec and others v. United Kingdom*, decision of 6 July 2005, *Reports* 2005-X; ECtHR, *Al-Saadoon and Mufdhi v. United Kingdom*, judgment of 2 March 2010, *unpublished*; ECtHR (GC), *Selmouni v. France*, judgment of 28 July 1999, *Reports* 1999-V; and famously the transsexual cases: ECtHR, *Cossey v. United Kingdom*, judgment of 27 September 1990, *Series* A No. 184; ECtHR, *Rees v. United Kingdom*, judgment of 17 October 1986, *Series* A No. 106; ECtHR, *B v. France*, judgment of 25 March 1992, *Series* A No. 232-C; ECtHR (GC), *Christine Goodwin v. United Kingdom*, judgment of 11 July 2002, *Reports* 2002-VI.

32 ECtHR, *Société Colas Est and others v. France*, judgment of 16 April 2002, *Reports* 2002-III, § 41.

non-pecuniary damage. In light of its evolutive approach, the Court considered that Article 8 should also be extended to include, under certain circumstances, a right for a company to respect its business premises.

Different uses of evolutive interpretation are visible in the Court's case law too. For example, in certain cases the Court has referred to an evolutive interpretation in order to justify explicitly overruling well-established previous cases.[33] The Convention system does not have a rule of binding precedent, but in practice the Court will respect its own precedents and will only overrule them when there are good reasons to do so.[34] In these situations there is a constant tension between on the one hand legal certainty and on the other hand the need for reform. When the Court considers that there is a need for reform, it refers to the need for a 'dynamic and evolutive approach'[35] as a justification for disregarding the principle of legal certainty. In this type of case, evolutive interpretation is usually not invoked to justify a new interpretation, like in the cases discussed above, but it rather serves to justify the overruling of a precedent. This means that a new meaning is often given as a result of the overruling, but the newly chosen interpretation in those cases is not always justified by evolutive arguments as such. The case of *Micallef* provides a good example of the Court's approach in such cases.[36] This case dealt with the question whether there were enough reasons to reconsider the case law that interim proceedings were excluded from the scope of Article 6. The Court argued that present-day conditions did warrant a new approach and thus the need for a new approach was justified by referring to the evolutive nature of the Convention. The criteria that were developed for the new approach were, however, not justified by referring to an evolutive approach.

There is also a small category of cases where the Court makes mention of the evolutive approach, but where in reality it does not appear to employ any evolutive arguments to underpin its conclusions. Interestingly enough this seems to be the case in *Tyrer*, which is elaborately discussed above as the first case where the Court

---

33 ECtHR (GC), *Micallef v. Malta*, judgment of 15 October 2009, *unpublished*; ECtHR (GC), *Mamatkulov and Askarov v. Turkey*, judgment of 4 February 2005, *Reports* 2005-I; ECtHR (GC), *Demir and Baykara v. Turkey*, judgment of 12 November 2008, *unpublished*; ECtHR (GC), *Stec and others v. United Kingdom*, decision of 6 July 2005, *Reports* 2005-X; ECtHR (GC), *Christine Goodwin v. United Kingdom*, judgment of 11 July 2002, *Reports* 2002-VI; ECtHR (GC), *Vilho Eskelinen and others v. Finland*, judgment of 19 April 2007, *unpublished*.

34 Supra note 23 (Chapter 1).

35 ECtHR (GC), *Vilho Eskelinen and others v. Finland*, judgment of 19 April 2007, *unpublished*, for the full excerpt, see note 1146. See also ECtHR (GC), *Mamatkulov and Askarov v. Turkey*, judgment of 4 February 2005, *Reports* 2005-I and ECtHR (GC), *Demir and Baykara v. Turkey*, judgment of 12 November 2008, *unpublished* .

36 ECtHR (GC), *Micallef v. Malta*, judgment of 15 October 2009, *unpublished*. The case of ECtHR (GC), *Vilho Eskelinen and others v. Finland*, judgment of 19 April 2007, *unpublished*, is also a good example.

referred to an evolutive approach. In another case, *Demades*, the Court had to decide whether a home where the applicant did not live could be considered 'home' in the context of Article 8. In both cases the Court recalled that the Convention is a living instrument, but does not refer to any evolutive arguments in its subsequent reasoning. Therefore it is difficult to see whether evolutive interpretation played any actual role in the reasoning of the Court.

The use of evolutive interpretation is not without its limits. It has already been mentioned that resorting to the principles of evolutive interpretation will not always lead to an evolutive approach. There are three different situations in which the ECtHR will generally not take an evolutive approach. Firstly, this is the case when other interpretation methods, like systematic and textual interpretation, clearly point in a different direction.[37] In *Pretty* the terminally ill applicant claimed that the refusal to grant her husband the guarantee that he would not be prosecuted for aiding her in committing suicide would lead to inhuman and degrading treatment, since she would have to suffer the final stages of her disease.[38] The Court recalled that it had to take a dynamic approach towards this issue, since the Convention is a living instrument, but it also pointed to the coherence of the Convention. Subsequently, it argued that Article 3 had to be interpreted in accordance with Article 2 and the latter did not confer a right to 'require a State to permit or facilitate his or her death'.[39] An evolutive approach was thus prevented by reliance on the system of the Convention.[40] Textual interpretation is, however, not always sacred. In the case of *Al-Saadoon* the Court had to determine whether in the light of recent circumstances Articles 2 and 3 should be interpreted to prohibit the death penalty at all times, even though the text of Article 2 explicitly allows the death penalty in some circumstances.[41] After careful consideration the Court took an evolutive approach and ignored the text of the Conven-

37 See Prebensen (2000), p. 1131, where he argues that the ECtHR will generally not take an evolutive approach when this is outweighed by primary means of interpretation.

38 ECtHR, *Pretty v. United Kingdom*, judgment of 29 April 2002, *Reports* 2002-III, § 54.

39 ECtHR, *Pretty v. United Kingdom*, judgment of 29 April 2002, *Reports* 2002-III, § 54.

40 A similar argument was made in ECtHR, *Soering v. United Kingdom*, judgment of 7 July 1989, *Series* A No. 161, § 103. In ECtHR (GC), *Ferrazzini v. Italy*, judgment of 12 July 2001, Reports 2001-VII, the text of the provision which included the word civil seemed to be an insurmountable obstacle; in ECtHR, *Quark Fishing Limited v. United Kingdom*, decision of 19 September 2006, *unpublished*, the Court indicated that it cannot unwrite a provision.

41 ECtHR, *Al-Saadoon and Mufdhi v. United Kingdom*, judgment of 2 March 2010, *unpublished*, § 120. Earlier in the case of ECtHR (GC), *Öcalan v. Turkey*, judgment of 12 May 2005, *Reports* 2005-IV a similar approach was taken with regard to the prohibition of the death penalty in peace time. The ECtHR held that the Contracting States had opted for the traditional method of amendment with regard to the prohibition of the death penalty at all times and did not consider it appropriate to adopt an evolutive approach in this latter context.

tion. This example should, however, be seen as an exception, since the Court in this case could find strong support in the existence of Protocol 13 which completely abolished the death penalty and which was ratified by a large majority of Contracting States. It is more common for the Court to regard a clear understanding of a certain Convention provision that is warranted on the basis of systemic and textual interpretation as an obstacle for an evolutive approach.

Secondly, in some cases there is not enough support to substantiate an evolutive interpretation, like in the case of *Vo*.[42] The question in *Vo* was whether a foetus fell within the scope of the right to life. The Court in this case held that there was no consensus in Europe and thus the Court did not take an evolutive approach. This can be a highly controversial limit on evolutive interpretation, since there are different views on the level of support needed for an evolutive approach.[43] This problematic aspect of finding a consensus has been discussed in section 6.1.6.2 on comparative interpretation. A somewhat contradictory situation seems to have presented itself in *F*. The question was whether Switzerland was allowed to impose a marriage ban after someone got a divorce. The Court acknowledged that no other country still had a marriage ban and thus in the light of an evolutive interpretation the practice should no longer be allowed. The Court, however, argued that states do not necessarily offend the Convention only due to the fact that they are the final state in a 'gradual evolution'. The Court thus did not interpret Article 12 in such a way that it prohibited remarriage bans, but it ultimately did conclude that the ban was disproportionate.

Finally, in some cases the intention of the drafters is very clear, which may lead the Court to consider that it cannot ignore this intention.[44] This was the reason for not taking an evolutive approach to the problem at hand in *Johnston* and *Banković*. In *Johnston* the *travaux préparatoires* indicated that Article 12 only protected the right to marry and not the right to divorce. The Court considered that:

> It is true that the Convention and its Protocols must be interpreted in light of present-day conditions. However, the Court cannot, by means of an evolutive interpretation, derive from these instruments a right that was not included therein at the outset. This is particularly so here, where the omission was deliberate.[45]

42 ECtHR (GC), *Vo v. France*, judgment of 8 July 2004, *Reports* 2004-VIII. See also: ECtHR, *Schalk and Kopf v. Austria*, judgment of 24 June 2010, *unpublished*, where the Court indicated that there was no consensus on opening the institution of marriage for homosexual couples.

43 See dissent in ECtHR (GC), *Vo v. France*, judgment of 8 July 2004, *Reports* 2004-VIII.

44 See ECtHR (GC), *Banković and others v. Belgium and others*, decision of 12 December 2001, *Reports* 2001-XII, § 65: '... the extracts of the *travaux préparatoires* detailed above constitute a clear indication of the intended meaning of Article 1 of the Convention, which cannot be ignored'.

45 ECtHR, *Johnston and others v. Ireland*, judgment of 18 December 1986, *Series* A No. 112, § 53.

Thus in some cases where *travaux préparatoires* are explicit about excluding a certain right or where they express a clear opinion the ECtHR will not adopt an evolutive interpretation, because it does not want to go against the deliberate intention of the drafters. Problematic in this regard is that it is not clear when the Court will regard the *travaux préparatoires* as being sufficiently clear to be able to override an evolutive approach. In *Sigurdur Sigurjónsson* the respondent government argued that it followed from the *travaux préparatoires* that a right not to be a member of an association was deliberately not included in the Convention.[46] The Court only stated that in a previous judgment no decisive importance was attached to the *travaux* and continued to discuss the present-day circumstances. By referring to the fact that in a previous judgment the *travaux* did not play a decisive role, the Court does not deny that the *travaux* indeed prove that a negative right of association was deliberately left out of the Convention. The practice of the Court with regard to respecting the *travaux* therefore risks becoming arbitrary, because there does not seem to be a clear pattern.

This section has demonstrated the various types of situations in which evolutive interpretation does play a role or when its limits are reached. There are no strict categories, but some patterns have been found, which help to get a clearer understanding of evolutive interpretation.

11.4 How does the Court find an 'evolution'?

The discussion so far has focused on the meaning of evolutive interpretation and the situations in which evolutive interpretation is used. An important question that has not yet been addressed is how an 'evolution' is established by the Court. Only referring to evolutive interpretation may not suffice to convincingly justify a certain interpretative outcome. Evolutive interpretation in that sense only points in a certain direction, but it cannot justify any substantive meaning of evolutive interpretation. This substantive evolutive meaning can only be established by using interpretation *methods*, such as teleological or comparative interpretation. Evolutive interpretation in this sense really has all the characteristics of an interpretative principle as discussed in section 4.1. This section will address the question whether the Court has realized that it needs to substantiate its reference to evolutive interpretation by using concrete methods of interpretation and, if so, how it has used the various methods of interpretation to do so.

46 ECtHR, *Sigurdur A. Sigurjónsson v. Iceland*, judgment of 30 June 1993, *Series* A No. 264. See also ECtHR (GC), *Scoppola v. Italy (No. 2),* judgment of 17 September 2009, *unpublished*, where the dissenters argued that the intention of the drafters was clear and that the decision of the majority to take an evolutive approach went beyond judicial interpretation.

In some cases the Court only summarily invokes evolutive interpretation without demonstrating the concrete existence of an evolution by the use of substantive arguments.[47] As a result it is not always clear whether the existence of an evolution has really been established and to what extent it has been taken into account in the reasoning in these cases. Moreover, without the use of any substantive arguments or methods of interpretation, the reference to evolutive interpretation is just a hollow phrase. A clear example of such lack of care in applying evolutive interpretation is, oddly enough, the case of *Tyrer*, which has been elaborately discussed in section 11.2.[48] The Court expressly stated for the first time in that case that it could not but be influenced by the 'developments and commonly accepted standards' in the Contracting States, but it never explained what these development and commonly accepted standards were.[49] This case therefore serves well as a judgment in which evolutive interpretation was introduced as an interpretative concept, but it is a poor example of how evolutive interpretation is used.

In many cases, however, the Court does substantiate the reference to evolutive interpretation.[50] The exercise to substantiate evolutive interpretation varies in the degree of elaboration from very succinct to rather thorough. In the overwhelming majority of the studied cases the Court resorts to comparative interpretation to sub-

47 ECtHR, *Pretty v. United Kingdom*, judgment of 29 April 2002, *Reports* 2002-III, § 54; ECtHR (GC), *Kress v. France*, judgment of 7 June 2001, *Reports* 2001-VI, § 70; ECtHR (GC), *Selmouni v. France*, judgment of 28 July 1999, *Reports* 1999-V, § 101; ECtHR, *S.A. Dangeville v. France*, judgment of 16 April 2002, *Reports* 2002-III, § 47; ECtHR, *Airey v. Ireland*, judgment of 9 October 1979, *Series* A No. 32, § 26; ECtHR, *Tyrer v. United Kingdom*, judgment of 25 April 1978, *Series* A No. 26, § 31.

48 ECtHR, *Tyrer v. United Kingdom*, judgment of 25 April 1978, *Series* A No. 26.

49 ECtHR, *Tyrer v. United Kingdom*, judgment of 25 April 1978, *Series* A No. 26, § 31.

50 ECtHR (GC), *Demir and Baykara v. Turkey*, judgment of 12 November 2008, *unpublished*; ECtHR, *Sigurdur A. Sigurjónsson v. Iceland*, judgment of 30 June 1993, *Series* A No. 264; ECtHR, *Soering v. United Kingdom*, judgment of 7 July 1989, *Series* A No. 161; ECtHR, *M.C. v. Bulgaria*, judgment of 4 December 2003, *Reports* 2003-XII; ECtHR (GC), *Stec and others v. United Kingdom*, decision of 6 July 2005, *Reports* 2005-X; ECtHR (GC), *T v. United Kingdom*, judgment of 16 December 1999, *unpublished*; ECtHR (GC), *Chapman v. United Kingdom*, judgment of 18 January 2001, *Reports* 2001-I; ECtHR, *Loizidou v. Turkey (preliminary objections)*, judgment of 23 March 1995, *Series* A No. 310; ECtHR (GC), *Mamatkulov and Askarov v. Turkey*, judgment of 4 February 2005, *Reports* 2005-I; ECtHR (GC), *Vilho Eskelinen and others v. Finland*, judgment of 19 April 2007, *unpublished*; ECtHR (GC), *Ferrazzini v. Italy*, judgment of 12 July 2001, Reports 2001-VII; ECtHR, *Van der Mussele v. Belgium*, judgment of 23 November 1983, *Series* A No. 70; ECtHR, *Société Colas Est and others v. France*, judgment of 16 April 2002, *Reports* 2002-III; the transsexual cases: ECtHR, *Cossey v. United Kingdom*, judgment of 27 September 1990, *Series* A No. 184; ECtHR, *Rees v. United Kingdom*, judgment of 17 October 1986, *Series* A No. 106; ECtHR, *B v. France*, judgment of 25 March 1992, *Series* A No. 232-C; ECtHR (GC), *Christine Goodwin v. United Kingdom*, judgment of 11 July 2002, *Reports* 2002-VI.

stantiate an evolutive argument, which is not surprising given the reference to present-day conditions.[51] Both comparative arguments resulting from material on the Contracting States and international materials are invoked in such cases. In the case of *M.C. v Bulgaria*, for example, the Court based itself on both the changing conditions in the Member States of the Council of Europe, on changes in countries outside Europe and on developments in international criminal law in order to show that the understanding of how rape is experienced by the victim has evolved.[52] As a result the Court held that the positive obligation for the State had to be interpreted in light of these developments.[53] Likewise, in *Sigurdur Sigurjónsson* the Court looked into developments in the Member States of the Council of Europe as well as into developments at the international level, as demonstrated by references to, among others, a (European) Community Charter on social rights for workers and the practice of one of the ILO Committees.[54] The Court thus makes full use of the comparative material available in order to support an evolutive interpretation.[55]

In only very few cases the Court does not refer to comparative interpretation in order to substantiate an evolutive interpretation.[56] In *Société Colas Est* the Court had to determine whether ‘the rights guaranteed by Article 8 of the Convention may be construed as including the right to respect for a company’s registered office, branches or other business premises’.[57] The Court held that the Convention is a living instrument and that the Court had to build on its dynamic interpretation of it when giving meaning to the right to respect for one’s private life. In doing so it did not

51 ECtHR (GC), *Demir and Baykara v. Turkey*, judgment of 12 November 2008, *unpublished*; ECtHR, *Sigurdur A. Sigurjónsson v. Iceland*, judgment of 30 June 1993, *Series* A No. 264; ECtHR, *Soering v. United Kingdom*, judgment of 7 July 1989, *Series* A No. 161; ECtHR, *M.C. v. Bulgaria*, judgment of 4 December 2003, *Reports* 2003-XII; ECtHR (GC), *Stec and others v. United Kingdom*, decision of 6 July 2005, *Reports* 2005-X; ECtHR (GC), *T v. United Kingdom*, judgment of 16 December 1999, *unpublished*; ECtHR (GC), *Chapman v. United Kingdom*, judgment of 18 January 2001, *Reports* 2001-I; ECtHR, *Loizidou v. Turkey (preliminary objections)*, judgment of 23 March 1995, *Series* A No. 310; ECtHR (GC), *Mamatkulov and Askarov v. Turkey*, judgment of 4 February 2005, *Reports* 2005-I; ECtHR (GC), *Ferrazzini v. Italy*, judgment of 12 July 2001, Reports 2001-VII; ECtHR, *Van der Mussele v. Belgium*, judgment of 23 November 1983, *Series* A No. 70; the transsexual cases: ECtHR, *Cossey v. United Kingdom*, judgment of 27 September 1990, *Series* A No. 184; ECtHR, *Rees v. United Kingdom*, judgment of 17 October 1986, *Series* A No. 106; ECtHR, *B v. France*, judgment of 25 March 1992, *Series* A No. 232-C; ECtHR (GC), *Christine Goodwin v. United Kingdom*, judgment of 11 July 2002, *Reports* 2002-VI.

52 ECtHR, *M.C. v. Bulgaria*, judgment of 4 December 2003, *Reports* 2003-XII, § 155-166.

53 ECtHR, *M.C. v. Bulgaria*, judgment of 4 December 2003, *Reports* 2003-XII, § 166.

54 ECtHR, *Sigurdur A. Sigurjónsson v. Iceland*, judgment of 30 June 1993, *Series* A No. 264, § 35.

55 For an extensive discussion of comparative interpretation, see Chapter 6 for a theoretical analysis and Chapter 10 for a case law analysis.

56 ECtHR, *Société Colas Est and others v. France*, judgment of 16 April 2002, *Reports* 2002-III.

57 ECtHR, *Société Colas Est and others v. France*, judgment of 16 April 2002, *Reports* 2002-III, § 41.

refer to comparative material, but it considered that for other Convention provisions the Court had already extended the scope to offer some guarantees for companies. The Court concluded that 'the time had come' to do the same for Article 8.[58] The present-day conditions were thus reflected in the approach of the Court to other Convention guarantees, which can be seen as a form of systemic interpretation. In the case of *Al-Saadoon* the Court adopted a combined approach.[59] The question was whether under present-day conditions the death penalty could be considered to be contrary to Article 3. Until the case of *Al-Saadoon*, Article 3 had always been interpreted not to prohibit the death penalty, since the text of Article 2 does allow for the death penalty in certain circumstances. In the meantime Protocol 13 abolishing the death penalty in all circumstances had been adopted and ratified by a large majority of Contracting States. The existence of this protocol and the practice in the Contracting States played a role in the conclusion of the Court in *Al-Saadoon* that the death penalty can in present-day conditions be regarded as a form of inhuman or degrading treatment.[60] The Court in this case thus combined a systemic and comparative interpretation to give shape to its desire to give an evolutive meaning to the Convention.

Despite these examples of a different approach to substantiate evolutive interpretation, the Court's predominant approach thus appears to be reliance on only comparative arguments. The situations in which a substantiated evolutive argument will not be sufficient for the Court to opt for an evolutive approach have been discussed when dealing with the limits of evolutive interpretation.[61] One of the situations in which the role of evolutive interpretation is limited, is when there is a lack of comparative support. The question whether in a certain case there is enough comparative material to support an evolutive interpretation is not a very objective one. The case that was used as an example, namely *Vo*, already illustrates this point. In that case the judges disagreed on whether the comparative findings supported an evolutive interpretation.[62] The fact that there is no guideline or minimum threshold for comparative arguments contributes to the disagreement on the question whether there is enough evidence to support an evolutive approach. The case law does not provide any help in this regard, rather confirming the theoretical observation that this is a complicated aspect of its case law by showing disagreement on the conclusions from the comparative

58 ECtHR, *Société Colas Est and others v. France*, judgment of 16 April 2002, *Reports* 2002-III, § 41.
59 ECtHR, *Al-Saadoon and Mufdhi v. United Kingdom*, judgment of 2 March 2010, *unpublished.*
60 ECtHR, *Al-Saadoon and Mufdhi v. United Kingdom*, judgment of 2 March 2010, *unpublished*, § 120.
61 See section 11.3.
62 ECtHR (GC), *Vo v. France*, judgment of 8 July 2004, *Reports* 2004-VIII.

results.[63] The problematic aspects of relying on consensus or comparative arguments have been discussed elaborately in the chapter on comparative interpretation. Having regard to the frequent use of comparative arguments in connection with evolutive interpretation, these problems are to some extent incorporated in evolutive interpretation too. At this point it is therefore important to realize that the persuasiveness and legitimacy of an evolutive approach depends on the quality of the use of comparative arguments by the Court.

11.5 Relation to other interpretative aids

In order to fully grasp the role evolutive interpretation plays in the case law of the Court, it is important to analyze the relation of this interpretative aid with the other aids, mainly those selected for the purpose of this thesis. Some of the sections in this chapter have already touched upon this relation of evolutive interpretation with other interpretative aids, whereby these other aids may either function as a limit to evolutive interpretation or as a way to substantiate evolutive interpretation. In *Soering,* for example, the Court concluded that it could not take an evolutive approach, since considerations based on systematic and textual interpretation strongly pointed in different directions and proved to be a clear reflection of the intentions of the drafters.[64] This case again shows the tense relation between the intention of the drafters and the living nature of the Convention. Only in relatively few cases will evolutive interpretation have to yield to the intention of the drafters.

The most important relation that has been discussed is that between comparative interpretation and evolutive interpretation. This relation has been elaborated upon in the previous section, which showed that comparative interpretation is often used to determine the present-day conditions in the light of which the Convention has to be interpreted. This tight relation is not very surprising, as it had already been observed in the theoretical chapter on the basis of academic literature.[65] Some authors, however, have equated evolutive interpretation to comparative interpretation and have failed to make a clear distinction between the two concepts.[66] While this

---

63 See for example: the dissenting opinions in ECtHR, *Sheffield & Horsham v. United Kingdom*, judgment of 30 July 1998, *Reports* 1998-V; ECtHR (GC), *T v. United Kingdom*, judgment of 16 December 1999, *unpublished*; ECtHR (GC), *V v. United Kingdom*, judgment of 16 December 1999, *Reports* 1999-IX.

64 ECtHR, *Soering v. United Kingdom*, judgment of 7 July 1989, *Series* A No. 161, § 102-103. Similar examples can be found in ECtHR, *Johnston and others v. Ireland*, judgment of 18 December 1986, *Series* A No. 112, § 53 and ECtHR (GC), *Banković and others v. Belgium and others*, decision of 12 December 2001, *Reports* 2001-XII, § 65.

65 See Chapter 6 on comparative interpretation, but mainly Chapter 7 on evolutive interpretation.

66 Most notably Helfer (1993); Rigaux (1998).

chapter (and the chapter on comparative interpretation) has illustrated that comparative interpretation and evolutive interpretation are closely connected, it has also tried to demonstrate that they are two separate concepts. Each concept plays a different role in the interpretation process and they can and have been applied independently as well. Evolutive interpretation indicates the direction in which an interpretation might go and comparative interpretation provides the substantive justification for a specific evolutive interpretation.

One of the other interpretative aids central to this thesis is autonomous interpretation. Only very few cases show both references to autonomous and evolutive interpretation to establish the meaning of a Convention provision, notable exceptions being the cases of *Stec* and *Ferrazzini*.[67] Indeed, in *Stec* the Court explained the relation between autonomous and evolutive interpretation in express terms:

> It is in the interests of the coherence of the Convention as a whole that the *autonomous concept* of "possessions" in Article 1 of Protocol No. 1 should be interpreted in a way which is consistent with the concept of pecuniary rights under article 6 § 1. It is moreover important to adopt an interpretation of Article 1 of Protocol No. 1 which avoids inequalities of treatment based on distinctions which, *at the present day*, appear illogical or unsustainable (emphasis added).[68]

Thus, also when the Court has adopted an autonomous meaning of one of the Convention provisions, it considers it necessary to keep it under review whether this autonomous meaning still meets the present-day standards. The Court indicated in *Ferrazzini*, this is not without its limitations:

> The principle according to which the autonomous concepts contained in the Convention must be interpreted in the light of present-day conditions in democratic societies does not give the Court power to interpret Article 6 § 1 as though the adjective "civil" (with the restriction that that adjective necessarily places on the category of "rights and obligations" to which that Article applies) were not present in the text.[69]

Evolutive interpretation can as a result be used to reform the autonomous understanding of some of the Convention concepts, however, within the limits of the wording of the provision. It should be underlined that this has happened in very few cases.

---

67 ECtHR (GC), *Stec and others v. United Kingdom*, decision of 6 July 2005, *Reports* 2005-X; ECtHR (GC), *Ferrazzini v. Italy*, judgment of 12 July 2001, Reports 2001-VII.

68 ECtHR (GC), *Stec and others v. United Kingdom*, decision of 6 July 2005, *Reports* 2005-X, § 49. In *Stec* the Court actually adopted an evolutive approach. In ECtHR (GC), *Ferrazzini v. Italy*, judgment of 12 July 2001, Reports 2001-VII, the Court in the end did not.

69 ECtHR (GC), *Ferrazzini v. Italy*, judgment of 12 July 2001, Reports 2001-VII, § 30.

Finally, the relation with teleological interpretation should be discussed. Contrary to the relation with other interpretative methods and principles, the link between evolutive and teleological interpretation exists at a more abstract level. It has already been pointed out that an evolutive approach is often justified by the Court on the basis of the need to interpret its provisions in a practical and effective manner and not leave them theoretical and illusory.[70] This need for a practical and effective approach is, according to the Court, required by the object and purpose of the Convention.[71] In justifying an evolutive approach the Court has linked evolutive interpretation with the need for practical and effective protection.[72] Evolutive interpretation seems to be one of the ways to keep the Convention guarantees practical and effective and as such it helps fulfil one of the objectives of the Convention. In that sense evolutive interpretation can be seen as one of the meta-teleological principles of the Convention and the justification provided by the Court seems to confirm this view. Even if the Court does not express itself on the nature of evolutive interpretation, it does consider it one of the purposes of the Convention.

11.6 Conclusion

Various questions that still remained after the theoretical analysis of the notion of evolutive interpretation have been addressed in the case law analysis, resulting in greater clarity as to its meaning and its use by the Court. The Court evidently is cautious not to let the European Convention become a dead letter and often refers to the need to interpret according to present-day circumstances. The question that was posed in this context in the theoretical analysis was whether this desire to interpret according to present-day circumstances in practice meant that the Court aimed for a higher standard of protection. This has been confirmed in many cases by the Court, where it indicated that the Convention should be interpreted according to increasingly higher standards. The question whether this is always possible with conflicting fundamental rights is something that has not been addressed by the Court, but should be kept in mind when thinking about this tendency of the ECtHR to aim for higher standards.

The Court has not expressly addressed the nature of evolutive interpretation, which means that it is difficult to conclude on the basis of the case law analysis whether

70 See footnote 1186 for the quote from ECtHR (GC), *Stec and others v. United Kingdom*, decision of 6 July 2005, *Reports* 2005-X.

71 See ECtHR (GC), *Mamatkulov and Askarov v. Turkey*, judgment of 4 February 2005, *Reports* 2005-I, § 101; ECtHR, *Soering v. United Kingdom*, judgment of 7 July 1989, *Series* A No. 161, § 87.

72 See among others: ECtHR (GC), *Stec and others v. United Kingdom*, decision of 6 July 2005, *Reports* 2005-X and ECtHR (GC), *Mamatkulov and Askarov v. Turkey*, judgment of 4 February 2005, *Reports* 2005-I.

the ECtHR considers evolutive interpretation to be an interpretative method or principle. Nevertheless, the justification it often provides for the choice for evolutive interpretation, namely that is necessary to keep the Convention practical and effective, supports the conclusion that it is based on a meta-teleological approach to the Convention. In light of the theoretical analysis, evolutive interpretation as it is used by the Court can therefore be considered a meta-teleological *principle*, even though the Court is unclear about its nature.

There is no clear trend in the type of case of situation types of the ECtHR in which the Court chooses to apply an evolutive approach. Some trends can, however, be found in the situations in which the ECtHR does consider an evolutive approach to be inappropriate. If a textual or systemic interpretation clearly points in a different direction, this will often trump an evolutive approach. Also when the ECtHR considers that it does not have enough evidence for an evolutive approach, it will not adopt an evolutive solution. Finally, in some cases a clear intention of the drafters can be discerned in the *travaux préparatoires*, which has sometimes (though not always) been respected by the Court. The ECtHR thus does seem to be aware of the limits of this approach, although it has to be stressed that it does not always consistently apply these limits.

A final point that has been analyzed is how an evolutive interpretation is established. This is often with the help of comparative interpretation. Reference is made to both internal and external comparative material.[73] The problems discussed in section 6.1.6.2 which relate to proving that a consensus can be found, also resonate when used to establish an evolution. The question whether an evolution exists is therefore not always clearly proven.

73 See section 6.1.3. for a discussion of this distinction.

Chapter 12
Autonomous interpretation in the case law of the ECtHR

This chapter will address the use of autonomous interpretation in the case law of the European Court of Human Rights. Autonomous interpretation has been identified in the theoretical chapter as one of the meta-teleological principles that are used in the case law of the Court. The theoretical chapter identified meta-teleological principles as principles that are based on the object and purpose of the Convention, thereby justifying the use of an interpretation that is in line with the main aims of the Convention. The question is whether this justification for the use of autonomous interpretation is actually visible in the case law of the Court, and so whether the Court really refers to the object and purpose of the Convention as a basis for autonomous interpretation. Related to this, it will be interesting to see whether the Court clarifies the nature of this interpretative aid, i.e. whether it can be gleaned from its case law if it considers autonomous interpretation to be either an interpretation method or an interpretative principle.[1]

The theoretical chapter revealed that much is still unclear about the use of autonomous interpretation by the Court. It is not known in what type of situations the Court relies on an autonomous approach. The theoretical analysis suggested, for example, that more technical terms, or terms related to the rule of law, are more likely to be interpreted in an autonomous manner than other terms. One of the questions to be answered therefore is whether this presupposition is supported by the case law analysis or whether another pattern can be found.

Furthermore, one of the characteristics of an interpretative principle is that it cannot on its own justify a specific interpretation.[2] The principles only indicate a specific interpretative approach and do not provide a specific substantive argument on which an interpretation can be based. Presupposing that the Court actually uses autonomous interpretation as a principle, rather than as a method of interpretation (see above), it is to be expected that it will refer to different interpretation methods in order to find an autonomous meaning of the Convention – an examination of this element will therefore also be made in this chapter. In addition, and regardless of the way the Court characterizes autonomous interpretation, the role of autonomous in relation

1 For a discussion on the difference, see section 4.1.
2 For an elaborate discussion, see section 4.1.

to other interpretative aids will be discussed in order to obtain a better understanding of the interpretative framework that is used by the ECtHR.

As indicated in the theoretical chapter on autonomous interpretation, this thesis will only address those cases where the Court has explicitly adopted or rejected an autonomous approach. The reason for this is that those cases will be most instructive for the question how autonomous interpretation is used in the case law of the ECtHR. The discussion of the analysis of these cases in this chapter will be structured along the lines of the questions and issues for examination that have been presented above. Thus, this chapter will address what autonomous interpretation means (section 12.1), how it is characterized (section 12.2), why it is used (section 12.3), when it is applied (section 12.4) and how the Court applied autonomous interpretation (section 12.5). The role of autonomous interpretation in relation to other interpretation principles and methods will be addressed throughout all these discussions.

12.1 What is autonomous interpretation?

Before going into an in-depth analysis of the role and use of autonomous interpretation in the case law of the ECtHR, it is useful to discuss what the Court means by autonomous interpretation. The Court in many cases refers to the 'autonomous meaning' of Convention provisions,[3] but only in few cases does it explicitly explain what this entails.[4] In *Stran Greek Refineries* the Court held that 'the concept of "civil rights and obligations" is not to be interpreted solely by reference to the respondent State's

3 See for example: ECtHR (GC), *Beyeler v. Italy*, judgment of 5 January 2000, *Reports* 2000-I, § 100; ECtHR (GC), *Iatridis v. Greece*, judgment of 25 March 1999, *Reports* 1999-II, § 54; ECtHR, *Zwierzynski v. Poland*, judgment of 19 June 2001, *Reports* 2001-VI, § 63; ECtHR, *Matos e Silva, Lda, and others v. Portugal*, judgment of 16 September 1996, *Reports* 1996-IV, § 75; ECtHR, *Gasus Dosier- und Fördertechnik GmbH v. the Netherlands*, judgment of 23 February 1995, *Series* A No. 306B, § 53; ECtHR, *Witold Litwa v. Poland*, judgment of 4 April 2000, *Reports* 2000-III, § 76; ECtHR (GC), *Jussila v. Finland*, judgment of 23 November 2006, *unpublished*, § 29; ECtHR (GC), *Chassagnou and others v. France*, judgment of 29 April 1999, *Reports* 1999-III, § 100; ECtHR, *James and others v. United Kingdom*, judgment of 21 February 1986, *Series* A No. 98, § 42; ECtHR (GC), *Öneryildiz v. Turkey*, judgment of 30 November 2004, *Reports* 2004-XII, § 124; ECtHR (GC), *Scoppola v. Italy (No. 2)*, judgment of 17 September 2009, *unpublished*; ECtHR (GC), *Depalle v. France*, judgment of 29 March 2010, *unpublished*, § 62; ECtHR, *Storbråten v. Norway*, decision of 1 February 2007, *unpublished*, § 7. In ECtHR (GC), *Stec and others v. United Kingdom*, decision of 6 July 2005, *Reports* 2005-X, § 49, the Court refers to autonomous *concepts*.

4 See ECtHR (GC), *Chassagnou and others v. France*, judgment of 29 April 1999, *Reports* 1999-III, § 100; ECtHR, *Stran Greek Refineries and Stratis Andreadis v. Greece*, judgment of 9 December 1994, *Series* A No. 301-B, § 39; separate opinion by Matscher in ECtHR, *König v. Germany*, judgment of 28 June 1978, *Series* A No. 27.

domestic law'.[5] Some of the terms in the Convention are thus expressly interpreted independently from the classification of these terms in the domestic law of the defending State. The meaning of autonomous interpretation has been most elaborately explained by Judge Matscher in his separate opinion in *König*:

> In my view, autonomous interpretation means, above all, that the provisions of international conventions must not be interpreted solely by reference to the meaning and scope which they possess in the domestic law of the contracting State concerned, but that reference must be made "first, to the objectives and scheme of the Convention, and, secondly, to the general principles which stem from the corpus of the national legal systems."[6]

This quote confirms the fact that autonomous interpretation means autonomy from national classifications. However, the opinion by Judge Matscher was a separate opinion and therefore not necessarily reflects the opinion of the Court. This might explain why the second point made by Matscher is not visible in the case law of the Court, as will be shown in this chapter.

From the two examples given above it is safe to conclude that autonomy refers only to the national classifications of particular terms and not to autonomy from, for example, the meaning of specific terms within the European Union.[7] The following examples can provide further support to this conclusion:

> In this connection the Court points out that the concept of 'possessions' in the first part of Article 1 has an autonomous meaning which is not limited to ownership of physical goods and is independent from the formal classification in domestic law.[8]

> The term 'association' therefore possesses an autonomous meaning; the classification in national law has only relative value and constitutes no more than a starting point.[9]

Thus, the general meaning of 'autonomous interpretation' seems to be relatively clear and uncontested in the Court's case law.

---

5 ECtHR, *Stran Greek Refineries and Stratis Andreadis v. Greece*, judgment of 9 December 1994, *Series* A No. 301-B, § 39.

6 Separate opinion by Matscher in ECtHR, *König v. Germany*, judgment of 28 June 1978, *Series* A No. 27. Judge Matscher subsequently referred to an CJEU judgment from which this quote was taken and explains that the latter part of his explanation means that the Court should look for the common denominator.

7 This aspect of autonomous interpretation, namely autonomy from the ECHR, does play a role in the context of the CJEU, as will be seen in Chapter 13. Vanneste (2010), p. 232, also emphasizes that the ECtHR only employs an autonomous approach in relation to the domestic classification.

8 ECtHR (GC), *Beyeler v. Italy*, judgment of 5 January 2000, *Reports* 2000-I, § 100.

9 ECtHR (GC), *Chassagnou and others v. France*, judgment of 29 April 1999, *Reports* 1999-III, § 100.

12.2 Autonomous interpretation: interpretative principle or method?

One of the objectives of this chapter is to analyze the role of autonomous interpretation in the interpretation process of the Court. In order to get a complete picture of the role of autonomous interpretation, it is necessary to discuss the nature of this interpretative aid as it is used by the ECtHR. The theoretical analysis showed that some authors recognize the special nature of autonomous interpretation as an interpretative aid, but the explicit distinction between interpretative principles and interpretation methods has hardly been made in this context. The question is how the ECtHR itself classifies this interpretative aid – can any indication be found in the case law as to whether the Court qualifies autonomous interpretation as an interpretative principle or rather as a method of interpretation.[10]

The Court is generally not very explicit on methodological issues, although indirect indications can sometimes be found.[11] As has already been indicated above, the Court in many cases stresses that particular terms in the Convention have an autonomous meaning: '[i]t recalls that the notion "possessions" (in French: "biens") in Article 1 of Protocol 1 has an autonomous meaning.'[12] The Court has also employed different formulations by referring to the autonomy of certain notions in Convention provisions:

> Having thus reaffirmed the 'autonomy' of the notion 'criminal' as conceived of under Article, what the Court must determine is whether or not the 'regulatory offence' committed by the applicant was a 'criminal' one within the meaning of that Article 6.[13]

These examples do not actually reveal how the Court qualifies autonomous interpretation, but they do to a certain extent reveal the nature of autonomous interpretation. The Court seems to consider autonomous interpretation as an objective that should be obtained, not so much as an interpretative technique. By invoking an autonomous meaning the Court adopts a particular *approach* towards some of the Convention terms, namely to take the national classification only as a starting point. The reference to autonomous interpretation or autonomous meaning does not indicate a certain technique to establish that autonomous or 'European' meaning. Indeed, referring to the autonomy of a notion seems to imply something about the character of the notion,

---

10 See section 4.1. for a discussion of the differences between an interpretative method and principle.

11 ECtHR, *Golder v. United Kingdom*, judgment of 21 February 1975, *Series* A No. 18 and ECtHR (GC), *Demir and Baykara v. Turkey*, judgment of 12 November 2008, *unpublished* are rare examples of the ECtHR addressing methodological issues.

12 ECtHR, *Matos e Silva, Lda, and others v. Portugal*, judgment of 16 September 1996, *Reports* 1996-IV, § 75.

13 ECtHR, *Öztürk v. Germany*, judgment of 21 February 1984, *Series* A No. 73, § 50. See also: ECtHR, *König v. Germany*, judgment of 28 June 1978, *Series* A No. 27, § 88.

rather than indicating a concrete interpretative technique that may be used to determine its meaning.

In a few cases the Court has even expressly referred to autonomous interpretation as a *principle* that should be applied:

> The Court has on several occasions affirmed the principle that this concept is 'autonomous', within the meaning of Article 6 § 1 of the Convention.[14]

> The Court confirms this case-law on the present occasion. Hence, it considers that the same principle of autonomy applies to the concept in question; any other solution might lead to results incompatible with the object and purpose of the Convention.[15]

It might be tempting to conclude that the Court considers autonomous interpretation as an interpretative principle, but that would perhaps be making too much out of these two references. However, even if the Court usually remains silent on the nature of autonomous interpretation, these references may certainly be regarded as an indication that the Court does not consider autonomous interpretation to be a regular interpretation method.

12.3 Why autonomous interpretation?

The Convention does not make reference to autonomous interpretation, nor does it contain any provision that indirectly allows for an autonomous approach. While this does not mean that such an interpretative approach does not fit the Convention scheme, it does beg for a justification for the introduction and use of this approach. As has been explained in the theoretical chapter on autonomous interpretation (Chapter 8), many authors invoke the Vienna Convention to justify the use of an autonomous approach by international judges. Perhaps rather surprisingly, however, the ECtHR itself has never invoked the VCLT to justify an autonomous approach (even though it has referred to the VCLT to justify its interpretative approach in general).

In a limited number of cases the ECtHR provided an explanation for relying on an autonomous approach.[16] In the case of *Öztürk,* one of the earlier cases in which the concept was invoked, Judge Matscher in his dissenting opinion explained why

14 ECtHR (GC), *Ferrazzini v. Italy*, judgment of 12 July 2001, Reports 2001-VII, § 24.

15 ECtHR, *König v. Germany*, judgment of 28 June 1978, *Series* A No. 27, § 88.

16 Most notably: ECtHR, *König v. Germany*, judgment of 28 June 1978, *Series* A No. 27; ECtHR, *Öztürk v. Germany*, judgment of 21 February 1984, *Series* A No. 73; ECtHR (GC), *Ferrazzini v. Italy*, judgment of 12 July 2001, Reports 2001-VII; ECtHR (GC), *Chassagnou and others v. France*, judgment of 29 April 1999, *Reports* 1999-III; ECtHR, *Storbråten v. Norway*, decision of 1 February 2007, *unpublished*; ECtHR (GC), *Sergey Zolotukhin v. Russia*, judgment of 10 February 2009, *unpublished.*

perhaps the Court has not always articulated the justifications for autonomous interpretation very clearly. He considered that:

> It goes without saying that autonomous interpretation is the method best suited to multilateral conventions, and particularly rule-making instruments, such as the European Convention on Human Rights.[17]

Matscher apparently considered the use of this interpretative aid self-evident. The ECtHR, however, in this and many other cases relied on teleological arguments to justify its autonomous approach as will be discussed below.

There are two related strands of problems that would result were the Court to defer to national classifications for the applicability of Convention provisions. The Court has referred to both to provide a more detailed elaboration of the general justification for relying on autonomous interpretation, namely that another approach would jeopardize the object and purpose of the Convention. In the first place, the Court does not want to grant the Contracting States the freedom to shift labels and thereby avoid having to comply with the Convention requirements. It would severely damage the effective protection of fundamental rights in Europe. The second problem would be that, in addition to this, the level of protection would differ per Contracting State. In States where the domestic and European classification would coincide, citizens would be afforded protection, while others citizens in similar situations would be denied this protection. Such an unequal result is undesirable according to the Court, which is why in cases like *Pellegrin*[18] the Court has adopted an autonomous interpretation. In *Pellegrin* the Court had to determine in what situations a legal dispute concerning a civil servant would be covered by the protection afforded by Article 6. The Court emphasized that it would be undesirable if the applicability of the Convention would depend on the specific national legal situation. The fact that different Contracting States had different approaches led the Court to adopt an autonomous approach. The following excerpts from both cases reflect this aim to afford equal protection:

> The Court accordingly considers that it is important, with a view to applying Article 6 § 1, to establish an autonomous interpretation of the term 'civil service' which would make it possible to afford *equal treatment* to public servants performing equivalent or similar duties in the States Parties to the Convention, irrespective of the domestic system of employment

17 ECtHR, *Öztürk v. Germany*, judgment of 21 February 1984, *Series* A No. 73, dissenting opinion by Matscher, § 2.

18 ECtHR (GC), *Pellegrin v. France,* judgment of 8 December 1999, *Reports* 1999-VIII. This is one of the few cases where the ECtHR explicitly mentioned the aspect of equal protection; in others cases this aspect is often implied in the reasoning.

> and, in particular, whatever the nature of the legal relation between the official and the administrative authority (emphasis added).[19]

The emphasis on equivalent protection is also visible in the case of *Stec* where the Court had to determine whether both contributory and non-contributory benefits were considered 'possessions' for the purpose of Article 1 Protocol No. 1. The case law had been contradictory on this point and there were many differences between the ways the social system was organized in the different Contracting States. Both aspects led the Court to adopt an autonomous approach.

> It is in the interest of the coherence of the Convention as a whole that the autonomous concept of "possessions" in Article 1 of Protocol No. 1should be interpreted in a way which is consistent with the concept of pecuniary rights under Article 6 § 1. It is moreover important to adopt an interpretation of Article 1 of Protocol No. 1 which avoids *inequalities of treatment* based on distinctions which, at the present day, appear illogical or unsustainable (emphasis added).
> ... Given the variety of funding methods, and the interlocking nature of benefits under most welfare systems, it appears increasingly artificial to hold that only benefits financed by contributions to a specific fund fall within the scope of Article 1 of Protocol No. 1.[20]

In conclusion one can say that the Court wants to control the applicability of the Convention in order to grant an equal minimum level of protection throughout Europe.[21]

In this context it is interesting to note that the ECtHR may sometimes also decide to revert to a more dependent and subsidiary approach. This is what happened in the case of *Vilho Eskelinen* in which the Court in its own words 'further developed' the criterion from *Pellegrin*, which determined in what situations a legal dispute concerning civil servants would be covered by Article 6. The Court in *Vilho Eskelinen* had to decide whether the autonomous criterion developed in *Pellegrin* was still workable. The majority concluded that it was not and it established new criteria to determine whether disputes concerning civil servants would fall under Article 6. According to the new approach a Member State is allowed to exclude a civil servant protection under Article 6 if two conditions are met, i.e. that the protection is expressly excluded under national law and the exclusion is justified on objective grounds. What is striking about this new approach is that the ECtHR has abandoned the autonomous approach taken in *Pellegrin* and opted for a more dependent and subsidiary approach whereby it still holds some control under the second condition. This new approach

19 ECtHR (GC), *Pellegrin v. France*, judgment of 8 December 1999, *Reports* 1999-VIII, § 63.

20 ECtHR (GC), *Stec and others v. United Kingdom*, decision of 6 July 2005, *Reports* 2005-X, § 49-50.

21 Matscher (1993), p. 73 and Vande Lanotte (2005), p. 186 point to the harmonizing effect of autonomous interpretation.

has been heavily criticized by the dissenters, who argue that this variable approach is an 'inappropriate step back'.[22] Why the ECtHR did not develop a different autonomous criterion, but instead afforded an important position to the domestic qualification is not clear. It would have been enlightening for the discussion on autonomous interpretation if the reasons behind this move had been made clearer.

This raises the question whether the ECtHR really wants to establish a harmonized, minimum level of protection in all situations. The new approach in *Vilho Eskelinen* already provides an answer to that question, but there are other cases that shed light on this question. There are two cases in which the ECtHR clearly refused to adopt an autonomous approach, because it would have been too sensitive to harmonize the different views on this issue. In *Kimlya* the question was whether Scientology could be considered a religion in the sense of Article 9 of the Convention.[23] In other cases, which have been discussed above, like *Pellegrin* and *Stec*, the fact that Contracting States differed in their qualification led the ECtHR to adopt an autonomous approach, so that individuals would be offered the same level of minimum protection. In *Kimlya* the ECtHR used the fact that Contracting States differ on the qualification of Scientology as a religion to argue against an autonomous approach. The ECtHR held that: 'In the absence of any European consensus on the religious nature of Scientology teachings, and being sensitive to the subsidiary nature of its role, the Court considers that it must rely on the position of the domestic authorities in the matter and determine the applicability of Article 9 of the Convention accordingly.'[24] The protection afforded in this case thus depends on the national classification.

A similar situation arose in the case of *Vo*, where the Court had to determine whether a foetus could be considered a person in the context of the right to life. The Court indicated that there was no consensus among Contracting States nor in scientific circles on the beginning of life.[25] The ECtHR subsequently held that it was 'convinced that it is neither desirable, nor even possible as matters stand, to answer in the abstract the question whether the unborn child is a person for the purposes of Article 2 of the Convention'.[26] Like in the case of *Kimlya* the ECtHR did not want to apply an autonomous approach due to the differences between Contracting States.

22 Dissenters in ECtHR (GC), *Vilho Eskelinen and others v. Finland*, judgment of 19 April 2007, *unpublished*.

23 ECtHR, *Kimlya and others v. Russia*, judgment of 1 October 2009, *unpublished*.

24 ECtHR, *Kimlya and others v. Russia*, judgment of 1 October 2009, *unpublished*, § 79. The ECtHR held that in Russia Scientology was recognized as a religion.

25 ECtHR (GC), *Vo v. France*, judgment of 8 July 2004, *Reports* 2004-VIII, § 82. The ECtHR exceptionally refers to the margin of appreciation of Contracting States in this case, but generally Contracting States are not granted a margin of appreciation when it comes to the interpretation of the Convention.

26 ECtHR (GC), *Vo v. France*, judgment of 8 July 2004, *Reports* 2004-VIII, § 85.

The reason the Court provides seems understandable, but it is more difficult to understand when compared with the approach in other cases that have been discussed above. The differences in the Contracting States triggered an autonomous approach in those cases.

In general, it is safe to conclude that teleological considerations are mainly at the basis of the choice for an autonomous approach. An autonomous approach is necessary to respect the object and purpose of the Convention either because it would prevent the States from shifting labels or because it would prevent inequality. This confirms the argument in the theoretical chapter that autonomous interpretation is one of the meta-teleological principles that has been introduced to protect the object and purpose of the Convention.[27]

12.4 When autonomous interpretation?

In the theoretical analysis it has been submitted that autonomous interpretation mainly plays a role in the context of Article 6 and Article 1 Protocol No. 1. The question is whether such preference is actually visible in the analyzed case law and, if so, whether any indications can be found in the case law to explain why an autonomous approach is adopted in specifically these situations.

There are two different situations in which the Court has applied autonomous interpretation. The differences between the situations are subtle, but to regard them as belonging to one and the same category would amount to overly generalizing. Firstly, many cases where the Court has adopted an autonomous meaning involved a dispute between the applicant and the government on the applicability of the right invoked by the applicant.[28] The issue in these cases is whether the applicant's complaint concerns a sufficient interest to fall within the scope of the Convention. The majority of these cases concern the question whether an applicant holds a 'possession' which brings the case under the protection of Article 1 First Protocol.[29] In these cases the Court recalls that the notion of 'possession' has an autonomous meaning under the Convention and tries to establish whether the facts of the case come within that meaning. This is not, however, a typical situation that does not occur in relation

27 See section 4.4.1.3. and the introduction to Chapter 8.

28 ECtHR (GC), *Öneryildiz v. Turkey*, judgment of 30 November 2004, *Reports* 2004-XII, § 124; ECtHR (GC), *Beyeler v. Italy*, judgment of 5 January 2000, *Reports* 2000-I; ECtHR, *Matos e Silva, Lda, and others v. Portugal*, judgment of 16 September 1996, *Reports* 1996-IV; ECtHR, *Gasus Dosier- und Fördertechnik GmbH v. the Netherlands*, judgment of 23 February 1995, *Series* A No. 306B; ECtHR (GC), *Iatridis v. Greece*, judgment of 25 March 1999, *Reports* 1999-II; ECtHR, *Posti and Rahko v. Finland*, judgment of 24 September 2002, Reports 2002-VII; ECtHR, *Zwierzynski v. Poland*, judgment of 19 June 2001, *Reports* 2001-VI.

29 Supra note 28 for references.

to any other Convention right, since it is basically a matter of applying the facts of the case. It is therefore not a characteristic situation that necessarily requires autonomous interpretation and may therefore explain a preference for autonomous interpretation in relation to Article 1 Protocol No. 1.

Secondly, the Court has often applied autonomous interpretation in cases where the domestic classification would prevent a certain case from being protected by the Convention.[30] If the Court would accept such a national classification, this would determine the applicability of the Convention and, accordingly, the Court's jurisdiction to decide on the complaint. While in the first category the dispute concerns the evaluation of the facts in light of the Convention, thus, in these cases the Court would not even get to that stage, since the classification under national law implies that the Convention is not applicable. In some of these cases the Court has explicitly said that if the Court were to defer to the national classifications 'the operation of the fundamental clauses of Articles 6 and 7 would be subordinated to their sovereign will'.[31] Such a control by the Contracting States would be incompatible with the object and purpose of the Convention according to the Court, as discussed above, and which can be seen by the following examples:

> If Contracting States were able, at their discretion, by classifying an association as "public" or "para-administrative", to remove it from the scope of Article 11, that would give them such latitude that it might lead to results incompatible with the object and purpose of the Convention, which is to protect rights that are not theoretical or illusory but practical and effective.[32]

> The Court has on several occasions affirmed the principle that this concept is "autonomous", within the meaning of article 6 § 1 of the Convention ... The Court confirms this case-law in the instant case. It considers that any other solution is liable to lead to results that are incompatible with the object and purpose of the Convention.[33]

The protection afforded by the Convention would be hampered if the application of the Convention depended on the discretion of the Contracting States. The Court does not want to play games with labels and therefore looks beyond the national classification. This general justification for the use of the principle could be relevant to all

30 See most importantly: ECtHR, *Engel and others v. the Netherlands*, judgment of 8 June 1976, *Series* A No. 22; ECtHR, *König v. Germany*, judgment of 28 June 1978, *Series* A No. 27; ECtHR, *Öztürk v. Germany*, judgment of 21 February 1984, *Series* A No. 73; ECtHR (GC), *Pellegrin v. France*, judgment of 8 December 1999, *Reports* 1999-VIII.

31 ECtHR, *Engel and others v. the Netherlands*, judgment of 8 June 1976, *Series* A No. 22, § 81. Similar statement made in ECtHR, *Öztürk v. Germany*, judgment of 21 February 1984, *Series* A No. 73, § 49.

32 ECtHR (GC), *Chassagnou and others v. France*, judgment of 29 April 1999, *Reports* 1999-III, § 100.

33 ECtHR (GC), *Ferrazzini v. Italy*, judgment of 12 July 2001, *Reports* 2001-VII, § 24.

rights protected by the Convention. It is difficult to see how this could be a problem that occurs mainly when interpreting the right to fair trial and the right to property, as has been implied in academic literature. In many other situations the Court needs to look beyond appearances and determine an interpretation that might be independent of the national interpretation. Nevertheless, the question remains as to why the ECtHR in these situations opts for an explicit acknowledgement of the autonomous approach in these cases. It appears from the case law analysis that the answer to this question might be that not only the situation in which an autonomous approach has been adopted is relevant, but that also the specific terms that have been labelled autonomous play a role in this regard.

The question is then whether an autonomous interpretation is specifically reserved for certain terms and not for others. The theoretical chapter indicated that not all terms have been explicitly recognized as having an autonomous meaning. There are only a relatively limited number of cases in which the Court has explicitly adopted an autonomous meaning.[34] What immediately attracts the attention when considering these cases is that they mainly concern the interpretation of two Convention rights, namely the right to a fair trial and the right to property.[35] It seems that in only few

---

34 ECtHR (GC), *Chassagnou and others v. France*, judgment of 29 April 1999, *Reports* 1999-III; ECtHR, *Witold Litwa v. Poland*, judgment of 4 April 2000, *Reports* 2000-III; ECtHR (GC), *Pellegrin v. France*, judgment of 8 December 1999, *Reports* 1999-VIII; ECtHR (GC), *Jussila v. Finland*, judgment of 23 November 2006, *unpublished*; ECtHR, *Öztürk v. Germany*, judgment of 21 February 1984, *Series* A No. 73; ECtHR, *Engel and others v. the Netherlands*, judgment of 8 June 1976, *Series* A No. 22; ECtHR, *König v. Germany*, judgment of 28 June 1978, *Series* A No. 27; ECtHR (GC), *Ferrazzini v. Italy*, judgment of 12 July 2001, Reports 2001-VII; ECtHR, *Stran Greek Refineries and Stratis Andreadis v. Greece*, judgment of 9 December 1994, *Series* A No. 301-B; ECtHR (GC), *Beyeler v. Italy*, judgment of 5 January 2000, *Reports* 2000-I; ECtHR, *Matos e Silva, Lda, and others v. Portugal*, judgment of 16 September 1996, *Reports* 1996-IV; ECtHR, *Gasus Dosier- und Fördertechnik GmbH v. the Netherlands*, judgment of 23 February 1995, *Series* A No. 306B;ECtHR (GC), *Iatridis v. Greece*, judgment of 25 March 1999, *Reports* 1999-II;ECtHR, *Posti and Rahko v. Finland*, judgment of 24 September 2002, Reports 2002-VII; ECtHR, *Zwierzynski v. Poland*, judgment of 19 June 2001, *Reports* 2001-VI; ECtHR (GC), *Stec and others v. United Kingdom*, decision of 6 July 2005, *Reports* 2005-X.

35 ECtHR (GC), *Pellegrin v. France*, judgment of 8 December 1999, *Reports* 1999-VIII; ECtHR (GC), *Jussila v. Finland*, judgment of 23 November 2006, *unpublished*; ECtHR, *Öztürk v. Germany*, judgment of 21 February 1984, *Series* A No. 73; ECtHR, *Engel and others v. the Netherlands*, judgment of 8 June 1976, *Series* A No. 22; ECtHR, *König v. Germany*, judgment of 28 June 1978, *Series* A No. 27; ECtHR (GC), *Ferrazzini v. Italy*, judgment of 12 July 2001, Reports 2001-VII; ECtHR, *Stran Greek Refineries and Stratis Andreadis v. Greece*, judgment of 9 December 1994, *Series* A No. 301-B; ECtHR (GC), *Beyeler v. Italy*, judgment of 5 January 2000, *Reports* 2000-I; ECtHR, *Matos e Silva, Lda, and others v. Portugal*, judgment of 16 September 1996, *Reports* 1996-IV; ECtHR, *Gasus Dosier- und Fördertechnik GmbH v. the Netherlands*, judgment of 23 February 1995, *Series* A No. 306B; ECtHR (GC), *Iatridis v. Greece*, judgment of 25 March 1999, *Reports* 1999-II;ECtHR, *Posti and Rahko v. Finland*, judgment of 24 September 2002, Reports 2002-VII; ECtHR,

other cases autonomous interpretation has expressly been applied to entirely different rights, namely the right to freedom of association, the right to respect for one's home and a specific aspect of the right to freedom of liberty.[36] In the case of *Chassagnou* the ECtHR had to establish whether French hunting associations were associations within the meaning of Article 11 of the Convention.[37] The Court held that the term 'association' has an autonomous meaning and concluded that the hunting association was indeed an association within the meaning of Article 11. In the case of *Witold Litwa* the Court determined that the term 'alcoholic' expressed in Article 5 of the Convention had an autonomous meaning.[38] In the cases of *Prokopovich* and *Hartung* the Court determined that the notion 'home' is an autonomous concept which does not depend on classification under domestic law.[39] The ECtHR has also relied on an autonomous interpretation in the context of the right not to be punished or tried.[40] In that case, however, the ECtHR had to establish the autonomous meaning of the term 'criminal' in the context of Article 4 Protocol 7, but in doing so referred to the autonomous meaning of the term 'criminal' in the context of fair trial. The latter example is thus not entirely disassociated from the autonomous interpretation of the right to fair trial. All other cases that have been studied either concern the interpretation of Article 6 of the Convention, more specifically the interpretation of the notions 'civil right' and 'criminal charge',[41] or the interpretation of the term 'possession'

Zwierzynski v. Poland, judgment of 19 June 2001, *Reports* 2001-VI; ECtHR (GC), *Stec and others v. United Kingdom*, decision of 6 July 2005, *Reports* 2005-X.

36 ECtHR (GC), *Chassagnou and others v. France*, judgment of 29 April 1999, *Reports* 1999-III; ECtHR, *Prokopovich v. Russia*, judgment of 18 November 2004, *Reports* 2004-XI, confirmed in ECtHR, *Hartung v. France*, decision of 3 November 2009, *unpublished*; ECtHR, *Witold Litwa v. Poland*, judgment of 4 April 2000, *Reports* 2000-III.

37 ECtHR (GC), *Chassagnou and others v. France*, judgment of 29 April 1999, *Reports* 1999-III, the applicant objected to the fact that by law he automatically became a member of a hunting association, without the possibility to undo this membership.

38 ECtHR, *Witold Litwa v. Poland*, judgment of 4 April 2000, *Reports* 2000-III, § 76 referring back to § 57-63.

39 In ECtHR, *Prokopovich v. Russia*, judgment of 18 November 2004, *Reports* 2004-XI, the respondent government argued that the applicant could not claim that the flat of her deceased partner was her 'home' for the purpose of Article 8, even though they had lived their together for 10 years. In ECtHR, *Hartung v. France*, decision of 3 November 2009, *unpublished,* the question was whether a dressing room of an artist could be considered 'home' in the context of Article 8. The Court did not rule out that possibility, but doubted whether Article 8 was applicable in the circumstances of this case. The case was finally dismissed on other grounds.

40 See ECtHR, *Storbråten v. Norway*, decision of 1 February 2007, *unpublished* and ECtHR (GC), *Sergey Zolotukhin v. Russia*, judgment of 10 February 2009, *unpublished.*

41 ECtHR (GC), *Pellegrin v. France*, judgment of 8 December 1999, *Reports* 1999-VIII; ECtHR (GC), *Jussila v. Finland*, judgment of 23 November 2006, *unpublished*; ECtHR, *Öztürk v. Germany*, judgment of 21 February 1984, *Series* A No. 73; ECtHR, *Engel and others v. the Netherlands*,

under Article 1 First Protocol.[42] Hence, the case law analysis confirms this trend that has been suggested in the theoretical analysis. It has been found that the ECtHR itself does not provide any such explanation. What is visible, though, is that an autonomous approach automatically leads to a minimum level of harmonization, which also may be an important explanation. In the theoretical analysis, it has also been assumed that the reason for an autonomous approach is that the terms in question are technical legal terms or that the explanation may be found in the nature of the rights concerned.[43] Contracting States might more easily accept a certain level of harmonization, and thus intrusion on its national sovereignty, when it concerns terms that do not have strong moral connotations, which is the case for the terms connected to the right to fair trial and the right to property.[44] Once again, even though this explanation is not expressly embraced by the Court, the cases of *Kimlya* and *Vo* seem to support this explanation.

Of course, however, this does not yet explain the occurrence of autonomous interpretation in cases that do not relate to technical terms as contained in Articles 6 or 1 First Protocol. In this respect it is interesting to note that most of these cases have been from relatively recent dates. *Chassagnou* dates from 1999, *Witold Litwa* from 2000, *Prokopovich* from 2004 and *Hartung* from 2009. This might justify the conclusion that the Court is now more willing to apply autonomous interpretation to other notions than it was before, but it is difficult to warrant such a conclusion in the light of contrary examples such as *Kimlya* and *Vo*.

---

judgment of 8 June 1976, *Series* A No. 22; ECtHR, *König v. Germany*, judgment of 28 June 1978, *Series* A No. 27; ECtHR (GC), *Ferrazzini v. Italy*, judgment of 12 July 2001, Reports 2001-VII; ECtHR, *Stran Greek Refineries and Stratis Andreadis v. Greece*, judgment of 9 December 1994, *Series* A No. 301-B. See also ECtHR (GC), *Micallef v. Malta*, judgment of 15 October 2009, *unpublished*, where the Court had to determine whether injunction proceedings fell within the scope of Article 6. The Court established two criteria, one of which is that the injunction proceedings have to concern civil rights and obligations in their autonomous meaning. The Court thus incorporated an autonomous concept in the criteria for determining whether injunction proceedings are covered by Article 6. The second criterion is not autonomous and indicates that the object and purpose of the injunction proceedings must be taken into account.

42 ECtHR (GC), *Beyeler v. Italy*, judgment of 5 January 2000, *Reports* 2000-I; ECtHR, *Matos e Silva, Lda, and others v. Portugal*, judgment of 16 September 1996, *Reports* 1996-IV; ECtHR, *Gasus Dosier- und Fördertechnik GmbH v. the Netherlands*, judgment of 23 February 1995, *Series* A No. 306B; ECtHR (GC), *Iatridis v. Greece*, judgment of 25 March 1999, *Reports* 1999-II; ECtHR, *Posti and Rahko v. Finland*, judgment of 24 September 2002, Reports 2002-VII; ECtHR, *Zwierzynski v. Poland*, judgment of 19 June 2001, *Reports* 2001-VI; ECtHR (GC), *Stec and others v. United Kingdom*, decision of 6 July 2005, *Reports* 2005-X.

43 See Letsas (2004), p. 285; Matscher (1993), p. 70; Harris, O'Boyle (1995), p. 16. This observations has, however, not been included in their most recent edition. See also section 8.2.

44 See section 8.2.

12.5 How is autonomous meaning established?

An important aspect that can prove to be very relevant to the discussion on autonomous interpretation relates to the way in which the Court establishes this meaning. The reference to the autonomous meaning of a certain notion or provision implies that there is a 'European' meaning of the term in question. How does the Court arrive at this 'European' or autonomous meaning? Can any clues be found in the case law? Does the Court invoke specific interpretation methods or is there another way to determine the autonomous meaning?

There is not one standard method to establish an autonomous meaning. In the case law two main trends can be discerned. In the first category of cases the Court develops a criterion or a set of criteria which will help the Court to look beyond the domestic classification and assess the true nature of a certain right.[45] This is mostly visible in the context of establishing the autonomous meaning of a 'criminal charge' or the meaning of 'civil service' to determine whether Article 6 is applicable. The case of *Engel*[46] was the first in which the Court employed this approach in order to establish the autonomous meaning of a 'criminal charge' and it has been a leading precedent ever since.[47] In that case the Court had to determine whether disciplinary sanctions for a conscript in the military constituted a criminal charge within the meaning of Article 6. After concluding that it had to adopt an autonomous approach in this case, the Court set itself to the task of specifying how it could determine whether a charge with a disciplinary character constituted a criminal charge within the meaning of Article 6. It first took the national classification into account, but it considered this as merely a starting point. Interestingly, the national classification of the respondent state had to be considered 'in light of the common denominator of the respective legislation of the various Contracting States'.[48] Subsequently, it considered that a crucial factor was the nature of the offence. Finally, the degree of severity of the penalty had to be taken into consideration. These three criteria determine the autonomous meaning of 'criminal charge' under Article 6. The autonomous

45 See for example: ECtHR, *König v. Germany*, judgment of 28 June 1978, *Series* A No. 27; ECtHR, *Engel and others v. the Netherlands*, judgment of 8 June 1976, *Series* A No. 22; ECtHR, *Öztürk v. Germany*, judgment of 21 February 1984, *Series* A No. 73; ECtHR (GC), *Jussila v. Finland*, judgment of 23 November 2006, *unpublished*; ECtHR (GC), *Ferrazzini v. Italy*, judgment of 12 July 2001, Reports 2001-VII. The same approach adopted in the context of establishing the autonomous interpretation of Article 4 Protocol 7. See also: ECtHR (GC), *Scoppola v. Italy (No. 2)*, judgment of 17 September 2009, *unpublished*.

46 ECtHR, *Engel and others v. the Netherlands*, judgment of 8 June 1976, *Series* A No. 22.

47 See ECtHR, *König v. Germany*, judgment of 28 June 1978, *Series* A No. 27; ECtHR (GC), *Jussila v. Finland*, judgment of 23 November 2006, *unpublished*; ECtHR, *Öztürk v. Germany*, judgment of 21 February 1984, *Series* A No. 73.

48 ECtHR, *Engel and others v. the Netherlands*, judgment of 8 June 1976, *Series* A No. 22, § 82.

meaning is thus not a specific meaning or definition, but rather a way to test whether the right at national level falls within the category of rights that the provision in question aims to protect.

It is interesting to note that the Court does not really explain how it established these criteria. It seems to derive the criteria from the nature of the right, but this analysis cannot really be supported by any indications from the case itself. The question how the Court has established the autonomous interpretation can thus hardly be answered since it is unclear how these criteria have been established.

The Court adopted a somewhat similar approach with regard to the autonomous meaning of 'civil service' in the context of Article 6.[49] The ECtHR established in its case law that 'disputes relating to the recruitment, careers and termination of service of civil servants' are not within the scope of applicability of Article 6, because they do not concern civil proceedings.[50] The question before the Court in *Pellegrin* was whether it was fair to exclude from the protection of Article 6 civil servants whose position was comparable to that of employees under a private law contract.[51] The Court held that a criterion was necessary in order to establish on the basis of the nature of the employee's duties and responsibilities whether Article 6 should be applicable, instead of the domestic label being decisive. The ECtHR adopts a functional criterion under which civil servants 'whose duties typify the specific activities of the public service in so far as the latter is acting as the depositary of public authority responsible for protecting the general interest of the State and other public authorities' are excluded from the protection of Article 6.[52] The Court did spend some time on explaining this criterion it established in this case, but it did not explicitly relate this criterion to, for example, the text or purpose of the article in question or the Convention scheme in general. Perhaps one could argue for this case that this is implicit in the Courts reasoning, but when establishing a criterion that should form the basis of an autonomous approach, it would be better if the Court is explicit about the origins of the criterion. This need for a better explanation on the origins or justification of this criterion is already visible in the judgment itself. Indeed, the dissenting judges explained that they failed to see the necessity of the criterion established by the majority and they provided a different solution, which, in their view, would be more

49 As pointed out by the dissenting judges in ECtHR (GC), *Pellegrin v. France,* judgment of 8 December 1999, *Reports* 1999-VIII, this term does not exist in the Convention, but the ECtHR uses this term to determine which cases concerning civil servants fall within Article 6 and which cases are excluded from the protection afforded by this provision.

50 ECtHR (GC), *Pellegrin v. France,* judgment of 8 December 1999, *Reports* 1999-VIII, § 59.

51 ECtHR (GC), *Pellegrin v. France,* judgment of 8 December 1999, *Reports* 1999-VIII.

52 ECtHR (GC), *Pellegrin v. France,* judgment of 8 December 1999, *Reports* 1999-VIII, § 66.

in line with the spirit and letter of Article 6.[53] While it might always be possible to disagree on the reasoning in a particular case, at least the starting point for each of the positions should be clear and that is not the case in *Pellegrin*.

In the cases concerning the autonomous interpretation of the concept 'home', the Court also formulated some criteria. The Court indicated that the question whether the notion 'home' is applicable depends on 'the factual circumstances, namely, the existence of sufficient and continuous links with a specific place'.[54] The choice of these criteria is justified with references to previous case law. Indeed, these criteria indicate which element in the factual situation of the case counts most for the question of applicability and thus provides some guidance for subsequent cases. Nevertheless, the criteria themselves are not often repeated in later case law and they do not seem to be of great importance to the practical use of autonomous interpretation.

In the second category of cases the Court does not formulate any clear criteria which reflect the autonomous meaning of the Convention provision or any particular term contained therein. Examples of this approach can be found when establishing the autonomous interpretation of 'civil rights and obligations',[55] 'possession'[56] and 'association'.[57] In the case of *König* the ECtHR held that the concept of 'civil rights and obligations' should also be treated autonomously, like the concept of a 'criminal charge'.[58] The ECtHR did provide some sort of criterion to establish when one can speak of a civil right or obligation, namely by looking at 'the substantive content and effects of the right under the domestic law of the State concerned'.[59] In that

53 ECtHR (GC), *Pellegrin v. France,* judgment of 8 December 1999, *Reports* 1999-VIII, dissenting opinion by Tulkens, Fischbach, Casadevall and Thomassen.

54 ECtHR, *Prokopovich v. Russia,* judgment of 18 November 2004, *Reports* 2004-XI, § 36 andECtHR, *Hartung v. France*, decision of 3 November 2009, *unpublished,* § 1.

55 In the context of Article 6, see: ECtHR, *König v. Germany,* judgment of 28 June 1978, *Series* A No. 27; ECtHR, *Stran Greek Refineries and Stratis Andreadis v. Greece*, judgment of 9 December 1994, *Series* A No. 301-B; ECtHR, *Posti and Rahko v. Finland*, judgment of 24 September 2002, Reports 2002-VII;ECtHR (GC), *Ferrazzini v. Italy*, judgment of 12 July 2001, Reports 2001-VII; ECtHR (GC), *Perez v. France*, judgment of 12 February 2004, *Reports* 2004-I.

56 In the context of Article 1 First Protocol, see: ECtHR (GC), *Iatridis v. Greece,* judgment of 25 March 1999, *Reports* 1999-II; ECtHR, *Matos e Silva, Lda, and others v. Portugal*, judgment of 16 September 1996, *Reports* 1996-IV; ECtHR, *Gasus Dosier- und Fördertechnik GmbH v. the Netherlands*, judgment of 23 February 1995, *Series* A No. 306B; ECtHR (GC), *Öneryildiz v. Turkey*, judgment of 30 November 2004, *Reports* 2004-XII; ECtHR, *Zwierzynski v. Poland*, judgment of 19 June 2001, *Reports* 2001-VI; ECtHR (GC), *Beyeler v. Italy*, judgment of 5 January 2000, *Reports* 2000-I; ECtHR (GC), *Depalle v. France*, judgment of 29 March 2010, *unpublished.*

57 In the context of Article 11, see ECtHR (GC), *Chassagnou and others v. France,* judgment of 29 April 1999, *Reports* 1999-III.

58 ECtHR, *König v. Germany,* judgment of 28 June 1978, *Series* A No. 27, § 88.

59 ECtHR, *König v. Germany,* judgment of 28 June 1978, *Series* A No. 27, § 89.

process, the ECtHR held, it must also take account of the object and purpose of the Convention and the law of the other Contracting States. Later cases show, however, that the ECtHR only looks at the effect of the right in question and does not address the object and purpose, or the situation in other Contracting States.[60] The difference with the criteria for establishing a criminal charge is that these criteria actually indicate what aspects play a role in assessing whether something is a criminal charge, while the 'criterion' established in *König* only indicates that the ECtHR must look beyond appearances. That is basically a different way of stating what it means to take an autonomous approach and therefore it does not provide much guidance.

In the cases concerning the interpretation of the term possession, the ECtHR took a similar approach. Often the ECtHR stated that the term 'possession' has an autonomous meaning and looked into the facts of the case to assess whether the interest claimed in the specific case could be regarded as possession.[61] The case of *Beyeler* can serve to illustrate this approach.[62] In this case the parties disagreed whether the applicant had a property interest that was protected under Article 1 First Protocol. The Court considered that:

> In that connection the Court points out that the concept of "possessions" in the first part of Article 1 has an autonomous meaning which is not limited to ownership of physical goods and is independent from the formal classification in domestic law: certain other rights and interests constituting assets can also be regarded as "property rights", and thus as "possessions" for the purposes of this provision. The issue that needs to be examined is whether the circumstances of the case, considered as a whole, conferred on the applicant title to a substantive interest protected by Article 1 of Protocol No. 1. The Court considers that that approach requires it to take account of the following points of law and of fact. [The Court went on to consider the facts of the case, which proved that the applicant had a proprietary interest over a painting, even though this right was revocable during a certain period.][63]

60 See ECtHR, *Stran Greek Refineries and Stratis Andreadis v. Greece,* judgment of 9 December 1994, *Series* A No. 301-B;ECtHR, *Posti and Rahko v. Finland*, judgment of 24 September 2002, Reports 2002-VII; ECtHR (GC), *Perez v. France*, judgment of 12 February 2004, *Reports* 2004-I. In ECtHR (GC), *Ferrazzini v. Italy*, judgment of 12 July 2001, Reports 2001-VII, the ECtHR took a more abstract approach and did refer to the situation in democratic societies, which can be seen as an abstract way of referring to the situation in the Member States, but the Court did not take into account the object and purpose.

61 See for example: ECtHR (GC), *Iatridis v. Greece,* judgment of 25 March 1999, *Reports* 1999-II; ECtHR, *Matos e Silva, Lda, and others v. Portugal*, judgment of 16 September 1996, *Reports* 1996-IV; ECtHR, *Gasus Dosier- und Fördertechnik GmbH v. the Netherlands*, judgment of 23 February 1995, *Series* A No. 306B; ECtHR (GC), *Öneryildiz v. Turkey*, judgment of 30 November 2004, *Reports* 2004-XII;ECtHR, *Zwierzynski v. Poland*, judgment of 19 June 2001, *Reports* 2001-VI; ECtHR (GC), *Beyeler v. Italy*, judgment of 5 January 2000, *Reports* 2000-I.

62 ECtHR (GC), *Beyeler v. Italy,* judgment of 5 January 2000, *Reports* 2000-I.

63 ECtHR (GC), *Beyeler v. Italy,* judgment of 5 January 2000, *Reports* 2000-I, § 100. See recently:ECtHR (GC), *Depalle v. France*, judgment of 29 March 2010, *unpublished*, confirming this approach.

The most important observation that can be made on the basis of this excerpt is that it does not provide a clear idea of what the autonomous meaning of 'possession' exactly is. There has to be a substantive interest protected by Article 1 First Protocol, but that in itself does not provide much guidance. In contrast, the criteria provided for establishing whether something can be considered a 'criminal charge' or whether a position can be considered to fall under 'civil service' provide more guidance by indicating which aspects are taken into account in the assessment. In order to establish whether something could be considered a substantive interest protected by the right to property the ECtHR has relied heavily on precedent, which does help in understanding what is and what is not covered by the autonomous meaning of 'possession'. Even then, it is still rather unclear what the autonomous meaning of 'possession' really entails, which makes the application of this concept difficult or at least very vague.

Similarly unclear is the approach by the ECtHR in the case of *Chassagnou*, where the Court had to establish whether a hunting association was an association in the autonomous understanding of Article 11 of the Convention.[64] The government in question argued that the hunting associations were public law associations and accordingly fell outside the scope of Article 11. The Court held that the domestic classification was only a starting point and subsequently looked at the facts of the case to assess the hunting association. The ECtHR concluded that it indeed could be considered as an association for the purpose of Article 11. The conclusion is clear, but the case does not help in getting a clear understanding of what an 'association' for the purpose of Article 11 means. No criteria were provided and therefore it seems to be a matter that is decided on the facts of each individual case.

The risk of the approach in the second category of cases is that it is rather strongly case-based. This is especially problematic, since the terms that are being explained by the Court, i.e. 'possession' in the right to property cases and 'association' in the *Chassagnou*-case, determine the scope of Convention provisions. Whether or not the case is covered by the Convention guarantees depends on the meaning given to these terms. For that reason the Court should be much clearer about the autonomous meaning of these terms, either by providing adequate criteria for their application, or by actually providing an autonomous meaning.

After having discussed these two categories of cases, it may be concluded that the answer to the question *how* the Court established the autonomous meaning, appears to be that the Court actually does not define any autonomous meaning at all. It really takes an autonomous *approach*, while the term 'meaning' has the connotation that there is one definition that constitutes the autonomous meaning – that is not what the Court does. The Court looks beyond the national classification and it has regard

64 ECtHR (GC), *Chassagnou and others v. France,* judgment of 29 April 1999, *Reports* 1999-III.

to the nature of the right in dispute. It thus interprets rights in an autonomous way, rather than giving its own particular definition. The Court's own reference to autonomous meaning therefore seems to be misleading.

The only two cases in which the Court actually adopted an autonomous meaning or definition are the case of *Stec* and *Witold Litwa*. As these are the only two cases, it would be perhaps too much to call this a category on its own. In *Stec* the Court was confronted with two distinct authoritative lines in its case law, which contradicted each other.[65] The question was whether welfare benefits in a non-contributory scheme could constitute 'possessions' for the purpose of Article 1 First Protocol. The answers given by the ECtHR in previous cases had been contradictory and unclear, because there was no criterion to provide guidance on what possession meant in this context. The Court therefore found that it needed to address this question anew and establish an unambiguous precedent. By invoking arguments from systematic, evolutive and comparative interpretation the Court finally determined the autonomous meaning of 'possession' in this context, namely that welfare benefits constituted a possession regardless of whether they were financed by a non-contributory or a contributory scheme.[66]

In the case of *Witold Litwa* the ECtHR had to determine the meaning of the term 'alcoholics' as expressed in Article 5. Reference is even made to the Vienna Convention in order to justify the use of textual and teleological interpretation in order to come to an understanding of the term 'alcoholics'. The Court also invokes the *travaux préparatoires* to support its autonomous interpretation of the term in question. The ECtHR finally holds that the term does not mean that for a person to be held under Article 5 this person needs to be addicted to alcohol, but the term 'alcoholics' also refers to persons abusing alcohol and thereby posing a danger to themselves or the public. The Court in this case thus clearly, by relying on several interpretation methods, establishes an autonomous meaning of a Convention term.

The discussion in the case of *Stec* is not only important to show that the Court has adopted an autonomous meaning in some of its cases, but also that there is a risk of diverging lines in the case law of the Court. Especially when hardly any guidance is provided on how this autonomous meaning should be established, as in the second category of cases discussed above, the risk of diverging interpretations becomes real. Judging only on the basis of the facts of each individual case without any criteria or indication on what is the crucial factor that determines whether a certain concept falls within the autonomous interpretation of a specific term risks being arbitrary and contradictory. It might not be possible in all cases to provide an answer as clear as

65 ECtHR (GC), *Stec and others v. United Kingdom,* decision of 6 July 2005, *Reports* 2005-X, § 46.

66 ECtHR (GC), *Stec and others v. United Kingdom,* decision of 6 July 2005, *Reports* 2005-X, § 53. The distinction between contributory and non-contributory schemes was no longer justified.

in the case of *Witold Litwa*, but some criteria as in the case of *Engel* might already provide more guidance.

12.6 Conclusion

In this chapter, some of the questions relating to autonomous interpretation could be answered on the basis of the case law analysis, while in respect to some other issues the case law did not provide enough information for clear conclusions. One such issue is whether the ECtHR regards autonomous interpretation as an interpretative principle or interpretation method, which the Court has not pronounced itself explicitly on. Nonetheless, the analysis presented in this chapter made clear which role the notion of autonomous interpretation plays in the interpretative framework of the Court. The cases indicate that the Court uses autonomous interpretation as an approach to indicate a specific aim for the interpretation of some Convention terms rather than a method that provides a substantive element that helps justify a particular interpretation. Viewing autonomous interpretation as an approach is in line with the concept of interpretative principles as discussed in this thesis. The fact that autonomous interpretation is justified with reference to the object and purpose of the Convention supports the assumption in the theoretical chapter that autonomous interpretation can be viewed as one of the meta-teleological principles of the Convention.

If autonomous interpretation is only an approach, the question *how* an autonomous interpretation is established becomes acute. The discussion in section 12.5 indicated that in some cases the ECtHR establishes criteria that help to determine whether a certain factual situation is covered by the scope of the autonomous concept. In other cases the Court takes account of the factual situation, but has not established criteria on which to assess the facts in a consistent manner. Only in a few cases has the Court established a real autonomous meaning of a Convention term. In these cases of *Stec* and *Witold Litwa* the Court explicitly resorted to other interpretative aids (most importantly systematic, comparative and evolutive interpretation).[67] In all other cases the Court did not explicitly link up with any interpretative aid at all, not even in those cases where the Court provided criteria.[68] The fact that the ECtHR not often invokes references to other interpretative aids, when using autonomous interpretation, is problematic in the sense that it risks an arbitrary interpretation, because no reference is made to a recognized interpretative aid that can justify the choices made.

---

67 ECtHR (GC), *Stec and others v. United Kingdom,* decision of 6 July 2005, *Reports* 2005-X; ECtHR, *Witold Litwa v. Poland*, judgment of 4 April 2000, *Reports* 2000-III.

68 Only in ECtHR, *König v. Germany,* judgment of 28 June 1978, *Series* A No. 27 and ECtHR, *Engel and others v. the Netherlands*, judgment of 8 June 1976, *Series* A No. 22, the Court mentioned that the criteria have to be applied in the light of the object and purpose *and* comparative material.

The theoretical analysis indicated that comparative interpretation plays an important role for autonomous interpretation. The case law does not seem to really support this assumption.

An important part of this chapter dealt with the question when autonomous interpretation was used. The case law did not provide an entirely clear picture here. To some extent it supports the theoretical assumption that autonomous interpretation is mainly used when interpreting legally technical terms, rather than terms that have strong moral connotations. Terms from Article 6 and Article 1 First Protocol have been identified in theoretical literature as most likely to be interpreted autonomously. However, the case law analysis also showed that in the past decade other terms have also been interpreted in an autonomous manner. The ECtHR might thus be inclined to explicitly adopt an autonomous interpretation in a wider range of cases than has always been assumed.

CHAPTER 13
INTERPRETATION IN THE CASE LAW OF THE CJEU[1]

After the case law analysis of the ECtHR it is now time to analyze the case law of the CJEU in detail, more in particular the use of interpretation methods and the reasoning by the CJEU. The aim of this chapter is to analyze in detail the use of comparative interpretation, teleological interpretation, evolutive interpretation and autonomous interpretation in the case law of the CJEU. These interpretation methods and interpretative principles have been discussed extensively in the theoretical part of this thesis. The present case law analysis will rely on this theoretical discussion and use that as a starting point. A thorough analysis of the different issues that have been identified in the theoretical discussion will provide more insight into the reasoning of the CJEU. Moreover, it will enable a discussion of the specific aspects that might be open for improvement.

It is important to keep in mind that this is not an exhaustive analysis of interpretation methods and principles employed by the CJEU. Other methods, like textual interpretation, play a role as well in the reasoning of the CJEU. The methods and principles in this thesis have, however, been selected for the reasons set out in Chapter 4, one of these reasons being the special role that these methods and principles play in reasoning in a multilevel legal system like the EU system. The other, non-selected, methods will only be discussed insofar as that would serve the discussion of the four interpretation methods and principles that are central to this thesis.

The case law analysis will, as has been indicated before, limit itself to a selection of cases in which the CJEU deals with fundamental rights. In the introductory Chapter 3 on the CJEU, the way in which fundamental rights were introduced into the European Community system was discussed. That discussion will serve as a basis for this chapter. This means that the emphasis in this chapter will not be on the different stages that the protection of fundamental rights went through in order to gain a permanent spot in the EU, but rather on the way in which the CJEU determines the existence and scope of individual fundamental rights.

The range of cases in which the CJEU deals with fundamental rights is rather wide. For that reason, it was necessary to introduce certain limiting criteria. Firstly,

1 The case law analysis includes judgments until 31.12.2010.

only cases have been selected in which fundamental rights played a role that have a counterpart in the European Convention on Human Rights. This approach enhances the possibility to compare the Strasbourg and Luxemburg case law approaches. Apart from the possible comparison, it seemed almost self-evident to limit the scope of analysis for both courts to the same type of case. As a consequence of this choice, rights that have been recognized only in the EU context will not be discussed. No attention will accordingly be paid to the rights attached to the status of citizen of the European Union,[2] such as the right to move and reside freely in the EU.[3]

Secondly, only cases in which the CJEU dealt with the *interpretation* or definition of fundamental rights have been selected. This means that the focus has been placed on cases in which the CJEU determined the scope of fundamental rights and not on cases in which the CJEU applied fundamental rights to particular situations. However, it proved to be challenging to find cases in which the CJEU expressly deals with the scope of a certain fundamental right. Section 13.1 will discuss this characteristic feature more elaborately and will explain its background. For here, it is more relevant to note that a narrow understanding of the notion of 'interpretation' would have resulted in a very small number of cases that could be analyzed in depth. After all, the particular context of the CJEU, which was discussed in Chapter 3 has as its most specific feature that only relatively recently has a catalogue of fundamental rights been formulated.[4] The CJEU for quite a period had to proceed without such a catalogue and it had to employ specific argumentative instruments to construe fundamental rights. In order to take this background sufficiently into account, the selection has been made on the basis of a somewhat broader understanding of interpretation, namely by looking more generally at cases in which the CJEU actually construes fundamental rights and which might provide information about the way in which it determines their scope. Incorporating these cases into the analysis is useful as it sheds light on this broader use of interpretation methods and argumentative instruments as well.

The selected cases have been drawn from a variety of sources in order to ensure that a representative selection could be made. The initial selection, most importantly, included cases which were mentioned in the Explanatory Report to the Charter of Fundamental Rights. The cases that have been incorporated in this Explanatory Report represent in the view of the drafters the most relevant cases from the CJEU concerning fundamental rights. The initial selection also included cases selected on the basis of two secondary sources. Firstly, references to fundamental rights cases have been taken

2 For an elaborate discussion, see Craig and De Burca (2008), Chapter 23.

3 See for example: C-200/02, *Kunqian Catherine Zhu and Man Lavette Chen v. Secretary of State for the Home Department* [2004] ECR I-09925; C-127/08, *Blaise Baheten Metock and Others v. Minister for Justice, Equality and Law Reform* [2008] I-06241.

4 On 1 December 2009 this catalogue became legally binding; see Chapter 3 for more details.

from secondary literature on EU law.[5] Secondly, the selection has been supplemented with references to CJEU cases drawn from another secondary source, namely a legal periodical on European human rights case law, in which a relevant selection of CJEU cases on fundamental rights is regularly published.[6]

The resulting, broad initial selection has then been narrowed down on the basis of the criteria mentioned above, namely the fact that the right at stake should have a counterpart in the European Convention and the case had to deal with the interpretation of that right (rather than only its application). These cases constitute the final selection and have been analyzed as to the meaning and use that is made therein of the four interpretative aids that are central to this thesis.

The discussion of the various cases that is presented in the following chapters will focus on both the judgments of the Court and the opinions of the Advocate General.[7] A general overview of the role of the Advocate General was provided in Chapter 3, where it was also explained that these opinions are of particular relevance in determining the use of certain methods or principles of interpretation. For the purposes of the present chapter, the opinions therefore have been studied in detail, focusing on the role of the Advocate General in the use of interpretation methods and principles. The discussion of both the judgments and the opinions will provide a complete picture of the use of interpretation methods before the CJEU.

The analysis to be presented here has been organized in a slightly different manner than the discussion of the ECtHR case law, which was provided in Chapters 9-12. One of the reasons for this is that the CJEU's work is not limited to fundamental rights and that fundamental rights have found their way into EU law in a rather different way than is the case in the context of the ECtHR. For that reason, the discussion of the CJEU will start by addressing some striking features that have emerged from analyzing the CJEU case law (section 13.1). The subsequent sections will deal with an analysis of how the CJEU and its Advocates General make use of the four selected interpretative aids: comparative interpretation (section 13.2), teleological interpretation (section 13.3), evolutive interpretation (section 13.4.1) and autonomous interpretation (section 13.4.2). Finally, some conclusions will be drawn on the basis of the overview presented in this chapter (section 13.5).

5 The well-known handbook on EU law by Craig & De Burca served as a source for selecting the relevant cases. Craig & De Burca (2008). This is a widely respected secondary source for EU law and as a result a reliable source for case law references.

6 *European Human Rights Cases*. As this journal focuses on presenting a representative selection of fundamental rights cases, it is a useful source to supplement the other two.

7 The focus will only be the cases of the Court of Justice and not the General Court.

13.1 The CJEU and the interpretation of fundamental rights

The main task of the CJEU is to interpret European Union law, which includes fundamental rights as general principles of EU law.[8] A few general comments need to be made about the interpretative approach of the CJEU to set the background for the discussion on the specific interpretation methods and principles. The case law analysis clearly revealed the difference in judicial style between the CJEU and the ECtHR. Even though the ECtHR is not always elaborate in its judgments, there is certainly a difference with the judgments of the CJEU. The ECtHR, when interpreting a Convention provision, usually provides a framework (ranging from rather cursory to rather extensive) in which some general considerations concerning the right in question are discussed. The CJEU is much more to the point and does not elaborate much on the meaning of a specific fundamental right. Indeed, the approach of the CJEU seems to be even more case-based than the approach by the ECtHR; the CJEU seems conscious not to go beyond what is necessary for answering the specific question.[9] This 'void' is to some extent filled by the opinions of the Advocate General, who often provides a more elaborate reasoning on the meaning of a specific right.[10]

To illustrate this, the case of *Kent Kirk* can be mentioned.[11] In this case, the Court was asked to decide whether a certain provision could have retroactive effect. In reply, the Court limited itself to stating that:

> The principle that penal provisions may not have retroactive effect is one which is common to all the legal orders of the Member States and is enshrined in Article 7 of the European Convention for the Protection of Human Rights and Fundamental Freedoms as a fundamental right.[12]

---

8 See former Article 220 EC Treaty on the competence of the CJEU and former Article 6 EU Treaty. Article 220 EC has been repealed and replaced in substance by Article 19 TEU. Article 6 EU remains Article 6 TEU.

9 For example in the case of *Booker Aquacultur*, where the Court not even mentioned that this case fell within the ambit of the rights to property, but only asked whether a violation had occurred, C-20/00, *Booker Aquacultur Ltd v. The Scottish Ministers* [2003] ECR I-07411. In the case of *Bosman* the Court referred to the freedom of association, but failed to elaborate on the meaning of this right in relation to the case at hand. Only mentioning a right followed by a extremely terse reaction does not help in clarifying the scope of fundamental rights for the Member States, C-415/93, *Union royale belge des sociétés de football association ASBL and others v. Jean-Marc Bosman* [1995] ECR I-04921.

10 See for an example of an extensive discussion of the meaning of a specific fundamental right, namely *ne bis in idem*, the opinion of Advocate General Ruiz-Jarabo Colomber in C-436/04, *Criminal proceedings against Leopold Henri Van Esbroeck* [2006] ECR I-02333.

11 C-63/83, *Regina v. Kent Kirk* [1986] ECR 02689.

12 C-63/83, *Regina v. Kent Kirk* [1986] ECR 02689, § 22.

Non-retroactivity of penal provision was thus recognized as one of the fundamental rights to be protected by the EU. The CJEU did not explain, however, what this fundamental right meant in the EU context, for example by addressing the question whether it is the national or the EU-qualification of the notion of 'penal' that counts. By using such a short and case-based approach, the CJEU does not provide much guidance to the Member States on the level of protection afforded under EU law.

In the case of *Promusicae* the CJEU left many questions open in a similar way.[13] *Promusicae* is an organization protecting the intellectual rights of music producers, who wanted to take action against illegal downloading. The question was whether EU law allowed Member States to limit the duty for internet providers to provide data on specific users of their services to criminal investigations or to protect public security and thus exclude civil proceedings. The CJEU concluded in its judgment that EU law did not oblige the Member States to extend the duty to provide data. The CJEU added that, when transposing the relevant directives, the Member State should strike a fair balance between all the fundamental rights at stake. Reference was made to the right to intellectual property and the right to an effective judicial remedy. The Court furthermore mentioned that the right to private life, namely protection of personal data, should play a role in the balance of interests to be struck. What the Court did not address, however, was the extent to which the circumstances of this case actually came within the scope of the fundamental rights mentioned. The right to private life does encompass the right to protection of personal data, but to what extent? What kind of data falls within the scope of this right? By not providing any kind of clarification as to the scope of the rights at stake the CJEU made it difficult for the national authorities to understand how these rights are balanced. Especially in such a relatively new context it would have provided much guidance to the Member States if the Court at least paid some attention to these aspects.

There are other cases, however, in which the Court provides more insight into the scope of a certain right, for example in the case of *Connolly*.[14] This case concerned the freedom of expression of an EU civil servant, who had published a critical book on the EU during his leave even though permission to publish the book had been denied on earlier occasions. The Court indicated, by citing a case of the ECtHR, that also expressions that offend, shock and disturb are protected by the freedom of expression.[15] Moreover, the Court expressly confirmed that 'officials and other employees of the European Communities enjoy the right of freedom of expression even in areas falling within the scope of the activities of the Community institu-

---

13 C-275/06, *Productores de Música de España (Promusicae) v. Telefónica de España SAU* [2008] ECR I-00271.

14 C-274/99, *Bernard Connolly v. Commission of the European Communities* [2001] ECR I-01611.

15 C-274/99, *Bernard Connolly v. Commission of the European Communities* [2001] ECR I-01611, § 39.

tions'.[16] The Court thus explicitly mentioned two elements of the scope of the right, namely the content of the right to freedom of expression and the persons protected by that right.

In the case of *Mary Carpenter*, the CJEU discussed the meaning of the right to family.[17] Even though it did so in a rather cursory manner, the CJEU did provide enough of a framework to understand why it considered this case to fall within the scope of family life. Mary Carpenter, a Philippines national, married an Englishman. Despite being married to a UK national she was not allowed to stay in the United Kingdom and was threatened with deportation. The question before the CJEU was whether her deportation was contrary to respect for the family life of Mr. Carpenter. The CJEU stated that this constituted an interference with the right to respect for family life. Subsequently, the CJEU paraphrased the doctrine of the ECtHR, holding that the right to family life does not entail a right to enter or reside, but also stated that removing someone from a country where that person has close family ties, may breach the right to respect for one's family life. This case thus provided some explanation on the scope of the right to family life.

It is clear, thus, that the focus of the CJEU when dealing with fundamental rights is generally not on determining the scope of these rights. Rather, the CJEU focuses on the question whether fundamental rights can be legitimately restricted. That observation warrants a more elaborate discussion. The CJEU often emphasizes that fundamental rights within the EU context are always relative and never absolute. In the case of *Wachauf* the Court made this clear in a general statement that: 'The fundamental rights recognized by the Court are not absolute (…) but must be considered in relation to their social function.'[18] The CJEU continued to emphasize that, accordingly, restrictions are allowed provided that they meet certain criteria and that the core of the right is not affected.[19] The same emphasis can be seen in the case of *Hauer*, where the applicant claimed that her right to property had been violated.[20] In this case the CJEU mentioned that the right to property is protected by EC law

16 C-274/99, *Bernard Connolly v. Commission of the European Communities* [2001] ECR I-01611, *Connolly*, § 43.

17 C-60/00, *Mary Carpenter v. Secretary of State for the Home Department* [2002] ECR I-06279.

18 C-5/88, *Hubert Wachauf v. Bundesamt für Ernährung und Forstwirtschaft* [1989] ECR 02609, § 18.

19 The rest of the specific paragraph reads: 'Consequently, restrictions may be imposed on the exercise of those rights, in particular in the context of a common organization of a market, provided that those restrictions in fact correspond to objectives of general interest pursued by the Community and do not constitute, with regard to the aim pursued, a disproportionate and intolerable interference, impairing the very substance of those rights'. C-5/88, *Hubert Wachauf v. Bundesamt für Ernährung und Forstwirtschaft* [1989] ECR 02609, § 18.

20 C-44/79, *Liselotte Hauer v. Land Rheinland-Pfalz* [1979] ECR 03727.

and it recalled the text of the right to property under the European Convention on Human Rights.[21] The CJEU subsequently stated that: 'Having declared that persons are entitled to the peaceful enjoyment of their property, that provision envisages two ways in which the rights of a property owner may be impaired'.[22] The Court thus did not discuss whether the right to property was actually applicable to the case at hand, nor did it provide information as to its meaning and scope. It limited itself to stating that the right to property as such is protected in the Community. It spent considerably more words in this case on the question whether the limitation of the right was justified. This structure can be seen in many more judgments by the CJEU as well,[23] which clearly reveals a different attitude towards fundamental rights than the European Court of Human Rights. Indeed, the ECtHR regularly emphasizes that justification clauses should be narrowly constructed.[24]

Nevertheless, there are some examples of cases in which the CJEU has actually differentiated between two phases, such as the case of *Österreichischer Rundfunk*.[25] This case raised the question whether Austrian local and regional authorities and public undertakings could be obliged to communicate data on the income of their employees to the National Audit Office. The CJEU first addressed the issue whether the collection of data on a person's income with a view to send it to third parties constituted an interference with the right to private life of that person. After quoting the ECtHR in saying that the notion of private life should not be interpreted restrictedly, the CJEU continued to address whether the case showed an interference with Article 8 ECHR. The CJEU held that the recording of data does not form an interference, but communicating it with third parties does:

21 C-44/79, *Liselotte Hauer v. Land Rheinland-Pfalz* [1979] ECR 03727, § 17-18.

22 C-44/79, *Liselotte Hauer v. Land Rheinland-Pfalz* [1979] ECR 03727, § 19.

23 See for example: C-341/05, *Laval un Partneri Ltd v. Svenska Byggnadsarbetareförbundet and others* [2007] ECR I-11767; C-438/05, *International Transport Workers' Federation and Finnish Seamen's Union v. Viking Line ABP and OÜ Viking Line Eesti* [2007] ECR I-10779; C-275/06, *Productores de Música de España (Promusicae) v. Telefónica de España SAU* [2008] ECR I-00271, where the Court does not speak expressly about limiting these rights, but about balancing these rights. Balancing involves a certain amount of limiting, therefore this case can be regarded as an example of this approach as well. See also: C-136/79, *National Panasonic (UK) Limited v Commission of the European Communities* [1980] ECR 02033; C-94/00, *Roquette Frères SA v. Directeur général de la concurrence, de la consommation et de la répression des fraudes, and Commission of the European Communities* [2002] ECR I-09011.

24 The case of C-275/06, *Productores de Música de España (Promusicae) v. Telefónica de España SAU* [2008] ECR I-00271, also revealed a similar approach.

25 C-465/00, *Rechnungshof v Österreichischer Rundfunk and Others* [2003] ECR I-04989.

> It necessarily follows that, while the mere recording by an employer of data by name relating to the remuneration paid to his employees cannot as such constitute an interference with private life, the communication of that data to third parties, in the present case a public authority, infringes the right of the persons concerned to respect for private life, whatever the subsequent use of the information thus communicated, and constitutes an interference within the meaning of Article 8 of the Convention.
>
> To establish the existence of such an interference, it does not matter whether the information communicated if of a sensitive character or whether the persons concerned have been inconvenienced in any way [reference to ECtHR judgment]. It suffices to find that data relating to the remuneration received by an employee or pensioner have been communicated by the employer to a third party.[26]

The Court, thus, first interpreted the right to private life as protecting data that were to be communicated to a third party. Subsequently, the CJEU discussed the justification for the interference. However, this bifurcated approach is only rarely visible in the CJEU's case law as it has been analyzed in this thesis.

Thus, it can be concluded that the CJEU generally marginalizes an important phase in the adjudicative process, namely the interpretative phase.[27] This does not render an analysis of the use of interpretation methods by the CJEU useless. Indeed, the terse judgments are inherent to the French inspired style of reasoning by the CJEU. The fact that the CJEU adheres to a different style of reasoning does not mean that there is no point in analyzing the interpretation process. It is, however, a factor that explains the perhaps more limited results of the case law analysis of the CJEU compared to those of the ECtHR. It also indicates the importance of taking the opinions of the Advocate General into consideration, since they may sometimes provide additional insight as to the scope and meaning of the rights at issue.

13.2 Comparative Interpretation

13.2.1 Introduction

As one of the main interpretation methods analyzed in this thesis, it is important to pay attention to the role of comparative interpretation in the case law of the CJEU. The use of the method should be particularly interesting in the case of the CJEU, as this court has been classified in the literature as the 'working laboratory for comparative law'.[28] Before delving into the analysis of the Court's use of this method,

---

26 C-465/00, *Rechnungshof v Österreichischer Rundfunk and Others* [2003] ECR I-04989, § 74-75.

27 Gerards & Senden (2009).

28 See Hilf (1986), p. 550, where he provides many more literature references.

it is useful to recall the main theoretical issues that play a role when applying comparative interpretation. Chapter 6 has defined comparative interpretation as interpretation whereby references are made to (or arguments are based on) the law as it stands in foreign legal systems. The term 'foreign' has been explained in the context of the two supranational courts discussed in this thesis (CJEU and ECtHR) as referring to any other legal system than the one in which the respective court has jurisdiction. This means for the CJEU that the term 'foreign' refers to any other system than the EU legal system. In the theoretical chapter, a distinction was furthermore made between external and internal comparative interpretation. In the context of the EU, this means that internal comparative interpretation takes place when the CJEU takes the national legal systems of the EU Member States into account in defining the scope and substance of fundamental rights, while external comparative interpretation means that reference is made to any legal system outside the EU (including international treaties to which the CJEU itself is not a party).

The present case law analysis will take this distinction as a starting point. First, the use of comparative material from within the Member States will be discussed. Subsequently, the role of material foreign in relation to the EU will be discussed. The latter category is itself divided into two different subcategories. On the one hand, the role of the European Convention on Human Rights will be discussed. Despite the fact that there is some overlap in Member States between the European Union and the Council of Europe, the legal system provided by the European Convention is regarded as external, since this legal system is set in a different organization, which, unlike the EU, covers almost the whole of Europe.[29] According to the CJEU 'special significance'[30] should be attached to the ECHR when dealing with fundamental rights, which is why the role of the European Convention should be dealt with separately.

---

29 The European Union presently has 27 Member States. The Council of Europe has 47 Member States that have all ratified the European Convention of Human Rights.

30 See for example: C-44/79, *Liselotte Hauer v. Land Rheinland-Pfalz* [1979] ECR 03727; C-46/87 *Hoechst AG v. Commission of the European Communities* [1989] ECR 02859; C-260/89, *Elliniki Radiophonia Tiléorassi (ERT) AE and Panellinia Omospondia Syllogon Prossopikou v. Dimotiki Etairia Pliroforissis and Sotirios Kouvelas and Nicolaos Avdellas and others* [1991] ECR I-02925; C-219/91, *Criminal proceedings against Johannes Stephanus Wilhelmus Ter Voort* [1992] ECR I-05485; C-299/95, *Friedrich Kremzow v Republik Österreich* [1997] I-02629; C-309/96, *Daniele Annibaldi v. Sindaco del Comune di Guidonia and Presidente Regione Lazio* [1997] ECR I-07493; C-17/98, *Emesa Sugar (Free Zone) NV v. Aruba* [2000] ECR I-00665; C-274/99, *Bernard Connolly v. Commission of the European Communities* [2001] ECR I-01611; C-94/00, *Roquette Frères SA v. Directeur général de la concurrence, de la consommation et de la répression des fraudes, and Commission of the European Communities* [2002] ECR I-09011; C-36/02, *Omega Spielhallen- und Automatenaufstellungs-GmbH v. Oberbürgermeisterin der Bundesstadt Bonn* [2004] ECR I-09609; C-540/03, *European Parliament v Council of the European Union* [2006] ECR I-05769.

The second subcategory consists of other international materials, which are either derived from other international organizations or the legal systems of third countries.

The discussion of the various categories of comparative sources will address the respective bases for the references to these different materials. This question has received much attention in theoretical discussions due to its importance for the acceptability of the method. Another critical issue is the question on the exact role of this method, namely whether the conclusions drawn from the comparative material play a decisive or a supportive role in the reasoning of the court. Answering these questions, however, would still leave some aspects unaddressed. A discussion of the relevant practical aspects relating to this method of interpretation may help to analyze to what extent the problematic issues identified in the theoretical chapter materialize in the reality of the case law of the CJEU. Therefore a closer look will be taken within each category of comparative interpretation at the kind of material that is used by the CJEU and at its sources.

Thus far, reference has been made in this chapter to the CJEU in general, referring to the institution as a whole. A distinction should, however, be made between the reasoning of the CJEU (the judgments) and the reasoning of the Advocate General (the opinions). As has been stressed before, for the purposes of the analysis presented in this chapter, the reasoning of the Advocate General will be looked at in detail, as well. By doing so, it will become clear that the approaches of the Advocate General and the CJEU differ with regard to comparative interpretation.

Ultimately, the presented analysis should facilitate a discussion of the purpose of the method before the CJEU, in particular on the questions whether the theoretical criticism of this method applies to the CJEU, whether something useful can be learned from the application of the method by the CJEU and whether some aspects should be adapted.

13.2.2 Role of national constitutional traditions

Ever since the case of *Internationale Handelsgesellschaft*, the CJEU refers to the constitutional traditions common to the Member States as a source of inspiration for defining fundamental rights.[31] In the case of *Nold* the CJEU confirmed these national traditions to be one of the main sources of inspiration[32] when it held that:

31 C-11/70, *Internationale Handelsgesellschaft mbH v. Einfuhr- und Vorratsstelle für Getreide und Futtermittel* [1970] ECR 01125.

32 The other main source is the European Convention on Human Rights, which will be discussed later on in section 13.2.3.

> The Court is bound to draw inspiration from constitutional traditions common to the Member States, and it cannot therefore uphold measures which are incompatible with fundamental rights recognized and protected by the Constitutions of those States.[33]

This reference to the constitutional traditions of Member States as a source of inspiration still features in recent cases and has become part and parcel of the fundamental rights case law of the CJEU.[34] A 2008 judgment in the *Sopropré* case is one recent example of a case in which the CJEU re-emphasized that it 'draws inspiration from the constitutional traditions of the Member States'.[35] This reference to common constitutional traditions has become so ingrained in the case law of the CJEU that one can question whether it still means anything or whether it is has become a hollow phrase or mere ornamentation. Several questions can be asked in order to try and provide an answer to this central question. What is the basis for these references (section 13.2.2.1)? How has the CJEU incorporated these references in its case law (section 13.2.2.2)? What has been the approach of the Advocates General in dealing with references to national constitutional traditions (section 13.2.2.3)? What are the main differences between the approach of the CJEU and the Advocates General (section 13.2.2.4)? What has been the purpose of these references (section 13.2.3.5) And, perhaps most importantly, is a *common* tradition necessary and what does this mean (section 13.2.2.6)? Where does the information come from (section 13.2.2.7)? What information is taken into consideration? Finally, the theoretical chapter paid much attention to the question whether references to comparative materials (either internal or external) are sufficiently justified. That question will be addressed at the end of this section in the conclusion. The fact that there might be a basis for the references to national constitutional traditions is not necessarily enough for a justified use of this method of interpretation.[36] The specific use of these references plays a role in answering that question as well.

These questions should be answered in order to be able to have some understanding of the role of this aspect of comparative interpretation in the case law of the CJEU. A short preview of the role of national constitutional traditions has already been given in the introductory Chapter 3 and in the theoretical analysis provided in

---

33 C-4/73, J. *Nold, Kohlen- und Baustoffgroßhandlung v. Ruhrkohle Aktiengesellschaft* [1974] ECR 00491, § 13.

34 See C-260/89, *Elliniki Radiophonia Tiléorassi (ERT) AE and Panellinia Omospondia Syllogon Prossopikou v. Dimotiki Etairia Pliroforissis and Sotirios Kouvelas and Nicolaos Avdellas and others* [1991] ECR I-02925, § 41; C-74/95, *Criminal Proceedings against X* [1996] ECR I-06609, § 25; C-411/04, *Salzgitter Mannesmann GmbH v. Commission of the European Communities*, [2007] ECR I-00959, § 41 as some examples throughout the years in which the CJEU has mentioned the constitutional traditions as a source of inspiration.

35 C-349/07, *Sopropé – Organizações de Calçado Lda v. Fazenda Pública* [2008] ECR I-10369, § 33.

36 See section 6.1.6.2. on practical criticism that also influences a justified use of this method.

Chapter 6. This slight overlap can hardly be avoided, given the particular way in which fundamental rights have found their way into the EU.

13.2.2.1 The basis for invoking national constitutional traditions

An aspect that has led to much debate in the legal-theoretical literature on comparative interpretation is whether the court in question has any legal basis for relying on comparative references.[37] This is a controversial issue in particular when discussing the external component of comparative interpretation, but it is also relevant in the context of the internal component.

The introductory chapter already referred to former Article 6 (3) TEU (former Article 6 (2) EU), which provides that:

> The Union shall respect fundamental rights, as guaranteed by the European Convention for the Protection of Human Rights and Fundamental Freedoms signed in Rome on 4 November 1950 and as they result from the constitutional traditions common to the Member States, as general principles of Community law.

This provision, which found its way into the EU legal order through the Maastricht Treaty in 1992,[38] explicitly lists the two main sources of inspiration, namely constitutional traditions and the European Convention on Human Rights. In fact, this provides a solid basis for the CJEU to rely on references to national constitutional traditions. Such an explicit basis for comparative interpretation is rather uncommon, but in the EU context its existence is quite understandable. Article 6 (3) TEU represents a codification of the practice of the CJEU at that point in time.[39] In most older fundamental rights cases the CJEU treated constitutional traditions and the European Convention as the main sources of inspiration.[40] For cases after the insertion of this

37 See section 6.1. dealing with various aspects related to the question whether there is a sufficient basis for comparative interpretation.

38 Initially this was Article F(2) in the Maastricht Treaty; the Treaty of Amsterdam changed this into the well-known Article 6(2) EU. The content of this particular aspect of the provision did not change as a result of Amsterdam.

39 In C-303/05, *Advocaten voor de Wereld VZW v. Leden van de Ministerraad* [2007] ECR I-03633 Advocate General Ruiz-Jarabo Colomber mentions this point in his Opinion, § 75. See also: Rainer (2008), p. 31.

40 See for example: C-44/79, *Liselotte Hauer v. Land Rheinland-Pfalz* [1979] ECR 03727; C-136/79, *National Panasonic (UK) Limited v Commission of the European Communities* [1980] ECR 02033; C-63/83, *Regina v. Kent Kirk* [1986] ECR 02689; C-222/84, *Marguerite Johnston v. Chief Constable of the Royal Ulster Constabulary* [1986] ECR 01651; C-222/86, *Union nationale des entraîneurs et cadres techniques professionnels du football (Unectef) v. Georges Heylens and others* [1987] ECR 04097; C-46/87 *Hoechst AG v. Commission of the European Communities* [1989] ECR 02859; C-374/87, *Orkem v. Commission of the European Communities* [1989] ECR 03283; C-260/89, *Elliniki*

provision, it is no longer an issue on what basis these references are made. The approach by the CJEU had already been accepted by the EU institutions in a joint declaration of the European Parliament, the Council and the Commission in 1977.[41] Finally, by ratifying then Article 6(2) EU the Member States accepted this approach as well.

However, the question remains on what basis the CJEU used these comparative references before the existence of former Article 6 (2) EU. The judgments by the CJEU do not really answer this question. In *Nold*, the Court stated that it 'is bound to draw inspiration from constitutional traditions',[42] but that hardly qualifies as a justification for relying on these references. Advocate General Dutheillet De Lamothe in *International Handelsgesellschaft* provided a rather more elaborate explanation for considering national constitutional traditions as a source of inspiration. He argued that national constitutional traditions provide a foundation from which fundamental rights emerge that should be protected in the EU:

> They [national constitutional traditions] contribute to forming that philosophical, political and legal substratum common to the Member States from which through the case-law an unwritten Community law emerges, one of the essential aims of which is precisely to ensure respect for the fundamental rights of the individual.
> In that sense, the fundamental principles of the national legal systems contribute to enabling Community law to find in itself the resources necessary for ensuring, where needed, respect for the fundamental rights which form the common heritage of the Member States.[43]

Thus, references to national constitutional traditions appear to be justified in the view of Advocate General Dutheillet De Lamothe since they help to shape the EU legal order in a field where no written EU law exists. No more explicit explanation has been given in the Court's case law or in opinions of the Advocates General.

While the CJEU remains silent on this matter, some attention has been given by legal commentators to the justification for resorting to comparative interpretation. Although some authors only refer to Article 6(3) TEU as the basis for incorporating references to national constitutional traditions,[44] others have paid attention to the

---

Radiophonia Tiléorassi (ERT) AE and Panellinia Omospondia Syllogon Prossopikou v. Dimotiki Etairia Pliroforissis and Sotirios Kouvelas and Nicolaos Avdellas and others [1991] ECR I-02925.

41 OJ 1977/C 103/1. See also: Dörte Hempfing (2004), p. 14; Lenaerts & De Smijter (2001), p. 275.

42 C-4/73, J. *Nold, Kohlen- und Baustoffgroßhandlung v. Ruhrkohle Aktiengesellschaft* [1974] ECR 00491, § 13.

43 Opinion by Advocate General Dutheillet de Lamothe in C-11/70, *Internationale Handelsgesellschaft mbH v. Einfuhr- und Vorratsstelle für Getreide und Futtermittel* [1970] ECR 01125, p. 1146. Rainer also refers to common constitutional traditions as an ideological basis for fundamental rights, (2008), p. 28.

44 Singer & Engel (2007), p. 499.

fact that this provision only came into existence after a few decades of fundamental rights case law before the CJEU. Some have argued that Article 19 TEU (which is similar in substance to former Article 220 EC) provides a basis for using comparative interpretation.[45] This provision requires the CJEU (and later also the General Court) 'to guarantee that in the interpretation and application of the Treaty the law is observed'. According to LENAERTS, comparative interpretation helps the CJEU to find 'the *ius commune* – i.e. 'the law'- whose observance they are to ensure in the interpretation and application of the Treaty'.[46] This justification is thus based on a wide interpretation of the notion of 'law' as contained in Article 19 TEU.[47]

Furthermore, reference is made in the literature to the fact that the CJEU has consistently held that the EU legal order is based on legal principles.[48] The national constitutional traditions are an accepted source of these common principles of law. Especially in the field of fundamental rights, where no written provisions existed, comparative interpretation may legitimately serve as a gap-filling method.[49]

Interestingly, these justifications for the use of comparative materials are interrelated in the sense that they all assume that principles common to the Member States can be considered as part of the 'law' that should be observed by the CJEU. In that sense they also fit the justification provided by the Advocate General in *Internationale Handelsgesellschaft*.[50]

13.2.2.2 CJEU and national constitutional traditions

In the previous section, it has been made clear that the CJEU often refers to the constitutional traditions of the Member States as a basis for its fundamental rights case law. An important question in regard to the central theme of this thesis is whether the CJEU only does do so in a general fashion, or whether it actually and in a concrete way discusses some or all of these traditions. This question is important for understanding how the references to common constitutional traditions are used in practice.

The CJEU's case law discloses roughly three different scenarios. First, in a substantial number of cases the CJEU does not provide any express reference to national constitutional traditions at all, neither in an abstract manner nor by very

45 See for example: Lenaerts (2003), p. 876; Wasensteiner (2004), p. 29; Kakouris (1994), p. 272-273.

46 Lenaerts (2003), p. 877.

47 See also Wasensteiner (2004), p. 30.

48 See for example: Kakouris (1991), p. 496-497; Wasensteiner (2004), p. 30.

49 Lenaerts (2003), p. 879 hints at this justification; Kakouris (1991), p. 496. Fairclothes-People (2008), p. 223.

50 C-11/70, *Internationale Handelsgesellschaft mbH v. Einfuhr- und Vorratsstelle für Getreide und Futtermittel* [1970] ECR 01125, Opinion by Advocate General Dutheillet De Lamothe.

concrete references to the situation in the Member States.[51] In these cases the reference to the constitutional traditions remains devoid of any real explanation, the CJEU solely mentioning that common constitutional traditions are a source of inspiration. In the case of *Kent Kirk*, for example, the question was whether the principle of non-retroactivity of criminal provisions could be considered one of the fundamental rights protected by the EU. In answer to this, the CJEU simply held that:

51 In C-11/70, *Internationale Handelsgesellschaft mbH v. Einfuhr- und Vorratsstelle für Getreide und Futtermittel* [1970] ECR 01125, both the CJEU and Advocate General Dutheillet de Lamothe only mention that constitutional traditions can play a role, but do not discuss any national constitutional traditions. In C-4/73, J. *Nold, Kohlen- und Baustoffgroßhandlung v. Ruhrkohle Aktiengesellschaft* [1974] ECR 00491, the CJEU only refers to constitutional traditions as a source of inspiration. Advocate General Trabucchi reaffirms the importance of constitutional traditions as a source of inspiration as well, but fails to provide any substance, apart from the reference to all countries of the free world, which is so general that it can hardly be considered to be an example of substantiating these references. In C-63/83, *Regina v. Kent Kirk* [1986] ECR 02689, the CJEU states that the principle of non-retroactivity is common to all legal orders of the Member States. In C-222/84, *Marguerite Johnston v. Chief Constable of the Royal Ulster Constabulary* [1986] ECR 01651, the CJEU solely states that the requirement of judicial control reflects a general principle of law which underlies the constitutional traditions common to the Member States. See also C-222/86, *Union nationale des entraîneurs et cadres techniques professionnels du football (Unectef) v. Georges Heylens and others* [1987] ECR 04097; C-260/89, *Elliniki Radiophonia Tiléorassi (ERT) AE and Panellinia Omospondia Syllogon Prossopikou v. Dimotiki Etairia Pliroforissis and Sotirios Kouvelas and Nicolaos Avdellas and others* [1991] ECR I-02925, only the reference to the ECHR is more elaborately dealt with. See in similar fashion: C-94/00, *Roquette Frères SA v. Directeur général de la concurrence, de la consommation et de la répression des fraudes, and Commission of the European Communities* [2002] ECR I-09011 (only the ECHR is extensively dealt with); C-465/00, *Rechnungshof v Österreichischer Rundfunk and Others* [2003] ECR I-04989, is also more detailed on the ECHR. Or C-74/95, *Criminal Proceedings against X* [1996] ECR I-06609; C-185/97, *Belinda Jane Coote v. Granada Hospitality Ltd.* [1998] ECR I-05199; C-7/98, *Dieter Krombach v. André Bamberski* [2000] ECR I-01935; C-17/98, *Emesa Sugar (Free Zone) NV v. Aruba* [2000] ECR I-00665; C-274/99, *Bernard Connolly v. Commission of the European Communities* [2001] ECR I-01611, only mentioning it as source of inspiration. See also: C-112/00, *Eugen Schmidberger, Internationale Transporte und Planzüge v. Republik Österreich* [2003] ECR I-05659; C-263/02, *Commission of the European Communities v. Jégo-Quéré & Cie SA* [2004] ECR I-03425; C-540/03, *European Parliament v Council of the European Union* [2006] ECR I-05769; C-411/04, *Salzgitter Mannesmann GmbH v. Commission of the European Communities*, [2007] ECR I-00959; C-370/05, *Criminal proceedings against Uwe Kay Festersen* [2007] ECR I-01129; C-432/05, *Unibet (London) Ltd and Unibet (International) Ltd v. Justitiekanslern* [2007] ECR I-02271; C-450/06, *Varec SA v. Belgian State* [2008] ECR I-00581; C-465/07, *Meki Elgafaji and Noor Elgafaji v. Staatssecretaris van Justitie* [2009] ECR I-00921;C-349/07, *Sopropé – Organizações de Calçado Lda v. Fazenda Pública* [2008] ECR I-10369. In C-308/07, *Koldo Gorostiaga Atxalandabaso v. European Parliament* [2009] ECR I-01059, the judgment does not mention any reference to constitutional traditions; the AG in this case does, but only lists them as a source of inspiration.

> The principle that penal provisions may not have retroactive effect is one which is common to all the legal orders of the Member States ...; it takes its place among the general principles of law whose observance is ensured by the Court of Justice.[52]

Another example is the equal treatment case of *Marguerite Johnston*, where one of the questions related to the right to a judicial remedy. The CJEU in this case did not do more than just stating that:

> The requirement of judicial control stipulated by that article reflects a general principle of law which underlies the constitutional traditions common to the Member States.[53]

In both examples neither the CJEU nor the Advocate General provided more insight into the basis for reaching the conclusion that these rights really formed part of the constitutional traditions in the various Member States.

The second scenario is when the CJEU itself does not address the fundamental rights issue or fails to substantiate the reference to national traditions, but the Advocate General does.[54] These cases will be discussed in depth in the subsequent section, which specifically deals with the approach of the Advocates General to comparative interpretation. The purpose of mentioning these types of cases here is to show that, when the CJEU does not address the common constitutional traditions at all, this does not automatically mean that no attention is paid to the substance of these constitutional traditions at all.

In the third and last scenario, the CJEU does provide some form of explanation on what the constitutional traditions entail. The extent and depth of this explanation

---

52 C-63/83, *Regina v. Kent Kirk* [1986] ECR 02689, § 22.

53 C-222/84, *Marguerite Johnston v. Chief Constable of the Royal Ulster Constabulary* [1986] ECR 01651, § 18.

54 See for example: C-130/75, *Vivien Prais v. Council of the European Communities* [1976] ECR 01589; C-20/00, *Booker Aquacultur Ltd v. The Scottish Ministers* [2003] ECR I-07411; C-17/74, *Transocean Marine Paint Association v. Commission of the European Communities* [1974] 01063; C-118/75, *Lynne Watson and Alessandro Belmann* [1976] ECR 01185; C-168/91, *Christos Konstantinidis v. Stadt Altensteig – Standesamt and Landratsamt Calw – Ordnungsamt* [1993] ECR I-01191; C-13/94, *P v. S and Cornwall County Council* [1996] ECRI-02143; C-50/00, *Unión de Pequeños Agricultores (UPA) v. Council of the European Union* [2002] ECR I-06677; C-117/01, *K.B. v National Health Service Pensions Agency and Secretary of State for Health* [2004] ECR I-00541. See also C-341/05, *Laval un Partneri Ltd v. Svenska Byggnadsarbetareförbundet and others* [2007] ECR I-11767, the judgment in this case only refers to the international instruments as a source of inspiration, while the AG refers to Member States as well. See also: C-341/06, *Chronopost SA and La Poste v. Union française de l'express (UFEX) and Others* [2008] ECR I-04777, where the AG responds to one of the arguments of the parties by discussing their references to constitutional traditions. To a very limited extent: C-136/79, *National Panasonic (UK) Limited v Commission of the European Communities* [1980] ECR 02033 (Advocate General Warner speaks in rather abstract terms).

differs per case. The CJEU seldom names individual Member States when discussing whether a common constitutional tradition exists.[55] In most cases the CJEU discusses the existence of a certain tradition at an abstract level, not mentioning any Member State in particular.[56] In the case of *Orkem* the CJEU discussed whether the Member States acknowledged a right not to incriminate oneself to legal persons in competition cases:

> In general, the laws of the Member States grant the right not to give evidence against oneself only to a natural person charged with an offence in criminal proceedings. A comparative analysis of national law does not therefore indicate the existence of such a principle, common to the laws of the Member States, which may be relied upon by legal persons in relation to infringements in the economic sphere, in particular infringements of competition law.[57]

The CJEU thus implied that it had undertaken a comparative analysis of which it only included the very brief conclusion in the judgment itself. The cited considerations do not deal with Member States individually, but, as can be seen, contain a rather concise and abstract reference to the situation in the Member States. Interestingly, Advocate General Darmon in his opinion to the case discussed the law of a number of individual Member States and concluded from this that no common principle could be found therein for legal persons not to incriminate themselves. This opinion will be discussed in more detail in the next section. At this point it is important to realize that the discussion of the Advocate General in this case provided a useful and elaborate foundation for the brief reasoning of the CJEU.

In the case of *Grant* the CJEU also discussed the situation in the Member States at a very abstract level.[58] The question was whether stable homosexual relationships

---

55 This is also the impression that is generally expressed in the literature. See for example: Lenaerts (2003), p. 874; Singer (2007), p. 498; Colneric (2007), p. 316; Hilf (1986), p. 561; Kakouris (1994), p. 276; Wasensteiner (2004), p. 41. Exceptionally in the case of C-44/79, *Liselotte Hauer v. Land Rheinland-Pfalz* [1979] ECR 03727, the CJEU did name individual Member States, § 20.

56 See for example: C-155/79, *AM & S Europe Limited v. Commission of the European Communities* [1982] ECR 01575, § 18-22; C-46/87 *Hoechst AG v. Commission of the European Communities* [1989] ECR 02859, § 17; C-374/87, *Orkem v. Commission of the European Communities* [1989] ECR 03283, § 29; C-249/96, *Lisa Jacqueline Grant v. South-West Trains Ltd* [1998] ECR I-00621, § 32; C-122/99, *D and Kingdom of Sweden v. Council of the European Union* [2001] ECR I-04319, § 35; C-341/05, *Laval un Partneri Ltd v. Svenska Byggnadsarbetareförbundet and others* [2007] ECR I-11767, § 92. The case of *Omega Spielhallen* (C-36/02, *Omega Spielhallen- und Automatenaufstellungs-GmbH v. Oberbürgermeisterin der Bundesstadt Bonn* [2004] ECR I-09609) differs from the other examples. In this judgment the judges explicitly refer back to the discussion by Advocate General Stix-Hackl and in that sense put some flesh on the bones of the reference to national constitutional traditions.

57 C-374/87, *Orkem v. Commission of the European Communities* [1989] ECR 03283, § 29.

58 C-249/96, *Lisa Jacqueline Grant v. South-West Trains Ltd* [1998] ECR I-00621.

outside marriage should be considered equal to stable heterosexual relationships outside marriage. The CJEU noted the following about the situation in the Member States:

> As for the laws of the Member States, while in some of them cohabitation by two persons of the same sex is treated as equivalent to marriage, although not completely, in most of them it is treated as equivalent to a stable heterosexual relationship outside marriage only with respect to a limited number of rights, or else it is not recognized in any particular way.[59]

There was thus no clear common tradition, but the Court clearly discerned some developments in the direction of a legal consensus. The CJEU, however, finally concluded that homosexual and heterosexual relations outside marriage did not have to be regarded as equivalent.

Finally, in the case of *AM & S* the CJEU had to decide on the confidentiality of written communications between a lawyer and his/her client in competition proceedings.[60] Here the CJEU spent a few more words on discussing what the national traditions entailed. The discussion dealt with these traditions at an abstract level, not mentioning any individual Member State. However, the CJEU did indicate that the scope and criteria for protecting this type of communication varied between the legal systems.[61] The CJEU mentioned some examples of these differences and concluded that common criteria were also to be found.[62] The following paragraphs may illustrate this point:

> As far as the protection of written communications between lawyer and client is concerned, it is apparent from the legal systems of the Member States that, although the principle of such protection is generally recognized, its scope and the criteria for applying it vary, as has, indeed, been conceded both by the applicant and by the parties who have intervened in support of its conclusions.
>
> Whilst in some of the Member States the protection against disclosure afforded to written communications between lawyer and client is based principally on a recognition of the very nature of the legal profession, inasmuch as it contributes towards the maintenance of the rule of law, in other Member States the same protection is justified by the more specific requirement (which, moreover, is also recognized in the first-mentioned States) that the rights of the defense must be respected.

---

59 C-249/96, *Lisa Jacqueline Grant v. South-West Trains Ltd* [1998] ECR I-00621, § 32.

60 C-155/79, *AM & S Europe Limited v. Commission of the European Communities* [1982] ECR 01575.

61 C-155/79, *AM & S Europe Limited v. Commission of the European Communities* [1982] ECR 01575, § 19-20

62 C-155/79, *AM & S Europe Limited v. Commission of the European Communities* [1982] ECR 01575, § 20-21

> Apart from these differences, however, there are to be found in the national laws of the Member States common criteria ... .[63]

In the end, the CJEU held that the common elements to the laws of the Member States were to be incorporated into EC law.[64]

The examples provided of the third scenario show that the Court is not very fond of referring to individual Member States, but prefers to discuss national traditions in a more general and abstract manner. HILF has provided an explanation for this approach by the CJEU, namely that the Court is aware of the practical difficulties inherent to this method. By refusing to discuss the Member States individually, the Court may want to avoid 'the reproach of "dilettantism" if it omitted or misunderstood one of the numerous national legal systems'.[65] The Court itself has not provided any clues as to why it prefers abstract references, but it is certainly likely that the explanation by HILF is correct.

The division into three scenarios made in this section may be useful for analytical purposes as it helps to shed light on the role of internal comparative interpretation by the Court. No substantive conclusions should, however, be attached to whether a judgment can be listed under the first, second or third scenario. The main reason for making this distinction is to gain some insight into the different forms in which common constitutional traditions are used in the different judgments.

The case law studied for the purposes of this thesis also clearly shows that not all scenarios occur equally frequently. In the majority of cases neither the Court nor the Advocate General refer to more than the fact that the common constitutional traditions are a source of inspiration.[66] Less common is the scenario in which the Court remains silent and the Advocate General to some extent tries to substantiate the reference to national constitutional traditions.[67] Finally, the Court will only rarely provide a more detailed account of what it perceives to be the national constitutional traditions.[68] Even when this occurs, the Court does do so in a rather abstract and concise manner.

---

63 C-155/79, *AM & S Europe Limited v. Commission of the European Communities* [1982] ECR 01575, § 19-20-21.

64 C-155/79, *AM & S Europe Limited v. Commission of the European Communities* [1982] ECR 01575, § 22

65 Hilf (1986), p. 561.

66 Supra note 51.

67 Supra note 54.

68 Supra note 55 and 56.

How can this difference between the use of the three scenarios be explained? The case law itself, unfortunately, does not provide any clues. One first explanation, however, may be that the reference to both constitutional traditions and the European Convention on Human Rights has become a standard part of most judgments on fundamental rights. In some cases it might therefore be mentioned as part of the standard reasoning, merely framing the legal context, without any intention to develop this in any way at some point in the reasoning. After the codification of this practice in Article 6(3) TEU (formerly Article 6(2) EU) it has become even more understandable that the Court refers to constitutional traditions as an acknowledged source of inspiration. A second explanation might be found in the fact that there are two main sources of inspiration, the European Convention being the second source. In cases where no attention is paid to national constitutional traditions, references may still be made to the European Convention or to other international material. In *K.B.*, for example, the Court only referred to the case law of the European Convention, without mentioning the national constitutional traditions at all.[69] A third possible explanation relates to the role of the European Convention and also the Charter of Fundamental Rights. It might appear, albeit rather implicitly, from the case law that these documents are regarded as an expression of the common constitutional traditions. Indeed, Advocate General Ruiz-Jarabo Colomber expressly stated in his opinion in the case of *Advocaten voor de Wereld*[70] that the Charter of Fundamental Rights 'codifies and reaffirms certain rights which are derived from the heritage common to the Member States'.[71] In a similar way the European Convention can be viewed as 'proof' of common constitutional traditions, since it has been ratified by all Member States of the EU.[72] This may well render an investigation into the national constitutional traditions superfluous in some (more recent) cases, especially if a certain right is clearly mentioned in the Convention or in the Charter. Only where it concerns rights not protected by the Charter or the European Convention might there be a more prominent role for national traditions. Another potential explanation is that in some cases the Court recalls the sources of inspiration for establishing fundamental rights in the EU context, but refers to a precedent in which it has already been decided that

69 C-117/01, *K.B. v National Health Service Pensions Agency and Secretary of State for Health* [2004] ECR I-00541, Advocate General Ruiz-Jarabo Colomer did refer to national constitutional traditions.

70 C-303/05, *Advocaten voor de Wereld VZW v. Leden van de Ministerraad* [2007] ECR I-03633 .

71 C-303/05, *Advocaten voor de Wereld VZW v. Leden van de Ministerraad* [2007] ECR I-03633, § 77. See also Reich (2005), p. 217.

72 A similar argument is made in Craig & De Burca (2008), p. 386. See also: Rainer (2008), p. 29 where he claims that the ECHR is an expression of a common European legal conviction binding the Member States. See also Reich (2005), p. 210 who argues that the CJEU considers the Convention to be a codification of the principles common to the Member States.

a certain right should be protected. This was the case in *UNECTEF v Heylens*,[73] where the Court referred back to the case of *Johnston*,[74] in which it had recognized the right to an effective judicial remedy:

> As the Court held in its judgment of 15 May 1986 in Case 222/84 *Johnston v Chief Constable of the Royal Ulster Constabulary* ..., that requirement reflects a general principle of Community law which underlies the constitutional traditions common to the Member States and has been enshrined in Articles 6 and 13 of the European Convention for the Protection of Human Rights and Fundamental Freedoms.[75]

A fresh examination of national constitutional traditions would evidently have been redundant in this case.

In summary, thus, it may be recalled that three different scenarios can be identified in the case law of the CJEU referring to national constitutional traditions. Most often the reference to national constitutional traditions is not substantiated. This seems to be a result of the fact that reference to common constitutional traditions and the European Convention of Human Rights as a source of inspiration has become a standard phrase in the judgments of the CJEU. Such references may seem to be of a rhetoric nature, rather than providing a substantive basis for a new interpretation or the recognition of a new right. The second scenario, whereby the Advocate General substantiates a reference and the CJEU remains silent, occurs less frequently. Least frequent is the third scenario in which the CJEU itself substantiates a reference to national constitutional traditions. These latter references are, moreover, mostly rather general in character, not at all mentioning specific national legislation or case law.

The discussion in this section has focused primarily on the reasoning of the Court. The following section will concentrate on the approach by the Advocate General. A subsequent discussion in section 13.2.2.4 will deal with the differences between the two approaches in more detail.

13.2.2.3 Advocate General and national constitutional traditions

The Advocate General plays an important role in the context of referring to national constitutional traditions. This has already been hinted at in the previous section, but

---

73 C-222/86, *Union nationale des entraîneurs et cadres techniques professionnels du football (Unectef) v. Georges Heylens and others* [1987] ECR 04097.

74 C-222/84, *Marguerite Johnston v. Chief Constable of the Royal Ulster Constabulary* [1986] ECR 01651.

75 C-222/86, *Union nationale des entraîneurs et cadres techniques professionnels du football (Unectef) v. Georges Heylens and others* [1987] ECR 04097, § 14.

it is also frequently noted in theoretical literature.[76] This assumption warrants a more detailed look at the opinions of the Advocates General in order to analyze their approach to national constitutional traditions. The discussion of the Advocate General's opinions in this section will focus on all opinions where references to the national constitutional traditions play a certain role. Mention will be made, whenever relevant, within which of the three scenarios an opinion appears to fall, since that can be relevant for the context in which a judgment by the CJEU has been given and it might explain the reasoning by the CJEU in some situations.

Some of the aspects identified in the theoretical chapter on comparative interpretation and briefly cited in the introduction to this section have been or will be addressed for both the Court and the Advocate General together. The discussion of the justification for references to national traditions in section 13.2.2.1 above, for example, did not distinguish between the Court and the Advocate General. By contrast, the way in which national constitutional traditions are being invoked and the way in which references to these traditions are substantiated, can be made more insightful by discussing the Court and the Advocates General separately. Moreover, discussing these approaches separately enables a comparison to be made between the approach taken by the Court and by the Advocates General.

An important conclusion from the analysis of references to national constitutional traditions reached in section 13.2.2.2. was that the CJEU either not really substantiates the reference, or only does so at a rather abstract level. The question is whether this conclusion is also valid with respect to the opinions of the Advocate General or whether a different approach can be detected there.

Indeed, in a certain number of cases the Advocates General does not refer at all to national constitutional traditions as a source of inspiration for fundamental rights.[77]

---

76 See Craig & De Burca (2008), p. 386; Faircloth Peoples (2008), p. 224; Ritter (2005), p. 758; Hilf (1986).

77 C-7/98, *Dieter Krombach v. André Bamberski* [2000] ECR I-01935; C-370/05, *Criminal proceedings against Uwe Kay Festersen* [2007] ECR I-01129; C-94/00, *Roquette Frères SA v. Directeur général de la concurrence, de la consommation et de la répression des fraudes, and Commission of the European Communities* [2002] ECR I-09011; C-465/00, *Rechnungshof v Österreichischer Rundfunk and Others* [2003] ECR I-04989; C-263/02, *Commission of the European Communities v. Jégo-Quéré & Cie SA* [2004] ECR I-03425; C-300/04, *M. G. Eman and O. B. Sevinger v. College van burgemeester en wethouders van Den Haag* [2006] ECR I-08055; C-436/04, *Criminal proceedings against Leopold Henri Van Esbroeck* [2006] ECR I-02333; C-438/05, *International Transport Workers' Federation and Finnish Seamen's Union v. Viking Line ABP and OÜ Viking Line Eesti* [2007] ECR I-10779; C-450/06, *Varec SA v. Belgian State* [2008] ECR I-00581; C-14/07, *Ingenieurbüro Michael Weiss und Partner GbR v. Industrie- und Handelskammer Berlin* [2008] ECR I-03367; C-6/75, *Ulrich Horst v. Bundesknappschaft* [1975] ECR 00823; C-63/83, *Regina v. Kent Kirk* [1986] ECR 02689; C-222/84, *Marguerite Johnston v. Chief Constable of the Royal Ulster Constabulary* [1986] ECR

For example, the Advocate General may not spend much time on analyzing the fundamental rights aspect of the case,[78] or he may only focus on the European Convention.[79]

In another range of cases the Advocates General refers to the standard phrase mentioned earlier, just stating that national constitutional traditions are a source of inspiration, without developing or substantiating this general reference to these traditions.[80] Once again, this may have a variety of explanations. In some cases the Advocate General simply recalls the content of Article 6 (3) TEU or refers to the well-established case law in order to indicate that fundamental rights are protected within the EU, like Advocate General Trsentjak did in the case of *Atxalandabaso*. In this case the Advocate General referred to the standard formula and subsequently devoted all his attention to the European Convention.[81]

The range of cases that is most interesting for the present purposes, however, are those cases in which the Advocate General provides a substantive discussion on the national constitutional traditions used as a basis for establishing or construing a fundamental right.[82] The discussions in these cases may be rather brief or very ela-

---

01651; C-49/88, *Al-Jubail Fertilizer Company (Samad) and Saudi Arabian Fertilizer Company (Safco) v. Council of the European Communities* [1991] ECR I-03187; C-222/86, *Union nationale des entraîneurs et cadres techniques professionnels du football (Unectef) v. Georges Heylens and others* [1987] ECR 04097; C-260/89, *Elliniki Radiophonia Tiléorassi (ERT) AE and Panellinia Omospondia Syllogon Prossopikou v. Dimotiki Etairia Pliroforissis and Sotirios Kouvelas and Nicolaos Avdellas and others* [1991] ECR I-02925; C-74/95, *Criminal Proceedings against X* [1996] ECR I-06609.

78 See for example: C-465/00, *Rechnungshof v Österreichischer Rundfunk and Others* [2003] ECR I-04989; C-263/02, *Commission of the European Communities v. Jégo-Quéré & Cie SA* [2004] ECR I-03425; C-63/83, *Regina v. Kent Kirk* [1986] ECR 02689.

79 See for example: C-94/00, *Roquette Frères SA v. Directeur général de la concurrence, de la consommation et de la répression des fraudes, and Commission of the European Communities* [2002] ECR I-09011; C-74/95, *Criminal Proceedings against X* [1996] ECR I-06609.

80 C-60/00, *Mary Carpenter v. Secretary of State for the Home Department* [2002] ECR I-06279; C-122/00, *Schmidberger*; C-540/03, *European Parliament v Council of the European Union* [2006] ECR I-05769; C-411/04, *Salzgitter Mannesmann GmbH v. Commission of the European Communities*, [2007] ECR I-00959; C-303/05, *Advocaten voor de Wereld VZW v. Leden van de Ministerraad* [2007] ECR I-03633; C-432/05, *Unibet (London) Ltd and Unibet (International) Ltd v. Justitiekanslern* [2007] ECR I-02271; C-308/07, *Koldo Gorostiaga Atxalandabaso v. European Parliament* [2009] ECR I-01059; C-465/07, *Meki Elgafaji and Noor Elgafaji v. Staatssecretaris van Justitie* [2009] ECR I-00921; C-11/70, *Internationale Handelsgesellschaft mbH v. Einfuhr- und Vorratsstelle für Getreide und Futtermittel* [1970] ECR 01125; C-149/77, *Gabrielle Defrenne v Société anonyme belge de navigation aérienne Sabena* [1978] ECR 01365.

81 C-308/07, *Koldo Gorostiaga Atxalandabaso v. European Parliament* [2009] ECR I-01059, § 54 et seq, Opinion by Advocate General Trstenjak.

82 C-122/99, *D and Kingdom of Sweden v. Council of the European Union* [2001] ECR I-04319; C-274/99, *Bernard Connolly v. Commission of the European Communities* [2001] ECR I-01611; C-20/00, *Booker Aquacultur Ltd v. The Scottish Ministers* [2003] ECR I-07411; C-117/01, *K.B. v National*

borately, as will be shown later on. First, the above will be further illustrated by a number of examples.

In one of the first cases to introduce the references to national constitutional traditions, *Nold*, Advocate General Trabucchi referred in a very abstract manner to the fact that the right to property was recognized by all Member States:

> It will be necessary to examine in particular whether there has been any violation of the general principle of protection of property which is recognized by all the Constitutions of the Member States and which, without doubt, is also an integral part of the Community order.[83]

The Advocate General did not support this statement with a reference to the law and legal practice of individual Member States, nor to any study that might have underpinned this conclusion. Other cases in which the Advocates General only marginally refers to the national constitutional traditions can easily be found. A similarly abstract reference was made in the case of *National Panasonic*, where Advocate General Warner had to interpret the powers of the Commission when carrying out investigations of infringements of competition law.[84] The Advocate General referred *in abstracto* to the laws of the Member States in order to show that '[i]n general, though not always, the laws of Member States require officers of a public

Health Service Pensions Agency and Secretary of State for Health [2004] ECR I-00541; C-36/02, *Omega Spielhallen- und Automatenaufstellungs-GmbH v. Oberbürgermeisterin der Bundesstadt Bonn* [2004] ECR I-09609; C-341/05, *Laval un Partneri Ltd v. Svenska Byggnadsarbetareförbundet and others* [2007] ECR I-11767; C-341/06, *Chronopost SA and La Poste v. Union française de l'express (UFEX) and Others* [2008] ECR I-04777; C-4/73, J. *Nold, Kohlen- und Baustoffgroßhandlung v. Ruhrkohle Aktiengesellschaft* [1974] ECR 00491; C-17/74, *Transocean Marine Paint Association v. Commission of the European Communities* [1974] 01063; C-118/75, *Lynne Watson and Alessandro Belmann* [1976] ECR 01185; C-130/75, *Vivien Prais v. Council of the European Communities* [1976] ECR 01589; C-44/79, *Liselotte Hauer v. Land Rheinland-Pfalz* [1979] ECR 03727; C-136/79, *National Panasonic (UK) Limited v Commission of the European Communities* [1980] ECR 02033; C-155/79, *AM & S Europe Limited v. Commission of the European Communities* [1982] ECR 01575; C-46/87 *Hoechst AG v. Commission of the European Communities* [1989] ECR 02859; C-374/87, *Orkem v. Commission of the European Communities* [1989] ECR 03283; C-168/91, *Christos Konstantinidis v. Stadt Altensteig – Standesamt and Landratsamt Calw – Ordnungsamt* [1993] ECR I-01191; C-13/94, *P v. S and Cornwall County Council* [1996] ECRI-02143.

83 C-4/73, J. *Nold, Kohlen- und Baustoffgroßhandlung v. Ruhrkohle Aktiengesellschaft* [1974] ECR 00491, Opinion by Advocate General Trabucchi.

84 C-136/79, *National Panasonic (UK) Limited v Commission of the European Communities* [1980] ECR 02033, Opinion by Advocate General Warner.

authority to have such a [search] warrant before they may enter private premises'.[85] This type of brief and abstract reference does not really shed much light on the question whether a common principle exists and as such does not provide much guidance on the actual use of the method of comparative interpretation.

In quite a large number of cases, the Advocates General provide a more substantial reference to national constitutional traditions.[86] This reference can still be rather short, like in the case of *D v Council*, where Advocate General Mischo was faced with the question whether the term spouse had to be interpreted broadly in order to include registered partners as well.[87] The Advocate General took into account the situation in the whole Community and concluded that there was no general consensus on the basis of which registered partnerships could be equated with marriage:

> At the time of the events in question, there existed in only three of the fifteen Member States the legal category of registered partnership assimilating, to a greater or lesser degree, the communal life of two persons of the same sex to that of two married persons in the traditional meaning of the term.[88]

---

85 C-136/79, *National Panasonic (UK) Limited v Commission of the European Communities* [1980] ECR 02033, p. 2068. See also the case of C-274/99, *Bernard Connolly v. Commission of the European Communities* [2001] ECR I-01611.

86 See, for example (note the difference in depth of the reference): C-17/74, *Transocean Marine Paint Association v. Commission of the European Communities* [1974] 01063, p. 1088-1089; C-118/75, *Lynne Watson and Alessandro Belmann* [1976] ECR 01185; C-130/75, *Vivien Prais v. Council of the European Communities* [1976] ECR 01589; C-44/79, *Liselotte Hauer v. Land Rheinland-Pfalz* [1979] ECR 03727, p. 3759-3761; C-155/79, *AM & S Europe Limited v. Commission of the European Communities* [1982] ECR 01575; C-46/87 *Hoechst AG v. Commission of the European Communities* [1989] ECR 02859, § 49-111; C-374/87, *Orkem v. Commission of the European Communities* [1989] ECR 03283, § 96-129; C-168/91, *Christos Konstantinidis v. Stadt Altensteig – Standesamt and Landratsamt Calw – Ordnungsamt* [1993] ECR I-01191, § 36-38; C-13/94, *P v. S and Cornwall County Council* [1996] ECRI-02143, § 9-11; C-122/99, *D and Kingdom of Sweden v. Council of the European Union* [2001] ECR I-04319, § 48; C-20/00, *Booker Aquacultur Ltd v. The Scottish Ministers* [2003] ECR I-07411, § 116-124; C-117/01, *K.B. v National Health Service Pensions Agency and Secretary of State for Health* [2004] ECR I-00541, § 28; C-36/02, *Omega Spielhallen- und Automatenaufstellungs-GmbH v. Oberbürgermeisterin der Bundesstadt Bonn* [2004] ECR I-09609, § 83; C-341/05, *Laval un Partneri Ltd v. Svenska Byggnadsarbetareförbundet and others* [2007] ECR I-11767; C-341/06, *Chronopost SA and La Poste v. Union française de l'express (UFEX) and Others* [2008] ECR I-04777; C-506/06, *Sabine Mayr v. Bäckerei und Konditorei Gerhard Flöckner OHG* [2008] ECR I-01017, § 44.

87 C-122/99, *D and Kingdom of Sweden v. Council of the European Union* [2001] ECR I-04319, Opinion by Advocate General Mischo.

88 C-122/99, *D and Kingdom of Sweden v. Council of the European Union* [2001] ECR I-04319, § 48, Opinion by Advocate General Mischo.

This is still an abstract reference to the law of the Member States, no states being mentioned specifically, but the statistics mentioned by the Advocate General provide some insight into the situation in the Community. What is problematic about the reference in this case, however, is that no source is provided on the basis of which this conclusion has been based, which makes it difficult to check the validity of the Advocate General's conclusions. This is different in the case of *Omega Spielhallen*, in which Germany endeavoured to justify an infringement of the freedom to provide services by expressing its desire and need to protect the right to human dignity.[89] In order to provide an answer to the preliminary questions asked in this case, Advocate General Stix-Hackl had to discuss the status of human dignity in the Community and the status of human dignity in the Member States formed part of that discussion. As a result the Advocate General stated that some form of protection of human dignity could be found in all Member States:

> As far as the constitutional systems of the Member States are concerned, therefore, the concept of human dignity enjoys full recognition in one form or another, especially when one considers ... that this concept can be expressed in different ways.[90]

Once again this reference seems to be of a rather abstract nature, but this time the Advocate General at least provided a source, namely two academic studies,[91] on which she could base her conclusions.

In the third category of cases, the Advocates General have referred to individual Member States in order to provide an overview of the situation in the Community.[92]

---

89 C-36/02, *Omega Spielhallen- und Automatenaufstellungs-GmbH v. Oberbürgermeisterin der Bundesstadt Bonn* [2004] ECR I-09609.

90 C-36/02, *Omega Spielhallen- und Automatenaufstellungs-GmbH v. Oberbürgermeisterin der Bundesstadt Bonn* [2004] ECR I-09609, Opinion by Advocate General Stix-Hackl, § 83.

91 C-36/02, *Omega Spielhallen- und Automatenaufstellungs-GmbH v. Oberbürgermeisterin der Bundesstadt Bonn* [2004] ECR I-09609, Opinion by Advocate General Stix-Hackl, footnote 55.

92 See for varying degrees of references: C-168/91, *Christos Konstantinidis v. Stadt Altensteig – Standesamt and Landratsamt Calw – Ordnungsamt* [1993] ECR I-01191; C-117/01, *K.B. v National Health Service Pensions Agency and Secretary of State for Health* [2004] ECR I-00541; C-13/94, *P v. S and Cornwall County Council* [1996] ECRI-02143; C-374/87, *Orkem v. Commission of the European Communities* [1989] ECR 03283; C-46/87 *Hoechst AG v. Commission of the European Communities* [1989] ECR 02859; C-155/79, *AM & S Europe Limited v. Commission of the European Communities* [1982] ECR 01575; C-44/79, *Liselotte Hauer v. Land Rheinland-Pfalz* [1979] ECR 03727; C-118/75, *Lynne Watson and Alessandro Belmann* [1976] ECR 01185; C-130/75, *Vivien Prais v. Council of the European Communities* [1976] ECR 01589; C-17/74, *Transocean Marine Paint Association v. Commission of the European Communities* [1974] 01063; C-341/06, *Chronopost SA and La Poste v. Union française de l'express (UFEX) and Others* [2008] ECR I-04777; C-341/05, *Laval un Partneri Ltd v. Svenska Byggnadsarbetareförbundet and others* [2007] ECR I-11767; C-20/

In the case of *K.B.*, for example, Advocate General Ruiz-Jarabo Colomer had to answer questions regarding the entitlement of transsexuals to a widow's or widower's pension.[93] The status of transsexuals' right to marry in the different Member States was relevant to answering these questions. In a brief overview Advocate General Ruiz-Jarabo Colomer referred to all (then) 15 Member States and provided a clear (though rather succinct) overview of the ways in which and the extent to which most of them accepted or allowed for marriage of transsexuals according to their acquired gender:

> A comparative study of the prevailing legal situation shows that the marriage of transsexuals in their acquired gender is generally accepted. Whether it is as a result of express action by the legislature (Germany, Greece, Italy, the Netherlands, Sweden), administrative practice (Austria, Denmark) or judicial interpretation (Belgium, Spain, Finland, France, Luxembourg, Portugal), registers can be amended following gender reassignment operations, so that transsexuals are able to marry. Only the Irish and United Kingdom legal systems appear to go against this general trend, which is not a bar to identifying a sufficiently uniform legal tradition capable of being a source of a general principle of Community law.[94]

Even though the references provided in this opinion are short and even though they are rather roughly divided into broad categories, they still offer a relatively complete

---

00, *Booker Aquacultur Ltd v. The Scottish Ministers* [2003] ECR I-07411; C-279/09, *DEB Deutsche Energiehandels- und Beratungsgesellschaft mbH v. Bundesrepublik Deutschland* [2010], § 77.

93 C-117/01, *K.B. v National Health Service Pensions Agency and Secretary of State for Health* [2004] ECR I-00541, Opinion by Advocate General Ruiz-Jarabo Colomer.

94 C-117/01, *K.B. v National Health Service Pensions Agency and Secretary of State for Health* [2004] ECR I-00541, § 28 Opinion by Advocate General Ruiz-Jarabo Colomer. The origin of the sources will be discussed in section 13.2.2.7. A more extensive version of this type of reference is provided by the case of C-13/94, *P v. S and Cornwall County Council* [1996] ECRI-02143. In this case Advocate General Tesauro discussed, among others things, the situation in Member States concerning the changing legal status of transsexuals. The Advocate General observed that in almost all Member States surgery to alter one's sex is permitted. Subsequently, the Advocate General discussed in general terms the different ways in which recognition of these operations had been guaranteed. Only a few Member States were mentioned individually, the rest being discussed as an abstract category, but the footnotes referred to individual Member States: 'Some States have given a legal response to transsexuality by adopting special legislation. As far as Member States of the Community are concerned this is so in the case of Sweden, the Federal Republic of Germany, Italy and the Netherlands. The laws concerned authorize transsexuals to correct their birth certificates so as to include a reference to their new sexual identity, with the result that they have the right to marry, adopt children and enjoy pension rights according to their *new* sexual identity. The fact that the other Member States do not have special laws on the subject does not mean that the position of transsexuals is ignored. As a matter of fact, in some States, the legality of surgery performed on transsexuals and of the resulting change of civil status is based on laws which themselves have nothing to do with the questions of transsexuality [footnote refers to Denmark]. In most of the other States the problem is, by contrast, resolved case by case by the courts, or even, much more simply, at the administrative level [Footnote refers to France, Belgium, Spain, Portugal, Luxembourg and Greece].'

overview which permits conclusions to be drawn about the situation in the Member States of the then Community.[95]

In other cases a more elaborate discussion of the situation in the different Member States is provided. A good example is the case of *Hoechst* in which the question was raised whether the inviolability of the home could be extended to the business premises of undertakings.[96] Advocate General Mischo discussed the situation in all (at the time 12) Member States at rather great length. To cite a part of this discussion would not be relevant, since that would require delving too deeply into the subject matter of the case and it would result in lengthy quotations. Indeed, the fact that the comparative discussion took up to nine pages of the opinion may already indicate that the situation in all of the Member States was discussed rather extensively.[97] The Advocate General concluded that the right to inviolability of the home was common to the traditions of the Member States, but that the situation was less clear when extending this protection to the business premises of legal persons.[98] The Advocate General, however, did discern a trend and he concluded that a fundamental right to inviolability of business premises existed at the time, but that it did not apply to the same extent as to private dwellings.[99]

In more recent cases, such an elaborate discussion of the state of law in the different Member States has never been given. This can probably be explained by the increase in Member States of the EU, since it would be perhaps too time-consuming to discuss all 27 Member States separately at such great length in an opinion on a concrete case.

95 A related type of references is made in the case of *Sabine Mayr*, where reference was made to the wide variety of provisions in the different Member States on the storing of fertilized ova. Some broad categories were mentioned and in this case only the two ends of the spectrum were mentioned, along with the Member State that was involved in the case. See C-506/06, *Sabine Mayr v. Bäckerei und Konditorei Gerhard Flöckner OHG* [2008] ECR I-01017, § 44.

96 C-46/87 *Hoechst AG v. Commission of the European Communities* [1989] ECR 02859, Opinion by Advocate General Mischo.

97 Similar approaches can be seen in the following cases: C-17/74, *Transocean Marine Paint Association v. Commission of the European Communities* [1974] 01063; C-44/79, *Liselotte Hauer v. Land Rheinland-Pfalz* [1979] ECR 03727; C-155/79, *AM & S Europe Limited v. Commission of the European Communities* [1982] ECR 01575 Opinion by Advocate General Slynn; C-374/87, *Orkem v. Commission of the European Communities* [1989] ECR 03283. To a somewhat lesser extent this is also visible in: C-130/75, *Vivien Prais v. Council of the European Communities* [1976] ECR 01589; C-168/91, *Christos Konstantinidis v. Stadt Altensteig – Standesamt and Landratsamt Calw – Ordnungsamt* [1993] ECR I-01191.

98 C-46/87 *Hoechst AG v. Commission of the European Communities* [1989] ECR 02859, § 97-101.

99 C-46/87 *Hoechst AG v. Commission of the European Communities* [1989] ECR 02859, § 103-106.

The preceding examples clearly show that when the Advocates General choose to substantiate the reference to national constitutional traditions, they generally prefer to do so at a rather concrete level. In most cases some reference is made to individual Member States,[100] while in only a few cases an abstract reference is made to general notions such as the existence of a common tradition.[101] It has already been noted above that the extensive references to national traditions can be found mainly in the older cases, but even in recent cases references to individual Member States can be found.[102]

The examples mentioned above correspond to both the second and third scenario identified in section 13.2.2.2. It does not need much explanation why cases belonging to the second group are discussed, since that scenario concerned the cases where only the Advocate General elaborated on the national constitutional traditions and where the CJEU remained silent on this aspect. In these cases the extent of the reference to national constitutional traditions by the Advocate General differs, as has been shown above. In the cases that fall within the third scenario, i.e. the cases where the Court itself also substantiates the reference to national constitutional traditions, the degree of reference by the Advocate General differs as well. It can be noted in this regard that the most elaborate references by the Advocates General have been given in those cases where subsequently the Court also invoked a more substantial reference to

---

100 C-17/74, *Transocean Marine Paint Association v. Commission of the European Communities* [1974] 01063; C-130/75, *Vivien Prais v. Council of the European Communities* [1976] ECR 01589; C-188/75, *Watson & Belmann*; C-44/79, *Liselotte Hauer v. Land Rheinland-Pfalz* [1979] ECR 03727; C-155/79, *AM & S Europe Limited v. Commission of the European Communities* [1982] ECR 01575; C-374/87, *Orkem v. Commission of the European Communities* [1989] ECR 03283; C-46/87 *Hoechst AG v. Commission of the European Communities* [1989] ECR 02859; C-168/91, *Christos Konstantinidis v. Stadt Altensteig – Standesamt and Landratsamt Calw – Ordnungsamt* [1993] ECR I-01191; C-13/94, *P v. S and Cornwall County Council* [1996] ECRI-02143; C-20/00, *Booker Aquacultur Ltd v. The Scottish Ministers* [2003] ECR I-07411; C-117/01, *K.B. v National Health Service Pensions Agency and Secretary of State for Health* [2004] ECR I-00541; C-341/05, *Laval un Partneri Ltd v. Svenska Byggnadsarbetareförbundet and others* [2007] ECR I-11767; C-341/06, *Chronopost SA and La Poste v. Union française de l'express (UFEX) and Others* [2008] ECR I-04777. C-122/99, *D and Kingdom of Sweden v. Council of the European Union* [2001] ECR I-04319 is a borderline case. In this case the Advocate General does not mention Member States individually, but does refer to numbers of Members States thereby indicating the division in the EU. The reference is thus neither concrete nor abstract.

101 C-4/73, J. *Nold, Kohlen- und Baustoffgroßhandlung v. Ruhrkohle Aktiengesellschaft* [1974] ECR 00491; C-136/79, *National Panasonic (UK) Limited v Commission of the European Communities* [1980] ECR 02033; C-36/02, *Omega Spielhallen- und Automatenaufstellungs-GmbH v. Oberbürgermeisterin der Bundesstadt Bonn* [2004] ECR I-09609.

102 See for example: C-341/05, *Laval un Partneri Ltd v. Svenska Byggnadsarbetareförbundet and others* [2007] ECR I-11767.

constitutional traditions.[103] This is not always the case, however, so no conclusions can be drawn from this observation. Nonetheless, it is striking that in only one case the Court invokes substantial references to national constitutional traditions, while the Advocate General does not.[104] This might imply that the discussions by the Advocate General play an important role for the substantial references in the reasoning of the Court, either as a basis for the analysis by the Court or as an indicator that references to constitutional traditions could be a relevant factor in a specific case.

13.2.2.4 Comparing approaches

The preceding two sections have addressed the approaches of the CJEU and the Advocates General in referring to national constitutional traditions. Two clearly different approaches have been identified. The Court itself prefers to be silent on national constitutional traditions. If a more substantial reference is made, this is most often a rather abstract reference which does not mention any individual Member States. At the most, reference is made to certain categories of Member States.[105] The Advocates General on the other hand, prefer to substantiate their references to national constitutional traditions, in most cases by making concrete references to the law of the Member States. Not seldom are individual Member States mentioned by the Advocates General. The difference is thus that the Advocates General more often rely on this form of comparative interpretation and, if so, they use concrete rather than abstract references.

The section on the CJEU's approach already provided some explanations for the attitude taken by this Court. The question here is whether an explanation can be found for the difference in attitude between the two. This difference can be explained from the difference in style between the Advocate General and the CJEU, which has been addressed in Chapter 3. The distinction made by Loth between the Advocates General, who contribute to the substantial debate, and the CJEU, who makes authoritive decisions, also appears to hold true in the context of comparative interpretation.[106]

13.2.2.5 The purpose of invoking national constitutional traditions

The previous sections have shown that in many cases the reference to national constitutional traditions does not stretch beyond the remark that they are an important source

103 See for example: C-155/79, *AM & S Europe Limited v. Commission of the European Communities* [1982] ECR 01575; C-374/87, *Orkem v. Commission of the European Communities* [1989] ECR 03283.

104 C-249/96, *Lisa Jacqueline Grant v. South-West Trains Ltd* [1998] ECR I-00621.

105 C-155/79, *AM & S Europe Limited v. Commission of the European Communities* [1982] ECR 01575.

106 Loth (2009), p. 274.

of inspiration. Thus in many cases the reference does not go further than a rhetorical reference to indicate the link with the Member States.

In those cases where the reference to national constitutional traditions is substantiated there seem to be three goals for the references to constitutional traditions. One purpose of relying on national constitutional traditions is to construe fundamental rights that deserve protection in the EU. As indicated before – see mainly Chapter 3 – the EU until 2000 did not have its own fundamental rights document, but EU law had to be interpreted in accordance with fundamental rights. The question was: Which fundamental rights? Those fundamental rights that could be found in the national constitutional traditions and the ECHR. Thus the purpose of the references was to fill the gap by providing a basis on which to decide which fundamental rights had to be protected within the EU or by providing a reason not to construe a fundamental right, when there was no sufficient support. This purpose is thus mainly visible in the earlier cases and not really in the more recent cases after the Charter of Fundamental Rights came into existence.[107] A rare, relatively recent example of this purpose would be the opinion of Advocate General Mengozzi in *Laval*, where he referred to national constitutional traditions to indicate that the right to collective action to defend trade union members is a fundamental right to be protected in the EU.[108] The example simultaneously explains why this purpose of referring to national constitutional traditions has become relatively seldom:

> As regards the constitutional traditions of the Member States, whilst I am not of the view that they must be examined exhaustively, in view of the fact that, as emphasized in point 68 of this Opinion, the Charter of Fundamental Rights, although not binding, is principally intended to reaffirm the rights resulting in particular from those traditions, I would nevertheless point out that the constitutional instruments of numerous Member States explicitly protect the right to establish trade unions and the defense of their interests by collective action, the

---

107 See for example: C-17/74, *Transocean Marine Paint Association v. Commission of the European Communities* [1974] 01063; C-130/75, *Vivien Prais v. Council of the European Communities* [1976] ECR 01589; C-44/79, *Liselotte Hauer v. Land Rheinland-Pfalz* [1979] ECR 03727; C-155/79, *AM & S Europe Limited v. Commission of the European Communities* [1982] ECR 01575; C-46/87 *Hoechst AG v. Commission of the European Communities* [1989] ECR 02859; C-374/87, *Orkem v. Commission of the European Communities* [1989] ECR 03283; C-168/91, *Christos Konstantinidis v. Stadt Altensteig – Standesamt and Landratsamt Calw – Ordnungsamt* [1993] ECR I-01191; C-13/94, *P v. S and Cornwall County Council* [1996] ECRI-02143; C-74/95, *Criminal Proceedings against X* [1996] ECR I-06609; C-341/05, *Laval un Partneri Ltd v. Svenska Byggnadsarbetareförbundet and others* [2007] ECR I-11767; C-438/05, *International Transport Workers' Federation and Finnish Seamen's Union v. Viking Line ABP and OÜ Viking Line Eesti* [2007] ECR I-10779.

108 C-341/05, *Laval un Partneri Ltd v. Svenska Byggnadsarbetareförbundet and others* [2007] ECR I-11767, opinion by Advocate General Mengozzi, § 77.

> right to strike being, in that connection, the method most regularly referred to. [In several footnotes the Advocate General referred to legislation in specific countries].[109]

This corresponds to the observation made before when addressing the question why substantiated references to national constitutional traditions have diminished. This does not, however, mean that the references have become irrelevant or vanished entirely, because that is not the only purpose for relying on references to the Member States.

References to the Member States are also used to solve interpretative problems that arise concerning rights that have already been recognized or that have been laid down in the Charter.[110] In *Booker Aquaculture*, for example, the question was whether a right to compensation existed for the destruction of fish.[111] The right to property had already been recognized on earlier occasions and the question as the right to compensation for the destruction of fish fell within its scope. Advocate General Mischo referred to some Member States and concluded that there was 'no constitutional principle common to the laws of the Member States'.[112] In *DEB*, the CJEU and Advocate General Mengozzi were trying to find an answer to the question whether Article 47 of the Charter included a right to legal aid for legal persons as well.[113] In answering that question they included a reference to a few Member States in order to show that no such common principle could be found. The final conclusion was that such a right was not necessarily excluded from the scope of Article 47 of the Charter. These two examples show that the references to Member States can still have a relevant function and the fact that it is also used for interpretative problems concerning the Charter indicates that in the future they might continue to play a role.

A final purpose of relying on references to Member States is to check the state of affairs in the Member States and thus to support an evolutive interpretation. As will be discussed in the section on evolutive interpretation this happens on a rather

---

109 C-341/05, *Laval un Partneri Ltd v. Svenska Byggnadsarbetareförbundet and others* [2007] ECR I-11767, opinion by Advocate General Mengozzi, § 77.

110 See for example: C-20/00, *Booker Aquacultur Ltd v. The Scottish Ministers* [2003] ECR I-07411; C-303/05, *Advocaten voor de Wereld VZW v. Leden van de Ministerraad* [2007] ECR I-03633; C-279/09, *DEB Deutsche Energiehandels- und Beratungsgesellschaft mbH v. Bundesrepublik Deutschland* [2010].

111 C-20/00, *Booker Aquacultur Ltd v. The Scottish Ministers* [2003] ECR I-07411, Opinion by Advocate General Mischo, § 119-124.

112 C-20/00, *Booker Aquacultur Ltd v. The Scottish Ministers* [2003] ECR I-07411, opinion by Advocate General Mischo, § 123-124.

113 C-279/09, *DEB Deutsche Energiehandels- und Beratungsgesellschaft mbH v. Bundesrepublik Deutschland* [2010].

small scale, but there are some examples of this purpose of comparative interpretation.[114] This will be discussed in more detail when dealing with evolutive interpretation, in section 13.4.1, but it is important to realize that this is one of the purposes of comparative references to the Member States as well.

A final question in this context that helps to shed light on the role of the references to Member States is whether the references have been used as the sole argument pleading for a specific interpretative conclusion or whether they have been used in conjunction with other arguments. In the majority of the cases in which either the CJEU or the Advocate General (or both) refer to Member States the outcome of that reference is supported by other arguments.[115] In most cases this other argument consists of a reference to the ECHR and its case law.[116] Only in some cases, mainly older cases, did the reference to the Member States seem to be the decisive argument.[117] The fact that these references are mainly used to support a specific argument is understandable, because both are placed on an equal footing with the ECHR in Article 6 TEU.

114 C-122/99, *D and Kingdom of Sweden v. Council of the European Union* [2001] ECR I-04319; C-117/01, *K.B. v National Health Service Pensions Agency and Secretary of State for Health* [2004] ECR I-00541; C-249/96, *Lisa Jacqueline Grant v. South-West Trains Ltd* [1998] ECR I-00621.

115 See for example: C-341/05, *Laval un Partneri Ltd v. Svenska Byggnadsarbetareförbundet and others* [2007] ECR I-11767, Opinion by Advocate General Mengozzi, § 77; C-20/00, *Booker Aquacultur Ltd v. The Scottish Ministers* [2003] ECR I-07411, Opinion by Advocate General Mischo, § 104-132; C-122/99, *D and Kingdom of Sweden v. Council of the European Union* [2001] ECR I-04319, where the references are supported by textual interpretation, § 31 and Opinion by Advocate General Mischo who supports the references to teleological interpretation, § 51; C-249/96, *Lisa Jacqueline Grant v. South-West Trains Ltd* [1998] ECR I-00621, § 36; C-117/01, *K.B. v National Health Service Pensions Agency and Secretary of State for Health* [2004] ECR I-00541, Opinion by Ruiz-Jarabo Colomer § 27-29.

116 C-341/05, *Laval un Partneri Ltd v. Svenska Byggnadsarbetareförbundet and others* [2007] ECR I-11767, Opinion by Advocate General Mengozzi, § 77; C-20/00, *Booker Aquacultur Ltd v. The Scottish Ministers* [2003] ECR I-07411, Opinion by Advocate General Mischo, § 104-132; C- 249/96, *Lisa Jacqueline Grant v. South-West Trains Ltd* [1998] ECR I-00621, § 36; C-117/01, *K.B. v National Health Service Pensions Agency and Secretary of State for Health* [2004] ECR I-00541, Opinion by Ruiz-Jarabo Colomer § 27-29.

117 C-17/74, *Transocean Marine Paint Association v. Commission of the European Communities* [1974] 01063, Opinion by Advocate General Warner; 155/79, *AM & S Europe Limited v. Commission of the European Communities* [1982] ECR 01575; C-168/91, *Christos Konstantinidis v. Stadt Altensteig – Standesamt and Landratsamt Calw – Ordnungsamt* [1993] ECR I-01191, Opinion by Advocate General Jacobs; C-46/87 *Hoechst AG v. Commission of the European Communities* [1989] ECR 02859; C-122/99, *D and Kingdom of Sweden v. Council of the European Union* [2001] ECR I-04319.

13.2.2.6 Common Traditions?

Several questions concerning the references to national constitutional traditions have already been answered in the above, namely both as regards the basis of and justification for using these references, and as regards the way in which the Court and the Advocates General express these references. An important question that has been identified in the theoretical chapter that still needs to be answered, is how these references are used. It has become clear from the analysis so far that when reference is made to the Member States, this is always done to establish a common constitutional tradition; no references to individual Member States have been found without these references being part of the search for common constitutional traditions. Against that background, it is particularly interesting to know if the CJEU is really looking for a 'common' tradition, i.e. to some kind of consensus within the European Union. Indeed, the term 'common' would seem to imply that the sought principle must be recognized in each Member State. The question is whether that is possible in the current European Union with its 27 members.[118] In a Union of this size, if a real common tradition can be found at all, such commonality will probably only exist on a very general level – as soon as more concrete elements of a certain right are concerned, opinions and laws will probably differ. Thus, even if a real common approach would be sought for, finding it would not provide much guidance as to the actual meaning and scope of the right at issue. It is thus unlikely that absolute unanimity among the Member States is intended when reference is made to 'common traditions'.

Leaving unanimity aside, however, the question still is when the CJEU considers a certain tradition sufficiently 'common' as to warrant a specific right to be recognized as part of the general principles of EU law. That is rather hard to distil from the reasoning in the CJEU's cases, since the Court only refers to Member States law in a rather abstract fashion. As has been explained before, however, the opinions of the Advocates General might be helpful in this respect. In the case of *Orkem* it became clear, for example, that the Court could not find a common principle or right not to incriminate oneself in competition proceedings, but it did not explain the basis for this conclusion.[119] The opinion of Advocate General Darmon does shed some light on this finding by the Court. In his opinion he discussed all Member States, painting a rather diverse picture. The Advocate General mentioned that in only two (of the then 12) Member States the right not to incriminate oneself was available in com-

---

118 The Advocate General in *AM & S* also refers to this practical problem: C-155/79, *AM & S Europe Limited v. Commission of the European Communities* [1982] ECR 01575, p. 1651 Opinion by Advocate General Slynn, p. 1650.

119 C-374/87, *Orkem v. Commission of the European Communities* [1989] ECR 03283, § 29.

petition cases. The conclusion from this legal mosaic, as he called it, was according to him that a right not to incriminate oneself could be regarded as a 'general' principle (of Community law). The analysis in the view of Advocate General Darmon, however, showed that the general principle found among the Member States was 'not of such "force" that it cannot be excluded in an area such as competition law'.[120] Thus, the framing of the conclusions reached by the Court and the Advocate General is different, but in substance they both disclose that the CJEU will not accept the existence of a common tradition when there is too much diversity in the national law on a certain issue.

Although this much may be clear, this does not yet answer the question as to how much consensus is needed for a common tradition to be found. Indeed, the Court appears to be very vague on this, the same lack of clarity as to the proper standard of consensus being visible not only in *Orkem*, but also in other cases. In *D*, for instance, the CJEU likewise concluded that, despite developments in an increasing number of Member States, there was still too much diversity, so no common principle could be found.[121] Again it was not clear what would have been necessary for a common tradition to arise.

Perhaps the CJEU does not even want to set a standard for consensus. One of the Advocates General in *AM & S* refers to a report from another CJEU-judge on interpretation methods by the CJEU. In this report by Judge Kutscher he states that:

> ... it [the CJEU] is not obliged to take the minimum which the national solutions have in common, or their arithmetic mean or solution produced by a majority of the legal systems as the basis of its decision. The Court has to weigh up and evaluate the particular problem and search for the best and most appropriate solution.[122]

Thus, the CJEU does not necessarily look for a 'common' solution, but rather for a solution it considers *appropriate*.[123] Advocate General Slynn in *AM* & S likewise stressed that unanimity was not required; a 'widely accepted' principle, even if only a very broad principle, may 'be found to be part of Community law'.[124] In his view, the CJEU must then decide how this principle works most appropriately in the Com-

120 C-374/87, *Orkem v. Commission of the European Communities* [1989] ECR 03283, Opinion by Advocate General Darmon, § 122.

121 C-122/99, *D and Kingdom of Sweden v. Council of the European Union* [2001] ECR I-04319, § 35-36.

122 C-155/79, *AM & S Europe Limited v. Commission of the European Communities* [1982] ECR 01575, p. 1649, Opinion by Advocate General Slynn.

123 See also: Lenaerts (2003), p. 883; Hilf(1986), p. 563; Kakouris (1994); Wasensteiner (2004), p. 35; Šišková (2008), p. 9.

124 C-155/79, *AM & S Europe Limited v. Commission of the European Communities* [1982] ECR 01575, p. 1650.

munity context.[125] Advocate General Warner has made a similar argument indicating that differences between Member States are not an insurmountable obstacle for establishing a common principle.[126] Nevertheless, if one considers the abovementioned reasoning of the CJEU in *D* or in *Orkem*, it becomes clear that at a certain point differences become fatal. It is understandable that the Court does not indicate when this point has been reached, since doing so would be difficult if not impossible – the degree of consensus required will obviously depend on the legal landscape in each individual case and on the perceived appropriateness of reaching a certain outcome. If, however, the reasoning of the CJEU was more explicit in this respect, perhaps some clues could be distilled and the transparency of the use of the method could be improved.

As has been established in the theoretical analysis, legal commentaries have likewise provided only limited guidance on this point. Legal commentators have made clear that unanimity or a majority is not required, but it remains obscure what is sufficient to constitute a 'common tradition'. HILF has argued that there is no standard solution in cases where no common principle can be found. The question will be whether a certain solution 'conforms to the aims and structure'[127] of the EU.[128] In this sense, teleological interpretation plays a role in this context as well.[129]

A separate question is at what level a common principle needs to be found. Is it sufficient that a broad and rather abstract legal concept is recognized by all Member States, or is it necessary that agreement or a trend is found on a more concrete level? Usually, it will be much more difficult to find a common approach on a concrete level, because at that level differences in form and practice might start to play a role. Has any indication been given by the CJEU? No, the Court has not provided any clues, but, once again, one of the Advocates General has. In his opinion in *AM&S*, Advocate General Slynn argued that consensus on the level of principle is sufficient:

> The fact that proceedings in one Member State may be criminal, in others civil, that judicial procedures differ, that for historical reasons different practices are adopted, different conditions apply, makes divergences inevitable. In my opinion, what has to be looked for is a general principle, even if broadly expressed. If that is widely accepted then it may, if relevant, be found to be part of Community law. It is then for the Court to declare how that principle is worked out in the best and most appropriate way, ..., in the context of Community pro-

---

125 C-155/79, *AM & S Europe Limited v. Commission of the European Communities* [1982] ECR 01575, p. 1650.

126 C-155/79, *AM & S Europe Limited v. Commission of the European Communities* [1982] ECR 01575, p. 1632, Opinion by Advocate General Warner.

127 Hilf (1986), p. 563.

128 Lenaerts (2003), p. 887.

129 See also: Lenaerts (2003), p. 879.

> ceedings. Nor is the fact that in some Member States the general principle may have been modified or excluded, in certain contexts covered by legislation, fatal to the existence of that principle.[130]

Accordingly, the fact that at a more concrete level Member States differ is not fatal to finding a common principle according to this statement. The broad principle should thus be recognized by the Member States, but *how* this recognition is framed in legal terms is not relevant.

The question when one can speak of common constitutional traditions can thus only be answered in the extreme situations when there is either no unanimity at all, or when such unanimity obviously exists. In all situations lying between these extremes, the case law does not provide any guidance on the question when one can speak of common constitutional traditions. It is suggested that differences at a concrete level do not prevent the existence of a common principle at a more abstract level. But the question when differences become fatal for finding a common tradition cannot be answered on the basis of the case law analysis undertaken in the context of this thesis.

13.2.2.7 Material

Discussions on comparative interpretation not only focus on the question whether this type of reasoning is justified. The practical side has received much attention as well.[131] The main questions in this respect concern the origin of the material (who supplies the comparative material?) and what kind of comparative material is taken into account. On both questions some indicative answers are provided by the judgments of the Court and by the opinions by the Advocates General.

The first source of information that is identified in the case law is the parties to a case. In *Booker Aquaculture* Advocate General Mischo explicitly indicated that one of the parties had provided references to national constitutional traditions:[132]

> Booker states that the constitutional texts of the Member States, which it reproduces in an annex to its observations, would enable it to obtain the payment of compensation for all or

130 Opinion by Advocate General Slynn in C-155/79, *AM & S Europe Limited v. Commission of the European Communities* [1982] ECR 01575, p. 1650.

131 See 6.1.6.2.

132 C-20/00, *Booker Aquacultur Ltd v. The Scottish Ministers* [2003] ECR I-07411, Opinion by Advocate General Mischo. See also: C-155/79, *AM & S Europe Limited v. Commission of the European Communities* [1982] ECR 01575; C-341/06, *Chronopost SA and La Poste v. Union française de l'express (UFEX) and Others* [2008] ECR I-04777 in which Advocate General Sharpston criticized the parties for referring to too few Member States.

part of the losses it has suffered in practically all of the Member States of the Community, except for the United Kingdom.[133]

The Advocate General went on to discuss some of the Member States mentioned in the comparison provided by *Booker*, but he did so in a critical manner. The Advocate General in the end did not reach the same conclusion as the party did who supplied the material. In *Orkem* Advocate General Darmon also indicated that the comparative information in that case was derived from the written submissions by the parties.[134] In the view of the Advocate General in *Orkem*, the parties used this comparison only to support their own conclusion. Of course, that is a quite natural attitude of parties in a legal process, but he added that the parties, invoking these references, used them to find what they 'had decided to find'.[135] This statement seems to imply that the comparative overview provided was not entirely objective.

This implication touches upon an important question that should be addressed, namely when comparative references are provided by the parties can they be considered sufficiently objective and who ensures their correctness? The two examples above show a critical attitude by the Advocates General towards this material. That attitude ensures a more objective approach towards the conclusion drawn from the different materials. In *AM & S*, a case that was elaborately dealt with in section 13.2.2.2, Advocate General Slynn commented on the information available as well, this time on the issue of correctness. He admitted that he felt some hesitation in referring to the report provided by the parties, since there had been some discussion at the hearing on the correctness of the described legal situation in some Member States.[136] The Advocate General explained that this was not fatal for the usefulness of the material, but that it indicated the difficulty of describing in detail the situation in Member States while, at the same time, trying to distil a common principle.[137] The critical approach that is visible in the opinions of the Advocates General is a necessary safeguard that helps to ensure the objectivity of the comparative references.

---

133 C-20/00, *Booker Aquacultur Ltd v. The Scottish Ministers* [2003] ECR I-07411, Opinion by Advocate General Mischo, § 116.

134 C-374/87, *Orkem v. Commission of the European Communities* [1989] ECR 03283, Opinion by Advocate General Darmon, § 97.

135 C-374/87, *Orkem v. Commission of the European Communities* [1989] ECR 03283, Opinion by Advocate General Darmon, § 97.

136 C-, *AM & S Europe Limited v. Commission of the European Communities* [1982] ECR 01575, p. 1651 Opinion by Advocate General Slynn. In this case the CJEU quite exceptionally reopened the procedure to hear the parties' view on the national constitutional traditions. See Lenaerts (2003), p. 875.

137 C-155/79, *AM & S Europe Limited v. Commission of the European Communities* [1982] ECR 01575, p. 1651 Opinion by Advocate General Slynn, p. 1651.

Other possible sources of comparative studies have not really been explicitly mentioned in the case law itself. One main source, however, appears to be the comparative knowledge which the CJEU or the Advocate General are able to generate themselves. In an older case, *Vivien Prais*, Advocate General Warner complained that the parties had provided too little information.[138] The Advocate General indicated that information had only been provided on the United Kingdom and therefore he had to find information on the other states himself.[139] This research apparently had its limits, since the Advocate General was careful to introduce his findings by stating: 'From such researches as I have been able to make, it appears to be as follows.'[140] While it is understandable that an Advocate General cannot undertake a very thorough analysis of all Member States, especially considering the number of Member States in the present European Union, it is not very convincing if the materials are only based on what the Advocate General could find and understand.

Situations like this one will, probably, no longer occur nowadays, since the CJEU now has a Research and Documentation Unit.[141] At the request of the Court or the Advocate General this unit can undertake comparative research.[142] The Advocates General will therefore no longer be forced to do comparative research themselves or to depend entirely on the information provided by the parties. In the case of *Laval*,[143] for example, the comparative information appears to have been provided by this unit. Advocate General Mengozzi in his opinion to the case referred in general to the situation in the Member States, mentioning specific Member States in the footnotes.[144] No explanation has been given for the origin of this information,[145] as is good practice if the information has been supplied by the parties; hence the conclusion might be that it has been supplied by the Research unit of the Court.

138 C-130/75, *Vivien Prais v. Council of the European Communities* [1976] ECR 01589.

139 C-130/75, *Vivien Prais v. Council of the European Communities* [1976] ECR 01589, Opinion by Advocate General Warner, p. 1605.

140 C-130/75, *Vivien Prais v. Council of the European Communities* [1976] ECR 01589, Opinion by Advocate General Warner, p. 1605.

141 See Singer & Engel (2007).

142 Singer & Engel (2007), p. 508.

143 C-341/05, *Laval un Partneri Ltd v. Svenska Byggnadsarbetareförbundet and others* [2007] ECR I-11767, opinion by Advocate General Mengozzi. See also: C-117/01, *K.B. v National Health Service Pensions Agency and Secretary of State for Health* [2004] ECR I-00541; C-117/01, *K.B. v National Health Service Pensions Agency and Secretary of State for Health* [2004] ECR I-00541, Opinion by Advocate General Ruiz-Jarabo Colomer.

144 C-341/05, *Laval un Partneri Ltd v. Svenska Byggnadsarbetareförbundet and others* [2007] ECR I-11767, opinion by Advocate General Mengozzi, § 77.

145 See Lenaerts who states that this research 'rarely transpire directly in the reasoning'. Lenaerts (2003), p. 875.

It is clear that the existence of a Research and Documentation Unit may prove to be an important factor in professionalizing comparative references. It ensures that references are not tainted by the position of the provider of information in the legal process, since the sources and materials are put forward by an independent unit. Moreover, with the expansion of the EU, having a specialized unit will help to ensure that all Member States are taken into consideration. Private parties or the Advocates General will, probably, be much more hampered by language and time concerns. This presumption that the existence of a Research and Documentation Unit enhances the quality of the references to Member States does not always hold. In a recent case, the CJEU explicitly referred back to the Advocate General to support the conclusion that no common principle can be found. In his opinion, Advocate General Mengozzi, supports this conclusion by referring to only four Member States in a Union of 27.[146] He acknowledges that this is not an exhaustive overview, but considers it sufficient for the conclusion that no common principle can be found. It is not really convincing that such a conclusion can be drawn on the basis of only four Member States, perhaps the situation in all other Member States points in the direction of a common principle. This example indicates that this is still a matter for concern.

One last possibility for the Court to assemble relevant materials is by asking the European Commission to undertake a comparative study.[147] The Commission can perform this study either as one of the parties to the proceedings or as an *amicus curiae*.[148] With the creation of the Research and Documentation unit one may wonder when there is still a need to ask the Commission for a comparative study. This question is clearly difficult to answer on the basis of case law analysis alone.

The second question to be addressed in this section concerns the *kind* of material that is taken into consideration. The reference to *constitutional traditions* already reveals the kind of information the CJEU takes into account when trying to establish a common principle, namely the constitutions or, more generally, the constitutional principles of the Member States. The CJEU does not refer to the kind of materials it takes into consideration in finding out what these constitutions contain. However, the Advocates General often mention in passing the kind of materials that played a role in their comparisons. In *Laval*, for example, Advocate General Mengozzi made reference in a footnote to constitutional provisions of the different Member States.[149] In *AM & S*, Advocate General Slynn indicated that legislation, case decisions and

146 C-279/09, *DEB Deutsche Energiehandels- und Beratungsgesellschaft mbH v. Bundesrepublik Deutschland* [2010], Opinion by Advocate General Mengozzi, § 76-78.

147 Lenaerts (2003), p. 875; Hilf (1986), p. 564-565.

148 Lenaerts (2003), p. 875.

149 C-341/05, *Laval un Partneri Ltd v. Svenska Byggnadsarbetareförbundet and others* [2007] ECR I-11767, opinion by Advocate General Mengozzi, footnote 31-32-33.

opinions of academic authors have been taken into consideration.[150] From the *Orkem* judgment it becomes clear that these same elements, but also draft legislation, had been considered in the comparison.[151] Thus, the category of materials taken into consideration is generally rather wide and undefined.[152] This does leave a lot of flexibility to the Court, but for a good comparative study to be made, it is at the least important that the same or equivalent materials are taken into account for each individual Member State that is being studied. Unfortunately, it is not clear if this is really done in practice by either the CJEU research unit or the parties providing comparative overviews.

13.2.2.8 Conclusion

The different elements mentioned in the introduction to this section (section 13.2.1) have been addressed as far as possible on the basis of the information provided in the judgments of the CJEU and the opinions of the Advocates General. Particularly the discussions on the way in which the CJEU and the Advocates General refer to national constitutional traditions have provided interesting insights. The CJEU prefers not to refer to national traditions in an explicit manner at all and, if it ever refers to them, it prefers to do so in a rather abstract fashion. The Advocates General are usually more inclined to refer to national traditions and they tend to do so in a more concrete manner, often by referring to individual Member States. What is perhaps most striking about this, is that still most authors claim that comparative interpretation plays an important role for the Court. In their view such comparisons take place more indirectly. It can be submitted, however, that if such comparisons take place and if they affect the reasoning of the Court, that should be done explicitly.[153] Especially in a field where the CJEU already is not very willing to elaborate on the concepts in question, namely the scope of fundamental rights.

From cases like *D v Council* and *Orkem* it has appeared that the references to national traditions indeed do play some role. The Court in those cases attached quite some weight to the fact that no common principle could be found, implying that in some cases these traditions can play a strong role in the reasoning of the Court. In the majority of the cases, however, it has been found that the references to the Member States play a supportive role often together with a reference to the ECHR.

---

150 C--155/79, *AM & S Europe Limited v. Commission of the European Communities* [1982] ECR 01575, p. 1651 Opinion by Advocate General Slynn, p. 1651.

151 C-374/87, *Orkem v. Commission of the European Communities* [1989] ECR 03283, Opinion by Advocate General Darmon, § 97-125.

152 See also: Lutzhoeft (2009), p. 44.

153 See also De Witte (1999), p. 882.

It has been shown that the frequency of substantive references in order to establish a common principle has diminished. Several reasons have been provided, one of them being that the Charter of Fundamental Rights provides a codification of those common principles. Still, in certain situations references to the Member States can be useful, and have proven to be useful, to solve an interpretative problem. The value of these references has therefore not been lost with the drafting of the Charter, but the purpose of relying on these references has changed. Instead of serving as a basis for establishing a fundamental right, they now provide help to find an answer to 'common' interpretative problems. In addition, the references are sometimes used to support an evolutive interpretation, but only in a limited type of case, as will be shown in section 13.4.1.

An area for improvement of the Court's reasoning relates to the question when one can speak of a common constitutional tradition. It would provide much insight into the use of this component of comparative interpretation if the CJEU or its Advocates General would be more open about the existence of a common constitutional tradition. There is no need to provide an exact standard, but if they would show more insight into the material taken into consideration for the analysis and the result of the analysis, this would already provide more insight into the existence of a common constitutional tradition. A related concern that still needs to be kept in mind when referring explicitly to a number of Member States is that at least a representative number of Member States is taken into consideration. Basing a firm conclusion on only four out of 27 Member States is not a convincing form of relying on common constitutional traditions.

13.2.3 Role of the ECHR

Apart from the role of national constitutional traditions in the comparative case law of the CJEU, an important source of inspiration is provided by the European Convention of Human Rights and the interpretation of the Convention as laid down in the judgments of the European Court of Human Rights.[154] One of the earliest references to the ECHR was made in the case of *Rutili*,[155] where the CJEU held that certain limitations on the powers of Member States were regarded as:

> [S]pecific manifestations of the more general principle, enshrined in Articles 8, 9, 10, 11 of the European Convention for the Protection of Human Rights and Fundamental Freedoms,

154 Lawson (2009) argues that the ECtHR is starting to taking more and more account of EU law and CJEU judgments, but it is not yet as widespread as the reliance from Luxembourg on Strassbourg.

155 C-36/75, *Roland Rutili v. Ministre de l'intérieur* [1975] ECR 01219.

> signed in Rome on 4 November 1950 and ratified by all Member States, and in Article 2 of Protocol No 4 of the same Convention ... .[156]

The CJEU here thus connected the fundamental rights protection within the EU with the protection under the ECHR. In later cases this became more explicit and more prominent and in many cases on fundamental rights at least reference is made to the ECHR.[157] A reference to the ECHR has been included in the standard phrase the CJEU commonly uses when referring to fundamental rights protection within the EU:

---

156 C-36/75, *Roland Rutili v. Ministre de l'intérieur* [1975] ECR 01219, § 32.

157 See for example: C-44/79, *Liselotte Hauer v. Land Rheinland-Pfalz* [1979] ECR 03727; C-222/84, *Marguerite Johnston v. Chief Constable of the Royal Ulster Constabulary* [1986] ECR 01651; C-222/86, *Union nationale des entraîneurs et cadres techniques professionnels du football (Unectef) v. Georges Heylens and others* [1987] ECR 04097; C-46/87 *Hoechst AG v. Commission of the European Communities* [1989] ECR 02859; C-260/89, *Elliniki Radiophonia Tiléorassi (ERT) AE and Panellinia Omospondia Syllogon Prossopikou v. Dimotiki Etairia Pliroforissis and Sotirios Kouvelas and Nicolaos Avdellas and others* [1991] ECR I-02925; C-415/93, *Union royale belge des sociétés de football association ASBL and others v. Jean-Marc Bosman* [1995] ECR I-04921; C13/94, *P v. S and Cornwall County Council* [1996] ECRI-02143; C-74/95, *Criminal Proceedings against X* [1996] ECR I-06609; C-185/95, *Baustahlgewebe GmbH v. Commission of the European Communities* [1998] ECR I-08417; C-299/95, *Friedrich Kremzow v Republik Österreich* [1997] I-02629; C-368/95, *Vereinigte Familiapress Zeitungsverlags- und vertriebs GmbH v Heinrich Bauer Verlag* [1997] ECR I-03689; C-249/96, *Lisa Jacqueline Grant v. South-West Trains Ltd* [1998] ECR I-00621; C-309/96, *Daniele Annibaldi v. Sindaco del Comune di Guidonia and Presidente Regione Lazio* [1997] ECR I-07493; C-185/97, *Belinda Jane Coote v. Granada Hospitality Ltd.* [1998] ECR I-05199; C-7/98, *Dieter Krombach v. André Bamberski* [2000] ECR I-01935; C-17/98, *Emesa Sugar (Free Zone) NV v. Aruba* [2000] ECR I-00665; C-274/99, *Bernard Connolly v. Commission of the European Communities* [2001] ECR I-01611; C-50/00, *Unión de Pequeños Agricultores (UPA) v. Council of the European Union* [2002] ECR I-06677; C-60/00, *Mary Carpenter v. Secretary of State for the Home Department* [2002] ECR I-06279; C-94/00, *Roquette Frères SA v. Directeur général de la concurrence, de la consommation et de la répression des fraudes, and Commission of the European Communities* [2002] ECR I-09011; C-112/00, *Eugen Schmidberger, Internationale Transporte und Planzüge v. Republik Österreich* [2003] ECR I-05659; C-465/00, *Rechnungshof v Österreichischer Rundfunk and Others* [2003] ECR I-04989; C-117/01, *K.B. v National Health Service Pensions Agency and Secretary of State for Health* [2004] ECR I-00541; C-36/02, *Omega Spielhallen- und Automatenaufstellungs-GmbH v. Oberbürgermeisterin der Bundesstadt Bonn* [2004] ECR I-09609; C-263/02, *Commission of the European Communities v. Jégo-Quéré & Cie SA* [2004] ECR I-03425; C-540/03, *European Parliament v Council of the European Union* [2006] ECR I-05769; C-411/04, *Salzgitter Mannesmann GmbH v. Commission of the European Communities*, [2007] ECR I-00959; C-436/04, *Criminal proceedings against Leopold Henri Van Esbroeck* [2006] ECR I-02333; C-303/05, *Advocaten voor de Wereld VZW v. Leden van de Ministerraad* [2007] ECR I-03633; C-370/05, *Criminal proceedings against Uwe Kay Festersen* [2007] ECR I-01129; C-432/05, *Unibet (London) Ltd and Unibet (International) Ltd v. Justitiekanslern* [2007] ECR I-02271; C-341/06, *Chronopost SA and La Poste v. Union française de l'express (UFEX) and Others* [2008] ECR I-04777; C-450/06, *Varec SA v. Belgian State* [2008] ECR I-00581; C-14/07, *Ingenieurbüro Michael Weiss und Partner GbR v. Industrie- und Handelskammer Berlin* [2008] ECR I-03367; C-308/07, *Koldo Gorostiaga Atxalandabaso v. European Parliament* [2009] ECR I-01059.

> [F]undamental rights form an integral part of the general principles of law, the observance of which it [the CJEU] ensures. For that purpose, the Court draws inspiration from the constitutional traditions common to the Member States and from the guidelines supplied by international treaties for the protection of human rights on which the Member States have collaborated or of which they are signatories. The European Convention for the Protection of Human Rights and Fundamental Freedoms of 4 November 1950 has *special significance* in that respect (emphasis added).[158]

The ECHR thus has a special status when it comes to the interpretation of fundamental rights by the CJEU. The CJEU refers to it as a source of inspiration, but the analysis below will address the question whether that really is the purpose of referring to the ECHR and the ECtHR case law.

Several questions will be addressed in this analysis on the role of the ECHR in comparative references by the CJEU. Several explanations on the reason why the CJEU relies on the ECHR and its case law were discussed in the theoretical analysis, but the question is whether the CJEU in its case law provides any indication on this reason as well. Furthermore, it should be addressed how references to the ECHR feature in the reasoning. How extensive are these references to the ECHR and its case law? And are they used as support in addition to other arguments or are they used as a decisive argument in the reasoning? It is also important to realize for which purpose they are used – as a source of inspiration or do they play a different role? In addition, the question whether the theoretical distinction made between external and internal comparative interpretation is visible in the reasoning with regard to the ECHR and whether the CJEU attaches any consequences to this distinction should be addressed. The previous section revealed a strong difference between the approach of the CJEU and its Advocates General. The question is whether the situation is the same in the context of references to the ECHR. Finally, the practical aspect of who collects the materials should be addressed.

An important question that warrants attention is why the CJEU has adopted this approach, i.e. what explanation had been given by the CJEU for this special status of the ECHR. The statement from *Rutili*,[159] cited above, suggests that the fact that this treaty has been ratified by all Member States is an important reason to take special note of this treaty. This seems to be the most important justification provided until the codification of the special status of the ECHR in the EU Treaty, as explained in the introductory Chapter 3. Of course, the fact that a treaty has been ratified by all Member States is an important indication that these rights are widely supported

---

158 C-309/96, *Daniele Annibaldi v. Sindaco del Comune di Guidonia and Presidente Regione Lazio* [1997] ECR I-07493, § 12, but a version of this phrase is visible in many judgments.

159 C-36/75, *Roland Rutili v. Ministre de l'intérieur* [1975] ECR 01219.

by the Member States. That does not necessarily mean, however, that respecting that treaty (*in casu* the European Convention) involves incorporating so much of the case law on that treaty literally.

In cases after the codification of the special status of the ECHR, the CJEU often refers to this codification if it mentions the relevance of the ECHR as a comparative source:

> [A]rticle 8 of the Convention for the Protection of Human Rights and Fundamental Freedoms ..., which is among the fundamental rights which according to the Court's settled case-law, restated by the Preamble to the Single European Act and by Article 6(2) EU, are protected in Community law.[160]

Even in the light of the codification of the special status of the ECHR it is still warranted to take a critical look at the extent of the references to the ECHR.

An important aspect to further the discussion is how the CJEU refers to the ECHR and ECtHR. Specifically relevant in this regard is the extent to which references are made to the ECHR and ECtHR. In some cases the reference does not go beyond the statement about the importance of the ECHR when interpreting fundamental rights, but in other cases the CJEU incorporates rather substantive references to the ECHR into its own judgments. Some examples may be mentioned to clarify this use of the Convention and the ECtHR's case law.

In some cases the CJEU only mentions that a certain right has been laid down in the ECHR, like in the case of *Jégo- Quéré*.[161] Here the CJEU held that:

> It should be noted that individuals are entitled to effective judicial protection of the rights the derive from the Community legal order, and the right to such protection is one of the general principles of law stemming from the constitutional traditions common to the Member States. That rights has also been enshrined in Articles 6 and 13 of the ECHR [reference to CJEU cases].[162]

In the remainder of the judgment the CJEU did not at all refer to the ECHR, so the reference was only made to indicate that a certain right exists in the ECHR. Given the special status of the ECHR as recognized in the Treaties, these references seem understandable as they provide extra support for the recognition of a certain right. The short references, however, do not provide any information on the scope and

160 See for example: C-60/00, *Mary Carpenter v. Secretary of State for the Home Department* [2002] ECR I-06279, § 41.

161 C-263/02, *Commission of the European Communities v. Jégo-Quéré & Cie SA* [2004] ECR I-03425. See also: C-74/95, *Criminal Proceedings against X* [1996] ECR I-06609, § 25.

162 C-263/02, *Commission of the European Communities v. Jégo-Quéré & Cie SA* [2004] ECR I-03425, § 29.

meaning of the right in question. In order to draw any convincing conclusions on the question whether a right has been violated in a certain case, like the right to effective judicial protection, the scope of that right should have been made clear. Only then would a proper discussion on the alleged violation be possible.

In quite a number of cases the CJEU refers to more than just a provision in the ECHR. Such references include interpretations given to the ECHR in the judgments of the Strasbourg Court.[163] The case of *Chronopost* is a good and elaborate example of the approach taken by the CJEU.[164] In this appeal case the CJEU had to decide whether Chronopost – a French postal company, which had been accused of receiving state aid – received a fair trial, since one of the judges acting as a Judge-Rapporteur at the General Court had been Judge-Rapporteur and president in a Chamber dealing with a parallel case. The CJEU endeavoured to answer this question by starting off with a reference to Article 6 ECHR and some general comments on what the right to fair trial entails.[165] In this discussion on the meaning to the right to fair trial and impartiality of judges, the CJEU made reference to an ECHR judgment in the same way as it usually refers to CJEU judgments:[166]

163 See for example: C-13/94, *P v. S and Cornwall County Council* [1996] ECRI-02143; C-185/95, *Baustahlgewebe GmbH v. Commission of the European Communities* [1998] ECR I-08417; C-368/95, *Vereinigte Familiapress Zeitungsverlags- und vertriebs GmbH v Heinrich Bauer Verlag* [1997] ECR I-03689; C-249/96, *Lisa Jacqueline Grant v. South-West Trains Ltd* [1998] ECR I-00621; C-7/98, *Dieter Krombach v. André Bamberski* [2000] ECR I-01935; C-17/98, *Emesa Sugar (Free Zone) NV v. Aruba* [2000] ECR I-00665; C-274/99, *Bernard Connolly v. Commission of the European Communities* [2001] ECR I-01611; C-60/00, *Mary Carpenter v. Secretary of State for the Home Department* [2002] ECR I-06279; C-94/00, *Roquette Frères SA v. Directeur général de la concurrence, de la consommation et de la répression des fraudes, and Commission of the European Communities* [2002] ECR I-09011; C-465/00, *Rechnungshof v Österreichischer Rundfunk and Others* [2003] ECR I-04989; C-117/01, *K.B. v National Health Service Pensions Agency and Secretary of State for Health* [2004] ECR I-00541; C-540/03, *European Parliament v Council of the European Union* [2006] ECR I-05769; C-411/04, *Salzgitter Mannesmann GmbH v. Commission of the European Communities*, [2007] ECR I-00959; C-303/05, *Advocaten voor de Wereld VZW v. Leden van de Ministerraad* [2007] ECR I-03633; C-432/05, *Unibet (London) Ltd and Unibet (International) Ltd v. Justitiekanslern* [2007] ECR I-02271; C-341/06, *Chronopost SA and La Poste v. Union française de l'express (UFEX) and Others* [2008] ECR I-04777; C-450/06, *Varec SA v. Belgian State* [2008] ECR I-00581; C-14/07, *Ingenieurbüro Michael Weiss und Partner GbR v. Industrie- und Handelskammer Berlin* [2008] ECR I-03367; C-308/07, *Koldo Gorostiaga Atxalandabaso v. European Parliament* [2009] ECR I-01059; C-279/09, *DEB Deutsche Energiehandels- und Beratungsgesellschaft mbH v. Bundesrepublik Deutschland* [2010].

164 C-341/06, *Chronopost SA and La Poste v. Union française de l'express (UFEX) and Others* [2008] ECR I-04777.

165 C-341/06, *Chronopost SA and La Poste v. Union française de l'express (UFEX) and Others* [2008] ECR I-04777, § 44-46.

166 C-341/06, *Chronopost SA and La Poste v. Union française de l'express (UFEX) and Others* [2008] ECR I-04777, § 46.

> [T]here are two aspects to the requirement of impartiality: (i) the members of the tribunal themselves must be subjectively impartial, that is, none of its members must show bias or personal prejudice, there being a presumption of personal impartiality in the absence of evidence to the contrary; and (ii) the tribunal must be objectively impartial, that is to say, it must offer guarantees sufficient to exclude any legitimate doubt in this respect (see, to that effect, in particular, Eur. Court HR, *Fey v. Austria*, judgment of 24 February 1993, Series A no. 255-A, p. 12, § 28; *Findlay v. United Kingdom*, judgment of 25 February 1997, *Reports of Judgments and Decisions* 1997-I, p. 281, § 73; and *Forum Maritime S.A. v. Roumanie*, judgment of 4 October 2007, nos. 63610/00 and 38692/05, not yet published in the *Reports of Judgments and Decisions*).

The CJEU thus incorporated the Strasbourg approach to judicial impartiality without providing any 'translation' of this practice into the EU context. That is not necessarily problematic, but it is a rather striking characteristic of the relation between the CJEU and the ECHR. The CJEU refers to ECHR cases in the same way as to its own cases. They are simply included in the judgment and thereby become part and parcel of the precedents of the CJEU. Given that it is an entirely different court, judging cases in a very different context, references to the ECHR fall into the category of external comparative interpretation. In that context this appears to be a quite far-reaching approach, but that will be discussed in more detail below.

The CJEU in this case went even further, however, by looking at the organization of the judicial process at the ECHR in order to support their conclusion that *Chronopost* in this case did not receive an unfair trial:[167]

> It must also be observed that, under article 27(3) of the ECHR, when a case if referred to the Grand Chamber of the Court of Human Rights, on a referral following a Chamber's judgment, no Judge from the Chamber which rendered the judgment is to sit in the Grand Chamber, with the exception of the President of the Chamber and the Judge who sat in respect of the State Party concerned. The ECHR thus accepts that Judges who heard and determined the case initially may sit in another formation hearing and determining the same case again, and that that is not in itself incompatible with the requirements of a fair trial.[168]

Thus, even the way in which the ECtHR itself is organized provided an argument for the CJEU to conclude that the circumstances in the case at hand did not involve a violation of the right to a fair trial.

A similar approach is visible in the case of *Connolly*, where the CJEU had to decide whether disciplinary sanctions for an EU employee who published without permission a critical book on EU policy during his leave was contrary to the freedom

167 C-341/06, *Chronopost SA and La Poste v. Union française de l'express (UFEX) and Others* [2008] ECR I-04777, § 59-60.

168 C-341/05, *Laval un Partneri Ltd v. Svenska Byggnadsarbetareförbundet and others* [2007] ECR I-11767, § 59.

of expression.[169] A large part of the reasoning of the CJEU switched between the case law of the ECtHR and its own precedents as if they were one and the same court.[170] The CJEU adopts the approach by the ECtHR to the full extent, at least so it seems.

There are more cases in which this approach is visible.[171] Even in the case of the most elaborate references to the ECHR, ECtHR judgments are not discussed at great length. One author has noted that the CJEU 'rarely discusses the facts of those cases nor discusses the rational basis of those decisions'.[172] An explanation for this approach may be found in that, if the Court would engage in such a discussion on the rational basis of the ECtHR judgments, this would lead to a much more fundamental discussion on the scope of fundamental rights. It would make it much more obvious why certain rights are protected in the EU and as a result provide more guidance to the Member States. Simultaneously, however, this might result in deviations between the Strasbourg and the Luxemburg case law.

In some cases, however, the CJEU has taken a different approach than Strasbourg. A clear example is the case of *Emesa Sugar*.[173] Sugar producer Emesa had requested to be granted the opportunity to respond to the Opinion of the Advocate General, relying on a judgment of the ECtHR in order to support that request.[174] In that case the ECtHR held that the impossibility of a Belgian national to respond to the submission of the *Procureur Général* resulted in a breach of Article 6 ECHR.[175] The CJEU emphasized the distinct nature of the judicial process at the Community level and the role of the Advocate General therein and concluded that this Strasbourg case law was not applicable to this situation.[176] The CJEU thus deliberately took a different approach than the ECtHR in this case, because of the specific nature of its own system. This is the most obvious example in which the two systems diverge on a certain issue. Why the CJEU adopted a diverging approach in specifically this case is not clear.

The discussion on the extent of the references to the ECHR and its case law indicate that these references play an important role in the reasoning of the CJEU.

169 C-274/99, *Bernard Connolly v. Commission of the European Communities* [2001] ECR I-01611.

170 C-274/99, *Bernard Connolly v. Commission of the European Communities* [2001] ECR I-01611, § 37-50.

171 Supra note 163.

172 Douglas-Scott (2006), p. 658.

173 C-17/98, *Emesa Sugar (Free Zone) NV v. Aruba* [2000] ECR I-00665. This case is used as an example in the literature. See Douglas-Scott 2006, p. 648.

174 ECtHR, *Vermeulen v. Belgium*, judgment of 20 February 1996, *Reports* 1996-I.

175 C-17/98, *Emesa Sugar (Free Zone) NV v. Aruba* [2000] ECR I-00665, § 5-6 referring to ECtHR, *Vermeulen v. Belgium*, judgment of 20 February 1996, *Reports* 1996-I.

176 C-17/98, *Emesa Sugar (Free Zone) NV v. Aruba* [2000] ECR I-00665, § 10-20.

The question is whether arguments based on the ECHR were used in addition to other arguments or whether these references are decisive for the CJEU's reasoning. The amount of cases where a substantive reference is made to the ECHR and its case law seem to indicate that these references play a decisive role.[177] Often when setting out the scope of a fundamental right reference is only made to the ECHR. A clear example of this phenomenon is the case of *Roquette Frères*, in which the CJEU determined that it had to review its own position on the scope of the protection of privacy afforded to business premises. The CJEU had established in *Hoechst* that the right to privacy and inviolability of the home could not be extended to legal persons. In *Roquette Frères* it had to revisit that position and the CJEU held that:

> For the purposes of determining the scope of that principle in relation to the protection of business premises, regard must be had to the case-law of the European Court of Human Rights subsequent to the judgment in *Hoechst*. According to that case-law, first, the protection of the home provided for in Article 8 of the ECHR may in certain circumstances be extended to cover such premises (see, in particular, the judgment of 16 April 2002 in *Colas Est and Others v. France*, not yet published in the *Reports of Judgments and Decisions*, § 41) and, second, the right of interference established by Article 8(2) of the ECHR 'might well be more far-reaching where professional or business activities or premises were involved than would otherwise be the case' (Niemietz v. Germany, cited above, § 31).[178]

No other arguments were presented to justify overruling the earlier judgment of the CJEU. Thus the case law of the ECtHR played a decisive role in the reasoning in this case. No questions were asked whether this development was in line with developments within the EU.

In other cases the CJEU refers to other arguments to support a conclusion and thus the ECHR in those cases plays a more supportive role.[179] A clear example of this supportive role of the ECHR is the case of *DEB*. The question was whether the right of legal persons to effective access to justice meant that legal persons should

177 See for example: C-274/99, *Bernard Connolly v. Commission of the European Communities* [2001] ECR I-01611; C-60/00, *Mary Carpenter v. Secretary of State for the Home Department* [2002] ECR I-06279; C-94/00, *Roquette Frères SA v. Directeur général de la concurrence, de la consommation et de la répression des fraudes, and Commission of the European Communities* [2002] ECR I-09011; C-465/00, *Rechnungshof v Österreichischer Rundfunk and Others* [2003] ECR I-04989; C-450/06, *Varec SA v. Belgian State* [2008] ECR I-00581; C-341/06, *Chronopost SA and La Poste v. Union française de l'express (UFEX) and Others* [2008] ECR I-04777.

178 C-94/00, *Roquette Frères SA v. Directeur général de la concurrence, de la consommation et de la répression des fraudes, and Commission of the European Communities* [2002] ECR I-09011, § 29.

179 See for example: C-249/96, *Lisa Jacqueline Grant v. South-West Trains Ltd* [1998] ECR I-00621; C-540/03, *European Parliament v Council of the European Union* [2006] ECR I-05769; C-436/04, *Criminal proceedings against Leopold Henri Van Esbroeck* [2006] ECR I-02333; C-279/09, *DEB Deutsche Energiehandels- und Beratungsgesellschaft mbH v. Bundesrepublik Deutschland* [2010].

be granted legal aid. In order to answer that question the CJEU relied, among others, upon textual arguments and arguments referring to both the Member States and the ECHR. Even though the references to the ECtHR play an important role, they are not solely decisive for the conclusion in this case, which was that granting legal aid to legal persons was not excluded from the right to effective access to justice.

In both situations, when the ECHR is used as a supportive reference or as a decisive reference, it is hard to deny the importance and prominence of the ECHR and its case law in the reasoning of the CJEU. Can the ECHR in those circumstances still be considered only a source of inspiration? The use of the ECHR by the CJEU goes beyond an inspirational use, because the judgments are invoked and referred to almost as if they are the CJEU's own. In many cases there is no 'translation' of the ECHR material to the EU context and thus to call it a source of inspiration would be an understatement. Looking at the different purposes identified in the theoretical analysis it can be assumed that the purpose of the CJEU of looking at the ECHR is to keep up with international (in this case European) standards.[180] The only peculiarity is that by doing this the CJEU does not keep its own fundamental rights law up to date, but often solely relies on external materials. Also different from the theoretical analysis is that the CJEU does seem to take the ECHR and its case law not only as persuasive, but almost as binding. Though there are of course exceptions, the references to the ECHR are taken so seriously and without much criticism that it seems to border on regarding them as binding. This is interesting given that the CJEU is not (yet) formally bound by the ECHR. It is even more interesting in light of the distinction between external and internal comparative interpretation.

The theoretical analysis presented a distinction between external and internal comparative interpretation.[181] According to that distinction references to the ECHR and its case law should be considered as external comparative interpretation, because the ECHR as a treaty originates from an organization external to the EU. It was also argued that a different or additional justification from the one provided for internal comparative interpretation could be warranted in the context of external comparative interpretation. The question at present is whether the CJEU acknowledges this distinction between internal and external comparative interpretation and whether it attaches any consequences relating to the justification for external references. There are hardly any indications that the CJEU seems to acknowledge the distinction between external and internal sources for comparative interpretation. The justification provided in *Rutili* that the ECHR had been ratified by all Member States does indicate that the CJEU was aware that it could not too easily conclude that the ECHR had some relevance. It would, however, be reading too much into this statement to conclude

180 See section 6.1.4. for a description of various purposes.
181 See section 6.1.3.

that this is an indication that the CJEU makes a distinction between external and internal sources of comparative interpretation. In light of this distinction the non-critical manner in which many judgments have been included in the reasoning of the CJEU is remarkable, as noted when discussing the purpose of referring to the ECHR as well. Are there sufficient reasons to justify this approach? At the beginning of this section some preliminary answers were provided, namely that the ECHR has been ratified by all Member States and that the special status of the ECHR has been codified. Given the analysis in the remainder of the section it is important to revisit the question. The fact that by codifying the role of the ECHR the Member States and the EU institutions accepted references to this specific external material is significant. This is significant, because this means that the EU legislator has approved the reference to this external source by the CJEU. It resembles the provision in the South African constitution that encourages the judges to look at (external) comparative materials. In addition several strategic factors have been discussed in the theoretical analysis to explain the reliance of the CJEU on the ECHR. The complex relationship between the EU, the ECHR and the Member States, the fact that the Member States can be held accountable in Strasbourg and the experience that the ECHR already has with fundamental rights protection in Europe are all factors explaining the strategic reliance of the CJEU on the ECtHR. Advocate General Ruiz-Jarabo Colomer in his opinion in *Advocaten voor de Wereld* addresses these strategic reasons for relying on the ECHR in a more covert way by indicating that:

> The protective role is exercised in three different spheres – national, Council of Europe and European Union – which are partly coextensive and, most importantly, are imbued with the same values. There are many points of intersection and overlapping is possible, but respect for other jurisdictions does not create any insurmountable problems where there is confidence that all parties exercise their jurisdiction while fully guaranteeing the system of coexistence. A dialogue between the constitutional courts of the European Union permits the foundations to be laid for a general discussion.
> Thus, ... the Court may refer if necessary, ... to the judgments of the European Court of Human Rights concerning ... .[182]

Advocate General Ruiz-Jarabo Colomer thus also stresses the co-existence of the different protection systems and the complex relation as a reason for taking account of the ECHR and its case law.

These special circumstances in which the CJEU has to provide an answer to the questions put before it, help to explain to some extent the role of the ECHR in the case law of the CJEU. The codification and the circumstances thus provide the

182 C-303/05, *Advocaten voor de Wereld VZW v. Leden van de Ministerraad* [2007] ECR I-03633, § 81-82, Opinion by Advocate General Ruiz-Jarabo Colomer.

additional explanation needed to justify the reliance on external comparative interpretation.

Two final questions still need to be answered. These questions played an important role in the previous section on the reference to common constitutional traditions, but do not seem to lead to much discussion in the context of the references to the ECHR. Firstly, it is important to analyze whether a different approach is visible in the opinions of the Advocates General. While the Advocates General are often more elaborate in their references to the ECHR, there is much less difference between their opinions and the CJEU's judgments when compared to the references to national constitutional traditions. The Court in some of its judgments refers to case law of the ECHR; so do the Advocates General. There is not really a difference in the level or quality of the references, as we have seen for the references to national constitutional traditions. The main difference concerns the extent of the discussion on the ECHR. That is not specific for this method, but it is characteristic for the difference between the judgments of the Court and the opinions of the Advocate General, as has been discussed in Chapter 3.

Secondly, a more practical issue should be addressed, namely who supplies the relevant information. That question is not often addressed in the case law with respect to the European Convention. Indeed, it does not appear to be a relevant issue, since the material is easier to access and is available in the same language as the CJEU.[183] That of course is an important difference from the information on national constitutional traditions. Moreover, the material is available from one source; no study has to be made as to whether a common principle can be found. The reference to the ECtHR should in this respect perhaps be compared to a national court referring to the ECHR.

While only some examples have been discussed here, there are many cases in which the ECHR plays an important role.[184] In the vast majority of the cases the CJEU follows the ECHR and its case law closely. A case like *Emesa Sugar,* however, shows that the CJEU does feel free to adopt a different approach which fits the EU system better. The CJEU thus seems to retain its flexibility by not considering the case law binding for the CJEU.[185] The examples discussed show that the special status of the ECHR is thus not just a 'friendly gesture', but is actually substantiated in many instances. One may question the far-reaching extent of the references given that the ECHR can be considered an external source for comparative interpretation, but the

183 See www.echr.coe.int.
184 Supra note 163.
185 Kirsch (2007), p. 20.

strategic explanations provided in the theoretical analysis and the reference to the ECHR in the EU treaty seem to provide for a sufficiently strong basis for this form of external comparative interpretation.

13.2.4 Role of other international instruments

In a limited number of cases the CJEU makes references to international instruments in the context of interpretation.[186] This has been done for a variety of purposes. In the cases of *Defrenne*[187] and *Laval,*[188] the reference to international treaties supported the conclusion reached by using other interpretative methods, i.e. that a certain right should be recognized as a fundamental right under EU law. In both cases the CJEU referred to the European Social Charter and an ILO Convention. The CJEU did not elaborate on why it made these references, merely stating that similar rights or concepts were also protected as fundamental rights under these instruments.[189] In a case on the family reunion directive the CJEU likewise referred to international instruments such as the Convention of the Rights of the Child, in this case to support its finding that the directive did not violate fundamental rights.[190] In the view of the CJEU, the Convention on children's rights did not warrant the far-reaching interpretation that was claimed by the European Parliament.[191] In this case the international reference thus provided support for the CJEU *not* to recognize a certain interpretation of a fundamental right. In both cases, however, the purpose was to find support for a conclusion already reached on other grounds.

186 See C-149/77, *Gabrielle Defrenne v Société anonyme belge de navigation aérienne Sabena* [1978] ECR 01365; C-374/87, *Orkem v. Commission of the European Communities* [1989] ECR 03283; C-249/96, *Lisa Jacqueline Grant v. South-West Trains Ltd* [1998] ECR I-00621; C-540/03, *European Parliament v Council of the European Union* [2006] ECR I-05769; C-436/04, *Criminal proceedings against Leopold Henri Van Esbroeck* [2006] ECR I-02333; C-341/05, *Laval un Partneri Ltd v. Svenska Byggnadsarbetareförbundet and others* [2007] ECR I-11767.

187 C-149/77, *Gabrielle Defrenne v Société anonyme belge de navigation aérienne Sabena* [1978] ECR 01365, § 28.

188 C-341/05, *Laval un Partneri Ltd v. Svenska Byggnadsarbetareförbundet and others* [2007] ECR I-11767, § 90.

189 C-149/77, *Gabrielle Defrenne v Société anonyme belge de navigation aérienne Sabena* [1978] ECR 01365, § 28; C-341/05, *Laval un Partneri Ltd v. Svenska Byggnadsarbetareförbundet and others* [2007] ECR I-11767, § 90.

190 C-540/03, *European Parliament v Council of the European Union* [2006] ECR I-05769, § 57.

191 C-540/03, *European Parliament v Council of the European Union* [2006] ECR I-05769, § 59. In the case of C-249/96, *Lisa Jacqueline Grant v. South-West Trains Ltd* [1998] ECR I-00621 the CJEU denied a far-reaching claim based on references to international instruments as well. Similarly in C-374/87, *Orkem v. Commission of the European Communities* [1989] ECR 03283.

A different version of this use of international instruments is presented by the case of *Van Esbroeck*.[192] In this case the CJEU had to interpret the *ne bis in idem* principle. This principle has been laid down in Article 54 of the Convention implementing the Schengen Agreement (CISA) and prevents someone being prosecuted twice for the same acts. The question was how the notion of 'the same acts' should be interpreted. By referring, among others, to the International Covenant on Civil and Political Rights the CJEU tried to distinguish the terminology used in those provisions from the terms used in Article 54 CISA:

> It must also be noted that the terms used in that article [article 54 CISA] differ from those used in other international treaties which enshrine the *ne bis in idem* principle. Unlike article 54 of the CISA, article 14(7) of the International Covenant on Civil and Political Rights ... use the term 'offence', which implies that the criterion of the legal classification of the acts is relevant as a prerequisite for the applicability of the *ne bis in idem* principle which is enshrined in those treaties.[193]

The fact that other treaties used different terms thus seemed to warrant a different interpretation of Article 54 CISA. The CJEU here thus used a combination of comparative and textual interpretation.

These examples show that references to international law have been used to support interpretative solutions that were also based on other arguments. The documents referred to varied per case. It is not clear for all cases why certain documents are invoked or why specifically these international documents are referred to. However, in some cases it is clear that the sources are derived from the submissions of the parties.[194] That could provide an important explanation for the choice of references; the CJEU will respond to the documents contained in those submissions. The CJEU, however, may not incorporate every reference to international instruments made by the parties to the case into its judgments. It has stated on more than one occasion that international instruments are also a source of inspiration for the interpretation of fundamental rights, but that it will only consider those international instruments that have some connection to the Member States:

---

192 C-436/04, Criminal proceedings against Leopold Henri Van Esbroeck [2006] ECR I-02333, § 28.
193 C-436/04, Criminal proceedings against Leopold Henri Van Esbroeck [2006] ECR I-02333, § 28.
194 C-249/96, *Lisa Jacqueline Grant v. South-West Trains Ltd* [1998] ECR I-00621; C-540/03, *European Parliament v Council of the European Union* [2006] ECR I-05769.

> ... the Court draws inspiration from ... the guidelines supplied by international instruments for the protection of human rights on which the Member States have collaborated or to which they are signatories.[195]

This raises the question whether the CJEU refers to international instruments on which *all* Member States have collaborated or which they have all signed or even ratified, or whether it is enough that *some* or a *significant number* of Member States have been involved in the drafting and signing of these international instruments. With regard to some of the international instruments the CJEU has referred to the binding effect for Member States, seemingly in order to enhance the strength of the reference:

> The Court has already had occasion to point out that the International Covenant on Civil and Political Rights is one of the international instruments for the protection of human rights of which it takes account in applying the general principles of Community law [refer to earlier CJEU cases]. That is also true of the Convention on the Rights of the Child referred to above which, like the Covenant, binds each of the Member States.[196]

The international instruments mentioned in this section are binding on all Member States and they are therefore considered relevant for the interpretation process. However, even though this seems to provide some clarity as to the situations in which international instruments can be used as a basis for interpretation by the Court, the CJEU does not address the generally binding character for each international instrument. So perhaps it is not necessary for each international reference to be binding in all Member States. The CJEU at least seems to be aware of the need for some relevant link to the Member States in order to make the reference convincing.

The previous section on the role of the ECHR indicated that the CJEU does not acknowledge the distinction between internal and external comparative interpretation. Given that these references can be considered as external comparative interpretation, it is relevant to question whether the justification provided for these references is sufficient. The analysis indicated that the CJEU tries to emphasize the link between the CJEU or its Member States and the international document it cites. That is, however, not the case for every reference. As indicated in the theoretical analysis, it diminishes the argument if the CJEU fails to do so. It would thus be an improvement if the CJEU indicated the relevance of references to international materials in every case in order to avoid criticism. It should, however, be noted that overall not many

195 C-540/03, *European Parliament v Council of the European Union* [2006] ECR I-057691, § 35. See also: C-36/02, *Omega Spielhallen- und Automatenaufstellungs-GmbH v. Oberbürgermeisterin der Bundesstadt Bonn* [2004] ECR I-09609, § 33; C-117/01, *K.B. v National Health Service Pensions Agency and Secretary of State for Health* [2004] ECR I-00541, § 27.

196 C-540/03, *European Parliament v Council of the European Union* [2006] ECR I-057691, § 37.

references are made to international materials; thus the impact on the CJEU's reasoning if it fails to provide a justification is relatively minor.

13.2.5 Conclusion

Comparative arguments are regularly used both by the CJEU and the Advocates General. Most often these comparative arguments consist of references to the European Convention on Human Rights and the case law of the ECtHR. To a lesser extent references to common constitutional traditions and other international instruments are invoked. Comparative references made by the Advocate General are often more elaborate, which is in line with the general style difference between the judgments and opinions. The difference between the Advocate General and the CJEU in their use of comparative arguments is mainly visible in the context of references to common constitutional traditions. The CJEU in its judgments remains rather abstract and does not refer to any specific Member State or indicate what kind of material served as a basis for the comparative analysis and the subsequent conclusion. The Advocates General, on the other hand, more often refer to specific Member States and mention the kind of material used to come to their conclusion. Even though the Advocates General do not provide a complete insight into their comparative analysis and the following conclusion, they provide more substantiation than the CJEU does in its judgments. This can, however, be seen as a logical consequence of the judicial setup of the CJEU, as discussed in the introduction in Chapter 3.

References to comparative materials have been used for all kinds of purposes. In the early days comparative references mainly served to fill the gap that was caused by the lack of an EU fundamental rights catalogue. Presently, comparative references are used to solve regular interpretative problems, but there are also some examples of comparative interpretation being used to support an evolutive approach. The discussion in this chapter indicates that the separate categories of comparative arguments are often used for support. This support is, however, often provided by another category of comparative arguments. Often references to common constitutional traditions and to the European Convention are combined in a specific reasoning. The separate categories can thus have a supportive function, but comparative interpretation in general often plays a decisive or at least rather important role in the reasoning.

The theoretical chapter indicated the importance of a legitimate basis for relying on comparative arguments and made a distinction between external and internal comparative arguments. The analysis has shown that the existence of Article 6(3) TEU plays an important role in this regard. This codification of the references to the ECHR is an example of an extra justification that is required in the context of external comparative interpretation. The references to the European Convention and the case law of the ECtHR in the cases analyzed in this chapter make clear, however, that these sources do not only provide inspiration, but that in many cases the interpretation of the ECtHR is almost literally copied. The use of the ECtHR is thus taken further than one might suggest on the basis of Article 6(3) TEU. The justifications for this that are provided in the literature are all of a strategic nature, arguing that the CJEU wants to avoid conflicting obligations for the Member States and that referring to the ECtHR has helped to boost the fundamental rights protection in the EU in the sense that it added authority. If the CJEU or its Advocates General would have discussed the justification for relying on the European Convention to the extent that is currently visible, this would have made it easier to understand why they almost literally copy the Strasbourg approach. It would also explain why only in exceptional cases like *Emesa Sugar*, the CJEU adopts an approach which is not in line with ECtHR case law.

Even though the justification for relying on the European Convention can be commented upon, hardly a justification is provided for referring to international instruments. This form of comparative interpretation does not occur often, but even then a justification for invoking these instruments that have no obvious connection to the EU would be welcome.

Finally, some more practical aspect of comparative interpretation warrants attention. Even though the Advocates General provide more insight into the comparative analysis, there is one important question, identified in the theoretical analysis that still cannot be fully answered. When can one speak of common traditions? Even in the opinions this remains unclear. Unanimity is of course an indication that one can speak of a common tradition, just like the complete lack of convergence is an indication that there are no common traditions; however, in the majority of the cases the answer will lie somewhere in the middle. It would make the reasoning more accessible or verifiable if more indications were available to understand the conclusions.

The opinions of the Advocates General address another aspect of finding common traditions, namely at what abstract level these common traditions should be found. The case law analysis of the ECtHR showed that judges sometimes disagree regarding at what level a consensus has to be found, at a rather specific level or at an abstract level. There does not seem to be much discussion on this aspect between the judges and the Advocates General in the CJEU. It has even been indicated that finding a common tradition at the level of an abstract principle would be sufficient.

13.3 Teleological interpretation

The CJEU has been called *the* teleological court with respect to its judicial approach.[197] This is a general statement not related to any specific area of law and therefore it is interesting to see whether this approach is visible in the area of funda-

197 See for example: Albors Llorens (2000).

mental rights as well. Teleological interpretation has been defined as the interpretation of a notion or concept in accordance with the object, purpose, aim or underlying rationale of the document or the provision in question.[198] That description already indicates a potential problem for the CJEU, at least in the cases before 2000. After all, before 2000 there was no document at all containing a catalogue of fundamental rights for the EU. After 2000 the Charter came into being, but it only recently became legally binding.[199] Therefore, for a relatively long time there was no document containing fundamental rights that could be interpreted in a (micro-) teleological manner.

Nevertheless, the case law analysis has disclosed that the CJEU, despite the lack of an EU fundamental rights text, still sometimes employs teleological arguments. In one of the early judgments on fundamental rights in the EU, *Internationale Handelsgesellschaft*, the CJEU concluded that fundamental rights were an integral part of the general principle of law protected by the CJEU. These fundamental rights had to be protected within the 'framework of the structure and the objectives of the Community'.[200] The objectives of the Community can therefore be regarded as one of the elements that play a role in determining the scope of fundamental rights. In subsequent cases, however, this reference to teleological interpretation has not been repeated. Only in very few fundamental rights cases, teleological arguments have visibly been used. Not surprisingly, these cases generally involve the interpretation of a directive, regulation or a provision from the TFEU in relation to which fundamental rights have a certain importance.

In some cases the CJEU has considered the objective of a directive or regulation in order to establish whether actions by Community institutions that were based on the directive or regulation led to a violation of fundamental rights. This was the case in *National Panasonic*, where the CJEU had to address the question whether the investigative powers of the Commission based on a regulation in an investigation on infringements of competition law were in conflict with Article 8 ECHR.[201] On the basis of a decision by the Commission an unannounced search took place at the office of the applicant. The applicant subsequently complained about an infringement of his right to be informed of the decision and his right to be heard before the decision was taken. The CJEU concluded that, considering the objective of the provision in question and of the regulation as a whole, the application of this provision could not

198 See Chapter 5. Henceforth the terms object and purpose will serve as general indicators of a teleological approach, solely for practical reasons. Indicators like aim or underlying rationale or principle have, however, been used to discover an explicit teleological approach as well.

199 See Chapter 3 for a more elaborate explanation.

200 C-11/70, *Internationale Handelsgesellschaft mbH v. Einfuhr- und Vorratsstelle für Getreide und Futtermittel* [1970] ECR 01125, § 4.

201 C-136/79, *National Panasonic (UK) Limited v Commission of the European Communities* [1980] ECR 02033.

be held to constitute a violation of fundamental rights.[202] Having regard to the aims of the investigative stage, it was not necessary that these rights of the defence were respected.[203] The teleological arguments in this case were thus used to limit the scope of fundamental rights.[204]

One of the main areas in which the CJEU has resorted to teleological arguments to determine the scope of a fundamental right is in cases concerning discrimination.[205] In these cases the CJEU often refers to the object or purpose of a directive or to one of the provisions of the former EC-treaty on the prohibition of discrimination. The fundamental right at issue in those cases is to a certain extent codified in a piece of EC legislation, which makes it easier to use teleological argumentation. In the case of *P v. S*, for example, the applicant complained that she was fired in violation of a non-discrimination directive. She claimed that the reason for her dismissal was the fact that she underwent a gender reassignment to become a woman.[206] The question was raised whether this ground for discrimination was included within the scope of the directive. The CJEU discussed the purpose of the directive and the relevant provisions; in combination with some other arguments this led to the following conclusion:

> The scope of the directive cannot be confined simply to discrimination based on the fact that a person if of one or the other sex. In view of the purpose and the nature of the rights which it seeks to safeguard, the scope of the directive is also such as to apply to discrimination arising, as in this case, from the gender reassignment of the person concerned.[207]

Thus, the purpose of the directive played an important role in determining the scope of the fundamental right.

A similar example can be found in the *Coleman* judgment.[208] Here the applicant complained that she had been subjected to discrimination at work because her son

202 C-136/79, *National Panasonic (UK) Limited v Commission of the European Communities* [1980] ECR 02033, § 20-21

203 C-136/79, *National Panasonic (UK) Limited v Commission of the European Communities* [1980] ECR 02033, § 20-21

204 A similar example can be found in C-155/79, *AM & S Europe Limited v. Commission of the European Communities* [1982] ECR 01575.

205 See for example: C-13/94, *P v. S and Cornwall County Council* [1996] ECRI-02143; C-249/96, *Lisa Jacqueline Grant v. South-West Trains Ltd* [1998] ECR I-00621; C-222/84, *Marguerite Johnston v. Chief Constable of the Royal Ulster Constabulary* [1986] ECR 01651; C-185/97, *Belinda Jane Coote v. Granada Hospitality Ltd.* [1998] ECR I-05199; C-303/06, *S. Coleman v. Attridge Law and Steve Law* [2008] ECR I-05603; C-506/06, *Sabine Mayr v. Bäckerei und Konditorei Gerhard Flöckner OHG* [2008] ECR I-01017.

206 C-13/94, *P v. S and Cornwall County Council* [1996] ECRI-02143.

207 C-13/94, *P v. S and Cornwall County Council* [1996] ECRI-02143, § 20.

208 C-303/06, *S. Coleman v. Attridge Law and Steve Law* [2008] ECR I-05603.

was disabled. The question before the CJEU was whether discrimination on the basis of disability included the disability of someone else. In order to answer that question the CJEU looked into the purpose and objective of the directive that had been invoked in this case. On several occasions the CJEU referred to the objective of the directive as it followed from the provisions and the preamble.[209] The CJEU concluded that discrimination on the basis of disability should not be interpreted restrictively and it held as follows:

> Where it is established that an employee in a situation such as in the present case suffers direct discrimination on ground of disability, an interpretation of Directive 200/78 limiting its application only to people who are themselves disabled is liable to deprive that directive of an important element of its effectiveness and to reduce the protection which it is intended to guarantee.[210]

Once again, teleological arguments, in addition to other arguments, played an important role in this case. What is interesting about the quoted passage is that the CJEU also referred to the effectiveness of the directive, which can also be regarded as a kind of teleological argument. After all, inherent to a claim based on effectiveness is an assumption that the objectives of the directive should be achieved. This example is a rare one, however – the argument based on effectiveness does not feature in many other fundamental rights cases and does not seem to play an important role in the context of fundamental rights interpretation.

Another area in which the CJEU sometimes invokes teleological arguments concerns the interpretation of the principle of *ne bis in idem*. This principle has been laid down in Article 54 of the Convention implementing the Schengen Agreement (CISA) and protects individuals against double jeopardy. In both *Van Esbroeck*[211] and *Bourquain*[212] the CJEU referred to the objective of this provision in order to establish the scope of the protection provided by this provision. Other arguments were also invoked, but in both cases the Court held that the conclusion on the scope of the protection was 'reinforced by the objective of Article 54 of the CISA, which is to ensure that no one is prosecuted for the same acts in several Member States on account of his having exercised his right to freedom of movement'.[213] Teleological arguments thus provided a source of support in this case.

---

209 See for example: C-303/06, *S. Coleman v. Attridge Law and Steve Law* [2008] ECR I-05603, § 34-38-47-49.

210 C-303/06, *S. Coleman v. Attridge Law and Steve Law* [2008] ECR I-05603, § 51.

211 C-436/04, *Criminal proceedings against Leopold Henri Van Esbroeck* [2006] ECR I-02333.

212 C-297/07, *Klaus Bourquain* [2008] ECR I-09425.

213 C-436/04, *Criminal proceedings against Leopold Henri Van Esbroeck* [2006] ECR I-02333, § 33; C-297/07, *Klaus Bourquain* [2008] ECR I-09425, § 49.

The theoretical analysis indicated that a distinction can be made between subjective and objective teleological interpretation.[214] Subjective teleological interpretation takes account of the object and purpose of the original drafter, while objective teleological interpretation looks at the object and purpose of the rational drafter. The question is how the object and purpose in these cases is established by the CJEU. The theoretical analysis indicated that subjective teleological interpretation was expected to play no or at most a minor role in the case law of the CJEU, given the lack of publicly available *travaux préparatoires*. Is this theoretical assumption supported by the case law?

In some cases, reference is simply made to a specific object and purpose of a provision or directive, without any indication how this has been established.[215] In most cases, however, some reference is made to the source of the conclusion on the object and purpose.[216] Many of these cases indicate that the object and purpose of a directive are established on the basis of the first provision of the directive, which often indicates the main aim of the directive.[217] Furthermore, the preamble of a directive plays an important role as well in establishing the object and purpose.[218] A third factor that plays a role in justifying how the object and purpose were established is a reference to earlier precedents.[219] It is interesting to note that hardly any reference is made to the intention of the drafters, which warrants the conclusion that the CJEU mainly relies on objective teleological interpretation.

In those cases where the CJEU indicates the source of the object and purpose of the provision or directive it seeks to interpret, the reference to the object and purpose is generally substantiated. This means that the CJEU specifies what the object and purpose entail in that specific situation. This can be seen as a logical consequence of the explicit reference to the source of the object and purpose. In *Coote*, where the

214 See section 5.1.3.

215 See for example: C-249/96, *Lisa Jacqueline Grant v. South-West Trains Ltd* [1998] ECR I-00621.

216 C-436/04, *Criminal proceedings against Leopold Henri Van Esbroeck* [2006] ECR I-02333; C-303/06, *S. Coleman v. Attridge Law and Steve Law* [2008] ECR I-05603; C-13/94, *P v. S and Cornwall County Council* [1996] ECRI-02143; C-222/84, *Marguerite Johnston v. Chief Constable of the Royal Ulster Constabulary* [1986] ECR 01651; C-506/06, *Sabine Mayr v. Bäckerei und Konditorei Gerhard Flöckner OHG* [2008] ECR I-01017; C-297/07, *Klaus Bourquain* [2008] ECR I-09425.

217 C-303/06, *S. Coleman v. Attridge Law and Steve Law* [2008] ECR I-05603; 222/85; C-13/94, *P v. S and Cornwall County Council* [1996] ECRI-02143.

218 C-506/06, *Sabine Mayr v. Bäckerei und Konditorei Gerhard Flöckner OHG* [2008] ECR I-01017; C-303/06, *S. Coleman v. Attridge Law and Steve Law* [2008] ECR I-05603; C-13/94, *P v. S and Cornwall County Council* [1996] ECRI-02143.

219 C-185/97, *Belinda Jane Coote v. Granada Hospitality Ltd.* [1998] ECR I-05199; C-436/04, *Criminal proceedings against Leopold Henri Van Esbroeck* [2006] ECR I-02333; C-506/06, *Sabine Mayr v. Bäckerei und Konditorei Gerhard Flöckner OHG* [2008] ECR I-01017; C-297/07, *Klaus Bourquain* [2008] ECR I-09425.

CJEU had to determine whether retaliatory measures against a former employee were covered by the directive on equal treatment as regards employment, the object and purpose are stated in the discussion of the legal framework at the beginning of the judgment, where it was held that:

> According to Article 1(1) of the Directive, its purpose is 'to put into effect in the Member States the principle of equal treatment for men and women as regards access to employment, including promotion, and to vocational training and as regards working conditions and, on the conditions referred to in paragraph 2, social security. This principle is hereinafter referred to as "the principle of equal treatment".'[220]

In its reasoning the CJEU later referred to the purpose of the directive without substantiating the purpose, but it had already done so at the beginning of the judgment.[221] In *Coleman*, discussed above, the CJEU included a reference to the purpose of a specific directive in the legal framework as well, but also explicitly recalled that purpose several times in its reasoning:

> So far as the objectives of Directive 2000/78 are concerned, as is apparent from paragraphs 34 and 38 of the present judgment, the directive seeks to lay down, as regards employment and occupation, a general framework for combating discrimination on one of the grounds referred to in Article 1- including in particular disability- with a view to putting into effect in the Member States the principle of equal treatment. It follows from recital 37 in the preamble to the directive that it also has the objective of creating within the Community a level playing field as regards equality in employment and occupation.[222]

In other judgments the object and purpose are substantiated as well, but not always when setting out the legal framework. In many other cases or opinions the object and purpose are set out whenever relevant for the specific teleological reasoning. In *Sabine Mayr* the CJEU had to decide whether a woman whose eggs had been fertilized, but not yet transferred into her uterus was considered pregnant within the meaning of EU law. In order to answer that question the CJEU discussed the object and purpose of the respective directive and held that:

> As regards Directive 92/85, it should be borne in mind that its objective is to encourage improvements in the safety and health at work of pregnant workers and workers who have recently given birth or are breastfeeding.

---

220 C-185/97, *Belinda Jane Coote v. Granada Hospitality Ltd.* [1998] ECR I-05199, § 3.

221 C-185/97, *Belinda Jane Coote v. Granada Hospitality Ltd.* [1998] ECR I-05199, § 24.

222 C-303/06, *S. Coleman v. Attridge Law and Steve Law* [2008] ECR I-05603, § 47. See similarly also Advocate General Ruiz-Jarabo Colomber in C-297/07, *Klaus Bourquain* [2008] ECR I-09425; Advocate General Ruiz-Jarabo Colomber in C-436/04, *Criminal proceedings against Leopold Henri Van Esbroeck* [2006] ECR I-02333.

> In that field, the Court has also pointed out that the objective pursued by the Community law rules governing equality as between men and women in regards to the rights of pregnant women and women who have given birth, is to protect female workers before and after they have given birth [reference to earlier judgments].[223]

The conclusion of the CJEU was that Sabine Mayr could not be considered pregnant for the purpose of the directive.

The examples given above aim to indicate the way in which the CJEU substantiates its references to object and purpose. The references remain rather abstract, but at least they do provide some direction for the interpretative problem at hand. The references determine the boundaries within which the solution should be found. The purpose of indicating at what point in the judgment the object and purpose are explained, is to indicate that even if it is not included in the reasoning itself, in most cases the legal framework fills this void.

One of the questions that still needs to be asked in order to get a more complete picture of teleological interpretation is what role this method plays in the reasoning. Is teleological reasoning used in a decisive manner, whereby it is the only argument used to reach a specific conclusion? Or is it used in addition to many other arguments and thus plays a supportive role? It is difficult to tell whether all arguments weigh equally in a final conclusion, but teleological arguments seem to be used mainly in addition to other arguments, thus indicating that it mainly plays a supportive role. Other arguments often refer to textual, comparative or systemic considerations to support a conclusion.[224] The force of the different arguments does seem to differ per case. In *Coleman*, for example the focus seems to be mostly on teleological interpretation, while in the case of *Van Esbroeck* the different arguments seem to be more in balance.

A final aspect that should be discussed is whether there is any difference in the way the Advocate General uses teleological interpretation and the way the CJEU relies on this method. No real distinction can be noted here. Of course, the Advocate General is often more elaborate in its discussions, but that is a general feature of the judicial style of the CJEU. These more elaborate discussions by the Advocates General, like in the case of *Van Esbroeck*, provide more insight into the aim or objective of the provision or directive at hand, but they do not necessarily shed more light on the use

---

223 C-506/06, *Sabine Mayr v. Bäckerei und Konditorei Gerhard Flöckner OHG* [2008] ECR I-01017, § 31-32.

224 C-436/04, *Criminal proceedings against Leopold Henri Van Esbroeck* [2006] ECR I-02333; see also the opinion of Advocate General Ruiz-Jarabo Colomber in this case; C-506/06, *Sabine Mayr v. Bäckerei und Konditorei Gerhard Flöckner OHG* [2008] ECR I-01017 and C-303/06, *S. Coleman v. Attridge Law and Steve Law* [2008] ECR I-05603 Opinion by Advocate General Poiares Maduro.

of teleological interpretation.[225] The Advocates General also rely on the provisions of a directive, on the preamble and precedent to establish the object and purpose and do not discuss other means to establish the object or purpose.

The main examples of teleological arguments in the fundamental rights case law of the CJEU that have been discussed in this section, all have one important element in common, namely that in all of them the fundamental right had been laid down in a written document. This might explain why these arguments do not play a bigger role in the context of fundamental rights, even though the CJEU is generally famous for its teleological approach.

13.4 Other interpretation methods and principles

Only two of the selected interpretation methods have been discussed so far. Evolutive interpretation and autonomous interpretation still warrant a discussion. The fact that they have not yet been discussed already indicates that these interpretative aids do not play a very prominent role in the CJEU's case law. In fact, the case law analysis has disclosed that they do not really play an explicit role where interpretation of fundamental rights is concerned. This last section, in which these interpretative aids are analyzed, will therefore necessarily be brief.

13.4.1 Evolutive interpretation

Evolutive interpretation has been defined in the theoretical literature as interpretation 'in the light of present day conditions', as opposed to interpretation of the ECHR in line with the standards at the time it was drafted. This definition already indicates why the role of evolutive interpretation is different in the context of the CJEU than in the context of the ECtHR. Fundamental rights in the EU have only recently been laid down in a written document, namely the Charter, which was adopted in 2000 and which only became binding in 2009.[226] Before that time, fundamental rights were developed in the CJEU's case law on the basis of common national constitutional traditions, with the ECHR as a strong source of inspiration. Consequently, there was no written document that needed to be interpreted 'in light of present-day conditions' and it is therefore logical and understandable that express references to such an evolutive approach are missing in the CJEU's fundamental rights case law.

225 C-436/04, *Criminal proceedings against Leopold Henri Van Esbroeck* [2006] ECR I-02333, § 23-36. See also C-506/06, *Sabine Mayr v. Bäckerei und Konditorei Gerhard Flöckner OHG* [2008] ECR I-01017 for elaborate discussions by Advocate General Ruiz-Jarabo Colomer on the object and purpose.

226 See Chapter 3 for a more detailed discussion of this topic.

This does not mean, of course, that the CJEU does not take an evolutive approach at all. Introducing the whole concept of fundamental rights as such can be regarded as the utmost expression of an evolutive approach – this would perhaps never have happened if the CJEU adopted a purely static approach to interpretation. Thus, it may be said that the CJEU indeed employs an evolutive approach, even though it hardly ever refers to it in its judgments and, as a result, this approach is less visible. The focus of this thesis is on those occasions where the CJEU adopted a visibly evolutive approach in the sense that it was possible to discern that the CJEU looked at developments and changes in the Member States or changes in other respects. This choice has been made, because only in those instances can it be actually assumed that an evolutive approach is taken and those instances can thus help to understand how evolutive interpretation is used in the reasoning. If there is no visibly evolutive approach it becomes the reader's interpretation that an evolutive approach has been taken, which makes it difficult to analyze the actual use of evolutive interpretation by the CJEU.

A rare example of an express reference to the evolutive approach is visible in the case law with regard to the applicability of the protection of the inviolability of the home to legal persons. In the case of *Hoechst* the CJEU held that the right to inviolability of the home could not be extended to cover legal persons as well, since no support for that extension could be found in the national constitutional traditions and the ECHR.[227] The CJEU did conclude that interferences with private activities of legal persons had to have a legal basis and be proportionate.[228] After this judgment the ECHR dealt with this similar issue and concluded that the protection of inviolability of the home could in some situations be extended to cover legal persons as well.[229] In the case of *Roquette Frères* the CJEU had to address this question of *Hoechst* again, but now in the light of the developments at the Strasbourg level.[230] The CJEU repeated the principle established in *Hoechst*, which has been mentioned above, and it continued to reason as follows with regard to the subsequent developments:

> For the purpose of determining the scope of that principle in relation to the protection of business premises, regard must be had to the case-law of the European Court of Human Rights subsequent to the judgment in *Hoechst*. According to that case-law, first the protection of

227 C-46/87 *Hoechst AG v. Commission of the European Communities* [1989] ECR 02859, § 17-18.

228 C-46/87 *Hoechst AG v. Commission of the European Communities* [1989] ECR 02859, § 19

229 The CJEU referred in this context to ECtHR, *Société Colas Est and others v. France*, judgment of 16 April 2002, *Reports* 2002-III.

230 C-94/00, *Roquette Frères SA v. Directeur général de la concurrence, de la consommation et de la répression des fraudes, and Commission of the European Communities* [2002] ECR I-09011.

> the home provided for in Article 8 of the ECHR may in certain circumstances be extended to cover such premises [reference to ECHR case law] and second, the right of interference established by Article 8(2) of the ECHR 'might well be more far-reaching where professional of business activities or premises were involved than would otherwise be the case [reference to ECHR case law].[231]

The CJEU thus adopted a new approach, based on developments in the case law of the ECtHR. In contrast to the ECtHR the CJEU does not expressly state that they take an evolutive approach or use evolutive interpretation to justify a new approach – it simply adopts a new approach.[232]

Another example of the willingness of the CJEU to take developments into account is visible in some discrimination cases. In the case of *D* the CJEU discussed the situation in the Member States and concluded that there were some developments, but not enough for an extensive interpretation.[233]

> It is equally true that since 1989 an increasing number of Member States have introduced, alongside marriage, statutory arrangements granting legal recognition to various forms of union between partners of the same sex or of the opposite sex and conferring on such unions certain effects which, both between the partners and as regards third parties, are the same as or comparable to those of marriage.[234]

231 C-94/00, *Roquette Frères SA v. Directeur général de la concurrence, de la consommation et de la répression des fraudes, and Commission of the European Communities* [2002] ECR I-09011, § 29.

232 An example that is less clear is provided by the case of *Orkem* (C-347/87), in which the CJEU determined that undertakings in competition proceedings could be forced to answer (the CJEU explicitly referred to Article 6 ECHR and argued that this did not include a right not to incriminate oneself), except to questions that would lead to an admission on its part of the existence of an infringement which the Commission has to prove. In a subsequent case by the ECtHR (ECtHR, *Funke v. France*, judgment of 25 February 1993, *Series* A No. 256-A) it addressed the right not to incriminate oneself and considered this to be covered by Article 6 ECHR. The General Court (then Court of First Instance) in *Mannesmannröhren-Werke* (T-112/98, *Mannesmannröhren-Werke AG v. Commission of the European Communities* [2001] ECR II-00729) held that the applicant could not directly invoke Article 6 ECHR which included a right not to incriminate oneself, but that the fundamental rights recognized within the EU offered equivalent protection. Not the CJEU in this case, but the General Court, thus provided a more protective approach based on developments in the ECtHR case law. See also Craig & De Burca (2008), p. 393-394.

233 C-122/99, *D and Kingdom of Sweden v. Council of the European Union* [2001] ECR I-04319, § 35-37. The case concerned recognition of registered relationships as equivalent to marriage. In the case of *Grant* a similar awareness of developments in Member States is visible. C-249/96, *Lisa Jacqueline Grant v. South-West Trains Ltd* [1998] ECR I-00621, § 32 & 35.

234 C-122/99, *D and Kingdom of Sweden v. Council of the European Union* [2001] ECR I-04319, § 35.

The fact that the CJEU notices a development clearly indicates that it takes the present situation into account and considers such developments relevant to its interpretation of fundamental rights.

In another case, concerning the question whether discrimination on the grounds of sex also included discrimination of someone who underwent a gender change, Advocate General Tesauro also referred to the need to keep an evolutive approach.[235]

> ... the law cannot cut itself off from society as it actually is, and must not fail to adjust to it as quickly as possible. Otherwise it risks imposing outdated views and taking on a static role. In so far as the law seeks to regulate relations in society, it must on the contrary keep up with social change, and must therefore be capable of regulating new situations brought to light by social change and advances in society.[236]

He thus stressed the need to keep pace with developments in society. He subsequently referred to clear tendencies in the Member States towards recognition of the rights of transsexuals.

The role of evolutive interpretation is thus visible to the extent that it does play a role whenever necessary as indicated by the examples provided above. The examples indicate that comparative arguments play a role in the context of evolutive interpretation either in the form of references to the Member States or in the form of references to the ECHR. It cannot be concluded on the basis of the examples provided above that this is always the case, but it seems safe to assume that comparative interpretation and evolutive interpretation are also closely linked in the context of the CJEU. The number of references is, however, insufficient to warrant any further analysis of the use of the principle. There can be instances of evolutive interpretation that have not been explicitly qualified as such by the CJEU.[237] However, without an explicit indication from the CJEU that an evolutive approach has taken place, it is not possible to use those supposed instances of evolutive interpretation for the present analysis. For that reason, it cannot be established on the basis of the case law analysis if the CJEU regards evolutive interpretation as an interpretative principle or rather as a method of interpretation, where it finds the basis or justification for its use, and what sources it uses to establish the existence of a (sufficient) evolution.

---

235 C-13/94, *P v. S and Cornwall County Council* [1996] ECRI-02143.

236 C-13/94, *P v. S and Cornwall County Council* [1996] ECRI-02143, Opinion by Advocate General Tesauro, § 9.

237 Advocate General Poiares Maduro in C-465/07, *Meki Elgafaji and Noor Elgafaji v. Staatssecretaris van Justitie* [2009] ECR I-00921, § 20, refers to the dynamic character of the interpretation by the ECtHR. Even though he mentions that in a different context, it does imply that the CJEU also incorporates this dynamic interpretation into its case law when relying on Strasbourg.

13.4.2 Autonomous interpretation

Autonomous interpretation has been defined in the theoretical part of this thesis as interpretation independent from the meaning of a certain term or right in, for example, the domestic context. The discussion on autonomous interpretation as used by the ECtHR has centred on autonomy from *national* interpretations. In the context of the CJEU an additional 'version' of autonomy may be distinguished, namely autonomy from the ECHR.[238] Autonomous interpretation will be discussed from both angles in this section.

Before discussing autonomous interpretation at the CJEU it is necessary to discuss what form of autonomous interpretation will be analyzed. The theoretical discussion on the ECtHR indicated that two forms of autonomous interpretation can be distinguished, namely weak autonomy and strong autonomy. Weak autonomy means that every interpretation coming from an international judicial body charged with the interpretation of a treaty can be considered autonomous. Strong autonomy, on the other hand, refers to those interpretative solutions that are 'expressly and intentionally interpreted in a real 'European' way, disconnected from the national qualification'.[239] Even though this distinction was discussed in the context of the ECtHR, it certainly has relevance for the discussion before the CJEU as well. The extra dimension that needs to be added to the concept of strong autonomy would be to regard strong autonomy as interpretation in a real 'European Union' way, thus disconnected from the ECtHR interpretation as well. The focus of the present analysis will be on forms of strong autonomy in the case law of the CJEU. Any interpretation by the CJEU can be regarded as weak autonomy; thus an analysis focusing on weak autonomy would not be much help for understanding autonomous interpretation.[240] The focus will therefore be on those instances where the CJEU itself indicated that it would take an autonomous approach, because those cases provide the most useful information on the use of autonomous interpretation.

There are not many instances in which the CJEU takes an explicitly autonomous approach in the context of fundamental rights adjudication. In a recent case concerning the principle of *ne bis in idem* the CJEU was challenged by the referring national court to indicate whether the term the 'same acts' was an autonomous concept.[241] The German court in question was in doubt whether it could oppose the execution of a European arrest warrant by Italy against Mr. Mantello. He had been convicted of a drug-related crime in Italy, but for strategic reasons the prosecuting authorities

238 Douglas-Scott (2006) mentions this form of autonomy.

239 See section 8.2.

240 This is confirmed by Advocate General Mischo in C-122/99, *D and Kingdom of Sweden v. Council of the European Union* [2001] ECR I-04319, § 44.

241 C-261/09, *Gaetano Mantello* [2010].

had not prosecuted him for the crimes laid down in the arrest warrant, while that could have been possible at the time of his conviction. The referring court first sought to find out whether the concept of the 'same act' had to be interpreted in an autonomous manner or whether the Italian or German interpretation prevailed. Subsequently, it requested to find out whether the fact that the prosecution authorities could have prosecuted Mr. Mantello at an earlier stage was enough to object to the execution of the arrest warrant.

In answering the first question the CJEU explicitly states that the concept 'the same acts' is an autonomous concept:

> In that regard, the concept of 'same acts' in Article 3(2) of the Framework Decision cannot be left to the discretion of the judicial authorities of each Member State on the basis of their national law. It follows from the need for uniform application of European Union law that, since that provision makes no reference to the law of the Member States with regard to that concept, the latter must be given an autonomous and uniform interpretation throughout the European Union (see, by analogy, Case C-66/08 *Kosz³owski* [2008] ECR I-6041, paragraphs 41 and 42).[242]

The CJEU in this statement also provides the reason for characterizing this as an autonomous concept, namely the need for uniformity and the fact that the wording of the specific provision does not refer to national law. In the subsequent paragraph the CJEU addresses the meaning of this autonomous concept. It refers to Article 54 CISA, which is similar in nature and includes the concept of the 'same acts' as well:

> It should be recalled that that concept of the 'same acts' also appears in Article 54 of the CISA. In that context, the concept has been interpreted as referring only to the nature of the acts, encompassing a set of concrete circumstances which are inextricably linked together, irrespective of the legal classification given to them or the legal interest protected (see Case C-436/04 *Van Esbroeck* [2006] ECR I-2333, paragraphs 27, 32 and 36, and Case C-150/05 *Van Straaten* [2006] ECR I-9327, paragraphs 41, 47 and 48).
>
> In view of the shared objective of Article 54 of the CISA and Article 3(2) of the Framework Decision, which is to ensure that a person is not prosecuted or tried more than once in respect of the same acts, it must be accepted that an interpretation of that concept given in the context of the CISA is equally valid for the purposes of the Framework Decision.[243]

The autonomous concept is thus interpreted by adopting a systemic and teleological interpretation. This is an important observation in light of the distinction between interpretative principles and interpretation methods that has been made in this thesis. Autonomous interpretation in this example seems to be an interpretative principle,

242 C-261/09, *Gaetano Mantello* [2010], § 38.
243 C-261/09, *Gaetano Mantello* [2010], § 39-40.

the content of which needs to be established by resorting to interpretation methods. This way of viewing autonomous interpretation is in line with the classification of autonomous interpretation as an interpretative principle in the theoretical discussion.

This one example of autonomous interpretation can, however, not provide a proper basis for any conclusions on this interpretative principle.

Another recent case provides an example of a situation in which the CJEU does not find it necessary to adopt an autonomous approach.[244] The question was whether a legal person should be entitled to legal aid in order to provide an effective legal remedy in situations where the legal person tries to establish state liability under EU law.[245] According to German law the company in this case was not entitled to legal aid. In answering the question the CJEU could have opted for a uniform autonomous approach, but instead it opted for a minimalistic approach. The CJEU looked at the text of Article 47 of the Charter, its place within the Charter and took comparative arguments into account. It concluded that Article 47 did not leave it impossible for a legal person to claim legal aid, but that it was up to national courts to determine whether denying legal aid would violate the core right of access to a court. The CJEU could have also adopted an autonomous, uniform interpretation indicating that everyone (including legal persons) fulfilling the criteria under Article 47 of the Charter should be provided legal aid. It is not entirely clear why the CJEU opted for this more reserved approach. It could be related to the economic consequences that an autonomous approach would have had in this latter case, but on the basis of these two cases it is not possible to draw any firm conclusions.

There are also not many instances of an autonomous approach in relation to the ECHR to be found in the case law of the CJEU. The discussion on comparative interpretation and the European Convention in section 13.2.3 has shown that the CJEU usually strictly follows the Convention and the interpretation given to the Convention rights by the ECtHR. The only case in which the CJEU did not follow the ECtHR is the case of *Emesa Sugar,* which has also been discussed in section 13.2.3, which discloses a clear difference in approach between the CJEU and the ECtHR.[246] The applicants in that case complained about the fact that they were not allowed to comment on the Opinion of the Advocate General. *Emesa Sugar* contained a reference to Article 6 of the European Convention and the *Vermeulen* judgment issued by the ECtHR. In that judgment the ECtHR held that Belgian law was contrary to the right to a fair

244 C-279/09, *DEB Deutsche Energiehandels- und Beratungsgesellschaft mbH v. Bundesrepublik Deutschland* [2010].

245 C-279/09, *DEB Deutsche Energiehandels- und Beratungsgesellschaft mbH v. Bundesrepublik Deutschland* [2010], § 25.

246 See section 13.2.3. C-17/98, *Emesa Sugar (Free Zone) NV v. Aruba* [2000] ECR I-00665.

trial as protected by Article 6, because of the fact that Mr. Vermeulen could not react to the opinion of the *Procureur Général*. The argument of the applicant was that the position of the *Procureur Général* resembled that of the Advocate General and they should accordingly be given the opportunity to react to the Opinion of the Advocate General. The CJEU did not agree. It started to discuss the way the position of the Advocate General is incorporated in the structure of the CJEU and found that:

> Having regard to both the organic and the functional link between the Advocate General and the Court, ... , the aforesaid case-law of the European Court of Human Rights does not appear to be transposable to the Opinion of the Court's Advocates General.

The CJEU thus relied on the specific nature and context of the Community judiciary and concluded from this that the ECtHR case law did not apply in this context.[247] In other words it adopted an approach that was really autonomous from the ECtHR. This is the only clear example of a diverging and independent approach of the CJEU. Although the CJEU itself did not qualify this as an autonomous approach, it has been qualified in literature as such. Moreover, the approach taken clearly corresponds to the description of autonomous interpretation as employed in this thesis.

The example of *Emesa Sugar* seems to be the main example of diverging approaches in the interpretation phase. Interestingly, the reasons for the Court's diversion have not been considered convincing by everyone.[248] The decision thus raises the question why the CJEU adopted an autonomous approach here, and also why it has thus far only done so in this particular case. Perhaps it did make this choice because the approach of the ECtHR threatened the judicial structure of the CJEU,[249] but it could also be that the CJEU genuinely considered the two cases to be different.

Since autonomous interpretation in the case law of the CJEU on fundamental rights is relatively rare, in the sense that the Court usually tends to follow national and ECtHR interpretations, rather than providing one of its own, few conclusions can be drawn from the case law as to the use of the principle of autonomous interpretation. Some very careful assumptions can be made on the basis of the few cases discussed in this context. The theoretical discussion indicated that uniformity is an important goal of adopting an autonomous interpretation and the reasoning in the case of *Mantello* confirms this underlying goal of autonomous interpretation. That might at the same time be the reason why the CJEU has not often relied on a strong autonomous approach in fundamental rights cases. Taking an autonomous approach in those sensitive cases might in many cases have been one step too far for the CJEU.

---

247 C-17/98, *Emesa Sugar (Free Zone) NV v. Aruba* [2000] ECR I-00665.

248 Van den Berghe (2010), p. 144, referring to Lawson.

249 Van den Berghe (2010), p. 143.

The case of *DEB* is one example where an autonomous approach might have had far-reaching consequences. It should also be recalled that the area of fundamental rights has been termed in academic literature 'one of the least autonomous parts of European law'.[250] It has been suggested however, that more diverging approaches between the ECtHR and the CJEU can be found in the application phase and that both courts given their different contextual setting reach a different conclusion on questions of proportionality.[251] To that extent, the *application* of the rights still seems to be autonomous – but the phase of application of rights is not under study in this thesis.

Another interesting aspect of one of the cases discussed above is that *Mantello* could have been the textbook example of autonomous interpretation as an interpretative principle as discussed in this thesis. The autonomous interpretation in this case is clearly supported by references to interpretation methods. Unfortunately, there are too few examples to draw solid conclusions on the nature of the autonomous interpretation, but it is interesting to note that at least the potential is present.

13.5 Conclusion

The case law analysis has shown that all selected interpretative aids selected for this thesis are visible in the case law of the CJEU. The extent to which they can be found, however, greatly differs. Comparative interpretation is often relied upon and to a lesser extent teleological interpretation can be found as well. Evolutive interpretation and autonomous interpretation, however, play a much more limited role. As has been explained this is probably mainly the result of the particular context in which the CJEU has developed its fundamental rights case law, which lead it to follow closely either national law or, most frequently, the case law of the European Court on Human Rights. It may be said, perhaps, that, as a result of this approach, the CJEU interprets in an autonomous and evolutive manner to the extent that the ECtHR also does so. Also, it has been concluded that the case law approach of the CJEU may generally be qualified as evolutive, since it tends to follow changes and recent developments in national and ECtHR case law when constructing its own body of fundamental rights. Nevertheless, for the purposes of this study it is important that references to an autonomous approach, independent from that taken by the Member States or the Strasbourg Court, are extremely rare, just like references to the need to adapt the scope of fundamental rights to meet the needs of present-day conditions. For that reason,

250 Douglas-Scott referring to Bogdandy. Van de Berghe (2010), p. 150, argues that the CJEU, by referring to and relying on the ECtHR judgments, itself chose a higher authority in the human rights field and argues that the CJEU might not consider this as a threat for EU autonomy.

251 Van den Berghe (2010), p. 116.

hardly any conclusions can be drawn from this case law as to the deeper meaning these interpretative aids have for the CJEU's case law, whether this concerns their classification as principles or as methods of interpretation, the purpose to which they are used and the way in which a certain interpretation can be found in concrete cases.

The analysis of teleological interpretation indicated that this method mainly plays a role when the fundamental rights concerned are laid down in a legal text, either a directive or a treaty concluded in the EU context. In those cases the object and purpose are generally explained both by the CJEU and the Advocates General. Of course the discussion on the object and purpose are more elaborate by the Advocates General, but the CJEU at least provides a short insight into the meaning of the object and purpose in a specific case and how it has established that meaning. It has proven difficult to comment on the strength of teleological arguments, because even though the analysis showed that teleological arguments are often supported by other arguments, it is questionable whether those other arguments are always of equal force.

Comparative interpretation seems to play the most important role in the context of interpretation of fundamental rights. Given the specific historical position of fundamental rights in the EU, this is not very surprising. The theoretical discussion on comparative interpretation revealed that the basis or justification for comparative references was one of the most important aspects of this method, even more so in light of the distinction between internal and external comparative interpretation. The CJEU does not seem to acknowledge this distinction between external and internal comparative references. The main form of external comparative interpretation used by the CJEU, namely references to the ECHR, is justified by an explicit reference to this source in the EU treaty. In addition to strategic arguments advanced in the literature and only hinted at by the Advocates General, this does provide a strong basis for this type of external reference. One may question whether these references should be used to the extent that is presently the case, but that is a different matter.

Another important aspect identified in the theoretical analysis, is the practical use of comparative interpretation. Is it sufficiently explained what materials have been used for the comparative references? When relying on the ECtHR the CJEU generally refers to the specific cases, and also in the context of other external references, the specific documents are mentioned. In the context of internal comparative interpretation, however, when looking for common traditions, it is not always clear on what basis the conclusions are made. The conclusions in this area could become more transparent by indicating the materials that have been taken into account. This approach is visible in some cases. The most important practical concern also involved the search for a common tradition and the question when such a common tradition can be found. The analysis of both the CJEU and the Advocates General approach did not provide a clear indication of a criterion that shows when there is enough ground to find a common tradition. The ECtHR analysis showed a similar lack of any guidance as to when a consensus can be found. This might be an indication that for both courts it is extremely difficult to develop any guidelines in that respect. That does leave the use of this particular form of comparative interpretation open to criticism for lack of consistency and transparency.

An interesting question that warrants attention after this discussion of the CJEU's case law approach is whether the fact that the Charter has become binding will change anything in the judicial reasoning of the CJEU. The introduction on the CJEU, which was given in Chapter 3, already dealt with the question whether the fact that the CJEU will henceforth be dealing with a legally binding text will pose any new challenges. The conclusion was reached in that chapter that the text of the Charter is so broad that it probably will not make much of a difference if compared to the present situation. Moreover, the text mainly contains a codification of rights that already have been recognized. Nevertheless, the question still remains to be answered whether any changes are to be expected with regard to the use of the methods and principles that have been discussed in this chapter. Perhaps the most important question in that regard is whether the CJEU will continue to rely so strongly on the case law of the ECtHR. Article 52(3) of the Charter provides that:

> In so far as this Charter contains rights which correspond to rights guaranteed by the Convention for the Protection of Human Rights and Fundamental Freedoms, the meaning and scope of those rights shall be the same as those laid down by the said Convention. This provision shall not prevent Union law providing more extensive protection.

Thus, the European Convention and corresponding judgments can be expected to continue to play an important role. This is even more relevant, because the strategic arguments mentioned in section 6.3, are still valid, even though the Charter has become binding. In all probability, however, there will be some changes in the use of the methods and principles of interpretation. The number of references to common constitutional traditions will diminish, since the Charter is a codification of those common traditions and now provides a more direct and concrete basis for the CJEU's case law. Thus, comparative analyses may become less prominent than they currently are. However, the impact of this predictable change should not be overestimated. As can be seen in the context of the European Convention, the ECtHR still refers to the Member States in order to see whether developments warrant a new interpretation even though these rights have been laid down in the Convention. This particular form of comparative interpretation might start to play a role in the context of the CJEU as well, but the Charter is of a much more recent date, so the question is whether that will happen in the near future. In addition, it is likely that teleological interpretation will start to play a more important role, since the text of the Charter and the information that is available about the object and purpose provides a good basis for doing so. Closely connected to this, it may well be predicted that the CJEU will more visibly and expressly take up an evolutive approach. It is important to note that the probable relevance of these methods and principles will also have impact on the justification for their use, and on the way in which they are practically employed. To this extent, similar questions may become relevant for the CJEU as have already been asked in respect to the ECtHR. Indeed, it may be important for the CJEU to be well aware of the difficulties related to the various methods and to take careful notice of the way in which both academic literature and the ECtHR itself have responded to these difficulties.

Whereas it is probable that comparative, evolutive and teleological interpretation will grow more important in the CJEU's fundamental rights case law as a result of the Charter, it remains questionable whether autonomous interpretation will take up a more prominent approach. The European Convention and its case law remain important and it is not likely, given the strategic reasons discussed in section 6.3, that the CJEU will take a bolder approach and divert much from the interpretations adopted in Strasbourg.

PART IV

CONCLUSION

CHAPTER 14
CONCLUSION

The aim of this research project undertaken for the purpose of the present book has been to analyze the use of four interpretative instruments (teleological, comparative, evolutive and autonomous interpretation) by the Court of Justice of the European Union and the European Court of Human Rights: two supranational courts dealing with fundamental rights cases in a multilevel legal context. This setting poses specific difficulties for these courts, because, as indicated in the introduction, their effectiveness depends in large part on the cooperation of national authorities in the Contracting States / Member States. Therefore it is important for these courts to persuade national authorities of the need and value to implement their judgments by means of national legislation, case law and policy. Only then will these courts be able to afford individuals effective protection of their fundamental rights. A crucial aspect in trying to engage national authorities is to convince them of the need to adhere to the fundamental rights judgments, even if they might not agree with the conclusion in specific cases. This requires sound, objective and transparent legal reasoning. After all, if outsiders can understand on which arguments the conclusion is based, it is easier to accept it.[1] The importance of transparency and objectivity of reasoning for the European Courts has been held to raise the question whether the reasoning of both courts provides sufficient insight into the factors that have led to the adopted conclusion. In the introduction, it was stressed that such insight is all the more important because of the multilevel setting in which both courts have to operate. Any subjectivity on the side of the courts should be prevented, since that might generate criticism of the courts' reasoning and therefore weaken the persuasiveness of the conclusions reached. Thus, the main value on which the analysis in this thesis is based is that interpretation methods and principles should be used in a such a manner that it is clear how the conclusion has been reached and what factors played a role in doing so.

The main aim of this research project has thus been to analyze the use of a selected number of interpretative aids in the context of fundamental rights adjudication at the European Court of Human Rights and the Court of Justice of the European Union from a theoretical and practical perspective. The first part of the book provides a theoretical analysis as to how the four selected interpretative instruments ought to be used in theory in order to provide a persuasive part of the Courts' legal reasoning.

1 See Chapter 1.

The analysis focused on a few main questions that have been addressed for each interpretative aid. What basis or justification can be found for relying on these interpretative instruments? The question how the use of the specific method or principle has been justified does not play an equally important role for each interpretative aid. What aspects play a role when courts use these interpretative instruments? The theoretical analysis indicated for each method and principle, the main aspects that should be addressed when using this particular interpretative aid. What are the pitfalls of using these interpretative instruments? What criticism has been expressed in theoretical literature on the use of these interpretative aids in general or at the use of these aids in practice? Have any solutions for improvement been suggested? Not in all situations have improvements been discussed in legal literature, but the aim has been to discuss all interpretative aids suggestions to enhance the use of interpretative aids in practice. On the basis of this theoretical analysis an image emerged of the ideal use of all four interpretative instruments. Subsequently, a case law analysis addressed the actual use of these interpretative aids in the judgments of both courts. The questions addressed in the theoretical analysis formed a structure for the case law analysis as well.

Against this background, this final conclusion aims to discuss the main findings of both the theoretical and the case law parts of this thesis. In particular, attention will thereby be given to the question to what extent the theoretical analysis can help to enhance the actual use of the interpretative instruments by the CJEU and the ECtHR. The consecutive sections will each deal with one of the four interpretation methods or principles. However, the first section will briefly recall the central theoretical and practical findings with respect to both courts. The discussion of the proposed framework will then be continued when dealing with the separate interpretation methods and principles and try to establish whether the CJEU and ECtHR could benefit from looking at each other. Finally some closing remarks will be made.

14.1 Interpretation methods and interpretative principles

One of the starting points of this thesis is that a distinction should be made between interpretation *methods* and interpretative *principles*. An interpretation method is a technique that clarifies which substantive argument has been used in order to support a specific reasoning and which helps the judge to objectify its reasoning. An interpretative principle serves as an objective or aim that can be taken into account when interpreting a provision with the help of an interpretation method. As explained in Chapter 4, interpretative principles and interpretation methods have a different function in the interpretation process. Comparative interpretation and teleological interpretation have been identified as interpretation methods. In the case of comparative interpretation the comparative materials used by the respective court constitute the substantive argument that justifies the interpretative choice. For teleological interpretation, the reference to the object and purpose comprises the substantive argument that indicates on what grounds the interpretative conclusion has been reached. On the other hand, evolutive interpretation and autonomous interpretation have been qualified as interpretative principles, because both primarily indicate a goal that a court wants to achieve. The aim of evolutive interpretation is to prevent fundamental rights from becoming dead letters, while the aim of autonomous interpretation is to prevent Member or Contracting States from circumventing fundamental rights protection. The aim of these interpretative principles can be achieved by relying on different interpretation methods. One could argue that this is not the case for evolutive interpretation, but that point will be addressed when dealing with evolutive interpretation below.

The distinction between interpretation methods and interpretative principles has been introduced in the theoretical discussion of interpretation methods and principles, which raised the question whether this distinction can be seen in the case law as well. Put differently: Is this distinction actually visible in practice or is its relevance mainly theoretical? It has appeared from the case law analysis that the ECtHR does not seem to acknowledge this distinction in its case law, at least not explicitly. Comparative and teleological interpretation are used in such a manner that it is clear that they are viewed by the ECtHR as interpretation *methods*. However, the potentially controversial aspect of this distinction is not so much whether comparative and teleological interpretation are recognized as interpretation methods, but whether evolutive and autonomous interpretation are recognized as interpretative *principles*. Moreover, the pertinent question is whether they are recognized as principles to the full extent of the distinction, meaning that the respective court acknowledges that a separate interpretation method is needed to establish the meaning of the evolutive or autonomous concept. The discussion of the specific interpretative principles below will aim to answer this question on the basis of the case law analysis of the ECtHR. The CJEU also employs comparative and teleological interpretation as interpretation methods. The use of evolutive and autonomous interpretation is hardly visible in the case law of the CJEU, as will be discussed below. That makes it difficult to draw conclusions on the question whether the CJEU acknowledges them as interpretative principles.

14.2 Teleological interpretation

Teleological interpretation has played a role at two levels in this thesis, i.e. both at a meta level and at a micro level. Micro-teleological interpretation refers to the well-known interpretation method whereby the object and purpose of a provision or treaty are used to justify an interpretative conclusion. Meta-teleological interpretation is a concept introduced by Lasser in the context of judicial reasoning by the CJEU. It refers to the phenomenon that certain interpretative principles are based on an understanding of the object and purpose of the treaty system as a whole. These principles are thus a reflection of some of the values that underlie the treaty system, in the case of this thesis either the EU or the Convention system. The case law analysis in this thesis has endeavoured to establish for both courts to what extent any reasoning based on such meta-teleological principles or values is visible. Even though the concept was developed in the context of the CJEU, the CJEU's fundamental rights case law did not really show clear signs of meta-teleological reasoning. Perhaps the peculiar role of fundamental rights in the EU can be regarded as an explanation for this. In the ECtHR case law, on the other hand, many signs of meta-teleological reasoning are visible. The overarching, meta-teleological principle of practical and effective interpretation has provided fertile ground for other interpretative principles, like evolutive interpretation and autonomous interpretation. Many judgments refer to the fact that the European Convention, as a human rights treaty, needs to be interpreted in a way that ensures the effectiveness of these rights and does not render them theoretical and illusory. Two of these principles have been discussed at length in this thesis and will be addressed below.

Micro-teleological interpretation is also visible in the case law of both courts. This method is regularly used to help to solve interpretative problems. An important question in understanding micro-teleological reasoning is whether the courts explain the meaning of the object and purpose and how this is established. In this regard, it is important to note that the theoretical analysis indicated that *objective* teleological interpretation can be considered to be the most important form of teleological interpretation in the context of fundamental rights adjudication, meaning that the object and purpose are mainly established on the basis of a 'rational' drafter, rather than the original drafters. The case law proves to correspond to this theoretical analysis. The object and purpose of the drafters play only a minor role in the reasoning of both courts, which is understandable given the importance of evolutive interpretation.

The analysis in the second part of this thesis has further disclosed that micro-teleological interpretation mainly plays a role in the case law of the CJEU when the CJEU is dealing with fundamental rights problems that have some basis in a legal text, like a directive, or a treaty that has been established in the EU context. In those situations the CJEU mostly substantiates the reference to the object and purpose of the text or provision in question and explains how it arrived at this conclusion. The Advocate General is often even more elaborate in explaining the object and purpose. The fact that micro-teleological interpretation mainly plays a role when a text is involved, may be regarded as an indication that the role of this method could increase in the future as a result of the binding nature of the Charter.

Within the case law of the ECtHR, the object and purpose of a particular treaty provision are not always substantiated, nor is it always explained how the object and purpose have been established. The reference to the object and purpose often remains rather vague and its helpfulness to reaching insightful conclusions remains unclear. In this respect, the ECtHR could take the CJEU as an example and put more effort into justifying the meaning of the object and purpose of a specific provision and explaining how it has been established. This 'carelessness' of the ECtHR in establishing the object and purpose has not led to much apparent discussion among the judges – hardly ever the issue of teleological interpretation is visible in concurring or dissenting opinion.

While in theory, however, it might seem an improvement of the reasoning of the ECtHR if it would pay more attention to the particular objectives of a Convention provision, the question is whether aiming to put more flesh on the bones of the object and purpose would be beneficial in practice. It might also make the Court's reasoning more vulnerable, because, if the object and purpose are substantiated to a larger extent, this opens the floor for more controversy or criticism of those who do not agree with the chosen path. Thus, the deliberate choice not to apply micro-teleological interpretation in great detail may have its advantages, even if it results in a lack of transparency and clarity as regards the way in which the Court has reached its decisions.

14.3 Comparative interpretation

Comparative interpretation has proven to be a method of interpretation that plays an important role in the reasoning of both the CJEU and the ECtHR. This thesis has taken comparative interpretation to mean a type of reasoning that is based on references to foreign materials. The comparative materials provide a substantive argument that can be used as a basis for a certain interpretative conclusion; for that reason, this use can be classified as a *method* of interpretation, rather than an interpretative principle. It has already been indicated that this is generally recognized in theoretical literature and the case law analysis seems to confirm the hypothesis that comparative materials are used as a method to arrive at certain conclusions. The qualification of comparative interpretation as a method of interpretation thus does not seem to be disputed.

On the other hand, open to debate appears to be whether comparative interpretation inevitably includes evolutive interpretation. A difference in perspective on this issue is mainly visible in scholarly literature on the ECtHR, where some authors consider comparative interpretation and evolutive interpretation to be one single concept. Nevertheless, it can also be considered that comparative and evolutive interpretation are essentially different interpretative aids and that they have different functions for the courts' interpretation. It is the latter perspective that has been adhered to in this thesis. For that reason, evolutive interpretation will be addressed separately in the subsequent section.

Comparative interpretation has been employed for a variety of purposes by the European Courts. Both courts use it to solve regular interpretative problems and to help it to give shape to an evolutive approach. Moreover, the CJEU has also used the method to construe fundamental rights when there was not yet an EU catalogue of fundamental rights. The ECtHR has used comparative interpretation as justification for its avoidance of certain interpretative matters (e.g. the question as to when the right to life begins) or to corroborate textual interpretation (e.g. the finding that certain elements are not included in the text of the Convention).

An important distinction put forward in this thesis is the distinction between *external* and *internal* comparative interpretation. Internal comparative interpretation takes place when references are made to legal materials or to the practice of the states that fall within the jurisdiction of the respective court, i.e., in the case of the CJEU, references to the Member States of the European Union, and, in case of the ECtHR, to the Contracting States of the European Convention. External comparative interpretation refers to all other foreign instruments that are used in a judicial reasoning, like references to UN treaties or judgments of the Canadian Supreme Court. This distinction is not necessarily only relevant for defining comparative interpretation at international or supranational courts. In a federal system, like the United States of America, this could be a useful distinction as well. The following discussion will first address the use of internal comparative interpretation, before dealing with external comparative interpretation.

The case law analysis has demonstrated that neither the ECtHR nor the CJEU explicitly acknowledges the distinction between internal and external comparative interpretation in their case law. They do, however, mostly refer to materials of the Member States or the Contracting States in a different manner than to materials from other jurisdictions or international systems. In the case law of the ECtHR, the internal component of comparative interpretation is almost exclusively used for the purpose of establishing a consensus. In many cases, the ECtHR refers to the Contracting States to show the existence of a consensus or the lack thereof and uses that to support a specific interpretative conclusion. Within the context of the CJEU, the common constitutional traditions that flow from the Member States are one of the main sources of inspiration firstly identified by the CJEU and later codified in the EU treaty. The purpose of internal comparative interpretation at the CJEU is also to attempt to find a common ground that can serve as a basis for an interpretative conclusion.

A problem noted in theoretical discussions on the practical side of establishing this internal consensus or common ground is that for neither court is it clear when there is sufficient evidence to conclude that one can speak of a consensus or common ground. There are no numerical guidelines that can help one to understand this process. The case law analysis of the courts did not provide much more clarity in this respect. Within the context of the CJEU, several Advocates General have indicated that the search for a common ground is not necessarily a search for a common solution, but one for the solution that best fits the EU system. This suggestion has also been made in academic literature. That would imply that the outcome of the references to the

Member States, so the outcome of comparative interpretation, is subjected to a teleological assessment before a final conclusion is reached as to the proper meaning of a certain fundamental right. Several judgments have demonstrated, however, that there is a line where there is so much diversity among the Member States that it cannot be used to support a specific conclusion. Accordingly it must be accepted that the search for a common ground cannot be equated to a matter of finding the best solution. The actual criterion remains a mystery, however. Similarly, within the context of the ECtHR, much remains unclear with regard to the question when one can speak of a consensus. The case law analysis did not provide much clarification in this respect. Rather, it revealed that even the various judges sometimes disagree on whether one can really speak of consensus. This obscurity in both courts when it comes to the use of an internal consensus or common ground makes it rather difficult to understand why in some cases a consensus or common tradition has been found, whilst in others there was not enough support for such a conclusion. This undoubtedly affects the objectivity of this particular use of this method, as it is not possible to check the consistency of the use of this method. An important aspect for improvement for both courts is thus to provide more insight into this aspect of internal comparative interpretation.

The question is, of course, how this should be done. Should the courts provide numerical guidelines that indicate when one can speak of sufficient evidence depending perhaps on the sensitivity of the rights in question? That seems hardly feasible and for strategic reasons it might not be possible or desirable to draft such guidelines. It is therefore not easy to find a way in which to explain in an insightful manner when the conclusions that result from an internal comparison should be accepted, and when they should be considered not strong enough to support a specific interpretation. A potential solution will be discussed below.

As has been mentioned above, external comparative interpretation refers to the use of comparative material that springs from all other foreign or international sources. Such sources may be materials from non-European countries, international treaties, other international documents (such as soft law), case law from other international or supranational courts, etc. Thus, a wide range of materials qualifies as a basis for external comparative interpretation. The case law analysis has demonstrated that both courts often refer to such external sources, like UN treaties, Council of Europe treaties or ILO conventions. The ECtHR has also on occasion (more often than the CJEU or its Advocates General) relied on references to third countries, like Canada or the United States of America. One specific type of 'external' reference is the reference made by the CJEU to the ECtHR or vice versa. This type of reference plays a more prominent role in the context of the CJEU than in that of the ECtHR. It is of course understandable for many different reasons that the CJEU looks at the ECtHR's case law, rather than the other way around, given the latter's experience with fundamental rights protection.

References to external sources are used by the courts in a different manner than references to internal sources. Usually, one or a few individual references are used to support a specific conclusion. Only the ECtHR in some cases relied on a consensus derived from external sources to support an evolutive interpretation. Of course, this raises the same practical problems as a search for an internal consensus. Moreover, this use of external sources may raise questions as to its legitimacy.

Indeed, the main reason for making the distinction between internal and external comparative interpretation, is that a different justification may be required for relying on internal or external comparative interpretation. Relying on internal sources can be seen as a way to keep a link with the countries in which the fundamental rights protection needs to be implemented. This justification cannot be used for external references, which therefore require a different justification. That justification needs to explain why these materials are relevant in the context of the respective system. Why is it relevant to look at the Inter-American Court of Human Rights, ILO Conventions or UN treaties? Or, in the case of the ECtHR, why is it relevant to rely on international soft law documents or on judgments of the United States Supreme Court? There can be different reasons for looking at each document, but the theoretical analysis indicated that many of these do not suffice to explain why external materials are relevant. The fact that some materials just seem to be helpful to support a specific reasoning is not sufficient from a theoretical perspective – indeed, it does hardly enhance the legitimacy of the judgments based on such interpretation.

Are the CJEU and ECtHR aware of the necessity to justify the use of external materials? It has been shown in Chapter 13 that the CJEU in some cases mentioned that the treaties referred to in its reasoning were ratified by all Member States. This seems to imply that the CJEU wants to stress the relevance of such an international treaty for all the Member States. The ECtHR, on the other hand, has even accepted novel interpretations on the basis of international treaties which were not signed or ratified by the respondent state. It has either not provided any justification for such reliance on external references, or it has limited itself to referring to the fact that the European Convention does not operate in a vacuum. That is certainly true and there can of course be strategic reasons for invoking references to these external materials. The question is whether these reasons sufficiently explain why obligations arising from treaties or conventions that have not been ratified by all Contracting States should be incorporated into fundamental rights obligations under the ECHR.

As was already mentioned, a special category of external comparative interpretation consists of the references by the CJEU to the ECHR and the corresponding case law. This form of external comparative interpretation plays a vital role in the case law of the CJEU. In many CJEU judgments, extensive reference is made to the ECHR and judgments of the ECtHR. Judgments from Strasbourg are thereby often referred to almost in the same manner as precedents from the CJEU itself. Only in rare cases has the CJEU opted for a different approach than the ECtHR. Since this form of external comparative interpretation has been incorporated in the EU treaty, as well as in the EU Charter, a strong justification is given for the use of such 'external' material.

It has to be admitted that the use of external comparative interpretation is more controversial in theory than in practice. However, given the criticism that has been directed at the ECtHR for its reliance on non-ratified international treaties that had not been ratified by the respondent Contracting State, there is certainly value in trying to enhance the justification provided for external comparative interpretation.

The main question is what kind of justification can be provided for the use of external materials that are presently not sufficiently justified. The theoretical analysis disclosed a specific mode of comparative interpretation that might offer good prospects in this regard, namely dialogical interpretation. This mode for external comparative interpretation was developed by CHOUDHRY and it was subsequently taken up by many scholars in the field of comparative interpretation. The main idea behind dialogical interpretation is that references to external comparative materials should be used to improve the judge's understanding of his or her own system. These external materials should thus be used as a means for self-reflection. By looking at another system or solution a judge will be triggered to think about his or her own system. As a result of this self-reflection it will be possible to argue on the basis of the judge's own system whether the external solution fits in. The reasons for adopting or refusing a solution will then come from one's own system, which enhances the legitimacy of referring to these external materials.

This approach may be visible in judgments from the Canadian Supreme Court, but how is this with the case law of the CJEU or ECtHR? It has been found that no clear signs of this approach to external comparative interpretation are visible in the case law of these two courts. That prompts the question whether this mode can actually be relevant in practice, or whether it is mainly an interesting theoretical concept. The thought that looking at other external solutions can help to increase the understanding of the values and principles underlying the judge's own system can certainly be valuable. If the reasons for looking at external comparative interpretation finally stem from *within* the judge's own system, this conception also may help to avoid some of the current problems, such as those related to non-ratification of an international treaty. Moreover, the conception might also be useful when dealing with internal comparative interpretation. Problematic in the context of finding an internal consensus is that there is no clear criterion that can justify why certain results of an internal comparison are relevant in one case and not in another. Of course in the obvious situations when there actually is a consensus, there is no problem. In the majority of situations, however, the results of an internal comparison are not that clear-cut.

Dialogical interpretation in this respect might provide a solution to the practical problems connected to consensus interpretation. The outcome of the internal comparison could force judges to consider whether that solution would be in line with their own systems (i.e. either the Convention system or the EU legal system). It thus resembles what two Advocates General have found to take place at the CJEU, namely finding the best or the most appropriate solution on the basis of inspiration drawn from the various national constitutional systems.

One of the consequences of a dialogical approach to comparative interpretation would be that it would lead the judges and Advocates General of the CJEU and the judges on the ECtHR to develop more fully the principles and values under their respective systems. The EU and Convention systems and the rights resulting from it would thus be further developed in terms of substance. It would also be necessary to consider what the system really stands for in order to make a proper assessment as to whether a specific foreign solution will fit within the system. In theory this may be highly desirable, but whether this is feasible in practice remains to be seen. After all, the ECHR only provides minimum norms and the ECtHR strives to leave sufficient leeway to the Contracting States to make their own decisions as regards the protection of fundamental rights. If the ECtHR were to make more substantive choices by adopting a dialogical approach, this might provide more insight into its reasoning. As has been submitted earlier, such might be desirable from a theoretical perspective, but it might also lead to even more controversy. Contracting States might object to a more substantive approach out of fear of losing even more terrain to the judges in Strasbourg. Moreover, states (or critics in general) may now not agree with the foreign sources used in the ECtHR's reasoning, but if these materials are used for self-reflection they might end up not agreeing with the Convention system as a whole. This same risk can be seen in the context of the CJEU. However, given that the CJEU operates within the context of the EU, which is a legal order with a specific aim and purpose, it might be easier for the CJEU to use dialogical interpretation as a means of self-reflection. Thus, the notion of dialogical interpretation might be regarded as a good way for the CJEU to deal with external instruments and it might be rather easy to fit in the notion with its current practice, especially since it has already been seen to form a part of this Court's approach by some of the Advocates General.

Thus, the preceding discussion should not be understood as an argument against dialogical interpretation. On the contrary, it is a valuable theoretical option that could help further the debate on the justification for (external) comparative interpretation. There is indeed an element of doubt, however, whether in practice this form of reasoning would solve problems or create additional ones, especially in the context of the ECtHR.

14.4 Evolutive interpretation

Evolutive interpretation is one of the meta-teleological principles that were central to this thesis. It indicates that the rights subjected to interpretation should not be viewed in a static manner and should be adapted to the changes of time. Both courts rely on this interpretative principle in their reasoning, but the ECtHR refers to it on a much larger scale than the CJEU. The ECtHR has justified its strongly evolutive approach by pointing to the need to keep rights practical and effective, rather than theoretical and illusory. Within the context of the CJEU, Advocate General Tesauro has also stressed the need to avoid taking a static role and to keep in pace with social change. Both courts thus recognize the need to take an evolutive approach, but in the case of the ECtHR this is most clearly linked to a meta-teleological approach by indicating that adopting an evolutive approach is necessary to attain the meta-purposes of the European Convention.

The nature of evolutive interpretation as a principle of interpretation did not become clear from the theoretical analysis. Especially in literature on the ECtHR, evolutive interpretation is often considered to be synonymous to comparative interpretation and thus it is often considered a method of interpretation. This thesis has defended the view that evolutive interpretation should be seen as a separate concept with a different function, namely as an interpretative goal, but not a substantive argument that can be used as a basis for a specific reasoning. Is this understanding of the nature of evolutive interpretation as an interpretative principle reflected in the case law of the CJEU and the ECtHR? The case law analysis of the CJEU provided too little materials from the CJEU or its Advocates General to provide a sufficient basis for drawing any conclusions on whether they regard evolutive interpretation as an interpretative principle. With regard to the ECtHR, it is also difficult to answer this question on the basis of the case law, since the ECtHR is rather unclear about the nature of evolutive interpretation. The fact that the use of evolutive interpretation is justified by referring to the object and purpose of the Convention as a whole in itself would seem to support the conclusion that the ECtHR considers it to be a meta-teleological principle. This is, however, a rather small basis for drawing that conclusion. Nevertheless, the way in which evolutive interpretation is used, generally fits the description of an interpretative principle as employed in this thesis, since the ECtHR almost always relies on a further interpretation *method* to support its final conclusion. There is still some reason for doubt as to the exact function of evolutive interpretation in the Strasbourg case law, however. Given the fact that the ECtHR most often relies on comparative interpretation, one may wonder whether the ECtHR views evolutive and comparative interpretation as two distinct interpretative aids (the one being a principle, the other a method), or just as one interpretative aid.

Why should we consider the distinction between evolutive interpretation as a principle and comparative interpretation as a method to be important? This may be explained by recalling the analysis of the purposes for which comparative arguments are used by both courts under study. As indicated in section 14.3 of this conclusion, comparative interpretation is used for several purposes in the case law of both courts, only one of which is to support an evolutive approach. Comparative interpretation is often used to solve an interpretative problem without there being any need to indicate that society has changed since a specific earlier point in time. In the context of the CJEU, comparative interpretation has also been used extensively to *construe* rights, rather than to interpret them in an evolutive manner. For both courts there are also cases in which comparative interpretation has been used to establish an evolutive interpretation. To view both concepts as synonymous would thus on the basis of the case law analysis not reflect the full extent of the various purposes of comparative interpretation and the justification that might be given for such use.

Even though this thesis argues that evolutive interpretation and comparative interpretation should be viewed as two separate concepts, there is an undeniably close relationship between the two. Evolutive interpretation as a principle does not provide a meaning to rights or terms. It indicates that instead of a static approach a more dynamic approach can be an important value in a certain legal order. In order to establish the evolutive meaning of a term or principle at a certain point in time interpretation methods are needed to provide substantive arguments. Comparative interpretation provides a useful method to establish an evolutive interpretation. In particular, internal comparative interpretation is regularly used to determine the evolutive meaning of a specific right or term. Problematic is that, as a result of this, the practical concerns related to comparative interpretation (being mainly that it is not clear when one can speak of a consensus or common ground), may also affect evolutive interpretation. By acknowledging the different functions of comparative and evolutive interpretation it at least channels the criticism to the correct interpretative aid. The close relation between comparative and evolutive interpretation does not mean that comparative interpretation is the only method that can help to establish the evolutive meaning of a specific term or right. Arguments based on textual or teleological interpretation could also be used. The objective purpose of a provision can change over time or through technological changes terms can gain a different meaning over time. In practice, however, these justifications for a specific evolutive meaning have not been provided by the CJEU or the ECtHR.

The theoretical analysis showed that evolutive interpretation is sometimes also criticized for its lack of a guiding principle that determines its application. However, in the framework proposed in this thesis evolutive interpretation should be seen as a guiding principle itself. As such, it is a principle that can be used to help the courts to make choices between potential conclusions that arise from teleological or comparative interpretation. Evolutive interpretation can thus help to choose between option A or B or C, even though it in itself cannot attach a specific meaning to a term or right.

As indicated above, some elements of this use of evolutive interpretation are visible in the case law, mainly in that of the ECtHR. Nonetheless, if this distinction were to be more fully embraced and applied in the reasoning of both courts, it would force the judges to explain more clearly what the evolutive meaning is of a specific term and, more importantly, to explain how they arrived at that conclusion. Especially in the context of ever-expanding fundamental rights, sound reasoning is required to indicate where to draw a certain line. The framework presented here might help to push for such sound reasoning.

14.5 AUTONOMOUS INTERPRETATION

Autonomous interpretation is an interpretative principle that is generally based on a desire for uniformity. To take an autonomous approach means that an international court does not let the qualification of a specific term under domestic law be decisive for its own interpretation. The international or supranational judge thus develops its own understanding of a specific term, separate and independently from any outside qualification, whether it is a domestic qualification or a qualification under another international regime. The theoretical analysis indicated that legal commentaries also suggest that there is a strategic reason for these courts to adopt an autonomous interpretation. By adopting an autonomous approach, the Court in question strengthens its jurisdictional power by taking explicit control over the interpretation of a specific term.

The form of autonomous interpretation that has been mostly found in the case law of the two courts is autonomous interpretation with regard to *domestic* qualifications. In the context of the CJEU autonomous interpretation has, however, also been used in relation to the ECtHR. This form of autonomous interpretation is rather rare. While autonomous interpretation in relation to domestic qualifications is mainly driven by the desire for uniformity, autonomous interpretation in relation to the ECtHR can perhaps best be explained on a more strategic basis, that in some cases the CJEU wants to keep control.

The analysis in this thesis has focused on those instances of 'strong' autonomy, meaning those cases where the CJEU or the ECtHR expressly indicated that they were adopting an autonomous approach. Both courts have confirmed, in one way or another, that the basic idea behind autonomous interpretation is that an autonomous approach is sometimes necessary to ensure uniform protection of fundamental rights, and thus to avoid states being able to hide behind domestic qualifications.

The theoretical analysis indicated that autonomous interpretation would mainly be used to determine the meaning of technical legal terms, like 'criminal charge' and 'property'. The case law analysis of the ECtHR has confirmed this perception, but it has also shown that, in recent years, autonomous interpretation has been used to interpret an increasing variety of non-technical legal terms, like 'home'. However, even though the Convention terms interpreted by means of autonomous interpretation may no longer all classify as solely technical legal terms, autonomous interpretation does seem to have been reserved for terms that do not have a strong moral connotation.

In the context of the CJEU, too few examples of an autonomous approach in fundamental rights cases have been found to draw the definite conclusion that it applies autonomous interpretation to a specific type of term. Nevertheless, the fact that uniformity is the driving force behind autonomous interpretation at the CJEU may be considered to imply that the CJEU, too, would avoid applying an autonomous interpretation to morally contested terms and rights, like 'life'.

Autonomous interpretation has been qualified as a meta-teleological principle, but is this nature of autonomous interpretation reflected in the case law of the CJEU and the ECtHR? There are indications in the reasoning of both courts that they acknowledge that autonomous interpretation has a distinct nature from regular interpretation methods. In a rare case where an explicitly autonomous approach was visible, the CJEU referred to an 'autonomous concept'. Moreover, the CJEU subsequently relied on several interpretation methods to establish the meaning of this 'autonomous concept'. Such a single case may not 'prove' that the CJEU acknowledges the distinction made in this thesis and the consequences flowing from it, but it at least provides an indication to this effect.

The ECtHR also seems to realize that the nature of autonomous interpretation is different from the nature of interpretation methods. It refers to autonomous interpretation as an approach that is justified with a reference to the object and purpose of the Convention as a whole. As a result it can be regarded as a meta-teleological principle in the Court's case law. As already explained, one of the characteristics of interpretative principles is that referring to an interpretative principle cannot justify a specific interpretation. It should be used in combination with an interpretation method. When applying autonomous interpretation, however, the ECtHR has been shown to invoke an interpretation method only in a few cases. This seems to imply that, even though the ECtHR acknowledges the special nature of autonomous interpretation, it does not attach the same consequences to this special nature as would be preferred from the perspective of transparent and clear judicial reasoning. The example of the CJEU could be instructive for the ECtHR in this respect. Such justification of an autonomous meaning by reference to distinct and clear interpretation methods will be helpful in borderline cases to arrive at a novel interpretation in a consistent and non-arbitrary manner.

14.6 General conclusion

Many of the problems discussed in this thesis were more clearly visible in the case law of the ECtHR. One explanation for this may be found in the historical lack of a legally binding catalogue of fundamental rights in the EU, which has resulted in a very particular approach to establishing fundamental rights. This may certainly change now that the Charter has become binding. In cases in which the CJEU had a text as a basis, it has already showed to be more explicit about its interpretative aids. The discussions of the use of such aids by the ECtHR are therefore certainly relevant for the CJEU. They are moreover also relevant from the perspective that the CJEU currently relies heavily on the ECHR and the case law of the ECtHR. Flawed reasoning at the ECtHR will thus resonate in the case law of the CJEU. Therefore, improvement of the legal reasoning at the ECtHR may also prove to be important for the CJEU.

The aim of this thesis has been, by analyzing both theory and practice, to point out the areas where such improvements can be made. The thesis has shown that it is difficult to suggest any concrete improvements to be made, given the complicated multilevel context in which both the CJEU and the ECtHR have to operate. Although it might be desirable to arrive at more transparent and revealing interpretative conclusions, this also often means that a more substantive approach has to be adopted. This could result in resistance from states that do not agree with such a more substantive approach, which raises the question whether that would really improve matters in the bigger picture. Nevertheless, one of the improvements that can be made without requiring a more substantive approach is to adopt the distinction between methods and principles of interpretation. By adopting this distinction courts are automatically forced to provide a proper explanation for establishing an evolutive or autonomous approach by relying on relevant interpretation methods. And, moreover, if the courts should show (express or implicit) awareness of the problems identified in this thesis, much would be gained already.

Samenvatting

De interpretatie van fundamentele rechten in een veellagig rechtssysteem

Fundamentele rechten zijn notoir vaag en algemeen geformuleerd. Als gevolg van deze algemene formulering bestaat er veel onduidelijkheid over de exacte betekenis van fundamentele rechten. De tekst zelf biedt meestal weinig houvast. Daarnaast hebben vragen over de betekenis van fundamentele rechten vaak betrekking op controversiële zaken waar zeer verschillend over kan worden gedacht. Door de vage formulering wordt de invulling van fundamentele rechten overgelaten aan rechters in individuele zaken. Rechters worden dus regelmatig geconfronteerd met vragen die betrekking hebben op de reikwijdte van fundamentele rechten. In de interpretatiefase, die in dit proefschrift wordt onderscheiden van de toepassingsfase, zal een rechter invulling moeten geven aan de betekenis van het fundamentele recht in kwestie. Een rechter dient de keuze voor een bepaalde interpretatie van een fundamenteel recht te verantwoorden, zodat inzichtelijk wordt hoe hij tot een bepaalde keuze is gekomen. Alleen dan kan er een zinvol debat plaatsvinden over de kwaliteit en de overtuigingskracht van de redenering en dus over de interpretatie van het fundamentele recht dat voorwerp is van het geschil. Interpretatieve instrumenten spelen een belangrijke rol bij de verantwoording van interpretatieve keuzes.

In dit proefschrift staat een aantal interpretatieve instrumenten centraal. De keuze voor juist die instrumenten wordt verklaard door de centraalstelling van de twee hoven die het onderwerp vormen van deze studie. De problematiek van juridische argumentatie wordt in dit proefschrift bekeken vanuit het Europees Hof voor de Rechten van de Mens (EHRM) en het Hof van Justitie van de Europese Unie (HvJ EU). Van laatstgenoemd rechtscollege is uitsluitend onderzoek gedaan naar zaken waarin fundamentele rechten een rol spelen. De hoven zijn gekozen om twee redenen. Allereerst opereren zij beide in een zeer complexe, veellagige juridische context. Als Europese rechters dienen zij rekening te houden met zowel de Europese context als de nationale context van de verschillende lidstaten. Daarnaast speelt het belang van de individuele klager een rol. Deze verschillende lagen en belangen vormen de complexe achtergrond waartegen het EHRM en het HvJ EU beslissingen moeten nemen. Vanwege die achtergrond is het belangrijk dat Europese rechters hun interpretatieve keuzes op inzichtelijke wijze verantwoorden. Voorts speelt een rol dat de beide hoven veel zijn bekritiseerd, zowel wat betreft hun algehele functioneren, als – meer specifiek – hun juridische argumentatie. Juist deze kritiek, gekoppeld aan het feit dat beide hoven voor een groot deel afhankelijk zijn van de medewerking van de lidstaten, maakt dat het relevant is om kritisch te kijken naar een onderdeel van de juridische argumentatie, namelijk de interpretatiefase.

Voor het onderzoek in dit proefschrift zijn interpretatieve instrumenten geselecteerd die kunnen helpen een balans te vinden tussen de verschillende belangen die spelen in een veellagig rechtssysteem. Teleologische, comparatieve, evolutieve en autonome interpretatie zijn de vier instrumenten die voor beide hoven zijn geanalyseerd. Alle vier de geselecteerde methoden zijn onderworpen aan een theoretische en een rechtspraakanalyse. Op grond van de theoretische analyse zijn vragen, hypotheses en analytische suggesties opgesteld die vervolgens zijn getoetst in de rechtspraakanalyse.

Voor de analyse van de vier interpretatieve instrumenten is een praktische benadering gekozen door te kijken naar de belangrijkste punten van kritiek. Er is, als gezegd, veel kritiek op de inzichtelijkheid van de redenering van de twee hoven, en, daaraan gekoppeld, is er ook kritiek op de objectiviteit van de redering. Als niet duidelijk is hoe een keuze tot stand is gekomen, kan er twijfel ontstaan of subjectieve factoren die betrekking hebben op de persoon van de rechter een rol hebben gespeeld. Het uitgangspunt is dat duidelijk moet zijn op welke gronden een keuze voor een bepaalde interpretatie is gemaakt.

Onderscheid tussen methoden en beginselen

Voorafgaand aan de discussie over de verschillende interpretatieve instrumenten is een onderscheid gemaakt tussen interpretatiemethoden en interpretatiebeginselen. In de literatuur wordt, zowel ten aanzien van interpretatie door beide hoven als ten aanzien van interpretatie in het algemeen, veelal onduidelijk gebruik gemaakt van de verschillende termen, terwijl er wel degelijk een verschil bestaat tussen de verschillende labels.

Een interpretatiemethode geeft aan op welk inhoudelijk element een argument kan worden gebaseerd. Bij tekstuele interpretatie wordt een argument bijvoorbeeld gebaseerd op de tekst, bij teleologische interpretatie op het doel van een bepaling en bij systematische interpretatie op de systematiek van het verdrag. Een interpretatiebeginsel geeft daarentegen het doel aan dat wordt nagestreefd bij de interpretatie van een bepaling, zoals effectieve of evolutieve interpretatie. Vaak wordt dit doel gerechtvaardigd door te verwijzen naar de bedoeling van het verdrag in kwestie.

In dit proefschrift wordt ervan uitgegaan dat het belangrijkste verschil tussen interpretatiemethoden en interpretatiebeginselen is gelegen in de rol die deze instrumenten spelen in de interpretatiefase. Een interpretatiemethode kan een bepaalde interpretatie dragen en rechtvaardigen, doordat duidelijk is op welk inhoudelijk element een argumentatie is gebaseerd. Bij een interpretatiebeginsel is duidelijk welk doel er wordt beoogd. Daardoor kunnen deze beginselen richting geven bij de interpretatie van fundamentele rechten, maar kunnen zij niet op zichzelf een interpretatie dragen.

Moet bijvoorbeeld voor een effectieve, evolutieve of autonome interpretatie worden gekeken naar de tekst, het doel van de bepaling of naar andere argumenten? De kwalificaties effectief, evolutief en autonoom bieden hiervoor geen houvast. Interpretatiebeginselen moeten derhalve worden ondersteund door interpretatiemethoden. De beginselen kunnen vervolgens een rol spelen in de keuze voor een argument gebaseerd op interpretatiemethode A, B, C of D.

Als gezegd wordt in de literatuur weinig aandacht besteed aan de kwalificatie van interpretatieve instrumenten en worden, voor zover er al een onderscheid wordt erkend, de termen interpretatiemethoden en interpretatiebeginselen door elkaar gebruikt. Bij de bespreking van de verschillende interpretatiebeginselen wordt duidelijk of het onderscheid in de rechtspraak zichtbaar is en of er op dit punt verbeteringen mogelijk zijn.

Teleologische interpretatie

Teleologische interpretatie speelt op twee niveaus een rol in de analyse in dit proefschrift, namelijk op meta-niveau en op micro-niveau. Meta-teleologische interpretatie is een concept dat is geïntroduceerd door LASSER. Met meta-teleologische interpretatie wordt bedoeld dat het gebruik van bepaalde interpretatieve instrumenten wordt gerechtvaardigd door een beroep te doen op de doelstellingen van het verdrag in kwestie. LASSER hanteert niet hetzelfde onderscheid tussen interpretatiemethoden en -beginselen als gehanteerd in dit proefschrift, maar zijn concept van meta-teleologische interpretatie is met name van belang voor interpretatiebeginselen. In de rechtspraak van het HvJ EU is meta-teleologische interpretatie niet duidelijk zichtbaar. Het EHRM daarentegen heeft bijvoorbeeld bepaald dat één van de doelstellingen van het Europees Verdrag voor de Rechten van de Mens (EVRM) als mensenrechtenverdrag is dat de hierin opgenomen rechten op een praktische en effectieve manier moet worden uitgelegd. Het gebruik van onder andere evolutieve interpretatie wordt onder verwijzing naar deze doelstelling gerechtvaardigd. In de rechtspraak van het EHRM is deze variant van teleologische interpretatie dus duidelijk aanwezig.

Micro-teleologische interpretatie is de benaming die door LASSER wordt gehanteerd voor teleologische interpretatie als interpretatiemethode. Teleologische interpretatie is een veelgebruikte methode zowel in nationale als internationale rechtspraak. De methode *an sich* is niet controversieel, maar het gebruik van de methode kan soms leiden tot beschuldigingen dat de rechter zijn taakopvatting te buiten gaat. In dit proefschrift is daarom met name gekeken naar het gebruik van deze methode.

Teleologische interpretatie gaat ervan uit dat wetgeving of een verdrag met een bepaald doel in het leven is geroepen. Een belangrijke vraag die opkomt bij teleologische interpretatie is wiens doel moet worden gerespecteerd: het doel dat de originele oprichter van het verdrag voor ogen stond of het doel van een rationele oprichter? In het eerste geval is sprake van subjectieve teleologische interpretatie en wordt gekeken naar het doel van de oprichter van het verdrag, door bijvoorbeeld sterk gebruik te maken van de *travaux préparatoires*. In het tweede geval is sprake van objectieve teleologische interpretatie en wordt daarentegen gekeken naar onder meer de preambule, om op grond daarvan vast te stellen wat het objectieve doel is van het verdrag of de specifieke bepaling. Bij beide hoven is een voorkeur voor objectieve teleologische interpretatie zichtbaar. Subjectieve teleologische interpretatie is met name in de rechtspraak van het EHRM nog op beperkte schaal aanwezig. In de rechtspraak van het HvJ EU is deze variant nauwelijks van belang. De beperkte beschikbaarheid van de *travaux préparatoires* speelt daarbij ongetwijfeld een rol.

Voor de analyse van het gebruik van teleologische interpretatie is gekeken naar de vraag of het EHRM of het HvJ EU verduidelijken waar het doel van de bepaling uit volgt. Dit is met name van belang bij objectieve teleologische interpretatie, omdat hierbij het doel van een 'rationele oprichter' van het desbetreffende verdrag als uitgangspunt wordt genomen. Indien niet duidelijk is *hoe* de rechter heeft vastgesteld wat het doel is, kan dit tot kritiek leiden.

Het HvJ EU maakt met name gebruik van teleologische interpretatie op het moment dat er een juridisch bindende tekst (bijvoorbeeld een verordening) is waarin fundamentele bepalingen zijn vastgelegd. In die gevallen geeft het HvJ EU, vaak aangevuld door de conclusie van de Advocaat Generaal, duidelijk aan hoe het tot de vaststelling van het doel is gekomen. Aangezien het Handvest van de Grondrechten van de EU (het Handvest) met het Verdrag van Lissabon bindende kracht heeft verkregen, kan worden verwacht dat teleologische interpretatie een grotere rol gaat spelen in de rechtspraak van het HvJ EU.

In de rechtspraak van het EHRM wordt veelvuldig gebruik gemaakt van teleologische interpretatie, maar hierbij wordt minder duidelijk aangegeven hoe het EHRM heeft vastgesteld wat het doel van een bepaling is. Het doel van een bepaling wordt vaak opgeworpen als een voldongen feit, terwijl niet duidelijk is hoe het EHRM tot die conclusie is gekomen. Zeker als een extensieve interpretatie wordt gestoeld op een teleologische interpretatie is het noodzakelijk dat duidelijk wordt uitgelegd hoe het doel is vastgesteld om beschuldigingen van rechterlijke wetgeving te voorkomen.

Het EHRM zou een voorbeeld kunnen nemen aan het HvJ EU en op een meer gedetailleerde manier gebruik kunnen maken van teleologische interpretatie door dieper in te gaan op het doel van een bepaling en uit te leggen hoe het dat doel heeft vastgesteld. De argumentatie van het EHRM zou daardoor inzichtelijker worden. Nadelig is echter dat het tegelijkertijd ook tot meer controverse kan leiden, indien het EHRM inhoudelijk dieper op teleologische interpretatie ingaat.

Comparatieve interpretatie

Comparatieve interpretatie houdt in dat bij de uitleg van een bepaling een rechter kijkt naar materialen uit andere systemen dan zijn of haar eigen systeem. Er is veel discussie over deze methode in theoretische literatuur. Meest fundamenteel is de discussie of comparatieve interpretatie überhaupt wel een rol mag spelen als interpretatiemethode. In deze discussie staat dus de legitimiteit van de methode centraal. Hierbij speelt met name de vraag waarom materialen uit andere rechtssystemen relevant zijn. In andere discussies wordt de waarde van deze methode erkend, maar worden er veel vraagtekens gezet bij de uitwerking ervan in de praktijk.

Om de discussie over comparatieve interpretatie vooruit te helpen is in dit proefschrift een onderscheid voorgesteld tussen interne en externe comparatieve interpretatie. Interne comparatieve interpretatie houdt in dat er wordt verwezen naar materialen, rechtspraak of wetgeving uit staten die binnen de jurisdictie van het desbetreffende supranationale hof vallen. In het geval van het EHRM zijn dat de verdragsstaten van het EVRM en in het geval van het HvJ EU de lidstaten van de EU. Onder externe comparatieve interpretatie vallen alle overige verwijzingen naar andere systemen. Dat kan variëren van een verwijzing naar de situatie in de Verenigde Staten, tot verwijzing naar een uitspraak van het Joegoslavië Tribunaal, of een verwijzing naar een verdrag van de Verenigde Naties. Een verwijzing door het EHRM naar het HvJ EU of andersom valt ook onder de externe component van comparatieve interpretatie.

Het onderscheid is van belang, omdat het gebruik van beide versies van comparatieve interpretatie een andere rechtvaardiging behoeft. Interne comparatieve interpretatie kan worden gerechtvaardigd door te wijzen op de wens om als supranationaal hof voeling te houden met de situatie in de lidstaten. Externe comparatieve interpretatie dient echter op een andere wijze te worden gerechtvaardigd. Waarom is het relevant om te kijken naar de Verenigde Staten of om in een specifieke zaak een door de betrokken verwerende staat bewust niet geratificeerd verdrag aan te halen? Het feit dat deze externe materialen nuttig kunnen zijn, is in de theoretische discussie afgedaan als geen afdoende verklaring, omdat daarmee niet wordt verklaard waarom het is gerechtvaardigd om er een beroep op te doen.

Naast bezwaren ten aanzien van de rechtvaardiging van (externe) comparatieve interpretatie is er veel kritiek op het gebruik van comparatieve interpretatie (zowel intern als extern). Een veel besproken probleem is dat het bij comparatieve interpretatie eigenlijk altijd mogelijk is om materiaal te vinden dat een bepaalde interpretatie ondersteunt. Dit probleem wordt ook wel *cherry-picking* genoemd en geeft aan dat de methode vatbaar is voor manipulatie. Dat maakt het des te belangrijker dat het inzichtelijk is hoe de methode wordt gehanteerd. Een ander veel besproken praktisch probleem heeft te maken met de specifieke manier waarop (met name interne) comparatieve interpretatie wordt gebruikt. In de rechtspraak van beide hoven wordt regelmatig gekeken of er sprake is van een Europese consensus. Indien er sprake is van een consensus, dan dient deze veelal als argument voor een bepaalde interpretatie. Het probleem is dat niet duidelijk is wanneer er sprake is van een consensus. Moet er sprake zijn van een oplossing die in de meerheid van de staten te vinden is of is er een andere standaard die wordt gehanteerd? Uit zowel de theoretische als rechtspraakanalyse blijkt dat er geen maatstaf voor te vinden is en dat de vraag of er sprake is van een consensus redelijk willekeurig wordt beantwoord. Beide problemen doen afbreuk aan de betrouwbaarheid van comparatieve argumenten.

Zowel interne als externe comparatieve interpretatie wordt veel toegepast door beide hoven. Geen van beide hoven maakt evenwel onderscheid tussen de interne en externe variant, waardoor het gebruik van deze methode niet in alle gevallen afdoende wordt gerechtvaardigd. Gelet op het belang van zowel interne als externe comparatieve interpretatie in een veellagig systeem, is het van belang om oplossingen te bedenken voor de problemen die deze methode met zich meebrengt, zodat de betrouwbaarheid ervankan worden vergroot.

CHOUDHRY heeft een voorstel gedaan voor een bepaalde manier van comparatieve interpretatie om tegemoet te komen aan het bezwaar dat er onvoldoende rechtvaardiging bestaat voor externe comparatieve interpretatie. Zijn voorstel is ook relevant in het kader van het vaststellen van een consensus, zoals vaak gebeurt bij interne comparatieve interpretatie. Hij spreekt over 'dialogical interpretation'. Daarmee bedoelt hij dat naar andere systemen kan worden gekeken om te bezien of de oplossingen die daar zijn gevonden binnen het eigen systeem passen. Het over de grens kijken moet leiden tot zelfreflectie. Door deze zelfreflectie is het mogelijk op grond van argumenten afkomstig uit het eigen systeem te concluderen of een oplossing uit een ander systeem wel of niet past. Het dwingt ertoe beter na te denken over de waarden die ten grondslag liggen aan het eigen systeem. Deze oplossing kan ook worden gebruikt om te beargumenteren of een oplossing die is gevonden in de lidstaten past binnen het internationale of supranationale systeem. Op die manier wordt de numerieke vraag die bij de consensus vaak problemen oplevert losgelaten. In Canada en Zuid-Afrika zijn voorbeelden van deze wijze van comparatieve interpretatie zichtbaar.

Een nadeel van dit voorstel is echter dat, wanneer rechters worden gedwongen om beter over hun eigen systeem en de waarden die daaraan ten grondslag liggen na te denken, zij er niet aan ontkomen meer inhoud te geven aan dat systeem. Dat leidt onherroepelijk tot meer inhoudelijke of politieke keuzes die binnen een verdeeld Europa tot controverse kunnen leiden. De vraag is dan wat beter is in een diverse, veellagige context: onduidelijkheid ten aanzien van een gekozen interpretatie of een meer inhoudelijke benadering die weer andere problemen zal oproepen?

Evolutieve interpretatie

Evolutieve interpretatie houdt in dat bepalingen worden uitgelegd in het licht van hedendaagse omstandigheden. Het is een van de meta-teleologische beginselen die een rol spelen in de interpretatie door beide hoven. Het EHRM motiveert het gebruik van evolutieve interpretatie door te wijzen op de doelstelling van het EVRM om fundamentele rechten een praktische en effectieve uitleg te geven. In het kader van het HvJ EU is een vergelijkbare uitleg gegeven, waarbij is gewezen op het streven om geen statische invulling te geven aan fundamentele rechten en bij te blijven bij sociale veranderingen.

Evolutieve interpretatie wordt vaak gelijkgesteld met comparatieve interpretatie. Deze visie gaat uit van een beperkte opvatting van comparatieve interpretatie (aangezien uit rechtspraak blijkt dat het breder wordt gebruikt dan enkel om een evolutieve invulling te geven aan een bepaling). Bovendien miskent deze opvatting het verschil in functie tussen comparatieve interpretatie als methode en evolutieve interpretatie als beginsel. Een evolutieve interpretatie kan in theorie worden gebaseerd op verschillende interpretatiemethoden. Het objectieve doel van een verdrag kan bijvoorbeeld in de loop der tijd veranderen. In de praktijk wordt een evolutieve interpretatie echter vaak gebaseerd op comparatieve argumenten. Ook al zijn het geen synoniemen; er is dus wel degelijk een hechte link tussen de twee interpretatieve instrumenten. In de rechtspraak zijn te weinig aanwijzingen te vinden op grond waarvan kan worden vastgesteld of het EHRM en het HvJ EU evolutieve interpretatie zien als een op zichzelf staand beginsel of als een variant van comparatieve interpretatie.

Indien evolutieve interpretatie als beginsel wordt erkend en toegepast, dwingt het beide hoven om beter dan nu het geval is te verantwoorden op grond van welke argumenten ze tot een evolutieve uitleg komen. Zeker in het licht van de immer uitdijende fundamentele rechten kan een zorgvuldig gebruik van het beginsel van evolutieve interpretatie een waarborg bieden tegen de kritiek hierop.

Autonome interpretatie

Onder autonome interpretatie door het EHRM of het HvJ EU wordt verstaan dat begrippen worden geïnterpreteerd, los van de betekenis die in het kader van andere internationale verdragen of nationale wetgeving aan deze begrippen wordt gegeven. Een beroep op autonome interpretatie wordt in de rechtspraak met name gerechtvaardigd door de wens om alle burgers in Europa een gelijk, minimaal beschermingsniveau te bieden. Naast dit streven naar een uniform minimumniveau van bescherming wordt er in de literatuur ook gesproken over een strategische reden om autonome interpretatie toe te passen. In dat geval wordt ervan uitgegaan dat het desbetreffende hof dit beginsel toepast om expliciet de controle over de interpretatie van een bepaald concept naar zich toe te trekken.

In de grote meerderheid van de gevallen heeft autonome interpretatie betrekking op autonomie ten opzichte van de (mogelijk afwijkende) nationale kwalificatie. In de context van het HvJ EU is soms sprake van een ander soort autonomie, namelijk autonomie ten opzichte van het EHRM. In deze gevallen kiest het HvJ EU expliciet voor een interpretatie die losstaat van de interpretatie die door het EHRM is gegeven. Het is aannemelijk dat aan deze vorm van autonomie voornoemde strategische reden ten grondslag ligt.

Op grond van het onderscheid tussen interpretatiemethoden en interpretatiebeginselen wordt autonome interpretatie in dit proefschrift gekwalificeerd als een interpretatiebeginsel. Het feit dat een autonome uitleg wordt gekozen zegt namelijk niets over welke argumenten invulling moeten geven aan die autonome uitleg. Er zijn aanvullende interpretatiemethoden nodig om de keuze voor een bepaalde interpretatie te rechtvaardigen. Dit aspect van autonome interpretatie wordt in de literatuur nauwelijks onderkend en het is de vraag of het door de twee hoven als zodanig wordt erkend of toegepast.

Het EHRM lijkt zich te realiseren dat autonome interpretatie geen interpretatiemethode is, maar het wordt uit de rechtspraak niet geheel duidelijk hoe het EHRM autonome interpretatie dan wel kwalificeert. In sommige gevallen wordt een autonome interpretatie ondersteund door een verwijzing naar interpretatiemethoden. In andere gevallen formuleert het EHRM criteria die helpen om tot een autonome uitleg te komen. Ook al is vaak niet duidelijk hoe deze criteria tot stand komen, zij geven in ieder geval enige duidelijkheid over het gebruik van autonome interpretatie door het EHRM. In de meerderheid van de gevallen is echter in het geheel niet duidelijk hoe een autonome interpretatie tot stand komt.

In de rechtspraak van het HvJ EU zijn minder gevallen van autonome interpretatie zichtbaar. Dat heeft, net als bij evolutieve interpretatie, te maken met het gedurende lange tijd ontbreken van een bindende catalogus van fundamentele rechten. De voorbeelden lijken de voorzichtige conclusie te rechtvaardigen dat het HvJ EU autonome interpretatie als een interpretatiebeginsel kwalificeert. In een aantal gevallen gaat het HvJ EU voorbeeldig te werk en wordt een autonome interpretatie gerechtvaardigd door een verwijzing naar argumenten gebaseerd op verschillende interpretatiemethoden. Die voorbeelden laten zien dat het toepassen van dit onderscheid leidt tot een meer inzichtelijke interpretatie waar het EHRM een voorbeeld aan zou kunnen nemen.

Conclusie

De discussies op grond van de theoretische en rechtspraakanalyse van de verschillende methoden en beginselen in dit onderzoek laten duidelijk zien op welke punten de huidige praktijk van het EHRM en het HvJ EU tekortschiet. Als rechters zich bewust worden van deze tekortkomingen is dat al een groot gewin. In dat verband is illustratief dat op het gebied van comparatieve interpretatie al verbeteringen zichtbaar zijn als gevolg van de theoretische discussies over de met die methode verbandhoudende tekortkomingen.

Er zijn zowel inhoudelijke als meer instrumentele voorstellen tot verbetering gedaan. Daarbij is aangegeven dat sommige verbeteringen weer eigen problemen met zich meebrengen. Dat is met name zo bij een aantal inhoudelijke voorstellen die de rechters van het EHRM en het HvJ EU ertoe dwingen meer inhoudelijke keuzes te maken teneinde beter inzicht te geven in de beslissingen die tot een bepaalde interpretatie hebben geleid. Met name in een veellagig rechtssysteem levert dit in potentie weer een heel nieuw scala aan problemen op.

Het belangrijkste voorstel tot instrumentele verbetering ziet op de erkenning van het onderscheid tussen interpretatiemethoden en interpretatiebeginselen en de volledige toepassing daarvan in de praktijk. Dit voorstel spoort rechters aan stil te staan bij de rol die de verschillende methoden en beginselen spelen in het interpretatieproces. Methoden en beginselen kunnen elkaar versterken en zo bijdragen aan een meer inzichtelijke interpretatie.

BIBLIOGRAPHY

A

ALBORS LLORENS (1999): "The European Court of Justice, More Than a Teleological Court" 2 *Cambridge Yearbook of Legal Studies* 1999, p. 373-398

ALEXY (1989): ALEXY, *A Theory of Legal Argumentation; The Theory of Rational Discourse as Theory of Legal Justification*, Oxford, Clarendon Press, 1989, p. 221-250

ALKEMA (2000): "The European Convention as a Constitution and its Court as a Constitutional Court" in MAHONY (ed.), *Protection des droits de l'homme: la perspective européenne*, Cologne, Heymans, 2000, p. 41-63

ARAI-TAKAHASHI (2002): ARAI-TAKAHASHI, *The Margin of Appreciation Doctrine and the Principle of Proportionality in the Jurisprudence of the ECHR*, Antwerp, Intersentia, 2002

ARNULL (2006): ARNULL, *The European Union and its Court of Justice* (2nd ed.), Oxford, Oxford University Press, 2006

AUST (2000): "Interpretation" in AUST, *Modern Treaty Law and Practice*, Cambridge, Cambridge University Press, 2000, p.184-206

AUST (2007): "Interpretation" in AUST, *Modern Treaty Law and Practice* (2nd ed.), Cambridge, Cambridge University Press, 2007, p. 230-255

B

BALCERZAK (2004-2005): "The Doctrine of Precedent in the International Court of Justice and the European Court of Human Rights", 27 *Polish Yearbook of International Law* 2004-2005, p. 131-144

BARAK (2005A): BARAK, *Purposive Interpretation in Law*, Princeton, Princeton University Press, 2005

BARAK (2005B): "Constitutional Interpretation" in Mélin-Soucramien (ed), *L'Interprétation Constitutionelle*, Paris, Dalloz, 2005, p. 91-118

BARBER & FLEMING (2007): BARBER & FLEMING, *Constitutional Interpretation; The Basic Questions*, New York, Oxford University Press, 2007

BAUDENBACHER (2003): "Judicial Globalization: New Development or Old Wine in New Bottles?", 38 *Texas International Law Journal* 2003, p. 505-526

BENTELE (2008): "Mining for Gold: The Constitutional Court of South Africa's Experience with Comparative Constitutional Law", *Brooklyn Law School Legal Studies Research Papers*, 2008, No. 113, www.ssrn.com

Berghe, van den (2010): "The EU and Issues of Human Rights Protection: Same Solutions to More Acute Problems?" 16 *European Law Journal*, 2010, p. 112-157

Besselink (1998): "Entrapped by the Maximum Standard: On Fundamental Rights, Pluralism and Subsidiarity in the European Union", 35 *Common Market Law Review* 1998, p. 629-680

Bernhardt (1967): "Interpretation and Implied (Tacit) Modification of Treaties", 27 *Zeitschrift für Ausländisches Öffentliches Recht und Völkerrecht* 1967, p. 491-506

Bernhardt (1988): "Thoughts on the Interpretation of Human-Rights Treaties" in Matscher, Petzold & Wiarda, *Protecting Human Rights: the European Dimension*, Cologne, Karl Heymans Verlag, 1988, p. 65-71

Bernhardt (1995): "Interpretation in International Law" in Bernhardt, *Encyclopedia of International Law,* Vol 2, Amsterdam, p. 1416-1425

Bernhardt (1999a): "Evolutive Treaty Interpretation, Especially of the European Convention on Human Rights", 42 *German Yearbook of International* Law 1999, p. 10-25

Bernhardt (1999b): "Comparative Law in the Interpretation and Application of the European Convention on Human Rights" in Busuttil, *Mainly Human Rights*, Valetta, Fondation Internationale Malte, 1999, p. 33-40

Blanke (2006): "Protection of Fundamental Rights afforded by the European Court of Justice in Luxembourg", in Blanke & Mangiamelli, *Governing Europe under a Constitution*, Berlin, Springer, 2006, p. 265-277

Blois, de (1994): "The Fundamental Freedom of the European Court of Human Rights" in Lawson & De Blois (ed.), *The Dynamics of the Protection of Human Rights in Europe*, Dordrecht, Nijhoff, 1994, p. 35-59

Bogdandy, von (2000): "The European Union as a Human Rights Organization? Human Rights and the Core of the European Union", 37 *Common Market Law Review* 2000, p. 1307-1338

Bossuyt (2005): Bossuyt & Wouters, *Grondlijnen van internationaal recht*, Antwerp, Intersentia, 2005, p. 75-82

brennan (1985-1986): "In Defense of Dissents", 37 *Hastings Law Journal* 1985-1986, p. 427-438

Brennan (1989): "Why Have a Bill of Rights?", 9 *Oxford Journal of Legal Studies* 1989, p. 425-440

Brown & Kennedy (2000): Brown & Kennedy, *The Court of Justice of the European Communities* (5th ed.), London, Sweet & Maxwell

Buffard & Zemanek (1998): "The 'Object and Purpose' of a Treaty: An Enigma", 3 *Austrian Review of International & European Law* 1998, p. 311-343

C

CAROZZA (1998): "Uses and Misuses of Comparative Law in International Human Rights: Some Reflections on the Jurisprudence of the European Court of Human Rights", 73 Notre Dame Law Review 1997-1998, p. 1217-1237

CAROZZA (2003): "Subsidiarity as a Structural Principle of International Human Rights Law", 97 *American Journal of International* Law 2003, p. 38-79

CAROZZA (2004): "The Member States" in PEERS & WARD (ed.), *The EU Charter of Fundamental Rights: politics, law and policy*, Portland, Hart, 2004, p. 35-59

CHRISTOFFERSEN (2009A): "The principle of proportionality" in CHRISTOFFERSEN, *Fair Balance: proportionality, subsidiarity and primarity in the European Convention on Human Rights*, Leiden, Nijhoff, 2009, p. 44-60

CHOUDHRY (1998): "Globalization in Search of Justification: Towards a Theory of Comparative Constitutional Interpretation", 74 *Indiana Law Journal* 1998-1999, p. 819-890

CHOUDHRY (2006): "Migration as a new Metaphor in Comparative Constitutional Law" in CHOUDHRY (ed.), *Migration of Constitutional Ideas*, Cambridge, Cambridge University Press, 2006, p. 1-37

CHRISTOFFERSEN (2009B): "Impact on General Principles of Treaty Interpretation" in KAMMINGA & SCHEININ (ed.), *The Impact of Human Rights Law on General International Law*, Oxford, Oxford University Press, 2009, p. 37-61

CLITEUR (2005): "Rechtsvinding" in CLITEUR, *Nederlands recht* (2nd ed.), Deventer, Kluwer, 2005, p. 157-180

COHN & KREMNITZER (2005): "Judicial Activism: A Multidimensional Model", 18 *Canadian Journal of Law and Jurisprudence* 2005, p. 333-356

COLNERIC (2007): "Die Rolle des Rechtsvergleichung in der Praxis des EuGH" in EPINAY, HAAG & HEINEMANN, *Die Herausforderung von Grenzen*, 2007, Baden Baden, Nomos, p.317-323

COMMENTARY TO ARTICLES OF THE VIENNA CONVENTION ON THE LAW OF TREATIES, *Yearbook of International Law Commission*, 1966, p. 217-226

CONWAY (2008): "Levels of Generality in the Legal Reasoning of the European Court of Justice", 14 *European Law Journal* 2008, p. 787-805

COPPEL & O'NEILL (1992): "The European Court of Justice: Taking Rights Seriously", 29 *Common Market Law Review* 1992, p. 669-692

CRAIG (2008): "Fundamental Rights" in MOSER & SAWYER, *Making Community Law*, Cheltenham, Edward Elger Publishing, 2008, p. 54-79

CRAIG & DE BURCA (2008): CRAIG & DE BURCA, *EU Law; Text Cases and Materials* (4th ed.), New York, Oxford University Press, 2008

CUETO-RUA (1981): "The Pragmatic and Teleological Elements in the Interpretation and Application of the Law", in CUETO-RUA, *Judicial Methods of Interpretation*, Louisiana State University Law Publishers, p. 176-191

Cunha Rodrigues (2010): "The Incorporation of Fundamental Rights in the Community Legal Order", in Poiares Maduro & Azoulai (ed.), *The Past and Future of EU Law; The Classics of EU Law Revisited on the 50th Anniversary of the Rome Treaty*, Portland, Hart, 2010, p. 89-97

D

Dammann (2001-2002): "The Role of Comparative Law in Statutory and Constitutional Interpretation", 14 *Saint Thomas Law Review* 2001-2002, p. 517-559

De Burca (2001): "The Drafting of the European Union Charter of Fundamental Rights", 26 *European Law Review* 2001, p. 126-138

Dorsen (2005): "The Relevance of Foreign Legal Materials in U.S. Constitutional Cases: A Conversation between Justice Antonin Scalia and Justice Stephen Breyer" 3 *ICON* 2005, p. 519-541

Dörte Hempfing (2004): "European Convention on Human Rights: Just a Source of Inspiration? Jurisprudence of the European Court of Justice" in Gries & Alleweldt, *Human Rights within the European Union*, Berlin, Berliner Wissenschafts-Verlag, 2004, p. 9-26

Douglas-Scott (2004): "The Charter of Fundamental Rights as a Constitutional Document", 1 *European Human Rights Law Review* 2004, p. 37-50

Douglas-Scott (2006): "A Tale of Two Courts: Luxembourg, Strasbourg and the Growing European Human Rights Acquis", 43 *Common Market Law Review* 2006, p. 629-665

Drooghenbroeck (2009): "Les frontières du Droit et le temps juridique: la Cour européenne des droits de l'homme repousse les limites. En marge de l'arrêt de Grande Chambre du 12 novembre 2008 rendu en l'affaire Demir et Baykara c. Turquie", *Revue trimestrielle des droits de l'Homme* 2009, p. 811-850

Due (1999): "Understanding the reasoning of the Court of Justice" in Rodríguez Iglesias (ed.), *Mélanges en hommage à Fernand Schockweiler*, Baden Baden, Nomos, 1999, p. 73-85

Dworkin (1986): Dworkin, *Law's Empire*, London, Fontana Press, 1986, ch. 9

Dumon (1976): "The Case Law of the European Court of Justice: A Critical Examination of the Methods of Interpretation", *Report: Judicial and Academic Conference 27 and 28 September 1976*, Luxembourg, Court of Justice of the European Communities, 1976

E

Evans (2010): Evans, *International Law* (3rd ed.), Oxford, Oxford University Press, 2010, p. 198-204

F

FAIGMAN(1992): "Reconciling Individual Rights and Government Interests: Madisonian Principles versus Supreme Court Practice", 78 *Virginia Law Review* 1991, p. 1521-1580

FAIRCLOTH PEOPLES (2008): "The use of Foreign Law by the Advocates General of the Court of Justice of the European Communities", 35 *Syracuse Journal of International Law and Commerce* 2008, p. 218-271

FENNELLY (1996-1997): "Legal Interpretation at the European Court of Justice", 20 *Fordham International Law Journal* 1996-1997, p. 656-679

FETERIS (2005): "The Rational Reconstruction of Argumentation Referring to Consequences and Purposes in the Application of Legal Rules: A Pragma-Dialectical Perspective", 19 *Argumentation* 2005, p. 459-470

FITZMAURICE (2008A): "Dynamic (Evolutive) Interpretation of Treaties Part I", 21 *Hague Yearbook of International Law* 2008, p. 101-153

FITZMAURICE (2009): "Dynamic (Evolutive) Interpretation of Treaties Part II", 22 *Hague Yearbook of International Law* 2008, p. 3-31

FONTANA (2001): "Refined Comparativism in Constitutional Law", 49 *UCLA Law Review* 2001, p. 539-623

FRANKEN (2003): FRANKEN, *Encyclopedie van de rechtswetenschap*, Deventer, Kluwer, 2003, p. 171-203

FRENCH (2006): "Treaty Interpretation and the Incorporation of Extraneous Legal Rules", 55 *ICLQ* 2006, p. 281-314

G

GANSHOF VAN DER MEERSCH (1988): "Le caractère «autonome» des termes et la «margin d'appréciation» des gouvernements dans l'interprétation de la Convention européenne des Droits de l'Homme" in MATSCHER, PETZOLD & WIARDA, *Protecting Human Rights: the European Dimension*, Cologne, Karl Heymans Verlag, 1988, p. 201-220

GARLICKI (2009): "Judicial Deliberations: The Strasbourg Perspective" in HULS, ADAMS & BOMHOFF (ed.), *The Legitimacy of Highest Courts' Rulings*, The Hague, T.M.C. Asser Press, 2009, p. 389-397

GERARDS (2005): GERARDS, *Judicial Review in Equal Treatment Cases,* Leiden, Nijhoff, 2005

GERARDS (2009): "Judicial Deliberations in the European Court of Human Rights" in HULS, ADAMS & BOMHOFF (ed.), *The Legitimacy of Highest Courts' Rulings*, The Hague, T.M.C. Asser Press, 2009, p. 407-437

GERARDS & SENDEN (2009): "The Structure of Fundamental Rights and the European Court of Human Rights", 7 *ICON* 2009, p. 619-653

GERARDS (2010): "Methoden en beginselen van interpretatie en toetsing, inclusief de margin of appreciation doctrine" in HERINGA & SCHOKKENBROEK (ed.), *EVRM*

Rechtspaak & Commentaar (supplement 88), Lelystad, Koninklijke Vermande, 2010

GOLSONG (1993): "Interpreting the European Convention on Human Rights Beyond the Confines of the Vienna Convention of the Law on Treaties?" in MACDONALD, MATSCHER & PETZOLD, The *European system for the Protection of Human Rights*, Dordrecht, Nijhoff, 1993, p. 147-162

GOMEZ-AROSTEGUI (2005): "Defining Private Life under the European Convention on Human Rights by Referring to Reasonable Expectations", 35 California Western International Law Journal 2005, p. 153-202

GREER (2008): "What's wrong with the European Convention on Human Rights?", 30 *Human Rights Quarterly* 2008, p. 680-702

H

HARDING (2003): "Comparative Reasoning and Judicial Review", 28 *Yale Journal of International Law* 2003, p. 409-464

HARMSEN (2007): "The European Court of Human Rights as a ' Constitutional Court': Definitional Debates and the Dynamics of Reform", in MORRISON, MCEVOY & ANTHONY (ed.), *Judges, Transition and Human Rights*, New York, Oxford University Press, 2007, p. 33-53

HARRIS, O'BOYLE & WARBRICK (1995): "The interpretation of the Convention" in HARRIS, O'BOYLE & WARBRICK (ed.), *Law of the European Convention on Human Rights*, London, Butterworths, p. 5-19

HARRIS, O'BOYLE & WARBRICK (2009): "The interpretation of the Convention" in HARRIS, O'BOYLE & WARBRICK (ed.), *Law of the European Convention on Human Rights* (2nd ed.), Oxford, Oxford University Press, p. 5-10

HARTLEY (2003): HARTLEY, *The foundations of European Community law: an introduction to the constitutional and administrative law of the European Community* (5th ed.), Oxford, Oxford University Press, 2003

HARVEY (2004): "Militant Democracy and the European Convention on Human Rights", 29 *European Law Review* 2004, p. 407-420

HERINGA (1996): "The 'Consensus Principle'. The Role of 'Common Law' in the ECHR Case Law", 3 *Maastricht Journal* 1996, p. 108-145

HELFER (1993): "Consensus, Coherence and the European Convention on Human Rights", 26 *Cornell International Law Journal* 1993, p. 133-165

HELFER (1997-1998): "Toward a Theory of Effective Supranational Adjudication", 107 *Yale Law Journal* 1997-1998, p. 273-390

HELFER (2003-2004): "Constitutional Analogies in the International Legal System", 37 *Loyola of Los Angeles Law Review* 2003-2004, p. 193-238

HIGGINS (2006): "A Babel of Judicial Voices? Ruminations from the Bench", 55 *ICLQ* 2006, p. 791-804

Hilf (1986): "The Role of Comparative Law in the Jurisprudence of the Court of Justice of the European Communities", in Mestral (ed.), *The Limitation of Human Rights in Comparative Constitutional Law*, Cowansville, Blais, 1986, p. 549-573

Hoffman, Lord (2009): "The Universality of Human Rights", *Judicial Studies Board Annual Lecture*, 2009

Huscroft (2004): "A Constitutional 'Work in Progress'? The Charter and the Limits of Progressive Interpretation", 23 *Supreme Court Law Review* 2004, p. 413-438

J

Jackson (2005-2006): "Constitutional Comparisons: Convergence, Resistance, Engagement", 119 *Harvard Law Review* 2005-2006, p. 109-128

Jackson (2006): "A recipe of Increased Legitimacy of the European Court of Human Rights as a Supranational Constitutional Court", 39 *Connecticut Law Review* 2006, p. 759-806

Jackson (2006-2007): "Constitutions as 'Living Trees'? Comparative Constitutional Law and Interpretive Metaphors", 75 *Fordham Law Review* 2006-2007, p. 921-960

Jacobi (2005): "The Subtle Unraveling of Federalism: The Illogic of Using State Legislation as Evidence of an Evolving National Consensus", *Northwestern University School of Law Public Law & Legal Theory Research Paper Series* 2005, no. 15, www.ssrn.com

Jacobs (1969): "Varieties of Approach to Treaty Interpretation: with Special Reference to the Draft Convention on the Law of Treaties before the Vienna Diplomatic Conference" 18 *International and Comparative Law Quarterly* 1969, p. 319-346

Jacobs (2001): "Human Rights in the European Union: The Role of the Court of Justice", 26 *European Law Review* 2001, p. 331-341

Jacobs (2003a): "Approaches to Interpretation in a Plurilingual Legal System" in Hoskins & Robinson, *A True European*, Oxford, Hart, 2003, p. 297-305

Jacobs (2003b): "Judicial Dialogue and the Cross-Fertilization of Legal Systems: The European Court of Justice", 38 Texas International Law Journal 2003, p. 547-556

Jacobs (2007): "Between Luxembourg and Strasbourg: Dialogue between the European Court of Human Rights and the European Court of Justice" in Epinay, Haag & Heinemann, *Die Herausforderung von Grenzen*, 2007, Baden Baden, Nomos, p. 205-214

Janssen (2003): Janssen, *Constitutionele interpretatie: Een rechtsvergelijkend onderzoek naar de vaststelling van de reikwijdte van het recht op persoonlijkheid*, The Hague, Sdu, 2003, p. 157-200

Jonas & Saunders (2010): "The Object and Purpose of a Treaty: Three Interpretative Methods", 43 *Vanderbilt Journal of Transnational Law* 2010, p. 565-609

K

KAHN (2002-2003): "Comparative Constitutionalism in a New Key", 101 *Michigan Law Review* 2002-2002, p. 2677-2706

KAHN-FREUD (1974): "On Uses and Misuses of Comparative Law", 37 *Modern Law Review* 1974, p. 1-27

KAKOURIS (1994): "Use of the Comparative Method by the Court of Justice of the European Communities", 6 *Pace International Law Review* 1994, p. 267-283

KASTANAS (1996): "Les fondements de l'interpretation autonome de la convention" in KASTANAS, *Unité et Diversité: notions autonomes et margin d'appréciation des états dans la jurisprudence de la Cour européenne des droits de l'homme*, Brussels, Bruylant, 1996, p. 333-354

KAVANAGH (2003): "The Idea of a Living Constitution", 16 *Canadian Journal of Law and Jurisprudence* 2003, p. 55-89

KHUSHAL MURKENS (2008): "Comparative Constitutional Law in the Courts: Reflections on the Originalists' Objections", *LSE Law, Society and Economy Working Papers* 2008, No. 15, www.ssrn.com

KIIKERI (2001); KIIKERI, *Comparative Legal Reasoning and European Law*, Dordrecht, Kluwer, 2001

KLABBERS (1997): "Some Problems Regarding the Object and Purpose of Treaties", 8 *Finnish Yearbook of International Law* 1997, p. 138-160

KOFFEMAN (2010): "(The right to) personal autonomy in the case law of the European Court of Human Rights", *report for the Dutch Governmental Commission on the Constitution,* Leiden, Leiden University, 2010.

KOOPMANS (1996): "Judicial Decision-Making" in CAMPBELL & VOYATZI (ed.), *Legal Reasoning and Judicial Interpretation of European Law*, Trenton Publishing, 1996

KOOPMANS (2000): "The Theory of Interpretation and the Court of Justice" in O'KEEFFE (ed.), *Judicial Review in European Union law*, The Hague, Kluwer, 2000, p. 45-58

KRISCH (2008): "The Open Architecture of European Human Rights Law", 71 *The Modern Law Review* 2008, p. 183-216

KÜHLING (2006): "Fundamental Rights" in VON BOGDANDY & BAST, *Principles of European Constitutional Law*, Oxford, Hart, 2006, p. 501-547

KUNER (1991): "The Interpretation of Multilingual Treaties: Comparison of Texts Versus the Presumption of Similar Meaning", 40 *International and Comparative Law Quarterly* 1991, p. 953-964

KUTSCHER (1976): "Methods of Interpretation: as Seen by a Judge at the Court of Justice", *Report: Judicial and Academic Conference 27 and 28 September 1976*, Luxembourg, Court of Justice of the European Communities, 1976

L

LANGENBUCHER (1998): "Argument by Analogy in European Law", 57 *Cambridge Law Journal* 1998, p. 481-521

LASOK (2004): "Principles of Interpretation of EU Law" in LASOK & MILLETT, *Judicial Control in the EU: procedures and principles*, Richmond, Richmond Law & Tax, 2004, p. 375-417

LASSER (2004): LASSER, *Judicial Deliberations, A Comparative Analysis of Judicial Transparency and Legitimacy*, New York, Oxford University Press, 2004

LASSER (2009): LASSER, *Judicial Transformations; The Rights Revolution in the Courts of Europe*, Oxford, Oxford University Press, 2009, p. 214-222

LAWSON (1996): "Adieu les travaux! Het afgenomen belang van de *travaux préparatoires* voor de uitleg van het EVRM", 21 *NJCM-Bulletin* 1996, p. 61-74

LAWSON (2009): "Ex Boreale Lux: On the Influence of the ECJ on the Interpretation of the ECHR" in BULTERMAN, HANCHER, MCDONNELL & SEVENSTER (eds.), *Views of European Law from the Mountain*, Alphen aan de Rijn, Kluwer Law International, 2009, p. 439-454

LEACH (2005): "Underlying Convention Principles" in LEACH, *Taking a case to the European Court of Human Rights*, Oxford, Oxford University Press, 2005, p. 161-178

LEE (2007): "International Consensus as Persuasive Authority in the Eights Amendment", 156 *University of Pennsylvania Law Review* 2007, p. 102-158

LENAERTS & DE SMIJTER (2001A): "A 'Bill of Rights' for the European Union", 38 *Common Market Law Review* 2001, p. 273-300

LENAERTS & DE SMIJTER (2001B): "The Charter and the Role of the European Courts", 8 *Maastricht Journal* 2001, p. 90-101

LENAERTS (2003): "Interlocking Legal Orders in the European and Comparative Law", 52 *ICLQ* 2003, p. 873-906

LENAERTS (2005): "The Relationship between the Actors" in LENAERTS & VAN NUFFEL (ed.), *Constitutional Law of the European Union, London*, Thomson Sweet & Maxwell, 2005, p. 557-565

LENAERTS (2007): "Interpretation and the Court of Justice: A Basis for Comparative Reflection", 41 *International Lawyer* 2007, p. 1011-1032

LETSAS (2004): "The Truth in Autonomous Concepts: How to Interpret the ECHR", 15 *E.J.I.L.* 2004, p. 279-305

LETSAS (2007): LETSAS, *A Theory of Interpretation of the European Convention on Human Rights*, New York, Oxford University Press, 2007

LETSAS (2010): "Intentionalism and the Interpretation of the ECHR" in FITZMAURIZE & ELIAS, *Treaty Interpretation and the Vienna Convention on the Law of Treaties: 30 Years On*, Leiden, Nijhoff, 2010, p. 257-272

LINDERFALK (2003): "On the Meaning of 'Object and Purpose' Criterion, in the Context of the Vienna Convention on the Law of Treaties, Article 19", 72 *Nordic Journal of International Law* 2003, p. 429-448

LINDERFALK (2007): "Using the Object and Purpose" in LINDERFALK, *On the Interpretation of Treaties: the Modern International Law as Expressed in the 1969 Vienna Convention on the Law of Treaties*, Dordrecht, Springer, 2007, p. 203-233

LINDERFALK (2008A): "Doing the Rights Thing for the Right Reason- Why Dynamic or Static Approaches Should be Taken in the Interpretation of Treaties", 10 *International Community Law Review* 2008, p. 109-141

LINDERFALK (2008B): "Who are 'the Parties'? Article 31, Paragraph 3(c) of the 1969 Vienna Convention and 'the Principle of Systemic Interpretation Revisited'", *Netherlands International Law Review* 2008, p. 343-364

LOCK (2009): "The CJEU and the ECtHR: The Future Relationship between the Two European Courts", 8 *The Law and Practice of International Courts and Tribunals* 2009, p. 375-398

LOTH (2009): "Courts in a Quest for Legitimacy: a Comparative Approach" in HULS, ADAMS & BOMHOFF (ed.), *The Legitimacy of Highest Courts' Rulings*, The Hague, T.M.C. Asser Press, 2009, p. 267-288

LUTZHOEFT (2009): "How do Texts Matter? The Impact of Texts in Human Rights Reasoning in Europe", *Columbia Law School Public Law and Legal Theory Working Paper Group* 2009, www.ssrn.com

M

MAHONEY (1990): "Judicial Activism and Self-Restraint in the European Court of Human Rights" 11 *Human Rights Law Journal* 1990, p. 57-88

MAHONEY (2002-2003): "New Challenges for the European Court of Human Rights Resulting from the Expanding Case Load and Membership" 21 *Pennsylvania State International Law Review* 2002-2003, p. 101-114

MAHONEY (2004): "The Comparative Method in Judgments of the European Court of Human Rights: Reference Back to National Law" in CANIVET & ANDENAS (ed.), *Comparative Law before the Courts*, London BIICL, 2004, p. 133-150

MANCINI (2000): "Safeguarding Human Rights: The Role of the European Court of Justice" in MANCINI, *Democracy and Constitutionalism in the European Union*, Oxford, Hart, 2000, p. 81-95

MARKESINIS & FEDTKE (2005-2006): "The Judge as Comparatist", 80 *Tulane Law Review* 2005-2006, p. 13-167

MARKS (1995): "The European Convention on Human Rights and its 'Democratic Society'", 66 *British Yearbook of International Law* 1995, p. 209-238

MATSCHER (1993): "Methods of Interpretation of the Convention" in MACDONALD, MATSCHER & PETZOLD, The *European system for the Protection of Human Rights*, Dordrecht, Nijhoff, 1993, p. 63-81

McCormick (1978): McCormick, *Legal Reasoning and Legal Theory*, New York, Oxford University Press, 1978

McCormick & Summers (1991): "Interpretation and Justification", in MacCormick & Summers, *Interpreting Statutes: A Comparative Study*, Darthmouth, Aldershot, 1991, p. 511-551

McCormick (1993): "Argumentation and Interpretation in Law", 6 *Ratio Juris* 1993, p. 16-29

McCormick (2005); McCormick, *Rhetoric and the Rule of Law: A Theory of Legal Reasoning*, New York, Oxford University Press, 2005

McCrudden (2002): "The Future of the EU Charter of Fundamental Rights", 2002, www.ssrn.com

McCrudden (2003): "Human Rights and Judicial Use of Comparative Law" in Örücü (ed.), *Judicial Comparativism in Human Rights Cases*, Glasgow, UKNCCL, 2003, p. 1-22

McCrudden (2007): "Judicial Comparativism and Human Rights", in Örücü & Nelken (ed.), *Comparative Law: A Handbook*, Oxford, Hart, 2007, p. 371-398

McCrudden (2008): "Human Dignity and Judicial Interpretation of Human Rights" 19 *EJIL* 2008, p. 655-724

McLachlan (2005): "The Principle of Systemic Integration and Article 31(3)(c) of the Vienna Convention", 54 *ICLQ* 2005, p. 279-320

McRae (2002): "The Search for Meaning: Continuing Problems with the Interpretation of Treaties", 33 *Victoria University Wellington Law Review* 2002, p. 209-260

Melchior (1988): "Notions vagues ou indéterminées et lacunes dans la Convention européenne des Droits de l'Homme", in Matscher, Petzold & Wiarda, *Protecting Human Rights: the European Dimension*, Cologne, Karl Heymans Verlag, 1988, p. 411-419

Merrills (1993): Merrills, *The Development of International Law by the European Court of Human Rights* (2nd ed.), Manchester, Manchester University Press, 1993

Mertens de Wilmars (1990): "Methodes van interpretatie van het Hof van Justitie van de Europese Gemeenschappen" Rotterdam, Erasmus Universiteit, 1990

Mertens & Vermeulen (2008): "Dissenting Opinions" in Buruma, *Op het rechte pad*, Nijmegen, Wolff, 2008, p. 47-62

Miller (2009): "Beguiled Metaphors: The 'Living Tree' and Originalist Constitutional Interpretation in Canada", 22 *Canadian Journal of Law & Jurisprudence* 2009, p. 331

Millett (1989): "Rule of Interpretation of E.E.C. Legislation", 10 Statute Law Review 1989, p. 163-182

Mowbray (1999): "The Role of the European Court of Human Rights in the Promotion of Democracy", *Public Law* 1999, p. 703-725

Mowbray (2005): "The Creativity of the European Court of Human Rights", 5 *Human Rights Law Review* 2005, p. 57-79

MOWBRAY (2009): "An Examination of the European Court of Human Rights Approach to Overruling its Previous Case Law", 9 *Human Rights Law Review* 2009, p. 179-201

N

NAPEL, TEN (2009): "The European Court of Human Rights and Political Rights: The Need for More Guidance", 5 *European Constitutional Law Review* 2009, p. 464-480

NI AOLAIN (1995-1996): "The Emergence of Diversity: Differences in Human Rights Jurisprudence", 19 *Fordham International Law Journal* 1995-1996, p. 101-142

NICOL (2005): "Original Intent and the European Convention on Human Rights", *Public Law* 2005, p. 152-172

O

ORAKHELASHVILI (2003): "Restrictive Interpretation of Human Rights Treaties in the Recent Jurisprudence of the European Court of Human Rights", 14 *EJIL* 2003, p. 529-568

ORAKHELASHVILI (2008): ORAKHELASHVILI, *The Interpretation of Acts and Rules in Public International Law*, Oxford, Oxford University Press, 2008

OST (1992): "The Original Canons of Interpretation of the European Court of Human Rights" in DELMAS-MARTY (ed.), *The European Convention for the Protection of Human Rights: International Protection versus National Restrictions*, Dordrecht, Nijhoff, 1992, p. 283-318

OVEY & WHITE (2006): "Principles of Interpretation" in OVEY & WHITE, *Jacobs and White, The European Convention on Human Rights* (4th ed.), Oxford, Clarendon Press, 2006, p. 38-55

P

PEERS (2003): "The European Court of Justice and the European Court of Human Rights: Comparative Approaches" in Örücü (ed.), *Judicial Comparativism in Human Rights Cases*, Glasgow, UKNCCL, 2003, p. 107-129

PELLONPÄÄ (2007): "Continuity and Change in the Case-Law of the European Court of Human Rights", in KOHEN, *Promoting, Justice, Human Rights and Conflict Resolution Through International Law,* Leiden, Nijhoff, 2007, p. 409-420

PETZOLD (1993): "The Convention and the Principle of Subsidiarity" in MACDONALD, MATSCHER & PETZOLD, The *European system for the Protection of Human Rights*, Dordrecht, Nijhoff, 1993, p. 41-62

POIARES MADURO (2007): "Interpretation European Law: Judicial Adjudication in a Context of Constitutional Pluralism", 1 *European Journal of Legal Studies* 2007, p. 1

PREBENSEN (2000): "Evolutive Interpretation of the European Convention on Human Rights" in MAHONY (ed.), *Protection des droits de l'homme: la perspective européenne*, Cologne, Heymans, 2000, p. 1123-1137

R

RAINER (2008): "Fundamental Rights in the European Union" in ŠIŠKOVÁ (ed.), *The Process of Constitutionalisation of the EU and Related Issues,* Groningen, Europa Law Publishing, 2008, p. 27-38

REHNQUIST (2006): "The Notion of a Living Constitution", 29 *Harvard Journal of Law & Public Policy* 2006, p. 401-415

REICH (2005): REICH, *Understanding EU Law: Objectives, Principles and Methods of Community Law* (2nd ed.), Antwerp, Intersentia, 2005

REID (2004): "Convention Principles and Approach" in REID, *A Practitioner's Guide to the European Convention on Human Rights*, London, Thomson/Sweet & Maxwell, 2004

RESS (2006): "The Legal Relationship between the European Court of Human Rights and the Court of Justice of the European Communities according to the European Court of Human Rights" in BLANKE & MANGIAMELLI, *Governing Europe under a Constitution*, Berlin, Springer, 2006, p. 279-296

RIETIKER (2010): "The Principles of 'Effectiveness' in the Recent Jurisprudence of the European Court of Human Rights: Its Different Dimensions and Its Consistency with Public International Law – No Need for the Concept of Treaty Sui Generis", 79 *Nordic Journal of International Law* 2010, p. 245-277

RIGAUX (1998): in SUDRE, PETTITI & TRECHSEL (ed.), *L' interprétation de la Convention Européenne des Droits de l' Homme*, Brussels, Bruylant, 1998, p. 41-62

RITTER (2005-2006): "A New Look at the Role and Impact of the Advocates-General-Collectively and Individually", 12 *Columbia Journal of European Law* 2005-2006, p. 751-774

ROOSEVELT III (2006): ROOSEVELT III, *The Myth of Judicial Activism*, New Haven, Yale University Press, 2006

ROSENFELD (2006): "Comparing Constitutional Review by the European Court of Justice and the U.S. Supreme Court", 4 *ICON* 2006, p. 618-651

ROZAKIS (2005-2006): "The European Judge as Comparatist", 80 *Tulane Law Review* 2005-2006, p. 257-279

RYSSDALL (1996): "The Coming of Age of the European Convention on Human Rights", *European Human Rights Law Review* 1996, p. 18-29

S

SCALIA (1997): SCALIA, *A Matter of Interpretation*, Princeton, Princeton University Press, 1997

Scalia (2004): "Foreign Legal Authority in the Federal Courts" 98 *American Society of International Law Proceedings* 2004, p. 305-310

Schermers & Waelbroeck (2001): "The Community Legal Order" in Schermers & Waelbroeck (ed.), *Judicial Protection in the European Union* (6th ed.), The Hague, Kluwer, 2001, p. 3-27.

Schokkenbroek (2000): "Methoden van interpretatie en toetsing: een overzicht van beginselen toegepast in de Straatsburgse Jurisprudentie" in Heringa & Schokkenbroek (ed.), *EVRM Rechtspaak & Commentaar* (supplement 18), Lelystad, Koninklijke Vermande, 2000

Senden (2009): "Het gebruik van niet-geratificeerde internationale instrumenten voor de interpretatie van het EVRM. Noot bij *Demir & Baykara t. Turkije", 34 NJCM-Bulletin* 2009, p. 407-427

Sévon (1999): "Experiencing the Court of Justice of the European Communities" in Rodríguez Iglesias (ed.), *Mélanges en hommage à Fernand Schockweiler*, Baden Baden, Nomos, 1999, p. 577-592

Sharma Aryal (2003): Sharma Aryal, *Interpretation of Treaties: Law and Practice*, New Delhi, Deep & Deep, 2003

Sharpston (2008): "The Changing Role of the Advocate General" in Arnull & Eeckhout (ed.), *Continuity and Change in EU Law*, Oxford, Oxford University Press, 2008, p. 20-33

Shaw (2008): Shaw, *International Law* (6th ed.), Cambridge, Cambridge University Press, 2008, p. 932-938

Shelton (1996-1997): "Reconcilable Differences? The Interpretation of Multilingual Treaties", 20 *Hastings International and Comparative Law Review* 1996-1997, p. 611-638

Singer & Engel (2007): "L'importance de la recherché comparative pour la justice communautaire", 134 *Journal de droit International* 2007, p. 497-513

Šišková (2008): "European Constitutionalism and its Human Rights Dimension" in Šišková (ed.), *The Process of Constitutionalisation of the EU and Related Issues,* Groningen, Europa Law Publishing, 2008, p. 3-23

Sitaraman (2009): "The Use and Abuse of Foreign Law in Constitutional Interpretation", 32 *Harvard Journal of Law and Public Policy* 2009, p. 653-693

Slaughter (1994-1995): "A Typology of Transjudicial Communication", 29 *University of Richmond Law Review* 1994-1995, p. 99-137

Slaughter (2003): "A Global Community of Courts", 44 *Harvard International Law Journal* 2003, p. 191-219

Slotboom (2001): "Do Different Treaty Purposes Matter for Treaty Interpretation", 4 *Journal of International Economic Law* 2001, p. 557-579

Smith (2005): Smith, *Regels van rechtsvinding*, Den Haag, Boom, 2005

Sottiaux & Van Der Schyff (2008): "Methods of International Human Rights Adjudication: Towards a More Structured Decision-Making Process for the European Court of Human Rights", 31 *Hastings International and Comparative Law Review* 2008, p. 115-156

STEINER (2006): "General Principles of Law" in STEINER, *EU Law*, Oxford, Oxford University Press, 2006, p. 114-144

SUDRE (1998): "Le recours aux «notions autonomes»", in SUDRE, PETTITI & TRECHSEL (ed.), *L' interprétation de la Convention Européenne des Droits de l' Homme*, Brussels, Bruylant, 1998, p. 93-131

SUDRE (2008): "La motivation des decisions de la Cour Europeenne des Droits de l'Homme", in RUIZ FABRI & SOREL, *La motivation des décisions des jurisdictions internationales*, Paris, Pedone, 2008, p. 171-189

T

THOMASSEN (2006): "Het geheim van de raadkamer en de dissenting opinion" *NJB* 2006, p. 686

TIZZANO (2008): "The Role of the CJEU in the Protection of Fundamental Rights" in ARNULL & EECKHOUT (ed.), *Continuity and Change in EU Law*, Oxford, Oxford University Press, 2008, p. 125-138

TOUFAYAN (2005): "Human Rights Treaty Interpretation: A Postmodern Account of Its Claim to 'Speciality'", *Center for Human Rights and Global Justice Working Paper*, 2005, No. 2 (www.chrgj.org/publications/wp.html)

TRIBE & DORF (1990): "Levels of Generality in the Definition of Rights", 57 *University of Chicago Law Review* 1990, p. 1057-1108

TRIDIMAS (1996): "The Court of Justice and Judicial Activism", 21 *European Law Review* 1996, p. 199-210

TSEN-TA LEE (2007): "Interpreting Bills of Rights: The Value of a Comparative Approach", 5 *ICON* 2007, p. 122-152

TUSHNET (2003-2004): "Transnational/Domestic Constitutional Law", 37 *Loyola of Los Angeles Law Review* 2003-2004, p. 239-269

V

VANDE LANOTTE (2005): "Interpretatie- en toepassingsbeginselen van het Europees Hof voor de Rechten van de Mens" in VANDE LANOTTE & HAECK, *Handboek EVRM* (deel 1), Antwerp, Intersentia, 2005, p. 177-225

VANNESTE (2010): VANNESTE, *General International Law before Human Rights Courts: Assessing the Specialty Claims of International Human Rights Law*, Antwerp, Intersentia, 2010

VILLIGER (2009): VILLIGER, Commentary on the 1969 Vienna Convention on the Law of Treaties, Leiden, Nijhoff, 2009

VINCENZI & FAIRHURST (2002): VINCENZI & FAIRHURST, *Law of the European Community*, Harlow, Longman, 2002

W

WAELE, DE (2009): DE WAELE, *Rechterlijk activisme en het Europees Hof van Justitie*, The Hague, Boom, 2009, p. 369-380

WALDRON (2005-2006): "Foreign Law and the Modern Ius Gentium", 119 *Harvard Law Review* 2005-2006, p. 129-147

WALUCHOW (2007): "Constitutional Interpretation and Constitutional Theories" in WALUCHOW, *A Common Law Theory of Judicial Review. The Living Tree*, Cambridge, Cambridge University Press, 2007, p. 52-73

WASENSTEINER (2004): "Common Tradition of all Member States: The Courts Method of Defining the EU Human Rights Standards" in GRIES & ALLEWELDT, *Human Rights within the European Union*, Berlin, Berliner Wissenschafts-Verlag, 2004, p.

WEILER & LOCKHART (1995): "'Taking Rights Seriously' Seriously: The European Court and its Fundamental Rights Jurisprudence- Part I", 32 Common Market Law Review 1995, p. 51-94

WEILER & LOCKHART (1995): "'Taking Rights Seriously' Seriously: The European Court and its Fundamental Rights Jurisprudence- Part II", 32 Common Market Law Review 1995, p. 579-627

WEILER (1999): "Fundamental Rights and Fundamental Boundaries: on the Conflict of Standards and Values in the Protection of Human Rights in The European Legal Space" in WEILER, *The Constitution of Europe: "Do the new clothes have an emperor?" and other essays on European integrat*ion, Cambridge, Cambridge University Press, 1999, p. 102-129

WEILER (2000): "Editorial: Does the European Union Truly Need a Charter of Rights?", 6 *European Law Journal* 2000, p. 95-97

WESSEL (2004): "Relational Contract Theory and Treaty Interpretation: End-Game Treaties v. Dynamic Obligations" 60 NYU *Annual Survey of American Law* 2004, p. 149-186

WHEATLEY (2007): "Minorities under the ECHR and the Construction of a 'Democratic Society'", *Public Law* 2007, p. 770-792

WILDHABER (2000): "Precedent in the European Court of Human Rights", in MAHONY (ed.), *Protection des droits de l'homme: la perspective européenne*, Cologne, Heymans, 2000, p. 41-63

WILDHABER (2002): "A Constitutional Future for the European Court of Human Rights?", 23 *Human Rights Law Journal*, 2002, p. 161-165

WITTE, DE (1999): "The Past and Future Role of the European Court of Justice in the Protection of Human Rights", in ALSTON, *The EU and Human Rights*, Oxford, Oxford University Press, 1999, p. 859-897

WHITE (2008): "The Strasbourg Perspective and its Effect on the Court of Justice: Is Mutual Respect Enough?" in ARNULL & EECKHOUT (ed.), *Continuity and Change in EU Law*, Oxford, Oxford University Press, 2008, p. 139-156

White (2009): "Judgments in the Strasbourg Court: Some Reflections", 2009, www.ssrn.com
White & Boussiakou (2008): "Separate Opinions in the European Court of Human Rights", 2008, www.ssrn.com
White & Boussiakou (2009): "Voices from the European Court of Human Rights", 27 *Netherlands Quarterly of Human Rights* 2009, p. 167-189
Wyatt & Dashwood (2006): Wyatt & Dashwood, *European Union Law* (5th ed.), London, Sweet & Maxwell, 2006, p. 404-414

Y

Young (2005-2006): "Foreign Law and the Common Denominator Problem", 119 *Harvard Law Review* 2005-2006, p. 148-167
Yourow (1996): Yourow, *The Margin of Appreciation Doctrine in the dynamics of European Human Rights Jurisprudence*, The Hague, Kluwer

List of Cases

Judgments from the European Court of Human Rights

ECtHR (GC), *A v. Croatia*, judgment of 14 October 2010, *unpublished*

ECtHR (GC), *A, B and C v. Ireland*, judgment of 16 December 2011, *unpublished*

ECtHR, *Abdulaziz, Cabales and Balkandi v. United Kingdom*, judgment of 28 May 1985, Series A No. 94

ECtHR, *Airey v. Ireland*, judgment of 9 October 1979, *Series* A No. 32

ECtHR, *Al-Saadoon and Mufdhi v. United Kingdom*, judgment of 2 March 2010, *unpublished*

ECtHR (GC), *Amann v. Switzerland*, judgment of 16 February 2000, *Reports* 2000-II

ECtHR, *B. v. France*, judgment of 25 March 1993, *Series* A No. 232-C

ECtHR (GC), *Banković and others v. Belgium and others*, decision of 12 December 2001, Reports 2001-VII

ECtHR (GC), *Beard v United Kingdom*, judgment of 18 January 2001, *unpublished*

ECtHR (GC), *Behrami & Behrami v. France*, decision of 2 May 2007, *unpublished*

ECtHR (GC), *Beyeler v. Italy*, judgment of 5 January 2000, *Reports* 2000-I

ECtHR (GC), *Bosphorus HavaYollari Turizm Ve Ticaret Anonim Şirketi v. Ireland*, judgment of 30 June 2005, *Reports* 2005-VI

ECtHR, *Botta v. Italy*, judgment of 24 February 1998, *Reports* 1998-I

ECtHR, *Buckley v. United Kingdom*, judgment of 25 September 1996, *Reports* 1996-IV

ECtHR, *Burghartz v. Switzerland*, judgment of 22 February 1992, *Series* A No. 280-B

ECtHR, *Case "Relating to certain aspects of the laws on the use of languages in education in Belgium" v. Belgium*, judgment of 23 July 1968, *Series* A No. 6, A/6

ECtHR (GC), *Chapman v. United Kingdom*, judgment of 18 January 2001, *Reports* 2001-I

ECtHR (GC), *Chassagnou and others v. France*, judgment of 29 April 1999, *Reports* 1999-III

ECtHR (GC), *Christine Goodwin v. United Kingdom*, judgment of 11 July 2002, *Reports* 2002-VI
ECtHR (GC), *Comingersoll S.A. v. Portugal*, judgment of 6 April 2000, *Reports* 2000-IV
ECtHR, *Cossey v. United Kingdom*, judgment of 27 September 1990, *Series* A No. 184
ECtHR, *Costello-Roberts v. United Kingdom*, judgment of 25 March 1993, *Series* A No. 247-C
ECtHR, *Cruz Varas and others v. Sweden*, judgment of 20 March 1991
ECtHR, *Demir & Baykara v. Turkey*, judgment of 21 November 2006, *unpublished*
ECtHR (GC), *Demir and Baykara v. Turkey*, judgment of 12 November 2008, *unpublished*
ECtHR (GC), *Depalle v. France*, judgment of 29 March 2010, *unpublished*
ECtHR, *Deweer v. Belgium*, judgment of 27 February 1980, *Series* A No. 35). Sudre (1998), p. 116-117
ECtHR (GC), *Dickson v. United Kingdom*, judgment of 4 December 2007, *unpublished*
ECtHR, *Engel and others v. the Netherlands*, judgment of 8 June 1976, *Series* A No. 22
ECtHR (GC), *Evans v. United Kingdom*, judgment of 10 April 2007, *unpublished*
ECtHR, *F v. Switzerland*, judgment of 18 December 1987, *Series* A No. 128
ECtHR, *Fägerskiöld v. Sweden*, decision of 26 February 2008, *unpublished*
ECtHR (GC), *Ferrazzini v. Italy*, judgment of 12 July 2001, Reports 2001-VII
ECtHR, *Funke v. France*, judgment of 25 February 1993, *Series* A No. 256-A
ECtHR, *Futro v. Poland*, decision of 12 December 2000, *unpublished*
ECtHR, *Gasus Dosier- und Fördertechnik GmbH v. the Netherlands*, judgment of 23 February 1995, *Series* A No. 306B
ECtHR, *Gaygusuz v. Austria*, judgment of 16 September 1996, *Reports* 1996-IV
ECtHR, *Gillow v. United Kingdom*, judgment of 24 November 1986, *Series* A 109
ECtHR, *Gitonas v Greece*, judgment of 1 July 1997, *Reports* 1997-IV
ECtHR, *Golder v United Kingdom*, judgment of 21 February 1975, *Series* A No. 18
ECtHR, *Hartung v. France*, decision of 3 November 2009, *unpublished*
ECtHR (GC), *Hatton and others v. United Kingdom*, judgment of 8 July 2003, *Reports* 2003-VII
ECtHR (GC) *Hirst (No.2.) v. United Kingdom*, judgment of 6 October 2005, *Reports* 2005-IX
ECtHR (GC), *I v. United Kingdom*, judgment of 11 July 2002, *Reports* 2002-VI

ECtHR (GC), *Iatridis v. Greece*, judgment of 25 March 1999, *Reports* 1999-II
ECtHR (GC), *Ilaşcu and others v. Moldova and Russia*, decision of 4 July 2001, *unpublished*
ECtHR (GC), *Incal v Turkije*, judgment of 9 June 1998, *Reports* 1998-IV
ECtHR, *Ireland v. United Kingdom*, judgment of 18 January 1978, *Series* A No. 25
ECtHR, *James and others v. United Kingdom*, judgment of 21 February 1986, *Series* A No. 98
ECtHR, *Johnston and others v Ireland*, judgment of 18 December 1986, *Series* A No. 112
ECtHR (GC), *Jussila v. Finland*, judgment of 23 November 2006, *unpublished*
ECtHR, *Kimlya and others v. Russia*, judgment of 1 October 2009, *unpublished*
ECtHR, *Kjeldsen, Busk Madsen and Pederson v Denmark*, judgment of 7 December 1976, *Series* A No. 23
ECtHR, *Klass and others v Germany*, judgment of 6 September 1978, *Series* A No. 28
ECtHR, *König v. Germany*, judgment of 28 June 1978, *Series* A No. 27
ECtHR, *Koua Poirrez v. France*, judgment of 30 September 2003, *Reports* 2003-X
ECtHR (GC), *Kress v. France*, judgment of 7 June 2001, *Reports* 2001-VI
ECtHR (GC), *Kudla v. Poland*, judgment of 26 October 2000, *Reports* 2000-XI
ECtHR, *Leander v Sweden*, judgment of 26 March 1987, *Series* A No. 116
ECtHR, *Le Compte, Van Leuven and De Meyere v Belgium*, judgment of 23 June 1981, *Series* A No. 34
ECtHR, *Lithgow and others v United Kingdom*, judgment of 8 July 1986, *Series* A No. 102
ECtHR, *Loizidou v. Turkey (preliminary objections)*, judgment of 23 March 1995, *Series* A No. 310
ECtHR (GC), *Maaouia v. France*, judgment of 5 October 2000, *Reports* 2000-X
ECtHR (GC), *Mamatkulov and Askarov v. Turkey*, judgment of 4 February 2005, *Reports* 2005-I
ECtHR, *Marckx v. Belgium*, judgment of 13 June 1979, *Series* A No. 31
ECtHR (GC), *Martinie v. France*, judgment of 12 April 2006, Reports 2006-VI
ECtHR, *Matos e Silva, Lda, and others v. Portugal*, judgment of 16 September 1996, *Reports* 1996-IV
ECtHR (GC), *Matthews v. United Kingdom*, judgment of 18 February 1999, *Reports* 1999-I
ECtHR, *M.C. v. Bulgaria*, judgment of 4 December 2003, *Reports* 2003-XII
ECtHR *McCann and others v United Kingdom*, judgment of 27 September 1995, Series A No. 324

ECtHR (GC), *Micallef v. Malta*, judgment of 15 October 2009, *unpublished*
ECtHR, *Mubilanzila Mayeka and Kaniki Mitunga v. Belgium*, judgment of 12 October 2006, *Reports* 2006-XI
ECtHR, *Niemietz v. Germany*, judgment of 16 December 1992, *Series* A No. 251-B
ECtHR (GC), *Öcalan v. Turkey*, judgment of 12 May 2005, *Reports* 2005-IV
ECtHR (GC), *Öneryildiz v. Turkey*, judgment of 30 November 2004, *Reports* 2004-XII
ECtHR (GC), *Osman v. United Kingdom*, judgment of 28 October 1998, *Reports* 1998-VIII
ECtHR, *Öztürk v. Germany*, judgment of 21 February 1984, *Series* A No. 73
ECtHR (GC), *Pellegrin v. France*, judgment of 8 December 1999, *Reports* 1999-VIII
ECtHR, *P.G. and J.H. v. United Kingdom*, judgment of 25 September 2001, *Reports* 2001-IX
ECtHR (GC), *Polacek & Polackova v. Czech Republic*, decision of 10 July 2002, *unpublished*
ECtHR, *Posti and Rahko v. Finland*, judgment of 24 September 2002, Reports 2002-VII
ECtHR, *Pretty v. United Kingdom*, judgment of 29 April 2002, *Reports* 2002-III.
ECtHR, *Prokopovich v. Russia*, judgment of 18 November 2004, *Reports* 2004-XI
ECtHR, *Quark Fishing Limited v. United Kingdom*, decision of 19 September 2006, *unpublished*
ECtHR, *Rantsev v. Cyprus and Russia*, judgment of 7 January 2010, *unpublished*
ECtHR, *Ringeisen v. Austria*, judgment of 16 July 1971, *Series* A No. 13
ECtHR, *Rees v. United Kingdom*, judgment of 17 October 1986, *Series* A No. 106
ECtHR, *Rotaru v. Romania*, judgment of 4 May 2000, Reports 2000-V
ECtHR (GC), *Saadi v. United Kingdom*, judgment of 29 January 2008, *unpublished*
ECtHR, *S.A. Dangeville v. France*, judgment of 16 April 2002, *Reports* 2002-III
ECtHR, *Schalk and Kopf v. Austria*, judgment of 24 June 2010, *unpublished*
ECtHR (GC), *Scoppola v. Italy (No. 2),* judgments of 17 September 2009, *unpublished*
ECtHR (GC), *Selmouni v. France*, judgment of 28 July 1999, *Reports* 1999-V
ECtHR (GC), *Senator Lines GmbH v. Austria and others*, decision of 10 March 2004, *Reports* 2004-IV
ECtHR, *Sheffield & Horsham v. United Kingdom*, judgment of 30 July 1998, *Reports* 1998-V

ECtHR, *Sigurdur A. Sigurjónsson v. Iceland*, judgment of 30 June 1993, *Series* A No. 264
ECtHR, *Smirnova v. Russia*, judgment of 24 July 2003, *Reports* 2003-IX
ECtHR, *Société Colas Est and others v. France*, judgment of 16 April 2002, *Reports* 2002-III
ECtHR, *Soering v United Kingdom*, judgment of 7 July 1989, *Series* A No. 161
ECtHR (GC), *Stec and others v. United Kingdom*, decision of 6 July 2005, *Reports* 2005-X
ECtHR, *Stjerna v. Finland*, judgment of 25 November 1994, *Series* A No. 299-B
ECtHR (GC), *Stoll v. Switzerland,* judgment of 10 December 2007, *unpublished*
ECtHR, *Storbråten v. Norway*, decision of 1 February 2007, *unpublished*
ECtHR, *Stran Greek Refineries and Stratis Andreadis v. Greece*, judgment of 9 December 1994, *Series* A No. 301-B
ECtHR (GC), *T v. United Kingdom*, judgment of 16 December 1999, *unpublished*
ECtHR, *Tyrer v. United Kingdom*, judgment of 25 April 1978, *Series* A No. 26
ECtHR, *Tre Traktörer Aktiebolag v. Sweden*, judgment of 7 July 1989, *Series* A No. 159
ECtHR (GC), *Üner v. the Netherlands*, judgment of 18 October 2006, *Reports* 2006-XII
ECtHR (GC), *United Communist Party of Turkey and others v. Turkey*, judgment of 30 January 1998, *Reports* 1998-I
ECtHR (GC), *V v. United Kingdom*, judgment of 16 December 1999, *Reports* 1999-IX.
ECtHR, *Van der Mussele v. Belgium*, judgment of 23 November 1983, *Series* A No. 70
ECtHR, *Vanjak v Croatia*, judgment of 14 January 2010, *unpublished*
ECtHR, *Vermeulen v. Belgium*, judgment of 20 February 1996, *Reports* 1996-I
ECtHR (GC), *Vilho Eskelinen and others v. Finland*, judgment of 19 April 2007, *unpublished*
ECtHR (GC), *Vo v. France*, judgment of 8 July 2004, *Reports* 2004-VIII
ECtHR, *Von Hannover v. Germany*, judgment of 24 June 2004, *Reports* 2004-VII
ECtHR, *Witold Litwa v. Poland*, judgment of 4 April 2000, *Reports* 2000-III
ECtHR, *Wemhoff v. Germany*, judgment of 27 June 1968, *Series* A No. 7
ECtHR, *Young James and Webster v. United Kingdom*, judgment of 13 August 1981, *Series* A No. 44
ECtHR (GC), *Yumak & Sadak v. Turkey*, judgment of 8 July 2008, *unpublished*
ECtHR (GC), *Zolotukhin v. Russia*, judgment of 10 February 2009, *unpublished*
ECtHR, *Zwierzynski v. Poland*, judgment of 19 June 2001, *Reports* 2001-VI

Reports from the European Commission on Human Rights

ECHR, *Svenska Lokmannaförbundet v. Sweden*, report of 27 May 1974, *Series* B No. 18
ECHR, *Tyrer v. United Kingdom*, report of 14 December 1976, *Series* B No. 24.

Judgments from the European Court of Justice

C-26/62, *NV Algemene Transport- en Expeditie Onderneming van Gend & Loos v. Netherlands Inland Revenue Administration* [1963] ECR 1
C-28/62, *Da Costa en Schaake NV and others v. Administratie der Belastingen* [1963] ECR 61
C-6/64, *Flaminio Costa v. E.N.E.L* [1964] ECR 585
C-29/69, *Erich Stauder v City of Ulm – Sozialamt* [169] ECR 419
C-11/70, *Internationale Handelsgesellschaft mbH v. Einfuhr- und Vorratsstelle für Getreide und Futtermittel* [1970] ECR 01125
C-22/70, *Commission v. Council (ERTA)*, [1971] ECR 263
C-4/73, J. *Nold, Kohlen- und Baustoffgroßhandlung v. Ruhrkohle Aktiengesellschaft* [1974] ECR 00491
C-17/74, *Transocean Marine Paint Association v. Commission of the European Communities* [1974] 01063
C-6/75, *Ulrich Horst v. Bundesknappschaft* [1975] ECR 00823
C-36/75, *Roland Rutili v. Ministre de l'intérieur* [1975] ECR 01219
C-118/75, *Lynne Watson and Alessandro Belmann* [1976] ECR 01185
C-130/75, *Vivien Prais v. Council of the European Communities* [1976] ECR 01589
C-149/77, *Gabrielle Defrenne v Société anonyme belge de navigation aérienne Sabena* [1978] ECR 01365
C-44/79, *Liselotte Hauer v. Land Rheinland-Pfalz* [1979] ECR 03727
C-136/79, *National Panasonic (UK) Limited v Commission of the European Communities* [1980] ECR 02033
C-155/79, *AM & S Europe Limited v. Commission of the European Communities* [1982] ECR 01575
C-53/81, *D.M. Levin v Staatssecretaris van Justitie* [1982] ECR 01035
C-283/81,*CILFIT v. Ministero della Sanità* [1982] ECR 3415
C-63/83, *Regina v. Kent Kirk* [1986] ECR 02689
C-294/83, *Parti écologiste "Les Verts" v. European Parliament* [1986] ECR 01339
C-222/84, *Marguerite Johnston v. Chief Constable of the Royal Ulster Constabulary* [1986] ECR 01651

C-222/86, *Union nationale des entraîneurs et cadres techniques professionnels du football (Unectef) v. Georges Heylens and others* [1987] ECR 04097
C-46/87, *Hoechst AG v. Commission of the European Communities* [1989] ECR 02859
C-374/87, *Orkem v. Commission of the European Communities* [1989] ECR 03283
C-5/88, *Hubert Wachauf v. Bundesamt für Ernährung und Forstwirtschaft* [1989] ECR 02609
C-49/88, *Al-Jubail Fertilizer Company (Samad) and Saudi Arabian Fertilizer Company (Safco) v. Council of the European Communities* [1991] ECR I-03187
C-260/89, *Elliniki Radiophonia Tiléorassi (ERT) AE and Panellinia Omospondia Syllogon Prossopikou v. Dimotiki Etairia Pliroforissis and Sotirios Kouvelas and Nicolaos Avdellas and others* [1991] ECR I-02925
C-159/90, *The Society for the Protection of Unborn Children Ireland Ltd v Stephen Grogan and others* [1991] ECR I-04685
C-168/91, *Christos Konstantinidis v. Stadt Altensteig – Standesamt and Landratsamt Calw – Ordnungsamt* [1993] ECR I-01191
C-219/91, *Criminal proceedings against Johannes Stephanus Wilhelmus Ter Voort* [1992] ECR I-05485
C-267/91, *Criminal proceedings against Keck and Mithouard* [1993] ECR I-6097.
C-415/93, *Union royale belge des sociétés de football association ASBL and others v. Jean-Marc Bosman* [1995] ECR I-04921.
C-13/94, *P v. S and Cornwall County Council* [1996] ECRI-02143
C-74/95, *Criminal Proceedings against X* [1996] ECR I-06609
C-185/95, *Baustahlgewebe GmbH v. Commission of the European Communities* [1998] ECR I-08417; C-299/95, *Friedrich Kremzow v Republik Österreich* [1997] I-02629
C-368/95, *Vereinigte Familiapress Zeitungsverlags- und vertriebs GmbH v Heinrich Bauer Verlag* [1997] ECR I-03689
C-249/96, *Lisa Jacqueline Grant v. South-West Trains Ltd* [1998] ECR I-00621
C-309/96, *Daniele Annibaldi v. Sindaco del Comune di Guidonia and Presidente Regione Lazio* [1997] ECR I-07493
C-185/97, *Belinda Jane Coote v. Granada Hospitality Ltd.* [1998] ECR I-05199
C-245/97, *Germany v. Commission* [2000] ECR I-11621
C-7/98, *Dieter Krombach v. André Bamberski* [2000] ECR I-01935
C-17/98, *Emesa Sugar (Free Zone) NV v. Aruba* [2000] ECR I-00665
C-310/98, *Met-Trans and Sagpol* [2000] ECR I-1797

C-122/99, *D and Kingdom of Sweden v. Council of the European Union* [2001] ECR I-04319
C-274/99, *Bernard Connolly v. Commission of the European Communities* [2001] ECR I-01611
C-20/00, *Booker Aquacultur Ltd v. The Scottish Ministers* [2003] ECR I-07411
C-50/00, *Unión de Pequeños Agricultores (UPA) v. Council of the European Union* [2002] ECR I-06677
C-60/00, *Mary Carpenter v. Secretary of State for the Home Department* [2002] ECR I-06279
C-94/00, *Roquette Frères SA v. Directeur général de la concurrence, de la consommation et de la répression des fraudes, and Commission of the European Communities* [2002] ECR I-09011
C-112/00, *Eugen Schmidberger, Internationale Transporte und Planzüge v. Republik Österreich* [2003] ECR I-05659
C-465/00, *Rechnungshof v Österreichischer Rundfunk and Others* [2003] ECR I-04989
C-117/01, *K.B. v National Health Service Pensions Agency and Secretary of State for Health* [2004] ECR I-00541
C-36/02, *Omega Spielhallen- und Automatenaufstellungs-GmbH v. Oberbürgermeisterin der Bundesstadt Bonn* [2004] ECR I-09609
C-200/02, *Kunqian Catherine Zhu and Man Lavette Chen v. Secretary of State for the Home Department* [2004] ECR I-09925
C-263/02, *Commission of the European Communities v. Jégo-Quéré & Cie SA* [2004] ECR I-03425
C-540/03, *European Parliament v Council of the European Union* [2006] ECR I-05769
C-300/04, *M. G. Eman and O. B. Sevinger v. College van burgemeester en wethouders van Den Haag* [2006] ECR I-08055
C-411/04, *Salzgitter Mannesmann GmbH v. Commission of the European Communities*, [2007] ECR I-00959
C-436/04, *Criminal proceedings against Leopold Henri Van Esbroeck* [2006] ECR I-02333
C-303/05, *Advocaten voor de Wereld VZW v. Leden van de Ministerraad* [2007] ECR I-03633
C-341/05, *Laval un Partneri Ltd v. Svenska Byggnadsarbetareförbundet and others* [2007] ECR I-11767
C-370/05, *Criminal proceedings against Uwe Kay Festersen* [2007] ECR I-01129
C-432/05, *Unibet (London) Ltd and Unibet (International) Ltd v. Justitiekanslern* [2007] ECR I-02271

C-438/05, *International Transport Workers' Federation and Finnish Seamen's Union v. Viking Line ABP and OÜ Viking Line Eesti* [2007] ECR I-10779
C-275/06, *Productores de Música de España (Promusicae) v. Telefónica de España SAU* [2008] ECR I-00271
C-303/06, *S. Coleman v. Attridge Law and Steve Law* [2008] ECR I-05603
C-341/06, *Chronopost SA and La Poste v. Union française de l'express (UFEX) and Others* [2008] ECR I-04777
C-450/06, *Varec SA v. Belgian State* [2008] ECR I-00581
C-14/07, *Ingenieurbüro Michael Weiss und Partner GbR v. Industrie- und Handelskammer Berlin* [2008] ECR I-03367
C-308/07, *Koldo Gorostiaga Atxalandabaso v. European Parliament* [2009] ECR I-01059
C-349/07, *Sopropé – Organizações de Calçado Lda v. Fazenda Pública* [2008] ECR I-10369
C-465/07, *Meki Elgafaji and Noor Elgafaji v. Staatssecretaris van Justitie* [2009] ECR I-00921
C-127/08, *Blaise Baheten Metock and Others v. Minister for Justice, Equality and Law Reform* [2008] I-06241
C-506/06, *Sabine Mayr v. Bäckerei und Konditorei Gerhard Flöckner OHG* [2008] ECR I-01017
C-261/09, *Gaetano Mantello* [2010]
C-279/09, *DEB Deutsche Energiehandels- und Beratungsgesellschaft mbH v. Bundesrepublik Deutschland* [2010]

Judgment from the General Court

T-112/98, *Mannesmannröhren-Werke AG v. Commission of the European Communities* [2001] ECR

Index

Terms followed by section

A

Advocate General, role of: 3.3; 13.2.2.3
Application phase: 1.1; 2.4; 3.3; 4.4.1.4; 10.2.1.3; 10.2.2; 13.4
Argumentative burden: 3.1
Article 31 VCLT: 4.2; 4.3.1; 4.3.2; 4.3.3; 4.4.1.2; 4.4.1.3; 5.1.3; 6.1.2; 7.2; 8.1; 9.1; 10.3; 10.6
Article 32 VCLT: 4.2; 4.3; 5.1.3
Article 33 VCLT: 4.3.1; 9.1
Autonomie organique: 8.2
Autonomie substantielle: 8.2
Autonomous interpretation, principle of: 4.4.1.3; 4.4.2.3; 8; 12.1; 12.2; 13.4.2; 14.5

B

Bielefelder Kreis: 4.2
Bifurcated structure: 2.3
Broad evolutieve interpretation: 7.1

C

Charter on fundamental rights: 3.1; 3.2; 4.3.1; 4.3.3; 4.4.2; 6.1.4; 7.5; 8.3; 13; 13.2.2.2; 13.3; 13.4
Cherry-picking: 6.1.6.2; 10.4.5; 10.6
Collegiate body: 3.3
Choudhry: 6.1.7
Common ground: 5.2.2; 6.1; 6.2; 8.2; 8.3; 10.1; 10.2.1.3
Common denominator: 6.1.6.2; 7.4.3; 12.5
Comparative interpretation: 4.3.5; 6; 6.1.1; 10; 10.1; 13.2; 14.3
Consensus: 4.3.5; 6.1.6.2; 7.4.3; 7.4.4; 8.2; 10.2.1.2; 10.4; 13.2.2.6
Constitutional court: 2.2; 7; 7.3
Constitutional justice: 2.2
Contractual treaties: 2.1; 4.4.1.2

D

Democracy, principle of: 4.4.1.4
Dialogical interpretation: 6.1.7; 6.4; 14.3
Dynamic interpretation: 4.3.4; 4.4.2.4; 7.4.5; 7.5; 11.1; 11.3; 11.4

E

Emergent purpose: 5.1.2.; 5.3
Effectiveness, principle of: 4.4.1.2; 4.4.2.2
Evolutive interpretation, principle of: 4.4.2.4; 4.5; 5.2.2; 6.2; 7; 9.3; 9.4; 9.6; 10.2; 10.3; 10.5; 11; 13.2.2.5; 13.4.1
External comparative interpretation: 6.1.3; 6.1.5; 6.1.6.1; 6.2; 6.3; 6.4; 10.3; 10.4.1; 10.4.2; 10.4.4; 10.6; 13.2.1; 13.2.2; 13.2.3; 13.2.4; 13.5

G

Genealogical interpretation: 6.1.7

General principles of Community law: 3.1; 4.3.5

H
Heuristic phase: 1
Hierarchy: 4.2; 4.3.1
Historical interpretation: 4.3.4; 4.3.6; 7.3
Human dignity, principle of: 4.4.1.5
Hypothetical intent: 5.1.1

I
Individual justice: 2.2
Internal comparative interpretation: 6.1.3; 6.1.5; 6.2; 6.3; 7.4.3; 10.3; 10.4.4; 10.6; 11.6; 13.2.1; 13.2.2; 13.2.2.2; 13.2.3; 13.2.5; 13.5; 14.3
International Law Commission: 4.2.4; 4.3.4; 4.4.1.2
Interpretation phase: 1.1
Interpretative aids: 1.2; 4.1

J
Judicial activism: 4.3.2; 5.1.3; 5.1.4; 5.2.2; 5.3; 6.1.6.1; 7.2; 7.3; 8.2; 8.3;
Judicial law-making: 1.3; 4.3.2; 4.4.1.2; 5.1.4; 5.3; 6.1.6.1; 7.2; 11.3
Judicial style: 3.3; 13.1; 13.3

L
Law-making treaty: 2.1; 2.5; 4.3.1; 4.3.2; 4.4.1.2; 9
Level of abstraction: 4.4.2.1; 5.1.2; 6.1.6.2; 9.4; 9.6
Level of generality: 6.1.6.2
Living constitution: 7.3
Living instrument: 4.1; 4.3.4; 4.4.1.1; 11.1; 11.2; 11.3; 11.4
Living tree: 7.3

M
Margin of appreciation: 1.1; 8.2; 10.2; 10.2.1.3; 10.2.2
Meaning originalism: 7.1
Meta-teleological interpretation: 4.1; 4.3.2; 4.4.1.2; 4.4.2.1; 5; 7.5; 8.2; 9.1; 9.2; 9.3; 9.6; 11.6; 13.3
Methods of interpretation: 4.1; 4.3
Micro-teleological interpretation: 4.1; 4.3.2; 4.4.2.1; 5; 7.4.3; 8.2; 13.3
Multilateral treaties: 4.3.4; 5.1.3; 6.1.2
Multilevel: 1.2; 2.4; 4.3.2; 4.5; 6.1.7; 6.3
Multilingual treaty: 4.3.1; 4.3.2

N
Narrow evolutive interpretation: 7.1
National constitutional traditions: 3.1; 4.4.2.3; 6.3; 13.2.2

O
Object and purpose: 2.1; 4.3.2; 4.4.1.2; 5.1.1; 5.1.2; 5.1.3; 5.2.2; 7.4.1; 7.4.4; 8.1; 9.1; 9.2; 9.3; 9.5; 12.4; 13.3
Objective teleological interpretation: 4.3.2; 5.1.1; 9.1; 9.3.1; 9.3.2; 13.3
Originalism: 6.1.6.1; 7.1; 7.3

P
Personal autonomy, principle of: 4.4.1.5
Practical and effective rights: 4.4.1.2; 7.4.1; 9.1; 9.3.3; 9.4; 11.2; 11.5; 14.2; 14.3
Precedent: 1.2; 9.3.3; 10.2.1.2
Present-day conditions: 4.4.1.1; 4.4.2.4; 6.2; 7.1; 7.4.1; 7.4.2; 11.1; 11.2; 11.3; 11.5
Primary means of interpretation: 7.4.4
Principle of interpretation: 4.1; 4.4

Problematic: 1.5; 7.4.2
Process of discovery: 1
Process of justification: 1
Publicly argumentative model: 2.3

R
Real purpose: 4.3.2; 5.1.1
Reasonable author: 4.3.2 ; 5.1.1; 5.1.2

S
Separate opinions: 2.3
Sovereignty: 3.1; 6.1.6.1; 6.1.6.2
Special nature: 4.4.1.2; 5.2.2; 7.4.1
Strong autonomy: 8.2; 13.4.2
Subjective interpretation: 4.3.4
Subjective school: 5.1.1
Subjective teleological interpretation: 4.3.2; 5.1.1; 9.1; 9.3.1; 9.3.2; 13.3
Subsequent agreement: 7.2
Subsequent practice: 7.2
Subsidiarity: 2.4; 3.3
Supplementary means of interpretation: 5.1.3; 7.2; 7.4.4
Systemic interpretation: 4.2; 4.3.; 8.2; 10.4.3; 11.4

T
Teleological interpretation: 4.2; 4.3.2; 4.4.2.2; 4.5; 5; 7.4.3; 9; 11.5; 13.3; 14.2
Teleological school: 5.1.1
Textual interpretation: 4.1; 4.2; 4.3.1; 4.3.2; 4.3.3; 9.3.1; 11.3; 13.2.4; 14.3
Textual school: 5.1.1
Travaux préparatoires: 4.3.2; 4.3.4; 5.1.3; 5.2.1; 7.2; 7.4.4; 7.5; 9.3.1; 9.3.2; 9.6; 10.2.1.1; 11.3; 12.5; 13.3
Treaty of Lisbon: 3.1; 3.2; 8.3

U
Unified structure: 2.3
Uniformity: 1.1; 4.4.2.3; 8.1; 8.3
Universalist interpretation: 6.1.7

V
Vienna Convention on the Law of Treaties: 4.2; 4.3.1; 4.3.2; 4.3.3; 4.4.1.2; 4.4.1.3; 4.4.2.3; 5.1.1; 5.1.3; 6.1.2; 7.2; 8.1; 9.1; 10.3

W
Weak autonomy: 8.2; 13.4.2

CURRICULUM VITAE

Hanneke Senden studied European Law School at the University of Maastricht, where she graduated in 2004. During her studies she spent one semester at the University of Uppsala in Sweden. After her graduation she was accepted to the European Master's Degree in Human Rights and Democratisation in Venice, Italy. In the context of this Master, she spent one semester in Venice taking part in inter-disciplinary courses on human rights and one semester in Graz, Austria, to complete her thesis (*Reforming the reforms; securing the sustainability of the European Court of Human Rights*). For her thesis she was awarded an internship (and accompanying grant) at Human Rights Watch in Brussels, Belgium for the duration of six months. From September 2006 until May 2011 she worked as a PhD candidate at the Department of Public Law of Leiden University. In the context of her PhD research she spent one semester at Boston University (2009). Since June 2011 she works as a lawyer at Van Doorne (Amsterdam, The Netherlands).

School of Human Rights Research Series

The School of Human Rights Research is a joint effort by human rights researchers in the Netherlands. Its central research theme is the nature and meaning of international standards in the fi eld of human rights, their application and promotion in the national legal order, their interplay with national standards, and the international supervision of such application. The School of Human Rights Research Series only includes English titles that contribute to a better understanding of the different aspects of human rights.

Published titles within the Series:

1 Brigit C.A. Toebes, *The Right to Health as a Human Right in International Law*
ISBN 90-5095-057-4

2 Ineke Boerefijn, *The Reporting Procedure under the Covenant on Civil and Political Rights. Practice and Procedures of the Human Rights Committee*
ISBN 90-5095-074-4

3 Kitty Arambulo, *Strengthening the Supervision of the International Covenant on Economic, Social and Cultural Rights. Theoretical and Procedural Aspects*
ISBN 90-5095-058-2

4 Marlies Glasius, *Foreign Policy on Human Rights. Its Infl uence on Indonesia under Soeharto*
ISBN 90-5095-089-2

5 Cornelis D. de Jong, *The Freedom of Thought, Conscience and Religion or Belief in the United Nations (1946-1992)*
ISBN 90-5095-137-6

6 Heleen Bosma, *Freedom of Expression in England and under the ECHR: in Search of a Common Ground. A Foundation for the Application of the Human Rights Act 1998 in English Law*
ISBN 90-5095-136-8

7 Mielle Bulterman, *Human Rights in the External Relations of the European Union*
ISBN 90-5095-164-3

8 Esther M. van den Berg, *The Infl uence of Domestic NGOs on Dutch Human Rights Policy. Case Studies on South Africa,Namibia, Indonesia and East Timor*
ISBN 90-5095-159-7

9 Ian Seiderman, *Hierarchy in International Law: the Human Rights Dimension*
ISBN 90-5095-165-1

10 Anna Meijknecht, *Towards International Personality: the Position of Minorities and Indigenous Peoples in International Law*
ISBN 90-5095-166-X

11 Mohamed Eltayeb, *A Human Rights Approach to Combating Religious Persecution. Cases from Pakistan, Saudi Arabia and Sudan*
ISBN 90-5095-170-8

12 Machteld Boot, *Genocide, Crimes Against Humanity, War Crimes: Nullum Crimen Sine Lege and the Subject Matter Jurisdiction of the International Criminal Court*
ISBN 90-5095-216-X

13 Corinne Packer, *Using Human Rights to Change Tradition. Traditional Practices Harmful to Women's Reproductive Health in sub-Saharan Africa*
ISBN 90-5095-226-7

14 Theo R.G. van Banning, *The Human Right to Property*
ISBN 90-5095-203-8

15 Yvonne M. Donders, *Towards a Right to Cultural Identity?*
ISBN 90-5095-238-0

16 Göran K. Sluiter, *International Criminal Adjudication and the Collection of Evidence: Obligations of States*
ISBN 90-5095-227-5

17 Nicola Jägers, *Corporate Human Rights Obligations: in Search of Accountability*
ISBN 90-5095-240-2

18 Magdalena Sepúlveda, *The Nature of the Obligations under the International Covenant on Economic, Social and Cultural Rights*
ISBN 90-5095-260-7

19 Mitsue Inazumi, *Universal Jurisdiction in Modern International Law: Expansion of National Jurisdiction for Prosecuting Serious Crimes under International Law*
ISBN 90-5095-366-2

20 Anne-Marie L.M. de Brouwer, *Supranational Criminal Prosecution of Sexual Violence: The ICC and the Practice of the ICTY and the ICTR*
ISBN 90-5095-533-9

21 Jeroen Gutter, *Thematic Procedures of the United Nations Commission on Human Rights and International Law: in Search of a Sense of Community*
ISBN 90-5095-557-6

22 Hilde Reiding, *The Netherlands and the Development of International Human Rights Instruments*
ISBN 978-90-5095-654-3

23 Ingrid Westendorp, *Women and Housing: Gender Makes a Difference*
ISBN 978-90-5095-669-7

24 Quirine A.M. Eijkman, *We Are Here to Serve You! Public Security, Police Reform and Human Rights Implementation in Costa Rica*
ISBN 978-90-5095-704-5

25 Antoine Ch. Buyse, *Post-conflict Housing Restitution. The European Human Rights Perspective with a case study on Bosnia and Herzegovina*
ISBN 978-90-5095-770-0

26 Gentian Zyberi, *The Humanitarian Face of the International Court of Justice. Its Contribution to Interpreting and Developing International Human Rights and Humanitarian Law Rules and Principles*
ISBN 978-90-5095-792-2

27 Dragoş Cucereanu, *Aspects of Regulating Freedom of Expression on the Internet*
ISBN 978-90-5095-842-4

28 Ton Liefaard, *Deprivation of Liberty of Children in Light of International Human Rights Law and Standards*
ISBN 978-90-5095-838-7

29 Laura van Waas, *Nationality Matters. Statelessness under International Law*
ISBN 978-90-5095-854-7

30 Jeroen Denkers, *The World Trade Organization and Import Bans in Response to Violations of Fundamental Labour Rights*
ISBN 978-90-5095-855-4

31 Irene Hadiprayitno, *Hazard or Right? The Dialectics of Development Practice and the Internationally Declared Right to Development, with Special Reference to Indonesia*
ISBN 978-90-5095-932-2

32 Michał Gondek, *The Reach of Human Rights in a Globalising World: Extraterritorial Application of Human Rights Treaties*
ISBN 978-90-5095-817-2

33 Jeff Handmaker, *Advocating for Accountability: Civic-State Interactions to Protect Refugees in South Africa*
ISBN 978-90-5095-910-0

34 Anna Oehmichen, *Terrorism and Anti-Terror Legislation: The Terrorised Legislator? A Comparison of Counter-Terror Legislation and Its Implications on Human Rights in the Legal Systems of the United Kingdom, Spain, Germany and France*
ISBN 978-90-5095-956-8

35 Simon Walker, *The Future of Human Rights Impact Assessments of Trade Agreements*
ISBN 978-90-5095-986-5

36 Fleur van Leeuwen, *Women's Rights Are Human Rights: The Practice of the United Nations Human Rights Committee and the Committee on Economic, Social and Cultural Rights*
ISBN 978-90-5095-980-3

37 Eva Rieter, *Preventing Irreparable Harm. Provisional Measures in International Human Rights Adjudication*
ISBN 978-90-5095-931-5

38 Desislava Stoitchkova, *Towards Corporate Liability in International Criminal Law*
ISBN 978-94-000-0024-7

39 Paulien Muller, *Scattered Families. Transnational Family Life of Afghan Refugees in the Netherlands in the Light of the Human Rights-Based Protection of the Family*
ISBN 978-94-000-0021-6

40 Bibi van Ginkel, *The Practice of the United Nations in Combating Terrorism from 1946 to 2008. Questions of Legality and Legitimacy*
ISBN 978-94-000-0076-6

41 Christophe Paulussen, *Male captus bene detentus? Surrendering suspects to the International Criminal Court*
ISBN 978-94-000-0100-8

42 Brianne McGonigle Leyh, *Procedural Justice? Victim Participation in International Criminal Proceedings*
ISBN 978-1-78068-020-0

43 Maria Ventegodt Liisberg, *Disability and Employment. A Contemporary Disability Human Rights Approach Applied to Danish, Swedish and EU Law and Policy*
ISBN 978-1-78068-028-6

44 Tarlach McGonagle, *Minority Rights, Freedom of Expression and of the Media: Dynamics and Dilemmas*
ISBN 978-94-000-0215-9

45 Marloes van Noorloos, *Hate Speech Revisited*
ISBN 978-1-78068-032-3